USING DATA TO IMPROVE STUDENT LEARNING IN SCHOOL DISTRICTS

VICTORIA L. BERNHARDT, Ph.D.
Executive Director
Education for the Future Initiative

Professor
Department of Professional Studies in Education
College of Communication and Education
California State University, Chico, CA

EYE ON EDUCATION
6 Depot Way West
Larchmont, NY 10538
(914) 833-0551
(914) 833-0761 Fax
www.eyeoneducation.com

Library of Congress Cataloging—in—Publication Data

Bernhardt, Victoria L., 1952-
Using data to improve student learning in school districts / Victoria L. Bernhardt.
p. cm.
Includes bibliographical references.
ISBN 1-59667-029-0
1. Educational evaluation--United States. 2. School improvement programs--United States--Statistical methods. 3. Educational planning--United States--Statistical methods. 4. School districts--United States--Statistics. I. Title.

LB2822.75.B437 2006
373.1'535021--dc22

2006013813

Acknowledgements

I am so lucky to have many wonderful, dedicated colleagues and friends all over the world who keep me going, and help me improve each day. I am particularly grateful for special colleagues from Arkansas, California, Colorado, Connecticut, Georgia, Iowa, Indiana, Maryland, Massachusetts, Michigan, Missouri, Montana, New Jersey, New York, North Dakota, Ohio, Pennsylvania, South Carolina, Texas, Vermont, Washington, Wisconsin, Ecuador, and Brazil who have helped make this book factual and useful. These dedicated reviewers give me powerful information for making the content useful and user-friendly. The reviewers are critical in the writing of this book for probably more reasons than they know. They give me the confidence and sense of urgency to finish.

Special thanks goes to Mesa County Colorado School District 51, Karen DeJarnette, Veronica Hilyard, Bill Johnston, Andy Mark, and Karen Raney. Special mention needs to be made of Joy Rose's contributions. Joy read and edited the manuscript in every phase. Joy, as always, made herself available to help with any task, any time. Joy, my editor "extraordinaire," is unsurpassed as a supporter and encourager of high-quality work. The nature of her editing goes beyond the proper uses of verbs and commas—her knowledge of continuous improvement provides insights and revelations that I do not always see. I know the final product is so much better because of her input. Thank you, thank you, and thank you, Joy.

Marcy Lauck's time and assistance with looking at the data was invaluable. You are so appreciated, Marcy. Thank you. Marcy also created the Learning Organization Questionnaire that is seen in the case studies.

A special thanks to the school districts that gave me data to use in this book. In concert with our agreements, I will not reveal who you are or your real locations. We all appreciate the opportunity to learn from you. To those who used any of these case studies in early form, thank you for your insights to help us continuously improve the final story.

I am appreciative and thankful everyday for my outstanding *Education for the Future* staff: Lynn Varicelli, Brad Geise, Sally Withuhn, Thiago Jorge, Patsy Schutz, and Marcy Lauck. Brad managed the completion of the CD and graphics with his usual elegance. Sally, Thiago, and Patsy do amazing work, every day, to keep us operating and on the cutting edge. They also helped to make this book a reality. Alicia Warren, former *Education for the Future* employee, deserves special acknowledgement for her help in getting the data prepared for layout, and for her assistance with the data warehouse, references, and graphing. Alicia's help was incredibly valuable to Lynn, as was Sally's help with graphing questionnaire results. Marcy, serving in San Jose Unified School District, helps us know that it is possible to do this on a large scale and that it can be sustained over time.

Once again, I am awestruck and indebted to Lynn Varicelli, for her careful and artistic work on the book layout and CD files. Her dedication to supporting these publications is unmatched in the history of the world! Thank you, Lynn, for your stellar work, for your commitment, loyalty, and long hours over countless days without a break. These books could never be done without you. This one, in particular, with four case studies was pretty intense, and took over a year to complete the layout. I am so proud of this product and of you, Lynn!

I am also grateful to *MC² Design Group*. Brian Curtis and Vanessa Wolfe created the CD design, artwork, and cover—I highly recommend them—and Tom Devol (that's *loved* spelled backwards), our outstanding professional photographer (even if HE cannot spell backwards).

I thank my husband, Jim Richmond, for again providing his brand of support for my work. He does a lot of what I should be doing around the house so I can pursue these publications and the work I can't not do—with few complaints.

A huge thanks to my publisher, affectionately known as *Cousin Bob*, Mr. Robert Sickles. I am grateful for all you do for us. Thank you.

This *Acknowledgement* section could not be complete without thanking you, the reader, and you, the school district personnel working on continuous improvement, who have believed in and tried *Education for the Future* products and processes.

I do hope this book exceeds your expectations and if it does, it is because of the continuous improvement that has resulted from your insights, direction, assistance, and support all along the way. Thank you.

In appreciation to all interested in continuous quality improvement, enjoy this fourth in a series of four books on *Using Data to Improve Student Learning.*

Sincerely,
Vickie Bernhardt
June 2006

About the Author

Victoria L. Bernhardt, Ph.D., is Executive Director of the *Education for the Future Initiative,* a not-for-profit organization whose mission is to build the capacity of all learning organizations at all levels to gather, analyze, and use data to continuously improve learning for all students. She is also a Professor in the Department of Professional Studies in Education, College of Communication and Education, at California State University, Chico, currently on leave. Dr. Bernhardt is the author of the following books:

- A four-book collection of using data to improve student learning—*Using Data to Improve Student Learning in Elementary Schools (2003); Using Data to Improve Student Learning in Middle Schools (2004); Using Data to Improve Student Learning in High Schools (2005);* and *Using Data to Improve Student Learning in School Districts (2006).* Each book shows real analyses focused on one education organizational level and provides templates on an accompanying CD-Rom for leaders to use for gathering, graphing, and analyzing data in their own learning organizations.
- *Data Analysis for Continuous School Improvement* (First Edition, 1998; Second Edition, 2004) helps learning organizations use data to determine where they are, where they want to be, and how to get there—sensibly, painlessly, and effectively.
- *The School Portfolio Toolkit: A Planning, Implementation, and Evaluation Guide for Continuous School Improvement,* and CD-Rom (2002), is a compilation of over 500 examples, suggestions, activities, tools, strategies, and templates for producing school portfolios that will lead to continuous school improvement.
- *The Example School Portfolio* (2000) shows what a completed school portfolio looks like and further supports schools in developing their own school portfolios.
- *The School Portfolio: A Comprehensive Framework for School Improvement* (First Edition, 1994; Second Edition, 1999). This first book by the author assists schools with clarifying the purpose and vision of their learning organizations as they develop their school portfolios.

Dr. Bernhardt is passionate about her mission of helping all educators continuously improve student learning in their classrooms, their schools, their districts, and states by gathering, analyzing, and using actual data—as opposed to using hunches and "gut-level" feelings. She has made numerous presentations at professional meetings and conducts workshops on the school portfolio, data analysis, data warehousing, and school improvement at local, state, regional, national, and international levels.

Dr. Bernhardt can be reached at:

Victoria L. Bernhardt
Executive Director, *Education for the Future Initiative*
400 West First Street, Chico, CA 95929-0230
Tel: 530-898-4482 — Fax: 530-898-4484
e-mail: vbernhardt@csuchico.edu
website: *http://eff.csuchico.edu*

Table of Contents

Foreword

TetraData Corporation is an education software and services company that focuses on breakthrough performance and continuous improvement through the analysis of intersecting sets of data. TetraData continues to be proudly associated with Victoria L. Bernhardt, one of the most dedicated, capable, and forward-thinking leaders in school improvement today. Our firm shares a common passion, i.e., that fact-driven decision making can provide each district, each school, each class and each student with a reliable way to facilitate breakthrough performance and continuous education improvement. We also share a common vision of a world where education is moving toward increased knowledge, increased caring, and where we focus resources on our real future, i.e., the children of highly communicating and networking societies.

Using Data to Improve Student Learning in School Districts, the fourth in the series of four *Using Data to Improve Student Learning* books is an excellent addition to the preceding books that explain how to establish a data-driven environment and how to build the data warehouse to support the needed data analysis. The four books in this series focus on what to do with a robust data warehouse, i.e., what analyses to prepare and how to interpret the analyses. In the several years that Dr. Bernhardt and TetraData have been building and using education-specific data warehouses, the quality of the data and design of the warehouses have grown significantly. Now we have much of the data that we have been seeking to properly assemble and the next step is addressed by this wonderful publication series. This latest book is perhaps one of the most important since it clearly delineates the need for a District Portfolio that weaves together with School Portfolios in order to provide clear "data-driven" direction to the central office team, as that team seeks to motivate and equip the schools to accomplish breakthrough performance, as well as sustain that breakthrough with continuous improvement.

What I enjoyed immensely about these four publications is that Dr. Bernhardt has used real data from real life situations, in this case the text show an 8,000 student district, while the CD shows three other school district examples (200, 1,300, and 32,000 students). This brings richness to the examples and the principles that Dr. Bernhardt provides since it is set forth in such a realistic environment. This realism approach has also enabled Dr. Bernhardt to provide both an insightful, as well as, practical description of how to prepare and interpret the analyses. Since there are four books, the publications deliver this information specific to the teachers and staff in elementary, middle, high school, and the district office. That was a wonderful decision by Dr. Bernhardt as she provides very specific content for each portion of the education spectrum.

One of the major education issues that Dr. Bernhardt addresses is embodied in the word "Focus." One of the first results of the early education datawarehousing and data analysis efforts was the *kid in the candy shop* syndrome. What I mean by that is the school data was finally available for examination, and educators starting producing queries and analyses, many of which were useful, but not necessarily pertinent to the focus of their educational team. Dr. Bernhardt, in this work, brings focus to all of our data analysis efforts, a focus on what is important to bring school improvement, a focus on what will bring results in our quality programs, a focus on the real problems and opportunities, and a focus on what really can effect positive change.

This fine set of works touches the needs of numerous individuals in the education network, from the teacher who needs to understand the demographics and capabilities of her/his individual students to school principals, counselors, instructional coordinators, testing and analysis coordinators, district researchers, and certainly the district executives. By virtue of her excellent skills, Dr. Bernhardt has given everyone in education, including the non-technologists among us, the opportunity to benefit from this fine edition. I encourage your reading of this newest edition to the library of Dr. Bernhardt's works and welcome you to embrace the passion of improving education by making objective education-enhancement decisions. After you have read this book, I challenge you as I challenge myself every day, to provide the leadership, the tenacity, and the discipline it takes to constantly live with your data, to be driven to make sound decisions based upon the data, and to always remember that each piece of data links to students. Enjoy this wonderful rich book and let it drive all of us to focus on our future—our children.

Martin S. Brutosky
Chairman and CEO
TetraData Corporation
150 Executive Center Drive
Box 127
Greenville, SC 29615
Tel: 864-458-8243
http://www.tetradata.com

Preface

With the enactment of *No Child Left Behind,* every school and district in the country need to analyze their data to ensure adequate yearly progress. Sometimes, looking at another's analyses makes it easier to see things you would not have seen while looking only at your own analyses.

When it comes to analyzing student achievement data, the first two questions educators ask are *Now that we have the data, what analyses should we make?* and *What do the analyses tell us?*

These questions are hard to answer on the spot, so I have taken up the challenge to develop a series of books with the purposes of showing what analyses can be made, describing what these analyses are telling us, and illustrating how to use these analyses in continuous improvement planning. This series of books includes:

- *Using Data to Improve Student Learning in Elementary Schools*
- *Using Data to Improve Student Learning in Middle Schools*
- *Using Data to Improve Student Learning in High Schools*
- *Using Data to Improve Student Learning in School Districts*

I believe that most of the time we must look at K-12 data (district level) to ensure a continuum of learning that makes sense for all students. I have purposefully separated building levels in these books so there would be ample space to do a fairly comprehensive job of data analysis at each organizational level and to make the point about needing to understand results beyond one school level.

Each of these four publications uses real data (with some slight alterations to blur identities and to fill gaps where data are missing) and shows the actual descriptive analyses I would perform if I were the person analyzing the data at that particular level. You will see that no matter how much or how little *data* your school or district has, the *data* can tell the story. The study questions at the end of each chapter serve as guides for the reader. I have described what I saw in the analyses following the study questions for readers who want the feedback.

For the purposes of this publication, I have not included facilities, food services, construction, and financial data. These data were not available. My goal with this book is for anyone to be able to set up these analyses, regardless of the statistical resources available. Therefore, in addition to showing the analyses in the text, the graphing templates, narratives, text templates, and supplementary tools appear on the accompanying CD.

Intended Audiences

This book is intended for school and district teachers and administrators who want to use data to continuously improve what they do for children; and for college and university professors who teach school administrators, teachers, and support personnel how to analyze school data. It is my belief that all professional educators must learn how to use data in this time of high-stakes accountability.

My hope is that you will find this book and the CD to be helpful as you think through the analyses of *your* data to improve learning for all students.

Victoria L. Bernhardt
Executive Director, *Education for the Future Initiative*
400 West First Street, Chico, CA 95929-0230
Tel: 530-898-4482 — Fax: 530-898-4484
e-mail: vbernhardt@csuchico.edu
website: *http://eff.csuchico.edu*

Introduction

Chapter 1

Districts that do not study their data in a comprehensive fashion cannot lead their schools through comprehensive data analyses or sustainable improvement.

School districts that gather, analyze, and use information about their organizations make better decisions, not only about what to improve, but also how to institutionalize systemic improvement. Districts that understand the needs of their students and schools are more successful in planning improvements and remain more focused during implementation. Districts that simply gather some data, but make no sustained effort to comprehensively analyze and use data, are at a substantial disadvantage. Districts that use data in a comprehensive manner understand the effectiveness of their continuous improvement efforts; those that do not use data can only assume that effectiveness.

Districts that do not study their data in a comprehensive fashion cannot lead their schools through comprehensive data analyses or sustainable improvement. School districts that look at the entire organization through data can guide their schools in data-driven decision making.

Districts committed to improving student learning analyze data in order to plan for the future through understanding—

- the ways in which the district and the community have changed and are continuing to change
- the current and future needs of the district, schools, students, teachers, parents, and community
- how well current processes meet these customers' needs
- if all groups of students within the district are being well-served
- the gaps between the results the schools within the district are getting and the results they want
- the root causes for the gaps
- the types of education programs, expertise, and process adjustments that will be needed to alleviate the gaps and to meet the needs of all customers
- how well the new processes being implemented meet the needs of the district, schools, students, teachers, parents, and community

The Importance of Data

Businesses typically use data to determine customers' wants and needs. No matter what occupation we, or our students, aspire to, everyone can appreciate that fact. We can also appreciate the fact that businesses not properly analyzing and using data, more often than not, are not successful. Those of us who work in the business of education, however, may not be as familiar with the ways that *businesses* use *educational* data.

In many states, the prison systems look at the number of students not reading on grade level in grades two, three, or four to determine the number of prison cells to build ten years hence (*Lawmakers Move to Improve Literacy,* 2001). The fact that the prison system can use this prediction formula with great accuracy should make us all cringe, but the critical point is that if businesses can use educational data for predictions, so can educators. Not only can we predict, we can use the same data to *prevent* undesirable results from occurring. Nothing would make educators happier than to hear that prison systems do not need as many cells because more students are being successful in school and, therefore, in life.

If businesses can use educational data for predictions, so can educators. Not only can we predict, we can use the same data to "prevent" undesirable results from happening.

School districts in the United States have a long history of adopting innovations one after another as they are introduced. Very few districts take the time to understand the needs of the children being served. Few take the time to understand the impact current processes have on these children. Few take the time to determine the root causes of recurring problems, or to measure and analyze the impact of implementing new approaches. Fewer still use sound information to build and stick with a solid long-term plan that will improve learning for all students. Across our country, we have found that schools in many districts spend an average of about two years engaged in their improvement efforts. The sad fact is that many districts are already requiring schools to change their improvement efforts before some of their schools start implementing the last efforts. Is it any wonder that nothing seems to generate results for these districts?

We find a different story among the school districts that measure and analyze the impact of *implementing* their approaches. These districts know if what they are doing is working and, if not, why not. These districts stick with their efforts to create improvement long after most districts have switched to new efforts. These districts show the patience needed to truly implement continuous improvement. These districts get results.

Using data can make an enormous difference in district continuous improvement efforts by improving district processes and student learning. Data can help to—

- replace hunches and hypotheses with facts concerning what changes are needed
- facilitate a clear understanding of the gaps between where the district is and where the district wants to be
- identify the root causes of these gaps, so the district can solve the problem and not just treat the symptom
- understand the impact of processes on the student population
- ensure equity in program and school participation

- assess needs to target services on important issues
- provide information to eliminate ineffective practices
- ensure the effective and efficient uses of dollars
- show if district goals and objectives are being accomplished
- ascertain if the district and school staffs are *walking the talk*
- promote understanding of the impact of efforts, processes, and progress
- generate answers for the community related to: *What are we getting for our children by investing in the district's methods, programs, and processes?*
- continuously improve all aspects of the learning organization
- predict and prevent failures
- predict and ensure successes

Barriers to Using Data

Districts do not deliberately ignore data. Typically, districts say, "We have lots of data; we just do not know what data to use, or how or when to use them." When district personnel first get interested in data and want to do more with the data they have, they often hit the proverbial brick wall.

While many districts gather data, barriers begin with attempts to analyze the data to help improve teaching and learning. Barriers can pop-up anywhere and for a variety of reasons:

- In contrast to the work culture in business, the work culture in education usually focuses on programs, and not results data.
- Few people in districts and schools are adequately trained to gather and analyze data or to establish and maintain databases.
    - Administrators (who are mostly former teachers) and teachers have not been trained in data analysis
    - Some teachers see data analysis as another thing that takes away from teaching
- Administrators and teachers do not see gathering and analyzing data as part of their jobs.
    - District personnel have job definitions that often do not include, as a priority, analyzing data.
    - District departments are afraid they will lose their power if they share their data with someone else.

- Gathering data is perceived to be a waste of time (after all, we are here every day—we know what the problems are!).
- School districts do not have databases/data warehouses that allow for easy access and analysis of data.
  - Computer systems are outdated and inadequate; appropriate, user-friendly software and hardware are not available.
- Professional learning for administrators and teachers to understand why data are important and how data can make a difference in their work is often sorely lacking.
- Data are not used systematically from the state to the regional and local levels, nor are they used particularly well at all levels.
  - State legislatures keep changing the rules.
- Some district personnel have had only negative experiences with data.
  - There is a perception that data are collected for someone else's purposes.
  - Confusion exists regarding which data should be the focus of analyses.
- There are not enough good examples of school districts gathering, maintaining, and benefiting from the use of data.

Whatever it is that keeps us from assessing our progress and products adequately, we must learn to listen, to observe, and to gather data from all sources that will help us *know* how we are doing, where we are going, and how we can get there.

The Purposes of this Book

This book has three purposes. The first is to provide a learning opportunity for readers. The analyses provided in these chapters and on the CD are laboratories for learning—authentic tasks, if you will. The analyses are case studies, complete with study questions. The second and main purpose is to show what it would look like if we were analyzing different size districts' data, comprehensively. The third purpose is to provide tools to do these analyses in your district. The analysis tools are found on the accompanying CD.

The Structure of this Book

Using Data to Improve Student Learning in School Districts begins with an overview of why data are important to continuous school district improvement. Chapter 2 defines what data are important to have in comprehensive data analysis. It also discusses the intersections of four major categories of data in terms of different levels of analyses that can be created using these measures.

Chapter 3 describes how to get started and how data fit into a continuous improvement planning model. Chapters 4 through 7 present an example district analysis of approximately 8,000 students, and show how the model assists in understanding what the district is doing that is working or not working for its students. Three other district examples are on the CD. These examples are of districts with 30,941; 1,373; and 200 students. Due to space constraints, we decided to show the "medium-sized" district in the text.

Chapter 4 focuses on the example district's demographic data to answer the question, *Who are we?*, and to establish the context of the district.

Chapter 5 uses the example district's perceptions and process data to answer the question, *How do we do business?*, in terms of its work culture and organizational climate.

Where are we now? is the heart of Chapter 6. Ways to measure student learning are defined; analyses that can be made with different measures and their uses are discussed in this chapter. The example district's data assist us with understanding how to analyze state assessment results.

Chapter 7 discusses and shows gap analyses, answering the question, *What are the gaps?*

Chapter 8 synthesizes the analyses conducted in Chapters 4 through 7 and provides implications for the example district's continuous improvement plan. A plan that grew out of this data analysis example is shown.

Questions to guide the study of the information presented in the chapters are included at the end of Chapters 2 through 7, followed by the author's analyses. These files are also found on the CD.

Chapter 9 provides a brief summary and discussion of the example district's results. As the book concludes, typical process issues, such as *data warehouses, who does the data analysis work, what school district leaders can do to ensure continuous improvement throughout the district,* and *recommendations on how to get student learning increases* are discussed.

The questionnaires, the *Continuous Improvement Continuums* for districts and schools, and related tools used by the example districts are found on the CD, along with complete analyses, analysis templates, and questionnaire narratives, and other *Education for the Future* questionnaires. Whenever CD-ROM appears in the text, it means that file is on the CD. The specific name of the file (in parenthesis) follows the CD icon. A list of CD files related to each chapter appears at the end of each chapter. A complete index of CD contents appears in Appendix A.

The *Continuous Improvement Continuums* for districts is shown in Appendix B. The *Continuums* for schools appears in Appendix C. Both sets of *Continuums* are also on the CD. CD-ROM (CICs_Dstrct.pdf and CICs_Schls.pdf) A comprehensive *Glossary of Terms* commonly used in data analysis and assessment, and other terms used in this book, is located just before the references and resources list.

Summary

Using Data to Improve Student Learning in School Districts illustrates the basic steps in conducting data analysis to inform continuous improvement planning in school districts. Readers will understand what data to gather when analyzing district level data, how to analyze the data, what the analyses look like, and how the analyses can inform a continuous improvement plan. Three other district examples and the tools to help any district do this work, regardless of enrollment or number of schools, are provided on the accompanying CD.

What Data Are Important?

Chapter 2

> ***Learning takes place neither in isolation, nor only at school. Multiple measures must be considered and used to understand the multifaceted world of learning from the perspective of everyone involved.***

If the purpose of school districts is to provide support and resources so that all their schools ensure that all students learn, what data will help districts understand if they are effectively carrying out their purpose? What data analyses will help districts know if all students are learning? What data analyses will help districts know if all schools are making a difference for their students?

Learning takes place neither in isolation, nor only at school. Multiple measures must be considered and used in an ongoing fashion (formative) to understand the multifaceted world of learning from the perspective of everyone involved. Using more than one method of assessment allows students to demonstrate their full range of abilities, and collecting data on *multiple occasions* provides students several opportunities to demonstrate their various abilities. If you want to know if the district is achieving its purpose and how to continually improve all aspects of the district, multiple measures—gathered from varying points of view—must be used.

The major job of every school district is *student learning.* Staff must think through the factors that impact student learning to determine other data requirements. We need to ask students what they like about the way they learn at school and how they learn best. *School processes,* such as programs and instructional strategies, need to be described to understand their impact in helping all staff optimize the learning of all students.

Because students neither learn only at school nor only through teachers, we need to know about the learning environment from the parent and community perspective. Districts may also need to know employer perceptions of the abilities and skills of former students.

But will these data provide enough information to determine how well the district is meeting the needs of all students? Other factors over which we have little or no control, such as background or *demographics,* impact student learning. These data are crucial to our understanding of whom we serve, and whether or not our educational services are meeting the needs of every student.

Analyses of *demographics, perceptions, student learning,* and *school processes* provide a powerful picture that will help us understand the district's impact on student achievement. When used together, these measures give districts the information they need to improve teaching and learning and to get positive results.

In Figure 2.1, these four major categories of data are shown as overlapping circles. CD-ROM (MMgraphic.pdf) This figure illustrates the different types of information one can gain from individual measures and the enhanced levels of analyses that can be gained from the intersections of the measures.

Figure 2.1

Multiple Measures of Data

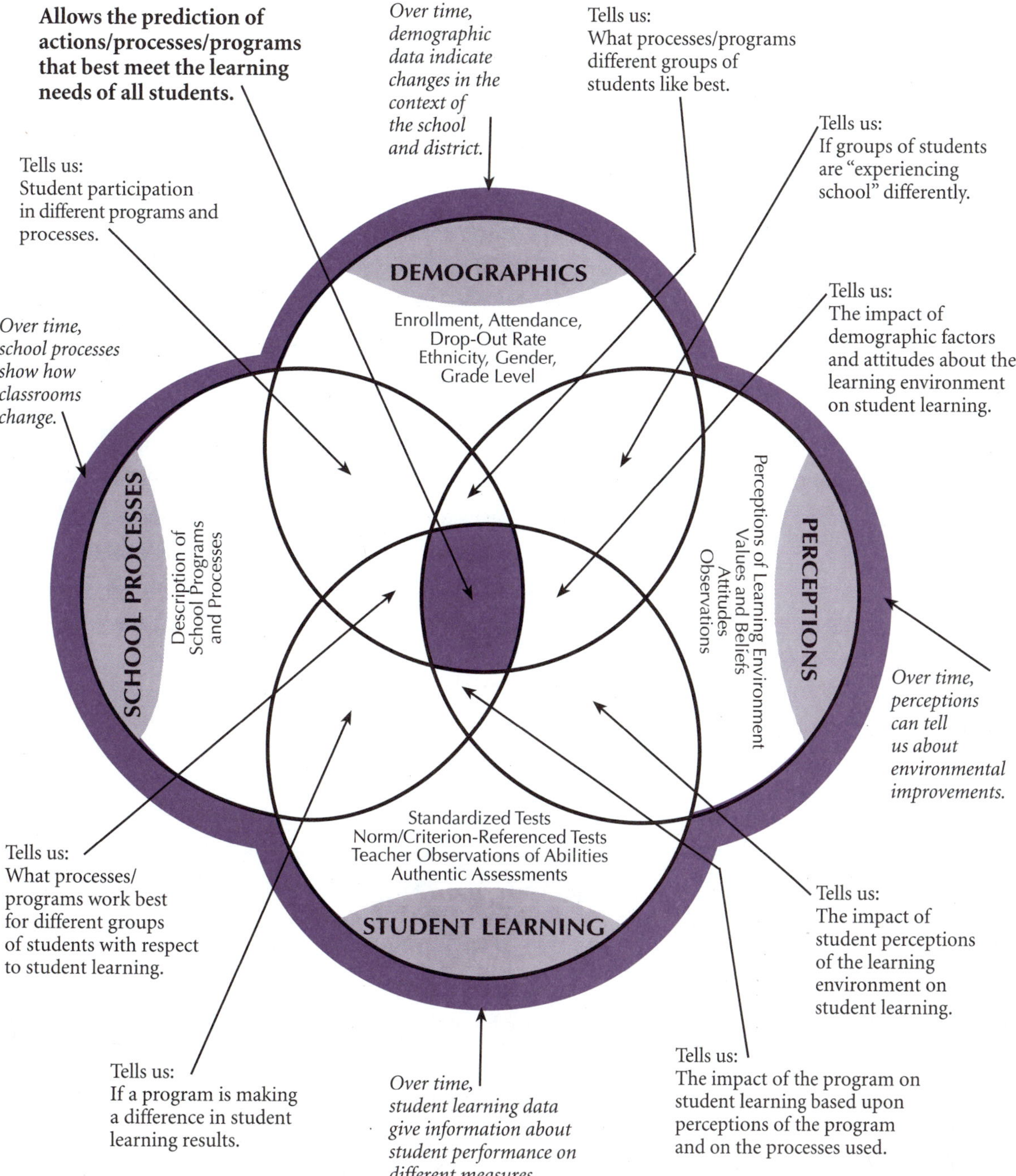

Allows the prediction of actions/processes/programs that best meet the learning needs of all students.
Over time, demographic data indicate changes in the context of the school and district.
Tells us: What processes/programs different groups of students like best.
Tells us: If groups of students are "experiencing school" differently.
Tells us: Student participation in different programs and processes.
Tells us: The impact of demographic factors and attitudes about the learning environment on student learning.
Over time, school processes show how classrooms change.
DEMOGRAPHICS
Enrollment, Attendance, Drop-Out Rate Ethnicity, Gender, Grade Level
SCHOOL PROCESSES
Description of School Programs and Processes
PERCEPTIONS
Perceptions of Learning Environment Values and Beliefs Attitudes Observations
Over time, perceptions can tell us about environmental improvements.
Standardized Tests Norm/Criterion-Referenced Tests Teacher Observations of Abilities Authentic Assessments
STUDENT LEARNING
Tells us: What processes/programs work best for different groups of students with respect to student learning.
Tells us: The impact of student perceptions of the learning environment on student learning.
Tells us: If a program is making a difference in student learning results.
Over time, student learning data give information about student performance on different measures.
Tells us: The impact of the program on student learning based upon perceptions of the program and on the processes used.

> *If administrators want to know if the district is achieving its purpose and how to continually improve all aspects of the district, multiple measures—gathered from varying points of view—must be used.*

One measure, by itself, gives useful information. Comprehensive measures, used together and over time, provide much richer information. Ultimately, districts need to be able to predict what they must do to meet the needs of all the students they have, or will have in the future. The information gleaned from the intersections of these four measures (*demographics, perceptions, student learning,* and *school processes*), helps us to define the questions we want to ask, and focuses us on what data are necessary in order to find the answers.

Levels of Analysis

Different levels of analysis reveal answers to questions at varying depths of understanding. Each of the four measures, on its own, gives valuable descriptive information. However, more and better quality information can be found by digging deeper into the data through different levels of analysis in which one type of measure is analyzed and compared with other measures, over time.

We will discuss ten levels of analysis. Each level builds on the previous one to show how past data and intersections of measures provide more comprehensive information than a single measure of data taken one time. If you feel you are only at level one, hang in there; this book and your own work will help you get to level ten.

Note: Unless otherwise specified, *over time* refers to no less than three years. Definitions of terms appear in the *Glossary* at the back of the book.

Level 1: Snapshots of Measures

Level one refers to the four major measures of data, shown in Figure 2.1, in their current state and independent of each other.

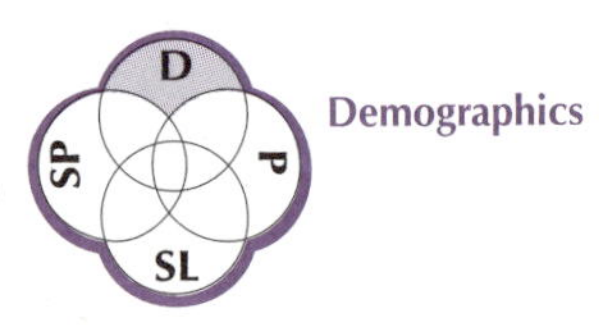

Demographic data provide descriptive information about the district community, such as enrollment, attendance, grade level, ethnicity, gender, and native language. Demographic data are the part of our educational system over which we have no control. From them, however, we can observe trends and glean information for purposes of prediction and planning. Demographic data give us a glimpse of the system and how the district organizes its system.

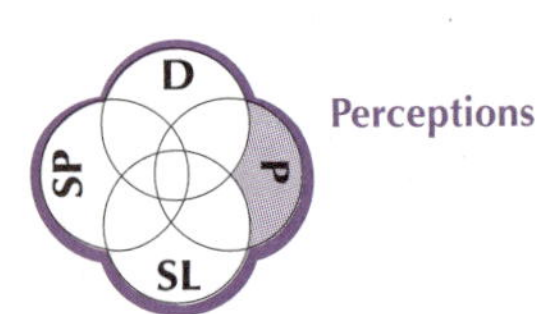

Perceptions data help us understand what students, parents, staff, and others think about the learning environment. Perceptions can be gathered through questionnaires, interviews, focus groups, and/or observations. Perceptions are important because peoples' actions reflect what they believe, perceive, or think about different topics. Perceptions data can also tell us what is possible.

Student Learning describes the outcomes of our educational system in terms of standardized test results, grade point averages, standards assessments, and authentic assessments. Districts often use a variety of student learning measurements separately, sometimes without thinking about how these measurements are interrelated. Districts normally think of multiple measures as looking only at different measures of student learning, rather than including demographics, perceptions, and school processes.

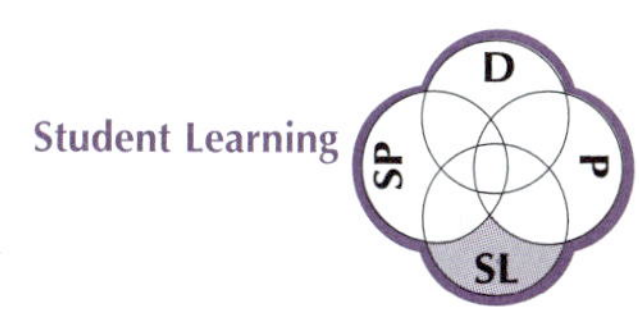

School Processes define what we are doing to help students learn: how we group, teach, and assess students. School processes include programs, instruction and assessment strategies, and other classroom practices. To change the results the district and schools are getting, administrators, teachers, and school personnel must document what processes are being *implemented* and align them with the results they are getting in order to understand what to improve to get different results, and to share their successes with others.

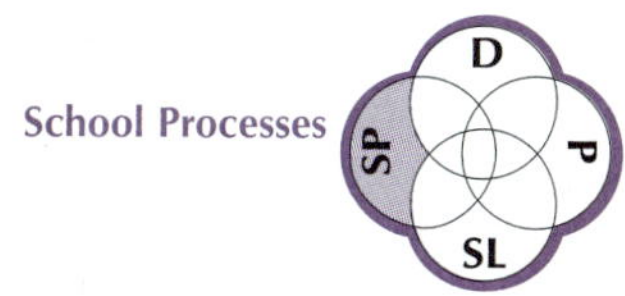

Looking at each of the four measures separately, we get snapshots of data in isolation from any other data at the district level. At this level we can answer questions such as—

- How many students are enrolled in the district and each school this year? *(Demographics)*
- How satisfied are parents, students, and/or staff with the learning environment? *(Perceptions)*
- How did students at each school score on a test? *(Student Learning)*
- What programs are operating in the district this year? *(School Processes)*

Level 2: Measures, Over Time

At the second level, we start digging deeper into each of the measures by looking *over time* (i.e., at least three years) to answer questions, such as, but not limited to—

- How has enrollment in the district and within each school changed over the past five years? *(Demographics)*
- How have student perceptions of the learning environment changed, over time? *(Perceptions)*
- Are there differences in student scores on state assessments over the years? *(Student Learning)*
- What programs have operated in the district during the past five years? *(School Processes)*

Different levels of analysis reveal answers to questions at varying depths of understanding.

Level 3: Two or More Variables Within Measures

Looking at *more than one type of data* within each of the circles gives us a better view of the learning organization (e.g., one year's state assessment subscores compared with performance assessment measures). We can answer questions such as—

- What percentage of the students currently in the district are fluent speakers of languages other than English? *(Demographics)*
- Are staff, student, and parent perceptions of the learning environment in agreement? *(Perceptions)*
- Are students' state assessment scores consistent with teacher-assigned grades and performance assessment rubrics? *(Student Learning)*
- What are the processes in the district's mathematics and science programs? *(School Processes)*

Level 4: Two or More Variables Within One Type of Measure, Over Time

Level 4 takes similar measures as Level 3, *across time* (e.g., state assessment subscores and performance assessment measures compared over the past four years), and allows us to answer deeper questions such as—

- How has the enrollment of non-English-speaking students changed in the past three years? *(Demographics)*
- Are staff, students, and parents more or less satisfied with the learning environment now than they were in previous years? *(Perceptions)*
- Over the past three years, how do teacher-assigned grades and state assessment scores compare? *(Student Learning)*
- How have the processes used in the district's mathematics and science programs changed over time? *(School Processes)*

Level 5: Intersection of Two Types of Measures

Level 5 begins the *intersections across two circles* (e.g., last year's state assessment results by ethnicity). Level 5 helps us to answer questions such as—

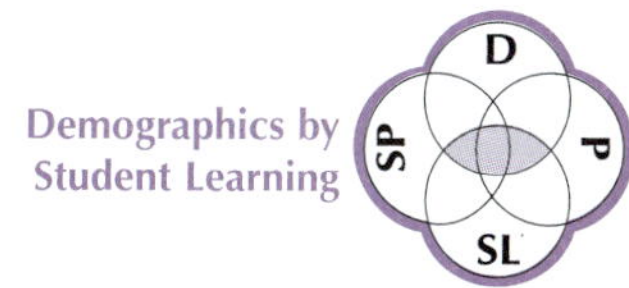

- Do students who attend school every day perform better on the state assessment than students who miss more than five days per month? *(Demographics by Student Learning)*

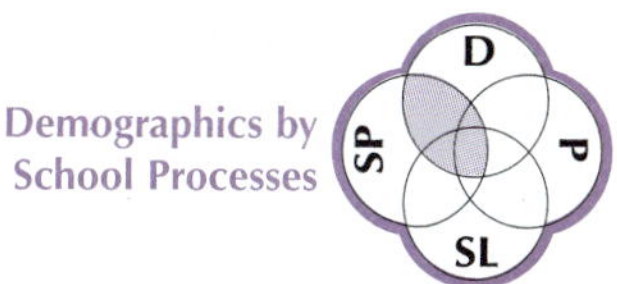

- How long does it take for non-English-speaking students to be redesignated as fluent English speakers? *(Demographics by School Processes)*

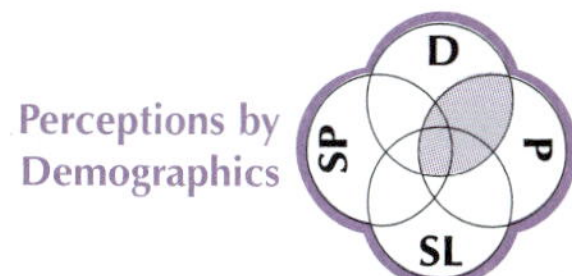

- Is there a gender difference in students' perceptions of the learning environment? *(Perceptions by Demographics)*
- Do students with positive attitudes about school do better academically, as measured by the state assessment? *(Perceptions by Student Learning)*

- Are there differences in how students enrolled in different programs perceive the learning environment? *(Perceptions by School Processes)*
- Do students identified as gifted get the highest scores on the state state assessment test? *(Student Learning by School Processes)*

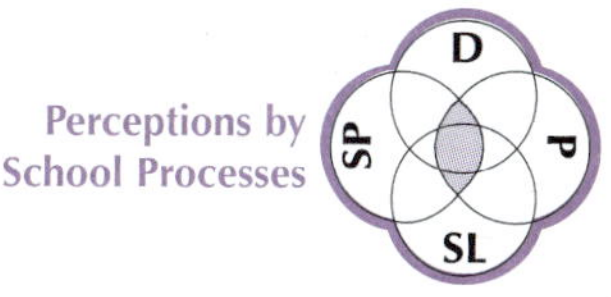

Level 6: Intersection of Two Measures, Over Time

Looking at the *intersection of two of the measures over time* allows us to see trends as they develop (e.g., state assessment test scores disaggregated by ethnicity over the past three years can help us see if the differences in score results, by ethnicity, is truly a trend or an initial fluctuation). This intersection also begins to show the relationship of the multiple measures and why it is so important to look at all the measures together.

At Level 6 we are looking at the intersection of two of the circles over time. The questions we can answer at this level include, as examples—

- How have students of different ethnicities scored on state assessments over the past three years? *(Demographics by Student Learning)*
- Are all student groups represented in special education, Title I, and gifted classes? *(Demographics by School Processes)*
- Have parent perceptions of the learning environment changed since the implementation of the new mathematics program? *(Perceptions by School Processes)*

Level 7: Intersection of Three Measures

As we *intersect three of the measures* at the district and school level (e.g., student learning measures disaggregated by ethnicity compared to student questionnaire responses disaggregated by ethnicity), the types of questions that we are able to answer include the following:

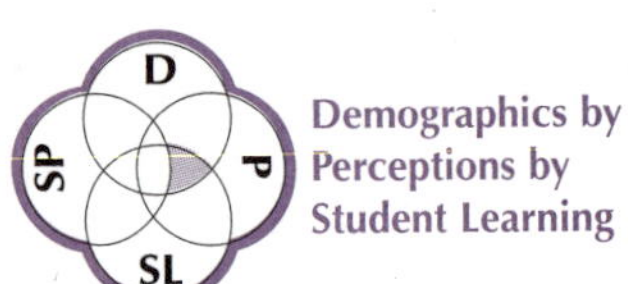

- Do students of different ethnicities perceive the learning environment differently, and are their scores on the state assessment consistent with these perceptions? *(Demographics by Perceptions by Student Learning)*

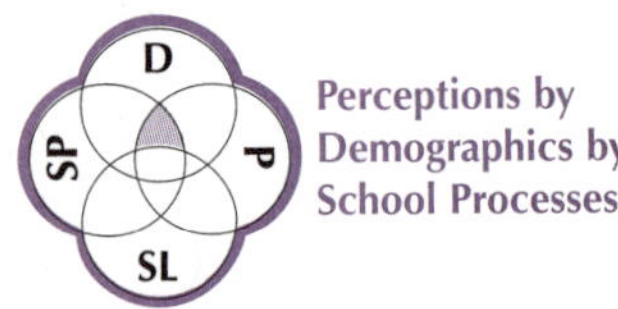

- What instructional process(es) did the students who were redesignated from English-learners to English-speaking enjoy most in their all-English classrooms this year? *(Perceptions by Demographics by School Processes)*

- Is there a difference in students' reports of what they like most about the school by whether or not they participate in extracurricular activities? Do students who participate in extracurricular activities have higher grade-point averages than students who do not participate in extracurricular activities? *(Perceptions by Student Learning by School Processes)*

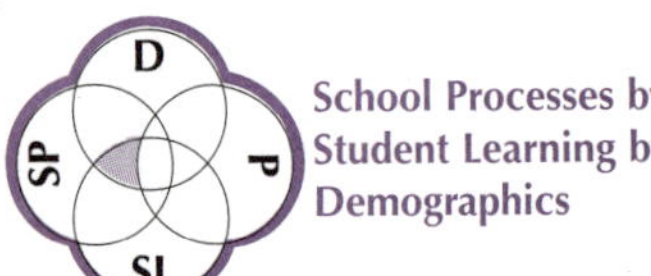

- Which program is making the biggest difference with respect to student achievement for at-risk students this year, and is one group of students responding "better" to the processes? *(School Processes by Student Learning by Demographics)*

Level 8: Intersection of Three Measures, Over Time

Looking at *three measures over time* allows us to see trends, to begin to understand the learning environment from the students' perspectives, and to know how to deliver instruction to get the desired results from and for *all* students.

Level 8 takes Level 7 intersections over time (e.g., state assessment scores disaggregated by ethnicity compared to student questionnaires disaggregated by ethnicity, for the past four years). Level 8 allows us to answer the following types of questions:

- What programs do all types of students like the most every year? *(Demographics by Perceptions by School Processes)*
- Have the processes used to teach English to English-learning students been consistent across schools and grade levels so each student is able to build on her/his abilities? *(Demographics by Student Learning by School Processes)*

Level 9: Intersection of All Four Measures

Our ultimate analysis is the *intersection of all four measures* at the district level (e.g., state assessment results disaggregated by program, by gender, within grade level, compared to questionnaire results for students by program, by gender, within grade level). These intersections allow us to answer questions such as—

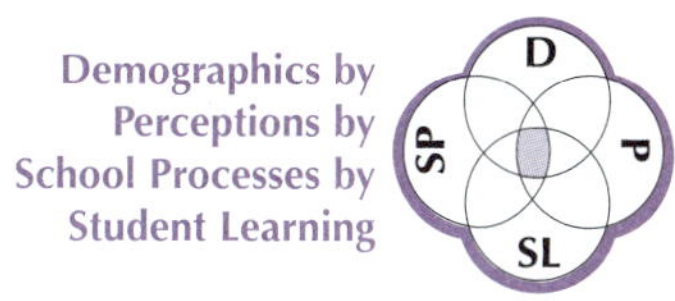

- Given the population that comes to this district, are our programs and strategies meeting their needs in every school and grade level, as measured by student learning results and everyone's perspective? *(Demographics by Perceptions by School Processes by Student Learning)*

Level 10: Intersection of All Four Measures, Over Time

It is not until we *intersect all four circles,* at the district level and *over time,* that we are able to answer questions that will predict if the actions, processes, and programs that we are establishing will meet the needs of all students. With this intersection, we can answer the ultimate question:

- Based on whom we have as students, how they prefer to learn, and what schools/programs they are in, are all students learning at the same rate? *(Student Learning by Demographics by Perceptions by School Processes)*

Do note that there might not always be a way to display these intersections in one comprehensive table or graph. Often, multiple graphs and/or tables are used together to observe intersection relationships.

It is important to look at each measure by itself to understand where the district and each school is right now and over time. Intersecting the measures can give a broader look at the data and help everyone understand all facets of the district. Figure 2.2 summarizes two, three, and four-way intersections. CD-ROM (IntrscTbl.pdf) On the CD are a *Data Discovery Activity* and two activities for creating questions from intersecting data, *Intersections Activity* and *Creating Intersections Activity.* CD-ROM (ACTDiscv.pdf, ACTIntrs.pdf, and ACTCreat.pdf) Also on the CD are the *Data Analysis Presentation,* a *Microsoft PowerPoint* slideshow overview to use with your staffs in getting started analyzing your data, and three articles entitled *Multiple Measures* (Bernhardt, 1998), *Intersections: New Routes Open when One Type of Data Crosses Another* (Bernhardt, 2000), and *No Schools Left Behind* (Bernhardt, 2003). CD-ROM (DASlides.ppt, MMeasure.pdf, Intersct.pdf, and NoSchls.pdf)

Figure 2.2

Summary of Data Intersections

Intersections	Can tell us —
Two-way Intersections	
• Demographics by student learning	• If student groups perform differently on student learning measures
• Demographics by perceptions	• If student groups are experiencing school differently
• Demographics by school processes	• If all student groups are represented in the different programs and processes offered by each school in the district
• Student learning by school processes	• If different programs are achieving similar student learning results
• Student learning by perceptions	• If student perceptions of the learning environment have an impact on their learning results
• Perceptions by school processes	• If people are perceiving programs and processes differently
Three-way Intersections	
• Demographics by student learning by perceptions	• The impact demographic factors and attitudes about the learning environment have on student learning
• Demographics by student learning by school processes	• What processes or programs work best for different student groups measured by student learning results
• Demographics by perceptions by school processes	• What programs or processes different students like best, or the impact different programs or processes have on student attitudes
• Student learning by school processes by perceptions	• The relationship between the processes students prefer and learning results
Four-way Intersections	
• Demographics by student learning by perceptions by school processes	• What processes or programs have the greatest impact on subgroups of students' learning, according to student perceptions, and as measured by student learning results

Input/Process/Outcome

Looking at the different types of data another way, Figure 2.3 shows these data in terms of *input, process,* and *outcome.* This figure helps us know why it is important to analyze all data. On the CD is an *Input, Process, Outcome (IPO) Activity* (and the *headings* and *data elements*) that allows staff to discuss data elements as input, process, or outcome elements. CD-ROM (ACTIPO.pdf, IPOHead.pdf, IPOElem.pdf)

Input

Input is made up of the elements that describe the "givens"—usually beyond our immediate control. The "givens" we have in districts and schools are—

- who the students are (e.g., gender, ethnicity, language fluency, free/reduced lunch status, disability, number of years in the system) (*Demographics*)
- characteristics of parents/community (*Demographics*)
- who the teachers are (e.g., gender, ethnicity, number of years teaching experience, qualifications, understanding of student needs) (*Demographics*)
- preconceived notions/expectations (*Perceptions*)
- learning preferences (*Perceptions*)
- teaching styles preferences (*Perceptions*)
- values and beliefs of everyone in the organization (*Perceptions*)
- student learning standards (*Processes*)

It behooves us to understand very clearly whom we are serving and to employ the best qualified people to best serve these students.

Input—data elements that describe the "givens"—usually beyond our immediate control.

Process—elements that describe the actions learning organizations plan for and implement to get the outcomes they are striving to achieve, given the input.

Outcome—the data elements that describe the results of a learning organization's processes, given the input.

Figure 2.3
Input, Process, Outcome Data Elements

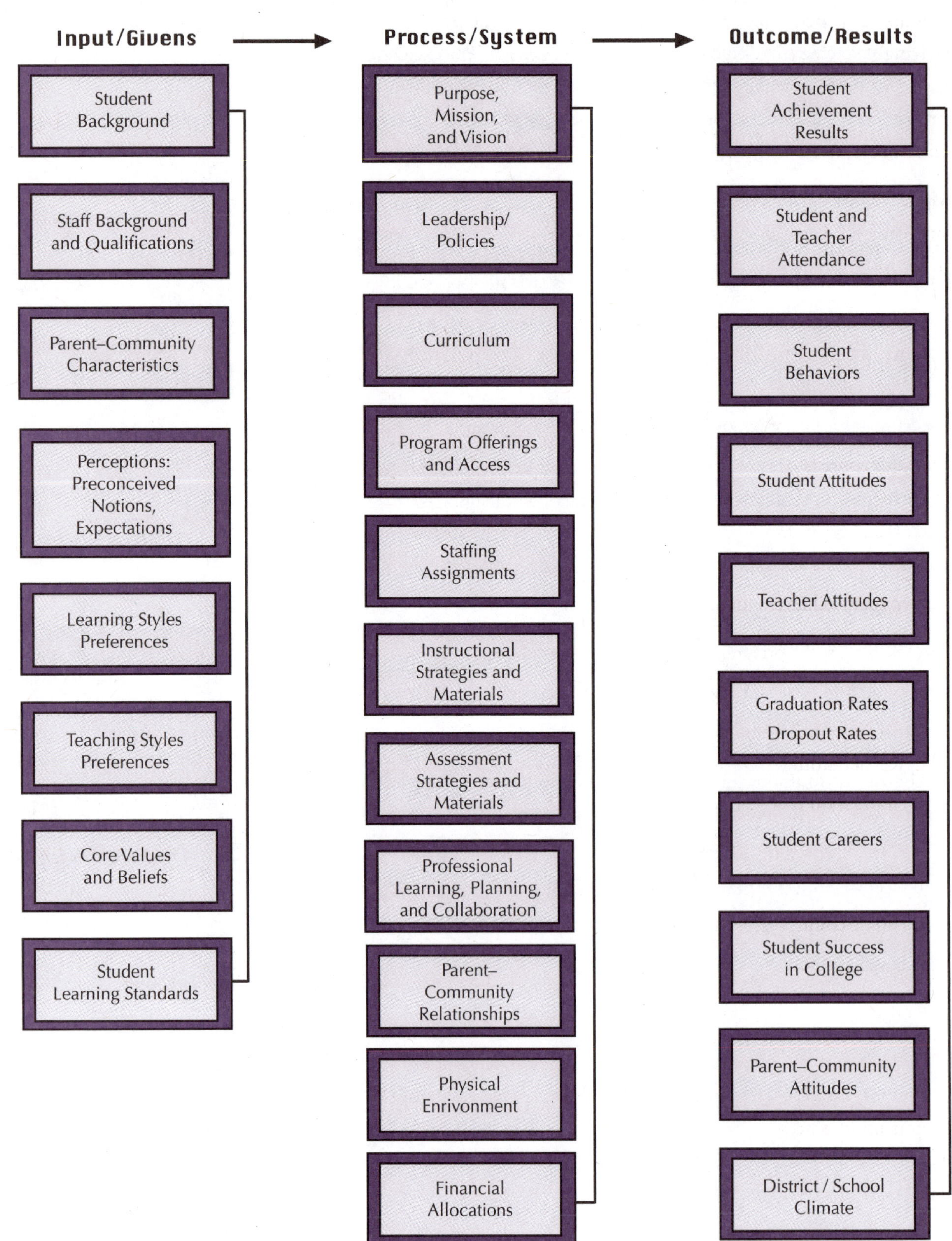
Input/Givens
Process/System
Outcome/Results
Student Background
Staff Background and Qualifications
Parent–Community Characteristics
Perceptions: Preconceived Notions, Expectations
Learning Styles Preferences
Teaching Styles Preferences
Core Values and Beliefs
Student Learning Standards
Purpose, Mission, and Vision
Leadership/ Policies
Curriculum
Program Offerings and Access
Staffing Assignments
Instructional Strategies and Materials
Assessment Strategies and Materials
Professional Learning, Planning, and Collaboration
Parent–Community Relationships
Physical Enrivonment
Financial Allocations
Student Achievement Results
Student and Teacher Attendance
Student Behaviors
Student Attitudes
Teacher Attitudes
Graduation Rates Dropout Rates
Student Careers
Student Success in College
Parent–Community Attitudes
District / School Climate

Process

Process is made up of the actions that contribute to the results that learning organizations need to plan for and implement to get the outcomes they are striving to achieve. Given whom we have as administrators, teachers, and students, what *processes* will get us to our outcomes? Clearly, a district purpose, mission, and vision should lead all efforts, and what we expect students to know and be able to do.

These guiding principles, along with strong leadership, effective policies, and sufficient financial allocations, guide the curriculum, instructional strategies, instructional materials, assessment strategies, program offerings and access, staffing assignments, professional learning, parent/community relations, and the district and school environments. Effective and high quality processes are based on an understanding of *input* data elements.

Data analysis should not be about just gathering data. It is very easy to get "analysis paralysis" by spending time pulling data together and not spending time using the data.

Outcome

Outcome consists of the data elements that describe the results of the processes a learning organization puts in place, given the *inputs.* In other words, the outcomes we get are dependent upon the processes we employ for whom we have as students and teachers. District and school *outcomes* include—

- Student achievement results *(Student Learning)*
- Student and teacher attendance *(Demographics)*
- Student behaviors *(Demographics)*
- Student attitudes *(Perceptions)*
- Teacher attitudes *(Perceptions)*
- Graduation rates, dropout rates *(Demographics)*
- Student careers *(Demographics)*
- Student success in college *(Demographics)*
- Parent-community attitudes *(Perceptions)*
- District/school climate *(Perceptions)*

Summary: Focusing the Data

It is important to pull together systematic and comprehensive data analyses, and keep it up to date over time. However, data analysis should not be about just gathering data. It is very easy to get *analysis paralysis* by spending time pulling data together and not spending time using the data. District-level data analyses should be about helping districts understand if the district and the schools within the district are achieving their guiding principles and meeting the needs of all students—and, if not, why not?

The guiding principles include the vision, created from the mission/purpose of the district and built from the values and beliefs of the district/school community, and standards—what we expect students to know and be able to do. Data analysis must focus on these guiding principles.

A focused data analysis process will enhance continuous improvement processes and provide comprehensive information about how the district is doing in relationship to its guiding principles.

A good way to avoid analysis paralysis is to consider using the input, process, outcome schema (Figure 2.3), or key questions that focus on the guiding principles, using the answers to these questions to guide your analyses.

The key questions used in this book are described in Chapter 3. The data we gather and analyze target the guiding principles of the district to achieve focused improvement. If this was not the case, the process could lead to nothing more than random acts of improvement, as shown in Figure 2.4.

These analyses flow comfortably from questions that administrators and staff naturally ask to learn if the purpose is being met. The good news is that, by looking at trends of the intersected four measures, the district and schools will have the same information required of program evaluations and needs analyses. These intersections can tell districts just about everything they would want to know, and the intersections are easy for everyone to understand.

Figure 2.4

Focusing the Data

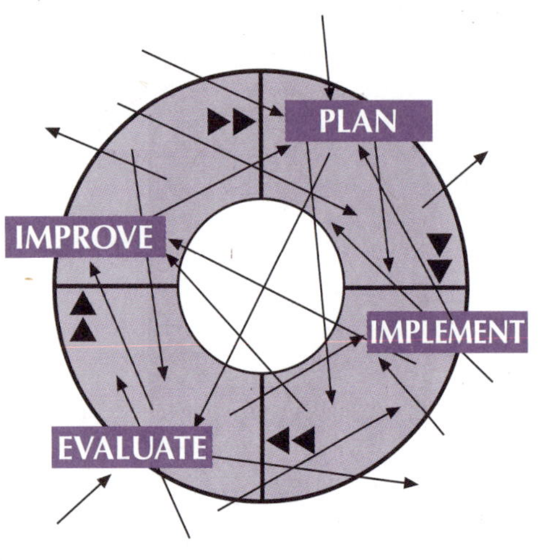

Random Acts of Improvement

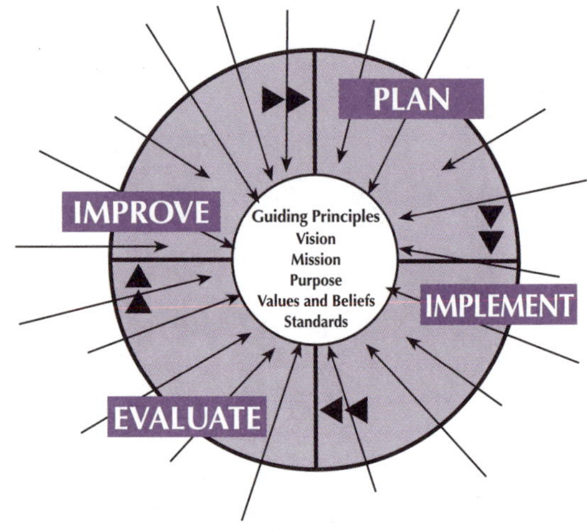

Focused Improvement

Study Questions for What Data Are Important?

As mentioned previously, the study questions at the end of the chapters are intended to guide your thinking about your own data analysis and/or to analyze the example district's results. CD-ROM (Ch2Qs.pdf) Take some time to consider these or other questions to get the maximum benefit from this publication.

Consider how you might identify intersections in your district's data and what those intersections could tell you. Use the spaces below to write at least one question you can answer about your school district with these intersections, and what data you need to answer these questions. (Examples appear in the table to get you started.)

Intersections	Questions	What data do you have or need to answer the questions?
Demographics by Student Learning D / SP / P / SL	*Is there a relationship between attendance and state assessment test results?*	*Number of days attended and state assessment results for each student.*
Demographics by School Processes D / SP / P / SL	*Is participation in special education representative of all students?*	*Special education enrollment by gender, ethnicity, language fluency, and indicators of poverty.*

Study Questions for What Data Are Important? (Continued)

Intersections	Questions	What data do you have or need to answer the questions?
Perceptions by Demographics 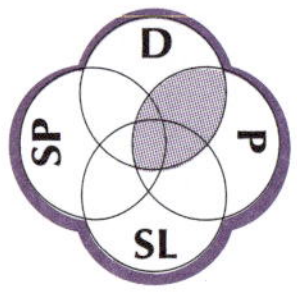	*Are all students perceiving the learning environment in the same way?*	*Student questionnaire results disaggregated by gender, by ethnicity, by grade level, and by school.*
Perceptions by Student Learning 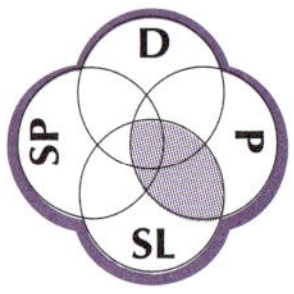	*Are the students who are getting the best grades the happiest with the learning environment?*	*Student grades by student perceptions.*
Perceptions by School Processes 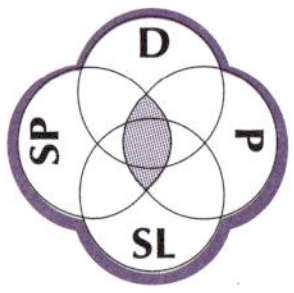	*Are there differences in how students perceive the learning environment, based on what school they attend?*	*Student perceptions disaggregated by school.*

Intersections	Questions	What data do you have or need to answer the questions?
Student Learning by School Processes 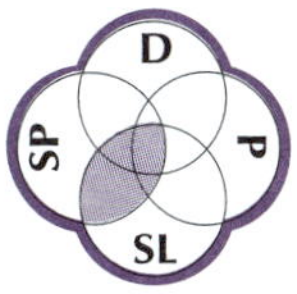	*Is there a difference in student achievement results by school?*	*Student achievement test results by school.*
Demographics by Perceptions by Student Learning 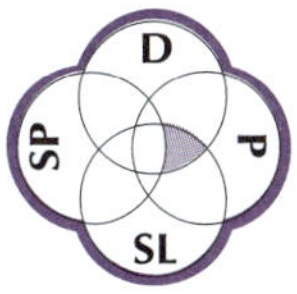	*What are the differences in student learning results based on whom we have as students and how they perceive the learning environment?*	*Student achievement test results disaggregated by gender and ethnicity, compared to student questionnaire results disaggregated by gender and ethnicity.*
Perceptions by Demographics by School Processes 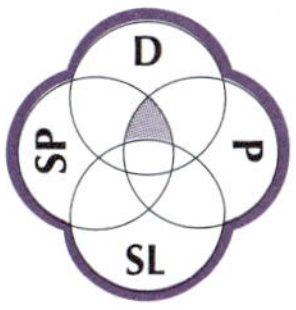	*Are the students most satisfied with school being taught differently from students not satisfied with school, and who are they?*	*Student questionnaires disaggregated by gender, ethnicity, grade level, and program participation, sorted by school.*

Study Questions for What Data Are Important? (Continued)

Intersections	Questions	What data do you have or need to answer the questions?
Perceptions by Student Learning by School Processes 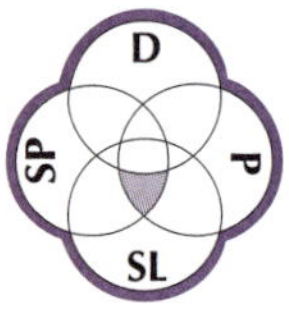	*What are the differences in student achievement results because of attitudes related to where they attend school?*	*Student achievement results disaggregated by school, compared to student questionnaire results disaggregated by school.*
Demographics by Student Learning by School Processes 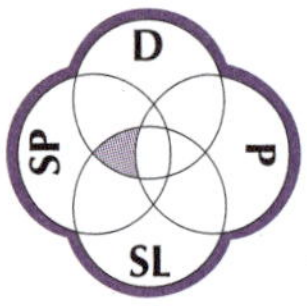	*What are the differences in student learning results based on who the students are and how they are taught to read?*	*Student achievement reading results, disaggregated by gender and ethnicity, and sorted by school.*
Student Learning by Demographics by Perceptions by School Processes 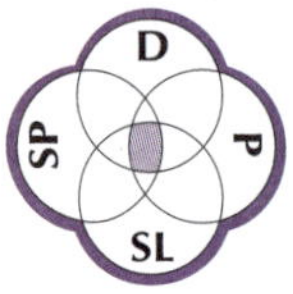	*What are the differences in the results we are getting, based on whom we have as students and how they are being taught? How would they prefer to learn?*	*Student achievement results, disaggregated by gender, ethnicity, grade level, and school, compared to student questionnaire results, disaggregated by gender, ethnicity, grade level, and school.*

Summary

Districts cannot use student achievement measures alone for continuous improvement. Why? Because the *context* is missing! Relying on only one measure can mislead districts into thinking they are analyzing student learning in a comprehensive fashion. Just looking at student learning measures alone could, in fact, keep districts, schools, and teachers from progressing and truly meeting the needs of students because they are not looking at the other elements that have a great impact on student learning and teaching.

If we want to get different results, we have to change the processes (e.g., instruction, system) that create the results. When we focus only on student learning measures, we see personnel using their time figuring out how to look better on the student learning measures. We want district and school personnel to use their time to determine how to *do* better for *all* students. In order to do that, we must look at intersections of *demographic, perceptual, student learning,* and *school process* data so we can understand the inter-relationships among these elements.

Just looking at student learning measures alone could, in fact, keep schools and teachers from progressing and truly meeting the needs of students, because they are not looking at the other elements that have a great impact on student learning and teaching.

On the CD Related to this Chapter

- *Multiple Measures of Data* Graphic (MMgraphc.pdf)
  This is Figure 2.1 in a PDF (portable document file) for printing.
- *Summary of Data Intersections* (IntrscTbl.pdf)
  This is Figure 2.2 in a PDF for your use with staff.
- *Data Discovery Activity* (ACTDiscv.pdf)
  The purpose of this activity is to look closely at examples of data and to discover specific information and patterns of information, both individually and as a group.
- *Intersections Activity* (ACTIntrs.pdf)
  The purpose of this activity is to motivate improvement teams to think about the questions they can answer when they cross different data variables. It is also designed to help teams focus their data-gathering efforts so they are not collecting everything and anything.
- *Creating Intersections Activity* (ACTCreat.pdf)
  This activity is similar to the *Intersections Activity.* The purpose is to have participants "grow" their intersections.
- *Data Analysis* Presentation (DASlides.ppt)
  This *Microsoft PowerPoint* presentation is an overview to use with your staffs in getting started with data analysis.

- Articles (Folder)

  These read-only articles, by Victoria L. Bernhardt, are useful in workshops or in getting started on data with staff.

  - *Multiple Measures* (MMeasure.pdf)

    This article summarizes why, and what, data are important to continuous district and school improvement.

  - *Intersections: New Routes Open when One Type of Data Crosses Another* (Intersct.pdf)

    This article, published in the *Journal of Staff Development* (Winter 2000), discusses how much richer your data analyses can be when you intersect multiple data variables.

  - *No Schools Left Behind* (NoSchls.pdf)

    This article, published in *Educational Leadership* (February 2003), summarizes how to improve learning for *all* students.

  - *It Takes More Than Test Scores* (TestScores.pdf)

    This article by Victoria L. Bernhardt, published in *ACSA Leadership* (Nov/Dec 2004), summarizes why analyzing state assessment results is only the beginning of effective data-driven decision making.

- Input/Process/Output (IPO) Diagram (IPODiagrm.pdf)

  This is Figure 2.3 in a PDF file that shows different types of data in terms of *input, process,* and *outcome.* This diagram helps us know why it is important to analyze all of these data. This read-only file is the handout graphic that goes with the *IPO Activity* (below).

- Input/Process/Output (IPO) Activity (ACTIPO.pdf)

  This is an activity that allows staffs to determine if different data elements are *input, process,* or *outcome* elements. With this activity, you will also need the *headings* and *elements* files below.

  - *IPO Headings* (IPOHead.pdf)

    This file contains the three *headings* to print and cut into strips for use when doing the *Input/Process/Output Activity* with staffs.

  - *IPO Elements* (IPOElem.pdf)

    This file contains the data *elements* to print and cut into strips for use when doing the *Input/Process/Output Activity* with staffs.

- Study Questions Related to *What Data are Important?* (Ch2Qs.doc)

  These study questions will help you understand the information provided in Chapter 2. This file can be printed for use with staffs as they think through the data questions they want to answer and the data they will need to gather to answer the questions.

Getting Started

On Data Analysis for Continuous Improvement

Chapter 3

We want to gather and analyze data that will help us understand the system that produces the results we are getting. We also want to move our district continuous improvement efforts from random acts of improvement to focused improvement that centers on our ultimate purpose—improving learning for all students.

How does a district get started with comprehensive data analysis work? How do you and others in your district know if what you are currently doing for students is making a difference with respect to what you expect students to know and be able to do? How do you know which strategies ought to be the focus of your district improvement efforts?

If your district is like 95% of the districts in this country, my hunch is that everyone on staff knows how to look at the state assessment results. But does your staff know which programs are working and which ones are not, across the district? Does staff know attendance, discipline, and retention rates and their relationship to student learning results? Is the manner in which students are placed into different programs consistent throughout the district?

We want to see data about all parts of the district and schools gathered and analyzed on a regular basis—not just when an external force requires it. We want members of the district community to understand how to use data to accurately inform their customers and other individuals of how the district and schools are doing. Finally, we especially want districts to analyze data to understand which strategies are not working and what to do differently to get different results.

This chapter describes a process for analyzing data at the district level. Data analysis in districts may be approached in many ways, and the effectiveness of district and school processes may be measured in many ways. The approach taken here is a systems approach: we want to gather and analyze data that will help districts understand the *system that produces the results they are getting.* We also want to move improvement efforts from random acts of improvement to focused improvement that centers on our ultimate purpose—improving learning for *all* students.

Analyzing Data Using a Continuous Improvement Planning Model

Data analysis is very logical. We need to think about what we want to know and why, gather the data we have or need, and analyze the data to answer the questions that will lead to understanding not only the effectiveness of what we are doing, but also what we need to do differently to get different results.

One approach to data analysis is to analyze and use data for continuous improvement planning. The *Multiple Measures of Data,* Figure 2.1 in Chapter 2, can be reorganized into a series of logical questions that can guide the analysis, as illustrated in the flowchart in Figure 3.1. If the data that are listed next to the questions in the boxes were gathered satisfactorily, one would be on the right track toward discovering how to continuously improve the district and schools within the district. Those questions, the data required, and discussion follow the flowchart.

Continuous Improvement Planning Via a District or School Portfolio

Figure 3.1 shows the logical questions one could ask to plan for continuous district improvement, the data needed to answer the questions, and where that data would be housed if a district or school was creating a district or school portfolio. CD-ROM (CSIPlang.pdf and CSIdscr.pdf) *The School Portfolio* is a framework for continuous school improvement (Bernhardt, 1999). A district portfolio, using the same process, can gather evidence in seven categories, tell the story of the district, and become a self-assessment. The seven categories of a district/school portfolio are:

- Information and Analysis
- Student Achievement
- Quality Planning
- Leadership
- Professional Development
- Partnership Development
- Continuous Improvement and Evaluation

On the CD is a *Microsoft PowerPoint* slideshow overview file, *The School Portfolio Presentation,* to use with your staffs in getting started on a district or school portfolio. CD-ROM (SPSlides.ppt)

Figure 3.1

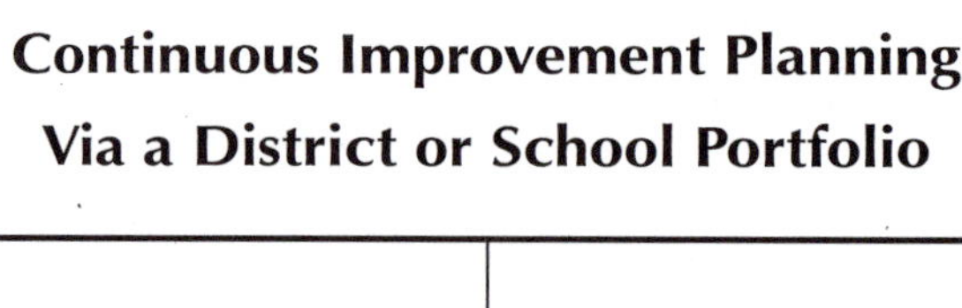

Who are we?
Demographics
- District
- Schools
- Students
- Staffs
- Community

How do we do business?
Perceptions
- Culture
- Climate
- Processes

Values & Beliefs

Where are we now?
Results
Strengths
Areas for Improvement

Information & Analysis

Why do we exist?
Purpose
Mission

Where do we want to be?
Vision
Goals
Objectives
Standards
State Vision & Goals
Federal Vision & Goals

Student Achievement

What are the gaps?
Difference between where we are now and where we want to be

How can we get to where we want to be?
Root Cause Analysis
Action Plan
Strategies
Activities
Finances

How will we implement?
Implementation Strategies

Quality Planning

Leadership
Professional Development
Partnership Development

How will we evaluate our efforts?

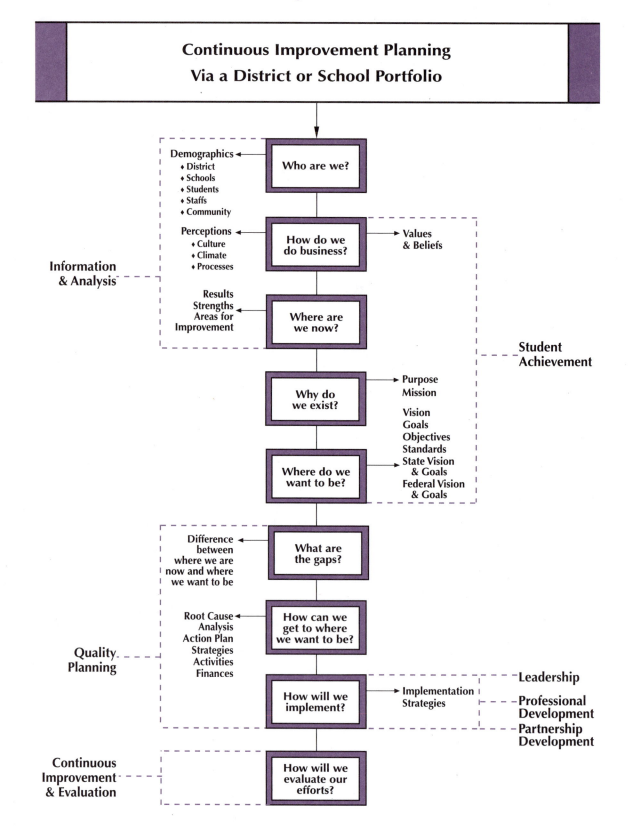

Continuous Improvement & Evaluation

Question 1: Who are we?

Continuous improvement planning begins by asking a question that can be answered with demographic data: *Who are we?* Specifically—

- *How is the district organized?*
- *How are our schools organized?*
- *Who are the students?*
- *Who is the staff?*
- *Who is the community?*

The answers to the first questions are important in understanding the district's organization, schools, students, staffs, and community, to determine future needs. These answers are critical for continuous improvement planning, as they establish the *context* of the district, schools, classrooms, and community. This is part of the *input* into the equation. It is important to understand how student and community populations have changed over time, as these changes are indicators of student characteristics to plan for in the future. Staff longevity within the system and plans for retirement might lead to establishing different types of improvement plans or assignments, as would staff experiences, certification, and levels of education. Demographic changes can also help explain results. This question is further studied in Chapter 4.

Question 2: How do we do business?

The second question, *How do we do business?*, is answered through data gathered to assess the district and school culture, climate, and organizational processes. Perceptual data, district and school processes, and values and beliefs fall into this category. Staff values and beliefs, most often assessed through questionnaires and/or determined during visioning processes, can tell a staff what is possible to implement and if team building or specific professional learning is necessary. Student and parent questionnaires can add different perspectives to the answers generated from staff data. An assessment on the *Education for the Future Continuous Improvement Continuums*[1] can provide an overview of where the staff believes the district or schools are, and where they can go with respect to continuous improvement. Chapter 5 reviews more on this question.

[1] *Note:* The *Education for the Future Continuous Improvement Continuums* (CICs) for districts and schools can be found in the back of this book (Appendices B and C) and on the accompanying CD. The CICs are a type of assessment rubric made up of seven key, interrelated, and overlapping components of systemic change, representing the theoretical flow of systemic district and/or school improvement. The *Continuums* take the theory and spirit of continuous improvement, interweave educational research, and offer practical meaning to the components that must change simultaneously and systemically. A CIC district analysis appears in Chapter 5.

If you don't know where you are going, you could wind up somewhere else.

Yogi Berra

Question 3: Where are we now?

The third data question, *Where are we now?,* requires a synthesis of student learning, perceptual, demographic, and school process data to describe results and to uncover strengths and areas for improvement. We examine data for patterns and trends across the four multiple measures. Chapter 6 reviews the student learning part of this question, including different types of student learning assessments and terms associated with them.

Question 4: Why do we exist?

Question number four, *Why do we exist?,* can be answered by determining the purpose/mission of the district. One can determine how well the district is meeting its purpose by revisiting the results collected in questions one through three. How to create a mission is discussed in-depth in other resources, such as, *The School Portfolio* (Bernhardt, 1999), and *The School Portfolio Toolkit* (Bernhardt, 2002).

Question 5: Where do we want to be?

A district defines its destination through its vision, goals, and standards. The district's destination falls under the umbrella of the state vision, goals, and standards; and, of course, the federal vision, goals, and mandates. One can determine how effective the vision is being implemented through the data used to answer questions one through four. This question is answered in-depth in other resources, such as, *The School Portfolio* (Bernhardt, 1999), and *The School Portfolio Toolkit* (Bernhardt, 2002).

Question 6: What are the gaps?

Gaps are the differences between *Where are we now?* and *Where do we want to be?* Gaps are determined by synthesizing the differences in the results the district/schools are getting with their current processes, and the results the district/schools want to be getting for their students. It is important to dig deeply into each gap to uncover root causes, or the gap cannot be eliminated. Gaps and root causes are studied in Chapter 7.

Question 7: How can we get to where we want to be?

The answer to *How can we get to where we want to be?* is key to unlocking how the vision will be implemented, and how gaps will be eliminated. An action plan, consisting of strategies, activities, people responsible, due dates, timelines, and resources, needs to be addressed to implement and achieve the vision and goals and to eliminate the root causes of the gaps. Chapter 8 shows how one can take the data analysis results and turn them into a continuous improvement plan.

Question 8: How will we implement?

This question is answered in the action plan. The action plan includes how the vision will be implemented, monitored, evaluated, and improved. Strategic plans need to clarify how decisions will be made, identify professional learning required to learn new skills and gain new knowledge, and clarify the use of partners to achieve the vision. A district's leadership structure, professional development strategies, and partnership development plan are important components of the answer to this question. Chapter 8 discusses what a plan would look like when it includes action for implementing, monitoring, evaluating, and improving the action plan.

Question 9: How will we evaluate our efforts?

Continuous Improvement and Evaluation are required to assess the alignment of all parts of the system to the vision and the results the learning organization is getting on an ongoing basis. All four data measures intersected to answer this question will assist with evaluating the continuously improving learning organization. Evaluation is a piece that needs to be built before implementation, not only at the end, to know if what the district and schools are doing is making a real difference. How the action plan will be evaluated is a part of the plan which can be pulled out, enhanced, and monitored. This piece is described in Chapter 8.

The chapters that follow show how one district answered the first six questions with data as it conducted data analyses and created its continuous improvement plan.

Study Questions for Getting Started

How will you get started with your district's continuous improvement planning? What data do you have, or need to gather, to answer the questions discussed in this chapter? Fill in the blank cells in the tables that follow to guide your work. CD-ROM (Ch3Qs.pdf) Examples appear in the table for guidance.

Questions	What data do you have or need to answer the questions?	What other data do you have or need to gather?
Who are we?	*Student enrollment by grade, by gender, by ethnicity, by free/reduced lunch status, for six years, for the district and by school.* *Number of teachers; number of years teaching by what grade level(s) and/or subject(s) they teach; which credentials teachers hold.*	Information about predicted community changes. Administrator information, such as number of years in current positions.
How do we do business?	*Perceptions: student, staff, parent, and former student questionnaires, for each school.* *Education for the Future Continuous Improvement Continuums Assessment.* *Organizational Learning Questionnaire for the district.*	
Where are we now?	*Student achievement results.* *Process data.*	

Questions	What data do you have or need to answer the questions?	What other data do you have or need to gather?
Why do we exist?	*Mission statement.* *Purpose of the district.*	
Where do we want to be?	*Vision.* *Goals.*	
What are the gaps? What are the root causes?	*Number and percentage of students not proficient in each subject area, sorted by school.* *Characteristics of the schools and students not meeting proficiency.* *How these students scored.* *What they know and do not know.* *How they were taught.*	

Study Questions for Getting Started (Continued)

Questions	What data do you have or need to answer the questions?	What other data do you have or need to gather?
How can we get to where we want to be?	*Changing what processes/programs get implemented.* *Professional Learning.* *Timeline.*	
How will we implement?	*Implementation strategies.* *Leadership structure.* *How we meet together to talk about the vision.*	
How will we evaluate our efforts?	*Rethinking our results data.* *Monitoring and evaluating the plan.* *Understanding the effectiveness of strategies already in place.*	

Summary

Districts that are not gathering, analyzing, and using comprehensive data in purposeful ways need to transform their thinking about data and start gathering, analyzing, and using data purposefully. Comprehensive data analyses focused on the continuous improvement of the entire learning organization will result in a continuous improvement plan that will improve learning for all students in all schools within the district.

Comprehensive data analyses focused on the continuous improvement of the entire learning organization will result in continuous improvement plans that will improve learning for all students.

Logical questions can be used to guide the gathering, analysis, and use of data. Recommended questions include:

- *Who are we?*
- *How do we do business?*
- *Where are we now?*
- *Why do we exist?*
- *Where do we want to be?*
- *What are the gaps?* and *What are the root causes?*
- *How can we get to where we want to be?*
- *How will we implement?*
- *How will we evaluate our efforts?*

On the CD Related to this Chapter

- *Continuous Improvement Planning Via a School or District Portfolio* Graphic (CSIPlang.pdf)
  This read-only file displays the questions that can be answered to create a continuous improvement plan. The data that can answer the questions, and where the answers would appear in a school or district portfolio, also appear on the graphic. In the book, it is Figure 3.1.
- *Continuous Improvement Planning Via a School or District Portfolio* Description (CSIdscr.pdf)
  This read-only file shows Figure 3.1, along with its description.
- *The School Portfolio Presentation* (SPSlides.ppt)
  This *PowerPoint* presentation is an overview to use with your staffs in getting started on a school or district portfolio.
- *Overview: The School Portfolio* (Overview.pdf)
  This read-only file summarizes what the school portfolio is, what it does, and describes the purposes for each of the sections of the school portfolio.
- *Purposes and Uses of a School Portfolio* (Purposes.pdf)
  This read-only file describes the purposes and uses for a school or district portfolio.
- Study Questions Related to *Getting Started* (Ch3Qs.doc)
  These study questions will help you understand the information provided in Chapter 3. This file can be printed for use with staffs as they begin continuous improvement planning. Answering the questions will help staff determine the data needed to answer the questions discussed in this chapter.

Analyzing the Data:

Who Are We?

Chapter 4

Demographic data are required to answer the question, "Who are we?"

Using the continuous district/school improvement planning model described in Chapter 3, our data analysis example begins with setting the context of the district by answering the question, *Who are we?* Demographic data are required to answer this question. Demographic data enable us to:

- *explain* and *understand* the district's context and results
- *disaggregate* other types of data, such as perceptual, process, and student learning data, to ensure all students are being served
- *predict* and *prepare* for the students we will have in the near future

In this chapter, you meet Canyon View School District with approximately 8,000 students, in 11 elementary, 2 middle, and 2 high schools. You will follow Canyon View's data throughout the rest of this book. Just in case Canyon View's size is different from your district's size, on the CD are templates for three additional case studies—

Three Rivers School District	30,941 students: 31 elementary, 8 middle, and 6 high schools
Table Mountain School District	1,373 students: 1 elementary, 1 middle, and 1 high school
Beachfront School District	180 students: 1 school (K-12)

Four different size districts are provided so you can build your own profile using templates from a district much like your own. Feel free to use any or all of these districts' stories as you think about what data you have and what it would look like if you analyzed these data in your own school district.

The table on the next page shows the number and percentage of districts in the United States by size, and the percentage of students represented at each district size as of 2001-02. One can see that although less than six percent of the districts in the country house more than 10,000 students, their populations represent over half of the country's students. Thirty-five per cent of the districts fall between 1,500 and 9,999, representing 39% of the student population. About 60% (8,443) of the districts in the country have fewer than 1,500 students. Of that 60%, 38% have between 1,499 and 300 students, while 22% (3,127 districts) have fewer than 300 students.

Distribution of Regular Public School Districts and Students, 2001-02
NCES Statistical Analysis Report of District Membership Size

District Membership Size	Number of Districts	Percentage of Districts	Percentage of Students
United States	14,229	100%	100%
100,000 or more	25	0.2%	12.5%
25,000 to 99,999	218	1.5%	20.2%
10,000 to 24,999	573	4.0%	18.7%
7,500 to 9,999	342	2.4%	6.3%
5,000 to 7,499	725	5.1%	9.4%
2,500 to 4,999	2,031	14.3%	15.2%
2,000 to 2,499	801	5.6%	3.8%
1,500 to 1,999	1,071	7.5%	4.0%
1,000 to 1,499	1,557	10.9%	4.1%
800 to 999	790	5.6%	1.5%
600 to 799	954	6.7%	1.4%
450 to 599	897	6.3%	1.0%
300 to 449	1,118	7.9%	0.9%
150 to 299	1,435	10.1%	0.7%
1 to 149	1,692	11.9%	0.2%

Note: Table includes the 50 states and the District of Columbia, and excludes 330 regular school districts for which no students were reported in membership. Detail may not sum to total because of rounding.

Source: U.S. Department of Education, National Center for Education Statistics, Common Core of Data (CCD), "Local Education Agency Universe Survey," 2001-02.

Adapted from *National Center for Education Statistics,* Institute of Education Sciences, U.S. Department of Education, 1990 K St., N.W., Washington, DC 20006.

The demographic analyses for Canyon View School District are on the pages that follow. Please note the study questions on page 105 to assist in studying the district's data. CD-ROM (Ch4Qs.doc) Also note that space is provided in the margins of the data pages to write your impressions about *strengths, challenges,* and *implications for the continuous improvement plan* as you review the data. It will help your work if you jot down your thoughts about what you are seeing in the data as you read. These first thoughts are placeholders until additional data validate the thoughts. When finished reading this chapter, think about other demographic data you wish the district would have had. At the end of the chapter, I share what I saw in the data, as well as typical demographic data that districts and schools have. Graphing templates are found on the CD-ROM to help you create your district's demographic profile. CD-ROM (DistrDemog.xls and DistrProfil.doc)

With so many charts and graphs, looking at district data can be mind-boggling. In addition to the study questions at the end of the chapter, above the graphs are some "Look Fors" and "Planning Implications" to assist you with the interpretation of the case study data and to provide reasons your district needs to pull these data together.

Demographic data set the context for understanding student learning results. Demographics also indicate how the district is set up to serve its clients. As you read and consider the data, consider the connections across the data elements as well.

Our Example District: Canyon View School District

Who Are We?

Canyon View School District is located in a major U.S. mountain range. The city in which the district is located is a hub of education and healthcare with a population of about 26,000. The county population is approximately 58,000, and the ethnicity is primarily White, with just under 5% representing Hispanic, Black, Native American, and other ethnicities. Over 91% of its residents have graduated from high school. Forty-four percent have some post-secondary education. The economy in this area is stable and viable. Unemployment is one of the lowest in the U.S. Average median household income in the county was just over $34,000 in 2000, with approximately 15% of the population classified as "below poverty." Many local, state, and federal agencies are located in the area, making the employment primarily in the government sector. Principal employment in the area includes federal, local, and state governments, colleges, agricultural operations, and various industrial, manufacturing, and commercial businesses. The work force is mostly professionals, white-collar workers, and employees of small business. The area has ready access to freight rail and airline services. The Regional Airport is only a few miles from the city center. The airport's modern facilities and the prevailing weather conditions make it the most reliable departure/arrival point in the state.

The school district, with an enrollment of just under 8,000, includes two high schools, one alternative high school, two middle schools, and 11 elementary schools. The district has total revenues of over $58 million, with 49% coming from local sources, 48% from the state, and 2% from the federal government. The district spends $7,377 per student. The district employs a staff of nearly 500. Canyon View School District has a long tradition of excellence in all areas—academics, the arts, technology, and sports. The schools encourage parental participation. More than 90% of middle school parents and 95% of elementary school parents routinely appear for parent/teacher conferences. The schools in the district currently have 30 school/business partnerships. High school students annually become involved in 14 major extracurricular activities. Scholarships and awards granted to graduating seniors reach well over $3 million annually. Approximately 57% of graduating seniors go on to four-year colleges or universities; another 22% go to two-year colleges, trade schools, or the military.

Canyon View School District

Canyon View School District currently serves 7,909 students. The overall district enrollment has decreased 13 students from six years ago, with fluctuations up and down in the intervening years. The highest district enrollment was 8,114 in 2002-03 (Figure 4.1), 205 more students than in 2005-06.

Look Fors:	**Increasing, steady, or decreasing enrollment.**
Planning Implications:	**Is there a need to expand or decrease facilities, services, and/or staff?**

Figure 4.1

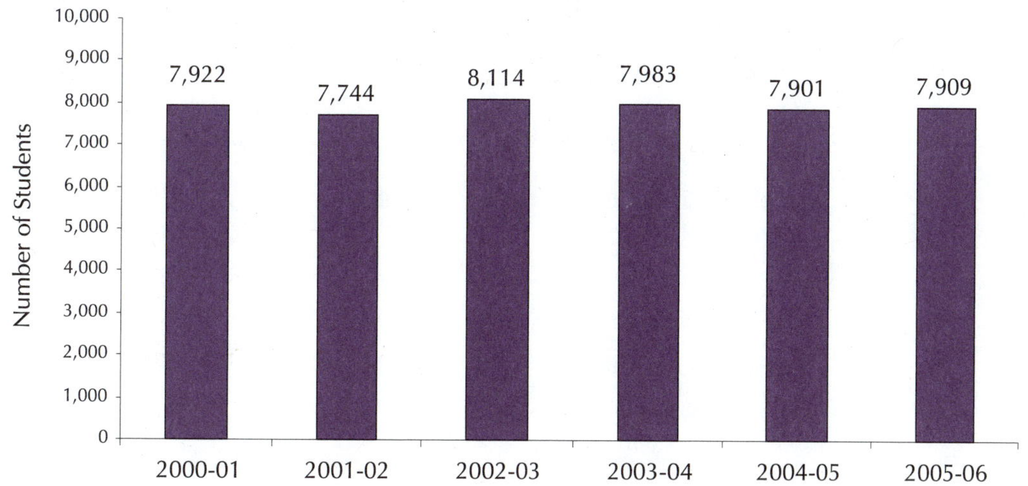

Traditionally, there have been more males than females enrolled at Canyon View School District. In fact, for each of the past six years, the district enrollment has been 49% female and 51% male (Figure 4.2).

Look Fors:	**More of one gender than the other.**
Planning Implications:	**Do instructional strategies and programs meet the needs of all students? Do teachers have the knowledge and skills to reach all students?**

Figure 4.2

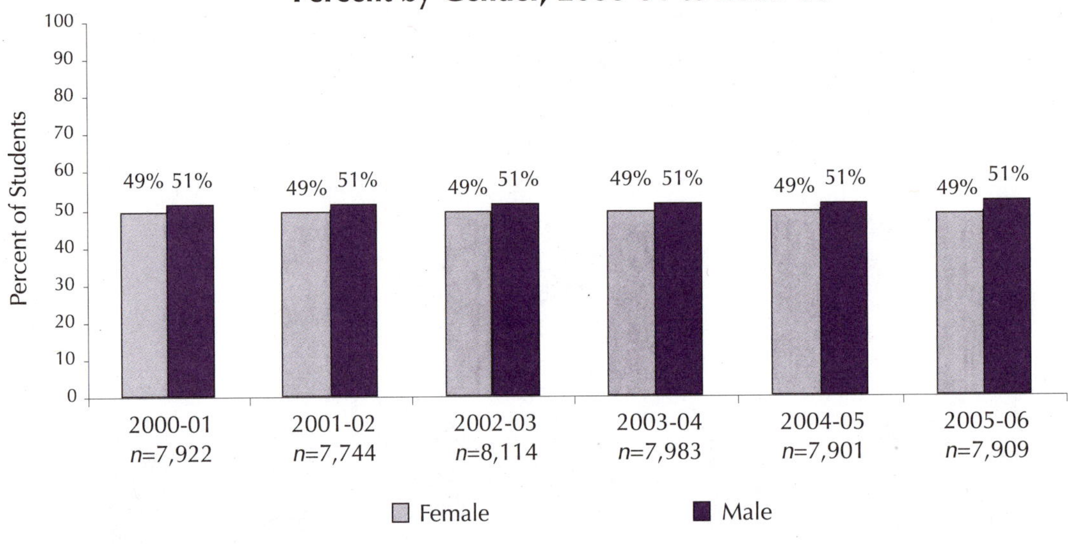

As shown in Figure 4.3, the current district student population consists of: 7,185 Whites (90.8%), 417 American Indians (5.3%), 137 Hispanics (1.7%), 98 Asians (1.2%), 65 Blacks (0.8%), and 7 Pacific Islanders (0.1%).

Look Fors:	**Degree of diversity in the district population.**
Planning Implications:	**Are teachers prepared to meet the needs of students from all backgrounds? Are instructional materials geared for all students? Is there a need for diversity programs?**

Figure 4.3

Canyon View School District
Student Enrollment by Percent Ethnicity[1]
2005-06 (N=7,909)

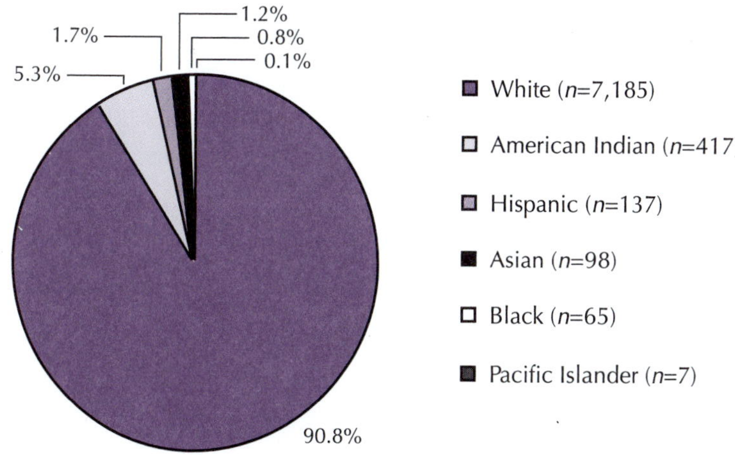

[1]The ethnicity/race categories used here, i.e., Black, White, Hispanic/Latino, Asian, are the federal categories used by this district and hopefully will not offend any ethnicity or race.

The percentage of White students has decreased steadily from 95.2% (n=7,534) in 2000-01 to 90.8% (n=7,185) in 2005-06. The percentage of American Indian students increased from 2.7% (n=211) to 5.3% (n=417) over the six years. The numbers of Hispanic, Asian, Pacific Islander, and Black students have remained comparatively small, although their percentages have slightly increased in recent years (Figure 4.4).

Look Fors: **Changes in diversity over time.**

Planning Implications: **Is staff equipped to meet the needs of a changing population? Do instructional materials meet the needs of all the district's students?**

Figure 4.4

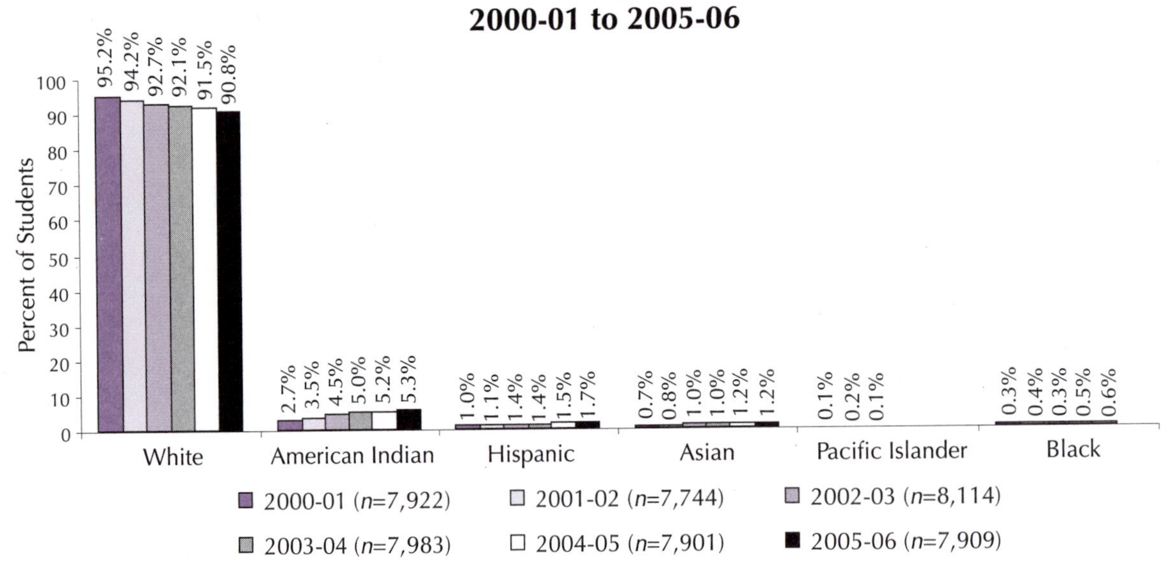

One can also see the grade-level population of this district attendance area over the last six years in Figures 4.5 and 4.6. In 2001-02, the Pre-K program was dropped because of lost funding, so pre-K and K figures for 2001-02 on are for Kindergarten only.

Note: Looking at the same grade level over time is called *grade level analysis. Also note:* The total Ns may not match across all graphs as the enrollment varies, depending upon the time of year the data were reported.

Look Fors:	**Consistency of numbers within and across grade levels.**
Planning Implications:	**Is there mobility within the district? Are enrollment fluctuations indicators of satisfaction with the services provided?**

Figure 4.5

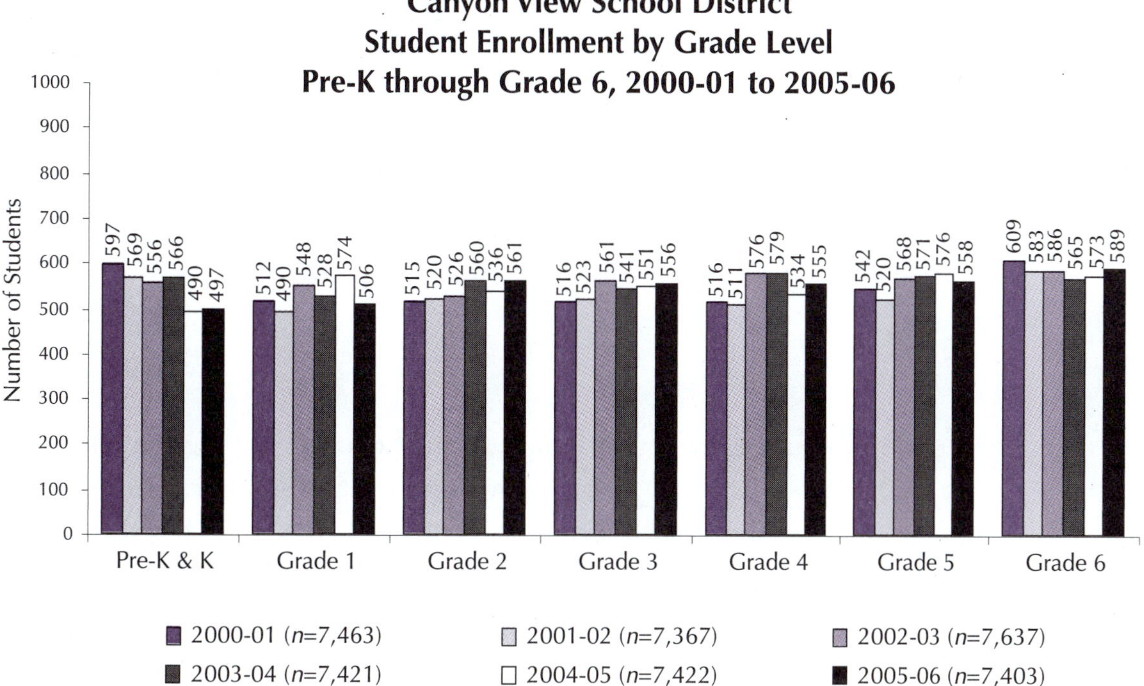

One can see the enrollment increase starting in grade nine (Figure 4.6). High schools get about 250 students from outside the district—mostly from a small rural K-8 district that feeds into Canyon View High Schools. The demographic characteristics of these students are similar to those of other students'.

Figure 4.6

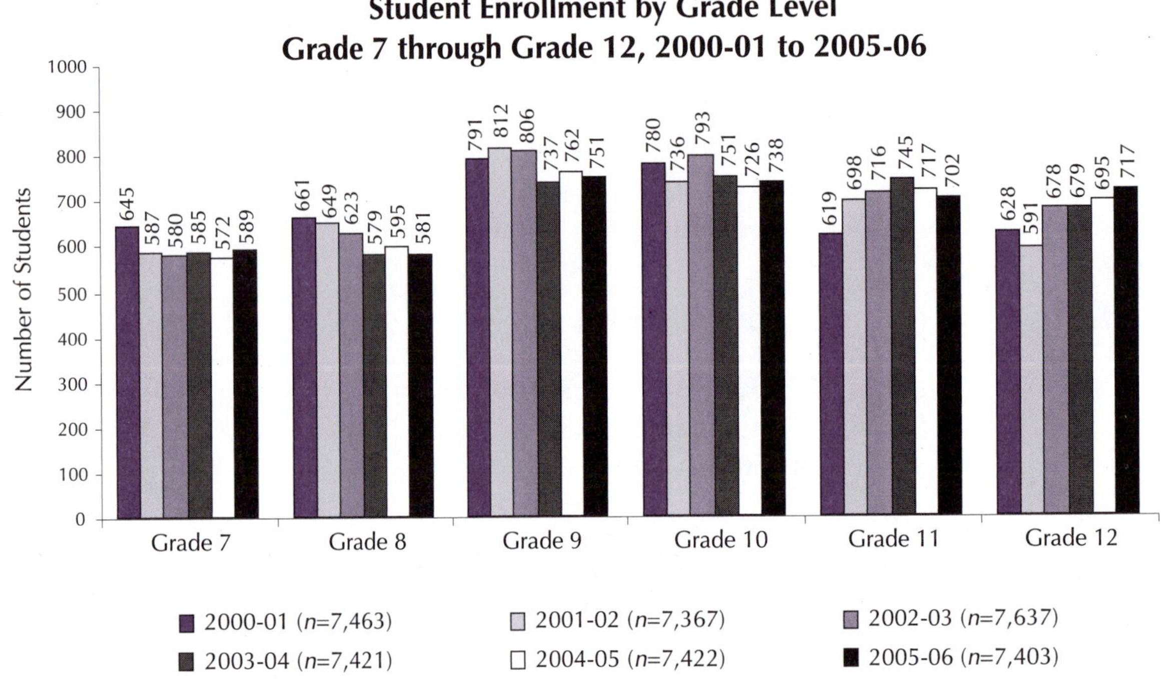

Reorganizing the data in Figures 4.5 and 4.6 to look at the groups of students progressing through the grades over time is called a *cohort analysis* (Figure 4.7 and 4.8). If we were looking at the same students (as opposed to the groups of students), the analyses would be called *matched cohort analyses.* The overall mobility rate for this district is calculated to be 17% and is further discussed later in this section.

Look Fors:	**Consistency in numbers within cohorts.**
Planning Implications:	**Are additional programs needed, including services to welcome new students to the school system? Does the district understand the mobility?**

Cohort A: Pre-K and K 2000-01, grade one 2001-02, grade two 2002-03, grade three 2001-02, grade four 2004-05, grade five 2005-06.

Cohort B: Grade one 2000-01, grade two 2001-02, grade three 2002-03, grade four 2001-02, grade five 2004-05, grade six 2005-06.

Cohort C: Grade two 2000-01, grade three 2001-02, grade four 2002-03, grade five 2001-02, grade six 2004-05, grade seven 2005-06.

Cohort D: Grade three 2000-01, grade four 2001-02, grade five 2002-03, grade six 2001-02, grade seven 2004-05, grade eight 2005-06.

Figure 4.7

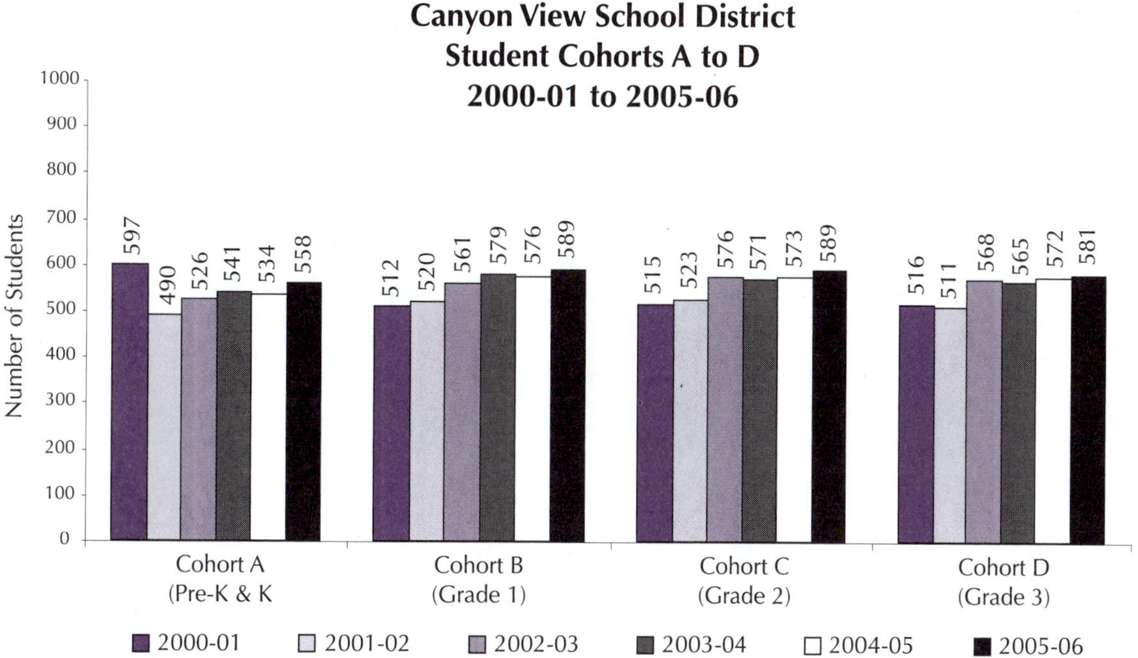

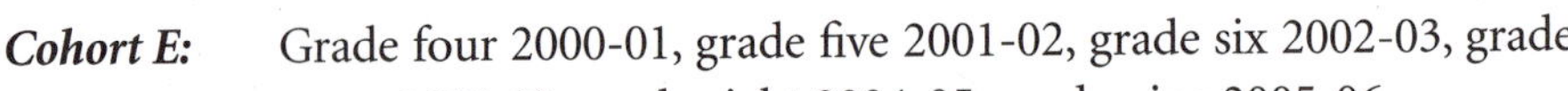

Cohort E: Grade four 2000-01, grade five 2001-02, grade six 2002-03, grade seven 2001-02, grade eight 2004-05, grade nine 2005-06.

Cohort F: Grade five 2000-01, grade six 2001-02, grade seven 2002-03, grade eight 2001-02, grade nine 2004-05, grade ten 2005-06.

Cohort G: Grade six 2000-01, grade seven 2001-02, grade eight 2002-03, grade nine 2001-02, grade ten 2004-05, grade eleven 2005-06.

Cohort H: Grade seven 2000-01, grade eight 2001-02, grade nine 2002-03, grade ten 2001-02, grade eleven 2004-05, grade twelve 2005-06.

Figure 4.8

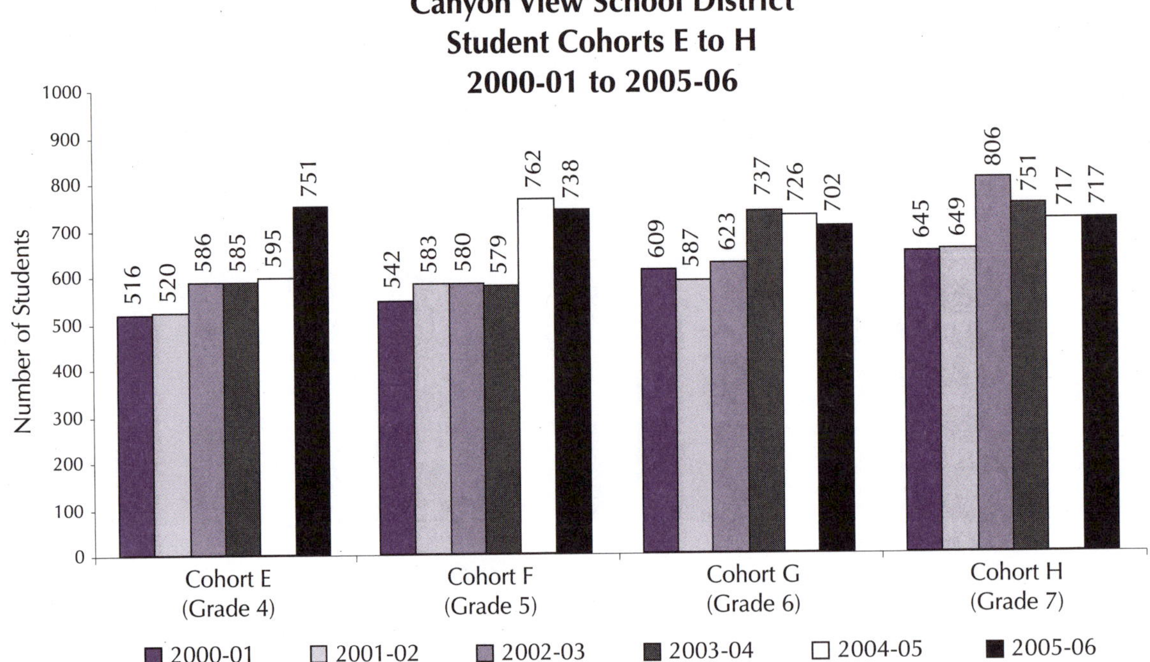

Figure 4.9 shows the number of students enrolled in Canyon View School District by type of school, school, and grade level. The names of the schools have been changed to anonymous labels. The number of *years of experience/years as principal of this school* (as of 2005-06) for each school's principal is shown below the school label. The schools with the shaded name squares in the table indicate one feeder pattern. The unshaded squares are another feeder pattern. Students go to the schools in their neighborhoods.

Because of fluctuations in enrollments during the year, we were unable to get/show reliable data for the alternative school. Therefore, this school does not appear in the remaining analyses. Building facilities are aged and well-maintained. The newest elementary school was built in the 1970's. The oldest in the 1800's. The high schools are old with additions in the 1990's.

Look Fors:	**Consistencies in enrollment within schools and grade levels, and across schools. Equal enrollment across schools. Longevity of the principals.**
Planning Implications:	**Are there enrollment fluctuations in the schools? Is there a need for boundary changes? Are the schools at capacity?**

Figure 4.9

Canyon View School District Student Enrollment By School and Grade Level, 2001-02 to 2005-06

	School	Grade Level	2001-02 (n=7,800)	2002-03 (n=8,142)	2003-04 (n=7,999)	2004-05 (n=7,922)	2005-06 (n=7,961)
ELEMENTARY	**Elementary 1** Principal Experience / Years at the School: 9 / 9 Years	Kindergarten	58	58	55	48	40
		Grade 1	45	41	41	54	45
		Grade 2	52	45	44	42	53
		Grade 3	39	48	45	43	37
		Grade 4	33	41	53	44	49
		Grade 5	47	33	43	50	46
		Total	**274**	**266**	**281**	**281**	**270**
	Elementary 2 Principal Experience / Years at the School: 12 / 12 Years	Kindergarten	32	34	42	42	46
		Grade 1	40	39	34	39	38
		Grade 2	40	38	44	33	38
		Grade 3	43	39	47	35	37
		Grade 4	38	43	47	45	35
		Grade 5	31	37	48	48	43
		Total	**225**	**230**	**263**	**242**	**238**
	Elementary 3 Principal Experience / Years at the School: 9 / 9 Years	Kindergarten	40	38	40	28	40
		Grade 1	57	52	49	47	34
		Grade 2	51	54	49	44	50
		Grade 3	47	49	58	50	48
		Grade 4	63	57	51	54	48
		Grade 5	61	67	50	48	53
		Total	**319**	**317**	**297**	**271**	**273**
	Elementary 4 Principal Experience / Years at the School: 12 / 3 Years	Kindergarten	99	91	79	79	79
		Grade 1	75	80	79	85	80
		Grade 2	80	74	82	87	89
		Grade 3	78	81	70	80	92
		Grade 4	77	78	80	73	79
		Grade 5	76	78	78	81	78
		Total	**485**	**482**	**468**	**485**	**497**
	Elementary 5 Principal Experience / Years at the School: 11 / 1 Years	Kindergarten	70	36	39	38	40
		Grade 1	38	40	36	39	40
		Grade 2	40	39	38	39	40
		Grade 3	43	44	44	44	41
		Grade 4	36	43	48	44	47
		Grade 5	38	33	47	49	53
		Total	**265**	**235**	**252**	**253**	**261**
	Elementary 6 Principal Experience / Years at the School: 9 / 2 Years	Kindergarten	38	35	38	35	33
		Grade 1	40	31	37	32	37
		Grade 2	41	39	34	34	27
		Grade 3	34	40	38	26	33
		Grade 4	49	35	39	34	30
		Grade 5	52	52	32	39	41
		Total	**254**	**232**	**218**	**200**	**201**

Figure 4.9 (Continued)

Canyon View School District Student Enrollment By School and Grade Level, 2001-02 to 2005-06

	School	Grade Level	2001-02 (*n*=7,800)	2002-03 (*n*=8,142)	2003-04 (*n*=7,999)	2004-05 (*n*=7,922)	2005-06 (*n*=7,961)
ELEMENTARY	**Elementary 7** Principal Experience / Years at the School: 1 / 1 Year	Kindergarten	41	40	40	41	41
		Grade 1	38	40	44	40	40
		Grade 2	36	38	41	44	40
		Grade 3	65	38	44	45	47
		Grade 4	52	63	40	42	43
		Grade 5	52	51	64	48	47
		Total	**284**	**270**	**273**	**260**	**258**
	Elementary 8 Principal Experience / Years at the School: 9 / 3 Years	Kindergarten		40	42	37	40
		Grade 1		40	37	40	37
		Grade 2		33	40	32	38
		Grade 3		39	37	42	32
		Grade 4		44	37	38	38
		Grade 5		50	41	39	38
		Total		**246**	**234**	**228**	**223**
	Elementary 9 Principal Experience / Years at the School: 2 / 2 Years	Kindergarten	85	90	90	53	72
		Grade 1	68	81	81	87	47
		Grade 2	79	77	81	88	86
		Grade 3	80	80	69	85	87
		Grade 4	65	80	78	68	79
		Grade 5	62	72	82	76	67
		Total	**439**	**480**	**481**	**457**	**438**
	Elementary 10 Principal Experience / Years at the School: 4 / 4 Years	Kindergarten	37	34	49	39	35
		Grade 1	52	50	44	53	53
		Grade 2	62	51	54	49	50
		Grade 3	54	56	55	46	54
		Grade 4	59	54	58	55	52
		Grade 5	52	57	48	51	53
		Total	**316**	**302**	**308**	**293**	**297**
	Elementary 11 Principal Experience / Years at the School: 9 / 3 Years	Kindergarten	69	60	52	50	40
		Grade 1	41	54	46	58	55
		Grade 2	39	38	53	44	50
		Grade 3	40	47	34	55	48
		Grade 4	40	38	47	37	54
		Grade 5	49	38	38	47	39
		Total	**278**	**275**	**270**	**291**	**286**
	Elementary All		**3,139**	**3,335**	**3,345**	**3,261**	**3,242**

Figure 4.9 (Continued)

Canyon View School District Student Enrollment By School and Grade Level, 2001-02 to 2005-06

	School	Grade Level	2001-02 (n=7,800)	2002-03 (n=8,142)	2003-04 (n=7,999)	2004-05 (n=7,922)	2005-06 (n=7,961)
MIDDLE	**Middle 1** Principal Experience / Years at the School: 16 / 10 Years	Grade 6	339	331	322	355	356
		Grade 7	337	337	338	340	373
		Grade 8	357	334	344	342	356
		Total	**1,033**	**1,002**	**1,004**	**1,037**	**1,085**
	Middle 2 Principal Experience / Years at the School: 13 / 10 Years	Grade 6	243	255	243	218	233
		Grade 7	250	240	247	232	216
		Grade 8	293	267	235	253	225
		Total	**786**	**762**	**725**	**703**	**674**
	Middle All		**1,819**	**1,764**	**1,729**	**1,740**	**1,759**
HIGH	**High 1** Principal Experience / Years at the School: 10 / 3 Years	Grade 9	357	350	342	351	360
		Grade 10	356	349	324	334	335
		Grade 11	326	336	316	308	327
		Grade 12	297	318	332	304	312
		Total	**1,336**	**1,353**	**1,314**	**1,297**	**1,334**
	High 2 Principal Experience / Years at the School: 2 / 2 Years	Grade 9	455	452	395	407	385
		Grade 10	378	435	408	378	387
		Grade 11	374	359	410	377	364
		Grade 12	296	352	338	387	391
		Total	**1,503**	**1,598**	**1,551**	**1,549**	**1,527**
	High All		**2,839**	**2,951**	**2,865**	**2,846**	**2,861**

By analyzing grade level by ethnicity and gender, one can see minor fluctuations in the number and percentage of females, males, and ethnic composition, over time, within and across grade levels (Figure 4.10).

Look Fors: **Changes in population over time within and across grade levels.**

Planning Implications: **Are programs and services appropriate for the students the district has now and will get in the future? Who is dropping out or leaving the district?**

Figure 4.10

Canyon View School District Student Enrollment By Grade Level, Ethnicity, and Gender, 2001-02 to 2005-06

Grade Level and Ethnicity		2001-02				2002-03				2003-04				2004-05				2005-06			
		Female	Male	Total	Percent	Female	Male	Total	Percent	Female	Male	Total	Percent	Female	Male	Total	Percent	Female	Male	Total	Percent
KINDERGARTEN	American Indian	7	14	21	4%	17	16	33	6%	14	9	23	4%	14	17	31	6%	10	9	19	4%
	Asian	1	1	2	0.4%	3	5	8	1%	3		3	1%	4	2	6	1%	1	4	5	1%
	Black	1	2	3	0.5%		1	1	.2%	2	2	4	1%	1	5	6	1%	3	6	9	2%
	Hispanic	4	5	9	1.6%	4	1	5	1%	3	2	5	1%	1	5	6	1%	3	4	7	1%
	White	231	300	531	93%	221	288	509	92%	248	282	530	94%	194	247	441	90%	221	243	464	92%
	Other		3	3	0.5%			0			1	1	.2%			0			2	2	.4%
	Total	**244**	**325**	**569**		**245**	**311**	**556**		**270**	**296**	**566**		**214**	**276**	**490**		**238**	**268**	**506**	
GRADE 1	American Indian	9	12	21	4%	16	17	33	6%	15	20	35	7%	16	13	29	5%	17	16	33	7%
	Asian	3	1	4	1%		1	1	.2%	3	5	8	2%	5		5	1%	5	2	7	1%
	Black	1	2	3	1%	2	2	4	1%	1	1	2	.4%	2	1	3	1%	1	7	8	2%
	Hispanic	5	7	12	2%	5	4	9	2%	6	2	8	2%	2	2	4	1%	1	8	9	2%
	White	211	240	451	92%	234	264	498	91%	212	263	475	90%	260	272	532	93%	201	248	449	89%
	Other			0		1	2	3	1%			0			1	1	.2%			0	
	Total	**229**	**262**	**491**		**258**	**290**	**548**		**237**	**291**	**528**		**285**	**289**	**574**		**225**	**281**	**506**	
GRADE 2	American Indian	16	10	26	5%	12	17	29	6%	20	19	39	7%	17	21	38	7%	19	11	30	5%
	Asian	2	4	6	1%	4	3	7	1%		1	1	.2%	2	3	5	1%	4		4	.7%
	Black	2	1	3	1%	2	2	4	1%	2	3	5	1%	1	1	2	.4%	2	2	4	.7%
	Hispanic	3	6	9	2%	3	7	10	2%	6	4	10	2%	4	3	7	1%	3	5	8	1%
	White	224	250	474	91%	234	242	476	90%	241	263	504	90%	222	262	484	90%	250	264	514	92%
	Other	248	272	520		255	271	526		269	291	560		246	290	536		278	282		
	Total	**248**	**272**	**520**		**255**	**271**	**526**		**269**	**291**	**560**		**246**	**290**	**536**		**278**	**283**	**561**	
GRADE 3	American Indian	10	13	23	4%	15	14	29	5%	17	18	35	6%	19	15	34	6%	14	20	34	6%
	Asian	2	1	3	1%	5	3	8	1%	4	3	7	1%		1	1	.2%	3	3	6	1%
	Black	4		4	1%	2	1	3	1%	4	5	9	2%	2	3	5	1%	2	1	3	.5%
	Hispanic	2	5	7	1%	3	4	7	1%	4	8	12	2%	7	5	12	2%	5	6	11	2%
	White	234	249	483	92%	242	271	513	91%	227	251	478	88%	251	247	498	90%	227	275	502	90%
	Other	3		3	1%	1		1	.2%			0			1	1	.2%			0	
	Total	**255**	**268**	**523**		**268**	**293**	**561**		**256**	**285**	**541**		**279**	**272**	**551**		**251**	**305**	**556**	

Figure 4.10 (Continued)

Canyon View School District Student Enrollment By Grade Level, Ethnicity, and Gender, 2001-02 to 2005-06

Grade Level and Ethnicity		2001-02				2002-03				2003-04				2004-05				2005-06			
		Female	Male	Total	Percent	Female	Male	Total	Percent	Female	Male	Total	Percent	Female	Male	Total	Percent	Female	Male	Total	Percent
GRADE 4	American Indian	10	13	23	5%	11	16	27	5%	17	15	32	6%	17	19	36	7%	20	18	38	7%
	Asian	4	4	8	2%	1	1	2	.3%	5	2	7	1%	2	3	5	1%	1	1	2	.4%
	Black	1	2	3	1%	5		5	1%	3	1	4	1%	6	2	8	1%	2	4	6	1%
	Hispanic	4	4	8	2%	5	7	12	2%	3	5	8	1%	4	9	13	2%	7	7	14	3%
	White	252	216	468	92%	263	265	528	92%	246	281	527	91%	223	249	472	88%	243	251	494	89%
	Other	1		1	.2%	2		2	.3%	1		1	.2%			0			1	1	.2%
	Total	**272**	**239**	**511**		**287**	**289**	**576**		**275**	**304**	**579**		**252**	**282**	**534**		**273**	**282**	**555**	
GRADE 5	American Indian	11	9	20	4%	17	19	36	6%	17	24	41	7%	14	14	28	5%	15	23	38	7%
	Asian	1	2	3	1%	2	4	6	1%	1	1	2	.4%	5	2	7	1%	2	3	5	.9%
	Black	1	2	3	1%	1	1	2	.4%	4	1	5	1%	2	1	3	1%	8		8	1%
	Hispanic	3	8	11	2%	5	6	11	2%	5	5	10	2%	4	3	7	1%	4	7	11	2%
	White	224	256	480	92%	273	240	513	90%	261	250	511	89%	247	283	530	92%	232	264	496	89%
	Other	1	2	3	1%			0		2		2	.4%	1		1	.2%			0	
	Total	**241**	**279**	**520**		**298**	**270**	**568**		**290**	**281**	**571**		**273**	**303**	**576**		**261**	**297**	**558**	
GRADE 6	American Indian	10	19	29	5%	13	18	31	5%	15	19	34	6%	17	22	39	7%	15	13	28	5%
	Asian	6	4	10	2%	4	4	8	1%	3	5	8	1%	1	3	4	1%	4	2	6	1%
	Black	1	1	2	.3%		2	2	.3%	2	1	3	1%	4	1	5	1%	2	2	4	.7%
	Hispanic	4	1	5	1%	4	7	11	2%	5	6	11	2%	6	6	12	2%	5	3	8	1%
	White	258	279	537	92%	248	285	533	91%	266	243	509	90%	265	247	512	89%	260	282	542	92%
	Other			0		1		1	.2%			0		1		1	.2%	1		1	.2%
	Total	**279**	**304**	**583**		**270**	**316**	**586**		**291**	**274**	**565**		**294**	**279**	**573**		**287**	**302**	**589**	
GRADE 7	American Indian	6	6	12	2%	14	17	31	5%	15	18	33	6%	17	19	36	6%	16	23	39	7%
	Asian	7	1	8	1%	8	6	14	2%	3	3	6	1%	3	3	6	1%	1	4	5	.8%
	Black	4		4	1%		1	1	.2%		3	3	1%	2	2	4	1%	5	1	6	1%
	Hispanic	1		1	.2%	4	2	6	1%	6	5	11	2%	8	5	13	2%	6	5	11	2%
	White	284	278	562	96%	248	280	528	91%	253	279	532	91%	270	243	513	90%	268	258	526	89%
	Other			0				0				0				0		2		2	.3%
	Total	**302**	**285**	**587**		**274**	**306**	**580**		**277**	**308**	**585**		**300**	**272**	**572**		**298**	**291**	**589**	

Figure 4.10 (Continued)

Canyon View School District Student Enrollment By Grade Level, Ethnicity, and Gender, 2001-02 to 2005-06

Grade Level and Ethnicity		2001-02				2002-03				2003-04				2004-05				2005-06			
		Female	Male	Total	Percent	Female	Male	Total	Percent	Female	Male	Total	Percent	Female	Male	Total	Percent	Female	Male	Total	
GRADE 8	American Indian	15	12	27	4%	15	10	25	4%	17	19	36	6%	12	17	29	5%	13	18	31	5%
	Asian	5	5	10	2%	7	3	10	2%	8	4	12	2%	3	4	7	1%	3	3	6	1%
	Black		3	3	.5%	2		2	.3%		2	2	.3%		4	4	1%	1	5	6	1%
	Hispanic	3	2	5	1%	4	2	6	1%	6	3	9	2%	5	6	11	2%	7	8	15	3%
	White	301	304	605	93%	292	288	580	93%	248	272	520	90%	252	292	544	91%	277	246	523	90%
	Other			0			1	1	.2%			0				0				0	
	Total	**324**	**326**	**650**		**320**	**304**	**624**		**279**	**300**	**579**		**272**	**323**	**595**		**301**	**280**	**581**	
GRADE 9	American Indian	9	6	15	2%	20	11	31	4%	11	7	18	2%	15	22	37	5%	16	24	40	5%
	Asian	2	1	3	.4%	5	6	11	1%	8	2	10	1%	7	7	14	2%	6	6	12	2%
	Black		1	1	.1%			0		1		1	.1%	1		1	.1%			5	.7%
	Hispanic	3	3	6	1%	5	4	9	1%	3	2	5	1%	6	7	13	2%	7	8	15	2%
	White	375	412	787	97%	383	372	755	94%	357	346	703	95%	335	362	697	91%	324	355	679	90%
	Total	**389**	**423**	**812**		**413**	**393**	**806**		**380**	**357**	**737**		**364**	**398**	**762**		**353**	**398**	**751**	
GRADE 10	American Indian	8	12	20	3%	12	8	20	3%	20	11	31	4%	14	7	21	3%	16	22	38	5%
	Asian			0		4	1	5	1%	4	6	10	1%	10	3	13	2%	9	5	14	2%
	Black	1		1	.1%		1	1	.1%		1	1	.1%	3	1	4	1%		1	1	.1%
	Hispanic		2	2	.3%	5	4	9	1%	5	3	8	1%	4	2	6	1%	5	9	14	2%
	White	366	347	713	97%	347	411	758	96%	353	348	701	93%	342	340	682	94%	323	348	671	91%
	Total	**375**	**361**	**736**		**368**	**425**	**793**		**382**	**369**	**751**		**373**	**353**	**726**		**353**	**385**	**738**	
GRADE 11	American Indian	10	13	23	3%	12	6	18	3%	13	6	19	3%	19	12	31	4%	15	7	22	3%
	Asian	1		1	.1%	1	1	2	.3%	3	1	4	1%	6	9	15	2%	8	4	12	2%
	Black			0			1	1	.1%			0			2	2	.3%	3		3	.4%
	Hispanic	1	1	2	.3%	4	2	6	1%	3	2	5	1%	6	2	8	1%	4	2	6	.9%
	White	323	349	672	96%	353	336	689	96%	343	374	717	96%	332	329	661	92%	328	331	659	94%
	Total	**335**	**363**	**698**		**370**	**346**	**716**		**362**	**383**	**745**		**363**	**354**	**717**		**358**	**344**	**702**	

Figure 4.10 (Continued)

Canyon View School District Student Enrollment
By Grade Level, Ethnicity, and Gender, 2001-02 to 2005-06

Grade Level and Ethnicity		2001-02				2002-03				2003-04				2004-05				2005-06			
		Female	Male	Total	Percent	Female	Male	Total	Percent	Female	Male	Total	Percent	Female	Male	Total	Percent	Female	Male	Total	
GRADE 12	American Indian	4	4	8	1%	8	11	19	3%	11	8	19	3%	13	5	18	3%	16	11	27	4%
	Asian			0		1		1	.1%	2	2	4	1%	4	2	6	1%	6	8	14	2%
	Black		1	1	.2%	1		1	.1%	1	1	2	.3%			0			2	2	.3%
	Hispanic	2	2	4	1%	7	2	9	1%	3	3	6	1%	4	2	6	1%	5	3	8	1%
	White	287	291	578	98%	317	332	649	96%	329	319	648	95%	316	349	665	96%	337	329	666	93%
	Total	**293**	**298**	**591**		**334**	**345**	**679**		**346**	**333**	**679**		**337**	**358**	**695**		**364**	**353**	**717**	
DISTRICT TOTAL	American Indian	125	143	268	3%	182	180	362	4%	202	193	395	5%	204	203	407	5%	202	215	417	5%
	Asian	34	24	58	1%	45	38	83	1%	47	35	82	1%	52	42	94	1%	43	45	98	1%
	Black	16	15	31	.4%	15	12	27	.3%	20	21	41	1%	24	23	47	1%	29	36	65	.8%
	Hispanic	35	46	81	1%	58	52	110	1%	58	50	108	1%	61	57	118	1%	62	75	137	2%
	White	3,570	3,771	7,341	94%	3,655	3,874	7,529	93%	3,584	3,771	7,355	92%	3,509	3,722	7,231	92%	3,491	3,694	7,185	91%
	Other	6	6	12	.2%	5	3	8	.1%	3	2	5	.1%	2	2	4	.1%	3	4	7	.1%
	Total	**3,786**	**4,005**	**7,791**		**3,960**	**4,159**	**8,119**		**3,914**	**4,072**	**7,986**		**3,852**	**4,049**	**7,901**		**3,840**	**4,069**	**7,909**	

Figure 4.11 shows enrollment by school, ethnicity, and gender, over time.

Look Fors:	**Changes in diversity within schools.** **Differences in diversity across schools.**
Planning Implications:	**Is diversity even and spread-out? Will changes in diversity require changes in instructional materials, services, and staff?**

Figure 4.11

Canyon View School District Student Enrollment By School, Ethnicity, and Gender, 2001-02 to 2005-06

School	Ethnicity	2001-02 Female #	2001-02 Male #	2001-02 Total #	2001-02 Percent %	2002-03 Female #	2002-03 Male #	2002-03 Total #	2002-03 Percent %	2003-04 Female #	2003-04 Male #	2003-04 Total #	2003-04 Percent %	2004-05 Female #	2004-05 Male #	2004-05 Total #	2004-05 Percent %	2005-06 Female #	2005-06 Male #	2005-06 Total #	2005-06 Percent %
ELEMENTARY 1	American Indian	6	9	15	5%	12	13	25	9%	12	14	26	9%	11	13	24	9%	10	9	19	7%
	Asian	2	4	6	2%	3	5	8	3%	2	3	5	2%	2	3	5	2%	1	3	4	1%
	Black	1	1	2	1%									1		1	.4%	2	2	4	1%
	Hispanic	3	10	13	5%	3	7	10	4%	3	4	7	2%	3	4	7	2%	4	6	10	4%
	White	110	127	237	86%	108	114	222	83%	123	119	242	86%	112	132	244	87%	111	122	233	86%
	Pacific Islander	1		1	.4%	1		1	.4%	1		1	.4%								
	Total	**123**	**151**	**274**		**127**	**139**	**266**		**141**	**140**	**281**		**129**	**152**	**281**		**128**	**142**	**270**	
ELEMENTARY 2	American Indian	10	12	22	10%	9	13	22	10%	17	15	32	12%	10	13	23	10%	12	17	29	12%
	Asian	3	1	4	2%	2	1	3	1%	1	1	2	1%		1	1	.4%		1	1	.4%
	Black		1	1	.4%	1	1	2	1%	3	4	7	3%	5	3	8	3%	5	2	7	3%
	Hispanic	1	3	4	2%	3	4	7	3%	6	2	8	3%	1	3	4	2%	1	4	5	2%
	White	93	99	192	85%	91	105	196	85%	89	125	214	81%	98	108	206	85%	75	121	196	82%
	Pacific Islander		2	2	.9%																
	Total	**107**	**118**	**225**		**106**	**124**	**230**		**116**	**147**	**263**		**114**	**128**	**242**		**93**	**145**	**238**	
ELEMENTARY 3	American Indian	11	7	18	6%	8	8	16	5%	5	12	17	6%	5	11	16	6%	5	13	18	7%
	Asian	2		2	1%	1	1	2	1%	3	1	4	1%	2	1	3	1%	3	2	5	2%
	Black	2		2	1%	4		4	1%	3		3	1%	2		2	1%	2	1	3	1%
	Hispanic	2	5	7	2%	2	4	6	2%	1	3	4	1%	1	3	4	1%	3	3	6	2%
	White	135	155	290	91%	140	149	289	91%	135	134	269	91%	127	119	246	91%	122	119	241	88%
	Total	**152**	**167**	**319**		**155**	**162**	**317**		**147**	**150**	**297**		**137**	**134**	**271**		**135**	**138**	**273**	
ELEMENTARY 4	American Indian	7	10	17	3%	7	7	14	3%	14	14	28	6%	14	14	28	6%	10	16	26	5%
	Asian		2	2	.4%		1	1	.2%		1	1	.2%		1	1	.2%		1	1	.2%
	Black	3	1	4	1%	2	2	4	1%	1	3	4	1%	1	5	6	1%	3	6	9	2%
	Hispanic	4	4	8	2%	3	3	6	1%	2	2	4	1%	5	1	6	1%	4	5	9	2%
	White	220	235	455	94%	227	230	457	95%	209	222	431	92%	215	229	444	92%	220	232	452	91%
	Total	**234**	**252**	**486**		**239**	**243**	**482**		**226**	**242**	**468**		**235**	**250**	**485**		**237**	**260**	**497**	
ELEMENTARY 5	American Indian	8	3	11	4%	7	3	10	4%	11	1	12	5%	7	4	11	4%	7	3	10	4%
	Asian	1	3	4	2%	4	4	8	3%	5	3	8	3%	7	2	9	4%	6	3	9	3%
	Black		2	2	1%	1	2	3	1%	1	1	2	1%		1	1	.4%	2	3	5	2%
	Hispanic	3	4	7	3%	5	3	8	3%	4	5	9	4%	4	4	8	3%	3	4	7	3%
	White	115	126	241	91%	94	112	206	88%	100	121	221	88%	99	125	224	89%	111	119	230	88%
	Total	**127**	**138**	**265**		**111**	**124**	**235**		**121**	**131**	**252**		**117**	**136**	**253**		**129**	**132**	**261**	

Figure 4.11 (Continued)

Canyon View School District Student Enrollment By School, Ethnicity, and Gender, 2001-02 to 2005-06

School and Ethnicity		2001-02				2002-03				2003-04				2004-05				2005-06			
		Female	Male	Total	Percent	Female	Male	Total	Percent	Female	Male	Total	Percent	Female	Male	Total	Percent	Female	Male	Total	Percent
		#	#	#	%	#	#	#	%	#	#	#	%	#	#	#	%	#	#	#	%
ELEMENTARY 6	American Indian	5	4	9	4%	4	5	9	4%	5	2	7	3%	5	2	7	4%	6		6	3%
	Asian	1		1	.4%		1	1	.4%		1	1	.5%	2	1	3	2%	2	1	3	1%
	Black	1	1	2	1%					1	2	3	1%						1	1	.5%
	Hispanic	3	1	4	2%	2		2	1%	1	2	3	1%		4	4	2%	1	3	4	2%
	White	101	137	238	94%	92	128	220	95%	72	132	204	94%	66	120	186	93%	62	125	187	93%
	Total	**111**	**143**	**254**		**98**	**134**	**232**		**79**	**139**	**218**		**73**	**127**	**200**		**71**	**130**	**201**	
ELEMENTARY 7	American Indian	2	6	8	3%	5	4	9	3%	9	6	15	5%	6	5	11	4%	7	6	13	5%
	Asian	1	1	2	1%	1	1	2	1%	1	1	2	1%	1	1	2	1%	1		1	.4%
	Black									1		1	.4%	1	1	2	1%	1	1	2	1%
	Hispanic		2	2	1%	1		1	.4%	1		1	.4%								
	White	134	134	268	94%	123	134	257	95%	118	136	254	93%	110	135	245	94%	99	143	242	94%
	Pacific Islander	2	2	4	1.4%		1	1	.4%												
	Total	**139**	**145**	**284**		**130**	**140**	**270**		**130**	**143**	**273**		**118**	**142**	**260**		**108**	**150**	**258**	
ELEMENTARY 8	American Indian					5	7	12	5%	1	5	6	3%	2	7	9	4%	6	5	11	5%
	Asian					1	2	3	1%	1	1	2	1%	1	1	2	1%		2	2	1%
	Black																	1	2	3	1%
	Hispanic									1		1	.4%	1		1	.4%	1		1	.4%
	White					125	106	231	94%	116	109	225	96%	110	106	216	95%	107	99	206	92%
	Total					**131**	**115**	**246**		**119**	**115**	**234**		**114**	**114**	**228**		**115**	**108**	**223**	
ELEMENTARY 9	American Indian	5	2	7	2%	11	18	29	6%	8	9	17	4%	11	13	24	5%	9	11	20	5%
	Asian	2		2	.5%	2		2	.4%	2		2	.4%	2		2	.4%	1		1	.2%
	Black	1	1	2	.5%	1	1	2	.4%	2	1	3	1%	2	1	3	1%	1		1	.2%
	Hispanic	3	3	6	1%	4	6	10	2%	3	6	9	2%	2	4	6	1%	3	6	9	2%
	White	213	209	422	96%	216	221	437	91%	220	231	451	94%	200	222	422	92%	205	202	407	93%
	Total	**224**	**215**	**439**		**234**	**246**	**480**		**235**	**247**	**482**		**217**	**240**	**457**		**219**	**219**	**438**	
ELEMENTARY 10	American Indian	5	13	18	6%	8	11	19	6%	9	16	25	8%	10	9	19	6%	12	9	21	7%
	Asian	1	2	3	1%		1	1	.3%									2		2	1%
	Black	1	2	3	1%	3	1	4	1%	4	2	6	2%	2	2	4	1%		2	2	1%
	Hispanic	1	1	2	1%	1	1	2	1%	5	1	6	2%	3	1	4	1%	3	4	7	2%
	White	139	148	287	91%	142	132	274	91%	137	132	269	87%	144	120	264	90%	137	126	263	89%
	Pacific Islander	2	1	3	.9%	2		2	.7%	1	1	2	.6%	1	1	2	.7%		2	2	.7%
	Total	**149**	**167**	**316**		**156**	**146**	**302**		**156**	**152**	**308**		**160**	**133**	**293**		**154**	**143**	**297**	

Figure 4.11 (Continued)

Canyon View School District Student Enrollment By School, Ethnicity, and Gender, 2001-02 to 2005-06

School	Ethnicity	2001-02				2002-03				2003-04				2004-05				2005-06			
		Female #	Male #	Total #	Percent %	Female #	Male #	Total #	Percent %	Female #	Male #	Total #	Percent %	Female #	Male #	Total #	Percent %	Female #	Male #	Total #	Percent %
ELEMENTARY 11	American Indian	4	5	9	3%	12	10	22	8%	9	11	20	7%	16	8	24	8%	11	8	19	7%
	Asian					1		1	.4%	1		1	.4%	1		1	.3%				
	Black	1		1	.4%													1		1	.3%
	Hispanic	1	2	3	1%	1	1	2	1%		1	1	.4%	2	3	5	2%		2	2	1%
	White	118	145	263	95%	109	139	248	90%	117	129	246	91%	116	144	260	89%	125	137	262	92%
	Pacific Islander	1	1	2	.7%	1	1	2	.7%	1	1	2	.7%		1	1	.3%		2	2	.7%
	Total	**125**	**153**	**278**		**124**	**151**	**275**		**128**	**142**	**270**		**135**	**156**	**291**		**137**	**149**	**286**	
MIDDLE 1	American Indian	10	17	27	3%	10	20	30	3%	13	24	37	4%	20	27	47	5%	22	30	52	5%
	Asian	9	4	13	1%	8	5	13	1%	5	8	13	1%	2	4	6	1%	4	4	8	1%
	Black	1	3	4	.4%	1		1	.1%	2	4	6	1%	3	5	8	1%	2	4	6	1%
	Hispanic	3	2	5	.5%	6	6	12	1%	11	6	17	2%	10	13	23	2%	12	10	22	2%
	White	508	478	986	95%	459	485	944	94%	472	459	931	93%	493	459	952	92%	509	488	997	92%
	Pacific Islander					1	1	2	.2%					1		1	.1%	1		1	.1%
	Total	**531**	**504**	**1,035**		**485**	**517**	**1,002**		**503**	**501**	**1,004**		**529**	**508**	**1,037**		**550**	**536**	**1,086**	
MIDDLE 2	American Indian	21	21	42	5%	32	25	57	7%	34	32	66	9%	26	31	57	8%	22	25	47	7%
	Asian	9	6	15	2%	11	8	19	2%	9	4	13	2%	5	6	11	2%	4	5	9	1%
	Black	4	1	5	1%	1	3	4	1%		2	2	.3%	3	2	5	1%	6	4	10	1%
	Hispanic	5	1	6	1%	6	4	10	1%	6	8	14	2%	9	4	13	2%	6	6	12	2%
	White	336	382	718	91%	317	355	672	88%	295	335	630	87%	294	323	617	88%	296	298	594	88%
	Total	**375**	**411**	**786**		**367**	**395**	**762**		**344**	**381**	**725**		**337**	**366**	**703**		**334**	**338**	**672**	
HIGH 1	American Indian	14	10	24	2%	15	10	25	2%	16	8	24	2%	19	16	35	3%	16	20	36	3%
	Asian	2		2	.1%	5	1	6	.4%	6	1	7	1%	10	9	19	1%	7	10	17	1%
	Black	1	1	2	.1%					1	1	2	.2%	1	1	2	.2%	1	5	6	.4%
	Hispanic	4	6	10	1%	5	8	13	1%	3	6	9	1%	11	8	19	1%	7	10	17	1%
	White	614	684	1,298	97%	662	671	1,333	97%	635	637	1,272	97%	590	633	1,223	94%	621	641	1,262	94%
	Total	**635**	**701**	**1,336**		**687**	**690**	**1,377**		**661**	**653**	**1,314**		**631**	**667**	**1,298**		**652**	**686**	**1,338**	
HIGH 2	American Indian	17	24	41	3%	34	23	57	4%	33	22	55	4%	40	28	68	4%	43	43	86	6%
	Asian	1	1	2	.1%	6	7	13	1%	11	10	21	1%	15	12	27	2%	21	13	34	2%
	Black		1	1	.1%	1	2	3	.2%	1	1	2	.1%	3	2	5	.3%	1	3	4	.3%
	Hispanic	2	2	4	.3%	16	5	21	1%	11	4	15	1%	9	5	14	1%	14	12	26	2%
	White	736	719	1,455	97%	728	776	1,504	94%	727	731	1,458	94%	714	721	1,435	93%	668	709	1,377	90%
	Total	**756**	**747**	**1,503**		**785**	**813**	**1,598**		**783**	**768**	**1,551**		**781**	**768**	**1,549**		**747**	**780**	**1,527**	

The percentage of students qualifying for free/reduced lunch is shown below in Figure 4.12. Over this six-year period, the total number of students in the district qualifying for free/reduced lunch has increased from 17% of the district population in 2000-01 to 23% in 2005-06. Elementary percentages varied from 27% to 30%, while middle school percentages varied from 19% to 26%. High schools, which have the hardest time getting families to return free/reduced lunch forms, had percentages from 3% to 12%. Free/reduced lunch is an indicator of family socio-economic status—providing insight into the number and percentage of families who live in poverty.

Look Fors: **Increases/decreases in the percentage of free/reduced lunch students.**

Planning Implications: **Free/reduced lunch count is an indicator of poverty—or an indicator of the degree to which the district is tracking paperwork to get all qualified students signed up to take advantage of free/reduced lunch. Have all students who qualify for free/reduced lunch returned their forms?**

Figure 4.12

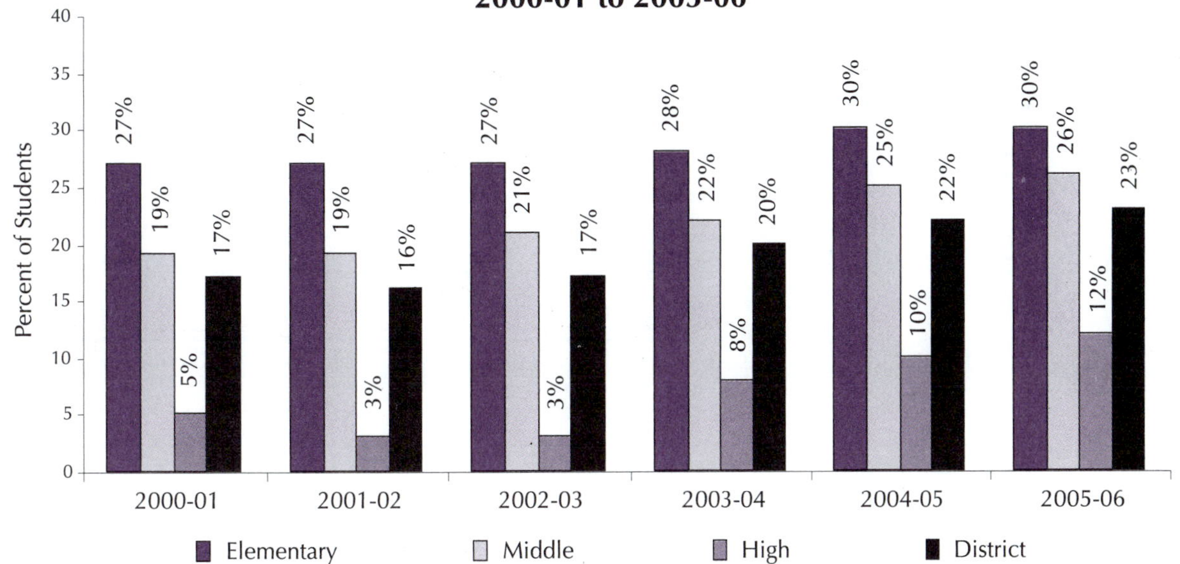

Figure 4.13 shows the number and percent of students qualifying for free/reduced lunch by school.

Look Fors: **Changes in free/reduced lunch over time within schools. Differences in free/reduced lunch percentages across schools.**

Planning Implications: **Do the schools need additional support to provide for their different populations (i.e., materials, staff, professional learning)?**

Figure 4.13

Canyon View School District
Students Qualifying for Free/Reduced Lunch by School, 2001-02 to 2005-06

	School	Lunch Status	2001-02 (*n*=7,800)		2002-03 (*n*=8,142)		2003-04 (*n*=7,999)		2004-05 (*n*=7,922)		2005-06 (*n*=7,961)	
			Number	Percent	Number	Percent	Number	Percent	Number	Percent	Number	Percent
ELEMENTARY	**Elementary 1**	Free/Reduced	95	35%	95	36%	111	40%	121	43%	114	42%
		Paid	179	65%	171	64%	169	60%	153	55%	140	52%
		Total	**274**		**266**		**281**		**281**		**270**	
	Elementary 2	Free/Reduced	126	56%	131	57%	160	61%	145	60%	149	63%
		Paid	99	44%	99	43%	102	39%	94	39%	86	36%
		Total	**225**		**230**		**263**		**242**		**238**	
	Elementary 3	Free/Reduced	105	33%	107	34%	91	31%	83	31%	79	29%
		Paid	214	67%	210	66%	206	69%	185	68%	187	69%
		Total	**319**		**317**		**297**		**271**		**273**	
	Elementary 4	Free/Reduced	88	18%	82	17%	96	21%	110	23%	100	20%
		Paid	385	79%	400	83%	369	79%	368	76%	372	75%
		Total	**486**		**482**		**468**		**485**		**497**	
	Elementary 5	Free/Reduced	50	19%	38	16%	45	18%	43	17%	58	22%
		Paid	215	81%	197	84%	207	82%	207	82%	196	75%
		Total	**265**		**235**		**252**		**253**		**261**	
	Elementary 6	Free/Reduced	47	19%	40	17%	35	16%	27	14%	37	18%
		Paid	207	82%	192	83%	183	84%	172	86%	159	79%
		Total	**254**		**232**		**218**		**200**		**201**	
	Elementary 7	Free/Reduced	82	30%	65	24%	71	26%	70	27%	55	21%
		Paid	202	70%	205	76%	202	74%	182	70%	189	73%
		Total	**284**		**270**		**273**		**260**		**258**	
	Elementary 8	Free/Reduced			59	24%	68	29%	63	28%	52	23%
		Paid			187	76%	166	71%	163	72%	164	74%
		Total			**246**		**234**		**228**		**223**	
	Elementary 9	Free/Reduced	82	19%	98	20%	95	20%	104	23%	98	22%
		Paid	360	81%	379	79%	385	80%	352	77%	338	77%
		Total	**442**		**480**		**482**		**457**		**438**	

Figure 4.13 (Continued)

Canyon View School District
Students Qualifying for Free/Reduced Lunch by School, 2001-02 to 2005-06

	School	Lunch Status	2001-02 (*n*=7,800)		2002-03 (*n*=8,142)		2003-04 (*n*=7,999)		2004-05 (*n*=7,922)		2005-06 (*n*=7,961)	
			Number	Percent	Number	Percent	Number	Percent	Number	Percent	Number	Percent
ELEMENTARY	Elementary 10	Free/Reduced	63	21%	66	22%	80	26%	81	28%	81	27%
		Paid	244	79%	236	78%	228	74%	212	72%	216	73%
		Total	**307**		**302**		**308**		**293**		**297**	
	Elementary 11	Free/Reduced	90	32%	111	40%	97	36%	117	40%	137	48%
		Paid	195	68%	164	60%	173	64%	167	57%	144	50%
		Total	**285**		**275**		**270**		**291**		**286**	
MIDDLE	Middle 1	Free/Reduced	165	16%	163	16%	185	18%	197	19%	224	21%
		Paid	875	85%	839	84%	819	82%	840	81%	861	79%
		Total	**1,035**		**1,002**		**1,004**		**1,037**		**1,086**	
	Middle 2	Free/Reduced	178	23%	197	26%	204	28%	225	32%	228	34%
		Paid	552	70%	503	66%	521	72%	444	63%	409	61%
		Total	**786**		**762**		**725**		**703**		**674**	
HIGH	High 1	Free/Reduced	90	7%	100	7%	83	6%	82	6%	122	9%
		Paid	1,246	93%	1,277	93%	1,231	94%	1,214	94%	1,213	91%
		Total	**1,336**		**1,377**		**1,314**		**1,298**		**1,338**	
	High 2	Free/Reduced					140	9%	197	13%	206	14%
		Paid	1,503	100%	1,506	100%	1,378	89%	1,318	85%	1,267	83%
		Total	**1,503**		**1,598**		**1,551**		**1,549**		**1,527**	

Mobility

The 2005-06 mobility rate for the district was approximately 17%. Figure 4.14 shows the mobility rates for each school, between 2001-02 and 2005-06. The highest mobility occurs in the elementary and high schools, then middle schools.

Look Fors: **Consistency in mobility within schools, over time. Differences in mobility percentages across schools.**

Planning Implications: **Do the schools with highest mobility rates need additional support or special services for students moving in and out? Does the district understand its mobility? Where do the students go? Does the district need a common curriculum? Are there effective transfer policies in place?**

Figure 4.14

Canyon View School District
Mobility by School, 2001-02 to 2005-06

School	2001-02		2002-03		2003-04		2004-05		2005-06	
	Number	Percent	Number	Percent	Number	Percent	Number	Percent	Number	Percent
Elementary 1	16	6%	71	27%	39	14%	41	15%	58	21%
Elementary 2	1	.4%	64	28%	55	21%	69	29%	74	31%
Elementary 3	69	22%	53	17%	38	13%	36	13%	39	14%
Elementary 4	45	9%	29	6%	37	8%	75	15%	69	14%
Elementary 5	8	3%	33	14%	13	5%	34	13%	34	13%
Elementary 6	41	16%	46	20%	18	8%	41	21%	61	30%
Elementary 7	29	10%	34	13%	19	7%	30	12%	50	19%
Elementary 8			20	8%	34	15%	34	15%	34	15%
Elementary 9	67	15%	60	13%	41	9%	67	15%	87	20%
Elementary 10	58	18%	53	17%	58	19%	56	19%	70	24%
Elementary 11	49	18%	22	8%	40	15%	29	10%	76	27%
Elementary All	**351**	**11%**	**343**	**10%**	**314**	**9%**	**430**	**13%**	**536**	**17%**
Middle 1	36	3%	43	4%	39	4%	51	5%	48	4%
Middle 2	59	8%	64	8%	53	7%	72	10%	85	13%
Middle All	**95**	**5%**	**107**	**6%**	**92**	**5%**	**123**	**7%**	**133**	**9%**
High 1	127	10%	142	10%	127	9%	113	9%	127	10%
High 2	257	17%	238	15%	231	15%	241	16%	214	14%
High All	**384**	**14%**	**380**	**13%**	**358**	**12%**	**354**	**12%**	**341**	**12%**

Attendance

Average percentage of days present for students is shown in Figure 4.15. The average daily attendance for the district was estimated to be 94% in 2005-06, consistent with previous years.

Look Fors: **High or low average student attendance. Decreasing or increasing attendance rates over time?**

Planning Implications: **Why is student attendance *high* or *low?* Why are students missing school? When are students missing school? What can be done to improve attendance?**

Figure 4.15

Canyon View School District
Average Percentage of Attendance Days in Year
2000-01 to 2005-06

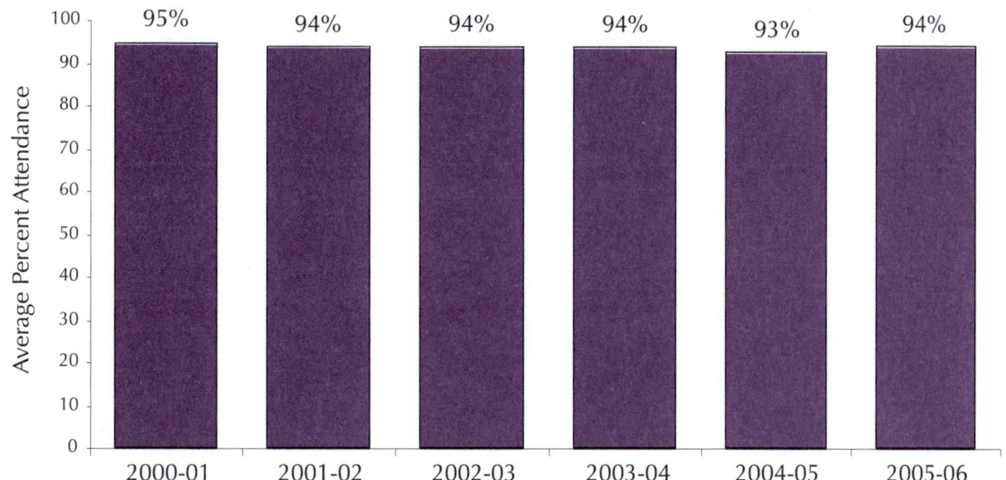

Figure 4.16 shows the average percent of days students are present by grade level, over time. Schools are open for 180 instructional days each year.

Look Fors: **Consistency of attendance rates within and across grade levels and over time.**

Planning Implications: **Why is attendance lower in some grade levels? Why are students not regularly attending? Are the current attendance policies effective? Are the policies being implemented consistently?**

Figure 4.16

Canyon View School District Students
Average Percentage of Days Present by Grade Level
2001-02 to 2005-06

Grade Level	2001-02	2002-03	2003-04	2004-05	2005-06
	Percent	Percent	Percent	Percent	Percent
Kindergarten	97%	95%	95%	93%	99%
Grade 1	95%	95%	94%	93%	93%
Grade 2	95%	95%	95%	93%	93%
Grade 3	96%	95%	95%	94%	93%
Grade 4	95%	95%	95%	93%	93%
Grade 5	95%	95%	95%	93%	93%
Grade 6	94%	94%	94%	93%	93%
Grade 7	94%	93%	94%	93%	93%
Grade 8	93%	90%	93%	94%	94%
Grade 9	94%	93%	94%	94%	94%
Grade 10	93%	93%	93%	94%	94%
Grade 11	91%	92%	92%	92%	93%
Grade 12	91%	92%	92%	93%	93%
Total Average	94%	94%	94%	93%	94%

Figure 4.17 shows the average percent rate of student attendance by school from 2001-02 to 2005-06.

Look Fors: **Consistency, decreases, or increases in attendance rates within and across schools, over time.**

Planning Implications: **Are the schools' attendance policies effective and being implemented consistently? Who are the students who are not attending, and why are they missing school? Why are there differences across schools?**

Figure 4.17

Canyon View School District Students Average Percentage of Days Present by School 2001-02 to 2005-06

School	2001-02	2002-03	2003-04	2004-05	2005-06
	Percent	Percent	Percent	Percent	Percent
Elementary 1	96%	96%	96%	94%	96%
Elementary 2	94%	94%	93%	94%	94%
Elementary 3	95%	95%	95%	95%	96%
Elementary 4	96%	96%	93%	92%	91%
Elementary 5	100%	96%	95%	91%	91%
Elementary 6	95%	95%	96%	92%	92%
Elementary 7	96%	95%	95%	95%	95%
Elementary 8		96%	96%	96%	96%
Elementary 9	94%	91%	94%	91%	92%
Elementary 10	95%	96%	95%	95%	95%
Elementary 11	96%	95%	94%	90%	90%
Middle 1	94%	94%	94%	94%	94%
Middle 2	93%	92%	92%	92%	91%
High 1	92%	91%	93%	94%	94%
High 2	92%	92%	92%	93%	93%

If available, student attendance percentage data could be shown by school and ethnicity for the district, over time. *Note:* the numbers that make up particular student groups can become very low. This type of table would never be shared with the public. However, the district needs to know this information.

Look Fors: **Differences in attendance rates by ethnicity. Changes over time.**

Planning Implications: **If there are differences in attendance by ethnicity, why and where? What can be done to increase attendance for all ethnicities?**

If the data are available, one could also show percentages of attendance by grade level, gender, and ethnicity, and school by gender and ethnicity.

Look Fors: **Differences in attendance rates by grade level, gender, and ethnicity, and schools, over time.**

Planning Implications: **Are there learning environment causes and/or implementations for low attendance? Is there one gender, or one or more ethnic groups, not feeling welcome or safe at school? Do attendance issues require new policies, a need for different instructional/curriculum resources, or staff professional learning ?**

An analysis of average percentage of days present and absent by grade level by lunch status, over time (not shown here), indicated that students who qualified for free/reduced lunch status had only slightly lower attendance rates.

Look Fors: **Differences in attendance rates by free/reduced lunch status within and across grade levels.**

Planning Implications: **Is there a need for family support to help students get to school?**

Completion and Dropout Rate

The 2005-06 completion rate for Canyon View School District high schools was 80%, down from 86% in 2004-05. The dropout rate was 20%, up from 14% in 2004-05. Digging deeper, the completion rate for High School 1 in 2004-05 was 85%, compared to 82% for High School 2. In 2005-06, the completion rate for High School 1 was 84% and 78% for High School 2.

Look Fors: **An acceptable and accurate graduation rate for the district and each high school.**

Planning Implications: **Who are the students who are dropping out? Why are students dropping out? What programs will assist in keeping students in school? Is there a way to predict dropouts and prevent them from happening?**

Discipline

Figure 4.18 shows the number of discipline referrals by grade level for the district. *Note:* these numbers only show the number of referrals; we do not know how many students were referred multiple times.

Look Fors: **Increase/decrease in discipline referrals over time within and across grade levels.**

Planning Implications: **Is the discipline policy appropriate? Is the policy being implemented consistently? Who are the students, and why are they being referred? How are students treated?**

Figure 4.18

Canyon View School District
Number of Discipline Referrals by Grade Level
2001-02 to 2005-06

Grade Level	2001-02	2002-03	2003-04	2004-05	2005-06
AM Kindergarten	9	13	9	22	14
PM Kindergarten	1	17	23	10	14
Pre-first	7	35			
Grade 1	97	128	164	250	386
Grade 2	164	171	230	266	177
Grade 3	263	290	213	240	198
Grade 4	206	447	294	263	232
Grade 5	198	391	379	362	316
Grade 6	856	467	585	492	272
Grade 7	1,197	830	798	1,082	628
Grade 8	2,133	1,414	1,097	1,193	743
Grade 9	682	816	734	1,113	876
Grade 10	542	1,168	634	802	789
Grade 11	571	654	807	779	609
Grade 12	881	882	1,172	1,232	806
Total	**7,807**	**7,723**	**7,139**	**8,106**	**6,060**

Figure 4.19 shows the number of discipline referrals for each school and grade level. The number of years each principal has been at their school has been added to this table to help study the impact of leadership.

Look Fors: **Changes within and across school and grade levels over time. Differences in numbers across schools and grade levels.**

Planning Implications: **Who are the students with the discipline referrals? Why and when are students being referred? How are the students treated? Are there policy implications?**

Figure 4.19

Canyon View School District
Number of Discipline Referrals by School and Grade Level
2001-02 to 2005-06

	School	Grade Level	2001-02	2002-03	2003-04	2004-05	2005-06
ELEMENTARY	**Elementary 1**	Grade 1					
	Principal Years at this School:	Grade 2	1				
	9 Years	Grade 3	4				
		Grade 4	8	4			
		Grade 5		6			
		Total	**13**	**10**			
	Elementary 2	AM Kindergarten			5	3	4
	Principal Years at this School:	PM Kindergarten			6	2	1
	12 Years	Grade 1	11	1	67	104	40
		Grade 2	9	14	41	91	36
		Grade 3	12	4	87	84	20
		Grade 4	17	23	39	158	42
		Grade 5	8	20	139	72	72
		Total	**57**	**62**	**384**	**514**	**225**
	Elementary 3	AM Kindergarten					
	Principal Years at this School:	Grade 1				13	
	9 Years	Grade 2				8	4
		Grade 3				7	
		Grade 4				2	
		Grade 5				30	6
		Total				**60**	**10**
	Elementary 4	AM Kindergarten					
	Principal Years at this School:	PM Kindergarten					1
	3 Years	Grade 1	3			2	7
		Grade 2	26			7	5
		Grade 3	21			4	6
		Grade 4	14			12	2
		Grade 5	22	1		15	28
		Grade 6	1				
		Total	**87**	**1**		**40**	**49**

Figure 4.19 (Continued)

Canyon View School District
Number of Discipline Referrals by School and Grade Level
2001-02 to 2005-06

	School	Grade Level	2001-02	2002-03	2003-04	2004-05	2005-06
ELEMENTARY	**Elementary 5**	AM Kindergarten			1		2
	Principal Years at this School:	PM Kindergarten			1		2
	1 Year	Grade 1	1	3	2	10	9
		Grade 2		9	1	13	15
		Grade 3	6	4	7	4	36
		Grade 4	4	11	2	11	12
		Grade 5		7	7	9	85
		Total	**11**	**34**	**19**	**47**	**157**
	Elementary 6	AM Kindergarten				5	
	Principal Years at this School:	PM Kindergarten				5	
	2 Years	Grade 1	13			30	193
		Grade 2	13	5		16	5
		Grade 3	27	12		15	8
		Grade 4	12	22		6	2
		Grade 5	12	12		14	17
		Total	**77**	**51**		**91**	**225**
	Elementary 7	PM Kindergarten			7	1	
	Principal Years at this School:	Grade 1			11	13	6
	1 Year	Grade 2	3	14	3	43	21
		Grade 3	13	14	7	20	10
		Grade 4	3	57	11	9	9
		Grade 5	11	27	30	40	8
		Total	**30**	**113**	**70**	**130**	**54**
	Elementary 8	AM Kindergarten				4	7
	Principal Years at this School:	PM Kindergarten			3		4
	3 Years	Grade 1		1	8	6	2
		Grade 2			15	19	9
		Grade 3			3	28	7
		Grade 4		2	19	8	28
		Grade 5		2	14	34	19
		Total		**5**	**62**	**99**	**76**
	Elementary 9	AM Kindergarten	1	6			
	Principal Years at this School:	PM Kindergarten		4			
	2 Years	Grade 1	29	32	25	5	27
		Grade 2	68	65	44	14	7
		Grade 3	54	81	60	1	57
		Grade 4	49	87	95	20	20
		Grade 5	34	78	112	10	46
		Total	**235**	**353**	**336**	**50**	**157**

Figure 4.19 (Continued)

Canyon View School District
Number of Discipline Referrals by School and Grade Level
2001-02 to 2005-06

	School	Grade Level	2001-02	2002-03	2003-04	2004-05	2005-06
ELEMENTARY	Elementary 10 Principal Years at this School: 4 Years	Grade 1				1	
		Grade 2	2			1	
		Grade 3				1	
		Grade 4	1			3	
		Grade 5	3			2	
		Total	**6**			**8**	
	Elementary 11 Principal Years at this School: 3 Years	AM Kindergarten	8	6	2	6	1
		PM Kindergarten	1	13	6	2	6
		Pre-First Grade	7	35			
		Grade 1	40	91	51	66	102
		Grade 2	42	64	126	54	75
		Grade 3	126	175	49	76	54
		Grade 4	98	241	128	34	107
		Grade 5	108	238	77	136	35
		Total	**430**	**863**	**439**	**374**	**380**
MIDDLE	Middle 1 Principal Years at this School: 10 Years	Grade 6	320	160	109	132	111
		Grade 7	367	228	346	306	293
		Grade 8	656	202	221	316	305
		Total	**1,343**	**590**	**676**	**754**	**709**
	Middle 2 Principal Years at this School: 10 Years	Grade 6	536	307	476	360	161
		Grade 7	830	602	452	776	335
		Grade 8	1,477	1,212	876	877	438
		Total	**2,843**	**2,121**	**1,804**	**2,013**	**934**
HIGH	High 1 Principal Years at this School: 3 Years	Grade 9	272	139	81	235	218
		Grade 10	160	250	117	291	209
		Grade 11	163	111	122	377	164
		Grade 12	133	112	103	440	130
		Total	**728**	**612**	**423**	**1,343**	**721**
	High 2 Principal Years at this School: 2 Years	Grade 9	410	677	653	878	658
		Grade 10	382	918	517	511	580
		Grade 11	408	543	685	402	445
		Grade 12	748	770	1,069	792	676
		Total	**1,948**	**2,908**	**2,924**	**2,583**	**2,359**

Special Programs

Over the past six years, Canyon View has been serving an increasing number of students classified as needing special education services. The majority of students receiving special education assistance were learning disabled and speech and language impaired. Figure 4.20 shows the special education numbers by gender for the district from 2001-02 to 2005-06. In 2001-02, 10% of the district population qualified for special education services. By 2005-06, that percentage increased to 15%.

Look Fors: **Changes in the number and percentage of students qualifying for special education services, in general, and by gender, over time. Changes in the number of students identified within primary learning disability, over time.**

Planning Implications: **Are the services provided meeting the needs of students with learning disabilities? Do teachers have the professional learning required to work with these students? Are the number and percentage increasing and decreasing reasonable?**

Figure 4.20

Canyon View School District
Special Education Numbers by Primary Disability by Gender
2001-02 to 2005-06

Primary Disability	2001-02			2002-03			2003-04			2004-05			2005-06		
	Female	Male	Total	Female	Male	Total	Female	Male	Total	Female	Male	Total	Female	Male	Total
Autistic	2	8	10	1	13	14	3	13	16	3	16	19	6	17	23
Cognitively Delayed	29	30	59	38	33	71	33	34	67	33	39	72	33	40	73
Deaf				1		1		1	1	1	1	2	1	1	2
Deaf and Blind	1		1												
Emotionally Disturbed	13	52	65	20	64	84	21	65	86	21	83	104	23	75	98
Hearing Disability	16	35	51	17	30	47	15	51	66	32	60	92	41	72	113
Learning Disability	122	278	400	128	286	414	133	278	411	140	304	444	157	325	482
Multiple Disabilities	8	9	17	6	12	18	2	4	6	2		2		1	1
Orthopedically Disabled	2	4	6	4	3	7	6	6	12	5	5	10	6	5	11
Other Health Disability	12	29	41	14	29	43	9	49	58	28	56	84	35	69	104
Speech and Language	30	72	102	55	86	141	62	139	201	83	143	226	89	167	256
Traumatic Brain Injury		2	2	1	2	3	1	1	2	2	1	3	2		2
Vision Disability		1	1	1	2	3	3		3	2	2	4	2	1	3
Total	**235**	**520**	**755**	**286**	**560**	**846**	**288**	**641**	**929**	**352**	**710**	**1,062**	**395**	**773**	**1,168**
Total by Gender	**31%**	**69%**	**755**	**34%**	**66%**	**846**	**31%**	**69%**	**929**	**33%**	**67%**	**1,062**	**34%**	**66%**	**1,168**
Total Percentage	**10%**			**10%**			**12%**			**13%**			**15%**		

Figure 4.21 shows special education disability numbers and percentages for the district by grade level and gender.

Look Fors:	**Changes in the number and percentage of students qualifying for special education services by primary disability, grade level, and gender, over time.**
Planning Implications:	**Is there one gender that is identified more than the other and, if so, how and why are students being identified for special education services? Is there an increase or decrease in special education disability numbers across grade levels?**

Figure 4.21

Canyon View School District
Special Education Numbers by Grade Level and Gender
2001-02 to 2005-06

Grade Level	Primary Disability	2001-02		2002-03		2003-04		2004-05		2005-06	
		Female	Male	Female	Male	Female	Male	Female	Male	Female	Male
Grade 1	Autistic		1		2		2	1	1		4
	Cognitively Delayed	2	3			2	1	1	3	1	5
	Deaf			1							
	Emotionally Disturbed		3	1	2	1	2		6	1	2
	Hearing Disabled	1	3		2		1	2	5	2	2
	Learning Disabled	1	8	3	4	5	7	5	10	6	11
	Multiple Disabilities					1					
	Orthopedically Disabled								1		
	Other Health Disability		3		2		1	2	4	1	2
	Speech and Language	2	13	7	14	7	19	8	23	20	33
	Vision Disabled							1			
	Total Females and Males	**6**	**34**	**12**	**26**	**16**	**33**	**20**	**53**	**31**	**59**
	All	**40 (8%)**		**38 (7%)**		**49 (9%)**		**73 (13%)**		**90 (18%)**	
Grade 2	Autistic	1	3		1		2		2	1	1
	Cognitively Delayed	2	2	3	2	1	2	2	3	1	5
	Emotionally Disturbed	1	5	1	7	2	4	2	4		4
	Hearing Disabled	1	3		2	1	5	1	8	5	8
	Learning Disabled	7	13	7	16	6	13	7	16	12	19
	Multiple Disabilities	1	1		1						
	Orthopedically Disabled		1								1
	Other Health Disability		3		2		5	1	8	4	7
	Speech and Language	4	16	7	15	10	21	12	24	15	25
	Traumatic Brain Injured							1			
	Total Females and Males	**17**	**47**	**18**	**46**	**20**	**52**	**26**	**65**	**38**	**70**
	All	**64 (12%)**		**64 (11%)**		**72 (13%)**		**91 (17%)**		**108 (19%)**	
Grade 3	Autistic			1	3		2				2
	Cognitively Delayed	1	1	2	1	2	2	3	1	2	4
	Deaf							1			
	Emotionally Disturbed		4	2	5	3	3	1	3	3	7
	Hearing Disabled	2	5	2	2		3	1	4	3	9
	Learning Disabled	8	25	12	23	10	26	8	19	9	17
	Multiple Disabilities		4	1	1		1				
	Orthopedically Disabled				1				1		
	Other Health Disability	1	5	1	2		3	1	4	2	9
	Speech and Language	5	11	10	20	10	29	18	21	13	27
	Traumatic Brain Injury									1	
	Total Females and Males	**17**	**55**	**31**	**58**	**25**	**69**	**33**	**53**	**33**	**75**
	All	**72 (14%)**		**89 (16%)**		**94 (17%)**		**86 (16%)**		**108 (19%)**	

Figure 4.21 (Continued)

Canyon View School District
Special Education Numbers by Grade Level and Gender
2001-02 to 2005-06

Grade Level	Primary Disability	2001-02		2002-03		2003-04		2004-05		2005-06	
		Female	Male	Female	Male	Female	Male	Female	Male	Female	Male
Grade 4	Autistic		1		1	1	2		2		
	Cognitively Delayed	1		1	2	5	3	2	2	2	1
	Deaf									1	
	Emotionally Disturbed	2	2	1	7	1	7	5	8	1	5
	Hearing Disabled	1	2	3	4	3	5	2	8	3	3
	Learning Disabled	12	22	11	36	14	30	13	28	11	24
	Multiple Disabilities	1			7						
	Orthopedically Disabled					1	1				
	Other Health Disability	1	1	2	4	2	5	2	8	3	3
	Speech and Language	5	7	15	11	8	23	11	22	9	20
	Vision Disabled			1							
	Total Females and Males	**23**	**35**	**34**	**72**	**35**	**76**	**35**	**78**	**30**	**56**
	All	**58 (11%)**		**106 (18%)**		**111 (19%)**		**113 (21%)**		**86 (15%)**	
Grade 5	Autistic				3		1	1	2		2
	Cognitively Delayed		3	3	1	1	3	5	3	3	3
	Emotionally Disturbed	1	4	5	5	1	12	3	9	4	8
	Hearing Disabled	2	3	2	2	4	10	6	4	2	10
	Learning Disabled	16	23	16	25	14	38	19	34	13	28
	Multiple Disabilities	2					2				
	Orthopedically Disabled	1	1					1			
	Other Health Disability	2	2	2	2	3	10	5	4	2	10
	Speech and Language	4	6	3	9	6	11	10	16	8	12
	Vision Disability					1					
	Total Females and Males	**28**	**42**	**31**	**47**	**30**	**87**	**50**	**72**	**32**	**73**
	All	**70 (13%)**		**78 (14%)**		**117 (20%)**		**122 (21%)**		**105 (19%)**	
Grade 6	Autistic								2	2	
	Cognitively Delayed	1	1	1	3	2		2	4	5	2
	Emotionally Disturbed	1	5	3	5	4	5		12	3	7
	Hearing Disabled		1	3	3		5	2	9	7	6
	Learning Disabled	17	34	21	30	17	25	19	37	18	33
	Multiple Disabilities			2							
	Orthopedically Disabled	1		2	1				1	1	
	Other Health Disability		1	3	3		5	2	9	7	6
	Speech and Language	1	5	4	4	3	4	4		5	10
	Vision Disability		1								
	Total Females and Males	**21**	**48**	**39**	**49**	**26**	**45**	**29**	**74**	**48**	**64**
	All	**69 (12%)**		**88 (15%)**		**71 (13%)**		**103 (18%)**		**112 (19%)**	

Figure 4.21 (Continued)

Canyon View School District
Special Education Numbers by Grade Level and Gender
2001-02 to 2005-06

Grade Level	Primary Disability	2001-02		2002-03		2003-04		2004-05		2005-06	
		Female	Male	Female	Male	Female	Male	Female	Male	Female	Male
Grade 7	Autistic	1	1			1			1		2
	Cognitively Delayed	3	1	1	1	3	3	3	1	1	5
	Emotionally Disturbed	3	9	1	6	2	4	5	7	2	12
	Hearing Disabled	4	9		1	2	2	4	2	2	11
	Learning Disabled	12	20	7	29	20	32	18	27	20	38
	Multiple Disabilities		2								
	Orthopedically Disabled			1		3	1				1
	Other Health Disability	4	8		1	2	2	2	1	2	11
	Speech and Language	3	1	1	4	4	4	4	1	2	1
	Vision Disabled				1						
	Total Females and Males	**30**	**51**	**11**	**43**	**37**	**48**	**36**	**40**	**30**	**81**
	All	**81 (14%)**		**54 (9%)**		**85 (15%)**		**76 (13%)**		**111 (19%)**	
Grade 8	Autistic		1		2			1		1	1
	Cognitively Delayed	2	2	3	4	1	1	3	2	3	2
	Emotionally Disturbed		7	2	9	3	4	2	5	2	8
	Hearing Disabled	1	1	5	8		4	4	5	3	4
	Learning Disabled	15	34	11	23	9	31	19	36	17	28
	Multiple Disabilities	1	1		1						
	Orthopedically Disabled					1		3	1		
	Other Health Disability	1	1	4	7		4	4	4	2	4
	Speech and Language	1	3	2		1	5	3	4	3	1
	Traumatic Brain Injury		1								
	Total Females and Males	**21**	**51**	**27**	**54**	**15**	**49**	**39**	**57**	**31**	**48**
	All	**72 (11%)**		**81 (13%)**		**64 (11%)**		**96 (16%)**		**79 (14%)**	
Grade 9	Autistic						1			2	1
	Cognitively Delayed	4	2	4	1	4	5	1	2	4	4
	Deaf						1		1		
	Emotionally Disturbed	2	10		5	1	11	2	14	2	4
	Hearing Disabled		2			2	6	1	3	4	4
	Learning Disabled	10	29	17	34	9	17	9	35	18	36
	Multiple Disabilities				1		1				
	Orthopedically Disabled		1			1		1		3	1
	Other Health Disability		2			1	5	1	3	4	3
	Speech and Language								3	3	2
	Traumatic Brain Injured			1	1						
	Vision Disability					1			1		
	Total Females and Males	**16**	**46**	**22**	**42**	**19**	**47**	**15**	**62**	**40**	**55**
	All	**62 (8%)**		**64 (8%)**		**66 (9%)**		**77 (10%)**		**95 (13%)**	

Figure 4.21 (Continued)

Canyon View School District
Special Education Numbers by Grade Level and Gender
2001-02 to 2005-06

Grade Level	Primary Disability	2001-02		2002-03		2003-04		2004-05		2005-06	
		Female	Male	Female	Male	Female	Male	Female	Male	Female	Male
Grade 10	Autistic						1		2		
	Cognitively Delayed	2	3	3	2	4	2	4	5	1	1
	Emotionally Disturbed	2	3	1	7		6	1	9	3	8
	Hearing Disabled	1		1	3		3	6	4	1	3
	Learning Disabled	10	26	6	23	15	25	9	22	8	33
	Multiple Disabilities	2	1	1				1			
	Orthopedically Disabled		1						1	1	
	Other Health Disability	1		1	3		3	5	3	1	3
	Speech and Language	1			1		1				2
	Traumatic Brain Injured					1	1				
	Vision Disabled							1			1
	Total Females and Males	**19**	**34**	**13**	**39**	**20**	**42**	**27**	**46**	**15**	**51**
	All	**53 (7%)**		**52 (7%)**		**62 (8%)**		**73 (10%)**		**66 (9%)**	
Grade 11	Autistic								1		2
	Cognitively Delayed	5	4	3	3	2	4	5	2	4	4
	Deaf										1
	Emotionally Disturbed	1		3	1	1	4		4	1	7
	Hearing Disabled	1	1		2	2		2	4	4	4
	Learning Disabled	9	26	9	20	8	17	11	28	11	25
	Multiple Disabilities				1						
	Orthopedically Disabled			1			1				1
	Other Health Disability	1			2	1		2	4	3	4
	Speech and Language		1	3	1		1		1		1
	Traumatic Brain Injury		1					1	1		
	Vision Disability									1	
	Total Females and Males	**17**	**33**	**19**	**30**	**14**	**27**	**21**	**45**	**24**	**49**
	All	**50 (7%)**		**49 (7%)**		**41 (6%)**		**66 (9%)**		**73 (10%)**	
Grade 12	Autistic		1						1		1
	Cognitively Delayed	3	4	6	5	4	4		2	4	3
	Deaf and Blind	1									
	Emotionally Disturbed				3	2			2		3
	Hearing Disabled	1	3	1			3	1	1	4	3
	Learning Disabled	4	17	8	21	5	16	2	8	13	29
	Multiple Disabilities	1		1		1		1			
	Orthopedically Disabled				1		2				
	Other Health Disability	1	1	1			2	1	1	4	3
	Speech and Language										2
	Traumatic Brain Injured				1					1	
	Vision Disability				1						
	Total Females and Males	**11**	**26**	**17**	**32**	**12**	**27**	**5**	**15**	**26**	**44**
	All	**37 (6%)**		**49 (7%)**		**39 (6%)**		**20 (3%)**		**70 (10%)**	

Figure 4.22 shows the special education numbers by school, primary disability, and gender from 2001-02 to 2005-06.

Look Fors:	**Differences in number of students by primary disability across schools. Increases/decreases within schools, over time.**
Planning Implications:	**Do teachers have the professional learning they need to meet the needs of students with disabilities? Is the manner in which students are being identified as requiring special education services consistent across schools?**

Figure 4.22

Canyon View School District
Special Education Numbers by School, Primary Disability, and Gender
2001-02 to 2005-06

	School	Primary Disability	2001-02		2002-03		2003-04		2004-05		2005-06	
			Female	Male	Female	Male	Female	Male	Female	Male	Female	Male
ELEMENTARY	Elementary 1	Autistic				3		1		1		1
		Cognitively Delayed	3	1	3		3	1	3		1	1
		Emotionally Disturbed			1	1		4		2		1
		Hearing Disabled						1		2		2
		Learning Disabled	1	10	1	11	4	8	4	8	3	7
		Multiple Disabilities				1						
		Other Health Disability						1		2		2
		Speech and Language	3	4	2	4	4	4	7	7	3	8
		Total	**7** (6%)	**15** (10%)	**7** (6%)	**20** (14%)	**11** (8%)	**20** (14%)	**14** (11%)	**22** (14%)	**7** (5%)	**22** (15%)
	Elementary 2	Autistic										1
		Cognitively Delayed	1	1	2	1	2	4	1	4		3
		Emotionally Disturbed	1	1	1	3	3	4	2	8	1	7
		Hearing Disabled	1			1		1	2	5	1	11
		Learning Disabled		6	3	7	5	11	3	5	5	6
		Multiple Disabilities						1				
		Orthopedically Disabled								1		
		Other Health Disability	1			1		1	2	5	1	11
		Speech and Language	2	7	5	7	8	18	13	10	12	15
		Total	**6** (6%)	**15** (13%)	**11** (10%)	**20** (16%)	**18** (16%)	**40** (27%)	**23** (20%)	**38** (30%)	**20** (22%)	**54** (37%)
	Elementary 3	Autistic		1		2		4		4		4
		Cognitively Delayed		1		1		1		3		5
		Deaf			1				1		1	
		Emotionally Disturbed				1		2		2		
		Hearing Disabled	2	5	1	3	2	3			1	2
		Learning Disabled	4	8	3	8		6	1	7	2	5
		Multiple Disabilities				1						
		Other Health Disability		5		3		3				2
		Speech and Language	6	17	4	11	4	21	6	20	8	20
		Total	**12** (8%)	**37** (22%)	**9** (6%)	**30** (19%)	**6** (4%)	**40** (27%)	**8** (6%)	**36** (27%)	**12** (9%)	**38** (28%)
	Elementary 4	Autistic					1		1		1	
		Cognitively Delayed			1		2	1	2	2	2	1
		Emotionally Disturbed						4		4	1	7
		Hearing Disabled	1	3	2	3	3	4	4	4	5	2
		Learning Disabled	10	15	10	14	9	16	14	13	8	15
		Multiple Disabilities	2	1	1	2						
		Orthopedically Disabled		1		1	1	1	1			
		Other Health Disability	1	3	2	3	3	4	4	4	5	2
		Speech and Language	1	4	3	6	3	11	7	15	8	22
		Total	**15** (6%)	**27** (11%)	**19** (8%)	**29** (12%)	**22** (10%)	**41** (17%)	**33** (14%)	**42** (17%)	**30** (13%)	**49** (31%)

Figure 4.22 (Continued)

Canyon View School District
Special Education Numbers by School, Primary Disability, and Gender
2001-02 to 2005-06

ELEMENTARY

School	Primary Disability	2001-02		2002-03		2003-04		2004-05		2005-06	
		Female	Male	Female	Male	Female	Male	Female	Male	Female	Male
Elementary 5	Autistic				2		2		2		2
	Cognitively Delayed	1							1		1
	Emotionally Disturbed	1		1		1	2	2	3	2	2
	Hearing Disabled		4		3		3	1	5	1	4
	Learning Disabled	2	2	4	7	2	6	1	4		3
	Other Health Disability		4		3		3	1	5	1	4
	Speech and Language	2	4	7	5	6	12	5	15	5	12
	Total	**6** (5%)	**14** (10%)	**12** (11%)	**20** (16%)	**9** (7%)	**28** (21%)	**10** (9%)	**35** (26%)	**9** (7%)	**28** (21%)
Elementary 6	Cognitively Delayed		1				1				1
	Emotionally Disturbed				4		1		1		1
	Hearing Disabled						2		1	1	5
	Learning Disabled	3	6	2	5	1	4	1	5		4
	Multiple Disabilities										1
	Orthopedically Disabled	1									1
	Other Health Disability						2		1	1	5
	Speech and Language	1	4	2	5	1	11	3	6	5	6
	Total	**5** (5%)	**11** (8%)	**4** (4%)	**14** (10%)	**2** (3%)	**21** (15%)	**4** (5%)	**14** (11%)	**7** (10%)	**24** (18%)
Elementary 7	Cognitively Delayed							1		1	
	Emotionally Disturbed		1	1		1					1
	Hearing Disabled						4	2	1	2	2
	Learning Disabled	10	10	7	10	5	8	7	11	9	8
	Multiple Disabilities	2	1	1	1	1					
	Other Health Disability						4	2	1	2	1
	Speech and Language		1	2	1	2	4	3	6	3	7
	Traumatic Brain Injured							1		1	
	Total	**12** (9%)	**13** (9%)	**11** (8%)	**12** (9%)	**9** (7%)	**20** (14%)	**16** (14%)	**19** (13%)	**18** (17%)	**19** (13%)
Elementary 8	Cognitively Delayed					2		2	1	2	1
	Emotionally Disturbed			1		1		1			
	Hearing Disabled			1		1	1			1	
	Learning Disabled			3	8	5	10	2	14	4	14
	Other Health Disability			1		1	1				
	Speech and Language			5	10	8	7	7	7	5	13
	Vision Disabled			1		1			1		
	Total			**12** (9%)	**18** (16%)	**19** (16%)	**19** (17%)	**12** (11%)	**23** (20%)	**12** (10%)	**28** (26%)
Elementary 9	Autistic	1	2	1	3	1	3	1	2		1
	Cognitively Delayed	1	3	3	2	2	1	1			1
	Emotionally Disturbed		2	1	1	1		1		2	
	Hearing Disabled		3	2	1		2		5	1	4
	Learning Disabled	10	25	12	29	13	31	12	28	12	22
	Orthopedically Disabled		1				1		1		1
	Other Health Disability		2	2	1		2		5	1	4
	Speech and Language	5	12	11	14	11	13	12	20	14	14
	Total	**17** (8%)	**50** (23%)	**32** (14%)	**51** (21%)	**28** (12%)	**53** (21%)	**27** (12%)	**61** (25%)	**30** (14%)	**47** (21%)

Figure 4.22 (Continued)

Canyon View School District
Special Education Numbers by School, Primary Disability, and Gender
2001-02 to 2005-06

	School	Primary Disability	2001-02		2002-03		2003-04		2004-05		2005-06	
			Female	Male	Female	Male	Female	Male	Female	Male	Female	Male
ELEMENTARY	Elementary 10	Autistic		2		1						
		Cognitively Delayed		1		1	1	1	2	2	3	1
		Emotionally Disturbed	2	14	3	18	1	13	5	10	4	7
		Hearing Disabled	3	3		2	1	4	1	5	3	2
		Learning Disabled		5	2	4	2	8	5	6	7	7
		Multiple Disabilities		1		2						
		Other Health Disability	2	2		2	1	4	1	5	1	2
		Speech and Language	2	4	3	7	5	13	5	13	7	13
		Total	**9 (6%)**	**32 (19%)**	**8 (5%)**	**37 (25%)**	**11 (7%)**	**43 (28%)**	**19 (12%)**	**41 (31%)**	**25 (16%)**	**32 (22%)**
	Elementary 11	Autistic										1
		Cognitively Delayed		1	1	2		3	1	5		4
		Emotionally Disturbed			1			1				
		Hearing Disabled	1		1		2	2	2	4	1	3
		Learning Disabled	5	5	2	3	3	7	3	10	2	12
		Multiple Disabilities		2		2		2				
		Orthopedically Disabled									1	
		Other Health Disabilities						2	1	3	1	2
		Speech and Language	2	5	1	6	2	10	4	15	6	18
		Vision Disabled					1		1			
		Total	**8 (6%)**	**13 (8%)**	**6 (5%)**	**13 (9%)**	**8 (6%)**	**27 (19%)**	**12 (9%)**	**37 (24%)**	**11 (8%)**	**40 (27%)**
	Elementary All	**Autistic**	**1**	**5**	**1**	**11**	**2**	**10**	**2**	**9**	**1**	**10**
		Cognitively Delayed	**6**	**9**	**10**	**7**	**12**	**13**	**13**	**18**	**9**	**19**
		Deaf			**1**				**1**		**1**	**3**
		Emotionally Disturbed	**4**	**18**	**10**	**28**	**8**	**31**	**11**	**30**	**10**	**26**
		Hearing Disabled	**8**	**18**	**7**	**13**	**9**	**27**	**12**	**32**	**17**	**37**
		Learning Disabled	**45**	**92**	**49**	**106**	**49**	**115**	**53**	**111**	**52**	**103**
		Multiple Disabilities	**4**	**5**	**2**	**9**	**1**	**3**				
		Orthopedically Disabled	**1**	**2**		**1**	**1**	**2**	**1**	**2**	**1**	**2**
		Other Health Disabilities	**4**	**16**	**5**	**13**	**5**	**27**	**11**	**31**	**13**	**35**
		Speech and Language	**24**	**62**	**45**	**76**	**54**	**124**	**72**	**134**	**76**	**148**
		Traumatic Brain Injured							**1**		**1**	**3**
		Vision Disabled			**1**		**2**		**1**	**1**		**5**
		Total	**97 30%**	**227 70%**	**131 33%**	**264 67%**	**143 29%**	**352 71%**	**178 33%**	**368 67%**	**181 32%**	**392 68%**

Figure 4.22 (Continued)

Canyon View School District
Special Education Numbers by School, Primary Disability, and Gender
2001-02 to 2005-06

Level	School	Primary Disability	2001-02		2002-03		2003-04		2004-05		2005-06	
			Female	Male	Female	Male	Female	Male	Female	Male	Female	Male
MIDDLE	Middle 1	Autistic				1	1		1	1	2	2
		Cognitively Delayed	2	1	2	5	4	3	4	4	7	3
		Deaf	2									
		Emotionally Disturbed		10	1	8	5	2	3	6	3	7
		Hearing Disabled	4	3	4	4	1	9	8	11	9	11
		Learning Disabled	27	43	22	41	28	47	38	65	41	69
		Multiple Disabiities	1	3	2	1						
		Orthopedically Disabled	1		1	1	2	1	1	1	1	
		Other Health Disabilities	4	3	3	4	1	9	6	9	8	11
		Speech and Language	1	1		1	1	5	7	3	4	5
		Vision Disabled									1	
		Total	**40 (8%)**	**64 (13%)**	**35 (7%)**	**66 (13%)**	**43 (9%)**	**76 (15%)**	**68 (13%)**	**100 (20%)**	**76 (14%)**	**108 (20%)**
	Middle 2	Autistic	1	2		1		1		2	1	1
		Cognitively Delayed	4	3	3	3	2	1	4	3	2	6
		Emotionally Disturbed	4	11	5	12	4	11	4	18	4	19
		Hearing Disabled	1	8	4	8	1	2	2	5	3	9
		Learning Disabled	17	45	17	41	18	41	18	35	14	30
		Orthopedically Disabled			2		2		2	1		1
		Other Health Disability	1	7	4	7	1	2	2	5	3	9
		Speech and Language	4	8	7	7	7	8	4	2	6	7
		Traumatic Brain Injured		1								
		Vision Disabled		1		1						
		Total	**32 (9%)**	**86 (21%)**	**42 (11%)**	**80 (20%)**	**35 (10%)**	**66 (17%)**	**36 (11%)**	**71 (19%)**	**33 (10%)**	**82 (24%)**
	Middle All	**Autistic**	**1**	**2**		**2**	**1**	**1**	**1**	**3**	**3**	**3**
		Cognitively Delayed	**6**	**4**	**5**	**8**	**6**	**4**	**8**	**7**	**9**	**9**
		Deaf	**2**									
		Emotionally Disturbed	**4**	**21**	**6**	**20**	**9**	**13**	**7**	**24**	**7**	**26**
		Hearing Disabled	**5**	**11**	**8**	**12**	**2**	**11**	**10**	**16**	**12**	**20**
		Learning Disabled	**44**	**88**	**39**	**82**	**46**	**88**	**56**	**100**	**55**	**99**
		Multiple Disabilities	**1**	**3**	**2**	**1**						**12**
		Orthopedically Disabled	**1**		**3**	**1**	**4**	**1**	**3**	**2**	**1**	**1**
		Other Health Disablity	**5**	**10**	**7**	**11**	**2**	**11**	**8**	**14**	**11**	**20**
		Speech and Language	**5**	**9**	**7**	**8**	**8**	**13**	**11**	**5**	**10**	**12**
		Traumatic Brain Injured		**1**								**1**
		Vision Disability		**1**		**1**					**1**	
		Total	**74 33%**	**150 67%**	**77 35%**	**146 65%**	**78 35%**	**142 65%**	**104 38%**	**171 62%**	**109 35%**	**203 65%**

Figure 4.22 (Continued)

Canyon View School District
Special Education Numbers by School, Primary Disability, and Gender
2001-02 to 2005-06

	School	Primary Disability	2001-02		2002-03		2003-04		2004-05		2005-06	
			Female	Male	Female	Male	Female	Male	Female	Male	Female	Male
HIGH	High 1	Autistic									1	
		Cognitively Delayed	3	8	4	8	3	6		6	2	6
		Emotionally Disturbed	2	5	2	10	1	10	1	8	1	7
		Hearing Disabled	1	1	1	2	1	1	5	6	7	9
		Learning Disabled	17	53	19	48	18	43	18	48	26	61
		Multiple Disabiities	2				1	1				
		Orthopedically Disabled		1	1			1	1	1	2	2
		Other Health Disabilities	1		1	2			4	6	6	6
		Speech and Language			1	1				1	1	3
		Vision Disabled								1		1
		Total	**26 (4%)**	**68 (10%)**	**29 (4%)**	**71 (10%)**	**24 (4%)**	**62 (9%)**	**29 (5%)**	**77 (12%)**	**46 (7%)**	**97 (14%)**
	High 2	Autistic		1				2		4	1	4
		Cognitively Delayed	11	5	12	3	11	9	9	5	11	6
		Deaf						1		1		1
		Deaf and Blind	1									
		Emotionally Disturbed	3	8	2	6	3	11	2	21	4	15
		Hearing Disabled	2	5	1	3	3	11	4	6	4	5
		Learning Disabled	16	45	21	50	19	32	11	41	19	57
		Multiple Disabilities	1	1	2	2			2			
		Orthopedically Disabled		1		1	1	2			2	
		Other Health Disability	2	3	1	3	2	10	4	5	4	5
		Speech and Language	1	1	2	1		2		3	2	4
		Traumatic Brain Injured		1	1	2	1	1	1	1	1	
		Vision Disabled				1	1		1		1	
		Total	**37 (5%)**	**71 (10%)**	**42 (5%)**	**72 (9%)**	**41 (5%)**	**81 (11%)**	**34 (4%)**	**87 (11%)**	**49 (7%)**	**97 (12%)**
	High All	**Autistic**		**1**				**2**		**4**	**2**	**4**
		Cognitively Delayed	**14**	**13**	**16**	**11**	**14**	**15**	**9**	**11**	**13**	**12**
		Deaf						**1**		**1**		**1**
		Deaf and Blind	**1**									
		Emotionally Disturbed	**5**	**13**	**4**	**16**	**4**	**21**	**3**	**29**	**5**	**22**
		Hearing Disabled	**3**	**6**	**2**	**5**	**4**	**12**	**9**	**12**	**11**	
		Learning Disabled	**33**	**98**	**40**	**98**	**37**	**75**	**29**	**89**	**45**	**118**
		Multiple Disabilities	**3**	**1**	**2**	**2**	**1**	**1**	**2**			**14**
		Orthopedically Disabled		**2**	**1**	**1**	**1**	**3**	**1**	**1**	**4**	**2**
		Other Health Disablity	**3**	**3**	**2**	**5**	**2**	**10**	**8**	**11**	**10**	**11**
		Speech and Language	**1**	**1**	**3**	**2**		**2**		**4**	**3**	**7**
		Traumatic Brain Injured		**1**	**1**	**2**	**1**	**1**	**1**	**1**	**1**	
		Vision Disability				**1**	**1**		**1**	**1**	**1**	**1**
		Total	**63 31%**	**139 69%**	**71 33%**	**143 67%**	**65 31%**	**143 69%**	**63 28%**	**164 72%**	**95 33%**	**192 67%**

Plan 504

Section 504 is part of the *Rehabilitation Act of 1973,* which is a civil rights act that protects the rights of people with disabilities. The law states that no person with a disability can be excluded from or denied benefits of any program receiving federal financial assistance; this includes all public schools. With the passage of the *Rehabilitation Act of 1973,* Congress required that school districts make their programs and activities accessible as well as usable to all individuals with disabilities.

Section 504 regulations require recipients of Federal financial assistance to provide to each qualified person with a disability a Free Appropriate Public Education (FAPE) designed to meet individual educational needs of persons with disabilities as adequately as the needs of non-disabled persons are met. This must be based on adherence to the procedural requirements of the regulation (educational setting, evaluation, placement, and procedural safeguards).

Section 504 falls under the management responsibility of the general, rather than special education program. No state or federal funding is provided to assist in complying with *Section 504.* All costs are the obligation of the local school.

Section 504 defines a person as disabled if she or he has (or is perceived to have) a mental or physical impairment which substantially limits one or more major life activities. This includes caring for one's self, performing manual tasks, walking, seeing, hearing, speaking, breathing, learning, and working. When a condition does not substantially limit a major life activity, the individual does not qualify for special accommodations under *Section 504.*

Figure 4.23 shows the number of students eligible for 504 services by grade level and gender between 2001-02 and 2005-06.

Look Fors: **Changes in the number of students eligible for 504 services, within grade levels by gender, and across grade levels, over time.**

Planning Implications: **Have more 504 services been required over time, and do teachers know how to provide the services? Is new professional learning necessary?**

Figure 4.23

Canyon View School District
Number of Students Eligible for Plan 504 Services by Grade Level and Gender
2001-02 to 2005-06

Grade Level	2001-02			2002-03			2003-04			2004-05			2005-06		
	Female	Male	Total	Female	Male	Total	Female	Male	Total	Female	Male	Total	Female	Male	Total
Morning Kindergarten							1		1						
Afternoon Kindergarten								1	1					1	1
Grade 1	2		2				1	1	2	2	2	4			
Grade 2	1	1	2	1		1		2	2	3	2	5	2	3	5
Grade 3	1		1		2	2	2	1	3	3	4	7	4	4	8
Grade 4		1	1				3	4	7	2	3	5	6	7	13
Grade 5	3	1	4		1	1	3		3	7	6	13	4	4	8
Grade 6	5	3	8	5	4	9	4	1	5	8	2	10	4	4	8
Grade 7	1		1	5	2	7	6	4	10	6	5	11	6	2	8
Grade 8	5	5	10	3		3	4	3	7	11	5	16	4	6	10
Grade 9	2	4	6	3	3	6	2		2	4	5	9	9	6	15
Grade 10	1	7	8	4	3	7	3	6	9	3	1	4	6	4	10
Grade 11	3	9	12	2	2	4	5	3	8	1	3	4	1	7	8
Grade 12	3	3	6	3	9	12		6	6	3	1	4	3	10	13
Total	**27**	**34**	**61**	**27**	**26**	**53**	**34**	**32**	**66**	**53**	**39**	**92**	**49**	**58**	**107**

Figure 4.24 shows the number of students eligible for *Section 504* services by school, gender, and grade level.

Look Fors: Changes in the number of students eligible for 504 services, within grade levels by gender, and across grade levels and schools, over time.

Planning Implications: Are there more services required over time, and do teachers know how to provide services? Is new professional learning necessary?

Figure 4.24

Canyon View School District
Number of Students Eligible for Plan 504 Services by School and Grade Level
2001-02 to 2005-06

	School	Grade Level	2001-02			2002-03			2003-04			2004-05			2005-06		
			Female	Male	Total	Female	Male	Total	Female	Male	Total	Female	Male	Total	Female	Male	Total
ELEMENTARY	**Elementary 1**	Grade 1	1		1												
		Grade 3					1	1									
		Grade 4							1	1	2				1		1
		Grade 5										1	2	3			
		Total	**1**		**1**		**1**	**1**	**1**	**1**	**2**	**1**	**2**	**3**	**1**		**1**
	Elementary 2	Grade 1											1	1			
		Grade 2											1	1		1	1
		Grade 3							1		1					2	2
		Grade 4										1	1				
		Grade 5													1		1
		Total							**1**		**1**	**1**	**2**	**3**	**1**	**3**	**4**
	Elementary 3	Grade 1										1		1			
		Grade 2	1	1	2												
		Grade 3	1		1		1	1	1		1						
		Grade 4		1	1					1	1						
		Grade 5	3	1	4		1	1	1		1	1	1	2			
		Total	**5**	**3**	**8**		**2**	**2**	**2**	**1**	**3**	**2**	**1**	**3**			
	Elementary 4	Grade 2										1		1			
		Grade 3										1		1	1		1
		Grade 5										1		1			
		Total										**3**		**3**	**1**		**1**
	Elementary 5	PM Kindergarten														1	1
		Grade 2													2		2
		Grade 4											1	1			
		Grade 5														1	1
		Total											**1**	**1**	**2**	**2**	**4**
	Elementary 6	Grade 1								1	1						
		Grade 2											1	1			
		Grade 3														1	1
		Grade 4							1	1	2	1	1	2	2		2
		Grade 5							1		1	1	2	3	2	1	3
		Total							**2**	**2**	**4**	**2**	**4**	**6**	**4**	**2**	**6**
	Elementary 7	Grade 4													1	1	2
		Total													**1**	**1**	**2**
	Elementary 8	Grade 4														1	1
		Total														**1**	**1**

Figure 4.24 (Continued)

Canyon View School District
Number of Students Eligible for Plan 504 Services by School and Grade Level
2001-02 to 2005-06

Level	School	Grade Level	2001-02			2002-03			2003-04			2004-05			2005-06		
			Female	Male	Total	Female	Male	Total	Female	Male	Total	Female	Male	Total	Female	Male	Total
ELEMENTARY	Elementary 9	AM Kindergarten				1		1	1		1						
		PM Kindergarten								1	1						
		Grade 1	1		1				1		1	1	1	2			
		Grade 2				1		1		2	2	2		2		1	1
		Grade 3								1	1	1	3	4	2	1	3
		Grade 4							1	1	2		1	1	1	3	4
		Grade 5							1		1	2	1	3	1	1	2
		Total	**1**		**1**	**2**		**2**	**4**	**5**	**9**	**6**	**6**	**12**	**4**	**6**	**10**
	Elementary 10	Grade 3											1	1	1		1
		Grade 4														1	1
		Total											**1**	**1**	**1**	**1**	**2**
	Elementary 11	Grade 2														1	1
		Grade 3										1		1			
		Grade 4													1	1	2
		Grade 5										1		1		1	1
		Total										**2**		**2**	**1**	**3**	**4**
MIDDLE	Middle 1	Grade 6	2	1	3							5	1	6	4	2	6
		Grade 7				1	1	2				2	4	6	3	1	4
		Grade 8							1	1	2	4	1	5	2	5	7
		Total	**2**	**1**	**3**	**1**	**1**	**2**	**1**	**1**	**2**	**11**	**6**	**17**	**9**	**8**	**17**
	Middle 2	Grade 6	3	2	5	5	4	9	4	1	5	3	1	4		2	2
		Grade 7	1		1	4	1	5	6	4	10	4	1	5	3	1	4
		Grade 8	5	5	10	3		3	3	2	5	7	4	11	2	1	3
		Total	**9**	**7**	**16**	**12**	**5**	**17**	**13**	**7**	**20**	**14**	**6**	**20**	**5**	**4**	**9**
HIGH	High 1	Grade 9	2	4	6		2	2	2		2		4	4	3	2	5
		Grade 10	1	7	8	4	3	7	1	5	6		1	1	2	2	4
		Grade 11	3	9	12	2	2	4	5	3	8	1	2	3		4	4
		Grade 12	3	3	6	3	9	12		6	6	3	1	4	2	5	7
		Total	**9**	**23**	**32**	**9**	**16**	**25**	**8**	**14**	**24**	**4**	**8**	**12**	**7**	**13**	**20**
	High 2	Grade 9				3	1	4				3	1	4	6	4	10
		Grade 10							2	1	3	2		2	3	1	4
		Grade 11											1	1	1		1
		Grade 12													1	1	2
		Total				**3**	**1**	**4**	**2**	**1**	**3**	**5**	**2**	**7**	**11**	**6**	**17**

Gifted Program

In 2005-06, there were 1,579 female and 1,481 male students enrolled in the district's gifted program. Figure 4.25 shows the number of students qualified to receive gifted services versus those students participating in the program by grade level and gender for 2005-06. The numbers prior to 2005-06 were not accurate, so they are not displayed here. There is no gifted program at the high school level.

Look Fors: **Changes in the number and percentage of students qualified for and participating in the gifted program by gender and grade levels, over time.**

Planning Implications: **Are there enough services for gifted students? Are the services effective? Is there a difference in the number qualified versus number enrolled? Why would students choose not to participate?**

Figure 4.25

Canyon View School District
Gifted Student Enrollment Numbers by Grade Level and Gender
2005-06

Grade Level	2005-06								
	Female			Male			Total		
	Qualified	Participated		Qualified	Participated		Qualified	Participated	
Grade 3	244	205	84%	468	439	94%	712	644	90%
Grade 4	430	270	63%	416	345	83%	846	615	73%
Grade 5	474	450	95%	555	486	88%	1,029	936	91%
Grade 6	428	183	43%	316	50	16%	744	233	31%
Grade 7	369	282	76%	165	147	89%	534	429	80%
Grade 8	278	189	68%	141	14	10%	419	203	48%
Total	2,224	1,579	71%	2,061	1,481	72%	4,285	3,060	71%
% of Population	58%	42%		58%	42%		58%	42%	

Figure 4.26 shows the number of qualified and participating gifted students by school, grade level, and gender for the same time period.

Look Fors: **Changes in the number and percentage of students qualified for and participating in the gifted program by school, gender, and grade level, over time.**

Planning Implications: **How are the students identified for participation in the gifted program? What services are offered gifted students in high school?**

Figure 4.26

Canyon View School District
Gifted Student Enrollment Numbers
By School, Grade Level, and Gender, 2005-06

School	Grade Level	2005-06			
		Female		Male	
		Qualified	Participated	Qualified	Participated
Elementary 1	Grade 3	40	40	7	7
	Grade 4	48	48	13	13
	Grade 5	1	1	6	6
	Total	**89**	**89**	**26**	**26**
Elementary 2	Grade 3	20	20	52	52
	Grade 4	13	13	12	12
	Grade 5			45	45
	Total	**33**	**33**	**109**	**109**
Elementary 3	Grade 3	13	13	101	101
	Grade 4	50	50	29	29
	Grade 5	66	66	44	37
	Total	**129**	**129**	**174**	**167**
Elementary 4	Grade 3	97	63	89	73
	Grade 4	9	9	109	76
	Grade 5	80	69	119	93
	Total	**186**	**141**	**317**	**242**
Elementary 5	Grade 3	30	30	58	58
	Grade 4	50	28	38	4
	Grade 5	140	140	113	113
	Total	**220**	**198**	**209**	**175**
Elementary 6	Grade 3			13	
	Grade 4			95	95
	Grade 5	76	76	133	133
	Total	**76**	**76**	**241**	**228**
Elementary 7	Grade 3	9	9	31	31
	Grade 4	8	8	15	15
	Grade 5	4	4	34	34
	Total	**21**	**21**	**80**	**80**

Figure 4.26 (Continued)

Canyon View School District
Gifted Student Enrollment Numbers
By School, Grade Level, and Gender, 2005-06

School	Grade Level	2005-06			
		Female		Male	
		Qualified	Participated	Qualified	Participated
Elementary 8	Grade 3	6	6		
	Grade 4	14	14		
	Grade 5	12	12	1	1
	Total	**32**	**32**	**1**	**1**
Elementary 9	Grade 3			32	32
	Grade 4	146	43	82	78
	Grade 5	42	31	43	24
	Total	**188**	**74**	**157**	**134**
Elementary 10	Grade 3	29	24	85	85
	Grade 4	51	16	6	6
	Grade 5	47	45	17	
	Total	**127**	**85**	**108**	**91**
Elementary 11	Grade 3				
	Grade 4	41	41	17	17
	Grade 5	6	6		
	Total	**47**	**47**	**17**	**17**
Elementary All	**Grade 3**	**244**	**205**	**468**	**439**
	Grade 4	**430**	**270**	**416**	**345**
	Grade 5	**474**	**450**	**555**	**486**
	Total	**1,148**	**925**	**1,439**	**1,270**
Middle 1	Grade 6	223	101	164	34
	Grade 7	248	188	54	41
	Grade 8	156	73	141	14
	Total	**627**	**362**	**359**	**89**
Middle 2	Grade 6	205	82	152	16
	Grade 7	122	94	111	106
	Grade 8	122	116		
	Total	**449**	**292**	**263**	**122**
Middle All	**Grade 6**	**428**	**183**	**316**	**50**
	Grade 7	**370**	**282**	**165**	**147**
	Grade 8	**278**	**189**	**141**	**14**
	Total	**1,076**	**654**	**622**	**211**

Advanced Placement Classes

Canyon View high schools have offered five advanced placement (AP) classes (American Government, American History, Biology II, English IV, and Spanish) for the past four years. Figure 4.27, below, shows the number of students enrolled in advanced placement classes, over time, by high school. Unfortunately, AP data by gender and/or ethnicity were not available.

Look Fors: **Increases or decreases in enrollment numbers over time. The number of advanced placement (AP) courses being offered. Differences in AP enrollment between high schools.**

Planning Implications: **Who is being served by AP, and who is not? Why are students not signing up for AP? Are other AP classes needed?**

Figure 4.27

Canyon View School District
Advanced Placement Subject Student Enrollment
2002-03 to 2005-06

AP Class	High School 1				High School 2			
	2002-03	2003-04	2004-05	2005-06	2002-03	2003-04	2004-05	2005-06
American Government	52	63	77	55	12	33	22	38
American History	26	62	42	74				
Biology II		59						
English IV		36	40	29	78	71	57	90
Spanish	3		3	8				1
Total	**81**	**220**	**162**	**166**	**90**	**104**	**79**	**129**

The Staff

Canyon View's superintendent, a White male, has been superintendent in this district for seven years. There were 476 teachers in the district in the 2005-06 school year, down from each of the previous years (Figure 4.28).

Look Fors:	**Increases/decreases in number of teachers over time, commensurate with student population.**
Planning Implications:	**Are there enough teachers to keep class sizes low?**

Figure 4.28

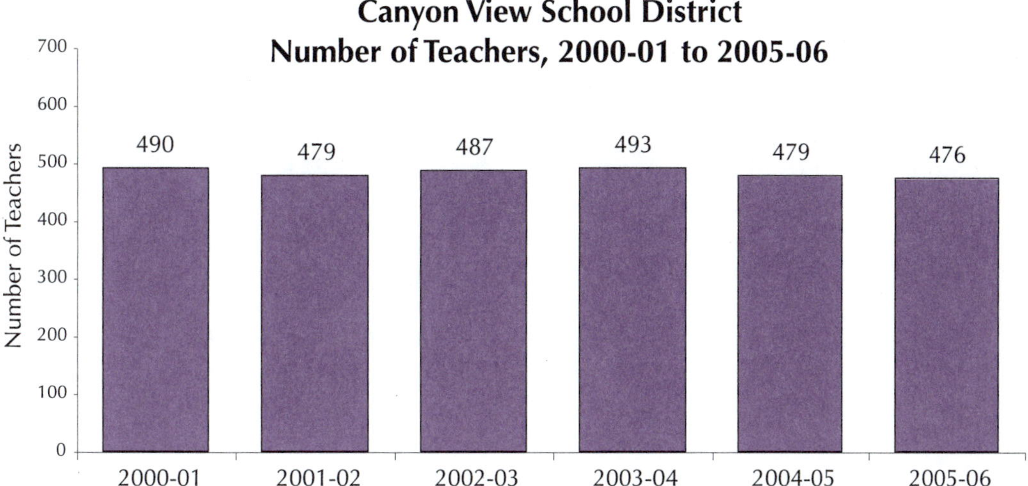

Figure 4.29 show that, in 2005-06, of the 476 teachers, 320 (69%) were female and 141 (31%) were male. All but 15 teachers in 2005-06 were White.

Look Fors:	Gender and ethnic balance.
Planning Implications:	Does the district need to recruit more teachers of a particular gender or ethnicity?

Figure 4.29

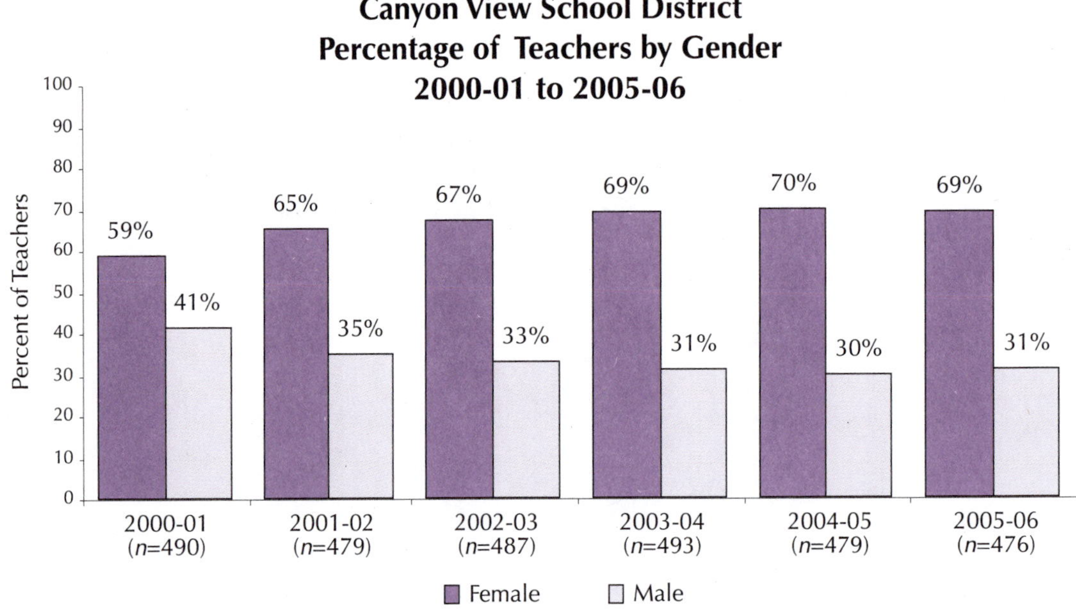

Figure 4.30 shows the number of full-time equivalent (FTE) teachers by school for the two years for which there is data—2004-05 and 2005-06.

Look Fors: **Increase/decreases in FTE over time within and across schools.**

Planning Implications: **Is there equality across schools? Are there any student-to-teacher ratios that are too high?**

Figure 4.30

Canyon View School District
Teacher FTE by School
2004-05 to 2005-06

School	2004-05	2005-06
Elementary 1	16.9	17.0
Elementary 2	18.6	18.2
Elementary 3	18.9	17.7
Elementary 4	29.5	26.5
Elementary 5	14.1	14.1
Elementary 6	11.9	11.9
Elementary 7	15.8	15.8
Elementary 8	14.0	14.2
Elementary 9	25.0	25.1
Elementary 10	20.7	20.3
Elementary 11	17.4	17.9
Elementary All	**202.8**	**198.7**
Middle 1	60.5	59.9
Middle 2	52.6	52.1
Middle All	**113.1**	**112.0**
High 1	87.8	88.5
High 2	112.7	112.1
High All	**200.5**	**200.6**
All	**516.4**	**511.3**

The student/teacher ratio is one of the lowest in the state with an average of 17 students per teacher in 2005-06. Figure 4.31 shows the average student-to-teacher ratio by school for 2001-02 through 2005-06.

Look Fors: **Increase/decreases in student-to-teacher ratios over time within and across schools.**

Planning Implications: **Is there equality across schools?**

Figure 4.31

Canyon View School District
Student to Teacher Ratio by School
2001-02 to 2005-06

School	2001-02			2002-03			2003-04			2004-05			2005-06		
	Students	Teachers	Total	Students	Teachers	Total	Students	Teachers	Total	Students	Teachers	Total	Students	Teachers	Total
Elementary 1	274	13	21.1	266	11	24.2	281	12	23.4	281	13	21.6	270	12	22.5
Elementary 2	225	10	22.5	230	12	19.2	263	12	21.9	242	12	20.2	238	12	19.8
Elementary 3	319	14	22.8	317	14	22.6	297	14	21.2	271	13	20.8	273	12	22.8
Elementary 4	486	24	20.3	482	23	21.0	468	22	21.3	485	22	22.0	497	23	21.6
Elementary 5	265	13	20.4	235	10	23.5	252	11	22.9	253	11	23.0	261	11	23.7
Elementary 6	254	11	23.1	232	11	21.1	218	10	21.8	200	9	22.2	201	9	22.3
Elementary 7	284	12	23.7	270	12	22.5	273	12	22.8	260	11	23.6	258	11	23.5
Elementary 8				246	12	20.5	234	12	19.5	228	11	20.7	223	11	20.3
Elementary 9	439	20	22.0	480	20	24.0	482	22	21.9	457	20	22.9	438	20	21.9
Elementary 10	316	16	19.8	302	14	21.6	308	14	22.0	293	14	20.9	297	14	21.2
Elementary 11	278	14	19.9	275	12	22.9	270	12	22.5	291	13	22.4	286	13	22.0
Elementary All	**3,140**	**147**	**21.4**	**3,335**	**151**	**22.1**	**3,346**	**153**	**21.9**	**3,261**	**149**	**21.9**	**3,242**	**148**	**21.9**
Middle 1	1,035	69	15.0	1,002	69	14.5	1,004	63	15.9	1,037	64	16.2	1,086	65	16.7
Middle 2	786	58	13.6	762	49	15.6	725	48	15.1	703	49	14.3	674	50	13.5
Middle All	**1,821**	**127**	**14.3**	**1,764**	**118**	**14.9**	**1,729**	**111**	**15.6**	**1,740**	**113**	**15.4**	**1,760**	**115**	**15.3**
High 1	1,336	96	13.9	1,377	102	13.5	1,314	100	13.1	1,298	95	13.7	1,338	94	14.2
High 2	1,503	118	12.7	1,598	122	13.1	1,551	123	12.6	1,549	118	13.1	1,527	118	12.9
High All	**2,839**	**214**	**13.3**	**2,975**	**224**	**13.3**	**2,865**	**223**	**12.8**	**2,847**	**213**	**13.4**	**2,865**	**212**	**13.5**

Figure 4.32 shows that the majority of district teachers (includes some part-time teachers) possess many years of teaching experience, with the highest number of teachers in any five-year span having taught for 6 to 10 years (*n*=105), 11 to 15 years (*n*=91), and 16 to 20 (*n*=85) years. Average number of years of teaching across the district is 18.

Look Fors: Number of years of teaching experience of the teaching staff.

Planning Implications: Will there be retirements in the near future? Is a new teacher mentoring program required?

Figure 4.32

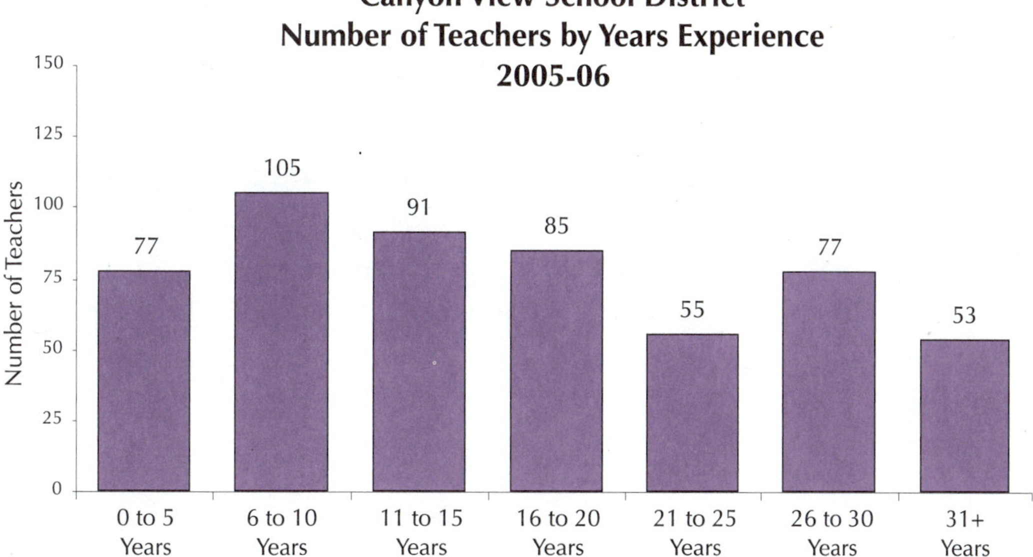

Figure 4.33 shows the current age of Canyon View's teaching staff for 2005-06.

Look Fors: **Relative ages of the teaching staff.**

Planning Implications: **Are there potential retirements on the horizon? How stable is staff? Is there a plan for recruitment of new teachers?**

Figure 4.33

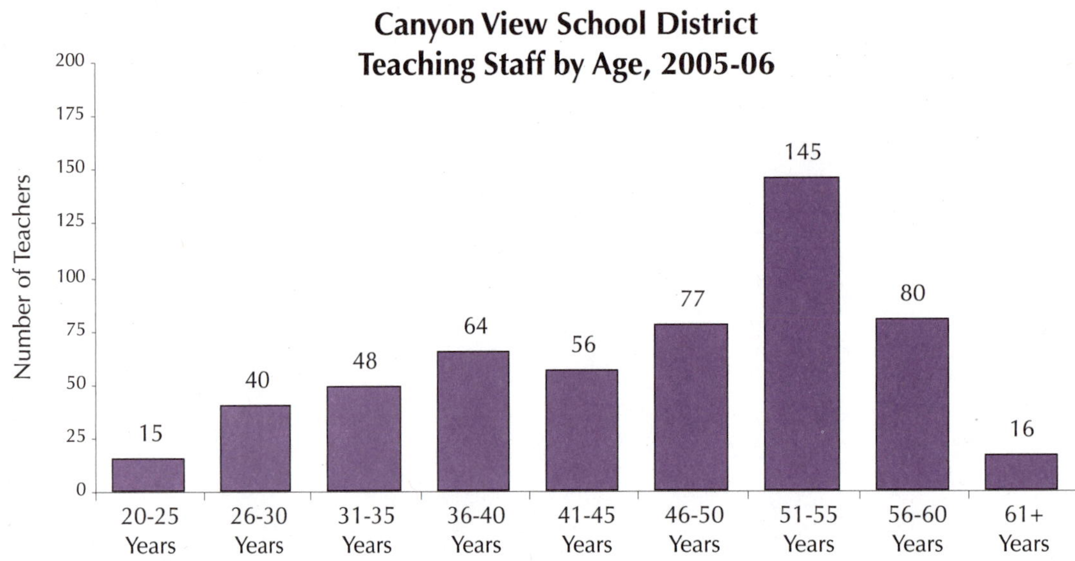

The mission of the school district is to challenge and empower each student to become a competent, productive, responsible, caring citizen. To accomplish this mission, the district employs a well-educated staff: 63% of certified staff have a M.A. or beyond; 28% have a B.A. plus one to three years of additional education; and 9% have a B.A. Figure 4.34 shows the educational qualifications for teachers in 2005-06.

Look Fors: The qualifications of staff.

Planning Implications: What are the costs of inexperienced versus experienced teachers? Do inexperienced teachers need additional college credits or training?

Figure 4.34

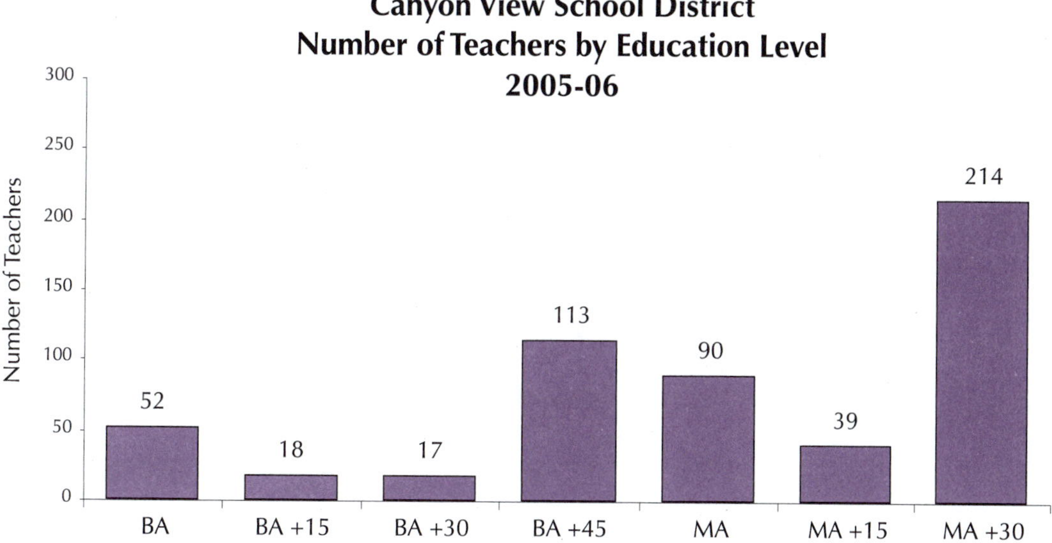

Figure 4.35 shows the average number of years of teaching experience by grade level, over time.

Look Fors: **Number of years of teaching experience within and across grade levels.**

Planning Implications: **Is a teacher mentoring program required within specific grade levels? Is teaching expertise even across grade levels?**

Figure 4.35

Canyon View School District Teachers Average Number of Years Experience by Grade Level 2001-02 to 2005-06

Grade Level	2001-02	2002-03	2003-04	2004-05	2005-06
Kindergarten	14.4	13.4	13.4	10.0	9.2
Grade 1	13.0	12.6	12.5	8.5	9.5
Grade 2	13.8	13.9	13.7	10.2	10.4
Grade 3	13.0	12.3	12.3	10.2	10.6
Grade 4	12.5	13.1	12.4	9.5	10.4
Grade 5	13.1	13.0	12.1	8.9	9.6
Grade 6	14.1	13.5	12.4	8.4	9.5
Grade 7	13.7	13.1	12.4	9.1	9.0
Grade 8	13.8	12.3	12.5	8.9	8.9
Grade 9	13.8	12.3	12.5	8.9	8.9
Grade 10	15.9	14.7	14.0	9.2	8.6
Grade 11	16.4	14.8	14.3	9.0	8.5
Grade 12	16.3	15.2	13.6	9.1	8.9

If the data are available, one would want to see the number of years of teaching by grade level for each school.

Look Fors: **The number of years of teaching experience across grade levels within schools.**

Planning Implications: **Are all grade levels adequately covered by number of years of teaching experience?**

Study Questions for Who Are We?

As you review Canyon View School District's data, use either the margins in the text, this page, or print this page from the CD-ROM to write down your thinking. (Ch4Qs.pdf) These notes, of course, are only placeholders until all the data are analyzed. If thinking about "strengths" and "challenges" is difficult, list "observations." It is important to jot down your thinking as you go through the data so you can see if additional data corroborate your first impressions.

1. What are the demographic *strengths* and *challenges* for Canyon View School District?	
Strengths	*Challenges*

2. What are some *implications* for the Canyon View's improvement plan?

3. Looking at the data presented, what other demographic data would you want to answer the question *Who are we?* for Canyon View School District?

What I Saw in the Example: Canyon View School District

At the end of each chapter, I add what I saw in the data, using the study questions. CD-ROM (Ch4Saw.pdf) When applicable, I have referenced the figure or page number that gave me my first impression of strengths and challenges.

Demographic Strengths	*Demographic Challenges*
• The Canyon View community sounds stable and economically viable, with low unemployment. Ninety-one percent of the residents have high school degrees, and 44% have some post-secondary education. (Page 44) • Canyon View is a medium-size school district with several schools. (Page 44) • Parent involvement sounds very good at elementary and middle school levels. (Page 44) • Schools have established partnerships with businesses. (Page 44-45) • Several extracurricular activities are offered at Canyon View. (Page 45) • About 80% of the graduates go onto college, trade schools, or the military. (Page 45) • The total enrollment by district has been relatively stable over time. (Figure 4.1) • Elementary school sizes are relatively small and stable. (Figure 4.9) • Some principals have lots of experience. (Figure 4.9) • The gender and ethnic enrollment by grade level and school have been relatively consistent over time. (Figures 4.10 and 4.11) • There is a relatively small percentage of students with families that qualify for free/reduced lunches. (Figure 4.12) • The largest schools tend to have some of the lowest percentages of free lunch students. (Figure 4.13)	• There is little diversity in the community. • There have been about 2% more male students than female students over time. (Figure 4.2) • The minorities in this school district are really in the minority. (Figures 4.3 and 4.4) • Enrollment surges in grade 9 with the influx of students from the rural K-8 district. (Figure 4.6) • The mobility rate is calculated to be 17%. (Page 68) • The elementary school enrollments are relatively small. Elementary students go to middle and high schools that are 4 to 6 times larger. (Figure 4.9) • Some schools have seen some enrollment fluctuations. Elementary schools 4 and 9 are almost twice the size of the other elementary schools. Middle school 1 is much larger than middle school 2. High school 2 has about 200 more students than high school 1. (Figure 4.9) • Elementary 9 looks like the only elementary school with the most declining enrollment in the past few years. (Figure 4.9) • Middle school 1 has increasing enrollment while middle school 2 is decreasing. (Figure 4.9) • Currently, 23% of the Canyon View school age population qualifies for free/reduced lunch. By school, the free/reduced lunch rates vary. (Figures 4.12 and 4.13) • It appears as though the high schools are not following up on students to return forms to qualify them for free/reduced lunches. (Figure 4.13) • The schools with the most challenging populations, with respect to free/reduced lunch, are Elementary 1, 2, and 11. (Figure 4.13) • The mobility rates for elementary schools increased in 2005-06. • Mobility rates are very different for the two middle schools. (Figure 4.14)

Demographic Strengths	Demographic Challenges
• Elementary school mobility is very small. (Figure 4.14) • Discipline referrals decreased from 2004-05 to 2005-06, especially in grades 6, 7, 8, 9, 11, and 12. (Figure 4.21) • Suspensions have decreased from grades 9 and 10 to grades 11 and 12. (Figure 4.18) • There is a program for gifted students. (Page 93) • Less than one-third of the teachers are male. (Figure 4.29) • The student/teacher ratio is fairly small, especially at the high schools. (Figure 4.31) • Teachers are experienced and well-educated. (Figures 4.32, 4.33, 4.34, and 4.35)	• The attendance rates are could be improved. (Figure 4.16) • The largest elementary schools have lower attendance rates. (Figure 4.17) • Elementary 11 has the lowest attendance rate for all schools. (Figure 4.17) • The high school completion rate is low and decreasing, especially for high school 2. (Page 72) • Discipline referrals are high. (Figures 4.18 and 4.19) • School leadership seems to be related to discipline numbers and suspensions. (Figure 4.19) • The number of students being identified for special education services has increased substantially over the past six years, with over twice as many males than females each year. (Figure 4.20) • There is an increase in special education in early grades. (Figure 4.21) • There are some elementary schools with very high Sp. Ed. percentages (2, 3, 4, 8, 11). (Figure 4.22) • There is an increase of students requiring 504 services. (Figure 4.23) • Gifted numbers are low, with none at the high school level. (Figures 4.25 and 4.26) • Elementary Schools 4, 5, 9, 10, and the middle schools have more students qualified than participating in the gifted program. (Figure 4.26) • There are not many AP classes offered at the high schools, especially high school 2. (Figure 4.27) • There are quite a few more females than male teachers in a district with a majority of male students each year. All but 15 teachers were white in 2005-06. (Figure 4.29) • Teaching experience has been going down at the high school level. (Figure 4.35) • Retirements will have an impact over the next few years. (Figure 4.33)

What I Saw in the Example: Canyon View School District (Continued)

Implications for Canyon View's continuous improvement plan

- Canyon View needs to clean its data better—especially attendance data.
- Is there a need for diversity training programs and materials?
- Is there a program to welcome the new students to Canyon View schools?
- Is there some way to get high school families to return forms for free/reduced lunch? This could translate into significant monies for the district.
- Who are the students that are mobile and where do they go?
- Attendance needs to be looked into—which students are not attending, why are they not attending, when are they not attending?
- Who are the students who are dropping out and why? What about a program to prevent dropouts?
- Why so many discipline referrals? Who, when, where and why the referrals are happening needs to be studied.
- It appears that where there are high discipline referrals, there is also high absenteeism and high special education in the elementary schools. What can be done about this relationship?
- How are students identified for special education services? What is the effectiveness of how they are being served? Why so many more males than females?
- What are the high schools doing to serve the students who were once identified for special education services?
- Are the high schools offering advanced programs for the higher achieving students?
- Can more male teachers and those of other ethnicities be recruited? Maybe younger teachers as well?
- Do teachers have the professional learning they need to work with students with special needs, classes with mostly males, and the tiny number of minorities that are in the school district?

Other desired demographic data or information

- Why is the student population at elementary schools 4 and 9 so much larger than at the other elementary schools? Why is middle school 2 smaller than middle school 1 and losing enrollment?
- Why are students dropping out? Where do they go?
- Need better data related to discipline.
- We want to know about the Alternative School.
- What happens to the students when they do not graduate?
- Why are some students electing not to participate in programs for the gifted?
- What other programs do the schools and district offer?
- Special education numbers by ethnicity.
- Advanced placement test results.
- Advanced placement enrollment by gender and ethnicity.
- Average attendance by school.
- The number of years of teaching by grade level for each school.

Summary

The first data required for continuous district improvement planning are demographic data. With demographic data, we are answering the basic question, *Who are we?* (Demodata.pdf) The answers to the question, *Who are we?*, set the context for the district, have huge implications for the direction the continuous district improvement plan will take, and can help explain how the district and schools get the results they are getting. Our main example district, Canyon View School District, showed how a demographic analysis could look. The accompanying CD-ROM has tools and templates to help your district create a comprehensive demographic profile. The CD also has 3 additional size district examples.

With demographic data, we are answering the basic question, "Who are we?" The answers to the question, "Who are we?", set the context for the district, have huge implications for the direction the continuous district improvement plan will take, and can help explain how the district and schools get the results they are getting.

Typical Demographic Data to Gather to Answer the Question, *Who Are We?*

Community

- Location and history
- Economic base, population trends, and community resources (*www.census.gov* is a great resource for getting information about the community, as is your local chamber of commerce)
- Community involvement
- Business partnerships

School District

- Description and history
- Number of schools, administrators, students and teachers over time, and by grade level

School

- Description and history, attendance area, location
- Type of school, e.g., magnet, alternative, charter, private, private management
- Number of administrators, students and teachers over time, and by grade level
- Number of students electing to come to the school from out of the attendance area
- Grants and awards received
- Title 1/Schoolwide
- Safety/crime data
- *State designation as a dangerous school
- Uniqueness and strengths
- Class sizes
- After-school programs/summer school
- Extracurricular activities
- Advisors for extracurricular activities
  - Are they teachers on staff who receive extra pay?
  - Are they teachers in district, but at other schools, who receive extra pay?
  - Are they non-teachers paid to be advisors?
- Tutoring/peer mentoring
- Community support-services coordinated
- Counseling opportunities
- *Facilities: equipped for networked computers and handicapped
- Facilities: age, capacity, maintenance
- Availability of necessities and other supplies

Students Over Time, and by Grade Level

- Living situation/family structure/family size
- Preschool/Head Start/Even Start
- Preschool attendance
- *Number of students
- Gender of students
- *Race/ethnicity numbers and percentages
- Free/reduced lunch numbers and percentages
- *Language fluency by language
- *Migrant/immigrants by country, home languages
- *Homeless
- *Special Education by disability, gender, ethnicity, language fluency, free/reduced lunch
- *Attendance/tardies
- Mobility (where students go/come from)
- Retention rates by gender, ethnicity, language fluency, free/reduced lunch
- *Dropout rates by gender, ethnicity, free/reduced lunch, migrant, special education (where students go/what they do)
- Number of students leaving school overall by gender, ethnicity, language fluency, free/reduced lunch
- Extracurricular activity participation/clubs/service learning by gender, ethnicity, language fluency, free/reduced lunch
- Number of participants in programs, such as AP, IB, Honors, Upward Bound, GEAR UP, college-prep, vocational
- Number of home schoolers associated with each school in the district, along with how they are associated with the school
- Number of students electing to come to the school from out-of-the-attendance area
- Number of bus riders and distances they ride
- Student employment
- *Discipline indicators (e.g., suspensions, referrals, types of incidences, number of students carrying weapons on school property)
- *Number of drugs on school property (offered, sold, or given illegal drugs)
- *Graduation rates by gender, ethnicity, language proficiency, free/reduced lunch, migrant, and special education (where students go/what they do)
- Number of high school students concurrently enrolled in college courses
- Number of students meeting college course entrance requirements by gender, ethnicity, language fluency, free/reduced lunch
- Number of middle students concurrently enrolled in high school courses
- Number of scholarships by gender, ethnicity, language proficiency, free/reduced lunch
- Number of students completing GEDs

- Adult education programs
- Number and percentage of students going on to college, post-graduate training, and/or employment
- Grade-point average in college
- Number of graduates ending up in college remedial classes

Staff Over Time

- *Number of teachers, administrators, instructional specialists, support staff by roles
- *Years of experience, by grade level and/or role, in this school/in teaching
- Ethnicity, gender, languages spoken
- Retirement projections
- *Types of certifications/licenses/teacher qualifications/percentage of time teaching in certified area(s)
- Grades/subjects teachers are teaching
- Degrees
- *Educational training of paraprofessionals
- Teacher-student ratios by grade level
- Teacher turnover rates
- Attendance rates
- Teacher involvement in extracurricular activities, program participation
- *Number of teachers receiving high-quality professional development
- *Percent of teachers qualified to use technology for instruction
- National Board for Professional Teaching Standards (NBPTS) teachers

Parents

- Educational levels, home language, employment, socioeconomic status
- Involvement with their child's learning
- Involvement in school activities
- Incarceration

*Required for *No Child Left Behind* (includes the numbers required to understand the disaggregated numbers required by NCLB).

On the CD Related to This Chapter

- Study Questions Related to *Who are we?* (Ch4Qs.doc)
  These study questions will help you understand the information provided in Chapter 4. This template file can be printed for use as you study the case study or to use with staff as they study demographic data.
- Canyon View Demographic Graphing Templates (DistrDemog1.xls and DistrDemog2.xls)
  All of the *Microsoft Excel* files that were used to create the demographic graphs in the Canyon View School District example (Chapter 4) appear on the CD. Use these templates by putting your data in the data source table and changing the title/labels to reflect your data. This file also explains how to use the templates.
- *Data Profile Template* (DistrProfil.doc)
  This *Microsoft Word* file provides a template for creating your own district data profile like the one for Canyon View School District, using the graphing and table templates provided. Create your graphs and tables in the graphing and table templates, then merge them into the *Data Profile Template.*
- Other-size District Demographic Profiles (Folder)
  These read-only profiles are examples of other-size districts. The graphing templates used to create these profiles are also provided in this section.
  - *Sample District A (30,941 students)* (District_A.pdf)
  - *Sample District B (1,373 students)* (District_B.pdf)
  - *Sample District C (180 students)* (District_C.pdf)
- Other-size District Demographic Templates (Folder)
  All of the *Microsoft Excel* files that were used to create the demographic graphs in the other-size district examples appear on the CD. Use the templates similar to your district size by putting your data in the *Excel* data source table and changing the title/labels to reflect your data. After you have created your graphs, merge them into the *Word* data profile template (DistrProfil.doc). After you create your tables, print and insert them in the profile document.
  - *Sample District A (30,941 students)* (District_A.xls)
  - *Sample District B (1,373 students)* (District_B.xls)
  - *Sample District C (180 students)* (District_C.xls)

- The following profile templates for gathering and organizing data, prior to graphing, can be adjusted to add data elements you feel are important to fully complete the profile. If you just need to graph your data, use the graphing templates. These are for optional use.
  - *School Profile* (ProfilSc.doc)
    The *School Profile* is an optional template for gathering and organizing data about your schools, prior to graphing, especially for districts without a central database system. Please adjust the profile to add data elements you feel are important for describing the context of your schools and district. This information is then graphed or tabled, and described in narrative form. If creating a district portfolio, the data graphs and narrative will appear in *Information and Analysis.* (If you already have your data organized and just need to graph it, you will want to skip this step.)
  - *Community Profile* (ProfilCo.doc)
    The *Community Profile* is an optional template for gathering and organizing data about your community, prior to graphing. Please adjust the profile to add data elements you feel are important for describing the context of your community. It is important to describe how the community has changed over time, and how it is expected to change in the near future. This information is then added to the narrative. If creating a district portfolio, the data graphs and narrative will appear in *Information and Analysis.* (If you already have your data organized and just need to graph it, you will want to skip this step.)
  - *Administrator Profile* (ProfilAd.doc)
    The *Administrator Profile* is an optional template for gathering and organizing data about your administrators, prior to graphing. Please adjust the profile to fully describe your administrators. This information is then graphed and written in narrative form. If creating a district portfolio, the data graphs and narrative will appear in the *Information and Analysis* and *Leadership* sections. (If you already have your data organized and just need to graph it, you might will to skip this step.)
  - *Teacher Profile* (ProfilTe.doc)
    The *Teacher Profile* is an optional template for gathering and organizing data about your teachers, prior to graphing. Please adjust the profile to fully describe your teachers. The synthesis of this information is then graphed and written in narrative form. If creating a district portfolio, the data graphs and narrative will appear in *Information and Analysis.* (If you already have your data organized and just need to graph it, you will want to skip this step.)

- *Staff (other than teacher) Profile* (ProfilSt.doc)
  The *Staff (other than teacher) Profile* is an optional template for gathering and organizing data about staff who are not teachers, prior to graphing. Please adjust the profile to fully describe your non teaching staff. The synthesis of this information is then graphed and written in narrative form. If creating a district portfolio, the data graphs and narrative will appear in *Information and Analysis.* (If you already have your data organized and just need to graph it, you will want to skip this step.)

- *History Gram Activity* (ACTHstry.pdf)
  The *History Gram* is a team-building activity that will "write" the history of the district or school, which could help everyone see what staff has experienced since coming to the district and how many continuous improvement initiatives have been started over the years. It is helpful for understanding what it will take to keep this continuous improvement effort going.

- *Questions to Guide the Analysis of Demographic Data* (QsDemogr.doc)
  This *Microsoft Word* file provides a guide for interpreting your demographic data. Adjust the questions to better reflect the discussion you would like to have with your staff about the gathered demographic data.

- *What I Saw in the Example* (Ch4Saw.pdf)
  What I Saw in the Example is a file, organized by the demographic study questions, that summarizes what the author saw in the demographic data provided by Canyon View School District.

- *Demographic Data to Gather to Create the Context of the District* (DemoData.pdf)
  This file defines the types of demographic data that are important to gather to create the context of the district and describe *Who are we?*

Analyzing the Data:
How Do We Do Business?

Chapter 5

> ***How a district does business can be ascertained through studying student, staff, administrator, and parent questionnaire results, and through assessing with tools that can tell how staff work together and with the larger community.***

The second question in our continuous improvement planning model, described in Chapter 3, is *How do we do business?* This question helps us understand organizational culture, shared assumptions, beliefs, and typical behaviors, which can be ascertained through studying student, staff, administrator, and parent questionnaire results regarding the district and all its schools, and through assessing with tools that can tell us how staffs work together and with the larger community. The answers to the question *How do we do business?* can inform school district staffs of what is possible as they plan for the future, and what actions will need to be taken to systemically improve how they work together.

Humans cannot act any differently from what they value, believe, or perceive. Since we all want staffs to act as the organizational vision directs, it seems wise to understand what staffs are perceiving about the learning environment and what they believe will improve student learning. Staff and administrator questionnaire results can tell us about needs for professional learning, team building, and motivation. Parent and student questionnaire results can point to needs that must also be considered in the continuous improvement plan.

The example district in this book used *Education for the Future* student, staff, administrator, and parent questionnaires to assess how it does business. CD-ROM (EFF_Qs Folder) The district also used the *Education for the Future District Continuous Improvement Continuums* (CICs) to assess the health of a district as a system. CD-ROM (CICs_Dstrct.doc) Canyon View schools used the *Education for the Future School Continuous Improvement Continuums* to understand the health of their school systems. CD-ROM (CICs_Schls.doc)

As we start on *How do we do business?* with Canyon View School District, please note the study questions on pages 128 and 197 to assist in studying the Canyon View data. CD-ROM (Ch5Qs_CICs.pdf and Ch5Qs_Qs.pdf) There is space in the margins on the data pages to write your impressions as you review the data. At the end of the sections (pages 129 and 198-199), I share what I saw in the data. CD-ROM (Ch5Saw_CICs.pdf and Ch5Saw_Qs.pdf) For reviewing your own data, you might want to use a comparison table to look across student, staff, administrator, and parent questionnaire results. CD-ROM (Distr_QTable.doc)

Our Example School: Canyon View School District

How Do We Do Business?

To get a better understanding of the learning environment, Canyon View School District administered student, staff, administrator, and parent questionnaires in December 2003 and again in Spring 2005. Staffs also assessed where the district and each school ranked on the *Education for the Future Continuous Improvement Continuums* (CICs). Summaries of the results follow, starting with the CICs.

School Processes

Canyon View School District Continuous Improvement Continuum Baseline Results

During the 2004-05 academic year, the district administrative team (district staff members and principals) met to conduct a baseline assessment of where the district is on the *Education for the Future Continuous Improvement Continuums.*

These Continuums, extending from *one* to *five* horizontally, represent a continuum of expectations related to continuous improvement with respect to an *approach* to the Continuum, *implementation* of the approach, and the *outcome* that results from the implementation. A *one* rating, located on the left of each Continuum, represents a district that has not yet begun to improve. *Five,* located on the right in each Continuum, represents a district that is one step removed from "world class quality." The elements between *one* and *five* describe how that Continuum is hypothesized to evolve in a continuously improving school. Each Continuum moves from a *reactive* mode to a *proactive* mode—from fire fighting to prevention. The *five* in *outcome* in each Continuum is the target.

Vertically, we have *Approach, Implementation,* and *Outcome,* for any number *one* through *five,* as hypotheses. In other words, the *implementation* statement describes how the *approach* might look when *implemented,* and the *outcome* is the "pay-off" for *implementing* the *approach.* If the hypotheses are accurate, the *outcome* will not be realized until the *approach* is actually *implemented.*

On January 16, 2005, 19 district administrative team members (district staff and principals) participated in the Canyon View's district baseline self-assessment continuum activities. After reading a Continuum, team members placed a dot on the Continuum to represent where she/he thought the district was with respect to *Approach, Implementation,* and *Outcome.* Following the discussion, team members came to consensus on a number that represented where the district is for each element, and created *Next Steps* for moving up the Continuums.

The ratings and brief discussions for each *District Continuous Improvement Continuum* follow.

Look Fors: **Is there a data system in place for use at the district and school levels? Is the district proactive or more reactive? Is there a district vision that is known and shared? Is there a district plan in place aligned to the vision? Does professional learning provided in the district help the district and schools implement their visions? Is the leadership structure known and helpful? Are parents, the community, and business partnerships sought to assist with the learning mission? Does the district evaluate all parts of the learning organization?**

Planning Implications: **How much do all staff members understand where the district is on these Continuums? To what degree are all staff on the same page?**

District Continuous Improvement Continuums

INFORMATION AND ANALYSIS

	One	Two	Three	Four	Five
Approach	Data or information about school student performance and needs are not gathered in any systematic way. The district does not provide assistance in helping schools understand what needs to change at the school and classroom levels, based on data.	There is no systematic process for data analysis across the district. Some school, teacher, and student information are collected and used to problem solve and establish student-learning standards across the district.	School district collects data related to school and student performance (e.g., attendance, enrollment, achievement), and surveys students, staff, and parents. The information is used to drive the strategic quality plan for district and school improvement.	There is systematic reliance on hard data (including data for subgroups) as a basis for decision making at the district, school, and classroom levels. Changes are based on the study of data to meet the educational needs of students and teachers.	Information is gathered in all areas of student interaction with the school. The district engages administrators and teachers in gathering information on their own performance. Accessible to all schools, data are comprehensive in scope and an accurate reflection of school and district quality.
Implementation	No information is gathered with which to make district or school changes. Student dissatisfaction with the learning process is seen as an irritation, not a need for improvement.	Some data are tracked, such as attendance, enrollment, and drop-out rates. Only a few individuals are asked for feedback about areas of schooling and district operations.	The district collects information on current and former students (e.g., student achievement and perceptions), analyzes and uses it in conjunction with future trends for planning. Identified areas for improvement are tracked over time.	Data are used to provide feedback to improve the effectiveness of teaching strategies on all student learning. Schools' historical performances are graphed and utilized for diagnosis by the district.	Innovative teaching processes that meet the needs of students are implemented across the district. Information is analyzed and used to prevent student failure. Root causes are known through analyses. Problems are prevented through the use of data.
Outcome	Only anecdotal and hypothetical information are available about student performance, behavior, and satisfaction. Problems are solved individually with short-term results.	Little data are available. Change is limited to some areas of the district and dependent upon individual administrators and their efforts.	Information collected about school needs, effective assessment, and instructional practices are shared with all school and district staff and used to plan for school and district improvement. Information helps staff understand pressing issues, analyze information for "root causes," and track results for improvement.	An information system is in place. Positive trends begin to appear in many schools and districtwide. There is evidence that these results are caused by understanding and effectively using the data collected.	Schools are delighted with their instructional processes and proud of their own capabilities to learn and assess their own growth. Good to excellent achievement is the result for all schools. Schools use data to predict and prevent potential problems. No student falls through the cracks.

Information and Analysis

Members of the district administrative team rated the district 2s in *Approach, Implementation,* and *Outcome* with respect to *Information and Analysis.*

Next Steps:

- Building administrators need to share more information with the staff in their buildings.
- Communication to all K-12 staff must outline what data are being collected and how the data are being collected.
- A process for surveying former students to determine what they thought of their educational experience in the schools needs to be developed.
- Transition data from ninth graders and sixth graders need to be gathered to gain insight into what they thought of their educational experience in their feeder schools.
- Administrators and teachers need training to effectively use the data being collected.

District Continuous Improvement Continuums
STUDENT ACHIEVEMENT

	One	Two	Three	Four	Five
Approach	Instructional and organizational processes critical to student success are not identified. Little distinction of student learning differences is made. Some schools believe that not all students can achieve.	Some data are collected on student background and performance trends. Learning gaps are noted to direct improvement of instruction. It is known that student learning standards must be identified.	Student learning standards are identified, and a continuum of learning is created across the district. Student performance data are collected and compared to the standards in order to analyze how to improve learning for all students.	Data on student achievement are used throughout the district to pursue the improvement of student learning. The district ensures that teachers collaborate to implement appropriate instruction and assessment strategies for meeting student learning standards articulated across grade levels. All teachers believe that all students can learn.	The district makes an effort to exceed student achievement expectations. Innovative instructional changes are made to anticipate learning needs and improve student achievement. District makes sure that teachers are able to predict characteristics impacting student achievement and to know how to perform from a small set of internal quality measures.
Implementation	All students are taught the same way. There is no communication between the district and schools about students' academic needs or learning styles. There are no analyses of how to improve instruction.	Some effort is made to track and analyze student achievement trends on a districtwide basis. District begins to understand the needs and learning gaps within the schools.	Teachers across the district study effective instruction and assessment strategies to implement standards and to increase students' learning. Student feedback and analysis of achievement data are used in conjunction with implementation support strategies.	There is a systematic focus on implementing student learning standards and on the improvement of student learning districtwide. Effective instruction and assessment strategies are implemented in each school. District supports teachers supporting one another with peer coaching and/or action research focused on implementing strategies that lead to increased achievement.	All teachers correlate critical instructional and assessment strategies with objective indicators of quality student achievement. A comparative analysis of actual individual student performance to student learning standards is utilized to adjust teaching strategies to ensure a progression of learning for all students.
Outcome	There is wide variation in student attitudes and achievement with undesirable results. There is high dissatisfaction among students with learning. Student background is used as an excuse for low student achievement.	There is some evidence that student achievement trends are available to schools and are being used. There is much effort, but minimal observable results in improving student achievement.	There is an increase in communication among district and schools, students, and teachers regarding student learning. Teachers learn about effective instructional strategies that will implement the shared vision, student learning standards, and how to meet the needs of students. The schools make some gains.	Increased student achievement is evident districtwide. Student morale, attendance, and behavior are good. Teachers converse often with each other about preventing student failure. Areas for further attention are clear.	Schools and teachers conduct self-assessments to continuously improve performance. Improvements in student achievement are evident and clearly caused by teachers' and students' understandings of individual student learning standards, linked to appropriate and effective instructional and assessment strategies. A continuum of learning results. No students fall through the cracks.

Student Achievement

District administrative team members rated the district 2s in *Approach, Implementation,* and *Outcome* with respect to *Student Achievement.*

Next Steps:

- Train all staff how to use and interpret data.
- Continue to develop confidence in how achievement data are collected.
- Ensure assessment consistency among schools.
- Develop an assessment tool to measure progress ensuring alignment in all curricular areas.
- Develop a systematic approach to analyzing school improvement goals, strategies, and assessment plans.
- Identify learning gaps that are hindering improved instruction.
- Make certain everyone has a shared vision regarding student achievement.
- Establish that all school program improvement days are concurrent with district goals.
- Align curriculum to standards, identify critical standards, and then offer professional learning in identified areas of need.

District Continuous Improvement Continuums
QUALITY PLANNING

	One	Two	Three	Four	Five
Approach	No quality plan or process exists. Data are neither used nor considered important in planning.	The district realizes the importance of a mission, vision, and one comprehensive action plan. Teams develop goals and timelines, and dollars are allocated to begin the process.	A comprehensive plan to achieve the district vision is developed. Plan includes evaluation and continuous improvement.	One focused and integrated districtwide plan for implementing a continuous improvement process is put into action. All district efforts are focused on the implementation of this plan that represents the achievement of the vision.	A plan for the continuous improvement of the district, with a focus on students, is put into place. There is excellent articulation and integration of all elements in the district due to quality planning. Leadership team ensures all elements are implemented by all appropriate parties.
Implementation	There is no knowledge of or direction for quality planning. Budget is allocated on an as-needed basis. Many plans exist.	School district community begins continuous improvement planning efforts by laying out major steps to a shared vision, by identifying values and beliefs, the purpose of the district, a mission, vision, and student learning standards.	Implementation goals, responsibilities, due dates, and timelines are spelled out. Support structures for implementing the plan are set in place.	The quality management plan is implemented through effective procedures in all areas of the district. Everyone commits to implementing the plan aligned to the vision, mission, and values and beliefs. All share responsibility for accomplishing district goals.	Districtwide goals, mission, vision, and student learning standards are shared and articulated throughout the district and with feeder schools. The attainment of identified student learning standards is linked to planning and implementation of effective instruction that meets students' needs. Leaders at all levels are developing expertise because planning is the norm.
Outcome	There is no evidence of comprehensive planning. Staff work is carried out in isolation. A continuum of learning for students is absent.	The school district community understands the benefits of working together to implement a comprehensive continuous improvement plan.	There is evidence that the district plan is being implemented in some areas of the district. Improvements are neither systematic nor integrated districtwide.	A districtwide plan is known to all. Results from working toward the quality improvement goals are evident throughout the district. Planning is ongoing and inclusive of all stakeholders.	Evidence of effective teaching and learning results in significant improvement of student achievement attributed to quality planning at all levels of the district organization. Teachers and administrators understand and share the district mission and vision. Quality planning is seamless and all demonstrate evidence of accountability.

Quality Planning

District administrative team members rated the district 2s in *Approach* and *Implementation,* and 3 in *Outcome* with respect to *Quality Planning.*

Next Steps:

- Continue to assess the status of quality planning.
- Continue work with Victoria Bernhardt and *Education for the Future.*
- Keep improvement process and issues before all teaching staff. Continue the dialogue at the building level.
- Communication from buildings to the district and from building to building is critical. We need to develop a means for sharing ideas and information between buildings.
- Research other planning models (e.g. the military, hospitals, etc.)
- District needs to support building implementation.
- Communicate, share, and integrate all stakeholders into the process.
- Consider using the school/community budget meeting model for school improvement. Consider this *focus group* model for seeking community input.
- Make a commitment to stay with the process.

District Continuous Improvement Continuums
PROFESSIONAL DEVELOPMENT

	One	Two	Three	Four	Five
Approach	There is no professional development. Teachers, principals, and staff are seen as interchangeable parts that can be replaced. Professional development is external and usually equated to attending a conference alone. Hierarchy determines "haves" and "have-nots."	The "cafeteria" approach to professional development is used, whereby individual teachers and administrators choose what they want to take, without regard to an overall district plan.	The shared vision, district plan and student needs are used to target focused professional development for all employees. Staff is inserviced on relevant instructional and leadership strategies.	Professional development and data-gathering methods are used by all teachers and administrators, and are directed toward the goals of the shared vision and the continuous improvement of the district and schools. Teachers have ongoing conversations about student achievement data. All staff members receive training in their content areas. Systems thinking is considered in all decisions.	Leadership and staff continuously improve all aspects of the learning organization through an innovative, data-driven, and comprehensive continuous improvement process that prevents student failures. Effective job-embedded professional development is ongoing for implementing the vision for student success. Traditional teacher evaluations are replaced by collegial coaching and action research focused on student learning standards. Policies set professional development as a priority budget line-item. Professional development is planned, aligned, and leads to the achievement of student learning standards.
Implementation	District staff, principals, teachers, and school staff performance is controlled and inspected. Performance evaluations are used to detect mistakes.	Teacher professional development is sporadic and unfocused, lacking an approach for implementing new procedures and processes. Some leadership training begins to take place.	The district ensures that teachers are involved in year-round quality professional development. The school community is trained in shared decision making, team building concepts, effective communication strategies, and data analysis.	Teachers, in teams, continuously set and implement student achievement goals. Leadership considers these goals and provides necessary support structures for collaboration. Teachers utilize effective support approaches as they implement new instruction and assessment strategies. Coaching and feedback structures are in place. Use of new knowledge and skills is evident.	Teams passionately support each other in the pursuit of quality improvement at all levels. Teachers make bold changes in instruction and assessment strategies focused on student learning standards and student learning styles. *A teacher as action researcher* model is implemented. Staffwide conversations focus on systemic reflection and improvement. Teachers are strong leaders.
Outcome	No professional growth and no staff or student performance improvement. There exists a high turnover rate of employees, especially administrators. Attitudes and approaches filter down to students.	The effectiveness of professional development is not known or analyzed. Teachers feel helpless and unsupported in making schoolwide changes.	Teachers, working in teams, feel supported by the district and begin to feel they can make changes. Evidence shows that shared decision making works.	A collegial school district is evident. Effective classroom strategies are practiced, articulated schoolwide. These strategies, focused on student learning standards, are reflective of professional development aimed at ensuring student learning and the implementation of the shared vision.	True systemic change and improved student achievement result because teachers are knowledgeable of and implement effective, differentiated teaching strategies for individual student learning gains. Teachers' repertoire of skills is enhanced and students are achieving. Professional development is driving learning at all levels.

Professional Development

The district administrative team rated the district a 3 in *Approach,* a 2 in *Implementation,* and a 3 in *Outcome* with respect to *Professional Development.*

Next Steps:

- Develop strategies that get everyone on board with the *School Portfolio.*
- Continue to allocate fiscal resources for planning.
- Develop a process that ensures that schools and curriculum committees are looking at curricular and school needs when proposing professional development.
- Research and plan to implement individual employee professional learning plans.
- Consider how to restructure time to allow for professional development during the work day (e.g., late start, early release, one professional development day per quarter).
- Develop a summer professional development series with the *Education Foundation.*
- Provide *TetraData* warehouse training and data analysis for teachers.
- Tie teacher professional learning goals to evaluation and the school improvement plan.
- Schedule time for teachers to talk about student instruction and improvement.

District Continuous Improvement Continuums

LEADERSHIP

	One	Two	Three	Four	Five
Approach	The School Board is decision maker. Decisions are reactive to state, district, and federal mandates. There is no knowledge of continuous improvement.	A shared decision-making structure is put into place and discussions begin on how to achieve a district vision. Most decisions are focused on solving problems and are reactive.	District leadership team is committed to continuous improvement. Leadership seeks inclusion of all school sectors and supports study teams by making time provisions for their work.	District leadership team represents a true shared decision-making structure. Study teams are reconstructed for the implementation of a comprehensive continuous improvement plan.	A strong continuous improvement structure is set into place that allows for input from all sectors of the district, school, and community, ensuring strong communication, flexibility, and refinement of approach and beliefs. The district vision is student focused, based on data and appropriate for district/school/community values, and meeting student needs.
Implementation	The School Board makes all decisions, with little or no input from administrators, teachers, the community, or students. Leadership inspects for mistakes.	District values and beliefs are identified; the purpose of district is defined; a district mission and student learning standards are developed with representative input. A structure for studying approaches to achieving student learning standards is established.	The district leadership team is active on study teams and integrates recommendations from the teams' research and analyses to form a comprehensive plan for continuous improvement within the context of the district mission. Everyone is kept informed.	Decisions about budget and implementation of the vision are made within teams, by the school board, by the leadership team, by the individual schools, and by the full staff, as appropriate. All decisions are communicated to the leadership team and to the full staff.	The vision is implemented and articulated across all grade levels and into feeder schools. Quality standards are reinforced throughout the district. All members of the district community understand and apply the quality standards. Leadership team has systematic interactions and involvement with district administrators, teachers, parents, community, and students about the district's direction. Necessary resources are available to implement and measure staff learning related to student learning standards.
Outcome	Although the decision-making process is clearly known, decisions are reactive and lack focus and consistency. There is no evidence of staff commitment to a shared vision. Students and parents do not feel they are being heard.	The mission provides a focus for all district and school improvement and guides the action to the vision. The school community is committed to continuous improvement. Quality leadership techniques are used sporadically.	The district leadership team is seen as committed to planning and quality improvement. Critical areas for improvement are identified. Faculty feel included in shared decision making.	There is evidence that the district leadership team listens to all levels of the organization. Implementation of the continuous improvement plan is linked to student learning standards and the guiding principles of the school. Leadership capacity for implementing the vision throughout the district is evident.	Site-based management and shared decision making truly exists. Teachers understand and display an intimate knowledge of how the school and district operate. Schools support and communicate with each other in the implementation of quality strategies. Teachers implement the vision in their classrooms and can determine how their new approaches meet student needs and lead to the attainment of student learning standards. Leaders are standards-driven at all levels.

Leadership

Canyon View staff rated the district 3s in *Approach, Implementation,* and *Outcome* with respect to *Leadership.*

Next Steps:

- Seek input from all school sectors to include parents and community.
- Define study teams and their role in communicating results and learnings to all staff.
- Ensure provisions are in place to support study teams; identify resources currently in place to support the work of study teams.
- Determine how to make study teams functional.
- Develop a plan to ensure the recommendations of study teams are implemented by all appropriate staff.
- Hold staff accountable once a decision is made—teachers, principals, Superintendent, District Administrators, and Board of Trustees.
- Create an environment that seeks input from all.

District Continuous Improvement Continuums

PARTNERSHIP DEVELOPMENT

	One	Two	Three	Four	Five
Approach	There is no system for input from parents, business, or community. Status quo is desired for managing the school district.	Partnerships are sought, but mostly for money and things.	School district has knowledge of why partnerships are important and seeks to include businesses and parents in a strategic fashion related to student learning standards for increased student achievement.	School district seeks effective win-win business and community partnerships and parent involvement to implement the vision. Desired outcomes are clearly identified. A solid plan for partnership development exists.	Community, parent, and business partnerships become integrated across all student groupings. The benefits of outside involvement are known by all. Parent and business involvement in student learning is refined. Student learning regularly takes place beyond the school and district walls.
Implementation	Barriers are erected to close out involvement of outsiders. Outsiders are managed for least impact on status quo.	A team is assigned to get partners and to receive input from parents, the community, and business in the school district.	Involvement of business, community, and parents begins to take place in some schools and after school hours related to the vision. Partners begin to realize how they can support each other in achieving district goals. District staff understand what partners need from the partnership.	There is systematic utilization of parents, community, and businesses districtwide. Areas in which the active use of these partnerships benefit student learning are clear.	Partnership development is articulated across all district groupings. Parents, community, business, and educators work together in an innovative fashion to increase student learning and to prepare students for the Twenty-first Century. Partnerships are evaluated for continuous improvement.
Outcome	There is little or no involvement of parents, business, or community at-large. The district is a closed, isolated system.	Much effort is given to establishing partnerships. Some spotty trends emerge, such as receiving donated equipment.	Some substantial gains are achieved in implementing partnerships. Some student achievement increases can be attributed to this involvement.	Gains in student satisfaction with learning and school are clearly related to partnerships. All partners benefit.	Previously non-achieving students enjoy learning with excellent achievement. Community, business, and home become common places for student learning, while school becomes a place where parents come for further education. Partnerships enhance what the school district does for students.

Partnership Development

Members of the district administrative team rated the district 3s in *Approach, Implementation,* and *Outcome* with respect to *Partnership Development.* Staff agreed the following steps are necessary to continue improvement in this area.

Next Steps:

- Survey all district schools and departments to gather specific information about current parent/business partnerships.
- Confirm the connection of these partnerships to the district vision.
- Reconfigure the guidelines and expectations for partnerships to include their connection to student curriculum standards and student achievement.
- Educate all stakeholders on the existence of the partnerships, their mutual benefits, and their connection to student standards and achievement.
- Recognize and acknowledge the partnerships with students, staffs, parents, businesses, and community as a district.
- Identify data collection needs that will assist in verifying student achievement as a result of partnerships.

District Continuous Improvement Continuums

CONTINUOUS IMPROVEMENT AND EVALUATION

	One	Two	Three	Four	Five
Approach	Neither goals nor strategies exist for the evaluation and continuous improvement of the district organization or for elements of the organization.	The approach to continuous improvement and evaluation is problem-solving. If there are no problems, or if solutions can be made quickly, there is no need for improvement or analyses. Changes in parts of the system are not coordinated with all other parts.	Some elements of the district organization are evaluated for effectiveness. Some elements are improved on the basis of the evaluation findings.	All elements of the district's operations are evaluated for improvement. Efforts are consistently made to ensure congruence of the elements with respect to the continuum of learning that students experience.	All aspects of the district organization are rigorously evaluated and improved on a continuous basis. Students, and the maintenance of a comprehensive learning continuum for students, become the focus of all aspects of the school district improvement process.
Implementation	With no overall plan for evaluation and continuous improvement, strategies are changed by individual schools, teachers, and/or administrators only when something sparks the need to improve. Reactive decisions and activities are a daily mode of operation.	Isolated changes are made in some areas of the district organization in response to problem incidents. Changes are not preceded by comprehensive analyses, such as an understanding of the root causes of problems. The effectiveness of the elements of the district organization is not known.	Elements of the district organization are improved on the basis of comprehensive analyses of root causes of problems, client perceptions, and operational effectiveness of processes.	Continuous improvement analyses of student achievement and instructional strategies are rigorously reinforced within each classroom and across learning levels to develop a comprehensive learning continuum for students and to prevent student failure.	Comprehensive continuous improvement becomes the way of doing business throughout the district. Teachers continuously improve the appropriateness and effectiveness of instructional strategies based on student feedback and performance. All aspects of the district organization are improved to support teachers' efforts.
Outcome	Individuals struggle with system failure. Finger pointing and blaming others for failure occur. The effectiveness of strategies is not known. Mistakes are repeated.	Problems are solved only temporarily and few positive changes result. Additionally, unintended and undesirable consequences often appear in other parts of the system. Many aspects of the school district are incongruent, keeping the district from reaching its vision.	Evidence of effective improvement strategies is observable. Positive changes are made and maintained due to comprehensive analyses and evaluation.	Teachers become astute at assessing and in predicting the impact of their instructional strategies on individual student achievement. Sustainable improvements in student achievement are evident at all grade levels due to continuous improvement supported by the district.	The district becomes a congruent and effective learning organization. Only instruction and assessment strategies that produce quality student achievement are used. A true continuum of learning results for all students and staff. The impact of improvements is increasingly measurable.

Continuous Improvement and Evaluation

District administrative team members rated their district a 3 in *Approach,* and 2s in *Implementation* and *Outcome* with respect to *Continuous Improvement and Evaluation.*

Next Steps:

- Identify what is to be evaluated and then develop a timeline/matrix.
- Develop a means to ensure communication among curriculum committees and the rest of the teaching population.
- Decide what to assess, how to assess it, and what to do with the data. All schools and departments need to be congruent—everyone going in the same direction.
- Develop a means to acquire client perception information (e.g. surveys, focus groups).
- Map the *Continuous Improvement Process* and be more mindful of where changes are made. Use a portion of every General Administrators' Meeting to discuss, share, and listen to what others are doing in relation to their building-level process work.
- Plan for both public and private celebrations when progress is made and goals are achieved.

Study Questions for How Do We Do Business? The District CIC Assessment

As you review Canyon View's *Continuous Improvement Continuums* data, use either the margins in the text, this page, or print this page from the CD to write down your early thinking. (Ch5Qs_CICs.pdf) These notes, of course, are only hunches or placeholders until all the data are analyzed.

What are some *implications* for the Canyon View improvement plan?

What I Saw in the Example: Canyon View School District CIC Assessment

Using the study questions as an outline, what I saw in the CIC data for Chapter 5 follows below.  (Ch5Saw_CICs.pdf)

Continuous Improvement Continuums Assessment

Implications for Canyon View's improvement plan

- It is time to reassess on the CICs.
- An alumni questionnaire could be administrated as well as a questionnaire that asks students about their transition to new schools.
- Staffs need training in data analysis and how to effectively use the data collected.
- An assessment tool to measure progress and curricular alignment is needed.
- Consistency among schools needs to improve with respect to assessments and curriculum alignment. A systematic approach to analyzing school improvement goals, strategies, and assessment plans is desirable.
- Administration needs to ensure a shared vision at each school, that curriculum is aligned to standards, and professional development is provided in the areas of need.
- Administration needs to keep the improvement process and issues active for all teaching staff.
- District needs to support the implementation of building plans.
- Administration might consider a focus group model for seeking community input.
- The district needs to get everyone on board with the School Portfolio and stick with the process.
- The administrative team feels the district needs to develop strategies and processes to ensure schools/curriculum connect the use of data to professional development goals and evaluation, and school improvement plans. Time needs to be restructured for professional development to include time during the work week to talk about student instruction and assessment.
- Staffs need to define study teams and their role in communicating results and learning to all staff, and determine how to make study teams functional.
- Administration needs to ensure provisions are in place to support study teams, and to identify resources currently in place to support the work of study teams.
- Administration needs to develop a plan to ensure the recommendations of study teams are implemented by all appropriate staff.
- Staffs need to be held accountable once a decision is made—that includes teachers, principals, the superintendent, district administrators, and Board of Trustees.
- The entire district needs to create an environment that seeks input from all.
- Staffs need to reconfigure the guidelines and expectations for partnerships to include their connection to student curriculum standards and student achievement. We need to confirm the connection of our partnerships to the district vision.
- Administration needs to educate all stakeholders of the existence of our partnerships, their mutual benefits, and their connection to student standards and achievement.
- Staffs need to recognize and acknowledge the partnerships with students, staffs, parents, and community as a district.
- Data collection that will assist in verifying student achievement, as a result of partnerships, needs to be identified.
- Administration needs to identify what is to be evaluated and then develop a timeline/matrix.
- The administrative team needs to develop a means to ensure communication among curriculum committees and the rest of the teaching population
- Staffs need to decide what to assess, how to assess it, and what to do with the data. All schools and departments need to be congruent—everyone going in the same direction.
- We need to acquire client perception information (e.g. surveys, focus groups).
- The administrative team needs to map the *Continuous Improvement Process* and be more mindful of where changes are made. We need to use a portion of every General Administrator's meeting to discuss, share, and listen to what others are doing in relation to their building level process work.
- Staffs need to plan for both public and private celebrations when progress is made and goals are achieved.
- Synthesizing the implications for the district plan indicates that some processes need to be established district-wide with reference to data, professional development, and partnerships.

Perceptions

Canyon View School District students, staffs, and parents completed *Education for the Future* questionnaires in March 2005. The results follow. (*Note:* School results are usually not compared in the same graph. Schools get their own data over time only, to avoid using the data to compete with other schools. We want schools to use the data to continuously improve their own school.)

Note: Education for the Future questionnaires and tools used to gather and assess perceptions, *similar* to the ones used by Canyon View School District, can be downloaded from the *Education for the Future* website:

http://eff.csuchico.edu/questionnaire_resources/

For more information about *designing* questionnaires, see *Data Analysis for Continuous School Improvement,* Second Edition (Bernhardt, 2004), and *Questionnaires Demystified: Using Perceptions Data for School Improvement* (Bernhardt and Geise, 2007, in press).

The icons in the graphs that follow show the average responses to each item by disaggregation indicated in the legend. The lines join the icons to help the reader know the distribution results for each disaggregation. The lines have no other meaning.

Note: Some of the subgroup numbers may not add up to the total number of respondents because some respondents did not identify themselves by this demographic, or identified themselves by more than one demographic.

Comparison of Student, Staff, and Parent Responses by School

Canyon View School District students, staffs, and parents responded to questionnaires designed to measure how they feel about their learning environment. Students were asked to respond to items using a five-point scale: 1 = strongly disagree; 2 = disagree; 3 = neutral; 4 = agree; and, 5 = strongly agree.

Responses were graphed by the totals by school and compared in the figures that follow. Average responses to each item on the questionnaire were graphed by the totals and disaggregated by school. In general, the average responses reveal few differences over time. A summary of results is shown below.

Student Responses by Elementary, Middle, and High Schools

When student responses were disaggregated by elementary, middle, and high schools, student responses to the items on the questionnaire revealed some differences by elementary school (Figure 5.1). Average student responses from elementary school students were in agreement with all statements, with the following exceptions:

- Elementary School 10 students were in disagreement with *Students are treated fairly by the people on recess duty,* while Elementary School 4 students responded neutral to this item.
- Elementary Schools 4 and 8 students responded neutral to: *I have choices in what I learn,* and *Students are treated fairly by the people on recess duty.*
- Elementary School 9 students responded in low agreement to: *Students are treated fairly by the people on recess duty, Students at my school treat me with respect,* and *Students at my school are friendly.*

Look Fors:	**Items which students, by school and across schools, are in agreement or disagreement.**
Planning Implications:	**Where can/should the district provide leadership, with respect to school/district environment?**

Canyon View School students were also asked to respond to two open-ended questions: *What do you like about your school?* and *What do you wish was different at your school?* The top ten responses, by school, follow the graphs. (*Note:* When analyzing open-ended results, one must keep in mind the number of responses that were written-in. Open-ended responses often help us understand the multiple choice responses, although caution must be exercised around small numbers of respondents. A file to help you analyze open-ended responses is on the CD.) CD-ROM (OEanalz.pdf)

Look Fors:	**The most often written-in responses to what students like about school and wish was different.**
Planning Implications:	**Perhaps issues regarding how students are treated in each school, or across schools.**

Figure 5.1

Canyon View School District Student Responses By Elementary School, March 2005

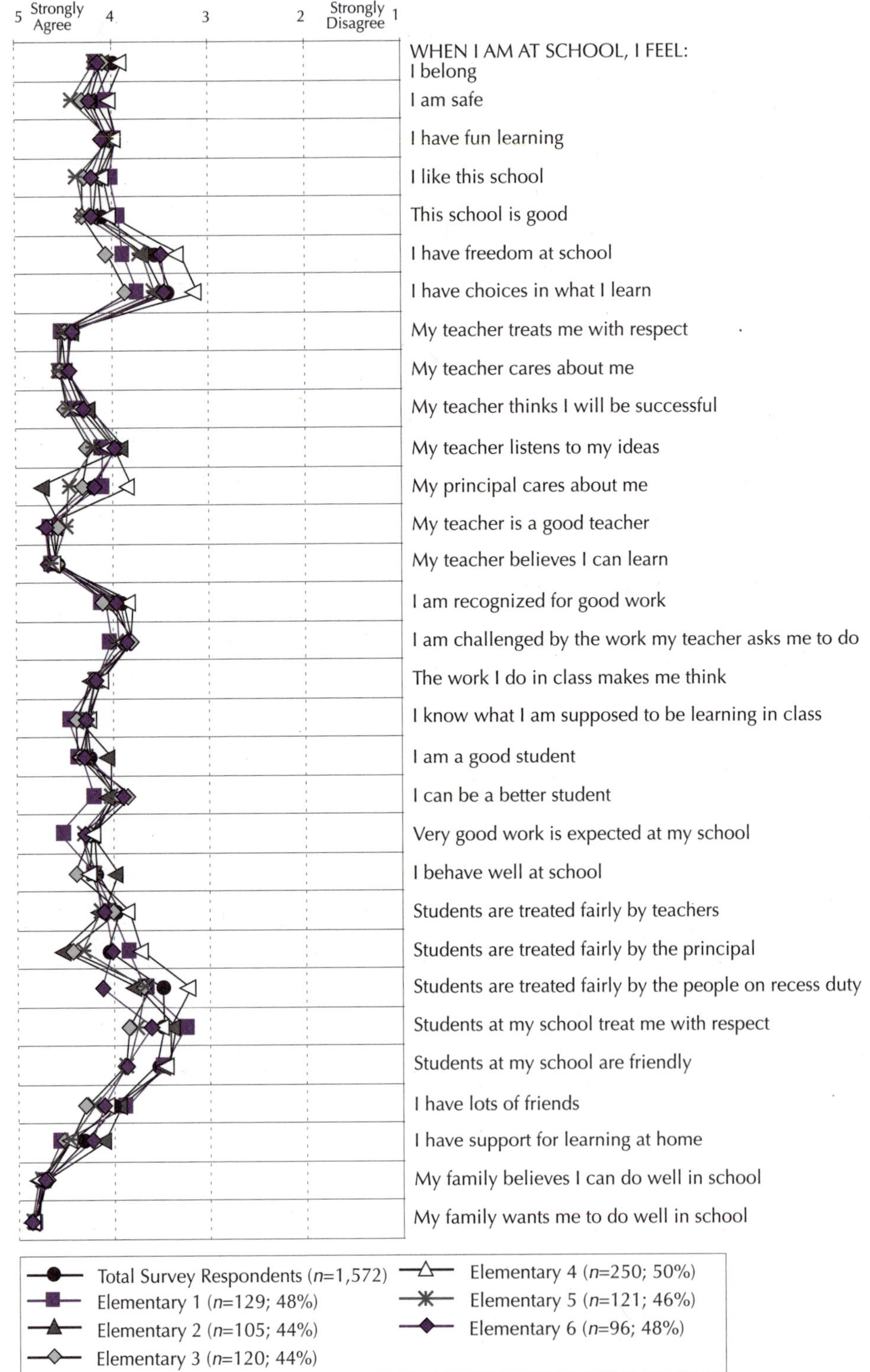
5 Strongly Agree
4
3
2
Strongly Disagree 1
WHEN I AM AT SCHOOL, I FEEL:
I belong
I am safe
I have fun learning
I like this school
This school is good
I have freedom at school
I have choices in what I learn
My teacher treats me with respect
My teacher cares about me
My teacher thinks I will be successful
My teacher listens to my ideas
My principal cares about me
My teacher is a good teacher
My teacher believes I can learn
I am recognized for good work
I am challenged by the work my teacher asks me to do
The work I do in class makes me think
I know what I am supposed to be learning in class
I am a good student
I can be a better student
Very good work is expected at my school
I behave well at school
Students are treated fairly by teachers
Students are treated fairly by the principal
Students are treated fairly by the people on recess duty
Students at my school treat me with respect
Students at my school are friendly
I have lots of friends
I have support for learning at home
My family believes I can do well in school
My family wants me to do well in school
Total Survey Respondents (n=1,572)
Elementary 1 (n=129; 48%)
Elementary 2 (n=105; 44%)
Elementary 3 (n=120; 44%)
Elementary 4 (n=250; 50%)
Elementary 5 (n=121; 46%)
Elementary 6 (n=96; 48%)

Figure 5.1 (Continued)

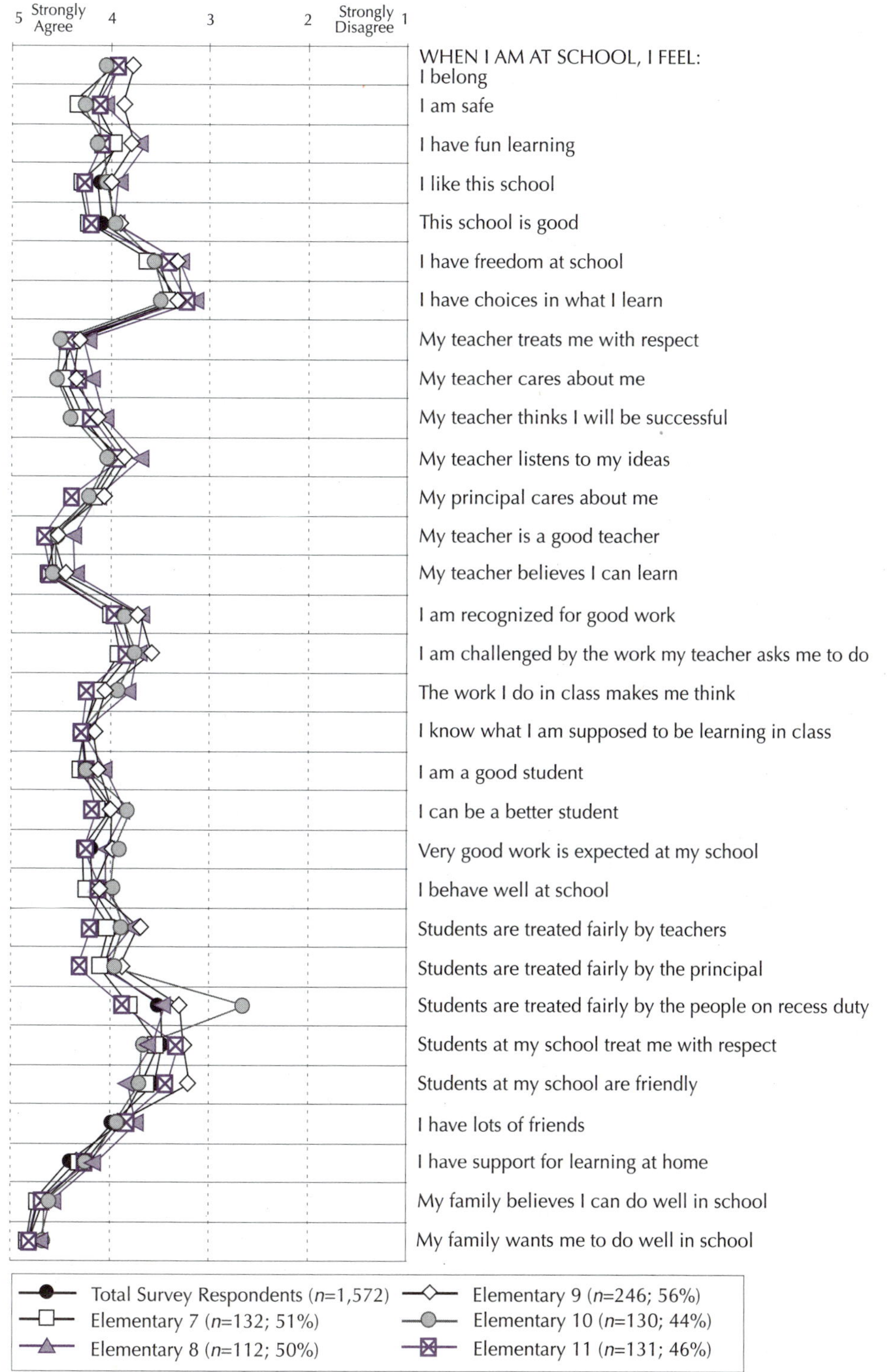

Elementary School 1 Student Open Ended Responses	
What do you like about this school?	***What do you wish was different at this school?***
• The teachers. (27) • Everything. (11) • It is fun. (9) • Most people are nice. (8) • Lunch. (7) • Recess. (7) • It is a good school. (6) • P.E. (6) • My friends. (5) • Art and Math. (4)	• Nothing. (15) • Better lunch. (11) • Lunch before recess. (9) • Kids would be nicer to me. (7) • It had new playground equipment. (7) • Longer recess. (4) • No little kids on the big kids' hill. (3) • The cafeteria would be a little cleaner. (2) • I want school to be different. (2) • Lunch rules. (2)

Elementary School 2 Student Open Ended Responses	
What do you like about this school?	***What do you wish was different at this school?***
• The nice teachers and staff. (33) • My friends. (15) • It is a good school/it is fun. (14) • The nice people. (10) • Recess. (7) • Learning. (7) • Principal. (6) • The playground. (4) • Reading. (3) • Math. (3)	• The playground equipment. (16) • Choices about what we want to learn. (4) • More music. (4) • Fewer rules. (4) • Longer recess. (3) • That we had P.E. everyday. (3) • Lunch. (2) • More respect. • A lot more man teachers. • Bigger library.

Elementary School 3 Student Open Ended Responses	
What do you like about this school?	***What do you wish was different at this school?***
• Teachers and staff. (55) • The principal. (15) • It is fun. (15) • My friends. (15) • The playground and equipment. (13) • Everything. (13) • It is a good place to learn. (11) • Everybody is nice. (10) • Having two or three recesses. (9) • People are treated with respect. (9)	• Nothing. (38) • More time for lunch. (12) • Recess was longer. (11) • The food. (8) • They would get new playground equipment. (8) • People were nicer. (6) • Lunch before recess. (5) • Redesign the girls' bathroom upstairs and down stairs. (4) • More trees and grass, less cement. (4) • No homework. (3)

Elementary School 4 Student Open Ended Responses

What do you like about this school?

- The teachers. (82)
- My friends and the kids. (30)
- The people are nice/everyone is treated with respect. (23)
- It's a good place to learn. (20)
- Recess. (19)
- Everything. (18)
- The principal. (17)
- It's fun. (17)
- The selection of books at the library. (14)
- Gym. (10)

What do you wish was different at this school?

- Nothing. (47)
- The food. (22)
- Kids should be nicer on the playground. No fighting. (21)
- We had more playground equipment. (19)
- The playground needs to be bigger and have more trees/grass. (14)
- Longer recess. (11)
- There was a bigger library with more books. (10)
- More respectful treatment. (9)
- The rules. (9)
- More choices in what we learn/more Math/more fun. (8)

Elementary School 5 Student Open Ended Responses

What do you like about this school?

- The teachers and staff. (63)
- Learning. (22)
- Everybody is nice. (20)
- My friends. (13)
- It is good and fun. (13)
- Recess/the playground. (10)
- Everything. (8)
- The principal. (7)
- Gym. (5)
- Playground aides. (5)

What do you wish was different at this school?

- Nothing. (37)
- The food. (28)
- We could play tackle football on the grassy side/the rules out at the playground. (10)
- Longer recess. (9)
- The rules out at the playground. (5)
- We had a bigger playground. (3)
- We had bigger classrooms. (2)
- I wish we could do more art. (2)
- Lockers for the fifth graders. (2)
- The library and the music room were a little closer. (2)

Elementary School 6 Student Open Ended Responses

What do you like about this school?

- Teachers. (29)
- Kids treat people with respect/all of the people are nice. (18)
- The kids/friends. (14)
- Learning. (12)
- Recess. (10)
- The fun. (8)
- Reading. (8)
- Friends. (6)
- It is good. (5)
- The playground. (5)

What do you wish was different at this school?

- Nothing. (19)
- Better food at lunchtime. (13)
- The equipment outside. (9)
- The playground teachers were nicer. (8)
- The kids were nicer/respectful. (8)
- More books in the library. (5)
- Some of the rules. (5)
- More computers in our classroom. (3)
- We could have more fun learning. (3)
- No homework club. (2)
- They'd allow trading cards. (2)

Elementary School 7 Student Open Ended Responses

What do you like about this school?

- The teachers. (51)
- Friends/students are nice. (34)
- Learning. (34)
- The playground and equipment. (23)
- It is fun/good. (17)
- P.E. (14)
- The principal. (11)
- Everything. (11)
- Everyone is treated with respect. (9)
- Library and books. (8)

What do you wish was different at this school?

- Nothing. (52)
- More equipment and bigger playground. (19)
- More and longer recess. (9)
- Longer time in specials like music, gym, library, and library skills. (9)
- The food. (7)
- That some kids were nicer. (5)
- The school had a bigger gym area. (4)
- More time to read/to do my work. (4)
- The boys could play tackle football. (3)
- Longer lunchtime. (3)

Elementary School 8 Student Open Ended Responses

What do you like about this school?

- People are friendly and respectful/friends. (26)
- The teachers. (16)
- Learning. (14)
- Recess. (6)
- P.E. is fun. (5)
- Good lunches. (5)
- It is very fun. (5)
- Conflict management program. (4)
- It is a very good school. (4)
- It feels safe. (4)

What do you wish was different at this school?

- Nothing. (13)
- New/more playground equipment. (10)
- People would treat others better. (4)
- That we could play tackle football. (4)
- That the playground aides weren't so strict. (3)
- We had more parties and more candy. (2)
- The food. (2)
- They would put grass on the soccer field. (2)
- More recess time. (2)
- More time to eat lunch. (2)

Elementary School 9 Student Open Ended Responses

What do you like about this school?

- Teachers and staff (84)
- Friends/nice people. (52)
- Recess. (32)
- The good food. (32)
- The playground and equipment. (25)
- The principal. (17)
- Learning is fun. (17)
- Everyone is treated nicely and with respect. (17)
- The library. (13)
- P.E. (11)

What do you wish was different at this school?

- More/new playground equipment/bigger playground. (38)
- Nothing. (34)
- More respectful/nicer kids. (23)
- Longer recess. (22)
- Better lunches. (19)
- The rules weren't as strict. (15)
- Some desserts at lunch. (13)
- My teacher will be nicer. (12)
- There was not a little kid's side and a big kid's side on the playground. (8)
- Less/easier work. (4)

Elementary School 10 Student Open Ended Responses	
What do you like about this school?	***What do you wish was different at this school?***
• The teachers and staff. (38) • Friends/everyone is friendly and respectful. (27) • I like this school. (12) • Learning. (10) • How many books we have/library. (9) • Kids. (9) • P.E. (7) • Everything. (5) • The playground equipment. (4) • Music. (4)	• Longer recess. (15) • Nicer/more helpful playground aides. (13) • Nothing. (11) • A longer lunch break. (10) • I wish some kids were a little nicer. (7) • The food. (6) • More books in the library. (5) • The playground rules. (4) • A better playground. (4) • Bring back the student council. (2)

Elementary School 11 Student Open Ended Responses	
What do you like about this school?	***What do you wish was different at this school?***
• Teachers and staff. (46) • My friends. (21) • Learning. (15) • The principal. (11) • Everybody is nice. (10) • Recess. (8) • It is fun. (6) • Gym. (5) • Everything. (2) • We have library skills. (2)	• Nothing. (15) • More kids treat other kids with respect. (13) • Rules. (6) • The playground was newer/bigger. (5) • More gym time. (3) • That we had grass. (2) • We could have more recess. (2) • Homework. (2) • Different playground aides. (2) • More reading time.

Middle and high school student responses mostly clustered around the overall average (Figure 5.2). Average middle school student responses fell below neutral (in disagreement) for both schools for the statement: *I have choices in what I learn.*

While students from Middle School 2 were in low agreement, Middle School 1 students were in disagreement with: *I have freedom at school.* Both middle schools received neutral average responses for:

- *Students at my school treat me with respect.*
- *Students at my school are friendly.*

Middle School 2 students' average was in low agreement with the items:

- *Students are treated fairly by teachers.*
- *Students are treated fairly by administrators.*

Figure 5.2

Canyon View School District Student Responses By Middle School, March 2005

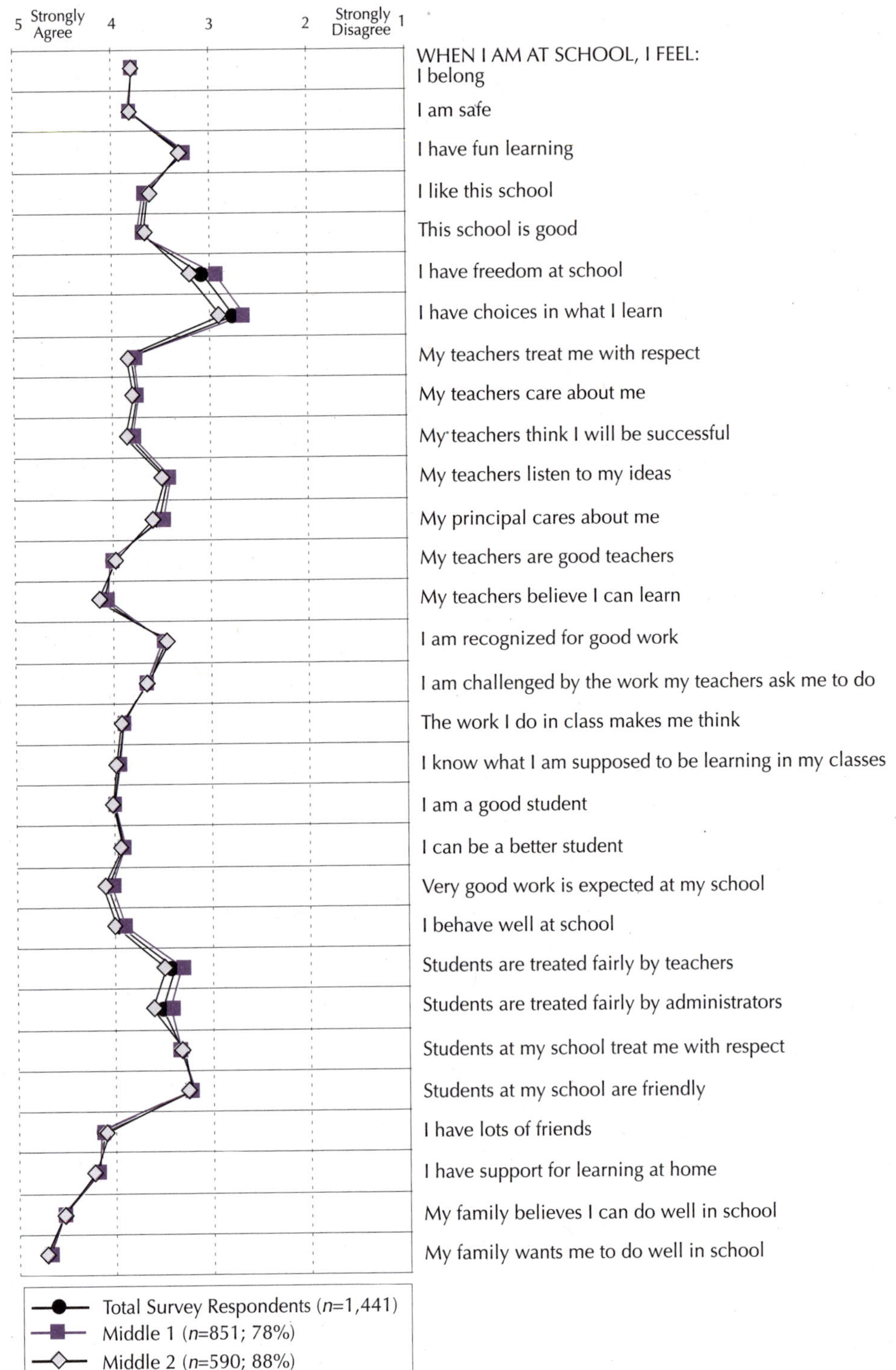

Middle School 1 Student Open Ended Responses	
What do you like about this school?	***What do you wish was different at this school?***
• The teachers/the principals. (503) • It is a fun place to learn. (196) • My friends. (164) • The people. (148) • Long lunch/the food is good/can socialize with friends. (116) • Everyone gets treated with respect. (85) • My classes. (53) • Freedom: opinions/clothes/classroom activities/to choose classes. (51) • I am getting a good education. (47) • I feel safe. (46)	• More lunch time/shorter lines. (185) • Students and teachers would be more kind/friendly/respectful to each other/teachers more caring. (156) • Better/more food/more choices/less expensive. (77) • Less homework. (75) • Nothing. (63) • That lunch was before recess. (59) • More time to get to classes. (59) • We could choose our classes/more choices. (58) • We should all get a longer study hall (advisor period). (47) • Schools needs to be more interesting/fun/more activities. (4)

Middle School 2 Student Open Ended Responses	
What do you like about this school?	***What do you wish was different at this school?***
• Teachers. (234) • Classes/the learning challenges/the programs, projects, and activities. (182) • All the nice/respectful people. (110) • The way we do the new lunch program and the food. (104) • Being with my friends. (87) • The learning/challenge. (67) • Having water bottles and snack breaks during the day. (62) • It is a fun school. (35) • Feeling safe. (31) • The principal. (29) • We can come inside earlier in the morning. (26)	• Longer lunch/better lunch program. (125) • Lunch was before recess. (96) • Students would be more respectful. (95) • Teachers would be more respectful/more encouragement/warmth from teachers. (61) • Nothing, I like how it is. (55) • No more violence/bullying. (39) • More choices in elective classes/more advanced science and language classes. (35) • Everything. (20) • We could have a study hall or advisor. (18) • We could chew gum during class. (18)

High school responses mostly clustered around the overall average of low agreement (Figure 5.3). Responses from high school students fell below neutral (in disagreement) with the statements:

- *I feel that I am in charge of what I learn.*
- *I find what I learn in school to be relevant to real life.*
- *In my classes, time is spent working in small groups.*
- *In my classes, time is spent doing work that I find meaningful.*
- *In my classes, time is spent using computers.*

High School 1 students also disagreed with the statement: *The office staff treat me fairly.* Average high school student responses indicated that time in their classes is spent: *listening to the teachers talk* and *answering questions from a book or worksheet.* Average high school student responses were neutral with respect to:

- *I have opportunities to choose my own projects.*
- *Teachers encourage me to assess the quality of my own work.*
- *This school is preparing me well for what I want to do after high school.*
- *This school is fun.*
- *My teachers are understanding when students have personal problems.*
- *My teachers help me gain confidence in my ability to learn.*
- *My teachers know me well.*
- *My teachers listen to my ideas.*
- *My teachers care about me.*
- *My teachers make learning fun.*
- *In my classes, time is spent in whole class discussions.*
- *In my classes, time is spent working on projects or research.*

Figure 5.3

Canyon View School District Student Responses By High School, March 2005

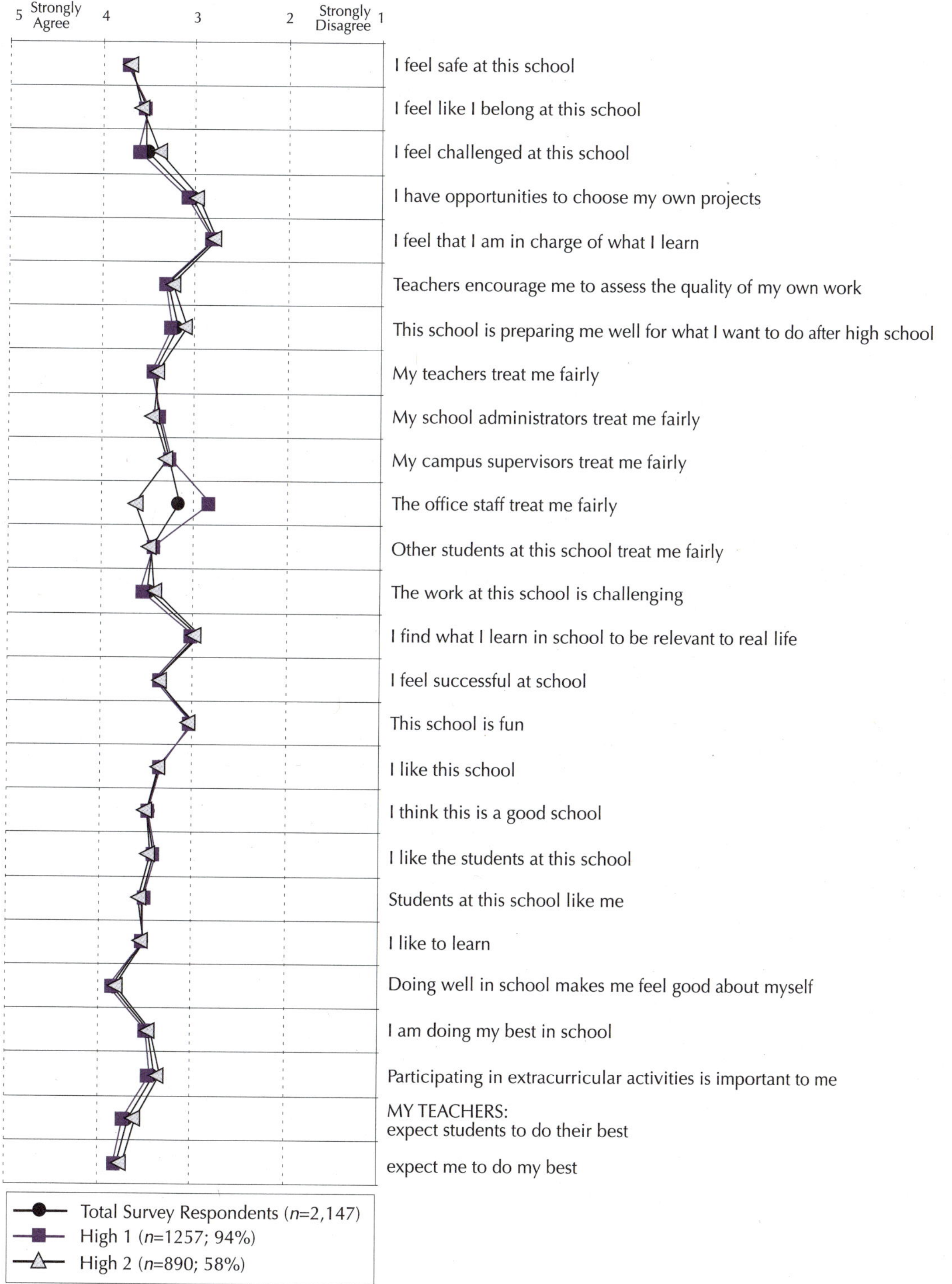

5 Strongly Agree
4
3
2
Strongly Disagree 1
I feel safe at this school
I feel like I belong at this school
I feel challenged at this school
I have opportunities to choose my own projects
I feel that I am in charge of what I learn
Teachers encourage me to assess the quality of my own work
This school is preparing me well for what I want to do after high school
My teachers treat me fairly
My school administrators treat me fairly
My campus supervisors treat me fairly
The office staff treat me fairly
Other students at this school treat me fairly
The work at this school is challenging
I find what I learn in school to be relevant to real life
I feel successful at school
This school is fun
I like this school
I think this is a good school
I like the students at this school
Students at this school like me
I like to learn
Doing well in school makes me feel good about myself
I am doing my best in school
Participating in extracurricular activities is important to me
MY TEACHERS:
expect students to do their best
expect me to do my best
Total Survey Respondents (n=2,147)
High 1 (n=1257; 94%)
High 2 (n=890; 58%)

Figure 5.3 (Continued)

Canyon View School District Student Responses By High School, March 2005

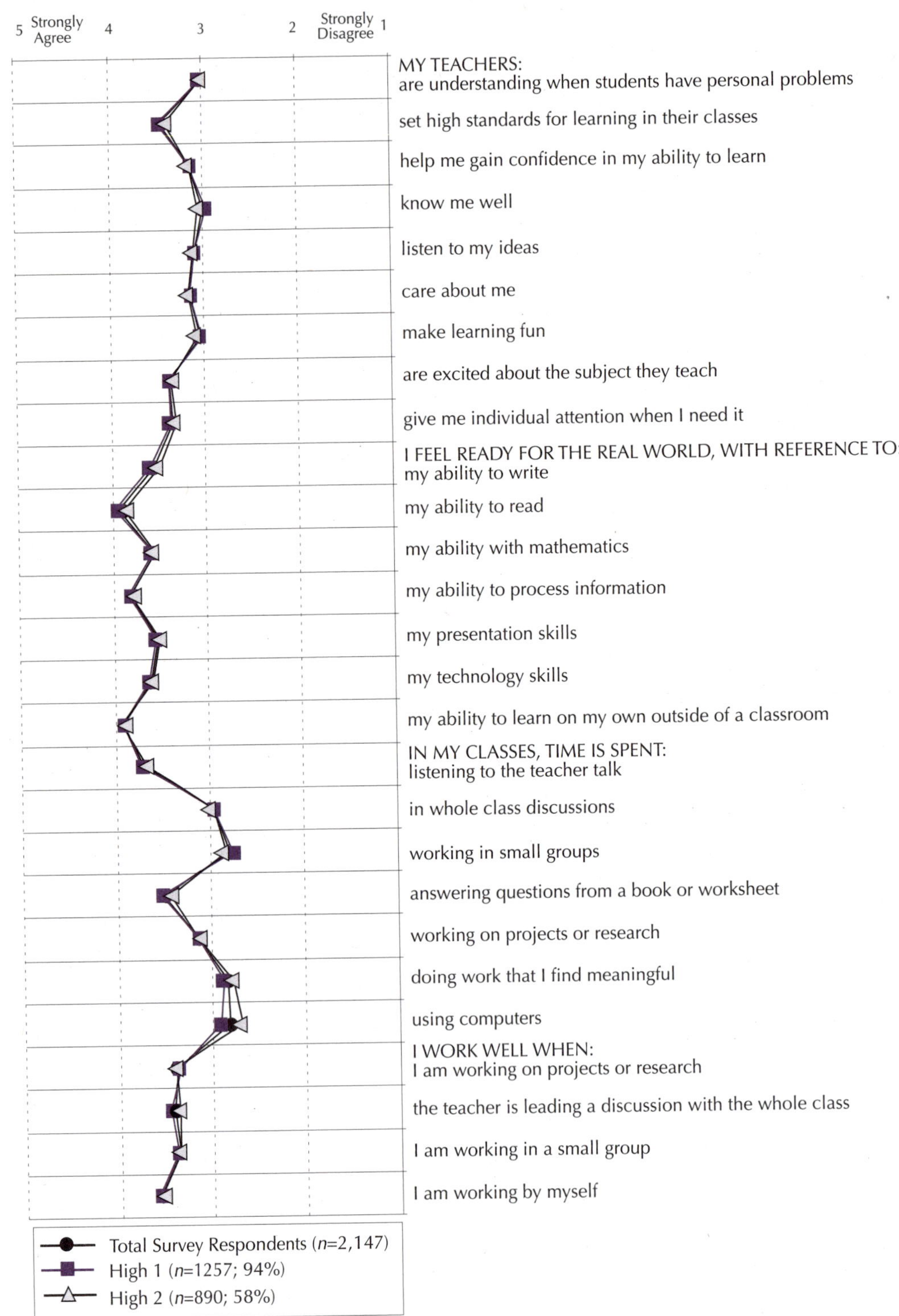

5 Strongly Agree
4
3
2
Strongly Disagree 1
MY TEACHERS:
are understanding when students have personal problems
set high standards for learning in their classes
help me gain confidence in my ability to learn
know me well
listen to my ideas
care about me
make learning fun
are excited about the subject they teach
give me individual attention when I need it
I FEEL READY FOR THE REAL WORLD, WITH REFERENCE TO:
my ability to write
my ability to read
my ability with mathematics
my ability to process information
my presentation skills
my technology skills
my ability to learn on my own outside of a classroom
IN MY CLASSES, TIME IS SPENT:
listening to the teacher talk
in whole class discussions
working in small groups
answering questions from a book or worksheet
working on projects or research
doing work that I find meaningful
using computers
I WORK WELL WHEN:
I am working on projects or research
the teacher is leading a discussion with the whole class
I am working in a small group
I am working by myself
Total Survey Respondents (n=2,147)
High 1 (n=1257; 94%)
High 2 (n=890; 58%)

High School 1 Student Open Ended Responses	
What do you like about this school?	***What do you wish was different at this school?***
• Teachers. (327) • Extracurricular activities/the athletics/sports programs. (300) • We get a good education/fun/challenging/the classes. (186) • Variety of good/elective classes. (112) • Nothing. (99) • The kids. (80) • Football program/team. (67) • The people. (61) • That every one is accepted/gets along/positive atmosphere/treats you fairly/with respect. (58) • The long/off campus lunch. (53)	• Better/nicer/more respectful teachers and staff. (265) • Longer lunch time. (199) • More recognition/funding for other sports/activities other than football. (139) • Nicer kids. (104) • More group/hands-on activities/class discussions/learning was more fun/somehow relate learning to real world. (90) • More choice of classes/variety of classes. (59) • Nothing. (55) • More freedom/fewer restrictions. (54) • More paved/assigned spots like at the other high school/better parking/no parking pass. (53) • Less homework. (52)

High School 2 Student Open Ended Responses	
What do you like about this school?	***What do you wish was different at this school?***
• Teachers and staff. (251) • The people. (151) • Everyone is accepted/everyone is friendly and treated fairly well. (125) • The many choices of electives. (73) • Extra curricular activities/clubs. (67) • It is a great place to learn/ the classes. (63) • The diversity. (60) • Open campus at lunch. (55) • The sports program. (55) • We have a lot of freedom and responsibility. (31)	• Teachers more understanding/respectful/friendly/helpful. (120) • People where more respectful, nicer, more tolerant and more understanding. (111) • We had more time at lunch. (105) • More groups/hands-on activities/learning more fun/less time listening to teachers lecture. (80) • Some of the rules/dress code/be able to wear hats. (46) • Nothing. (39) • School offered a wider variety of sports/activities/fairer. (37) • Equal representation of the different activities at this school, less focus on sports. (37) • Less structured, a little bit more lenient with tardies/attendance/etc. (31) • More electives to choose from/available to freshmen. (29)

Staff Responses by Elementary, Middle, and High Schools

When staff responses were disaggregated by elementary, middle, and high schools, responses to the items on the questionnaire revealed some differences; however, most responses clustered around the overall average (Figures 5.4 through 5.6).

All staff members were in strong agreement with most items on the first part of the questionnaire results shown in Figure 5.4, except for Elementary School 7, who disagreed with:

- *My administrators are effective instructional leaders.*
- *My administrators facilitate communication effectively.*

The other items related to administrators were additionally lower for Elementary School 7 than for the other schools (low agreement).

Look Fors:	**Items which staff members, by school and across schools, are in agreement or disagreement.**
Planning Implications:	**Where can/should the district provide leadership, with respect to school/district environment?**

Figure 5.4

Canyon View School District Staff Responses By Elementary School, March 2005

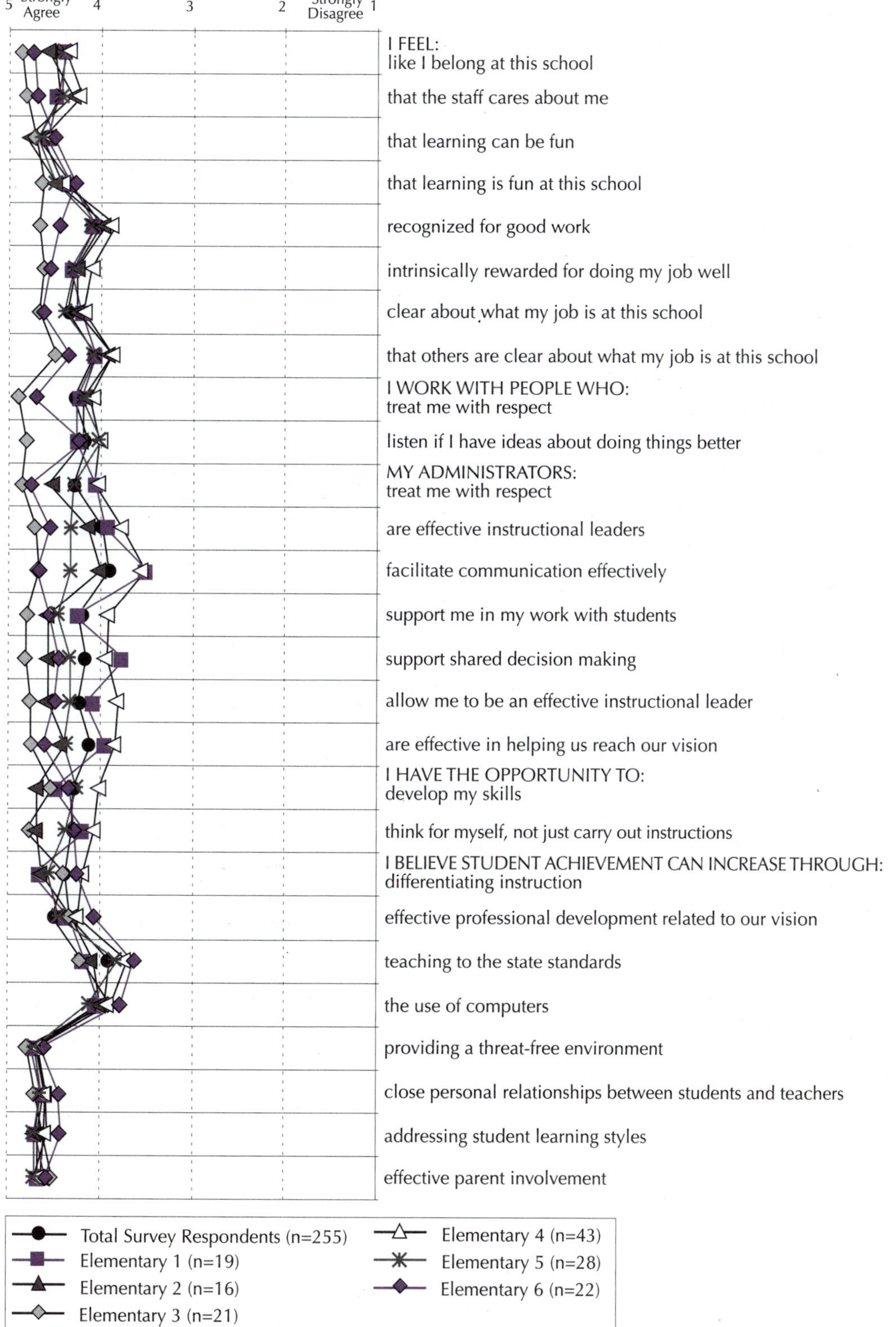

5 Strongly Agree
4
3
2
Strongly Disagree 1
I FEEL:
like I belong at this school
that the staff cares about me
that learning can be fun
that learning is fun at this school
recognized for good work
intrinsically rewarded for doing my job well
clear about what my job is at this school
that others are clear about what my job is at this school
I WORK WITH PEOPLE WHO:
treat me with respect
listen if I have ideas about doing things better
MY ADMINISTRATORS:
treat me with respect
are effective instructional leaders
facilitate communication effectively
support me in my work with students
support shared decision making
allow me to be an effective instructional leader
are effective in helping us reach our vision
I HAVE THE OPPORTUNITY TO:
develop my skills
think for myself, not just carry out instructions
I BELIEVE STUDENT ACHIEVEMENT CAN INCREASE THROUGH:
differentiating instruction
effective professional development related to our vision
teaching to the state standards
the use of computers
providing a threat-free environment
close personal relationships between students and teachers
addressing student learning styles
effective parent involvement
Total Survey Respondents (n=255)
Elementary 1 (n=19)
Elementary 2 (n=16)
Elementary 3 (n=21)
Elementary 4 (n=43)
Elementary 5 (n=28)
Elementary 6 (n=22)

Figure 5.4 (Continued)

Canyon View School District Staff Responses By Elementary School, March 2005

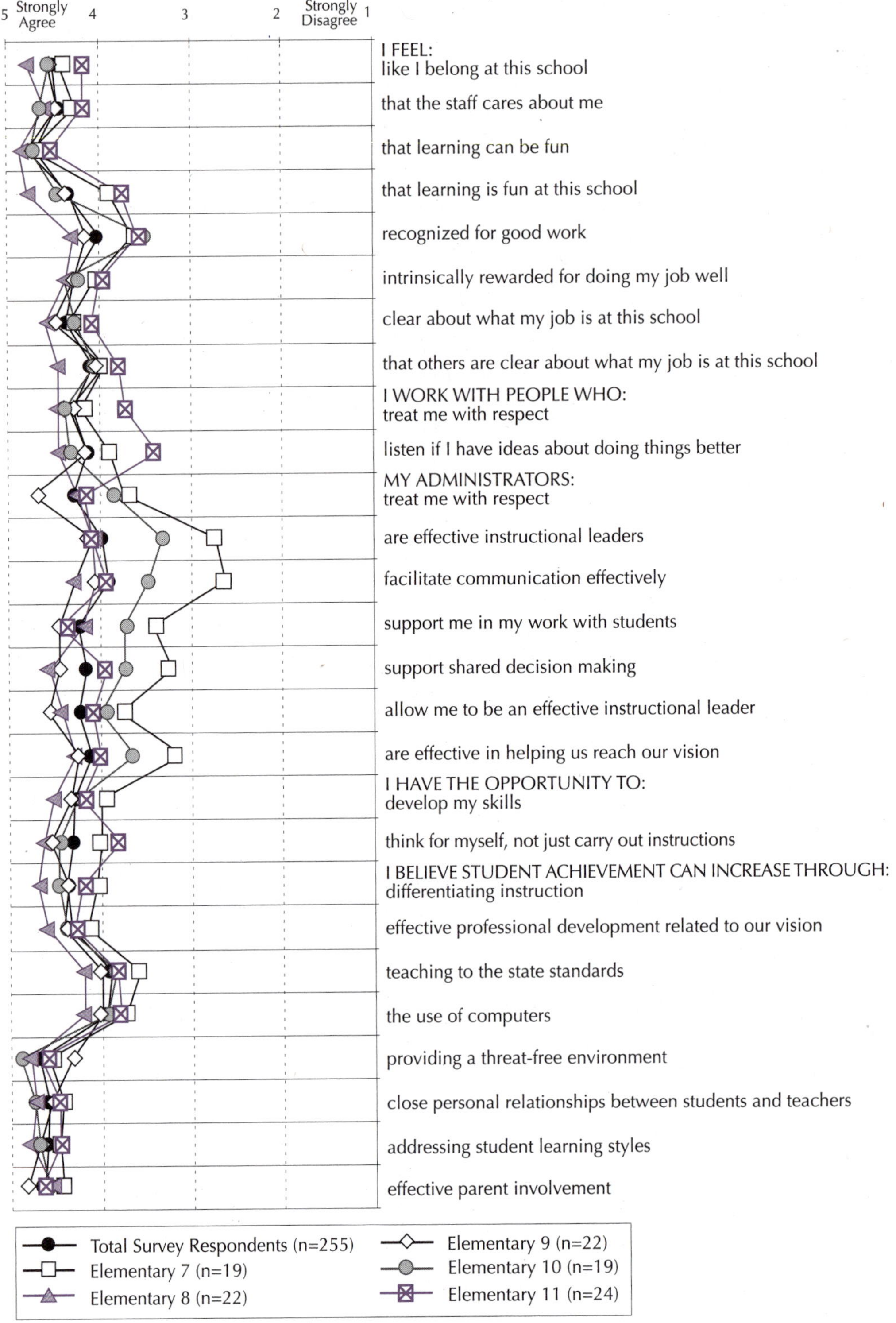

In Figure 5.5 (the results of the second part of the questionnaire), while other schools agreed, staff members from Elementary School 1 were neutral about the item: *I believe this school has a good public image.* Elementary School 7 staff members' responses were in disagreement with *Morale is high on the part of teachers* and *Morale is high on the part of support staff.* Elementary School 11 staff member's responses were in low agreement with *Morale is high on the part of teachers* and *I believe the vision for this school is shared.*

Figure 5.5

Canyon View School District Staff Responses By Elementary School, March 2005

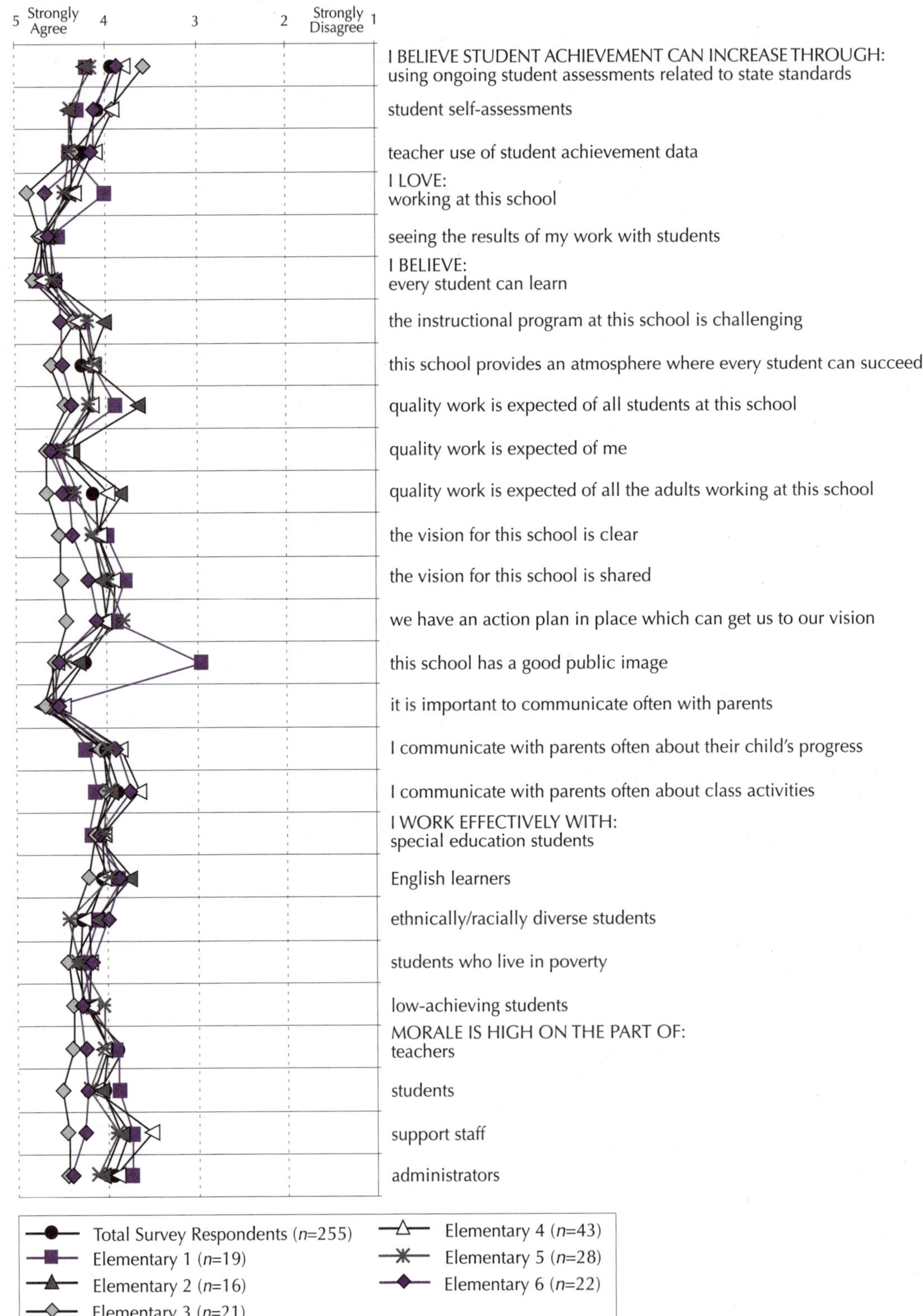

5 Strongly Agree
4
3
2
Strongly Disagree 1
I BELIEVE STUDENT ACHIEVEMENT CAN INCREASE THROUGH:
using ongoing student assessments related to state standards
student self-assessments
teacher use of student achievement data
I LOVE:
working at this school
seeing the results of my work with students
I BELIEVE:
every student can learn
the instructional program at this school is challenging
this school provides an atmosphere where every student can succeed
quality work is expected of all students at this school
quality work is expected of me
quality work is expected of all the adults working at this school
the vision for this school is clear
the vision for this school is shared
we have an action plan in place which can get us to our vision
this school has a good public image
it is important to communicate often with parents
I communicate with parents often about their child's progress
I communicate with parents often about class activities
I WORK EFFECTIVELY WITH:
special education students
English learners
ethnically/racially diverse students
students who live in poverty
low-achieving students
MORALE IS HIGH ON THE PART OF:
teachers
students
support staff
administrators
Total Survey Respondents (n=255)
Elementary 1 (n=19)
Elementary 2 (n=16)
Elementary 3 (n=21)
Elementary 4 (n=43)
Elementary 5 (n=28)
Elementary 6 (n=22)

Figure 5.5 (Continued)

Canyon View School District Staff Responses By Elementary School, March 2005

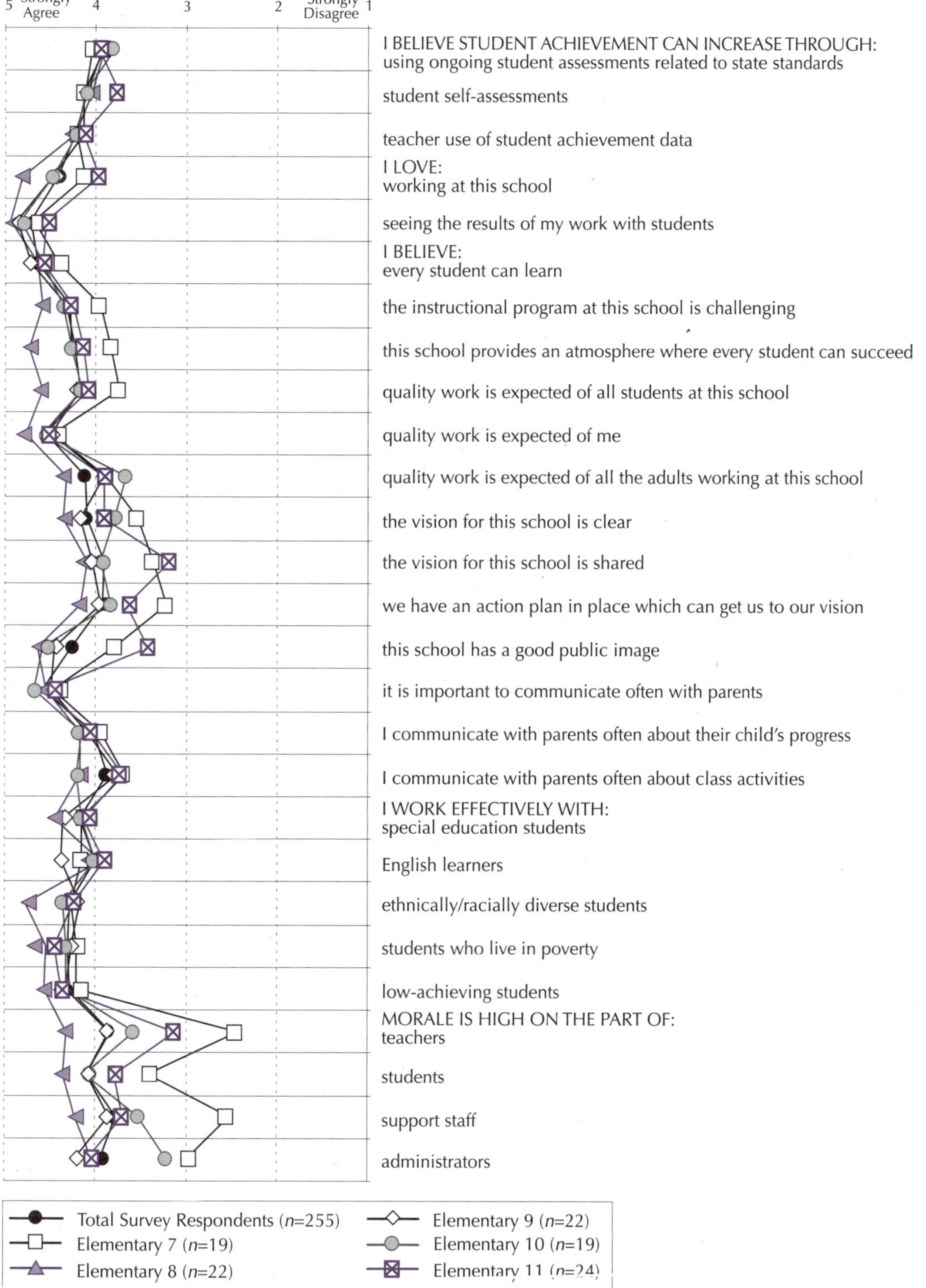

In Figure 5.6 (the last part of the staff questionnaire), all schools were in agreement with the five items, with the exception of Elementary School 11 staff who were in low agreement with *Teachers in this school communicate with each other to make student learning consistent across grades.*

Canyon View staff were asked to respond to three open-ended questions: *What would it take to improve student learning at this school?, What are the strengths at this school?,* and *What needs to be improved?* The top ten staff responses, by school, follow the graphs.

Look Fors:	**The most often written-in responses to what staff thinks would improve student learning, what they like about school, and what needs to be improved.**
Planning Implications:	**Perhaps issues in how students and teachers are treated in each school, or across schools.**

Figure 5.6

Canyon View School District Staff Responses Items for Teachers By Elementary School March 2005

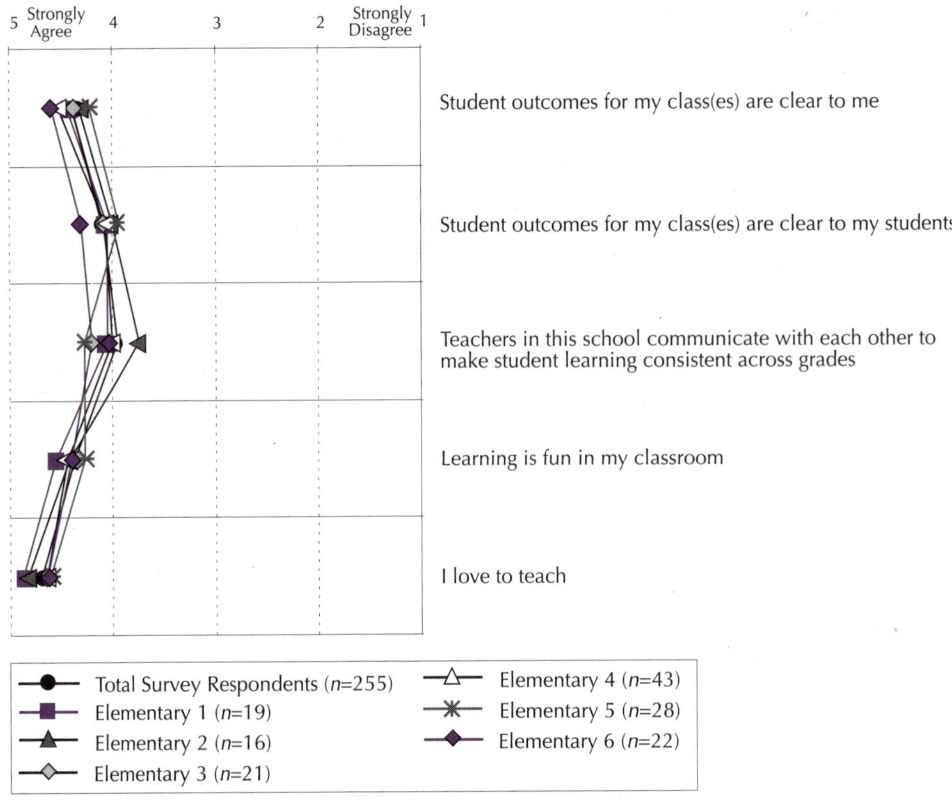

Figure 5.6 (Continued)

Canyon View School District Staff Responses Items for Teachers By Elementary School March 2005

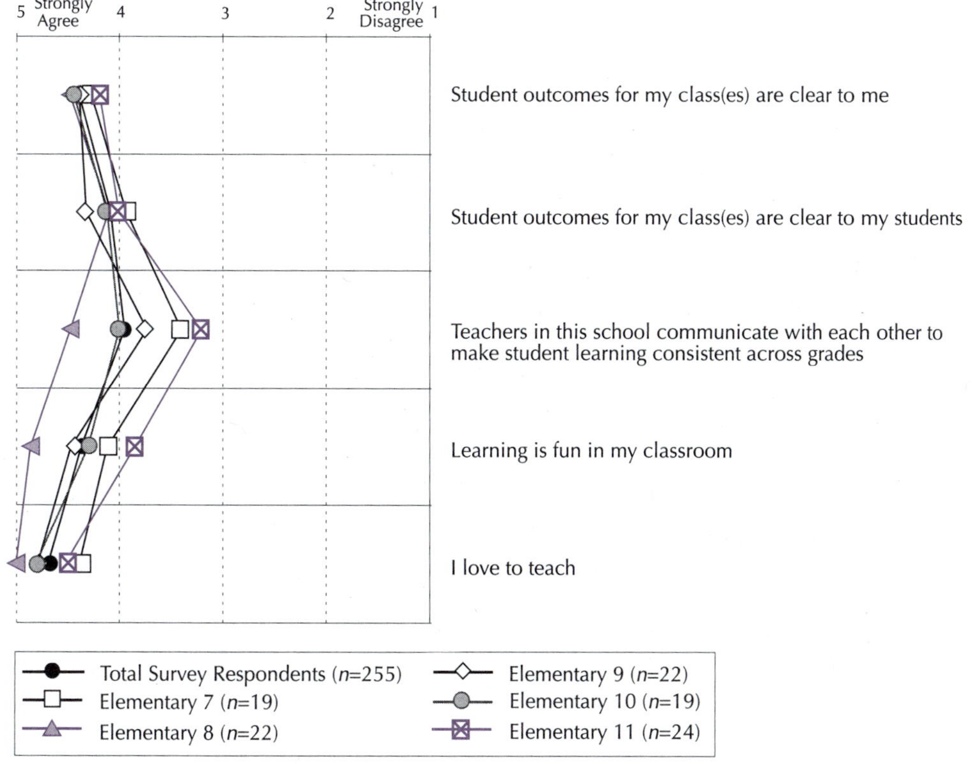

Elementary School 1 Staff Open Ended Responses	
What would it take to improve student learning in this school?	
♦ Articulate between the grade levels to make sure that students are being challenged. (4) ♦ The willingness of educators to think out of the box and try new things. (3) ♦ Parent involvement. (2) ♦ The district does not give the support needed in this school. (2) ♦ Teach less, better. (2) ♦ Constant evaluation of lesson design and assessment work to determine the needs of each child. ♦ Smaller class sizes would improve learning. ♦ Team approach to learning. ♦ Leadership that is more consistent. ♦ Realign the developmental expectations to the expectations of the standards.	
What are the strengths of this school?	***What needs to be improved?***
♦ The staff/educators who are willing to go out on a limb to try new approaches. (12) ♦ We have a developmental learning report card and everyone knows the standards. (9) ♦ Great work environment. (9) ♦ Putting the students' needs above all things. (9) ♦ Staff friendships. (8) ♦ The principal. (7) ♦ Great organization and support between the staff and administration. (4) ♦ Very kind and grounded students. ♦ We have parents who work with us in most cases.	♦ Administration. (6) ♦ Communication. (2) ♦ More professional development. (2) ♦ Time is not available for staff to align curriculum vertically. (2) ♦ Help from district staff. ♦ More support staff. ♦ Parent involvement. ♦ Time in our classrooms to do our jobs. ♦ Cut out the nonproductive meetings we have to attend. ♦ Better understanding of other standards.

Elementary School 2 Staff Open Ended Responses

What would it take to improve student learning in this school?

- More qualified staff to help with individualized instruction.
- Smaller class sizes. (6)
- More paraprofessionals. (5)
- No combination classes. (4)
- Cross-grade-level meetings. (3)
- Continue with our summer programs and make sure attendance is high. (3)
- Focusing on Math, Reading, and Language. (2)
- More parent involvement. (2)
- Full-time use of our trained Reading Recovery Specialists. (2)
- Poverty is a huge factor in student achievement at this school. Students often enter this school already at a deficit. We spend the next six years playing catch-up. (2)
- Knowing how to match instruction to testing.

What are the strengths of this school?

- Excellent teachers. (9)
- Supportive administrator. (4)
- Strong support staff. (3)
- Our Reading Recovery Program is a big boost to our low readers. (2)
- Staff and administration dedication to the children. (2)
- The staff remains committed to the challenge despite the obstacles. (2)
- Safe and caring environment. (2)
- Very supportive parents. (2)
- Good reputation in the public eye.
- Strong supportive community.
- Our social service coordinator is always willing to offer support

What needs to be improved?

- Communication. (6)
- All staff needs to have more time to work together on student success. (5)
- We need more computers. (4)
- Professional training with special education students and how the whole staff can work together to support these students. (4)
- Cohesive programs within our school. (3)
- Training of specialized staff/professional development opportunities on state standards. (3)
- More of a say on how our budget allotment is spent. (2)
- More paraprofessionals to supervise the playground and lunchroom.
- More supportive lunchroom servers, the students are afraid of the head server in the kitchen.
- Simplifications of state standards into clear essential skills.

Elementary School 3 Staff Open Ended Responses	
What would it take to improve student learning in this school?	
• More opportunity and time for meetings with administrators and other teachers, school-wide and district-wide. (5) • More training in working with special needs students would help the classes to be more effectively taught. The placement of high needs students in regular education is harming the learning of regular education students. (2) • Instructional assistants to assist student learning in deficit areas. (2) • Continued parental support. (2) • Even more cross-curricular work to improve the reinforcement of classroom skills in my music classes. • Diverse instruction to meet the needs of each child. • Student, teacher, and parent commitment to learning.	
What are the strengths of this school?	***What needs to be improved?***
• Staff gets along, creating a good environment. (20) • Respect for each other. (11) • Staff cares about students. (7) • Parent involvement. (5) • Caring, positive and supportive administrator. (4) • Diversified instruction. (3) • Continuous collaboration and sharing to make learning fun and effective. (2) • Keeping a positive attitude when times seem tough. • School-wide consistency using the same language and behavior expectations.	• Training and support for both the special needs students and the gifted. (4) • Computation skills. (3) • Time for grade levels to meet and plan together. (3) • Work to make learning better, more efficient, and effective, as well as social concerns. (2) • More training for paraprofessionals on how to work with special needs kids. (2) • Reading skills. • The follow through of actually accomplishing and sticking with the tasks and processes we start. • Provide larger, longer blocks of teaching time with fewer interruptions. • More assistance with differentiation of instruction. • Smaller class sizes.

Elementary School 4 Staff Open Ended Responses

What would it take to improve student learning in this school?

- Additional direct instruction for individual needs by trained adults to reinforce, reteach concepts and lessons. (10)
- Professional development. (8)
- More community and collaboration. (7)
- More planning time. (4)
- More parent involvement. (4)
- Smaller class size. (3)
- Training regarding standards. (3)
- Diagnostic testing. (3)
- Student study groups and mentors. (2)
- Fewer interruptions.

What are the strengths of this school?	*What needs to be improved?*
• Strong teaching staff. (22) • Parent/community support. (10) • Administrative support. (5) • Positive environment. (5) • Great staff of supporting teachers and para-professionals. (4) • Students who like learning. (3) • This is a beautiful building. We would like it to remain in good condition. (2) • Our school goals are in place. • Use of new programs/techniques	• All the staff should be required to do their jobs effectively. This school truly needs some new blood. (9) • More time for planning. (5) • Communication. (4) • Training opportunities. (3) • Do not interrupt the teaching day. Fewer meetings and more time for preparing. (3) • Smaller class room sizes for the upper levels 4th and 5th graders. (3) • The administration should be more supportive of the staff, and stick to the new policies. (3) • Window air conditioners. (2) • Our school needs to be cleaner. The door jams and windows are filthy. (2) • Parent and school relationship, when it comes to crossing guards. (2)

Elementary School 5 Staff Open Ended Responses

What would it take to improve student learning in this school?

- Cross-grade-level meetings about standards. More informed about what the state standards are at my grade level and how to meet them. (10)
- Each student comes to school ready and prepared to learn. (3)
- Continue to work as an entire staff to teach each child and make kids more responsible for their actions, let them know they are expected to do their best and hold them accountable for getting their work done on time. (3)
- Trained individuals for one on one with At-risk kids. (2)
- Programs and materials to teach the curriculum. (2)
- More emphasis on modifying distracting behavior on the parts of a small number of students who disrupt learning for others.
- Parental involvement and support.
- An organized reading program for low readers and additional teacher support for low readers.
- Quality feedback from school administration.
- Creating a vision we all believe in and facilitate in our classrooms.

What are the strengths of this school?

- Teachers who are committed. (24)
- Collaboration among all of the staff. (11)
- Positive, supportive, fun working environment. (7)
- Supportive parents. (5)
- High staff and student morale. (4)
- Great support from administrator. (4)
- Staff willing to change, learn new approaches, and take risks. (3)
- School has good reputation in the community and still feels like a small neighborhood school. (3)
- Full time principal.
- The facility is very clean and welcoming.
- Kids are awesome.

What needs to be improved?

- Work on professional development. (3)
- More assemblies in this area, clearer expectations for children, visual reminders throughout the school. (2)
- Teachers need more contact time with each other to plan in and across grade levels/support for teachers who have lost their love for teaching. (2)
- There is not enough staff to serve the needs of the students.
- The physical space of the office could be enlarged and more accommodating to gatherings of more than two people.
- Phone system in place for each educator.
- The principal could be more flexible and willing to allow teachers to share their opinions.
- Respect: student-to-student, student-to-adult, and adult-to-adult.
- Keep up-to-date on all of the new ideas concerning school legislation and updates on the state standards.
- More communication with principal and staff regarding what exactly is expected.

Elementary School 6 Staff Open Ended Responses	
What would it take to improve student learning in this school?	
• More programs to support our students who have learning difficulties. (2) • Time and effort to communicate and collaborate with each other. (2) • Continued in-service in all areas relating to standards and strategies would be great. • A different setting for the severe behavior problems. • More parents working with their kids at home rather than us trying to find things for parents to do at school. • Consistent behavior expectations.	
What are the strengths of this school?	***What needs to be improved?***
• An excellent staff. (9) • Parent involvement. (3) • Motivated students. (3) • A very strong administrator. (3) • Good communication. (2) • This school spends little time in staff meetings that are not beneficial to meeting student's needs. • We are always open to further skill acquisition and in-service training in order to further expertise. • The staff and parents work closely together. • Team atmosphere.	• Time to work on standards and teaching strategies. (2) • Communication. • We need to have further assistance in dealing with students below grade level or struggling at level. • Class configurations. • Limiting the amount of time that is spent trying to come up with ideas of things to do for the parents who want to be at school. • Willingness to embrace change and seek out change in an effort to improve learning. • School-wide conflict resolution plan with all adults using the same approach and verbiage. • Noise level.

Elementary School 7 Staff Open Ended Responses	
What would it take to improve student learning in this school?	
• More resources. (3) • Parental support. (3) • Knowing exactly what the standards are in every subject. Time to review, react, and reassess the standards and how we are going to most effectively get students where they should be. (3) • More student choices about learning. More experiential learning opportunities. (3) • More para assistance time in the classrooms. (2) • Smaller class size. • Time for planning with other teachers to share ideas, best practices. • Someone who can bring in speakers and or videos on effective teaching practices. • More alignment to school adopted texts so that skills are not missed. • More compassion for a students' situations outside the school and finding ways to better reach and talk to those troubled students.	
What are the strengths of this school?	***What needs to be improved?***
• Staff. (10) • Teachers are willing to work hard with students and to work at school improvement. (3) • Support staff. (2) • Parents and community. (2) • Principal. • ibook computers. • Good kids. • Respect is taught daily by all staff and good behavior is expected. • A caring atmosphere. We also believe in having fun. • Everyone is included in decision-making.	• Communication about effective strategy and practices. (5) • Strengthen relationships with parents. (3) • Make each school equal in resources and monies. (2) • Being consistent with our testing. • Fewer nonteaching assignments and projects. • There is always room for improvement.

Elementary School 8 Staff Open Ended Responses

What would it take to improve student learning in this school?

- Small class sizes. (3)
- Teacher training. (2)
- We need time to plan and collaborate with other teachers. (2)
- Vertical alignment of curriculum.
- More, newer, reliable PCs and printers.
- Less time fixing phone problems and PC hook ups to the Internet.
- Continue to support learning through title programs.
- Continued support from special education help in the building.
- An ongoing commitment to improvement. We are, as a staff, willing to make any changes necessary to facilitate student learning.
- Put into action the Plan the staff has created.

What are the strengths of this school?	*What needs to be improved?*
• Dedicated staff. (10) • Sense of community. (5) • A wonderful and diverse student population. (3) • Respect teachers have for support staff and visa versa. (3) • Flexibility. (2) • Good humor. (2) • Setting a goal and making a plan to improve student outcomes. (2) • Families. • Ensuring that every adult strives to make this a place of welcome and safety and learning. • Good morale.	• Communication. (4) • Dialogue between grade levels to ensure that all the concepts are being covered. (3) • Staff training. • More time to work collaboratively within the school day. • Continuous focus on early success in primary classrooms will reduce future need to remedy problems. This is done through small class size, support learning through Title Programs, etc. • The cleanliness of our facility. • We're here to serve the students and their families, and I will work to promote any positive effort that encourages this. • The physical facility is old; many things need to be fixed, but we are getting there. • Knowledge of the standards so the Plan can happen. • Playground safety.

Elementary School 9 Staff Open Ended Responses

What would it take to improve student learning in this school?

- Grade level meetings with our level and the teachers that teach the level before us and the level after us. (17)
- More cooperative planning between specialists, administrators, and classroom teachers with students performing below grade level. (7)
- Parents who take an active role in students' progress. (4)
- More resource time for needy students. More feedback as to what they are working on. (3)
- Letting go of old ideals and realizing that the student population is changing. Classrooms will be more difficult to manage and need to be kept as small as possible. (2)
- Better leadership at the administrative level.
- A positive attitude and work for what is the best for all students.
- Less emphasis on "No Child Left Behind" data gathering, more emphasis on good lessons.
- A school counselor that is willing to spend the majority of time with students in need and that communicates well with the classroom teacher.
- Schedules of all teachers, including specialists, outside their doors so we can use our time wisely for student conferences.

What are the strengths of this school?

- Great, dedicated staff. (24)
- Parent support. (4)
- Administration is supportive. (3)
- We have has always been a close-knit school. The parents feel it as well, and are pleased to have their children go to such a good school. (2)
- Willingness to try new things.
- Excellent instruction in the primary grades in reading foundations.
- Change has come, and others are starting to be less reactive and more proactive.
- Respect of individuality of faculty, staff, and students.
- Attitude that each child is important and all can learn.
- Commitment to students overall growth as individuals.

What needs to be improved?

- Communication. (8)
- Faculty meetings allowing enough time for teacher concerns. (7)
- Shared decision-making where everyone has an equal voice. (4)
- The new standards being set by the federal and state government are forcing us to think, work, and adjust out of our box, comfort zone. (2)
- Teacher morale, student effort in those that need it the most, parental support instead of excuses for why effort isn't being made. (2)
- School safety.
- People willing to attend meetings on time and stay the length of the meeting.
- More in-service training paid for by administration.
- A school psychologist willing to get more involved with students.
- Understanding the laws under IDEA rather than assume children need Resource because they are not performing in the classroom.

Elementary School 10 Staff Open Ended Responses

What would it take to improve student learning in this school?

- Increase amount of cross grade level discussion regarding standards, assessment tools, and collaboration. (10)
- More qualified support staff. (2)
- Better training available to teachers and support staff. (2)
- A total commitment from all (parents, teachers, administration, and students) to work toward higher standards. (2)
- Quality time, patience, keeping the interest in the subject and fun in learning and teaching. (2)
- The financial resources to implement our strategies.
- More instructional time, with fewer interruptions to the daily routine. More days in school. (2)
- Increased parental involvement.
- Better assessment tools.
- Continuous and informative communication with the parents on how their child is proceeding and ideas on how parents may help at home

What are the strengths of this school?

- Committed staff. (13)
- Supportive parent community. (9)
- A good administrator. (6)
- Collaborative attitude shared by most staff. (6)
- Support staff. (5)
- Very strong sense of collaboration, common vision/mission, willingness to do the work necessary for ongoing improvement. (3)
- Flexibility. (2)
- Incredible belief in the goodness of kids.
- Expertise.

What needs to be improved?

- Time to work together and learn from each other. (10)
- More training/more Paraprofessionals. (5)
- Communication among the staff needs to be improved. (4)
- More time for administrators to be in the classroom. (2)
- Parent input is important but should not be the standard by which instruction is delivered. (2)
- Students, parents, and teachers many times feel that the playground rules are too burdensome and extensive. Continued effort in promoting a safe environment for all students in the school. (2)
- Keep on working to increase learning effectiveness and school climate. Need to feel safe as a staff member. (2)
- Attitudes of a few staff.
- Assessment piece needs continued work.
- Support for special education.

Elementary School 11 Staff Open Ended Responses	
What would it take to improve student learning in this school?	
• Better home environments and more parent involvement at home with academics and behavior. (13) • We need to have a systematic approach to our curriculum and instruction that we all follow. (8) • Analysis of the assessment data and diagnosis of problems. An implementation plan for all students, high achieving and low achieving, followed by all teachers. (5) • The administrator to make sure that all teachers are teaching and assessing effectively. (3) • Time to teach uninterruptedly. (2) • Money for appropriate texts and materials. (2) • An essential skills list like we used to have for each grade level teacher to refer to. • Monthly grade level meetings. • Students behavior not disrupting class.	
What are the strengths of this school?	***What needs to be improved?***
• Professional caring staff. (26) • Principal. (10) • Good kids who are eager to learn. (3) • High expectations for students and staff. (3) • A warm, caring atmosphere provided by the office staff. (3) • It is a very nice place to work. (2) • Some very caring parents. • Willingness to make this the one constant safe place for our students.	• Parental support at home. (6) • Communication. (5) • We need to keep going on the goals that we have set and need to work together to meet those goals. We need to keep involving our parents and getting their support for the things we do to improve the curriculum for their children. (4) • Much more help for special education and low students. (3) • Equipment and resources; monetary support from the district. (2) • Staff development by grade level. (2) • There is a need to reteach skills after assessing. (2) • Accountability for teachers who are not teaching what everyone else is. (2) • The belief that all children must learn in exactly the same way with the exact same materials/texts. • Keep making sound research-based decisions in every thing we do to help our children succeed.

In Figures 5.7, 5.8, and 5.9, middle and high school staff members were in agreement with most items on the questionnaire, except for staff from High School 2, who disagreed with:

- *I believe the vision for this school is shared.*
- *I believe we have an action plan in place which can get us to our vision.*
- *I communicate with parents often about class activities.*
- *Morale is high on the part of teachers.*
- *Teachers in this school communicate with each other to make student learning consistent across grades.*

High School 2 staff responses averaged neutral for:

- *My administrators are effective instructional leaders.*
- *My administrators facilitate communication effectively.*
- *My administrators are effective in helping us reach our vision.*
- *I believe quality work is expected of all students at this school.*
- *I believe quality work is expected of all the adults working at this school.*
- *I believe the vision for this school is clear.*
- *Morale is high on the part of students.*
- *Morale is high on the part of support staff.*
- *Morale is high on the part of administrators.*

High School 1 staff responded in low agreement/neutral to:

- *I communicate with parents often about class activities.*

Figure 5.7

Canyon View School District Staff Responses By Middle and High School, March 2005

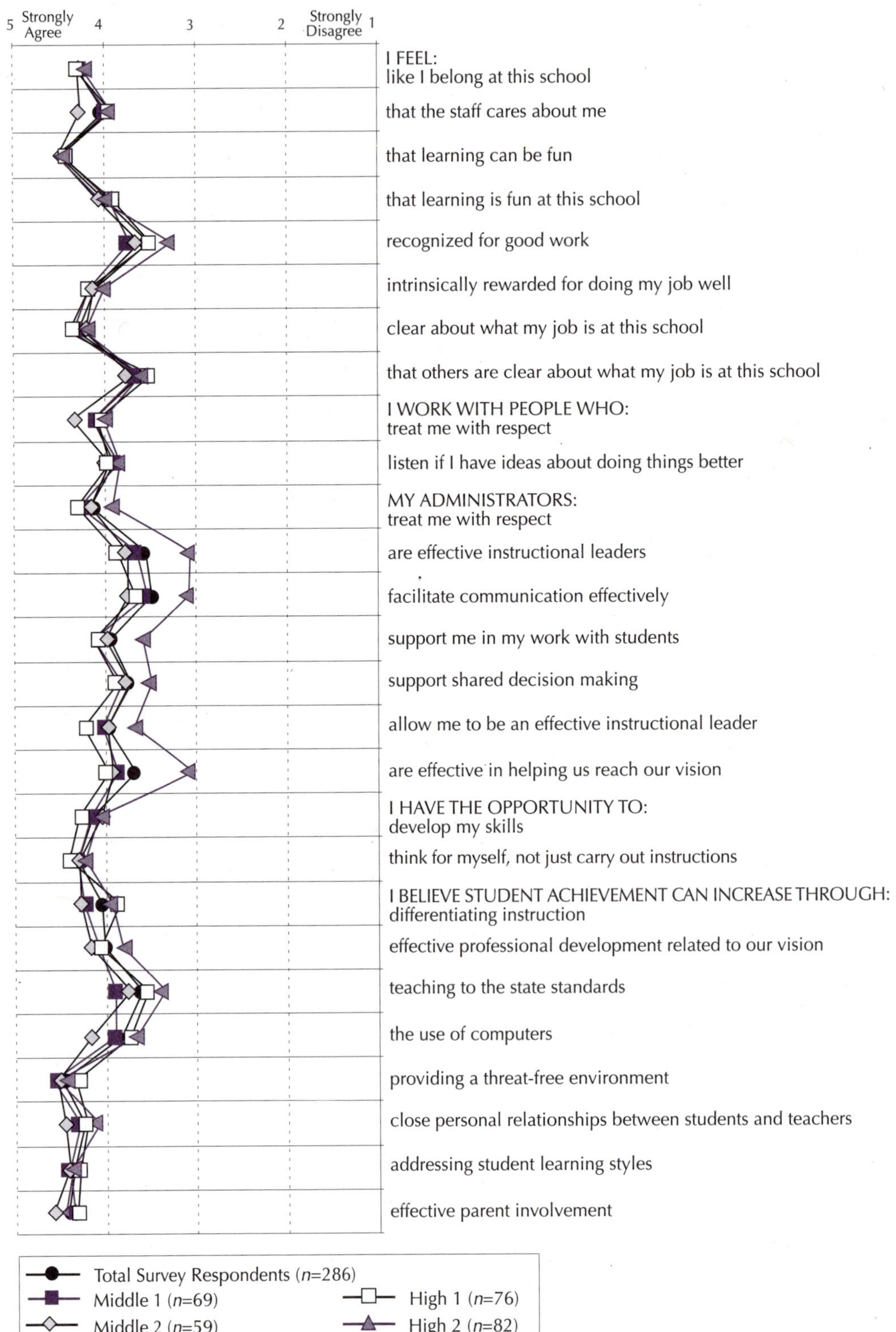

Figure 5.8

Canyon View School District Staff Responses By Middle and High School, March 2005

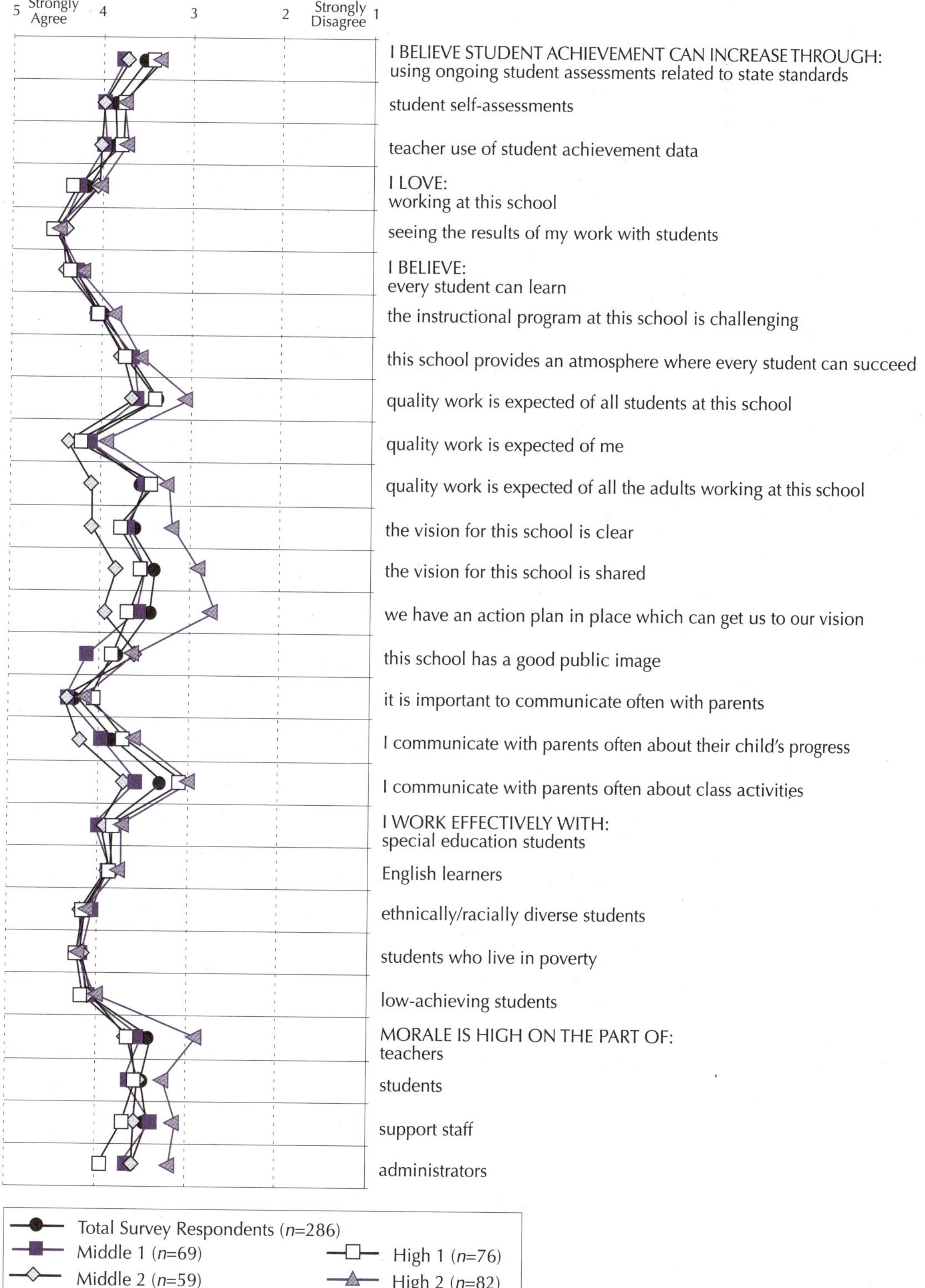

Figure 5.9

Canyon View School District Staff Responses
Items for Teachers by Middle and High School
March 2005

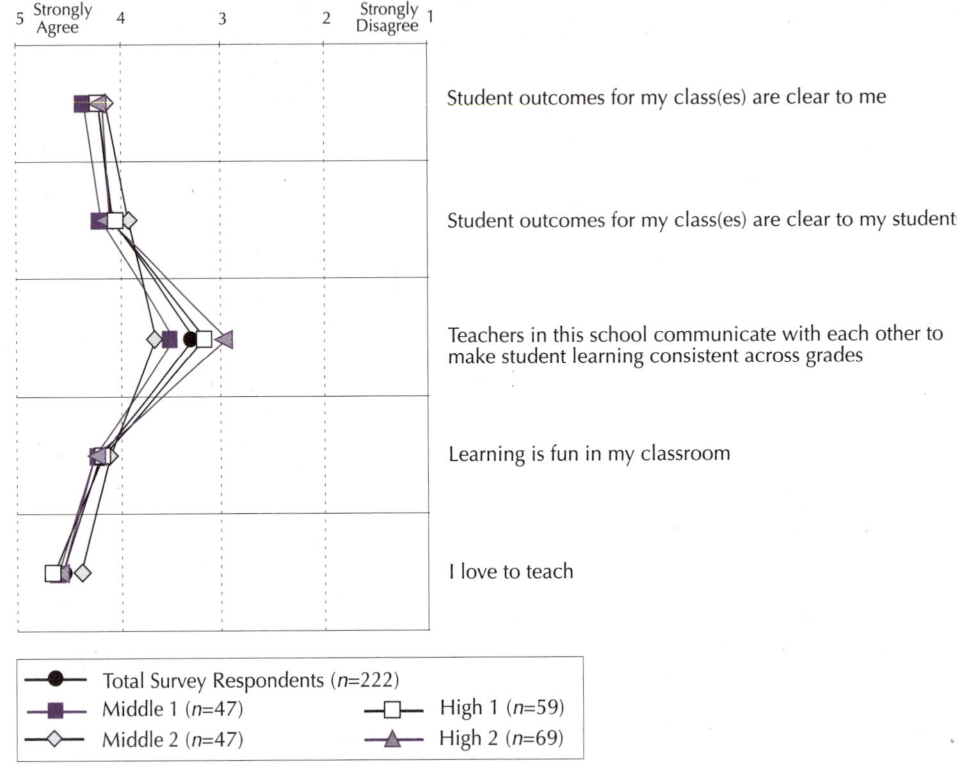

Middle School 1 Staff Open Ended Responses

What would it take to improve student learning in this school?

- Smaller class size. (11)
- Ability to differentiate curriculum for student levels/ability grouping. (6)
- More parent support. (5)
- More paraprofessional help. (4)
- Committed adults working together toward the same vision using compatible assessments to measure learning and evaluate teaching. (4)
- District administrative support for retention of students who have not met grade level expectations. (3)
- Hold the teachers to a higher level of instruction. Consistent student expectations from all teachers at all grade levels. (3)
- Student respect of their peers. (3)
- Professional development on teaching to the standards for all staff. (3)
- More study skills classes offered, increased counseling services. (3)

What are the strengths of this school?

- Staff. (14)
- The administration backs the teachers. (7)
- Involved students. (7)
- Good reputation. (5)
- Good parent support. (5)
- Team teaching. (2)
- Bully-proofing. (2)
- A caring environment where expectations for students are high. (2)
- We have fewer behavioral problems than many schools. (2)

What needs to be improved?

- Smaller class size. (10)
- Better communication. (7)
- Consistency in discipline from administrators. (7)
- Administrator knowledge of what goes on in classrooms and the courage to force change if necessary for student success. (6)
- Team time to do interdisciplinary units and discuss students we have in common. (6)
- Meeting the needs of the students who "fall between the cracks" and do not qualify for Sp. Ed. or 504s. (5)
- More training with regard to Sp. Ed. law on everybody's part so that we don't run into any legal battles. (4)
- Lockers of appropriate size for students' books, backpacks, and gym clothes that are in good working order. (4)
- Teacher morale. (3)
- Students' showing respect to other students and staff. (3)

Middle School 2 Staff Open Ended Responses

What would it take to improve student learning in this school?

- Parent involvement at home; early in the students' school life. Our students and their families need more social support. (14)
- Instructional consistency between and among content area grade level teams. (10)
- Staff members need to be committed to teaching students with compassion and high standards of excellence, committed to improving their own teaching skills. (8)
- Students must believe our school is safe. (5)
- Keep class size down. (4)
- More money for materials and services. (3)
- Positive relationships must be developed and nurtured among students, staff, administration, and community. (3)
- Disruptive students that interfere with the learning of others happens daily without any remediation. (2)
- A core subject called Reading. (2)
- We need more social worker, therapist, counselor, and positive behavior support staff for our students. (2)

What are the strengths of this school?

- Great staff. Most of the people in this school have the students' best interest in mind. They want to teach. They believe all students can learn. (37)
- Enthusiastic administrators. (12)
- Tackling the safety issue at our school. (3)
- Team teaching is strong here. (3)
- Many students are learning and enjoying school. (2)
- Parent communication is strong here. (2)
- Good class size. (2)
- All of our content area teachers have received writing training.
- Strong Special Education Department.
- Diverse population that can enrich all student learning.

What needs to be improved?

- Communication. (6)
- More parent involvement. (4)
- More focus on options and choices for middle school students. (4)
- More focus on reading. (2)
- The image of the school. (2)
- More preparation time. (2)
- More teachers dedicated to doing what is best for students. (2)
- School funding needs to be improved. (2)
- Staff willingness to be flexible and change. (2)
- A shared responsibility in educating our students that includes regular ed and special ed working together to help students achieve. (2)

High School 1 Staff Open Ended Responses

What would it take to improve student learning in this school?

- Teachers to care about all students. (8)
- A concerted focus on teaching and assessing to state standards. (4)
- Higher expectations and accountability. (3)
- More involvement from parents. (3)
- Better attendance of some students. (3)
- Consistency with grading. (3)
- Continuing ways to include parental and community resources for those students who struggle or need extra help. (2)
- Consistent expectations from all teachers in all subject areas. (2)
- Mutual respect between students and teachers. (2)
- Have students self-evaluate. (2)

What are the strengths of this school?

- Good teachers. (23)
- Good Administration team. (20)
- Caring, professional staff. (8)
- Good learning environment. (7)
- Students are motivated to learn. (4)
- Good reputation. (3)
- Our high school offers many options and opportunities for students. (3)
- Overall respect and support across staff. (3)
- Parent and community support. (3)
- Good morale. (2)

What needs to be improved?

- Communication. (9)
- More time. (5)
- Evaluate staff to make sure that teachers are doing their jobs. Address grade inflation and high standards. (4)
- Improve the attitudes of some teachers. (3)
- More support and emphasis on teaching to state standards. (3)
- Identify struggling students before they fail a class. (2)
- Administrative support for the teaching staff. (2)
- Classrooms need to have more hands-on, fun learning.
- Scheduling innovations and team teaching would help tremendously.
- Do more morale building.

High School 2 Staff Open Ended Responses

What would it take to improve student learning in this school?

- Better communication among administrators and teachers, departments, and individuals. A cultural commitment to consistent excellence. We sometimes fail our students by not being challenging enough, across all areas of the curriculum. (22)
- Student attendance. Limit school-sponsored and/or school-endorsed absences. (15)
- All teachers teaching to the standards. (10)
- More parental support. (9)
- Keep class sizes low. (6)
- More instructional time and fewer meetings. (6)
- Greater support and direction from our instructional leaders. (6)
- More activities that improve the climate at the school. (4)
- All teachers need to be evaluated appropriately and held accountable. (4)

What are the strengths of this school?

- The teaching staff (82)
- Diverse student body. (15)
- Good administrators. (9)
- Sense of community. (8)
- Caring environment. (6)
- Teachers willing to work together to do the work necessary. (5)
- Variety of classes offered. (4)
- Intrinsically motivated teachers and students. (2)
- There seems to be a place for everybody. (2)
- Its commitment to diversity, realization that we need to change in order to keep up with a changing student population. (2)

What needs to be improved?

- Communication. (28)
- Staff cohesiveness and professionalism needs to be improved—trust of each other is lacking. (17)
- Attendance—less time with students out of the classroom for other activities. (16)
- Improved curriculum and instruction. (15)
- Administration. (14)
- Discipline. Administration and teachers should be in the hallways. (7)
- There is a lot of resentment among staff. Some teachers are not being on time and leaving early and no consequences. We do have a contracted school day. (7)
- More classrooms. (7)
- Teachers need to be treated as valued and respected professionals by the administrators and by the community. (3)
- Opportunity for professional development. (3)

Parent Responses by Elementary, Middle, and High Schools

Parent questionnaire responses were disaggregated by elementary, middle, and high schools and revealed few differences, with most responses clustering around the overall average (Figures 5.10, 5.11, and 5.12).

Elementary and middle school parents were in agreement with all items on the questionnaire with the exception of two neutral items from parents of Middle School 1:

- *My child knows what his/her teachers expect of him/her.*
- *My child's teacher helps me to help my child learn at home.*

High school parents were in disagreement with one statement: *Teachers help me know how to support my child's learning at home.*

High School 1 and 2 parent responses averaged neutral for the items:

- *The school provides adequate information about non-college options after graduation.*
- *The school clearly communicates how parent volunteers can help.*
- *Parent volunteers are made to feel appreciated.*

High School 2 parents were also neutral with respect to:

- *Students are treated fairly by other students.*
- *I am informed about my child's progress at school.*

Look Fors:	**Items which parents, by school and across schools, are in agreement or disagreement.**
Planning Implications:	**Where can/should the district provide leadership, with respect to school/district environment?**

Canyon View parents were asked to respond to two open-ended questions: *What are the strengths at this school?* and *What needs to be improved?* The top ten parent responses, by school, follow the graphs.

Look Fors:	**The most often written-in responses to what parents like about school and what they believe needs to be improved.**
Planning Implications:	**Perhaps issues in how students are treated in each school, or across schools.**

Figure 5.10

Canyon View School District Parent Responses By Elementary School, March 2005

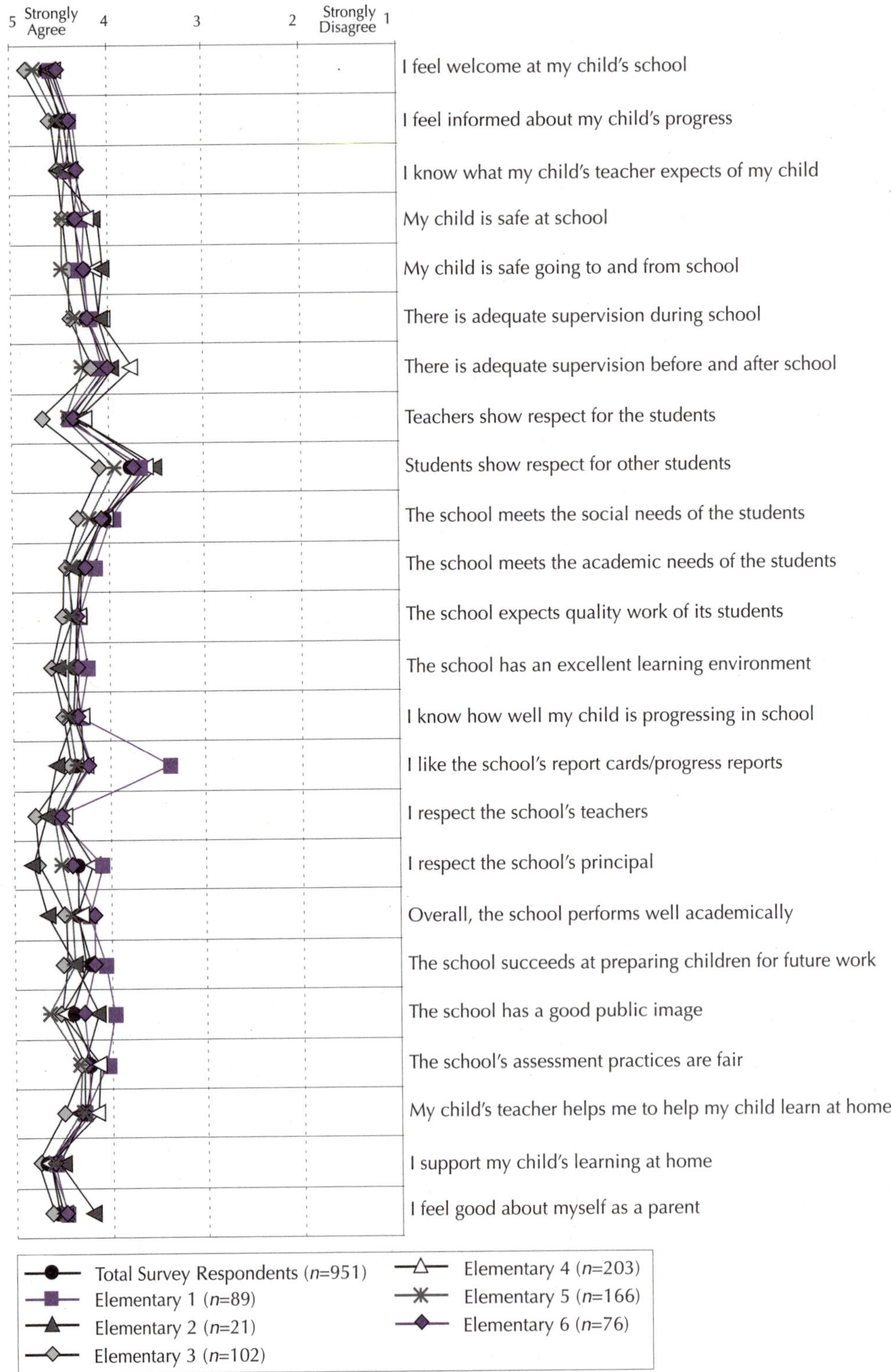

5 Strongly Agree
4
3
2
Strongly Disagree 1
I feel welcome at my child's school
I feel informed about my child's progress
I know what my child's teacher expects of my child
My child is safe at school
My child is safe going to and from school
There is adequate supervision during school
There is adequate supervision before and after school
Teachers show respect for the students
Students show respect for other students
The school meets the social needs of the students
The school meets the academic needs of the students
The school expects quality work of its students
The school has an excellent learning environment
I know how well my child is progressing in school
I like the school's report cards/progress reports
I respect the school's teachers
I respect the school's principal
Overall, the school performs well academically
The school succeeds at preparing children for future work
The school has a good public image
The school's assessment practices are fair
My child's teacher helps me to help my child learn at home
I support my child's learning at home
I feel good about myself as a parent
Total Survey Respondents (n=951)
Elementary 1 (n=89)
Elementary 2 (n=21)
Elementary 3 (n=102)
Elementary 4 (n=203)
Elementary 5 (n=166)
Elementary 6 (n=76)

Figure 5.10 (Continued)

Canyon View School District Parent Responses By Elementary School, March 2005

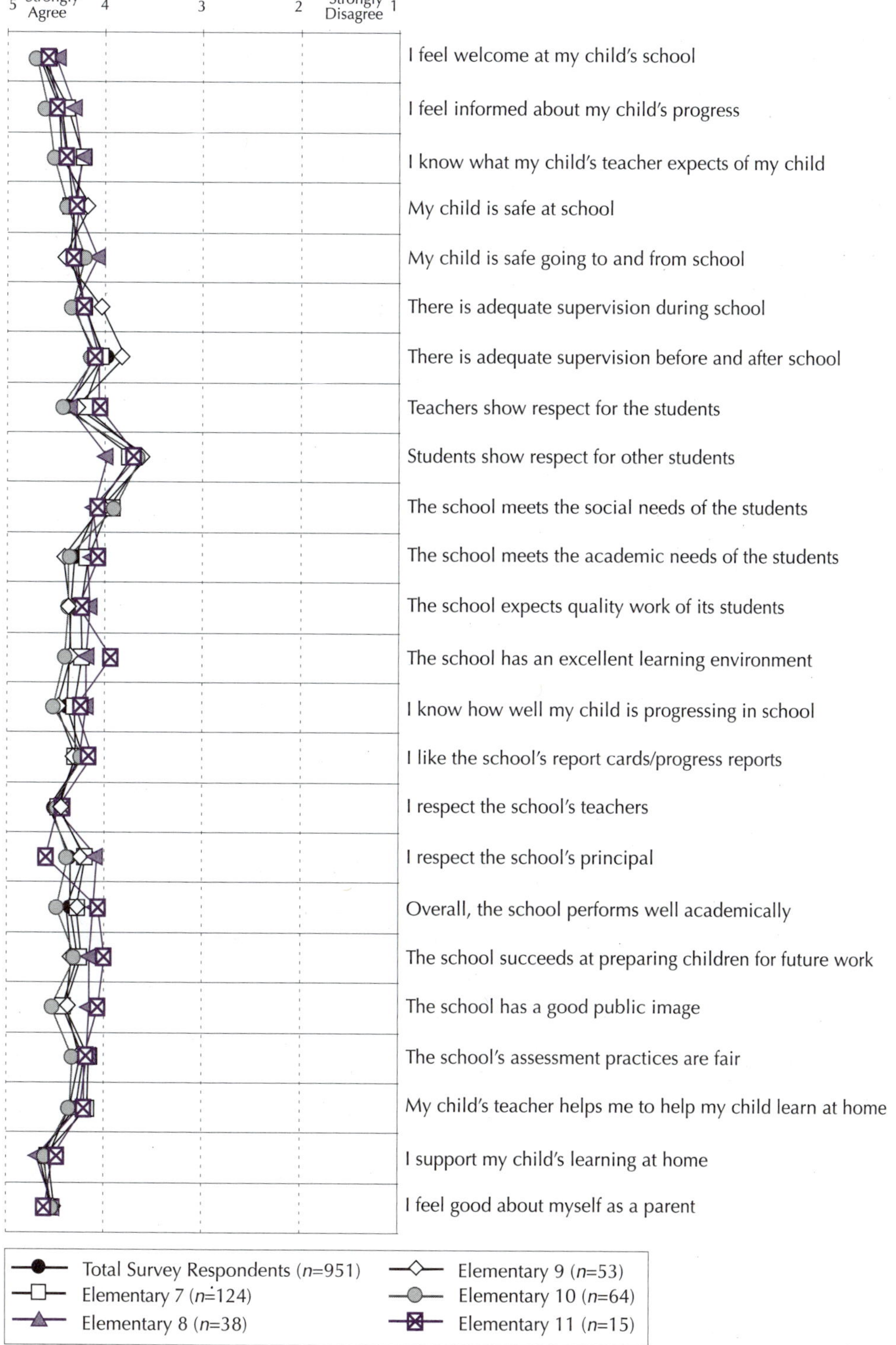

Elementary School 1 Parent Open Ended Responses

What are the strengths of this school?	What needs to be improved?
• Teachers and staff. (74) • Community atmosphere. (13) • Good communication. (8) • The principal. (7) • Student teacher ratio. (6) • Students' social and academic needs are met. (5) • Respect for the students. (4) • Students. (4) • The parent councils/parent interest. (4) • Unique learning ideas. (3)	• The principal. (18) • Nothing. (12) • Better playground supervision. (9) • The report cards. (6) • End bullying. (6) • Communication. (5) • More time to eat lunch. (4) • Better resources. (3) • Smaller class sizes. (2) • More empathy for the students. (2)

Elementary School 2 Parent Open Ended Responses

What are the strengths of this school?	What needs to be improved?
• Wonderful teachers and staff. (27) • The principal. (5) • The extra teachings on getting along with others, respecting self, and adults. (3) • The students are recognized for their attitudes and accomplishments with the assemblies. (2) • Parent involvement/a real sense of community. (2) • My children were integrated quickly from another school. Their academic levels were quickly assessed, and they were accepted nicely. • The school teaches the students strong school pride. • All students are treated as equals. • The teachers show respect for the parents involved. • The curriculum.	• Nothing. (8) • Playground safety. (5) • More playground aids. (2) • Pickup and drop off. (2) • Communication could be improved. (2) • More family meetings with other parents. • More field trips. • There needs to be more involvement with the school principal. • Time to eat lunch. • More computers.

Elementary School 3 Parent Open Ended Responses

What are the strengths of this school?	What needs to be improved?
• Teachers. (51) • Community spirit. (30) • Great parent involvement/encourages family involvement. (17) • Principal/administration. (14) • Respect for others is taught. (12) • Learning environment. (10) • Excellent reputation. (10) • The size. (6) • Communication with home. (6) • The curriculum. (6)	• Update playground. (15) • Funding. (11) • More teachers' aides on the playground at recess time. (11) • Nothing. (9) • Smaller class size. (5) • More respect for others. (5) • More basic math skills. (4) • Upkeep, improvements. (3) • More adequate parking or pick up/drop off area. (3) • Services for gifted students—the program should be in the students' own school. (2)

Elementary School 4 Parent Open Ended Responses

What are the strengths of this school?	*What needs to be improved?*
♦ Teachers and staff. (83) ♦ Positive learning environment. (19) ♦ Sense of community. (15) ♦ Wide variety of educational options. (14) ♦ Respect between staff, parents and students. (12) ♦ Opportunities for the parents to get involved. (10) ♦ Communication between teachers and parents. (8) ♦ Public image. (8) ♦ Safe. (4) ♦ Location. (4)	♦ Parking/pickup/drop-off are safety concerns that are getting worse. (25) ♦ More supervision on the playground. (11) ♦ Nothing. (7) ♦ Better before/after school supervision. (6) ♦ Crossing guards. (6) ♦ Communication. (5) ♦ More school sponsored activities. (4) ♦ Playground improvement. Remove rocks, put in trees and vegetation. (4) ♦ Smaller class size. (3) ♦ Some teachers and aides appear not to like children much. (3)

Elementary School 5 Parent Open Ended Responses

What are the strengths of this school?	*What needs to be improved?*
♦ Teachers and staff. (98) ♦ Parent involvement. (46) ♦ Sense of community/welcoming attitude. (36) ♦ Small neighborhood school. (24) ♦ Small class size. (19) ♦ Good communication with parents. (14) ♦ Principal. (12) ♦ Great learning atmosphere. (12) ♦ Outstanding reputation. (9) ♦ High academic standards. (9)	♦ Nothing. (27) ♦ More communication with the parents. (15) ♦ More classroom/playground aides should be hired. (11) ♦ Studies/classes for gifted students. (7) ♦ The playground. (6) ♦ A more current and usable website. (4) ♦ More nutritional items offered at lunch. (4) ♦ Playground aids response to children's' needs. (3) ♦ The pick up and parking area around the school. (3) ♦ Teachers respect for students. (3)

Elementary School 6 Parent Open Ended Responses

What are the strengths of this school?	*What needs to be improved?*
♦ Teachers and staff. (94) ♦ Good learning environment. (47) ♦ Parent involvement. (23) ♦ Principal. (19) ♦ Small class size. (18) ♦ Sense of community. (12) ♦ Good communication. (11) ♦ Respect for self and others is taught. (7) ♦ Location. (7) ♦ Activities. (6)	♦ Monitoring on the playground. (16) ♦ The playground needs to be fenced and have more grass and less asphalt. (14) ♦ Art on a more regular schedule. (9) ♦ The traffic, parking, and pickup situation. (8) ♦ More parent involvement/electronic communication included as part of the school's communications. (7) ♦ More respect for each other. (6) ♦ More music. (5) ♦ Smaller class sizes. (5) ♦ Better teacher salaries. (5) ♦ More opportunities for gifted and talented studies. (4)

Elementary School 7 Parent Open Ended Responses

What are the strengths of this school?	*What needs to be improved?*
• Teachers and staff. (64) • Small community environment. (32) • Fun learning environment. (19) • Principal. (10) • Communication. (8) • Fun, family activities. (6) • Parent involvement/wonderful P.T.A. (6) • Feels safe. (4) • The kids look forward to going. (4) • Attention to the special needs of individual students. (3)	• The parking lot. (16) • Need a bigger school. (7) • Parent involvement. (5) • More computer time. (4) • More supervision on recess. (3) • Before and after school supervision. (3) • The whole class lumped in one for discipline purposes. (3) • Better communication between teacher/parent on weekly work being done in class and weekly assignments. (2) • More challenging classes. (2) • Teachers' respect for students. (2)

Elementary School 8 Parent Open Ended Responses

What are the strengths of this school?	*What needs to be improved?*
• Teachers and staff. (55) • Great environment. (10) • Small school atmosphere. (8) • Strong sense of school community. (7) • Parent Involvement. (6) • The small class size. (5) • Principal. (4) • Excellent academic reputation. (3) • Safety. (3) • Good communication to home. (3)	• Playground. (14) • Teacher information to parents. (6) • Pickup and drop off areas. (5) • Parking. (3) • School facilities. (2) • Principal needs to be here more. (2) • More accommodation for working parents—with opportunities in the evening to interact with staff. (2) • Upgrade teaching methods. (2) • Teachers should expect parental involvement and make it a priority for every child. (2) • School politics.

Elementary School 9 Parent Open Ended Responses

What are the strengths of this school?	*What needs to be improved?*
• Teachers and staff. (102) • Parent involvement and communication. (36) • Good atmosphere. (25) • Good learning environment. (19) • Principal. (16) • The variety of fun activities/programs. (14) • The parent council does a wonderful job. (8) • Strong academics. (7) • A safe environment. (6) • Good public image. (5)	• Better supervision on the playground and before and after school. (23) • Better ongoing communication. (14) • Winter program needs to include all of the students. (11) • Improved drop off and pick up area. (5) • Better access by bicycle and footpath to the school. (4) • Friendliness of staff and teachers. (3) • Raise academic performance. (3) • More school activities. (3) • A little less homework at times. (3) • Smaller class size. (2)

Elementary School 10 Parent Open Ended Responses	
What are the strengths of this school? • Caring teachers and staff. (59) • Outstanding learning environment. (20) • Friendly atmosphere. (10) • Principal. (7) • Sense of community. (7) • Safe environment. (5) • Music program. (5) • Easy access to teachers and principal. (3) • Good communication. (3) • Location. (3)	***What needs to be improved?*** • Parking lot and pick up after school situation. (5) • Communication of students' progress in between parent-teacher conferences. (4) • Student respect for students and teachers. (4) • Include more kids in elite programs: school plays, officers, PEAK, school store, etc. (3) • Full time music and art teachers. (2) • Safety. (2) • Some of the playground aides. (2) • Be more efficient at solving recess spats. (2) • Higher academic standards for everyone. (2) • Would like a survey form to evaluate the teaching staff. (2)

Elementary School 11 Parent Open Ended Responses	
What are the strengths of this school? • Teachers and staff. (13) • Everyone is very positive with the children. (5) • Children excited about school. (2) • Positive atmosphere for learning. (2) • Principal is accessible. • Academically, this school is top notch. • It works a lot with values and respect. • The school knows each child by name and who the parents are. • The way they teach the children behavior and the school rules. • Communication with the parents.	***What needs to be improved?*** • Nothing that I can see. (4) • Playground needs more grass. (2) • More of an open door for parents. • Getting the parents more involved with their children. • A general meeting of the teachers with the parents to explain what is expected of the students in 4th and 5th grade. • Appropriate discipline of the children who are repetitive troublemakers. • The teaching of peer pressure should be stressed a bit better; there is an awful lot going around. • The kids enjoy taking the tests in the library. I hope this will continue and expand. • Supervision at the crosswalk at the end of the playground. • Before and after school care programs need to be established.

Figure 5.11

Canyon View School District Parent Responses By Middle School, March 2005

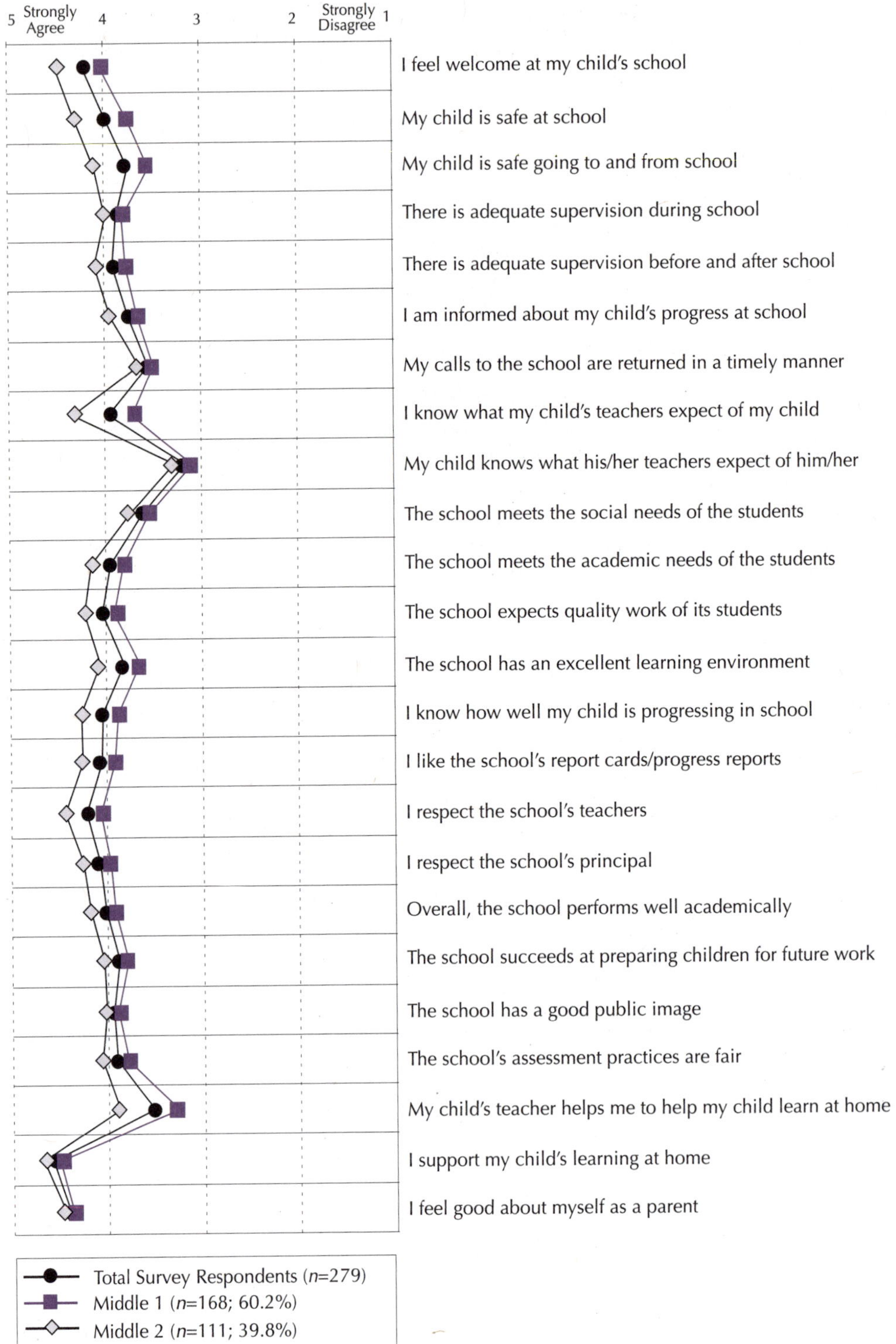

Middle School 1 Parent Open Ended Responses	
What are the strengths of this school? ♦ Teachers and staff. (63) ♦ The Vice-principal/administration. (24) ♦ Teaching teams. (10) ♦ E-mail progress reports. (13) ♦ Academic standards. (8) ♦ Regular contact with parents. (9) ♦ Organization. (8) ♦ My child is offered a variety of educational options. (5) ♦ Good extra-curricular activities. (4) ♦ After school program. (2)	***What needs to be improved?*** ♦ Teacher to parent communication/e-mail progress reports/ Parent teacher conferences need major improvement. (38) ♦ Overcrowding. (15) ♦ More time for the students to eat their lunches. (13) ♦ The level of bullying and disrespectful attitudes by too many students. (10) ♦ School needs its own sports program. (5) ♦ More after school activities. (5) ♦ A web page with term assignments, due dates, and daily assignments in each class. (4) ♦ Sufficient lockers (1/2 Lockers) so each student has her/his own. (4) ♦ Teachers need to make time during lunch, or before, or after school to help students. (4) ♦ Teachers need to stop bullying students. (4)

Middle School 2 Parent Open Ended Responses	
What are the strengths of this school? ♦ Great teachers and staff. (61) ♦ The team concept. (17) ♦ Administration/principal. (16) ♦ The greeter program. (6) ♦ Excellent food program. (6) ♦ Opening early. (4) ♦ A comfortable environment for the children to learn in. (4) ♦ Changes to lunch period. (4) ♦ Parent-teacher-child conferences. (3) ♦ Good student/teacher interaction/involvement. (2)	***What needs to be improved?*** ♦ More communication. (7) ♦ More intervention with problem students and bullies. (6) ♦ After school sports or intramural sports. (5) ♦ Less homework/better homework information and teachers that need to retire. (4) ♦ Study halls, so kids do not need to bring home 30 pound packs. (3) ♦ Academically gifted programs. (2) ♦ Better way to teach kids that have a harder time learning. (2) ♦ Non-caring attitude in the school. (2) ♦ Challenge the students who are academically bored. (2) ♦ Teachers need to have a communication system in place where they can easily report to each other significant information on a child. (2)

Figure 5.12

Canyon View School District Parent Responses By High School, March 2005

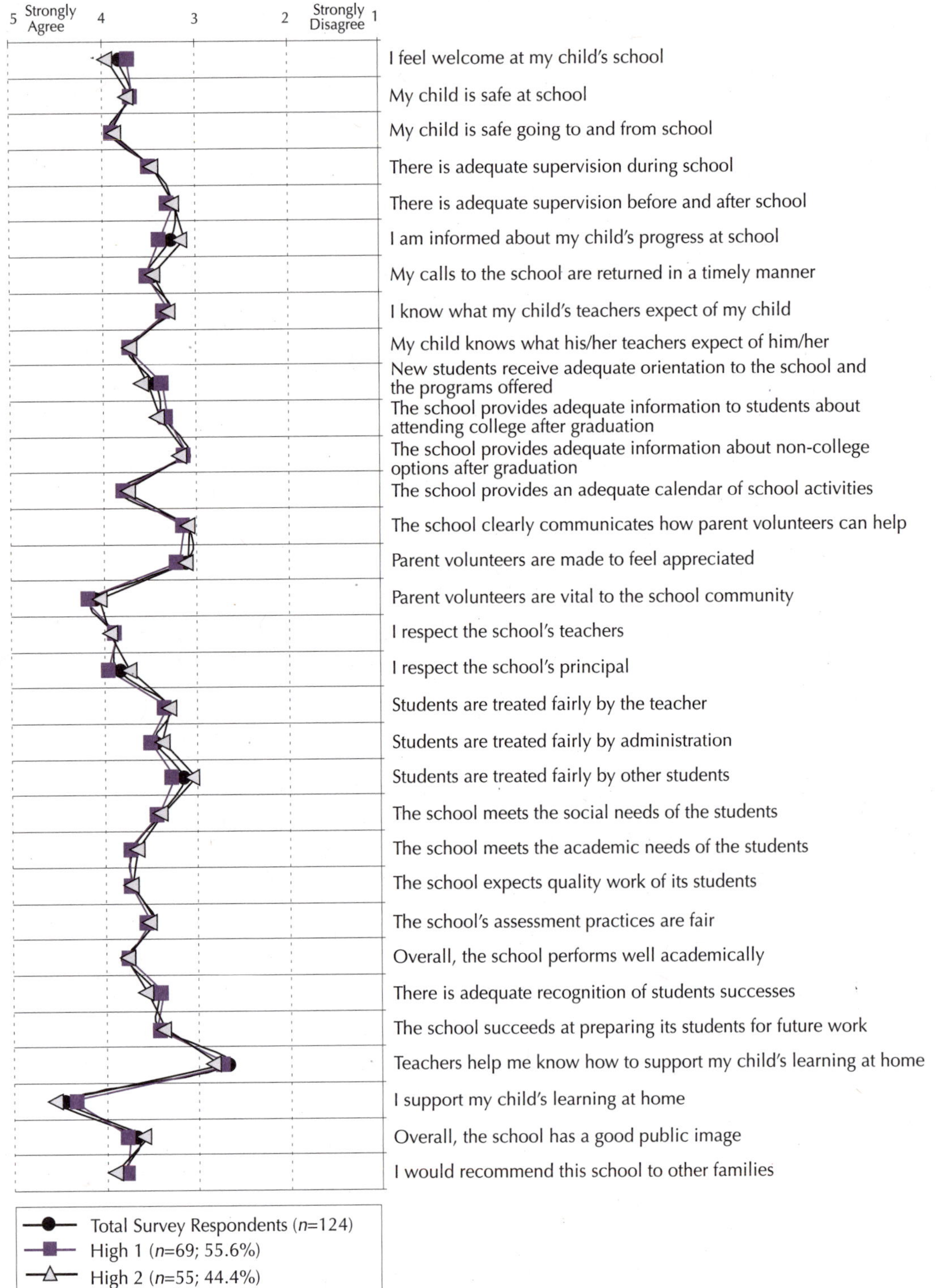

5 Strongly Agree
4
3
2
Strongly Disagree 1
I feel welcome at my child's school
My child is safe at school
My child is safe going to and from school
There is adequate supervision during school
There is adequate supervision before and after school
I am informed about my child's progress at school
My calls to the school are returned in a timely manner
I know what my child's teachers expect of my child
My child knows what his/her teachers expect of him/her
New students receive adequate orientation to the school and the programs offered
The school provides adequate information to students about attending college after graduation
The school provides adequate information about non-college options after graduation
The school provides an adequate calendar of school activities
The school clearly communicates how parent volunteers can help
Parent volunteers are made to feel appreciated
Parent volunteers are vital to the school community
I respect the school's teachers
I respect the school's principal
Students are treated fairly by the teacher
Students are treated fairly by administration
Students are treated fairly by other students
The school meets the social needs of the students
The school meets the academic needs of the students
The school expects quality work of its students
The school's assessment practices are fair
Overall, the school performs well academically
There is adequate recognition of students successes
The school succeeds at preparing its students for future work
Teachers help me know how to support my child's learning at home
I support my child's learning at home
Overall, the school has a good public image
I would recommend this school to other families
Total Survey Respondents (n=124)
High 1 (n=69; 55.6%)
High 2 (n=55; 44.4%)

High School 1 Parent Open Ended Responses	
What are the strengths of this school?	***What needs to be improved?***
• Teachers and staff. (42) • Good academics. (24) • Sports. (13) • Administration. (11) • Extracurricular opportunities. (9) • The facility. (7) • Community oriented. (5) • Communication. (5) • Variety of courses offered. (4) • Good computers. (3)	• Better web page/newsletter communication. (20) • Less emphasis on sports. (8) • The equal enforcement of the drug/alcohol policy. (6) • Greater focus on student academic achievements (speech & debate, language classes, chorus, etc.) (6) • Organized guidance in preparing for and selecting colleges. (4) • Need a friendly/informed office staff. (4) • Parking lot issues. (4) • Teachers keeping up on the most current teaching techniques. (4) • Harassment of students by other students. (3) • Grading should be consistent with all classes. (3)

High School 2 Parent Open Ended Responses	
What are the strengths of this school?	***What needs to be improved?***
• Teachers and staff. (61) • Good academic standards. (26) • Diverse class offerings. (15) • Students. (14) • Administrators. (10) • Good reputation with students, parents and the community. (8) • Variety of activities. (8) • Great communication between parents, students, and teachers. (7) • Prepares students for college experience. (4) • The counselors. (4)	• Communication to parents. (17) • More one-on-one counseling for students, especially seniors about college and scholarships. (8) • Supervision in halls and locker rooms between scheduled class times. (7) • More recognition for academics and clubs. (5) • Students are not treated with respect by staff. (4) • Intervention with inadequate teachers. (4) • Use website to the full advantage. (4) • Students do not seem to have a great deal of respect for the principal. (3) • Front office staff. (2) • More time for lunch. (2)

Administrator Questionnaire Results

District administrators (n=27) responded to a questionnaire in December 2005 designed to measure their perceptions of the district environment. Members of the district administration were asked to respond to items using a five-point scale: 1 = strongly disagree; 2 = disagree; 3 = neutral; 4 = agree; and 5 = strongly agree.

Average responses to each item on the questionnaire were graphed. Overall, the average responses to the items in the administrator questionnaire were in agreement and very positive (Figure 5.13). Almost all administrators strongly agreed with the comments *I believe: every student can learn, it is important to communicate often with parents,* and *quality work is expected of me.* Responses regarding morale, while still positive, were closer to neutral than other items.

Look Fors: **Items with which administrators are in agreement or disagreement.**

Planning Implications: **What do the questionnaire results tell administrators about improvements that are needed in the district?**

Figure 5.13

Canyon View School District Administrator Responses December 2005

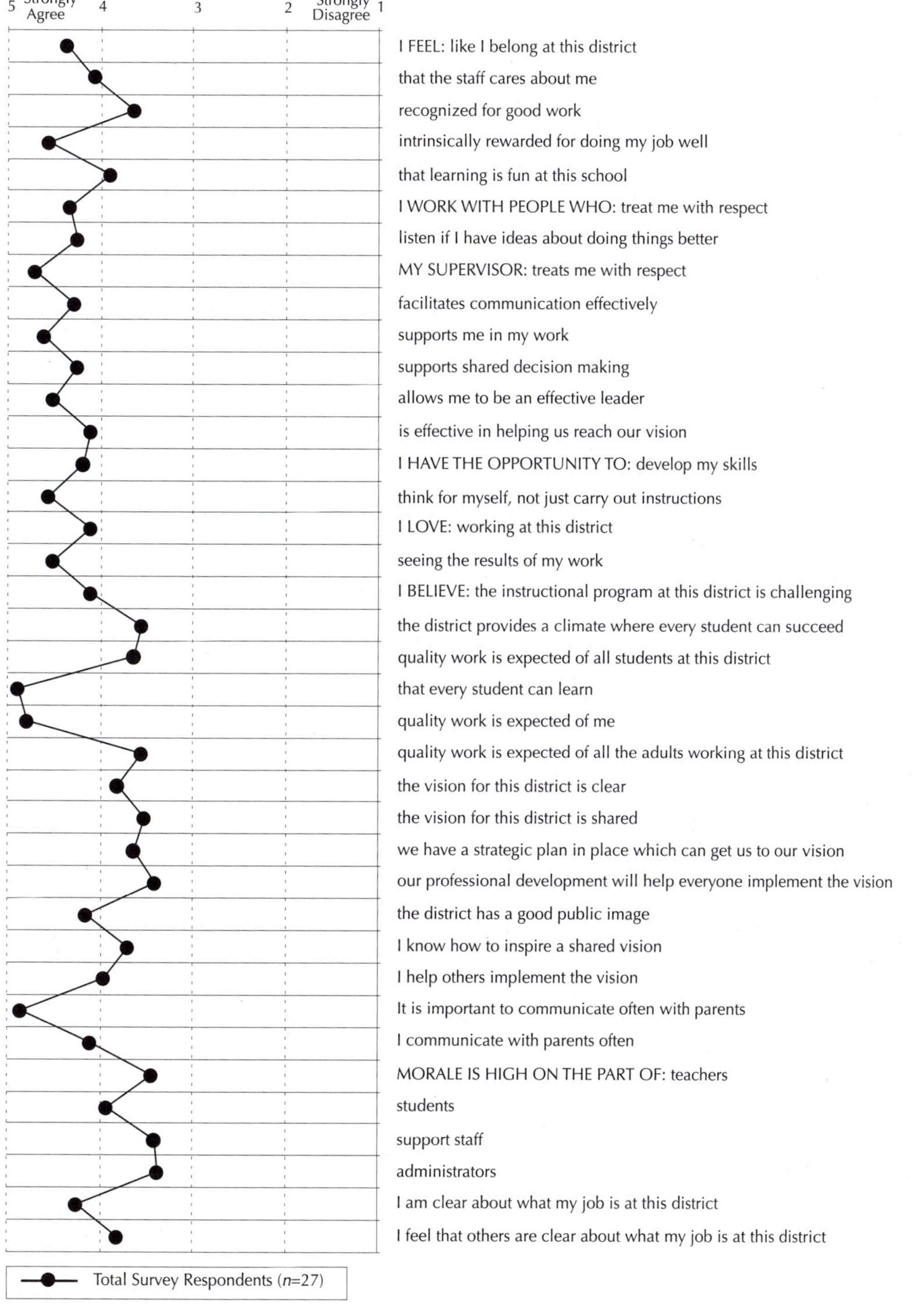

5 Strongly Agree
4
3
2
Strongly Disagree 1
I FEEL: like I belong at this district
that the staff cares about me
recognized for good work
intrinsically rewarded for doing my job well
that learning is fun at this school
I WORK WITH PEOPLE WHO: treat me with respect
listen if I have ideas about doing things better
MY SUPERVISOR: treats me with respect
facilitates communication effectively
supports me in my work
supports shared decision making
allows me to be an effective leader
is effective in helping us reach our vision
I HAVE THE OPPORTUNITY TO: develop my skills
think for myself, not just carry out instructions
I LOVE: working at this district
seeing the results of my work
I BELIEVE: the instructional program at this district is challenging
the district provides a climate where every student can succeed
quality work is expected of all students at this district
that every student can learn
quality work is expected of me
quality work is expected of all the adults working at this district
the vision for this district is clear
the vision for this district is shared
we have a strategic plan in place which can get us to our vision
our professional development will help everyone implement the vision
the district has a good public image
I know how to inspire a shared vision
I help others implement the vision
It is important to communicate often with parents
I communicate with parents often
MORALE IS HIGH ON THE PART OF: teachers
students
support staff
administrators
I am clear about what my job is at this district
I feel that others are clear about what my job is at this district
Total Survey Respondents (n=27)

Staff Standards Assessment Questionnaire

Staff members were asked about how well they are implementing their state/district content standards.

Figure 5.14 shows elementary teacher responses to the first set of questions. Elementary teachers seem to know most about the state/district English/Language Arts and Math standards. Figure 5.15 shows the percentage of teachers who answered the question, *How well would you say you know what it would look like, sound like, and feel like if you were teaching to the standards 100% of the time?* The majority of teachers responded *Well* and *Getting There.*

Figures 5.16 and 5.17 show middle and high school teacher responses to similar questions.

Look Fors:	**The degree to which staff members are knowledgeable about state content standards, and indications that they are implementing them.**
Planning Implications:	**Is there professional learning required to help staffs learn the standards and to enable them to implement the standards? Do staff members have opportunities to share best practices to implement the standards?**

Figure 5.14

Canyon View School District Elementary Teacher Responses March 2005

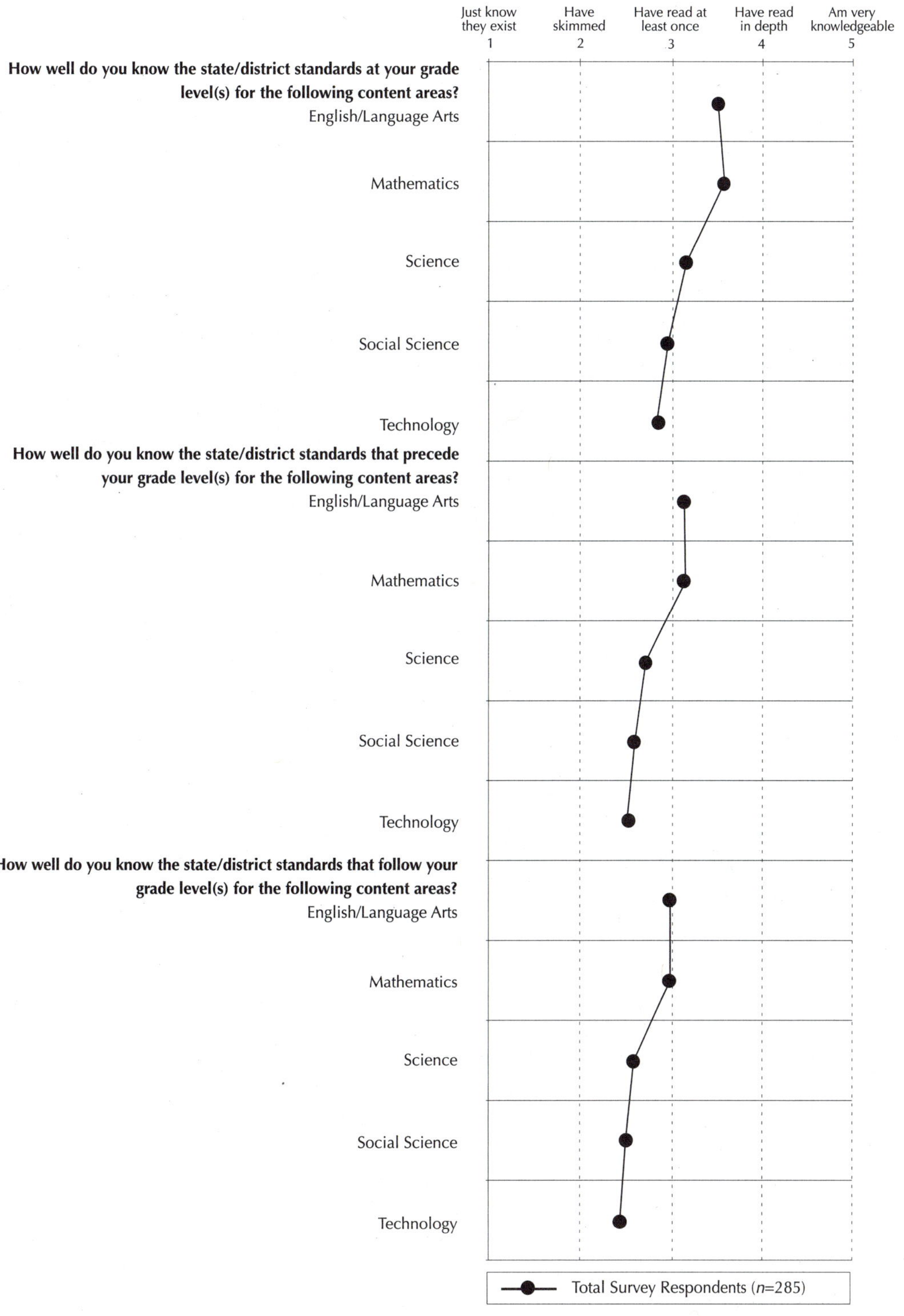

Figure 5.15

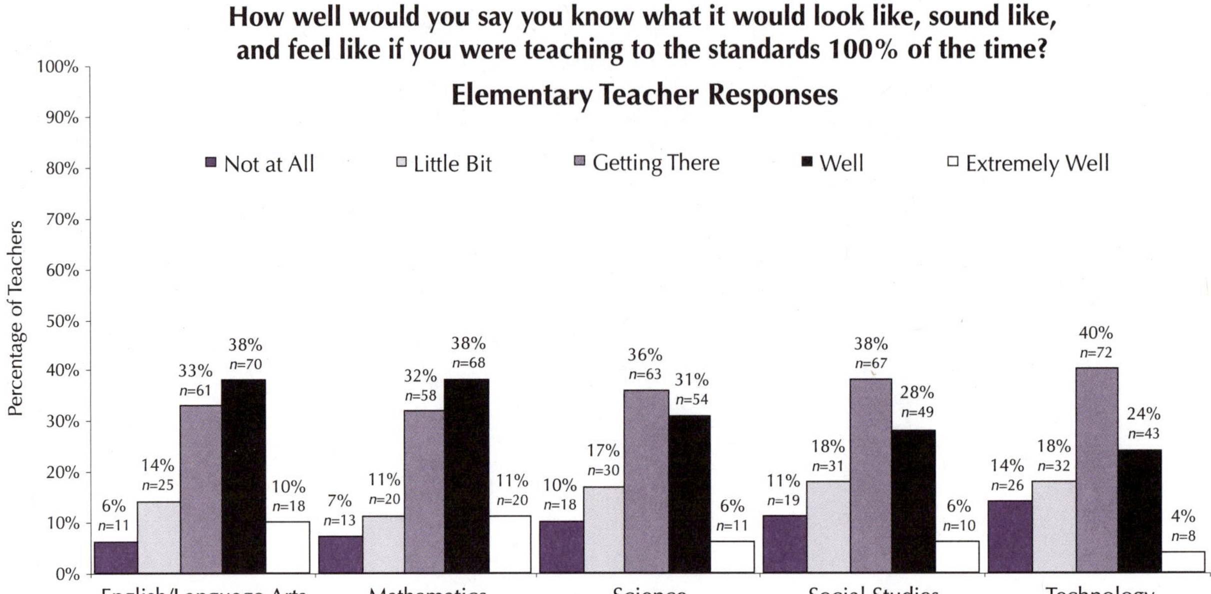
How well would you say you know what it would look like, sound like, and feel like if you were teaching to the standards 100% of the time?
Elementary Teacher Responses
Not at All
Little Bit
Getting There
Well
Extremely Well
Percentage of Teachers
100%
90%
80%
70%
60%
50%
40%
30%
20%
10%
0%
6% n=11
14% n=25
33% n=61
38% n=70
10% n=18
7% n=13
11% n=20
32% n=58
38% n=68
11% n=20
10% n=18
17% n=30
36% n=63
31% n=54
6% n=11
11% n=19
18% n=31
38% n=67
28% n=49
6% n=10
14% n=26
18% n=32
40% n=72
24% n=43
4% n=8
English/Language Arts
Mathematics
Science
Social Studies
Technology

Figure 5.16

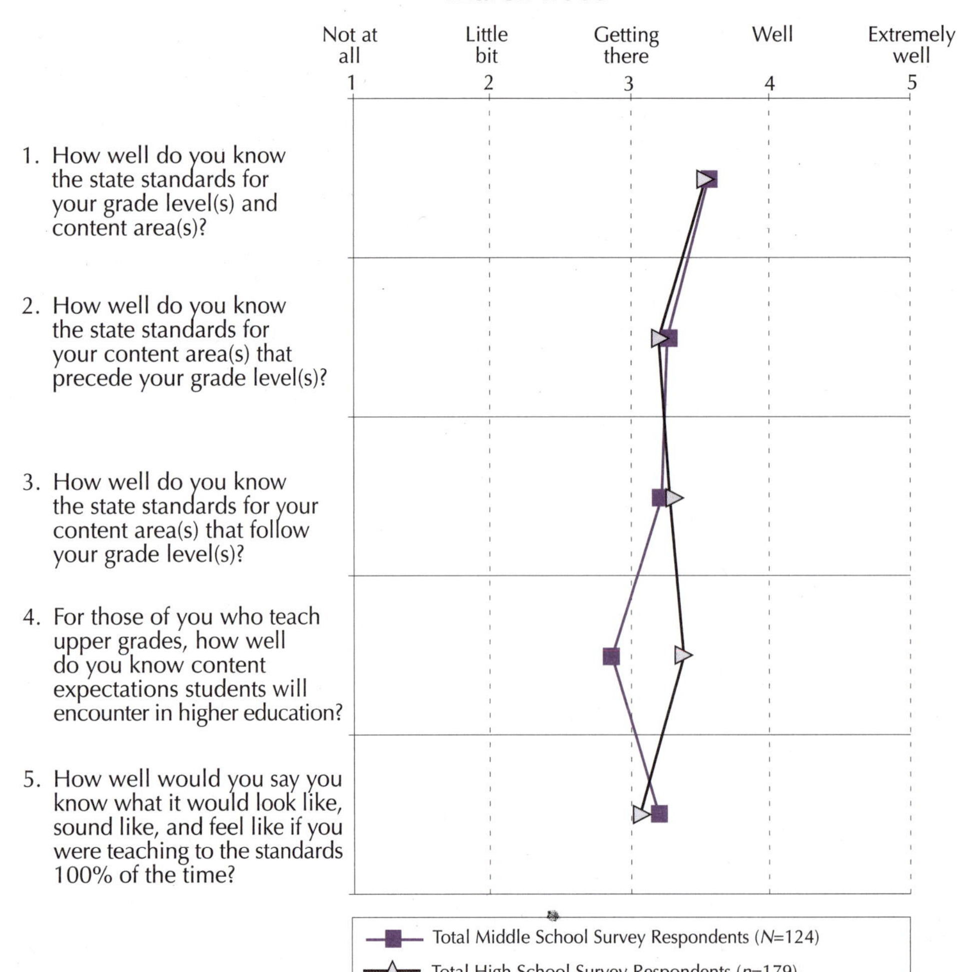
Canyon View School District Middle/High Teacher Responses
March 2005
Not at all
Little bit
Getting there
Well
Extremely well
1
2
3
4
5
1. How well do you know the state standards for your grade level(s) and content area(s)?
2. How well do you know the state standards for your content area(s) that precede your grade level(s)?
3. How well do you know the state standards for your content area(s) that follow your grade level(s)?
4. For those of you who teach upper grades, how well do you know content expectations students will encounter in higher education?
5. How well would you say you know what it would look like, sound like, and feel like if you were teaching to the standards 100% of the time?
Total Middle School Survey Respondents (N=124)
Total High School Survey Respondents (n=179)

Figure 5.17

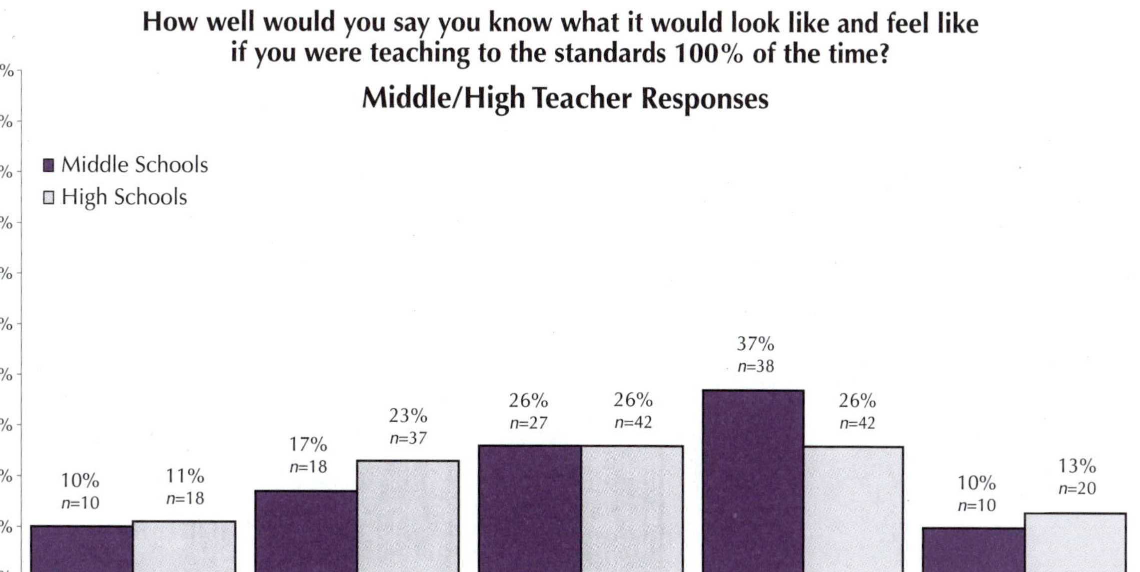
How well would you say you know what it would look like and feel like if you were teaching to the standards 100% of the time?
Middle/High Teacher Responses
Middle Schools
High Schools
Percentage of Teachers
100%
90%
80%
70%
60%
50%
40%
30%
20%
10%
0%
10% n=10
11% n=18
17% n=18
23% n=37
26% n=27
26% n=42
37% n=38
26% n=42
10% n=10
13% n=20
Not at All
Little Bit
Getting There
Well
Extremely Well

Figure 5.18 shows all three schools levels on a graph that asks staff members what would help them know the standards for their grade levels better.

Staff members were asked about how much support they received from their principal and colleagues. Figure 5.19 shows elementary, middle, and high school teachers responses.

Figure 5.18

How much would each of the following help you to better know the standards for your grade level(s)?

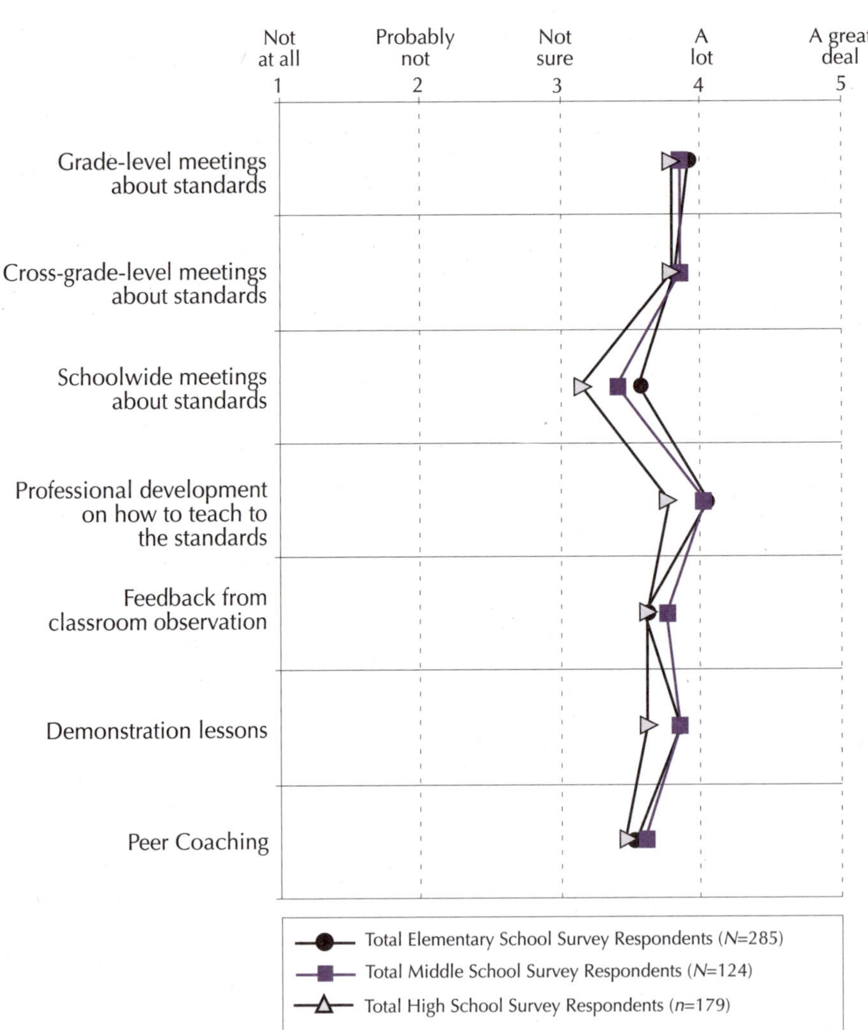

Figure 5.19

Canyon View School District Teacher Responses March 2005

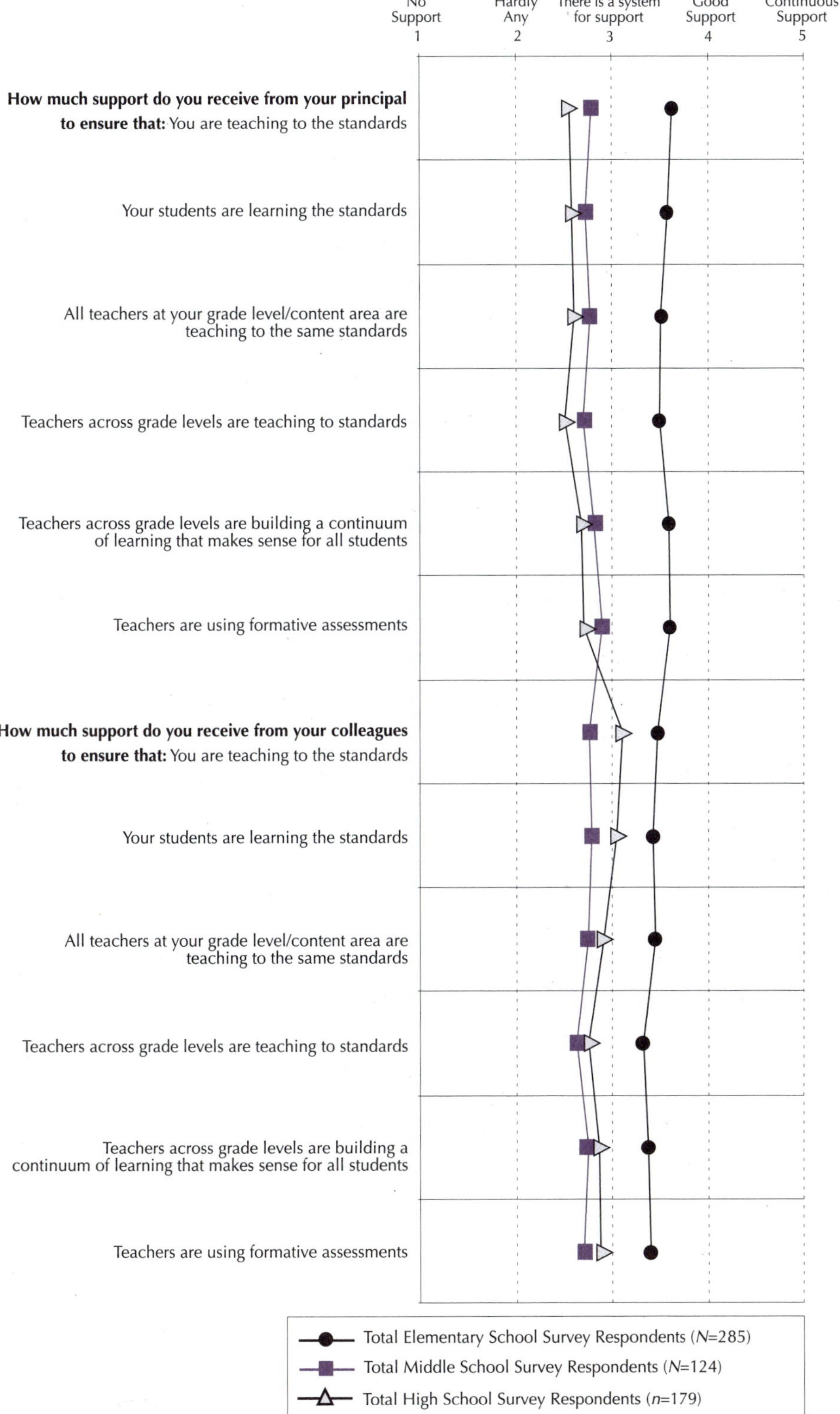

Teachers were asked to indicate which statements best describe how they use standards to design instruction. Results are shown in Figure 5.20.

Figure 5.20

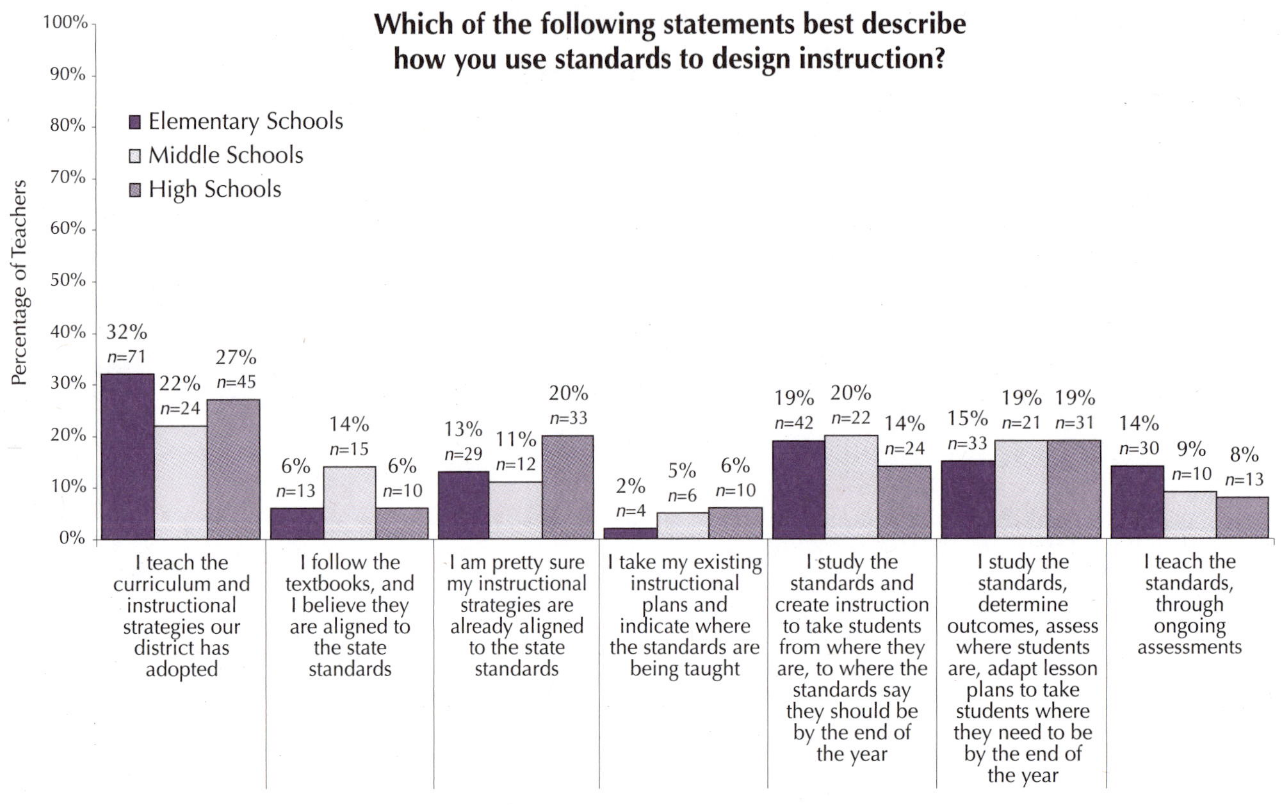

Teachers were asked to indicate which statements best describe how they use standards to design assessment. Results are shown in Figure 5.21 below.

Figure 5.21

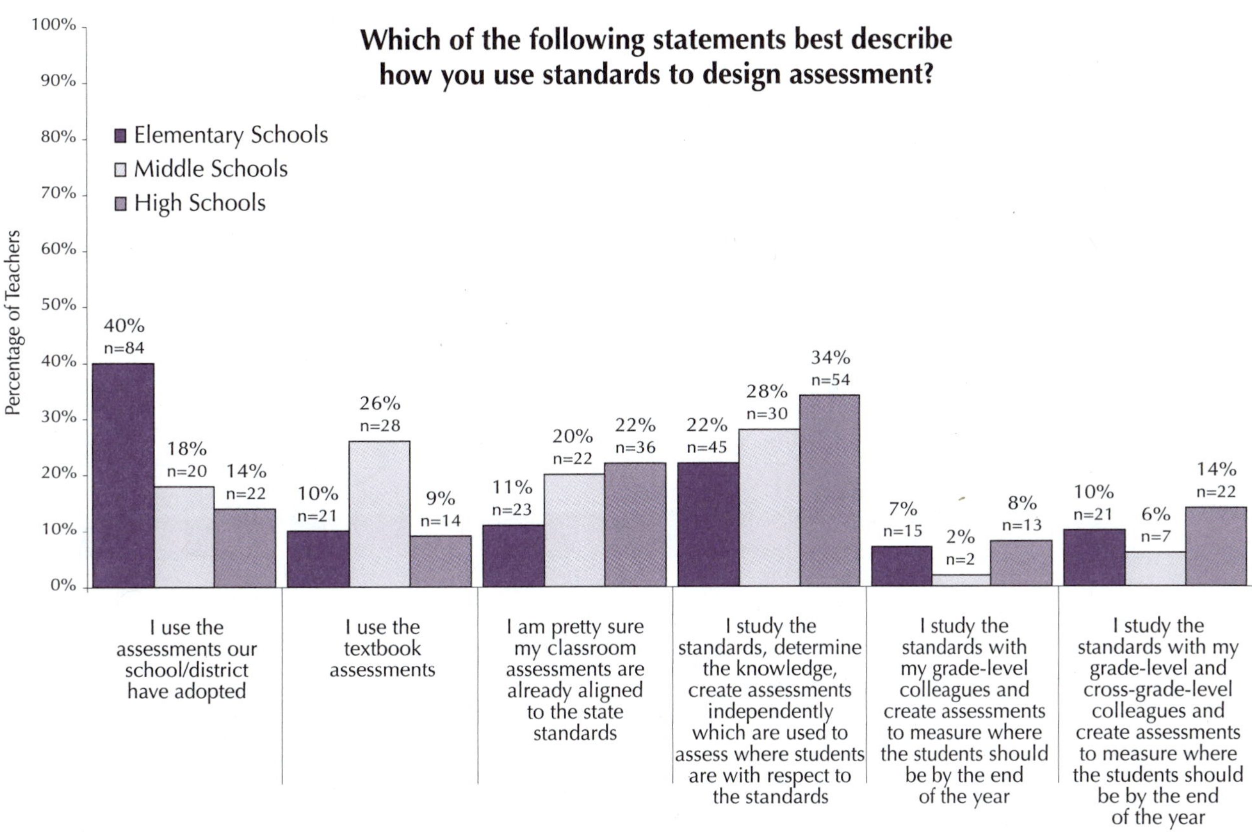

Teachers were asked what percentage of their students will meet the standards by the end of the school year. Results are shown in Figure 5.22.

Figure 5.22

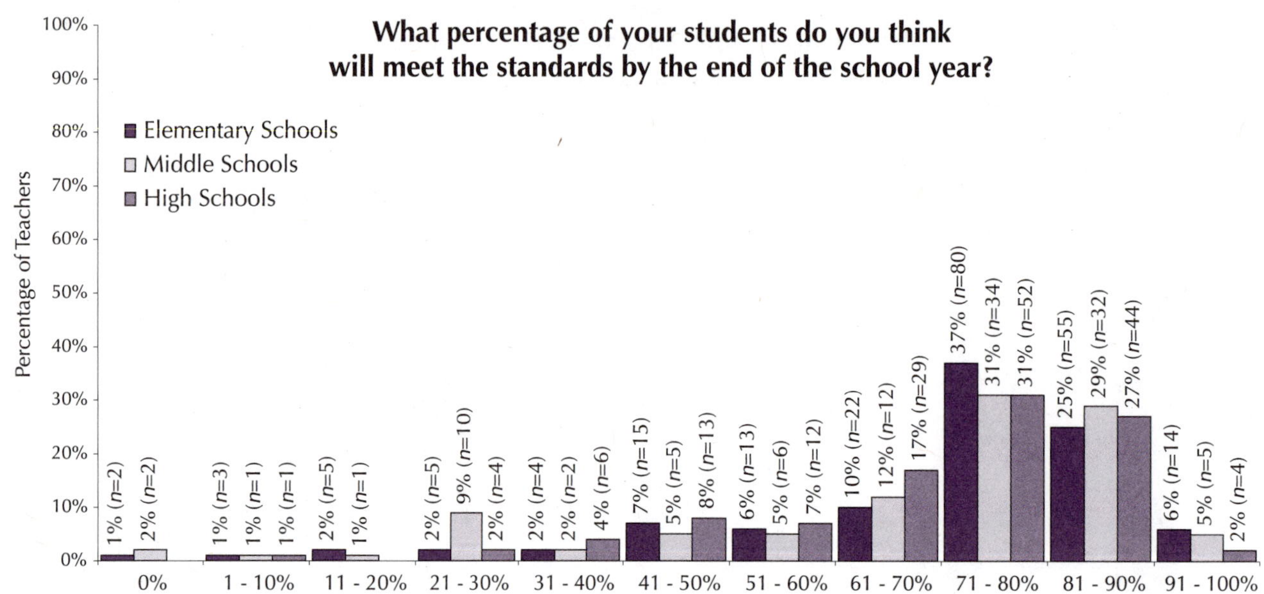

Teachers were asked what they do when students do not learn the standards and to select all response options that apply. Results are shown in Figure 5.23.

Figure 5.23

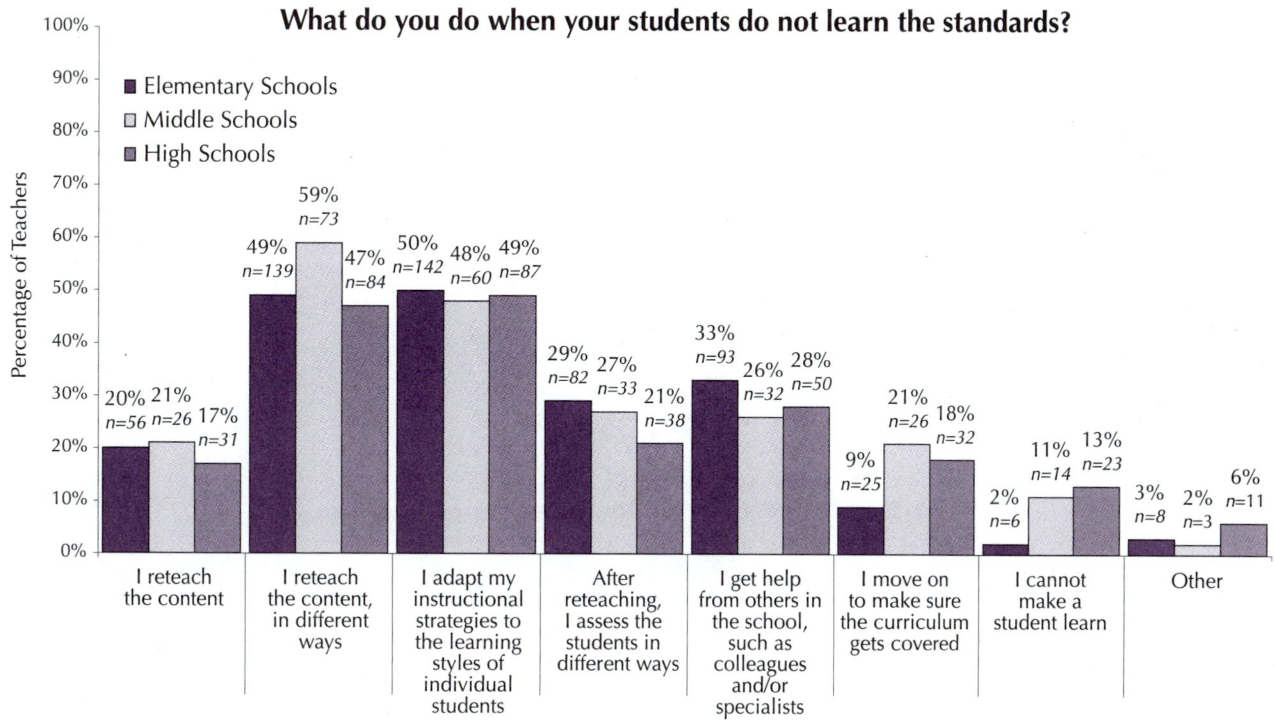

Teachers were asked to what extent they believe teachers and instructional staff can make the necessary changes to improve student learning. Results are shown in Figure 5.25.

Figure 5.24

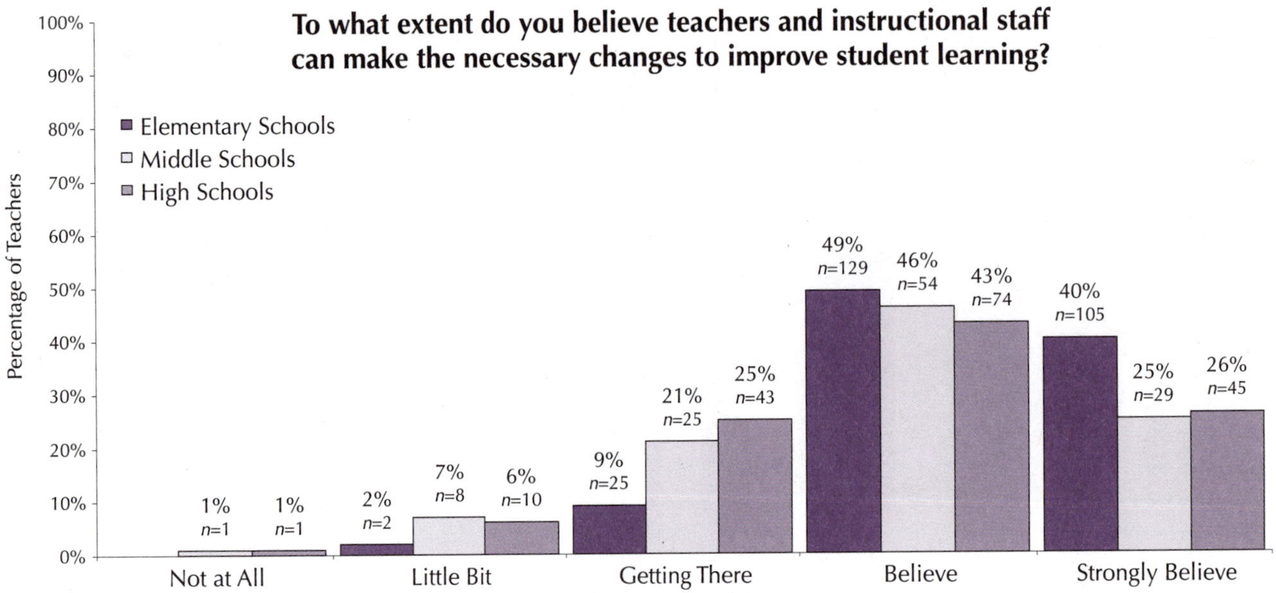

Teachers were asked to what extent they believe school leadership can facilitate the necessary changes to improve student learning. Results are shown in Figure 5.26.

Figure 5.25

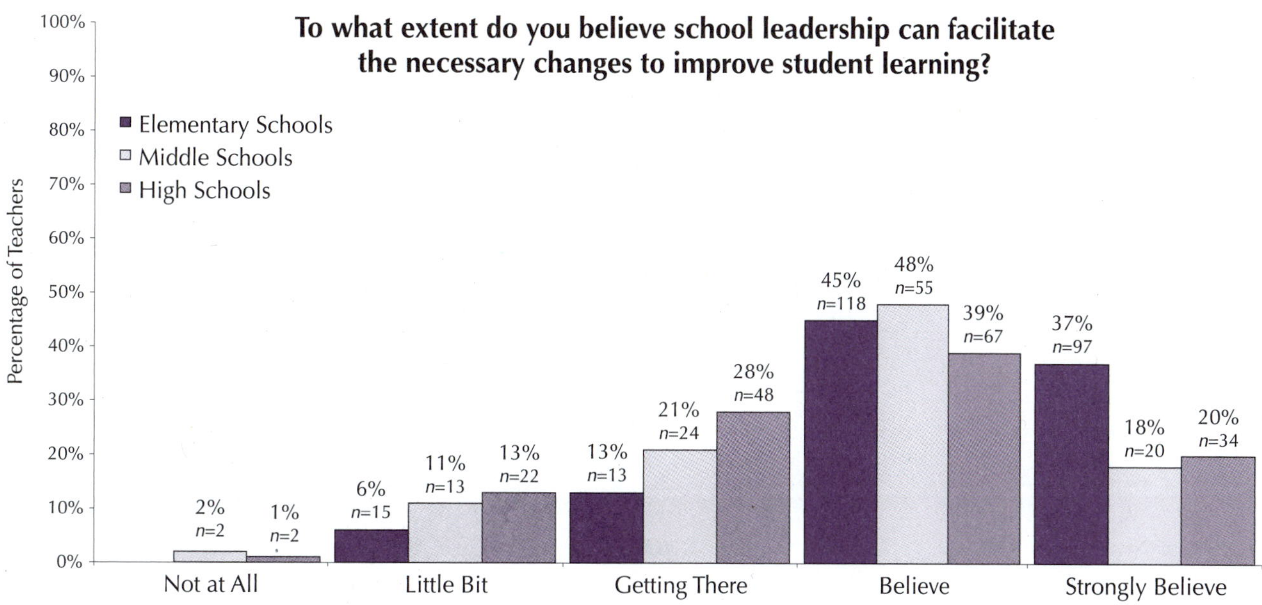

Teachers were asked how committed they are to making necessary changes to improve student learning. Results are shown in Figure 5.27

Figure 5.26

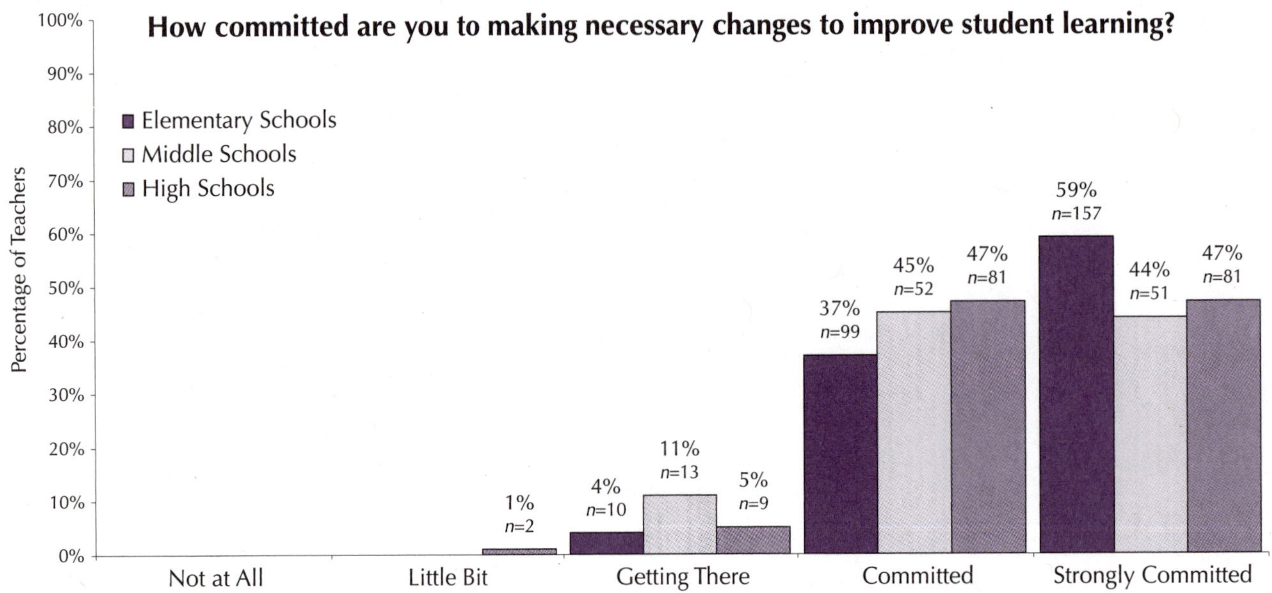

Study Questions for How Do We Do Business? Canyon View School District Questionnaires

As you review Canyon View's perceptual and standards assessment data, use either the margins in the text, this page, or print this page from the CD to write down your early thinking. (Ch5Qs_Qs.pdf) These notes, of course, are only hunches or placeholders until all the data are analyzed.

1. What are the perceptual *strengths* and *challenges* for Canyon View School District?	
Strengths	*Challenges*

2. What are some *implications* for the Canyon View improvement plan?

3. Looking at the data presented, what other perceptual data would you want to answer the question *How do we do business?* for Canyon View School District.

What I Saw in the Example: Canyon View School District Questionnaires

Using the study questions as an outline, what I saw in the data for Chapter 5 follows on the next two pages.

(Ch5Saw_Qs.pdf)

Questionnaire Data

Perceptual Strengths	*Perceptual Challenges*
• Student responses were overall positive, with the exception of some middle and high school responses. • Open-ended responses of Elementary School students showed that the teachers were the first thing they liked the most about school, except for Elementary School 8, teachers were written in second behind people and friends. • All but two schools had "nothing" as their number one written in response to the question, *What do you wish was different at this school?* The other two had "nothing" as their second and their most written in response to the question. • Middle school open-ended responses revealed that the number one thing the students who wrote in liked were the teachers (and the principals in Middle School 1). • High school open-ended responses revealed that the number one thing the students liked were the teachers and staff. • Elementary staff responses were quite positive. All school staffs aggregate responses showed that they were in strong agreement with the three items that indicate that teachers got into teaching for the right reasons: *I love to teach, I love seeing the results of my work with students,* and *I believe every student can learn.* • Middle and high staff responses were positive overall, but not as positive as elementary. • Staff open-ended responses showed teachers or staff as the number one strength of each of the schools. • Each school staff was able to identify what it would take to improve student learning in her/his school. • Parents were pretty positive overall. • Parent open-ended responses showed that they feel the greatest strengths in each of the schools are the teacher and staff. • Administrative staff items were all in agreement.	• Some students from Elementary 4 and 8 seem to be struggling with freedom and choices. In addition, Elementary 4 and 10 students do not feel they are being treated fairly by the people on recess duty. • Playground rules and wanting better food seem to be the main issues that students wished was better at their schools, according to the open-ended responses. • According to the middle school multiple choice item responses, they also seem to be struggling with freedom and choices, in addition to students and adults treating them fairly and with respect. • Middle school open-ended responses revealed that the number one thing the students wished was different was a better lunch program with more time. • Both middle school students' open-ended responses indicated that students wanted more choices and more respectful teachers. • High school students are not feeling cared for by the adults in the schools. They do not feel teachers know them well, that they are in charge of what they learn, that classtime is spent doing work they find meaningful, and that school is fun. Both the multiple choice and open-ended responses revealed these feelings. • Elementary School 7 staff multiple-choice responses indicate that they do not have effective leadership in place. Their morale is also very low, a by-product of the low responses about administration. This school also had relatively low responses for *the vision for the school is shared* and *we have an action plan in place that can get us to our vision.* • Elementary School 11 multiple-choice responses indicate that teachers' morale is fairly low and that there is not a vision in the school that is shared. Additionally, this staff was in low agreement with the item, *Teachers in this school communicate with each other to make student learning consistent across grades.* • Middle and high school staffs multiple choice responses were mostly in agreement with all items, with the exception of High School 2. High school 2 appears to need work on its vision, plan, and leadership. • Parent open-ended indicates that the parents would like to see improvements in the principal at Elementary School 1. Other than that, most elementary parent ideas about what needs to improve focus on supervision, playground, and the drop-off center and parking lots. • Middle school and high school parents want to see teacher-to-parent communication improved. • High school parents do not feel that high school teachers are helping them know how to support their child's learning at home. • High School 2 parents want more communication about their childs' progress and after school options.

Questionnaire Data *(Continued)*

Implications for Canyon View's improvement plan

- Perhaps some diversity and respect training for the adults and students need to be put into place.
- It appears as though high school classes need to be "spiced up," made more relevant to "real world" work and life. Teachers must still be suing mostly lecture and worksheets in many classes.
- Teacher-student relationships need to improve at middle and high schools.
- Elementary School 7 and High School 2 principals might need to be changed or supported with leadership support.
- High School 2 and the district need to revisit their visions and plans.
- District staff members need to review the school staffs' open-ended responses with respect to *What it would take to improve student learning* and *What needs to be improved.* If staffs are committed to these statements and plan to do something about it, they will get improvements.

Other desired perceptual data or information

- It would be good to know what graduates say about their experiences in the district and how well their Canyon View education prepared them for the world of work or post-secondary education.
- It would be good to hear from *all* students—not just a sample, especially from High School 2.

Standards Assessment Data

Perceptual Strengths	*Perceptual Challenges*
• Staff members assessed where they are with respect to standards implementation. • Staff said that professional development on how to teach to the standards, grade-level and cross-grade level meetings, and demonstration lessons would help all teachers better know the standards. • Teachers believe they can make the necessary changes to improve student learning and, for the most part, that leadership is in place to facilitate the changes—especially at the elementary level. • Staff is strongly committed to making the necessary changes to improve student learning.	• Teachers do not seem to know the standards that precede and follow their grade-levels or even the ones at their grade levels. • Elementary teachers seem to know a little about ELA and Math standards at their grade levels and nothing else. • All three levels felt schoolwide meetings about standards would be the least helpful in helping teachers better know standards. • Middle and high school staffs are not feeling supported with standards implementation. • Most of the teachers appear to be relying on the district's curriculum and instruction strategies to design instruction. • Sixty-eight percent of elementary, 65% middle, and 60% high school are committed.

Implications for Canyon View's improvement plan

- Professional learning related to how to teach to the standards, along with grade-level and cross-grade-level meetings.
- Figure out strategies to monitor and measure how standards are being implemented.
- Structures need to be put into place to support middle and high school teachers in their implementation of the standards.

> ***Understanding how the organization does business can help a school district know what is possible, what is appropriate, and what is needed in the continuous improvement plan.***

Summary

The second question in our continuous improvement planning approach is *How do we do business?* The answer to this question tells us about perceptions of the learning environment from student, staff, administrator, and parent perspectives. Multiple-choice questionnaires can give us a quick snapshot of different groups' perspectives. Open-ended responses, used with the multiple choice responses, and *Continuous Improvement Continuums* assessments, help paint the picture of the school district. Understanding how the organization does business can help a school district know what is possible, what is appropriate, and what is needed in the continuous improvement plan.

On the CD Related to this Chapter

- *Continuous Improvement Continuum* Tools (Folder)
  These files are tools for assessing on the CICs and for writing the CIC report.
  - *Continuous Improvement Continuums* for Districts (CICs_Dstrct.pdf)
    This read-only file contains the seven *Education for the Future District Continuous Improvement Continuums.* These can be printed as is or enlarged for showing individual staff opinions during staff assessments.
  - *Canyon View School District Baseline CIC Results* (CViewBase.pdf)
    This read-only file is the summary of Canyon View's baseline assessment on the *Education for the Future District Continuous Improvement Continuums,* as an example for you to use to create your CIC report.
  - *Continuous Improvement Continuums* for Schools (CICs_Schls.pdf)
    This read-only file contains the seven *Education for the Future School Continuous Improvement Continuums.* These can be printed as is or enlarged for posting individual staff opinions during staff assessments.
  - *Continuous Improvement Continuums Self-Assessment Activity* (ACTCIC.pdf)
    Assessing on the *Continuous Improvement Continuums* will help staffs see where their systems are right now with respect to continuous improvement and ultimately will show they are making progress over time. The discussion has major implications for the *Continuous Improvement Plan.*
  - *Coming to Consensus* (Consenss.pdf)
    This read-only file provides strategies for coming to consensus, useful when assessing on the *Continuous Improvement Continuums.*

- *Continuous Improvement Continuums Report Example* (ExReprt1.pdf)
  This read-only file shows a real school's assessment on the *Education for the Future School Continuous Improvement Continuums,* as an example.
- *Continuous Improvement Continuums Report Example for Follow-up Years* (ExReprt2.pdf)
  This read-only file shows a real school's assessment on the *Education for the Future School Continuous Improvement Continuums* over time, as an example.
- *Continuous Improvement Continuums Baseline Report Template* (ReptTemp.doc)
  This *Microsoft Word* file provides a template for writing your district's report of its assessment on the *Education for the Future Continuous Improvement Continuums.*
- *Continuous Improvement Continuums Graphing Templates* (CICGraph.xls)
  This *Microsoft Excel* file is a template for graphing your assessments on the seven *Education for the Future Continuous Improvement Continuums.*

▼ Study Questions Related to *How Do We Do Business?: The District CIC Assessment* (Ch5Qs_CICs.doc)
These study questions will help you understand the information provided in Chapter 5. This template file can be printed for use with staffs as they answer the question, *How do we do business?,* through analyzing Canyon View's CIC assessment data.

▼ *What I Saw in the Example: CIC Assessment* (Ch5Saw_CICs.pdf)
What I Saw in the Example is a file, organized by the CIC assessment data study questions, that summarizes what I saw in the CIC data provided by Canyon View School District.

▼ Study Questions Related to *How Do We Do Business?: The District Questionnaires* (Ch5Qs_Qs.doc)
These study questions will help you understand the information provided in Chapter 5. This template file can be printed for use with staffs as they answer the question, *How do we do business?,* through analyzing Canyon View's perceptual data.

▼ *What I Saw in the Example: Questionnaires* (Ch5Saw_Qs.pdf)
What I Saw in the Example is a file, organized by the perceptual study questions, that summarizes what I saw in the perceptual data provided by Canyon View School District.

- ▼ *Analysis of Questionnaire Data Table* (Distr_QTable.doc)
  This *Microsoft Word* file is a tabular guide for interpreting your district student, staff, and parent questionnaires, independently and interdependently. It will help you see the summary of your results and write the narrative.

- ▼ *Education for the Future* Questionnaires: (Folder)
  These PDF files are for content review purposes only—*not* intended for use in questionnaire administration. For more information about administering and analyzing *Education for the Future* questionnaires, please visit *http://eff.csuchico.edu/questionnaire_resources/*.
  - ◆ *Student (Kindergarten to Grade 3) Questionnaire* (StQKto3.pdf)
  - ◆ *Student (Grades 1 to 12) Questionnaire* (StQ1to12.pdf
  - ◆ *Student (Middle/High School) Questionnaire* (StQMidHS.pdf)
  - ◆ *Teaching Staff Questionnaire* (TeachStaffQ.pdf)
  - ◆ *Organizational Learning Questionnaire* (OrgLearnQ.pdf)
  - ◆ *Administrator Questionnaire* (AdminQ.pdf)
  - ◆ *Parent Questionnaire* (ParntK12Q.pdf)
  - ◆ *High School Parent Questionnaire* (ParntHSQ.pdf)
  - ◆ *Alumni Questionnaire* (AlumniQ.pdf)

Visit *http://eff.csuchico.edu* for information about, and to download, questionnaire tools and *Education for the Future* questionnaires.

- ▼ *Assessing Perceptions Using EFF Questionnaires* (EFF_AssessQs.pdf)
  This read-only file is a document that details the development of *Education for the Future's* questionnaire content, and specifically provides reliability and validity information.

- ▼ *How to Analyze Open-ended Responses* (OEanalz.pdf)
  This read-only file discusses how to analyze responses to the open-ended questions on questionnaires.

- ▼ *Questions to Guide the Analysis of Perceptions Data* (PerceptQ.doc)
  This *Microsoft Word* file is a tabular guide for interpreting your district perceptions data. You can change the questions if you like or use the file to write in the responses. It will help you write the narrative for your results.

Analyzing the Data:
Where Are We Now?
Chapter 6

> ***Most often, school districts and schools determine their results through student learning measures only.***

What are the results of current processes? Where are we now? The results from the demographic data collection and analysis, reviewed in Chapter 4, provide a context for understanding student performance data. Further, the understanding of district and school culture through the analyses of beliefs, values, and perceptions contribute to a richer understanding of the environment within which student learning takes place. We must remember, however, that the overall purpose of the continuous improvement model is to *get results:* to improve learning for all students in every classroom in every school in the district.

Most school districts determine their results through student learning measures only. More often than not, schools throughout a district use a simple student learning measure, usually a state-required assessment. While this is clearly a good starting point, generating a sound understanding of how well students are learning *requires multiple measures* that are disaggregated by school, across demographic groups, and over time. Only by understanding the different types of assessment data, analyzed for detail, can we get to an understanding of what we need to do to continuously improve our results.

Why do we measure student learning?
We measure student learning to know—

- if students have particular skills and knowledge
- if students have attained a level of proficiency/competence/mastery
- if instructional strategies are making a difference for all students
- the effectiveness of instructional strategies and curricula
- how to improve instructional strategies
- how to classify students into instructional groups
- that students are ready to graduate or proceed to the next level of instruction
- if school processes are making the intended progress

Unfortunately, student learning results are not always used in these ways. Most of the time it is because district and school personnel struggle with the way student learning is measured and the analyses to display the results. The purpose of this chapter is to show different ways of measuring, analyzing, and reporting student learning results.

We start with discussions of different ways to measure student learning; then the example, Canyon View School District, is shown. Please note the study questions on page 282 to assist in interpreting the data. CD-ROM (Ch6Qs.pdf) Also note that there is space in the margins on the data pages to write your impressions as you review the data. At the end of the chapter, I have shared what I saw in the data.

How Can School Districts Measure Student Learning?

School districts use a variety of means to assess student learning. Most districts are in states that use standardized tests at grades 3–8, or all grade levels. Other common means of assessing student learning are more classroom-based, such as standards and performance assessments, portfolio assessments, teacher-given grades, and teacher observations. Different means of assessing student learning are defined below, followed by the example analyses, Canyon View School District, created with its state criterion-referenced assessment.

Standardized Tests

Standardized tests are assessments that have uniformity in content, administration, and scoring. They can be used for comparing results across students, classrooms, schools, school districts, and states. Norm-referenced, criterion-referenced, and diagnostic tests (which can be normed and criterion-referenced) are the most commonly used standardized tests. Arguments *for* and *against* standardized testing appear in Figure 6.1. CD-ROM (TestArgu.pdf)

Figure 6.1

Arguments For and Against Standardized Testing

Arguments For Standardized Testing

- Standardized testing can be designed to measure performance, thinking, problem solving, and communication skills.
- The process students use to solve a problem can be tested, rather than just the result.
- Standardized tests can be developed to match state standards.
- Standardized tests can help drive the curriculum standards that are supposed to be taught.
- Ways need to be developed to determine if students have the skills to succeed in society; standardized tests can ensure all students, across a state or the entire country, have essential skills.
- Employers and the public need to know if students are able to apply skills and knowledge to everyday life; standardized testing can help with that assurance.
- Standardized testing may be helping to raise the bar of expectations for students in public schools—especially the lowest performing schools.
- Many schools, districts, and states have seen achievement levels rise in recent years which they attribute to higher expectations of students because of standardized tests.
- Standardized tests provide data that show which skills students are lacking, giving educators the information necessary to tailor classes and instructional strategies to student needs.
- Standardized tests can tell how the school or student is doing in comparison to a norming group, which is supposed to represent the typical students in the country.
- With most standardized tests, one can follow the same students over time.

Arguments Against Standardized Testing

- Standardized testing often narrows student learning to what is tested; what is tested is usually only a sample of what students should know.
- Standardized tests typically focus on what is easy to measure, not the critical thinking skills students need to develop.
- Standardized tests do not always match the state standards.
- To make standardized tests align to the state standards requires expertise and can be costly.
- The quality of standardized tests is a concern.
- Standardized tests are better at measuring rote learning than evaluating thinking skills.
- Too much instructional time is used to prepare students for multiple-choice tests, to the detriment of other uses of instructional time.
- Standardized tests could be culturally biased, drawing primarily upon the experiences of one socio-economic group.
- Decisions are sometimes made about a student's promotion from grade to grade or graduation based solely on one multiple-choice test.
- It is not fair to hold students accountable on one test when the schools might not be providing students with quality teachers, curricula, and time to master concepts.
- Students are not always provided with time to master what is expected on the standardized tests.
- There is a concern with standardized tests over getting the right answers.
- Standardized tests sometimes measure only what students know, not what they understand.
- Standardized testing is expensive.
- Testing is costly in teaching time and student time.

Norm-referenced Tests

Norm-referenced tests are also standardized tests. Norm-referenced test scores create meaning through comparing the test performance of a district, school, group, or individual with the performance of a norming group. A norming group is a representative group of students whose results on a norm-referenced test help create the scoring scales with which others compare their performance. Norming groups' results are professed to look like the normal curve, shown in Figure 6.2 below.

Figure 6.2

The Normal Curve and Scores

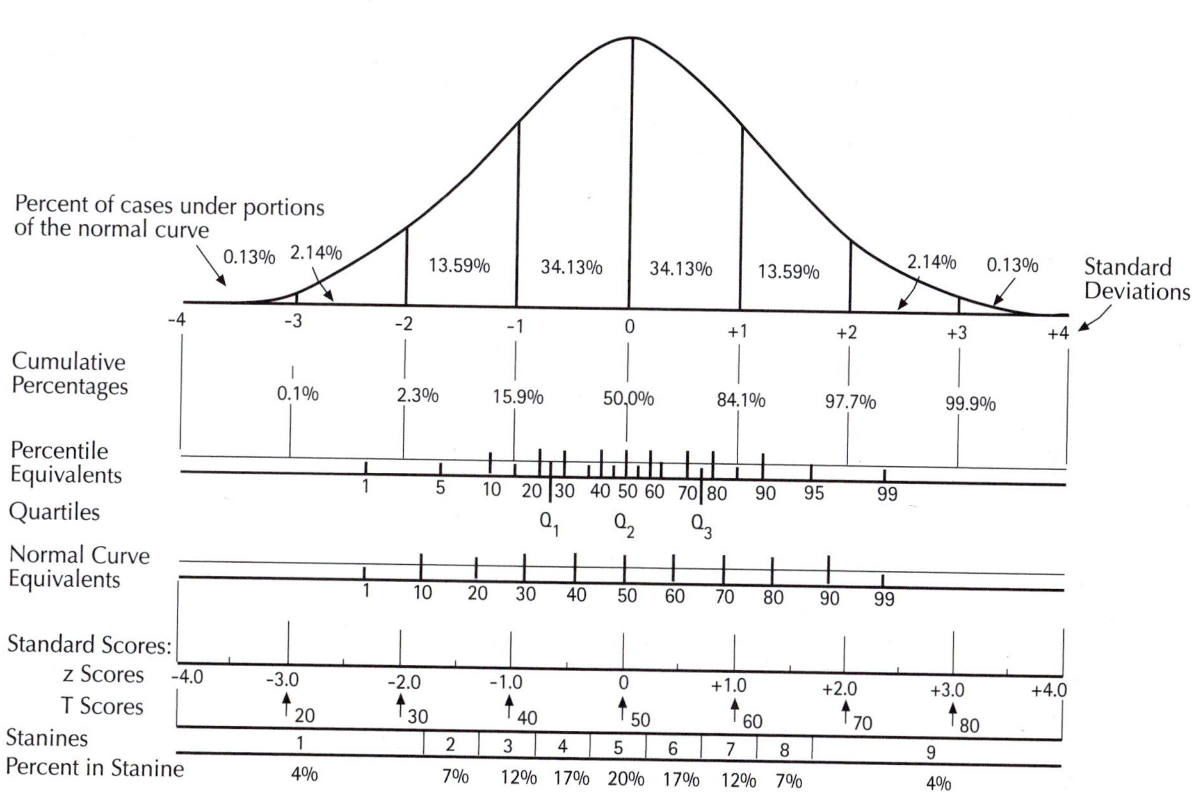

The national percentile rank is one of the most used scales; it is also misused the most.

Normal curve equivalent scores are excellent for looking at scores over time.

The normal curve is a distribution of scores or other measures that in graphic form has a distinctive bell-shaped appearance. In a normal distribution, the measures are distributed symmetrically about the mean, or average score. Most results are near the mean and decrease in frequency the farther one departs from the mean. Stated another way—the theory of the normal curve basically says that when test publishers give a test to a representative sample of students, most students score around the mean with very few students scoring very high or very low. Using this theory, test publishers are able to create scales that are useful for districts and schools to compare their scores with the norming group.

National Percentile Ranks. The two most commonly used and useful normed scales, or score types, are national percentile ranks and normal curve equivalents. The national percentile rank (NPR), also known as the national percentile equivalent, ranges from 1 to 99, with a midscore of 50. The NPR is one of the most used scales; it is also misused the most. The misuse of this scale stems from the fact that it is an unequal interval scale, which *prohibits* adding, subtracting, multiplying, and dividing the scores. *One should not look at gains, losses, or averages with percentile ranks.* Median scores, or the middle scores, are the most appropriate means of describing the typical performance of a whole district or school.

Normal Curve Equivalent Scores. Normal curve equivalent (NCE) scores were created to alleviate the problem of unequal interval scales presented by percentile ranks. This equal interval scale has a mean of 50, and range of 1 to 99, just like the NPR. A standard deviation of 21.06 forces the intervals to be equal, spreading the scores away from the mean. NCEs have the same meaning across students, subtests, grade levels, classrooms, schools, and school districts. Fifty (50) is what one would expect for an average year's growth. You can look at how close your scores are to expected performance, averages, gains, losses, highest, and lowest scores. NCEs are excellent for looking at scores over time.

Grade-level Equivalent Scores. Another score type used with norm-referenced tests is grade-level equivalent. Grade-level equivalent scores result in an interesting scale that shows the grade and month of the school year for which a given score is the actual or estimated average. Its meaning is that the student obtained the same score that one would expect average x^{th} grade students in their x^{th} month to score if they took the xth grade test. Based on a ten-month school year, scores would be noted as 9.1 for ninth grade, first month, or 10.7 for tenth grade, seventh month. For example, if a ninth grader scored a 10.8 on a subtest, that does not mean that she/he should be doing tenth grade, eighth-month work. It only means that the student obtained the same score that one would expect average tenth grade students to score if they took the same ninth-grade test during the eighth month of grade nine. Grade-level equivalent scores are okay for a snapshot in time, but they should not be averaged or taken literally.

Grade-level equivalent scores are okay for a snapshot in time, but they should not be averaged or taken literally.

Standard Scores. Standard scores, or scaled scores, refer to scores that have been *transformed* for reasons of convenience, comparability, and ease of interpretation. Ranges vary depending upon the test, and sometimes even the subtest. The best uses of standard scores are averages calculated over time allowing for the study of change. These scores are good to use for calculations because of their equal intervals and their easy conversions to other score types. The downsides are that, with the various ranges, it is difficult to look across subtests, grade levels, and years. It is often hard for the layperson to create meaning from these scores. The normal curve is needed to interpret the results with respect to other scores and people. The NCE is a standard score and probably one of the best to use because of the constant range and mean.

The best uses of standard scores are averages calculated over time allowing for the study of change.

Anticipated Achievement/Cognitive Abilities Scores. Occasionally, norm-referenced tests provide indicators of ability, such as anticipated achievement scores, cognitive abilities, or cognitive skills indexes. The anticipated achievement score is an estimate of the average score for students of a similar age, grade, and academic aptitude. It can be computed in grade-level equivalents, normal curve equivalents, standard scores, and national percentiles. The higher the student scores on sequences, analogies, memory, and verbal reasoning tests, the higher the student is expected to score on standardized tests.

A cognitive abilities or cognitive skills index is also created from the same four tests mentioned above, and assesses the student's academic aptitude. The range of this scale is 58 to 141, with a mean of 100. Two-thirds of the scores will fall between 84 and 118. Anticipated Achievement/Cognitive Abilities scores can tell teachers if they are teaching to students' potential, as measured by that test.

Anticipated Achievement/ Cognitive Abilities scores can tell teachers if they are teaching to the students' potential.

Criterion-referenced assessments tell us how well students are performing on specific criteria, goals, or standards.

Criterion-referenced Tests

Criterion-referenced tests compare an individual's performance to a specific learning objective or performance standard and not to the performance of other test takers. Criterion-referenced assessments tell us how well students are performing on specific criteria, goals, or standards. For district and school level analyses, criterion-referenced tests are usually scored in terms of the number or percentage of students meeting the standard or criterion, or the number or percentage of students falling in typical descriptive categories, such as *far below basic, below basic, basic, proficient,* and *advanced.* Criterion-referenced tests can be standardized or not, and they can also have norming groups.

Diagnostic tests can help teachers know the nature of students' difficulties, but not the cause of the difficulty.

Diagnostic Tests

Diagnostic tests, usually standardized and normed, are given before instruction begins to help the instructor(s) understand student learning needs. Diagnostic tests can help teachers know the nature of students' difficulties, but not the cause of the difficulty. Many different score types are used with diagnostic tests.

These tests, score types, and other frequently used terms are defined in Figure 6.3, along with a description of most effective uses and cautions for use. CD-ROM (TestTerm.pdf)

Figure 6.3

Standardized Test Score Terms, Their Most Effective Uses, and Cautions for Their Uses			
Score	**Definition**	**Most Effective Uses**	**Cautions**
Anticipated Achievement Scores	A student's anticipated achievement score is an estimate of the average score for students of similar ages, grade levels, and academic aptitude. It is an estimate of what we would expect the student to score on an achievement test.	Anticipated achievement scores can be used to see if a student is scoring "above" or "below" an expected score, indicating whether or not she/he is being challenged enough, or if her/his needs are being met.	It is easy to think of these scores as "IQ" scores. They are just achievement indicators on a standardized test.
Cognitive Abilities or Skills Index	The cognitive skills index is an age-dependent normalized standard score based on a student's performance on a cognitive skills test with a mean of 100 and standard deviation of 16. The score indicates a student's overall cognitive ability or academic aptitude relative to students of similar age, without regard to grade level.	Cognitive skills index scores can be used to see if a student is scoring "above" or "below" an expected score, indicating whether or not she/he is being challenged enough, or if her/his needs are being met.	It is easy to think of these scores as "IQ" scores. They are just achievement indicators on a standardized test.
Criterion-referenced Tests	Tests that judge how well a test-taker does on an explicit objective relative to a predetermined performance level.	Tell us how well students are performing on specific criteria, goals, or standards.	CRTs test only what was taught, or planned to be taught. CRTs can not give a broad estimate of knowledge.
Deciles	Deciles divide a distribution into ten equal parts: 1–10; 11–20; 21–30; 31–40; 41–50; 51–60; 61–70; 71–80; 81–90; 91–99. Just about any scale can be used to show deciles.	Deciles allow districts and schools to show how all students scored throughout the distribution. One would expect a school's distribution to resemble a normal curve. Watching the distribution move to the right, over time, could imply that all students in the distribution are making progress.	One must dig deeper to understand if all students and all groups of students are moving forward.
Diagnostic Tests	Diagnostic tests, usually standardized and normed, are given before instruction begins to help the instructor(s) understand student learning needs. Many different score types are used with diagnostic tests.	Help teachers know the nature of students' difficulties, but not the cause of the difficulty.	Make sure the diagnostic test is measuring what you want it to measure and that it can be compared to formative and summative assessments used.

Figure 6.3 (Continued)

Standardized Test Score Terms, Their Most Effective Uses, and Cautions for Their Uses			
Score	**Definition**	**Most Effective Uses**	**Cautions**
Grade-level Equivalents	Grade-level equivalents indicate the grade and month of the school year for which a given score is the actual or estimated average. Based on a ten-month school year, scores would be noted as 9.1 for ninth grade, first month, or 11.10 for eleventh grade, tenth month.	Grade-level equivalents are most effectively used as a snapshot in time. Scores are comparable across subtests.	These scores should not be taken literally. If a ninth grader scored a 11.8 on a subtest, that does not mean that she/he should be doing eleventh grade, eighth-month work. It only means that the student obtained the same score that one would expect average eleventh-grade students in their eighth month of school to score if they took the ninth-grade test.
Latent-trait Scale	A latent-trait scale is a scaled score obtained through one of several mathematical approaches collectively known as Latent-Trait Procedures or Item Response Theory. The particular numerical values used in the scale are arbitrary, but higher scores indicate more knowledgeable students or more difficult items.	Latent-trait scales have equal intervals allowing comparisons over time.	These are scores set up by testing professionals. Laypeople typically have difficulty understanding their meaning.
NCE (National or Local)	Normal Curve Equivalent (NCE) scores are standard scores with a mean of 50, a standard deviation of 21.06, and a range of 1 to 99. The term National would indicate that the norming group was national; local usually implies a state or district norming group.	NCEs have equal intervals so they can be used to study gains over time. The scores have the same meaning across subtests, grade levels, and years. A 50 is what one would expect in an average year's growth.	This score, just like all scores related to norm-referenced tests, cannot be taken literally. The score simply shows relative performance of a student group or of students to a norming group.
Percent Passing	Percent passing is a calculated score implying the percentage of the student group meeting and exceeding some number, usually a cut score, proficiency/mastery level, or a standard.	With standards-based accountability, it is beneficial to know the percentage of the population meeting and exceeding a standard and to compare a year's percentages with the previous year(s) to understand progress being made.	This is a very simple statistic, and its interpretation should be simple as well. Total numbers (n=) of students included in the percentage must always be noted with the percentage to assist with the understanding.

Figure 6.3 (Continued)

Standardized Test Score Terms, Their Most Effective Uses, and Cautions for Their Uses			
Score	**Definition**	**Most Effective Uses**	**Cautions**
Percentile / Percentile Rank (PR) (National or Local)	Percentile ranks indicate the percentage of students in a norm group (e.g., national or local) whose scores fall below a given score. The range is from 1 to 99. 50th percentile ranking would mean that 50 percent of the scores in the norming group fall below a specific score. The term National would indicate that the norming group was national; local usually implies a state or district norming group.	One-year comparison to the norming group. Districts and schools can see the relative standing of a student or group in the same grade to the norm group who took the test at a comparable time.	Percentile rank is not a score to use over time to look for gains because of unequal intervals, unless the calculations are made with equal interval scores and then converted to percentile ranks. One cannot calculate averages using NPR because of the unequal intervals. Medians are the most appropriate statistic to use.
Quartiles	There are three quartiles points—Q1, Q2, Q3 — that divide a distribution into four equal groups: Q1=25th percentile Q2=50th percentile (Median) Q3=75th percentile	Quartiles allow districts and schools to see the distribution of scores for any grade level, for instance. Over time, districts and schools trying to increase student achievement would want to monitor the distribution to ensure that all students are making progress.	With quartiles, one cannot tell if the scores are at the top of a quartile or the bottom. There could be "real" changes taking place within a quartile that would not be evident.
Raw Scores	Raw scores are the number of questions answered correctly on a test or subtest. A raw score is simply calculated by adding the number of questions answered correctly. The raw score is a person's observed score.	The raw score provides information about the number of questions answered correctly. To get a perspective on performance, raw scores must be used with the average score for the group and/or the total number of questions. Alone, it has no meaning.	Raw scores do not provide information related to other students taking the test or to other subtests. One needs to keep perspective by knowing the total number possible. Raw scores should never be used to make comparisons between performances on different tests unless other information about the characteristics of the tests are known and identical.
RIT Scale Scores	RIT scores, named for George Rasch who developed the theory of this type of measurement, are scaled scores that come from a series of tests created by the Northwest Evaluation Association (NWEA). The tests, which draw from an item bank, are aligned with local curriculum and state/local standards.	RIT scores provide ongoing measurement of curriculum standards and a way for students to see progress in their knowledge. The scores can also be shown as percentiles to know performance related to other students of similar ages and/or grades. You will most probably see gains each time a measurement is taken with a group of students.	RIT scores are great as long as the test was carefully designed to measure standards.

Figure 6.3 (Continued)

Standardized Test Score Terms, Their Most Effective Uses, and Cautions for Their Uses			
Score	**Definition**	**Most Effective Uses**	**Cautions**
Scaled Scores	A scaled score is a mathematical transformation of a raw score, resulting in interval scores within a defined range. Scaled scores take item difficulty into account.	The best uses of scaled scores are averages and averages calculated over time allowing for the study of change. These scores are good to use for calculations because of equal intervals. The scores can be applied across subtests within most tests. Scaled scores facilitate conversions to other score types.	Ranges vary, depending upon the test. Watch for the minimum and maximum values. It is sometimes hard for laypeople to create meaning from these scores. The normal curve is needed to interpret the results with respect to other scores and people.
Standard Scores	Standard score is a general term referring to scores that have been "transformed" for reasons of convenience, comparability, ease of interpretation, etc., to have a predefined mean and standard deviation. z-scores and T-scores are standard scores.	The best uses of standard scores are averages and averages calculated over time, allowing for the study of change. These scores are good to use for calculations because of equal intervals. The scores can be applied across subtests on most tests. Standard scores facilitate conversions to other score types.	Ranges vary, depending upon the test. Watch for the minimum and maximum values. It is sometimes hard for laypeople to create meaning from these scores. The normal curve is needed to interpret results with respect to other scores and people.
Standards-based Assessments	Standards-based assessments measure students' progress toward mastering local, state, and/or national content standards.	The way standards-based assessments are analyzed depends upon the scales used. The most effective uses are in revealing the percentage of students achieving a standard.	One has to adhere to the cautions of whatever test or score type used. It is important to know how far from mastering the standard the students were when they did not meet the standard.
Stanines	Stanines are a nine-point standard score scale. Stanines divide the normal curve into nine equal points: 1 to 9.	Stanines, like quartiles, allow districts and schools to see the distribution of scores for any grade level, for instance. Over time, districts and schools trying to increase student achievement would want to monitor the distribution to ensure that all student scores are improving.	Often, the first three stanines are interpreted as "below average," the next three as "average," and the top three as "above average." This can be misleading. As with quartiles, one cannot tell if the scores are at the top of a stanine or the bottom. There could be "real" changes taking place within a stanine that would not be evident.

Figure 6.3 (Continued)

Standardized Test Score Terms, Their Most Effective Uses, and Cautions for Their Uses			
Score	**Definition**	**Most Effective Uses**	**Cautions**
T-scores	A T-score is a standard score with a mean of 50 and a standard deviation of 10. T-scores are obtained by the following formula: $T=10z + 50$	The most effective uses of T-scores are averages and averages calculated over time. T-scores are good to use for calculations because of their equal intervals. T-scores can be applied across subtests on most tests because of the forced mean and standard deviation.	T-scores are rarely used because of the lack of understanding on the part of most test users.
z-scores	A z-score is a standard score with a mean of zero and a standard deviation of one. z-scores are obtained by the following formula: $z= \frac{\text{raw score (x)} - \text{mean}}{\text{standard deviation (sd)}}$	z-scores can tell one how many standard deviations a score is away from the mean. z-scores are most useful, perhaps, as the first step in computing other types of standard scores.	z-scores are rarely used by the lay public because of the difficulty in understanding the score.

The term "performance assessment" refers to assessments that measure skills, knowledge, and ability directly—such as through "performance."

Performance Assessments

The term *performance assessment* refers to assessments that measure skills, knowledge, and ability directly—such as through *performance.* In other words, if you want students to learn to write, you assess their ability on a writing activity. One must find a way to score these results and make sense for individual students and groups of students. Scoring is usually done through development of rubrics and extensive training of scorers. Some of the arguments for and against performance assessments are listed in Figure 6.4. CD-ROM (PerfArgu.pdf) (See *References* for sources.)

Figure 6.4

Arguments For and Against Performance Assessments

Arguments For Performance Assessments

- Performance assessments can be designed to measure performance, thinking, problem solving, and communication skills.
- Performance assessments can be used to measure the process students use to solve problems.
- Performance assessments can be developed to match state standards.
- Many schools, districts, and states have seen achievement levels rise in recent years, which they attribute to higher expectations of students and what they can do, attributed to the use of performance assessments.
- Performance assessments provide data that show what students are lacking, giving educators the information necessary to tailor classes and instructional strategies to student needs.
- Students can learn during a performance task.
- Some teachers believe that when students participate in developing a rubric for evaluating their performance, they come to appreciate high-quality work.
- Performance assessments provide opportunities for students to reflect on their own work.
- Performance assessments can allow students to work until standards are met—to ensure quality work from all students.
- Performance assessments can help the teacher improve instructional strategies.
- Performance assessments allow students to perform in the learning style that suits them best.

Arguments Against Performance Assessments

- Designing good performance assessments that accurately measure performance, thinking, problem solving, and communication skills is difficult.
- Designing good performance assessments that accurately measure performance, thinking, problem solving, and communication skills is very costly.
- Some performance tasks require long periods of time to complete, such as graduation or end-of-course exhibitions.
- To be effective, skills and performances being assessed should be taught in the same way they are measured.
- The quality of performance assessments is a concern.
- It is not fair to hold students accountable on one test when the district or schools might not be providing students with quality teachers, curricula, and time to master concepts.
- Scoring criteria requires analyzing performance into its components, such as breaking out the craft of writing into developmental elements.
- Many scoring criteria are no different from giving grades or norm-referenced scoring.
- Good scoring criteria could take a long time to develop.
- It is very difficult to design performance assessments that can be compared across grade levels in other than descriptive terms.

Teachers use number or letter grades to judge the quality of a student's performance on a task, unit, or during a period of time.

Grades

Teachers use number or letter grades to judge the quality of a student's performance on a task, unit, or during a period of time. Grades are most often given as A, B, C, D, F, with pluses and minuses given by some teachers for the first four to distinguish among students. Grades mean different things to different teachers. Needless to say, grades can be subjective. "It appears that teachers consider grading to be a private activity, thus 'guarding practices with the same passion with which one might guard an unedited diary' (Kain, 1996, p. 569)" (O'Connor, 2000, p. 11). Some of the arguments for and against teacher grading are shown in Figure 6.5. CD-ROM (GradeArg.pdf)

Figure 6.5

Arguments For and Against Teacher Grading

Arguments For Teacher Grading

- Grades can be designed to reflect performance, thinking, problem solving, and communication skills.
- Teachers can grade the process students use to solve a problem, rather than just the result.
- Grades can communicate to students, parents, and administrators the student's level of performance.
- Grading can allow teachers to be very flexible in their approaches to assessing student performance.
- Grades can match teaching.
- Grades can be given for team work and not just individual work.
- Grades can be effective if students are aware of expectations.
- Grades can cover multiple standards.
- Certain teacher-developed tests can be graded quickly.
- Most people believe they know what grades mean.

Arguments Against Teacher Grading

- It is difficult to convert activities, such as performance, thinking, and problem solving, into numbers or letters and have them hold true for all students in a class.
- Grading can be very subjective.
- Grading can be distorted by effort, extra credit, attendance, behavior, etc.
- To be beneficial, students must trust the grader and the grading process, have time to practice and complete an assessment, and have choices in how they are assessed—all of which make it time-consuming for teachers to do this type of assessment well.
- To be beneficial, grading assessments must be meaningful and promote learning.
- Grades must include a variety of assessment techniques to get to all areas of student understanding and performance.
- Often parents, students, and teachers focus on grades and not on learning.
- Grading is not reflective of instructional strategies.
- Grades are not always motivators; in fact, they can demoralize students on the low end, and on the high end.
- Grades tell little about student strengths and areas for improvement.
- Grading can mean many different things within a grade level, across grade levels by teacher, subject area, and school.
- Some teachers' highest priorities with grading are to use techniques where the grades can be calculated quickly.
- Grading is not always compatible with all instructional strategies.
- Grades often are given for more than achievement.
- Grading is not essential for learning.

Descriptive statistics summarize the basic characteristics of a particular distribution, without making any inferences about population parameters.

Analyzing the Results, Descriptively

Descriptive statistics (i.e., mean, median, percent correct) can give districts and schools very powerful information. It is imperative that the appropriate analyses be used for the specific score type. Figure 6.6 summarizes terms of analyses, their definitions, their most effective uses, and cautions for their uses in analyzing student learning scores descriptively. CD-ROM (SAterms1.pdf) Descriptive statistics are used in the examples in this chapter largely because they can show a district how its students are doing, and because anyone can do the calculations.

Descriptive statistics summarize the basic characteristics of a particular group of students, without making any inferences about any larger group that may include the one from which the scores are taken. Graphing the information can also be considered descriptive.

Figure 6.6

Terms Related to Analyzing Student Learning Results, Descriptively, Their Most Effective Uses, and Cautions for Their Uses			
Term	**Definition**	**Most Effective Uses**	**Cautions**
Disaggregate	Disaggregation is breaking a total score into groups for purposes of seeing how subgroups performed. One disaggregates data to make sure all subgroups of students are learning.	Disaggregating student learning scores by gender, ethnicity, backgrounds, etc., can show how different subgroups performed.	Disaggregations are for helping districts and schools understand how to meet the needs of all students, not to say, "This group always does worse than the other group and always will." We must exercise caution in reporting disaggregations with small numbers in a subgroup.
Gain	Gain scores are the change or difference between two administrations of the same test. Gain scores are calculated by subtracting the previous score from the most recent score. One can have negative gains, which are actually losses.	One calculates gains to understand improvements in learning for groups of students and for individual students.	Gain scores should not be calculated using unequal interval scores, such as percentiles. The quality of gain score results is dependent upon the quality of the assessment instrument; the less reliable the assessment tool, the less meaningful the results. One needs to make sure the comparisons are appropriate, e.g., same students, same score types.
Maximum	A maximum is the highest score achieved, or the highest possible score on a test.	Maximum possible scores and highest received scores are important for understanding the relative performance of any group or individual, especially when using scaled or standard scores.	A maximum can tell either the highest score possible or the highest score received by a test-taker. One needs to understand which maximum is being used in the analysis. It is best to use both.
Mean	A mean is the average score in a set of scores. One calculates the mean, or average, by summing all the scores and dividing by the total number of scores.	A mean can be calculated to provide an overall average for the group, and/or student, taking a specific test. One can use any equal interval score to get a mean.	Means should not be used with unequal interval scores, such as percentile ranks. Means are more sensitive to extreme results when the size of the group is small.
Median	A median is the score that splits a distribution in half: 50 percent of the scores fall above and 50 percent of the scores fall below the median. If the number of scores is odd, the median is the middle score. If the number of scores is even, one must add the two middle scores and divide by two to calculate the median.	Medians are the way to get a midpoint for scores with unequal intervals, such as percentile ranks. The median splits all scores into two equal parts. Medians are not sensitive to outliers, like means are.	Medians are relative. Medians are most effectively interpreted when reported with the possible and actual maximum and minimum.
Minimum	A minimum is the lowest score achieved, or the lowest possible score on the test.	Minimum possible scores and lowest received scores are important for understanding the relative performance of any group or individual.	A minimum tells either the lowest score possible or the lowest score received by a test-taker. One needs to understand which minimum is being used. It is best to use both.

Figure 6.6 (Continued)

Terms Related to Analyzing Student Learning Results, Descriptively, Their Most Effective Uses, and Cautions for Their Uses			
Term	**Definition**	**Most Effective Uses**	**Cautions**
Mode	The mode is the score that occurs most frequently in a scoring distribution.	The mode basically tells which score or scores appear most often.	There may be more than one mode. The mode ignores other scores.
Percent Correct	Percent correct is a calculated score implying the percentage of students meeting and exceeding some number, usually a cut score, or a standard.	This calculated score can quickly tell educators how well the students are doing with respect to a specific set of items. It can also tell educators how many students need additional work to become proficient.	Percent correct is a calculated statistic, based on the number of items given. When the number of items given is small, the percent correct can be deceptively high or low.
Percent Proficient ***Percent Passing*** ***Percent Mastery***	Percent proficient, passing, or mastery represent the percentage of students who passed a particular test at a "proficient," "passing," or "mastery" level, as defined by the test creators or the test interpreters.	With standards-based accountability, it is beneficial to know the percentage of the population meeting and exceeding the standard and to compare a year's percentage with the previous year(s) to understand progress being made.	This is a very simple statistic, and its interpretation should be simple as well. Total numbers (N=) of students included in the percentage must always be noted with the percentage to assist in understanding the results. Ninety percent passing means something very different for 10 or 100 test-takers.
Range	Range is a measure of the spread between the lowest and the highest scores in a distribution. Calculate the range of scores by subtracting the lowest score from the highest score. Range is often described as end points also, such as the range of percentile ranks is 1 and 99.	Ranges tell us the width of the distribution of scores. Educators working on continuous improvement will want to watch the range, of actual scores, decrease over time.	If there are outliers present, the range can give a misleading impression of dispersion.
Raw Scores	Raw scores refer to the number of questions answered correctly on a test or subtest. A raw score is simply calculated by adding the number of questions answered correctly. The raw score is a person's observed score.	The raw score provides information only about the number of questions answered correctly. To get a perspective on performance, raw scores must be used with the average score for the group and the total number of questions. Alone, raw scores have little meaning.	Raw scores do not provide information related to other students taking the test or to other subtests or scores. One needs to keep perspective by knowing the total number possible. Raw scores should never be used to make comparisons between performances on different tests unless other information about the characteristics of the tests are known and identical.

Figure 6.6 (Continued)

Terms Related to Analyzing Student Learning Results, Descriptively, Their Most Effective Uses, and Cautions for Their Uses			
Term	**Definition**	**Most Effective Uses**	**Cautions**
Relationships	Relationships refer to looking at two or more sets of analyses to understand what they mean to each other without using extensive statistical techniques.	Descriptive statistics lend themselves to looking at the relationships of different analyses to each other; for instance, student learning results disaggregated by ethnicity, compared to student questionnaire results disaggregated by ethnicity.	This type of analysis is general and the results should be considered general as well. This is not a "correlation."
Rubric	A rubric is a scoring tool that rates performance according to clearly stated levels of criteria. The scales can be numeric or descriptive, or both.	Rubrics are used to give teachers, parents, and students an idea of where they started, where they want to be with respect to growth, and where they are right now.	Students need to know what the rubrics contain or, even better, help with the development of the rubrics.
Standard Deviation	The standard deviation is a measure of variability in a set of scores. The standard deviation indicates how far away scores are from the mean. The standard deviation is the square root of the variance. Unlike the variance, the standard deviation is stated in the original units of the variable. Approximately 68 percent of the scores in a normal distribution lie between plus one and minus one standard deviation of the mean. The more scores cluster around the mean, the smaller the variance.	Tells us about the variability of scores. Standard deviations indicate how spread-out the scores are without looking at the entire distribution. A low standard deviation would indicate that the scores of a group are close together. A high standard deviation would imply that the range of scores is wide.	Often this is a confusing statistic for laypeople to understand. There are more descriptive ways to describe and show the variability of student scores, such as with a decile graph. Standard deviations only make sense with scores that are distributed normally.
Triangulation	Triangulation is a term used for combining three or more measures to get a more complete picture of student learning.	If students are to be retained based on standards proficiency, educators must have more than one way of knowing if the students are proficient or not. Some students perform well on standardized measures and not on other measures, while others do not do well with standardized measures. Triangulation allows students to display what they know on three different measures.	It is sometimes very complicated to combine different measures to understand proficiency. When proficiency standards change, triangulation calculations will need to be revised. Therefore, all the calculations must be documented so they can be recalculated when necessary.

Inferential statistics help generalize the results of data analysis, when one is not using the entire population in the analysis.

Analyzing the Results, Inferentially

Many district and building administrators and teachers have taken statistics courses that taught them that it is important to have control groups, experimental designs, and to test for significant differences. These terms fall in the category of *inferential statistics.* Inferential statistics are concerned with measuring a sample from a population, and then making estimates, or inferences, about the population from which the sample was taken. Inferential statistics help generalize the results of data analysis, when one is not using the entire population in the analysis.

The main purpose of this book is to model analyses that district and school personnel can perform *without* the assistance of statisticians. Descriptive analyses provide helpful and useful information and can be understood by a majority of people. When using the entire district or school population in your analyses, there is no need to generalize to a larger population—you have the whole population.

Districts with research departments are able to perform sophisticated analyses to understand better the relationship of all variables to each other and to share these analyses with building administrators and teachers.

Inferential statistical methods, such as analyses of variance, correlations, and regression analyses, are complex and require someone who knows statistics to meet the conditions of the analyses. Since there are times when a statistician is available to perform inferential statistics, some of the terms the statistician might use with tests include those listed in Figure 6.7. CD-ROM (SAterms2.pdf)

A Note About "Scientifically-based Research." With the passage of the *No Child Left Behind* (NCLB) *Act of 2001,* which reauthorized the *Elementary and Secondary Education Act of 1965,* school districts and schools are required to gather, analyze, and use data to ensure adequate yearly progress (AYP). While increased accountability is just one part of NCLB, all districts and schools must gather data and overcome the barriers to analyzing and using the data.

Figure 6.7

Terms Related to Analyzing Student Learning Results, Inferentially, Their Most Effective Uses, and Cautions for Their Uses			
Term	**Definition**	**Most Effective Uses**	**Cautions**
Analysis of Variance (ANOVA)	Analysis of variance is a general term applied to the study of differences in the application of approaches, as opposed to the relationship of different levels of approaches to the result. With ANOVAs, we are testing the differences of the means of at least two different distributions.	ANOVAs can be used to determine if there is a difference in student learning scores between one school and another, keeping all other variables equal. It cannot tell you what the differences are, per se, but one can compute confidence intervals to estimate these differences.	Very seldom are the conditions available to study differences in education in this manner. Too many complex variables get in the way, and ethics may be involved. There are well-defined procedures for conducting ANOVAs to which we must adhere.
Correlation Analyses	Correlation is a statistical analysis that helps one understand the relationship of scores in one distribution to scores in another distribution. Correlations show magnitude and direction. Magnitude indicates the degree of the relationship. Correlation coefficients have a range of -1.0 to +1.0. A correlation of around zero would indicate little relationship. Correlations of .8 and higher, or -.8 and lower would indicate a strong relationship. When the high scores in one distribution are also high in the comparing distribution, the direction is positive. When the high scores in one distribution are related to the low scores in the other distribution, the result is a negative correlational direction.	Correlations can be used to understand the relationship of different variables to each other, e.g., attendance and performance on a standardized test; .40 to .70 are considered moderate correlations. Above .70 is considered to be high correlations.	It is wise to plot the scores to understand if the relationship is linear or not. One could misinterpret results if the scores are not linear. Pearson correlation coefficient requires linear relationships. A few outliers could skew the results and oppositely skewed distributions can limit how high a Pearson coefficient can be. Also, one must remember that correlation does not suggest causation.
Regression Analyses	Regression analysis results in an equation that describes the nature of the relationship between variables. Simple regression predicts an object's value on a response variable when given its value on one predictor variable. Multiple regression predicts an object's value on a response variable when given its value on each of several predictor variables. Correlation tells you strength and direction of relationship. Regression goes one step further and allows you to predict.	A regression equation can be used to predict student learning results, for example. Regression can determine if there is a relationship between two or more variables (such as attendance and student background) and the nature of those relationships. This analysis helps us predict and prevent student failure, and predict and ensure student successes.	One needs to truly understand the statistical assumptions that need to be in place in order to perform a regression analysis. This is not an analysis to perform through trial and error.

Figure 6.7 (Continued)

Terms Related to Analyzing Student Learning Results, Inferentially, Their Most Effective Uses, and Cautions for Their Uses			
Term	**Definition**	**Most Effective Uses**	**Cautions**
Control Groups	During an experiment, the control group is studied the same as the experimental group, except that it does not receive the treatment of interest.	Control groups serve as a baseline in making comparisons with treatment groups. Control groups are necessary when the general effectiveness of a treatment is unknown.	It may not be ethical to hold back from students some method of learning that we believe would be useful.
Experimental Design	Experimental design is the detailed planning of an experiment, made beforehand, to ensure that the data collected are appropriate and obtained in a way that will lead to an objective analysis, with valid inferences.	Experimental designs can maximize the amount of information gained, given the amount of effort expended.	Sometimes it takes statistical expertise to establish an experimental design properly.
Tests of Significance	Tests of significance use samples to test claims about population parameters.	Tests of significance can estimate a population parameter, with a certain amount of confidence, from a sample.	Often laypeople do not know what *statistically significant* really means.

The term *scientifically-based research* (Title IX, General Provisions, Part A, Section 9101, Definitions) means (A) research that involves the application of rigorous, systematic, and objective procedures to obtain reliable and valid knowledge relevant to education activities and programs; and (B) includes research that:

- employs systematic, empirical methods that draw on observation or experiment
- involves rigorous data analyses that are adequate to test the stated hypotheses and justify the general conclusions drawn
- relies on measurements or observational methods that provide reliable and valid data across evaluators and observers, across multiple measurements and observations, and across studies by the same or different investigators
- is evaluated using experimental or quasi-experimental designs in which individuals, entities, programs, or activities are assigned to different conditions and with appropriate controls to evaluate the effects of the condition of interest, with a preference for random-assignment experiments, or other designs to the extent that condition controls
- ensures that experimental studies are presented in sufficient detail and clarity to allow for replication or, at a minimum, offer the opportunity to build systematically on their findings
- has been accepted by a peer-reviewed journal or approved by a panel of independent experts through a comparably rigorous, objective and scientific review

While NCLB calls for scientific and experimental procedures, such as control groups and experimental designs, in reality, they are not always possible. Over time, well-documented case studies have become accepted as powerful designs as well.

The Canyon View School District example that follows shows a sampling of descriptive analyses the school district performed using its state criterion-referenced test. Later in the book you will see more sophisticated analyses the district used to look across all the data categories.

Our Example District: Canyon View School District

What are our results?

Canyon View School District uses the *State Test of Basic Skills* (STBS) criterion-referenced test as its main basis for assessing student performance. The test is given for state accountability purposes in grades four, eight, and eleven. It is given at grade two for gifted placement.

Student results are provided by proficiency levels. The definition of the proficiency levels follow:

- *Novice*
  A student who performs at the *Novice* level on the STBS has not met minimum expectations for student performance based on the curriculum standards approved by the State Board of Education. The student is not prepared for work at the next grade.
- *Nearing Proficiency*
  Performance at the *Nearing Proficiency* level on the STBS means a student has met minimum expectations for student performance based on the curriculum standards approved by the State Board of Education. The student is minimally prepared for work at the next grade.
- *Proficient*
  A student who performs at the *Proficient* level on the STBS has met expectations for student performance based on the curriculum standards approved by the State Board of Education. The student is well prepared for work at the next grade. The *Proficient* level represents the long-term goal for student performance.
- *Advanced*
  A student who performs at the *Advanced* level on the STBS has exceeded expectations for student performance based on the curriculum standards approved by the State Board of Education. The student is very well prepared for work at the next grade.

Students in this state must score *Proficient* or *Advanced* to be considered "proficient." Figures 6.8 through 6.31 show the Reading and Math proficiency levels for the 15 schools and the district.

Reading Proficiency

Figure 6.8 shows the Reading proficiency levels for the district by grade level from 2002-03 to 2005-06.

Look Fors: **Changes in percentage of students in each proficiency level by grade and over time.**

Planning Implications: **Does the continuous improvement plan for the district focus on all proficiency levels or just the lowest end? Are all the students moving up?**

Figure 6.8

Canyon View School District Reading Proficiency Levels Number and Percentage by Grade Level, 2002-03 to 2005-06

Grade Level	Year	Novice		Nearing Proficiency		Proficient		Advanced		Total Proficient	
		Number	Percent	Number	Percent	Number	Percent	Number	Percent	Number	Percent
Grade 4	2002-03 (*n*=523)	35	7%	41	8%	306	59%	141	27%	**447**	**85%**
	2003-04 (*n*=529)	33	6%	50	9%	334	63%	112	21%	**446**	**84%**
	2004-05 (*n*=494)	31	6%	39	8%	289	59%	135	27%	**424**	**86%**
	2005-06 (*n*=527)	30	6%	50	9%	296	56%	151	29%	**447**	**85%**
Grade 8	2002-03 (*n*=555)	40	7%	59	11%	326	59%	130	23%	**456**	**82%**
	2003-04 (*n*=535)	46	9%	63	12%	321	60%	105	20%	**426**	**80%**
	2004-05 (*n*=551)	56	10%	71	13%	312	57%	112	20%	**424**	**77%**
	2005-06 (*n*=562)	52	9%	66	12%	337	60%	107	19%	**444**	**79%**
Grade 11	2002-03 (*n*=652)	50	8%	59	9%	352	54%	191	29%	**543**	**84%**
	2003-04 (*n*=694)	41	6%	81	12%	393	57%	179	26%	**572**	**82%**
	2004-05 (*n*=684)	61	9%	71	10%	377	55%	175	26%	**552**	**81%**
	2005-06 (*n*=655)	51	8%	65	10%	369	56%	170	26%	**539**	**82%**

Figure 6.9 shows the Reading proficiency levels for the district by grade level and gender, over time.

Look Fors: **Differences by gender within grade levels. Student proficiency changes over time.**

Planning Implications: **Are Reading strategies meeting the needs of males and females at each grade level?**

Figure 6.9

Canyon View School District Reading Proficiency Levels
Number and Percentage by Grade Level and Gender, 2002-03 to 2005-06

Grade Level	Gender	Year	Novice		Nearing Proficiency		Proficient		Advanced		Total Proficient	
			Number	Percent	Number	Percent	Number	Percent	Number	Percent	Number	Percent
Grade 4	Female	2002-03 (*n*=266)	17	6%	15	6%	161	61%	73	27%	**234**	**88%**
		2003-04 (*n*=247)	14	6%	17	7%	157	64%	59	24%	**216**	**87%**
		2004-05 (*n*=235)	14	6%	20	9%	135	57%	66	28%	**201**	**86%**
		2005-06 (*n*=261)	14	5%	19	7%	149	57%	79	30%	**228**	**87%**
	Male	2002-03 (*n*=257)	18	7%	26	10%	145	56%	68	26%	**213**	**83%**
		2003-04 (*n*=282)	19	7%	33	12%	177	63%	53	19%	**230**	**82%**
		2004-05 (*n*=259)	17	7%	19	7%	154	59%	69	27%	**223**	**86%**
		2005-06 (*n*=266)	16	6%	31	12%	147	55%	72	27%	**219**	**82%**
Grade 8	Female	2002-03 (*n*=287)	13	5%	35	12%	169	59%	70	24%	**239**	**84%**
		2003-04 (*n*=260)	16	6%	29	11%	165	63%	50	19%	**215**	**83%**
		2004-05 (*n*=251)	25	10%	26	10%	145	58%	55	22%	**200**	**80%**
		2005-06 (*n*=287)	24	8%	25	9%	192	67%	46	16%	**238**	**83%**
	Male	2002-03 (*n*=268)	27	10%	24	9%	157	59%	60	22%	**217**	**81%**
		2003-04 (*n*=275)	30	11%	34	13%	156	57%	55	20%	**211**	**78%**
		2004-05 (*n*=300)	31	10%	45	15%	167	56%	57	19%	**224**	**75%**
		2005-06 (*n*=275)	28	10%	41	15%	145	53%	61	22%	**206**	**75%**
Grade 11	Female	2002-03 (*n*=341)	22	6%	35	10%	188	55%	96	28%	**284**	**84%**
		2003-04 (*n*=338)	13	4%	41	12%	193	57%	91	27%	**284**	**84%**
		2004-05 (*n*=348)	24	7%	29	8%	200	57%	95	27%	**295**	**85%**
		2005-06 (*n*=332)	14	4%	35	11%	189	57%	94	28%	**283**	**85%**
	Male	2002-03 (*n*=311)	28	9%	24	8%	164	53%	95	31%	**259**	**84%**
		2003-04 (*n*=356)	28	8%	40	11%	200	56%	88	25%	**288**	**81%**
		2004-05 (*n*=336)	37	11%	42	13%	177	53%	80	24%	**257**	**76%**
		2005-06 (*n*=323)	37	11%	30	9%	180	56%	76	24%	**256**	**79%**

Figure 6.10 shows the Reading proficiency levels for the district by school, grade level, and gender for the same time period.

Look Fors: **The percentages of proficient students by school. Changes in the schools' percentages of proficient students over time.**

Planning Implications: **Are there particular schools that need support in increasing student learning results? Are programs that are being implemented effective? How are students being taught to read at each school?**

Figure 6.10

Canyon View School District Reading Proficiency Levels
Number and Percentage by School and Grade Level, 2002-03 to 2005-06

School	Grade Level	Year	Novice		Nearing Proficiency		Proficient		Advanced		Total Proficient	
			Number	Percent	Number	Percent	Number	Percent	Number	Percent	Number	Percent
Elementary 1	Grade 4	2002-03 (*n*=35)	3	9%	2	6%	23	66%	7	20%	**30**	**86%**
		2003-04 (*n*=49)	3	6%	8	16%	29	59%	9	18%	**38**	**78%**
		2004-05 (*n*=36)	2	6%	3	8%	23	64%	8	22%	**31**	**86%**
		2005-06 (*n*=46)	6	13%	7	15%	24	52%	9	20%	**33**	**72%**
Elementary 2	Grade 4	2002-03 (*n*=39)	6	15%	6	15%	20	51%	7	18%	**27**	**69%**
		2003-04 (*n*=44)	5	11%	3	7%	35	80%	1	2%	**36**	**82%**
		2004-05 (*n*=41)	7	17%	3	7%	22	54%	9	22%	**31**	**76%**
		2005-06 (*n*=30)	3	10%	2	7%	17	57%	8	27%	**25**	**83%**
Elementary 3	Grade 4	2002-03 (*n*=48)	7	15%	2	4%	24	50%	15	31%	**39**	**81%**
		2003-04 (*n*=42)	2	5%	2	5%	26	62%	12	29%	**38**	**90%**
		2004-05 (*n*=49)	2	4%	1	2%	30	61%	16	33%	**46**	**94%**
		2005-06 (*n*=46)	2	4%	4	9%	27	59%	13	28%	**40**	**87%**
Elementary 4	Grade 4	2002-03 (*n*=77)	1	1%	8	10%	43	56%	25	32%	**68**	**88%**
		2003-04 (*n*=74)	1	1%	3	4%	54	73%	16	22%	**70**	**95%**
		2004-05 (*n*=70)			6	9%	40	57%	24	34%	**64**	**91%**
		2005-06 (*n*=77)	2	3%	4	5%	40	52%	31	40%	**71**	**92%**
Elementary 5	Grade 4	2002-03 (*n*=41)	2	5%	4	10%	20	49%	15	37%	**35**	**85%**
		2003-04 (*n*=46)			3	7%	29	63%	14	30%	**43**	**93%**
		2004-05 (*n*=43)	5	12%	3	7%	22	51%	13	30%	**35**	**81%**
		2005-06 (*n*=42)	1	2%	6	14%	24	57%	11	26%	**35**	**83%**
Elementary 6	Grade 4	2002-03 (*n*=31)			1	3%	15	48%	15	48%	**30**	**97%**
		2003-04 (*n*=37)			2	5%	22	59%	13	35%	**35**	**95%**
		2004-05 (*n*=33)			2	6%	19	58%	12	36%	**31**	**94%**
		2005-06 (*n*=29)			2	7%	19	66%	8	28%	**27**	**93%**
Elementary 7	Grade 4	2002-03 (*n*=58)	2	3%	9	16%	41	71%	6	10%	**47**	**81%**
		2003-04 (*n*=31)	4	13%	2	6%	19	61%	6	19%	**25**	**81%**
		2004-05 (*n*=39)	3	8%	3	8%	26	67%	7	18%	**33**	**85%**
		2005-06 (*n*=43)	2	5%	5	12%	25	58%	11	26%	**36**	**84%**
Elementary 8	Grade 4	2002-03 (*n*=38)	3	8%	2	5%	20	53%	13	34%	**33**	**87%**
		2003-04 (*n*=35)	2	6%	3	9%	20	57%	10	29%	**30**	**86%**
		2004-05 (*n*=35)	1	3%	5	14%	20	57%	9	26%	**29**	**83%**
		2005-06 (*n*=36)	1	3%	2	6%	21	58%	12	33%	**33**	**92%**
Elementary 9	Grade 4	2002-03 (*n*=73)	4	5%	3	4%	49	67%	17	23%	**66**	**90%**
		2003-04 (*n*=73)	2	3%	9	12%	47	64%	15	21%	**62**	**85%**
		2004-05 (*n*=61)	4	7%	4	7%	34	56%	19	31%	**53**	**87%**
		2005-06 (*n*=78)	6	8%	7	9%	44	56%	21	27%	**65**	**83%**

Figure 6.10 (Continued)

Canyon View School District Reading Proficiency Levels Number and Percentage by School and Grade Level, 2002-03 to 2005-06

School	Grade Level	Year	Novice		Nearing Proficiency		Proficient		Advanced		Total Proficient	
			Number	Percent	Number	Percent	Number	Percent	Number	Percent	Number	Percent
Elementary 10	Grade 4	2002-03 (*n*=48)	2	4%	3	6%	24	50%	19	40%	**43**	**90%**
		2003-04 (*n*=53)	7	13%	6	11%	29	55%	11	21%	**40**	**75%**
		2004-05 (*n*=51)	3	6%	6	12%	27	53%	15	29%	**42**	**82%**
		2005-06 (*n*=48)	3	6%	2	4%	24	50%	19	40%	**43**	**90%**
Elementary 11	Grade 4	2002-03 (*n*=35)	5	14%	1	3%	27	77%	2	6%	**29**	**83%**
		2003-04 (*n*=45)	7	16%	9	20%	24	53%	5	11%	**29**	**64%**
		2004-05 (*n*=36)	4	11%	3	8%	26	72%	3	8%	**29**	**81%**
		2005-06 (*n*=52)	4	8%	9	17%	31	60%	8	15%	**39**	**75%**
Middle 1	Grade 8	2002-03 (*n*=313)	17	5%	36	12%	180	58%	80	26%	**260**	**83%**
		2003-04 (*n*=315)	23	7%	38	12%	190	61%	64	20%	**254**	**81%**
		2004-05 (*n*=315)	26	8%	46	15%	180	57%	63	20%	**243**	**77%**
		2005-06 (*n*=338)	29	9%	40	12%	204	60%	65	19%	**269**	**80%**
Middle 2	Grade 8	2002-03 (*n*=239)	22	9%	23	10%	144	60%	50	21%	**194**	**81%**
		2003-04 (*n*=220)	23	11%	25	11%	131	60%	41	19%	**172**	**79%**
		2004-05 (*n*=235)	30	13%	25	11%	132	56%	48	21%	**180**	**77%**
		2005-06 (*n*=220)	23	10%	26	12%	133	60%	38	17%	**171**	**78%**
High 1	Grade 11	2002-03 (*n*=317)	21	7%	22	7%	170	55%	94	31%	**264**	**86%**
		2003-04 (*n*=293)	16	5%	29	10%	163	56%	85	29%	**248**	**85%**
		2004-05 (*n*=297)	20	7%	30	10%	180	61%	67	23%	**247**	**83%**
		2005-06 (*n*=317)	16	5%	34	11%	175	55%	92	29%	**267**	**84%**
High 2	Grade 11	2002-03 (*n*=327)	24	7%	33	10%	174	54%	96	30%	**270**	**83%**
		2003-04 (*n*=380)	23	6%	45	12%	219	58%	93	24%	**312**	**82%**
		2004-05 (*n*=355)	31	9%	35	10%	182	51%	107	30%	**289**	**81%**
		2005-06 (*n*=332)	35	11%	28	8%	191	58%	78	23%	**269**	**81%**

Figure 6.11 shows the Reading proficiency levels for the district by grade level from 2002-03 to 2005-06.

Look Fors: **Student learning differences by gender within and across schools, and over time.**

Planning Implications: **Are all schools effective in serving males and females, at all grade levels? Are the scores consistent over time?**

Figure 6.11

Canyon View School District Reading Proficiency Levels
Number and Percentage by School, Grade Level, and Gender, 2002-03 to 2005-06

School and Grade Level			Gender	Year	Novice		Nearing Proficiency		Proficient		Advanced		Total Proficient	
					Number	Percent	Number	Percent	Number	Percent	Number	Percent	Number	Percent
ELEMENTARY	Elementary 1	Grade 4	Female	2002-03 (*n*=22)	1	5%			14	64%	7	32%	**21**	**95%**
				2003-04 (*n*=27)	1	5%	4	20%	11	55%	4	20%	**15**	**75%**
				2004-05 (*n*=14)	1	7%	2	14%	10	71%	1	7%	**11**	**79%**
				2005-06 (*n*=27)	3	11%	4	15%	14	52%	6	22%	**20**	**74%**
			Male	2002-03 (*n*=13)	2	15%	2	15%	9	69%			**9**	**69%**
				2003-04 (*n*=29)	2	7%	4	14%	18	62%	5	17%	**23**	**79%**
				2004-05 (*n*=22)	1	5%	1	5%	13	59%	7	32%	**20**	**91%**
				2005-06 (*n*=19)	3	16%	3	16%	10	53%	3	16%	**13**	**68%**
	Elementary 2	Grade 4	Female	2002-03 (*n*=13)	2	15%			10	77%	1	8%	**11**	**85%**
				2003-04 (*n*=24)	3	13%	1	4%	19	79%	1	4%	**20**	**83%**
				2004-05 (*n*=17)	5	29%	1	6%	9	53%	2	12%	**11**	**65%**
				2005-06 (*n*=10)			1	10%	7	70%	2	20%	**9**	**90%**
			Male	2002-03 (*n*=26)	4	15%	6	23%	10	38%	6	23%	**16**	**62%**
				2003-04 (*n*=20)	2	10%	2	10%	16	80%			**16**	**80%**
				2004-05 (*n*=24)	2	8%	2	8%	13	54%	7	29%	**20**	**83%**
				2005-06 (*n*=20)	3	15%	1	5%	10	50%	6	30%	**16**	**80%**
	Elementary 3	Grade 4	Female	2002-03 (*n*=27)	5	19%	1	4%	12	44%	9	33%	**21**	**78%**
				2003-04 (*n*=20)	1	5%	1	5%	10	50%	8	40%	**18**	**90%**
				2004-05 (*n*=26)			1	4%	18	69%	7	27%	**25**	**96%**
				2005-06 (*n*=22)	1	5%	1	5%	14	64%	6	27%	**20**	**91%**
			Male	2002-03 (*n*=21)	2	10%	1	5%	12	57%	6	29%	**18**	**86%**
				2003-04 (*n*=22)	1	5%	1	5%	16	73%	4	18%	**20**	**91%**
				2004-05 (*n*=23)	2	9%			12	52%	9	39%	**21**	**91%**
				2005-06 (*n*=24)	1	4%	3	13%	13	54%	7	29%	**20**	**83%**
	Elementary 4	Grade 4	Female	2002-03 (*n*=39)	1	3%	3	8%	22	56%	13	33%	**35**	**90%**
				2003-04 (*n*=28)			1	4%	21	75%	6	21%	**27**	**96%**
				2004-05 (*n*=38)			2	5%	21	55%	15	39%	**36**	**95%**
				2005-06 (*n*=34)	1	3%	3	9%	16	47%	14	41%	**30**	**88%**
			Male	2002-03 (*n*=38)			5	13%	21	55%	12	32%	**33**	**87%**
				2003-04 (*n*=46)	1	2%	2	4%	33	72%	10	22%	**43**	**93%**
				2004-05 (*n*=32)			4	13%	19	59%	9	28%	**28**	**88%**
				2005-06 (*n*=43)	1	2%	1	2%	24	56%	17	40%	**41**	**95%**
	Elementary 5	Grade 4	Female	2002-03 (*n*=20)	1	5%	2	10%	8	40%	9	45%	**17**	**85%**
				2003-04 (*n*=25)			1	4%	17	68%	7	28%	**24**	**96%**
				2004-05 (*n*=18)	1	6%	2	11%	10	56%	5	28%	**15**	**83%**
				2005-06 (*n*=26)	1	4%	3	12%	15	58%	7	27%	**22**	**85%**
			Male	2002-03 (*n*=21)	1	5%	2	10%	12	57%	6	29%	**18**	**86%**
				2003-04 (*n*=21)			2	10%	12	57%	7	33%	**19**	**90%**
				2004-05 (*n*=25)	4	16%	1	4%	12	48%	8	32%	**20**	**80%**
				2005-06 (*n*=16)			3	19%	9	56%	4	25%	**13**	**81%**

Figure 6.11 (Continued)

Canyon View School District Reading Proficiency Levels
Number and Percentage by School, Grade Level, and Gender, 2002-03 to 2005-06

School and Grade Level	Gender	Year	Novice		Nearing Proficiency		Proficient		Advanced		Total Proficient	
			Number	Percent	Number	Percent	Number	Percent	Number	Percent	Number	Percent
ELEMENTARY — Elementary 6 — Grade 4	Female	2002-03 (*n*=10)					6	60%	4	40%	**10**	**100%**
		2003-04 (*n*=17)			1	6%	12	71%	4	24%	**16**	**94%**
		2004-05 (*n*=13)			2	15%	7	54%	4	31%	**11**	**85%**
		2005-06 (*n*=7)					5	71%	2	29%	**7**	**100%**
	Male	2002-03 (*n*=21)			1	5%	9	43%	11	52%	**20**	**95%**
		2003-04 (*n*=20)			1	5%	10	50%	9	45%	**19**	**95%**
		2004-05 (*n*=20)					12	60%	8	40%	**20**	**100%**
		2005-06 (*n*=22)			2	9%	14	64%	6	27%	**20**	**91%**
Elementary 7 — Grade 4	Female	2002-03 (*n*=31)			3	10%	25	81%	3	10%	**28**	**90%**
		2003-04 (*n*=16)	1	6%	1	6%	10	63%	4	25%	**14**	**88%**
		2004-05 (*n*=20)	1	5%	2	10%	14	70%	3	15%	**17**	**85%**
		2005-06 (*n*=20)	2	10%			13	65%	5	25%	**18**	**90%**
	Male	2002-03 (*n*=27)	2	7%	6	22%	16	59%	3	11%	**19**	**70%**
		2003-04 (*n*=15)	3	20%	1	7%	9	60%	2	13%	**11**	**73%**
		2004-05 (*n*=19)	2	11%	1	5%	12	63%	4	21%	**16**	**84%**
		2005-06 (*n*=23)			5	22%	12	52%	6	26%	**18**	**78%**
Elementary 8 — Grade 4	Female	2002-03 (*n*=21)	3	14%	1	5%	11	52%	6	29%	**17**	**81%**
		2003-04 (*n*=16)					11	69%	5	31%	**16**	**100%**
		2004-05 (*n*=14)	1	7%	3	21%	6	43%	4	29%	**10**	**71%**
		2005-06 (*n*=20)					12	60%	8	40%	**20**	**100%**
	Male	2002-03 (*n*=17)			1	6%	9	53%	7	41%	**16**	**94%**
		2003-04 (*n*=19)	2	11%	3	16%	9	47%	5	26%	**14**	**74%**
		2004-05 (*n*=21)			2	10%	14	67%	5	24%	**19**	**90%**
		2005-06 (*n*=16)	1	6%	2	13%	9	56%	4	25%	**13**	**81%**
Elementary 9 — Grade 4	Female	2002-03 (*n*=39)	1	3%	3	8%	27	68%	9	23%	**36**	**90%**
		2003-04 (*n*=39)	2	5%	3	8%	23	59%	11	28%	**34**	**87%**
		2004-05 (*n*=28)	1	4%	1	4%	14	50%	12	43%	**26**	**93%**
		2005-06 (*n*=44)	4	9%	2	5%	24	55%	14	32%	**38**	**86%**
	Male	2002-03 (*n*=33)	3	9%			22	67%	8	24%	**30**	**91%**
		2003-04 (*n*=34)			6	18%	24	71%	4	12%	**28**	**82%**
		2004-05 (*n*=33)	3	9%	3	9%	20	61%	7	21%	**27**	**82%**
		2005-06 (*n*=34)	2	6%	5	15%	20	59%	7	21%	**27**	**79%**
Elementary 10 — Grade 4	Female	2002-03 (*n*=22)	1	5%	2	9%	9	41%	10	45%	**19**	**86%**
		2003-04 (*n*=24)	2	8%			15	63%	7	29%	**22**	**92%**
		2004-05 (*n*=29)	2	7%	2	7%	14	48%	11	38%	**25**	**86%**
		2005-06 (*n*=28)	2	7%	2	7%	11	39%	13	46%	**24**	**86%**
	Male	2002-03 (*n*=26)	1	4%	1	4%	15	58%	9	35%	**24**	**92%**
		2003-04 (*n*=29)	5	17%	6	21%	14	48%	4	14%	**18**	**62%**
		2004-05 (*n*=22)	1	5%	4	18%	13	59%	4	18%	**17**	**77%**
		2005-06 (*n*=20)	1	5%			13	65%	6	30%	**19**	**95%**

Figure 6.11 (Continued)

Canyon View School District Reading Proficiency Levels
Number and Percentage by School, Grade Level, and Gender, 2002-03 to 2005-06

School and Grade Level			Gender	Year	Novice		Nearing Proficiency		Proficient		Advanced		Total Proficient	
					Number	Percent	Number	Percent	Number	Percent	Number	Percent	Number	Percent
ELEMENTARY	Elementary 11	Grade 4	Female	2002-03 (*n*=21)	2	10%			17	81%	2	10%	**19**	**90%**
				2003-04 (*n*=18)	4	22%	4	22%	8	44%	2	11%	**10**	**56%**
				2004-05 (*n*=18)	2	11%	2	11%	12	67%	2	11%	**14**	**78%**
				2005-06 (*n*=23)			3	13%	18	78%	2	9%	**20**	**87%**
			Male	2002-03 (*n*=14)	3	21%	1	7%	10	71%			**10**	**71%**
				2003-04 (*n*=27)	3	11%	5	19%	16	59%	3	11%	**19**	**70%**
				2004-05 (*n*=18)	2	11%	1	6%	14	78%	1	6%	**15**	**83%**
				2005-06 (*n*=29)	4	14%	6	21%	13	45%	6	21%	**19**	**66%**
MIDDLE	Middle 1	Grade 8	Female	2002-03 (*n*=155)	4	3%	23	15%	86	56%	42	27%	**128**	**83%**
				2003-04 (*n*=162)	11	7%	16	10%	102	63%	33	20%	**135**	**83%**
				2004-05 (*n*=141)	9	6%	19	13%	83	59%	30	21%	**113**	**80%**
				2005-06 (*n*=176)	12	7%	17	10%	121	69%	26	15%	**147**	**84%**
			Male	2002-03 (*n*=158)	13	8%	13	8%	94	59%	38	24%	**132**	**84%**
				2003-04 (*n*=153)	12	8%	22	14%	88	58%	31	20%	**119**	**78%**
				2004-05 (*n*=174)	17	10%	27	16%	97	56%	33	19%	**130**	**75%**
				2005-06 (*n*=162)	17	10%	23	14%	83	51%	39	24%	**122**	**75%**
	Middle 2	Grade 8	Female	2002-03 (*n*=132)	9	7%	12	9%	83	63%	28	21%	**111**	**84%**
				2003-04 (*n*=98)	5	5%	13	13%	63	64%	17	17%	**80**	**82%**
				2004-05 (*n*=109)	16	15%	7	6%	62	57%	24	22%	**86**	**80%**
				2005-06 (*n*=110)	12	11%	8	7%	71	65%	19	17%	**90**	**82%**
			Male	2002-03 (*n*=107)	13	12%	11	10%	61	57%	22	21%	**83**	**78%**
				2003-04 (*n*=122)	18	15%	12	10%	68	57%	24	20%	**92**	**77%**
				2004-05 (*n*=126)	14	11%	18	14%	70	56%	24	19%	**94**	**75%**
				2005-06 (*n*=110)	11	10%	18	16%	62	56%	19	17%	**81**	**74%**
HIGH	High 1	Grade 11	Female	2002-03 (*n*=164)	8	5%	12	7%	88	54%	56	34%	**144**	**88%**
				2003-04 (*n*=139)	5	4%	17	12%	71	51%	46	33%	**117**	**84%**
				2004-05 (*n*=153)	7	5%	11	7%	94	61%	41	27%	**135**	**88%**
				2005-06 (*n*=159)	4	3%	23	14%	78	49%	54	34%	**132**	**83%**
			Male	2002-03 (*n*=143)	13	9%	10	7%	82	57%	38	27%	**120**	**84%**
				2003-04 (*n*=154)	11	7%	12	8%	92	60%	39	25%	**131**	**85%**
				2004-05 (*n*=144)	13	9%	19	13%	86	60%	26	18%	**112**	**78%**
				2005-06 (*n*=158)	12	8%	11	7%	97	61%	38	24%	**135**	**85%**
	High 2	Grade 11	Female	2002-03 (*n*=165)	11	7%	21	13%	93	57%	40	24%	**133**	**81%**
				2003-04 (*n*=190)	7	4%	20	11%	118	62%	45	24%	**163**	**86%**
				2004-05 (*n*=174)	10	6%	14	8%	96	55%	54	31%	**150**	**86%**
				2005-06 (*n*=169)	10	6%	10	6%	109	65%	40	24%	**149**	**88%**
			Male	2002-03 (*n*=162)	13	8%	12	7%	81	50%	56	35%	**137**	**85%**
				2003-04 (*n*=190)	16	8%	25	13%	101	53%	48	25%	**149**	**78%**
				2004-05 (*n*=181)	21	12%	21	12%	86	48%	53	29%	**139**	**77%**
				2005-06 (*n*=163)	25	15%	18	11%	82	50%	38	23%	**120**	**74%**

Figure 6.12 shows the Reading proficiency levels for the district by grade level and ethnicity from 2002-03 to 2005-06. *Note:* the numbers in some of the student groups are very small. These analyses are for district/school review only. These tables would never be shown to the public.

Look Fors: **Differences in Reading performance by ethnicity. Proficiency increasing and gaps decreasing over time.**

Planning Implications: **Are the instructional needs of all ethnicities being met at each grade level?**

Figure 6.12

Canyon View School District Reading Proficiency Levels
Number and Percentage by Grade Level and Ethnicity, 2002-03 to 2005-06

Grade Level	and Ethnicity	Year	Novice		Nearing Proficiency		Proficient		Advanced		Total Proficient	
			Number	Percent	Number	Percent	Number	Percent	Number	Percent	Number	Percent
GRADE 4	American Indian	2002-03 (*n*=23)	6	26%	3	13%	13	57%	1	4%	**14**	**61%**
		2003-04 (*n*=28)	2	7%	6	21%	17	61%	3	11%	**20**	**71%**
		2004-05 (*n*=30)	6	19%	4	13%	18	58%	3	10%	**21**	**68%**
		2005-06 (*n*=33)	3	9%	3	9%	18	55%	9	27%	**27**	**82%**
	Asian	2002-03 (*n*=2)					2	100%			**2**	**100%**
		2003-04 (*n*=7)	1	14%			5	71%	1	14%	**6**	**86%**
		2004-05 (*n*=5)					4	80%	1	20%	**5**	**100%**
	Black	2002-03 (*n*=2)					2	100%			**2**	**100%**
		2003-04 (*n*=4)					4	100%			**4**	**100%**
		2004-05 (*n*=7)					7	100%			**7**	**100%**
		2005-06 (*n*=6)			5	83%	1	17%			**1**	**17%**
	Hispanic	2002-03 (*n*=11)					9	82%	2	18%	**11**	**100%**
		2003-04 (*n*=8)					6	75%	2	25%	**8**	**100%**
		2004-05 (*n*=11)	2	18%			8	73%	1	9%	**9**	**82%**
		2005-06 (*n*=12)	3	25%	2	17%	5	42%	2	17%	**7**	**58%**
	Pacific Islander	2002-03 (*n*=2)					1	50%	1	50%	**2**	**100%**
		2003-04 (*n*=1)					1	100%			**1**	**100%**
		2005-06 (*n*=1)					1	100%			**1**	**100%**
	White	2002-03 (*n*=483)	29	6%	38	8%	279	58%	137	28%	**416**	**86%**
		2003-04 (*n*=481)	30	6%	44	9%	301	63%	106	22%	**407**	**85%**
		2004-05 (*n*=440)	23	5%	35	8%	252	57%	130	30%	**382**	**87%**
		2005-06 (*n*=475)	24	5%	40	8%	271	57%	140	29%	**411**	**87%**

Figure 6.12 (Continued)

Canyon View School District Reading Proficiency Levels
Number and Percentage by Grade Level and Ethnicity, 2002-03 to 2005-06

Grade Level and Ethnicity		Year	Novice		Nearing Proficiency		Proficient		Advanced		Total Proficient	
			Number	Percent	Number	Percent	Number	Percent	Number	Percent	Number	Percent
GRADE 8	American Indian	2002-03 (*n*=18)	4	22%	2	11%	10	56%	2	11%	**12**	**67%**
		2003-04 (*n*=32)	6	19%	2	6%	20	63%	4	13%	**24**	**75%**
		2004-05 (*n*=22)	4	18%	5	23%	10	45%	3	14%	**13**	**59%**
		2005-06 (*n*=31)	5	16%	8	26%	15	48%	3	10%	**18**	**58%**
	Asian	2002-03 (*n*=9)			1	11%	6	67%	2	22%	**8**	**89%**
		2003-04 (*n*=12)					9	82%	3	27%	**12**	**100%**
		2004-05 (*n*=7)	1	14%	1	14%	5	71%			**5**	**71%**
		2005-06 (*n*=6)	1	17%			4	67%	1	17%	**5**	**83%**
	Black	2002-03 (*n*=2)					1	50%	1	50%	**2**	**100%**
		2003-04 (*n*=2)					1	50%	1	50%	**2**	**100%**
		2004-05 (*n*=4)			1	25%	3	75%			**3**	**75%**
		2005-06 (*n*=6)	1	17%			4	67%	1	17%	**5**	**83%**
	Hispanic	2002-03 (*n*=4)	1	25%			2	50%	1	25%	**3**	**75%**
		2003-04 (*n*=8)			4	50%	2	25%	2	25%	**4**	**50%**
		2004-05 (*n*=7)	1	14%	2	29%	3	43%	1	14%	**4**	**57%**
		2005-06 (*n*=13)	2	15%	2	15%	9	69%			**9**	**69%**
	Pacific Islander	2002-03 (*n*=1)	1	100%							**0**	
	White	2002-03 (*n*=521)	34	7%	56	11%	307	59%	124	24%	**431**	**83%**
		2003-04 (*n*=481)	40	8%	57	12%	289	60%	95	20%	**384**	**80%**
		2004-05 (*n*=511)	50	10%	62	12%	291	57%	108	21%	**399**	**78%**
		2005-06 (*n*=506)	43	9%	56	11%	305	60%	102	20%	**407**	**80%**
GRADE 11	American Indian	2002-03 (*n*=14)	2	14%	3	21%	5	36%	4	29%	**9**	**64%**
		2003-04 (*n*=19)	3	16%	3	16%	9	47%	4	21%	**13**	**68%**
		2004-05 (*n*=27)	4	15%	4	15%	16	59%	3	11%	**19**	**70%**
		2005-06 (*n*=19)	2	11%	2	11%	11	58%	4	21%	**15**	**79%**
	Asian	2002-03 (*n*=2)					2	100%			**2**	**100%**
		2003-04 (*n*=4)					3	75%	1	25%	**4**	**100%**
		2004-05 (*n*=15)	3	20%	1	7%	5	33%	6	40%	**11**	**73%**
		2003-04 (*n*=11)	2	18%			8	73%	1	9%	**9**	**82%**
	Black	2002-03 (*n*=1)					1	100%			**1**	**100%**
		2004-05 (*n*=2)	1	50%			1	50%			**1**	**50%**
		2005-06 (*n*=2)			1	50%			1	50%	**1**	**50%**
	Hispanic	2002-03 (*n*=4)	1	25%			1	25%	2	50%	**3**	**75%**
		2003-04 (*n*=5)			1	20%	4	80%			**4**	**80%**
		2004-05 (*n*=8)					7	88%	1	13%	**8**	**100%**
		2005-06 (*n*=6)	3	50%			1	17%	2	33%	**3**	**50%**
	White	2002-03 (*n*=631)	47	7%	56	9%	343	55%	185	29%	**528**	**84%**
		2003-04 (*n*=666)	38	6%	77	12%	377	57%	174	26%	**551**	**83%**
		2004-05 (*n*=632)	53	8%	66	10%	348	55%	165	26%	**513**	**81%**
		2005-06 (*n*=617)	44	7%	62	10%	349	57%	162	26%	**511**	**83%**

Figure 6.13 shows the Reading proficiency levels for the district by school, grade level, and ethnicity from 2002-03 to 2005-06. *Note:* the numbers in some of the student groups are very small. These analyses are for district/school review only.

Look Fors:	**Differences in Reading performance by ethnicity. Proficiency increasing and gaps decreasing over time.**
Planning Implications:	**Are the instructional needs of all ethnicities being met at each grade level and in each school?**

Figure 6.13

Canyon View School District Reading Proficiency Levels
Number and Percentage by School, Grade Level, and Ethnicity, 2002-03 to 2005-06

School, Grade Level, and Ethnicity			Year	Novice		Nearing Proficiency		Proficient		Advanced		Total Proficient	
				Number	Percent	Number	Percent	Number	Percent	Number	Percent	Number	Percent
ELEMENTARY 1	Grade 4	American Indian	2002-03 (*n*=2)			1	50%	1	50%			**1**	**50%**
			2003-04 (*n*=3)			1	33%	2	67%			**2**	**67%**
			2004-05 (*n*=2)							2	100%	**2**	**100%**
			2005-06 (*n*=7)	1	14%	1	14%	5	71%			**5**	**71%**
		Asian	2002-03 (*n*=1)					1	100%			**1**	**100%**
			2003-04 (*n*=2)					2	100%			**2**	**100%**
		Black	2004-05 (*n*=1)					1	100%			**1**	**100%**
			2005-06 (*n*=1)			1	100%					**0**	
		Hispanic	2002-03 (*n*=3)					3	100%			**3**	**100%**
			2003-04 (*n*=2)					1	50%	1	50%	**2**	**100%**
			2005-06 (*n*=2)	2	100%							**0**	
		Pacific Islander	2002-03 (*n*=1)							1	100%	**1**	**100%**
		White	2002-03 (*n*=29)	3	10%	1	3%	19	66%	6	21%	**25**	**87%**
			2003-04 (*n*=43)	3	7%	7	16%	25	58%	8	19%	**33**	**77%**
			2004-05 (*n*=31)	2	6%	3	10%	20	65%	6	19%	**26**	**84%**
			2005-06 (*n*=36)	3	8%	5	14%	19	53%	9	25%	**28**	**78%**
ELEMENTARY 2	Grade 4	American Indian	2002-03 (*n*=2)	1	50%	1	50%					**0**	
			2003-04 (*n*=3)					3	100%			**3**	**100%**
			2004-05 (*n*=5)	2	40%			2	40%	1	20%	**3**	**60%**
			2005-06 (*n*=3)					1	33%	2	67%	**3**	**100%**
		Asian	2002-03 (*n*=2)					2	100%			**2**	**100%**
		Black	2002-03 (*n*=1)					1	100%			**1**	**100%**
			2003-04 (*n*=3)					3	100%			**3**	**100%**
		Hispanic	2003-04 (*n*=1)					1	100%			**1**	**100%**
			2004-05 (*n*=1)					1	100%			**1**	**100%**
			2005-06 (*n*=1)					1	100%			**1**	**100%**
		White	2002-03 (*n*=35)	5	14%	5	14%	18	51%	7	20%	**25**	**71%**
			2003-04 (*n*=39)	5	13%	3	8%	30	77%	1	3%	**31**	**79%**
			2004-05 (*n*=32)	5	16%	3	9%	16	50%	8	25%	**24**	**75%**
			2005-06 (*n*=26)	3	12%	2	8%	15	58%	6	23%	**21**	**81%**
ELEMENTARY 3	Grade 4	American Indian	2002-03 (*n*=5)	3	60%			2	40%			**2**	**40%**
			2004-05 (*n*=2)					2	100%			**2**	**100%**
			2005-06 (*n*=3)	1	33%	1	33%	1	33%			**1**	**33%**
		Black	2004-05 (*n*=1)					1	100%			**1**	**100%**
			2005-06 (*n*=1)			1	100%					**0**	
		Hispanic	2003-04 (*n*=2)					2	100%			**2**	**100%**
			2004-05 (*n*=2)	1	50%			1	50%			**1**	**50%**
		White	2002-03 (*n*=43)	4	9%	2	5%	22	51%	15	35%	**37**	**86%**
			2003-04 (*n*=40)	2	5%	2	5%	24	60%	12	30%	**36**	**90%**
			2004-05 (*n*=44)	1	2%	1	2%	26	59%	16	36%	**42**	**95%**
			2005-06 (*n*=42)	1	2%	2	5%	26	62%	13	31%	**39**	**93%**

Figure 6.13 (Continued)

Canyon View School District Reading Proficiency Levels
Number and Percentage by School, Grade Level, and Ethnicity, 2002-03 to 2005-06

School	Grade Level	Ethnicity	Year	Novice		Nearing Proficiency		Proficient		Advanced		Total Proficient	
				Number	Percent	Number	Percent	Number	Percent	Number	Percent	Number	Percent
ELEMENTARY 4	Grade 4	American Indian	2002-03 (*n*=2)					2	100%			**2**	**100%**
			2003-04 (*n*=3)					3	100%			**3**	**100%**
			2004-05 (*n*=6)			2	33%	4	67%			**4**	**67%**
			2005-06 (*n*=3)					1	33%	2	67%	**3**	**100%**
		Asian	2003-04 (*n*=1)	1	100%							**0**	
		Black	2002-03 (*n*=1)					1	100%			**1**	**100%**
			2005-06 (*n*=2)			1	50%	1	50%			**1**	**50%**
		Hispanic	2002-03 (*n*=2)					1	50%	1	50%	**2**	**100%**
			2003-04 (*n*=1)					1	100%			**1**	**100%**
			2005-06 (*n*=4)	1	25%	1	25%			2	50%	**2**	**50%**
		White	2002-03 (*n*=75)	1	1%	8	11%	39	54%	24	33%	**63**	**88%**
			2003-04 (*n*=69)			3	4%	50	72%	16	23%	**66**	**96%**
			2004-05 (*n*=64)			4	6%	36	56%	24	38%	**60**	**94%**
			2005-06 (*n*=68)	1	1%	2	3%	38	56%	27	40%	**65**	**96%**
ELEMENTARY 5	Grade 4	American Indian	2002-03 (*n*=2)			1	50%			1	50%	**1**	**50%**
			2003-04 (*n*=2)			1	50%	1	50%			**1**	**50%**
			2004-05 (*n*=2)			1	50%	1	50%			**1**	**50%**
			2005-06 (*n*=2)					1	50%	1	50%	**2**	**100%**
		Asian	2003-04 (*n*=1)					1	100%			**1**	**100%**
			2004-05 (*n*=2)					1	50%	1	50%	**2**	**100%**
		Black	2002-03 (*n*=1)					1	100%			**1**	**100%**
			2005-06 (*n*=1)			1	100%					**0**	
		Hispanic	2003-04 (*n*=1)							1	100%	**1**	**100%**
			2004-05 (*n*=3)	1	33%			2	67%			**2**	**67%**
			2005-06 (*n*=2)			1	50%	1	50%			**1**	**50%**
		White	2002-03 (*n*=38)	2	5%	3	8%	19	50%	14	37%	**33**	**87%**
			2003-04 (*n*=42)			2	5%	27	64%	13	31%	**40**	**95%**
			2004-05 (*n*=36)	4	11%	2	6%	18	50%	12	33%	**30**	**83%**
			2005-06 (*n*=37)	1	3%	4	11%	22	59%	10	27%	**32**	**86%**
ELEMENTARY 6	Grade 4	American Indian	2003-04 (*n*=2)					2	100%			**2**	**100%**
			2004-05 (*n*=1)					1	100%			**1**	**100%**
		Hispanic	2002-03 (*n*=1)					1	100%			**1**	**100%**
		White	2002-03 (*n*=30)			1	3%	14	47%	15	50%	**29**	**97%**
			2003-04 (*n*=35)			2	6%	20	57%	13	37%	**33**	**94%**
			2004-05 (*n*=32)			2	6%	18	56%	12	38%	**30**	**94%**
			2005-06 (*n*=29)			2	7%	19	66%	8	28%	**27**	**93%**

Figure 6.13 (Continued)

Canyon View School District Reading Proficiency Levels
Number and Percentage by School, Grade Level, and Ethnicity, 2002-03 to 2005-06

School, Grade Level, and Ethnicity			Year	Novice		Nearing Proficiency		Proficient		Advanced		Total Proficient	
				Number	Percent	Number	Percent	Number	Percent	Number	Percent	Number	Percent
ELEMENTARY 7	Grade 4	American Indian	2002-03 (*n*=2)					2	100%			**2**	**100%**
			2003-04 (*n*=1)							1	100%	**1**	**100%**
			2004-05 (*n*=1)					1	100%			**1**	**100%**
			2005-06 (*n*=3)					3	100%			**3**	**100%**
		Asian	2003-04 (*n*=1)					1	100%			**1**	**100%**
		Black	2005-06 (*n*=1)			1	100%					**0**	
		White	2002-03 (*n*=56)	2	4%	9	16%	39	70%	6	11%	**45**	**80%**
			2003-04 (*n*=29)	4	14%	2	7%	18	62%	5	17%	**23**	**79%**
			2004-05 (*n*=38)	3	8%	3	8%	25	66%	7	18%	**32**	**84%**
			2005-06 (*n*=39)	2	5%	4	10%	22	56%	11	28%	**33**	**85%**
ELEMENTARY 8	Grade 4	American Indian	2003-04 (*n*=1)	1	100%							**0**	
		Asian	2003-04 (*n*=1)					1	100%			**1**	**100%**
		Hispanic	2005-06 (*n*=1)					1	100%			**1**	**100%**
		White	2002-03 (*n*=38)	3	8%	2	5%	20	53%	13	34%	**33**	**87%**
			2003-04 (*n*=33)	1	3%	3	9%	19	58%	10	30%	**29**	**88%**
			2004-05 (*n*=35)	1	3%	5	14%	20	57%	9	26%	**29**	**83%**
			2005-06 (*n*=35)	1	3%	2	6%	20	57%	12	34%	**32**	**91%**
ELEMENTARY 9	Grade 4	American Indian	2002-03 (*n*=4)	1	25%			3	75%			**3**	**75%**
			2003-04 (*n*=3)			1	33%	2	67%			**2**	**67%**
			2004-05 (*n*=5)	2	40%	1	20%	2	40%			**2**	**40%**
			2005-06 (*n*=6)	1	17%	1	17%	2	33%	2	33%	**4**	**67%**
		Asian	2003-04 (*n*=1)					1	100%			**1**	**100%**
			2004-05 (*n*=1)					1	100%			**1**	**100%**
		Black	2003-04 (*n*=2)					2	100%			**2**	**100%**
			2004-05 (*n*=1)					1	100%			**1**	**100%**
		Hispanic	2002-03 (*n*=3)					2	67%	1	33%	**3**	**100%**
			2004-05 (*n*=3)					2	67%	1	33%	**3**	**100%**
			2005-06 (*n*=1)					1	100%			**1**	**100%**
		White	2002-03 (*n*=66)	3	5%	3	5%	44	67%	16	24%	**60**	**91%**
			2003-04 (*n*=67)	2	3%	8	12%	42	63%	15	22%	**57**	**85%**
			2004-05 (*n*=51)	2	4%	3	6%	28	55%	18	35%	**46**	**90%**
			2005-06 (*n*=71)	5	7%	6	8%	41	58%	19	27%	**60**	**85%**

Figure 6.13 (Continued)

Canyon View School District Reading Proficiency Levels
Number and Percentage by School, Grade Level, and Ethnicity, 2002-03 to 2005-06

School, Grade Level, and Ethnicity			Year	Novice		Nearing Proficiency		Proficient		Advanced		Total Proficient	
				Number	Percent	Number	Percent	Number	Percent	Number	Percent	Number	Percent
ELEMENTARY 10	Grade 4	American Indian	2002-03 (*n*=3)					3	100%			**3**	**100%**
			2003-04 (*n*=5)			1	20%	3	60%	1	20%	**4**	**80%**
			2004-05 (*n*=2)	1	50%			1	50%			**1**	**50%**
			2005-06 (*n*=5)					3	60%	2	40%	**5**	**100%**
		Black	2003-04 (*n*=1)					1	100%			**1**	**100%**
			2004-05 (*n*=1)					1	100%			**1**	**100%**
		Hispanic	2002-03 (*n*=2)					2	100%			**2**	**100%**
			2003-04 (*n*=1)					1	100%			**1**	**100%**
			2004-05 (*n*=1)					1	100%			**1**	**100%**
			2005-06 (*n*=1)					1	100%			**1**	**100%**
		Pacific Islander	2003-04 (*n*=1)					1	100%			**1**	**100%**
		White	2002-03 (*n*=43)	2	5%	3	7%	19	44%	19	44%	**38**	**88%**
			2003-04 (*n*=45)	7	16%	5	11%	23	51%	10	22%	**33**	**73%**
			2004-05 (*n*=47)	2	4%	6	13%	24	51%	15	32%	**39**	**83%**
			2005-06 (*n*=42)	3	7%	2	5%	20	48%	17	40%	**37**	**88%**
ELEMENTARY 11	Grade 4	American Indian	2002-03 (*n*=1)	1	100%							**0**	
			2003-04 (*n*=5)	1	20%	2	40%	1	20%	1	20%	**2**	**40%**
			2004-05 (*n*=5)	1	20%			4	80%			**4**	**80%**
			2005-06 (*n*=1)					1	100%			**1**	**100%**
		Asian	2003-04 (*n*=1)							1	100%	**1**	**100%**
		Hispanic	2004-05 (*n*=1)					1	100%			**1**	**100%**
		Pacific Islander	2002-03 (*n*=1)					1	100%			**1**	**100%**
			2005-06 (*n*=1)					1	100%			**1**	**100%**
		White	2002-03 (*n*=33)	4	12%	1	3%	26	79%	2	6%	**28**	**85%**
			2003-04 (*n*=39)	6	15%	7	18%	23	59%	3	8%	**26**	**67%**
			2004-05 (*n*=30)	3	10%	3	10%	21	70%	3	10%	**24**	**80%**
			2005-06 (*n*=50)	4	8%	9	18%	29	58%	8	16%	**37**	**74%**

Figure 6.13 (Continued)

Canyon View School District Reading Proficiency Levels
Number and Percentage by School, Grade Level, and Ethnicity, 2002-03 to 2005-06

School, Grade Level, and Ethnicity			Year	Novice		Nearing Proficiency		Proficient		Advanced		Total Proficient	
				Number	Percent	Number	Percent	Number	Percent	Number	Percent	Number	Percent
MIDDLE 1	Grade 8	American Indian	2002-03 (*n*=7)					7	100%			**7**	**100%**
			2003-04 (*n*=8)	1	13%			7	88%			**7**	**88%**
			2004-05 (*n*=9)	1	11%	3	33%	5	56%			**5**	**56%**
			2005-06 (*n*=18)	4	22%	3	17%	8	44%	3	17%	**11**	**61%**
		Asian	2002-03 (*n*=4)					2	50%	2	50%	**4**	**100%**
			2003-04 (*n*=7)					5	71%	2	29%	**7**	**100%**
			2004-05 (*n*=3)					3	100%			**3**	**100%**
			2005-06 (*n*=3)					3	100%			**3**	**100%**
		Black	2002-03 (*n*=1)					1	100%			**1**	**100%**
			2003-04 (*n*=1)					1	100%			**1**	**100%**
			2004-05 (*n*=2)			1	50%	1	50%			**1**	**50%**
			2005-06 (*n*=3)					2	67%	1	33%	**3**	**100%**
		Hispanic	2002-03 (*n*=2)					2	100%			**2**	**100%**
			2003-04 (*n*=5)			3	60%	1	20%	1	20%	**2**	**40%**
			2004-05 (*n*=4)	1	25%	1	25%	1	25%	1	25%	**2**	**50%**
			2005-06 (*n*=10)	1	10%	2	20%	7	70%			**7**	**70%**
		Pacific Islander	2002-03 (*n*=1)	1	100%							**0**	
		White	2002-03 (*n*=298)	16	5%	36	12%	168	57%	78	26%	**246**	**83%**
			2003-04 (*n*=294)	22	7%	35	12%	176	60%	61	21%	**237**	**81%**
			2004-05 (*n*=297)	24	8%	41	14%	170	57%	62	21%	**232**	**78%**
			2005-06 (*n*=304)	24	8%	35	12%	184	61%	61	20%	**245**	**81%**
MIDDLE 2	Grade 8	American Indian	2002-03 (*n*=11)	4	36%	2	18%	3	27%	2	18%	**5**	**45%**
			2003-04 (*n*=24)	5	21%	2	8%	13	54%	4	17%	**17**	**71%**
			2004-05 (*n*=13)	3	23%	2	15%	5	38%	3	23%	**8**	**62%**
			2005-06 (*n*=13)	1	8%	5	38%	7	54%			**7**	**54%**
		Asian	2002-03 (*n*=5)			1	20%	4	80%			**4**	**80%**
			2003-04 (*n*=5)					4	80%	1	20%	**5**	**100%**
			2004-05 (*n*=4)	1	25%	1	25%	2	50%			**2**	**50%**
			2005-06 (*n*=3)	1	33%			1	33%	1	33%	**2**	**67%**
		Black	2002-03 (*n*=1)							1	100%	**1**	**100%**
			2003-04 (*n*=1)							1	100%	**1**	**100%**
			2004-05 (*n*=2)					2	100%			**2**	**100%**
			2005-06 (*n*=3)	1	33%			2	67%			**2**	**67%**
		Hispanic	2002-03 (*n*=2)	1	50%					1	50%	**1**	**50%**
			2003-04 (*n*=3)			1	33%	1	33%	1	33%	**2**	**67%**
			2004-05 (*n*=3)			1	33%	2	67%			**2**	**67%**
			2005-06 (*n*=3)	1	33%			2	67%			**2**	**67%**
		White	2002-03 (*n*=220)	17	8%	20	9%	137	62%	46	21%	**183**	**83%**
			2003-04 (*n*=187)	18	10%	22	12%	113	61%	34	18%	**147**	**79%**
			2004-05 (*n*=213)	26	12%	21	10%	121	57%	45	21%	**166**	**78%**
			2005-06 (*n*=198)	19	10%	21	11%	121	61%	37	19%	**158**	**80%**

Figure 6.13 (Continued)

Canyon View School District Reading Proficiency Levels
Number and Percentage by School, Grade Level, and Ethnicity, 2002-03 to 2005-06

School, Grade Level, and Ethnicity			Year	Novice		Nearing Proficiency		Proficient		Advanced		Total Proficient	
				Number	Percent	Number	Percent	Number	Percent	Number	Percent	Number	Percent
HIGH 1	Grade 11	American Indian	2002-03 (*n*=4)			2	50%	2	50%			**2**	**50%**
			2003-04 (*n*=9)	2	22%	1	11%	4	44%	2	22%	**6**	**67%**
			2004-05 (*n*=6)	1	17%	1	17%	4	67%			**4**	**67%**
			2005-06 (*n*=9)	1	11%			7	78%	1	11%	**8**	**89%**
		Asian	2002-03 (*n*=1)					1	100%			**1**	**100%**
			2003-04 (*n*=2)					2	100%			**2**	**100%**
			2004-05 (*n*=5)	1	20%			2	40%	2	40%	**4**	**80%**
			2005-06 (*n*=3)					2	67%	1	33%	**3**	**100%**
		Black	2004-05 (*n*=1)					1	100%			**1**	**100%**
			2005-06 (*n*=1)			1	100%					**0**	
		Hispanic	2003-04 (*n*=3)			1	33%	2	67%			**2**	**67%**
			2004-05 (*n*=4)					4	100%			**4**	**100%**
			2005-06 (*n*=2)					1	50%	1	50%	**2**	**100%**
		White	2002-03 (*n*=302)	21	7%	20	7%	167	55%	94	31%	**261**	**86%**
			2003-04 (*n*=279)	14	5%	27	10%	155	56%	83	30%	**238**	**85%**
			2004-05 (*n*=281)	18	6%	29	10%	169	60%	65	23%	**234**	**83%**
			2005-06 (*n*=302)	15	5%	33	11%	165	55%	89	29%	**254**	**84%**
HIGH 2	Grade 11	American Indian	2002-03 (*n*=8)	1	13%	1	13%	2	25%	4	50%	**6**	**75%**
			2003-04 (*n*=9)	1	11%	2	22%	4	44%	2	22%	**6**	**67%**
			2004-05 (*n*=17)	2	12%	2	12%	10	59%	3	18%	**13**	**76%**
			2005-06 (*n*=10)	1	10%	2	20%	4	40%	3	30%	**7**	**70%**
		Asian	2002-03 (*n*=1)					1	100%			**1**	**100%**
			2003-04 (*n*=2)					1	50%	1	50%	**2**	**100%**
			2004-05 (*n*=9)	1	11%	1	11%	3	33%	4	44%	**7**	**78%**
			2005-06 (*n*=7)	2	29%			5	71%			**5**	**71%**
		Black	2002-03 (*n*=1)					1	100%			**1**	**100%**
			2004-05 (*n*=1)	1	100%							**0**	
			2005-06 (*n*=1)							1	100%	**1**	**100%**
		Hispanic	2002-03 (*n*=4)	1	25%			1	25%	2	50%	**3**	**75%**
			2003-04 (*n*=2)					2	100%			**2**	**100%**
			2004-05 (*n*=4)					3	75%	1	25%	**4**	**100%**
			2005-06 (*n*=4)	3	75%					1	25%	**1**	**25%**
		White	2002-03 (*n*=313)	22	7%	32	10%	169	54%	90	29%	**259**	**83%**
			2003-04 (*n*=367)	22	6%	43	12%	212	58%	90	25%	**302**	**82%**
			2004-05 (*n*=324)	27	8%	32	10%	166	51%	99	31%	**265**	**82%**
			2005-06 (*n*=310)	29	9%	26	8%	182	59%	73	24%	**255**	**82%**

Figure 6.14 shows the Reading proficiency levels for the district by grade level and lunch status from 2002-03 to 2005-06.

Look Fors: **Differences in Reading proficiency levels for students who pay for their lunches, versus those who receive free/reduced priced lunches.**

Planning Implications: **Do teachers at the different grade levels know how to teach students who live in poverty how to read?**

Figure 6.14

Canyon View School District Reading Proficiency Levels Number and Percentage by Grade Level and Lunch Status, 2002-03 to 2005-06

Grade Level	Lunch Status	Year	Novice		Nearing Proficiency		Proficient		Advanced		Total Proficient	
			Number	Percent	Number	Percent	Number	Percent	Number	Percent	Number	Percent
Grade 4	Paid	2002-03 (*n*=384)	14	4%	22	6%	216	56%	132	34%	**348**	**91%**
		2003-04 (*n*=376)	18	5%	33	9%	229	61%	96	26%	**325**	**86%**
		2004-05 (*n*=331)	10	3%	19	6%	191	58%	111	34%	**302**	**91%**
		2005-06 (*n*=353)	9	3%	22	6%	197	56%	125	35%	**322**	**91%**
	Free/Reduced	2002-03 (*n*=138)	21	15%	19	14%	89	64%	9	7%	**98**	**71%**
		2003-04 (*n*=152)	15	10%	17	11%	104	68%	16	11%	**120**	**79%**
		2004-05 (*n*=155)	21	14%	19	12%	92	59%	23	15%	**115**	**74%**
		2005-06 (*n*=156)	20	13%	28	18%	87	56%	21	13%	**108**	**69%**
Grade 8	Paid	2002-03 (*n*=452)	23	5%	38	8%	271	60%	120	27%	**391**	**87%**
		2003-04 (*n*=450)	26	6%	53	12%	277	62%	94	21%	**371**	**83%**
		2004-05 (*n*=433)	32	7%	46	11%	258	60%	97	22%	**355**	**82%**
		2005-06 (*n*=429)	24	6%	47	11%	260	61%	98	23%	**358**	**83%**
	Free/Reduced	2002-03 (*n*=81)	15	19%	18	22%	40	49%	8	10%	**48**	**59%**
		2003-04 (*n*=89)	20	24%	10	12%	44	52%	11	13%	**55**	**65%**
		2004-05 (*n*=106)	22	21%	23	22%	47	45%	14	13%	**61**	**58%**
		2005-06 (*n*=119)	26	22%	19	16%	66	55%	8	7%	**74**	**62%**
Grade 11	Paid	2002-03 (*n*=633)	49	8%	55	9%	344	55%	185	29%	**529**	**84%**
		2003-04 (*n*=643)	34	5%	70	11%	367	57%	169	26%	**536**	**84%**
		2004-05 (*n*=626)	45	7%	63	10%	349	56%	169	27%	**518**	**83%**
		2005-06 (*n*=591)	36	6%	60	10%	339	57%	156	26%	**495**	**84%**
	Free/Reduced	2002-03 (*n*=19)	1	5%	4	21%	8	42%	6	32%	**14**	**74%**
		2003-04 (*n*=49)	7	14%	9	18%	23	47%	10	20%	**33**	**67%**
		2004-05 (*n*=53)	15	28%	7	13%	25	47%	6	11%	**31**	**58%**
		2005-06 (*n*=47)	11	23%	4	9%	19	40%	13	28%	**32**	**68%**

Figure 6.15 shows the Reading proficiency levels for the district by school, grade level, and lunch status, over time.

Look Fors:	**Particular schools that are being more or less effective with respect to teaching students who live in poverty how to read.**
Planning Implications:	**How well are the schools teaching all students to read?**

Figure 6.15

Canyon View School District Reading Proficiency Levels
Number and Percentage by School, Grade Level, and Lunch Status, 2002-03 to 2005-06

School	Grade Level	Lunch Status	Year	Novice		Nearing Proficiency		Proficient		Advanced		Total Proficient	
				Number	Percent	Number	Percent	Number	Percent	Number	Percent	Number	Percent
ELEMENTARY 1	Grade 4	Paid	2002-03 (*n*=24)	2	8%	1	4%	14	58%	7	29%	**21**	**88%**
ELEMENTARY 1	Grade 4	Paid	2003-04 (*n*=29)	1	3%	5	17%	15	52%	8	28%	**23**	**79%**
ELEMENTARY 1	Grade 4	Paid	2004-05 (*n*=24)	1	4%	1	4%	15	63%	7	29%	**22**	**92%**
ELEMENTARY 1	Grade 4	Paid	2005-06 (*n*=22)	1	5%	4	18%	11	50%	6	27%	**17**	**77%**
ELEMENTARY 1	Grade 4	Free/Reduced	2002-03 (*n*=11)	1	9%	1	9%	9	82%			**9**	**82%**
ELEMENTARY 1	Grade 4	Free/Reduced	2003-04 (*n*=20)	2	10%	3	15%	14	70%	1	5%	**15**	**75%**
ELEMENTARY 1	Grade 4	Free/Reduced	2004-05 (*n*=12)	1	8%	2	17%	8	67%	1	8%	**9**	**75%**
ELEMENTARY 1	Grade 4	Free/Reduced	2005-06 (*n*=20)	5	25%	3	15%	10	50%	2	10%	**12**	**60%**
ELEMENTARY 2	Grade 4	Paid	2002-03 (*n*=18)	2	11%	1	6%	10	56%	5	28%	**15**	**83%**
ELEMENTARY 2	Grade 4	Paid	2003-04 (*n*=20)			2	10%	17	85%	1	5%	**18**	**90%**
ELEMENTARY 2	Grade 4	Paid	2004-05 (*n*=16)			2	13%	9	56%	5	31%	**14**	**88%**
ELEMENTARY 2	Grade 4	Paid	2005-06 (*n*=11)					7	64%	4	36%	**11**	**100%**
ELEMENTARY 2	Grade 4	Free/Reduced	2002-03 (*n*=21)	4	19%	5	24%	10	48%	2	10%	**12**	**57%**
ELEMENTARY 2	Grade 4	Free/Reduced	2003-04 (*n*=23)	5	22%	1	4%	17	74%			**17**	**74%**
ELEMENTARY 2	Grade 4	Free/Reduced	2004-05 (*n*=25)	7	28%	1	4%	13	52%	4	16%	**17**	**68%**
ELEMENTARY 2	Grade 4	Free/Reduced	2005-06 (*n*=19)	3	16%	2	11%	10	53%	4	21%	**14**	**74%**
ELEMENTARY 3	Grade 4	Paid	2002-03 (*n*=28)	1	4%	1	4%	14	50%	12	43%	**26**	**93%**
ELEMENTARY 3	Grade 4	Paid	2003-04 (*n*=29)	2	7%	1	3%	19	66%	7	24%	**26**	**90%**
ELEMENTARY 3	Grade 4	Paid	2004-05 (*n*=35)	1	3%	1	3%	19	54%	14	40%	**33**	**94%**
ELEMENTARY 3	Grade 4	Paid	2005-06 (*n*=30)			3	10%	16	53%	11	37%	**27**	**90%**
ELEMENTARY 3	Grade 4	Free/Reduced	2002-03 (*n*=20)	6	30%	1	5%	10	50%	3	15%	**13**	**65%**
ELEMENTARY 3	Grade 4	Free/Reduced	2003-04 (*n*=13)			1	8%	7	54%	5	38%	**12**	**92%**
ELEMENTARY 3	Grade 4	Free/Reduced	2004-05 (*n*=11)	1	9%			9	82%	1	9%	**10**	**91%**
ELEMENTARY 3	Grade 4	Free/Reduced	2005-06 (*n*=15)	2	13%	1	7%	11	73%	1	7%	**12**	**80%**
ELEMENTARY 4	Grade 4	Paid	2002-03 (*n*=65)			8	12%	34	52%	23	35%	**57**	**88%**
ELEMENTARY 4	Grade 4	Paid	2003-04 (*n*=61)	1	2%	2	3%	44	72%	14	23%	**58**	**95%**
ELEMENTARY 4	Grade 4	Paid	2004-05 (*n*=50)			1	2%	31	62%	18	36%	**49**	**98%**
ELEMENTARY 4	Grade 4	Paid	2005-06 (*n*=58)			2	3%	30	52%	26	45%	**56**	**97%**
ELEMENTARY 4	Grade 4	Free/Reduced	2002-03 (*n*=12)	1	8%			9	75%	2	17%	**11**	**92%**
ELEMENTARY 4	Grade 4	Free/Reduced	2003-04 (*n*=13)			1	8%	10	77%	2	15%	**12**	**92%**
ELEMENTARY 4	Grade 4	Free/Reduced	2004-05 (*n*=19)			5	26%	8	42%	6	32%	**14**	**74%**
ELEMENTARY 4	Grade 4	Free/Reduced	2005-06 (*n*=15)	1	7%	2	13%	9	60%	3	20%	**12**	**80%**
ELEMENTARY 5	Grade 4	Paid	2002-03 (*n*=35)	2	6%	3	9%	15	43%	15	43%	**30**	**86%**
ELEMENTARY 5	Grade 4	Paid	2003-04 (*n*=42)			1	2%	27	64%	14	33%	**41**	**98%**
ELEMENTARY 5	Grade 4	Paid	2004-05 (*n*=33)	3	9%	2	6%	18	55%	10	30%	**28**	**85%**
ELEMENTARY 5	Grade 4	Paid	2005-06 (*n*=30)			2	7%	19	63%	9	30%	**28**	**93%**
ELEMENTARY 5	Grade 4	Free/Reduced	2002-03 (*n*=6)			1	17%	5	83%			**5**	**83%**
ELEMENTARY 5	Grade 4	Free/Reduced	2003-04 (*n*=4)			2	50%	2	50%			**2**	**50%**
ELEMENTARY 5	Grade 4	Free/Reduced	2004-05 (*n*=9)	2	22%	1	11%	3	33%	3	33%	**6**	**67%**
ELEMENTARY 5	Grade 4	Free/Reduced	2005-06 (*n*=11)	1	9%	4	36%	5	45%	1	9%	**6**	**55%**

Figure 6.15 (Continued)

Canyon View School District Reading Proficiency Levels
Number and Percentage by School, Grade Level, and Lunch Status, 2002-03 to 2005-06

School, Grade Level, and Lunch Status			Year	Novice		Nearing Proficiency		Proficient		Advanced		Total Proficient	
				Number	Percent	Number	Percent	Number	Percent	Number	Percent	Number	Percent
ELEMENTARY 6	Grade 4	Paid	2002-03 (*n*=36)					11	42%	15	58%	**26**	**100%**
			2003-04 (*n*=33)			2	6%	19	58%	12	36%	**31**	**94%**
			2004-05 (*n*=29)			2	7%	16	55%	11	38%	**27**	**93%**
			2005-06 (*n*=25)					17	68%	8	32%	**25**	**100%**
		Free/Reduced	2002-03 (*n*=5)			1	20%	4	80%			**4**	**80%**
			2003-04 (*n*=4)					3	75%	1	25%	**4**	**100%**
			2004-05 (*n*=4)					3	75%	1	25%	**4**	**100%**
			2005-06 (*n*=3)			2	67%	1	33%			**1**	**33%**
ELEMENTARY 7	Grade 4	Paid	2002-03 (*n*=42)	2	5%	3	7%	31	74%	6	14%	**37**	**88%**
			2003-04 (*n*=24)	4	17%	1	4%	15	63%	4	17%	**19**	**79%**
			2004-05 (*n*=24)	1	4%			17	71%	6	25%	**23**	**96%**
			2005-06 (*n*=26)			3	12%	12	46%	11	42%	**23**	**88%**
		Free/Reduced	2002-03 (*n*=16)			6	38%	10	63%			**10**	**63%**
			2003-04 (*n*=7)			1	14%	4	57%	2	29%	**6**	**86%**
			2004-05 (*n*=13)	2	15%	2	15%	8	62%	1	8%	**9**	**69%**
			2005-06 (*n*=12)	2	17%	2	17%	8	67%			**8**	**67%**
ELEMENTARY 8	Grade 4	Paid	2002-03 (*n*=29)			1	3%	15	52%	13	45%	**28**	**97%**
			2003-04 (*n*=23)			3	13%	11	48%	9	39%	**20**	**87%**
			2004-05 (*n*=23)			2	9%	13	57%	8	35%	**21**	**91%**
			2005-06 (*n*=28)			1	4%	17	61%	10	36%	**27**	**96%**
		Free/Reduced	2002-03 (*n*=9)	3	33%	1	11%	5	56%			**5**	**56%**
			2003-04 (*n*=12)	2	17%			9	75%	1	8%	**10**	**83%**
			2004-05 (*n*=11)	1	9%	3	27%	6	55%	1	9%	**7**	**64%**
			2005-06 (*n*=8)	1	13%	1	13%	4	50%	2	25%	**6**	**75%**
ELEMENTARY 9	Grade 4	Paid	2002-03 (*n*=63)	3	5%	2	3%	41	65%	17	27%	**58**	**92%**
			2003-04 (*n*=53)	1	2%	8	15%	29	55%	15	28%	**44**	**83%**
			2004-05 (*n*=43)	1	2%	3	7%	22	51%	17	40%	**39**	**91%**
			2005-06 (*n*=62)	5	8%	4	6%	34	55%	19	31%	**53**	**85%**
		Free/Reduced	2002-03 (*n*=9)	1	11%	1	11%	7	78%			**7**	**78%**
			2003-04 (*n*=20)	1	5%	1	5%	18	90%			**18**	**90%**
			2004-05 (*n*=18)	3	17%	1	6%	12	67%	2	11%	**14**	**78%**
			2005-06 (*n*=15)	1	7%	3	20%	9	60%	2	13%	**11**	**73%**
ELEMENTARY 10	Grade 4	Paid	2002-03 (*n*=36)			2	6%	16	44%	18	50%	**34**	**94%**
			2003-04 (*n*=39)	4	10%	4	10%	22	56%	9	23%	**31**	**79%**
			2004-05 (*n*=37)	1	3%	4	11%	19	51%	13	35%	**32**	**86%**
			2005-06 (*n*=37)	1	3%			19	51%	17	46%	**36**	**97%**
		Free/Reduced	2002-03 (*n*=12)	2	17%	1	8%	8	67%	1	8%	**9**	**75%**
			2003-04 (*n*=14)	3	21%	2	14%	7	50%	2	14%	**9**	**64%**
			2004-05 (*n*=14)	2	14%	2	14%	8	57%	2	14%	**10**	**71%**
			2005-06 (*n*=11)	2	18%	2	18%	5	45%	2	18%	**7**	**64%**

Figure 6.15 (Continued)

Canyon View School District Reading Proficiency Levels
Number and Percentage by School, Grade Level, and Lunch Status, 2002-03 to 2005-06

School, Grade Level, and Lunch Status			Year	Novice		Nearing Proficiency		Proficient		Advanced		Total Proficient	
				Number	Percent	Number	Percent	Number	Percent	Number	Percent	Number	Percent
ELEMENTARY 11	Grade 4	Paid	2002-03 (*n*=18)	2	11%			15	83%	1	6%	**16**	**89%**
			2003-04 (*n*=23)	5	22%	4	17%	11	48%	3	13%	**14**	**61%**
			2004-05 (*n*=17)	2	12%	1	6%	12	71%	2	12%	**14**	**82%**
			2005-06 (*n*=24)	2	8%	3	13%	15	63%	4	17%	**19**	**79%**
		Free/Reduced	2002-03 (*n*=17)	3	18%	1	6%	12	71%	1	6%	**13**	**76%**
			2003-04 (*n*=22)	2	9%	5	23%	13	59%	2	9%	**15**	**68%**
			2004-05 (*n*=19)	2	11%	2	11%	14	74%	1	5%	**15**	**79%**
			2005-06 (*n*=27)	2	7%	6	22%	15	56%	4	15%	**19**	**70%**
MIDDLE 1	Grade 8	Paid	2002-03 (*n*=280)	14	5%	28	10%	164	59%	74	27%	**238**	**85%**
			2003-04 (*n*=277)	16	6%	30	11%	174	63%	57	21%	**231**	**84%**
			2004-05 (*n*=262)	19	7%	31	12%	159	61%	53	20%	**212**	**81%**
			2005-06 (*n*=284)	20	7%	30	11%	174	61%	60	21%	**234**	**82%**
		Free/Reduced	2002-03 (*n*=33)	3	9%	8	24%	16	48%	6	18%	**22**	**67%**
			2003-04 (*n*=38)	7	18%	8	21%	16	42%	7	18%	**23**	**61%**
			2004-05 (*n*=53)	7	13%	15	29%	21	40%	10	19%	**31**	**60%**
			2005-06 (*n*=54)	9	17%	10	19%	30	56%	5	9%	**35**	**65%**
MIDDLE 2	Grade 8	Paid	2002-03 (*n*=170)	9	5%	10	6%	105	62%	46	27%	**151**	**89%**
			2003-04 (*n*=173)	10	6%	23	13%	103	60%	37	22%	**140**	**82%**
			2004-05 (*n*=170)	13	8%	15	9%	99	59%	43	25%	**142**	**84%**
			2005-06 (*n*=141)	4	3%	17	12%	86	61%	34	24%	**120**	**85%**
		Free/Reduced	2002-03 (*n*=47)	11	23%	10	21%	24	51%	2	4%	**26**	**55%**
			2003-04 (*n*=47)	13	28%	2	4%	28	60%	4	9%	**32**	**68%**
			2004-05 (*n*=53)	15	28%	8	15%	26	49%	4	8%	**30**	**57%**
			2005-06 (*n*=65)	17	26%	9	14%	36	55%	3	5%	**39**	**60%**
HIGH 1	Grade 11	Paid	2002-03 (*n*=289)	20	7%	18	6%	163	56%	88	30%	**251**	**87%**
			2003-04 (*n*=278)	15	5%	27	10%	154	55%	82	30%	**236**	**85%**
			2004-05 (*n*=282)	18	6%	29	10%	171	61%	64	23%	**235**	**83%**
			2005-06 (*n*=302)	13	4%	33	11%	166	55%	90	30%	**256**	**85%**
		Free/Reduced	2002-03 (*n*=18)	1	6%	4	22%	7	39%	6	33%	**13**	**72%**
			2003-04 (*n*=15)	1	7%	2	13%	9	60%	3	20%	**12**	**80%**
			2004-05 (*n*=15)	2	13%	1	7%	9	60%	3	20%	**12**	**80%**
			2005-06 (*n*=14)	3	21%	1	7%	8	57%	2	14%	**10**	**71%**
HIGH 2	Grade 11	Paid	2002-03 (*n*=327)	24	7%	33	10%	174	54%	96	30%	**270**	**83%**
			2003-04 (*n*=342)	18	5%	36	11%	202	59%	86	25%	**288**	**84%**
			2004-05 (*n*=322)	22	7%	30	9%	166	52%	104	32%	**270**	**84%**
			2005-06 (*n*=286)	23	8%	25	9%	172	60%	66	23%	**238**	**83%**
		Free/Reduced	2003-04 (*n*=33)	5	15%	7	21%	14	42%	7	21%	**21**	**64%**
			2004-05 (*n*=29)	8	28%	5	17%	13	45%	3	10%	**16**	**55%**
			2005-06 (*n*=30)	8	27%	2	7%	9	30%	11	37%	**20**	**67%**

Figure 6.16 shows the Reading proficiency levels for the district by gifted status from 2004-05 to 2005-06.

Look Fors: **The percentage of students who participate in the gifted program scoring *Proficient* or *Advanced* in Reading. More gifted students scoring *Advanced*, over time.**

Planning Implications: **If not all gifted students are proficient, what needs to be changed to improve their performance? How are gifted students taught?**

Figure 6.16

Canyon View School District Reading Proficiency Levels
Number and Percentage by Grade Level and Gifted Status, 2004-05 to 2005-06

Grade Level	Year	Novice		Nearing Proficiency		Proficient		Advanced		Total Proficient	
		Number	Percent	Number	Percent	Number	Percent	Number	Percent	Number	Percent
Grade 4	2004-05 (*n*=56)					15	27%	41	73%	**56**	**100%**
	2005-06 (*n*=42)					6	14%	36	86%	**42**	**100%**

Figure 6.17 shows the Reading proficiency levels for gifted students in the district by school and grade level for the same time period.

Look Fors: **Differences by school in gifted students scoring *Proficient* or *Advanced*.**

Planning Implications: **Are all teachers able to meet the needs of their gifted students?**

Figure 6.17

Canyon View School District Reading Proficiency Levels
Number and Percentage by School, Grade Level, and Gifted Status, 2004-05 to 2005-06

School	Grade Level	Year	Novice		Nearing Proficiency		Proficient		Advanced		Total Proficient	
			Number	Percent	Number	Percent	Number	Percent	Number	Percent	Number	Percent
Elementary 1	Grade 4	2004-05 (*n*=3)							3	100%	**3**	**100%**
		2005-06 (*n*=4)							4	100%	**4**	**100%**
Elementary 2	Grade 4	2004-05 (*n*=1)							1	100%	**1**	**100%**
		2005-06 (*n*=3)					2	67%	1	33%	**3**	**100%**
Elementary 3	Grade 4	2004-05 (*n*=17)					7	41%	10	59%	**17**	**100%**
		2005-06 (*n*=7)					1	14%	6	86%	**7**	**100%**
Elementary 4	Grade 4	2004-05 (*n*=4)					1	25%	3	75%	**4**	**100%**
		2005-06 (*n*=4)							4	100%	**4**	**100%**
Elementary 5	Grade 4	2004-05 (*n*=8)					3	38%	5	63%	**8**	**100%**
		2005-06 (*n*=3)							3	100%	**3**	**100%**
Elementary 6	Grade 4	2004-05 (*n*=7)					2	29%	5	71%	**7**	**100%**
		2005-06 (*n*=4)							4	100%	**4**	**100%**
Elementary 7	Grade 4	2004-05 (*n*=3)							3	100%	**3**	**100%**
		2005-06 (*n*=2)							2	100%	**2**	**100%**
Elementary 8	Grade 4	2004-05 (*n*=2)					1	50%	1	50%	**2**	**100%**
		2005-06 (*n*=2)							2	100%	**2**	**100%**
Elementary 9	Grade 4	2004-05 (*n*=5)					1	20%	4	80%	**5**	**100%**
		2005-06 (*n*=8)					3	38%	5	63%	**8**	**100%**
Elementary 10	Grade 4	2004-05 (*n*=5)							5	100%	**5**	**100%**
		2005-06 (*n*=3)							3	100%	**3**	**100%**
Elementary 11	Grade 4	2004-05 (*n*=1)							1	100%	**1**	**100%**
		2005-06 (*n*=2)							2	100%	**2**	**100%**

Figure 6.18 shows the Reading proficiency for the district by grade level and IEP students from 2003-04 to 2005-06.

Look Fors:	**Percentage of students with IEPs meeting Reading proficiency.**
Planning Implications:	**Is Reading instruction meeting the needs of all students with IEPs? Do teachers know how to teach Reading to students with IEPs?**

Figure 6.18

Canyon View School District Reading Proficiency Levels
Number and Percentage of IEP Students by Grade Level, 2002-03 to 2005-06

Grade Level	Year	Novice		Nearing Proficiency		Proficient		Advanced		Total Proficient	
		Number	Percent	Number	Percent	Number	Percent	Number	Percent	Number	Percent
Grade 4	2002-03 (*n*=80)	18	23%	19	24%	39	49%	4	5%	**43**	**54%**
	2003-04 (*n*=79)	20	25%	19	24%	34	43%	6	8%	**40**	**51%**
	2004-05 (*n*=76)	21	28%	13	17%	34	45%	8	11%	**42**	**55%**
	2005-06 (*n*=63)	20	32%	17	27%	18	29%	8	13%	**26**	**41%**
Grade 8	2002-03 (*n*=50)	20	40%	8	16%	16	32%	6	12%	**22**	**44%**
	2003-04 (*n*=54)	22	42%	14	26%	17	32%	1	2%	**18**	**33%**
	2004-05 (*n*=72)	28	39%	18	25%	23	32%	3	4%	**26**	**36%**
	2005-06 (*n*=56)	25	45%	11	20%	19	34%	1	2%	**20**	**36%**
Grade 11	2002-03 (*n*=35)	16	46%	7	20%	11	31%	1	3%	**12**	**34%**
	2003-04 (*n*=34)	14	41%	12	35%	8	24%			**8**	**24%**
	2004-05 (*n*=52)	21	40%	12	23%	18	35%	1	2%	**19**	**37%**
	2005-06 (*n*=48)	19	40%	9	19%	17	35%	3	6%	**20**	**42%**

Figure 6.19 shows the Reading proficiency of IEP students by school and grade level, over time.

Look Fors:	**Student learning differences across schools for students with IEPs.**
Planning Implications:	**Are all schools effective in assuring that IEP goals are attainable? Are schools improving the percentage of students with IEPs meeting proficiency?**

Figure 6.19

Canyon View School District Reading Proficiency Levels
Number and Percentage of IEP Students by School and Grade Level, 2002-03 to 2005-06

School	Grade Level	Year	Novice		Nearing Proficiency		Proficient		Advanced		Total	
			Number	Percent	Number	Percent	Number	Percent	Number	Percent	Number	Percent
Elementary 1	Grade 4	2002-03 (*n*=4)	1	25%	1	25%	2	50%			**2**	**50%**
		2003-04 (*n*=5)			2	40%	3	60%			**3**	**60%**
		2004-05 (*n*=2)	2	100%							**0**	
		2005-06 (*n*=5)	3	60%	1	20%	1	20%			**1**	**20%**
Elementary 2	Grade 4	2002-03 (*n*=9)	2	22%	3	33%	4	44%			**4**	**44%**
		2003-04 (*n*=7)	4	57%	2	29%	1	14%			**1**	**14%**
		2004-05 (*n*=13)	6	46%	1	8%	5	38%	1	8%	**6**	**46%**
		2005-06 (*n*=6)	2	33%			2	33%	2	33%	**4**	**67%**
Elementary 3	Grade 4	2002-03 (*n*=6)	3	50%			2	33%	1	17%	**3**	**50%**
		2003-04 (*n*=6)	1	17%			4	67%	1	17%	**5**	**83%**
		2004-05 (*n*=4)	1	25%			1	25%	2	50%	**3**	**75%**
		2005-06 (*n*=6)	1	17%	2	33%	2	33%	1	17%	**3**	**50%**
Elementary 4	Grade 4	2002-03 (*n*=15)	1	7%	5	33%	8	53%	1	7%	**9**	**60%**
		2003-04 (*n*=9)			1	11%	7	78%	1	11%	**8**	**89%**
		2004-05 (*n*=12)			4	33%	8	67%			**8**	**67%**
		2005-06 (*n*=8)	2	25%	2	25%	2	25%	2	25%	**4**	**50%**
Elementary 5	Grade 4	2002-03 (*n*=7)	2	29%	4	57%	1	14%			**1**	**14%**
		2003-04 (*n*=7)			2	29%	3	43%	2	29%	**5**	**71%**
		2004-05 (*n*=5)	3	60%	1	20%	1	20%			**1**	**20%**
		2005-06 (*n*=6)	1	17%	3	50%			2	33%	**2**	**33%**
Elementary 6	Grade 4	2002-03 (*n*=4)			1	25%	3	75%			**3**	**75%**
		2003-04 (*n*=3)			1	33%			2	67%	**2**	**67%**
		2004-05 (*n*=5)					3	60%	2	40%	**5**	**100%**
		2005-06 (*n*=4)					3	75%	1	25%	**4**	**100%**
Elementary 7	Grade 4	2002-03 (*n*=10)	2	20%	4	40%	2	20%	2	20%	**4**	**40%**
		2003-04 (*n*=1)	1	100%							**0**	
		2004-05 (*n*=5)	3	50%	1	17%	2	33%			**2**	**33%**
		2005-06 (*n*=4)	1	25%	3	75%					**0**	
Elementary 8	Grade 4	2002-03 (*n*=5)	1	20%	1	20%	3	60%			**3**	**60%**
		2003-04 (*n*=8)	2	25%	3	38%	3	38%			**3**	**38%**
		2004-05 (*n*=5)			1	20%	3	60%	1	20%	**4**	**80%**
		2005-06 (*n*=5)	1	20%	1	20%	3	60%			**3**	**60%**
Elementary 9	Grade 4	2002-03 (*n*=11)	2	18%			9	82%			**9**	**82%**
		2003-04 (*n*=17)	2	12%	5	29%	10	59%			**10**	**59%**
		2004-05 (*n*=11)	2	18%	1	9%	6	55%	2	18%	**8**	**73%**
		2005-06 (*n*=10)	6	60%	1	10%	3	30%			**3**	**30%**
Elementary 10	Grade 4	2002-03 (*n*=4)					4	100%			**4**	**100%**
		2003-04 (*n*=9)	7	78%	2	22%					**0**	
		2004-05 (*n*=9)	2	22%	3	33%	4	44%			**4**	**44%**
		2005-06 (*n*=5)	2	40%	1	20%	2	40%			**2**	**40%**
Elementary 11	Grade 4	2002-03 (*n*=5)	4	80%			1	20%			**1**	**20%**
		2003-04 (*n*=7)	3	43%	1	14%	3	43%			**3**	**43%**
		2004-05 (*n*=4)	2	50%	1	25%	1	25%			**1**	**25%**
		2005-06 (*n*=4)	1	25%	3	75%					**0**	

Figure 6.19 (Continued)

Canyon View School District Reading Proficiency Levels
Number and Percentage of IEP Students by School and Grade Level, 2002-03 to 2005-06

School	Grade Level	Year	Novice		Nearing Proficiency		Proficient		Advanced		Total	
			Number	Percent	Number	Percent	Number	Percent	Number	Percent	Number	Percent
Middle 1	Grade 8	2002-03 (*n*=22)	8	36%	4	18%	7	32%	3	14%	**10**	**45%**
		2003-04 (*n*=35)	12	34%	10	29%	13	37%			**13**	**37%**
		2004-05 (*n*=47)	15	32%	13	28%	16	34%	3	6%	**19**	**40%**
		2005-06 (*n*=32)	16	50%	7	22%	9	28%			**9**	**28%**
Middle 2	Grade 8	2002-03 (*n*=28)	12	43%	4	14%	9	32%	3	11%	**12**	**43%**
		2003-04 (*n*=19)	10	56%	4	22%	4	22%	1	6%	**5**	**26%**
		2004-05 (*n*=25)	13	52%	5	20%	7	28%			**7**	**28%**
		2005-06 (*n*=24)	9	38%	4	17%	10	42%	1	4%	**11**	**46%**
High 1	Grade 11	2002-03 (*n*=14)	7	50%	4	29%	3	21%			**3**	**21%**
		2003-04 (*n*=17)	8	47%	4	24%	5	29%			**5**	**29%**
		2004-05 (*n*=21)	6	29%	7	33%	8	38%			**8**	**38%**
		2005-06 (*n*=17)	5	29%	5	29%	6	35%	1	6%	**7**	**41%**
High 2	Grade 11	2002-03 (*n*=21)	9	43%	3	14%	8	38%	1	5%	**9**	**43%**
		2003-04 (*n*=17)	6	35%	8	47%	3	18%			**3**	**18%**
		2004-05 (*n*=27)	13	48%	5	19%	8	30%	1	4%	**9**	**33%**
		2005-06 (*n*=31)	14	45%	4	13%	11	35%	2	6%	**13**	**42%**

Math Proficiency

Figure 6.20 shows the Math proficiency levels for the district by grade level from 2002-03 to 2005-06.

Look Fors: **Changes in the percentage of students in each proficiency level by grade and over time.**

Planning Implications: **Does the continuous improvement plan for the district focus on all proficiency levels, or just the lowest end? Are all students moving up?**

Figure 6.20

**Canyon View School District Math Proficiency Levels
Number and Percentage by Grade Level, 2002-03 to 2005-06**

Grade Level	Year	Novice		Nearing Proficiency		Proficient		Advanced		Total Proficient	
		Number	Percent	Number	Percent	Number	Percent	Number	Percent	Number	Percent
Grade 4	2002-03 (*n*=523)	50	10%	65	12%	316	60%	92	18%	**408**	**78%**
	2003-04 (*n*=530)	52	10%	58	11%	329	62%	91	17%	**420**	**79%**
	2004-05 (*n*=495)	38	8%	62	13%	300	61%	95	19%	**395**	**80%**
	2005-06 (*n*=527)	48	9%	61	12%	310	59%	108	20%	**418**	**79%**
Grade 8	2002-03 (*n*=555)	59	11%	72	13%	309	56%	115	21%	**424**	**76%**
	2003-04 (*n*=521)	68	13%	63	12%	303	58%	87	17%	**390**	**75%**
	2004-05 (*n*=546)	73	13%	70	13%	292	53%	111	20%	**403**	**74%**
	2005-06 (*n*=546)	62	11%	68	12%	286	52%	130	24%	**416**	**76%**
Grade 11	2002-03 (*n*=646)	48	7%	78	12%	385	60%	135	21%	**520**	**80%**
	2003-04 (*n*=691)	70	10%	69	10%	397	57%	155	22%	**552**	**80%**
	2004-05 (*n*=685)	86	13%	61	9%	414	60%	124	18%	**538**	**79%**
	2005-06 (*n*=658)	90	14%	67	10%	380	58%	121	18%	**501**	**76%**

Figure 6.21 shows the Math proficiency levels for the district by grade level and gender from 2002-03 to 2005-06.

Look Fors: **Differences by gender within grade levels. Student learning increases/decreases by gender.**

Planning Implications: **Are Math strategies meeting the needs of males and females at each grade level?**

Figure 6.21

Canyon View School District Math Proficiency Levels Number and Percentage by Grade Level and Gender, 2002-03 to 2005-06

Grade Level	Gender	Year	Novice		Nearing Proficiency		Proficient		Advanced		Total Proficient	
			Number	Percent	Number	Percent	Number	Percent	Number	Percent	Number	Percent
Grade 4	Female	2002-03 (*n*=265)	24	9%	33	12%	170	64%	38	14%	**208**	**78%**
		2003-04 (*n*=246)	21	9%	26	11%	170	69%	29	12%	**199**	**81%**
		2004-05 (*n*=235)	18	8%	33	14%	138	59%	46	20%	**184**	**78%**
		2005-06 (*n*=260)	21	8%	34	13%	154	59%	51	20%	**205**	**79%**
	Male	2002-03 (*n*=258)	26	10%	32	12%	146	57%	54	21%	**200**	**78%**
		2003-04 (*n*=284)	31	11%	32	11%	159	56%	62	22%	**221**	**78%**
		2004-05 (*n*=260)	20	8%	29	11%	162	62%	49	19%	**211**	**81%**
		2005-06 (*n*=267)	27	10%	27	10%	156	58%	57	21%	**213**	**80%**
Grade 8	Female	2002-03 (*n*=288)	20	7%	37	13%	170	59%	61	21%	**231**	**80%**
		2003-04 (*n*=248)	27	11%	29	12%	156	63%	36	15%	**192**	**77%**
		2004-05 (*n*=247)	30	12%	31	13%	142	58%	44	18%	**186**	**76%**
		2005-06 (*n*=279)	32	11%	27	10%	159	57%	61	22%	**220**	**79%**
	Male	2002-03 (*n*=267)	39	15%	35	13%	139	52%	54	20%	**193**	**72%**
		2003-04 (*n*=273)	41	15%	34	13%	147	54%	51	19%	**198**	**73%**
		2004-05 (*n*=299)	43	14%	39	13%	150	50%	67	22%	**217**	**73%**
		2005-06 (*n*=267)	30	11%	41	15%	127	48%	69	26%	**196**	**73%**
Grade 11	Female	2002-03 (*n*=341)	26	8%	42	12%	219	64%	54	16%	**273**	**80%**
		2003-04 (*n*=335)	27	8%	33	10%	213	64%	62	19%	**275**	**82%**
		2004-05 (*n*=348)	33	9%	34	10%	222	64%	59	17%	**281**	**81%**
		2005-06 (*n*=332)	32	10%	31	9%	220	66%	49	15%	**269**	**81%**
	Male	2002-03 (*n*=305)	22	7%	36	12%	166	55%	81	27%	**247**	**81%**
		2003-04 (*n*=356)	43	12%	36	10%	184	52%	93	26%	**277**	**78%**
		2004-05 (*n*=337)	53	16%	27	8%	192	57%	65	19%	**257**	**76%**
		2005-06 (*n*=326)	58	18%	36	11%	160	49%	72	22%	**232**	**71%**

Figure 6.22 shows the Math proficiency levels for the district by school and grade level from 2002-03 to 2005-06.

Look Fors:	**Percentages of proficient students increasing or decreasing by school. Schools' achievement percentages are increasing over time.**
Planning Implications:	**Are there particular schools that need support in increasing student learning results? Are Math programs being implemented effectively? What Math programs are in place at each school?**

Figure 6.22

Canyon View School District Math Proficiency Levels
Number and Percentage by School and Grade Level, 2002-03 to 2005-06

School	Grade Level	Year	Novice		Nearing Proficiency		Proficient		Advanced		Total Proficient	
			Number	Percent	Number	Percent	Number	Percent	Number	Percent	Number	Percent
Elementary 1	Grade 4	2002-03 (*n*=35)	2	6%	5	14%	24	69%	4	11%	**28**	**80%**
		2003-04 (*n*=49)	6	12%	8	16%	27	55%	8	16%	**35**	**71%**
		2004-05 (*n*=36)	1	3%	4	11%	26	72%	5	14%	**31**	**86%**
		2005-06 (*n*=45)	8	18%	6	13%	26	58%	5	11%	**31**	**69%**
Elementary 2	Grade 4	2002-03 (*n*=39)	8	21%	6	15%	22	56%	3	8%	**25**	**64%**
		2003-04 (*n*=44)	6	14%	10	23%	23	52%	5	11%	**28**	**64%**
		2004-05 (*n*=41)	7	17%	6	15%	26	63%	2	5%	**28**	**68%**
		2005-06 (*n*=30)	3	10%	1	3%	21	70%	5	17%	**26**	**87%**
Elementary 3	Grade 4	2002-03 (*n*=49)	10	20%	7	14%	28	57%	4	8%	**32**	**65%**
		2003-04 (*n*=44)	7	16%	6	14%	25	57%	6	14%	**31**	**70%**
		2004-05 (*n*=51)	5	10%	9	18%	32	63%	5	10%	**37**	**73%**
		2005-06 (*n*=46)	6	13%	11	24%	24	52%	5	11%	**29**	**63%**
Elementary 4	Grade 4	2002-03 (*n*=77)	2	3%	4	5%	50	65%	21	27%	**71**	**92%**
		2003-04 (*n*=75)	4	5%	3	4%	51	68%	17	23%	**68**	**91%**
		2004-05 (*n*=69)	4	6%	3	4%	40	58%	22	32%	**62**	**90%**
		2005-06 (*n*=77)	4	5%	4	5%	50	65%	19	25%	**69**	**90%**
Elementary 5	Grade 4	2002-03 (*n*=42)	2	5%	8	19%	26	62%	6	14%	**32**	**76%**
		2003-04 (*n*=46)	2	4%	1	2%	33	72%	10	22%	**43**	**93%**
		2004-05 (*n*=43)	2	5%	8	19%	23	53%	10	23%	**33**	**77%**
		2005-06 (*n*=42)	3	7%	4	10%	24	57%	11	26%	**35**	**83%**
Elementary 6	Grade 4	2002-03 (*n*=31)	1	3%	2	6%	18	58%	10	32%	**28**	**90%**
		2003-04 (*n*=37)	1	3%	2	5%	21	57%	13	35%	**34**	**92%**
		2004-05 (*n*=33)	1	3%	1	3%	20	61%	11	33%	**31**	**94%**
		2005-06 (*n*=29)	1	3%	1	3%	13	45%	14	48%	**27**	**93%**
Elementary 7	Grade 4	2002-03 (*n*=57)	4	7%	8	14%	38	67%	7	12%	**45**	**79%**
		2003-04 (*n*=31)	2	6%	2	6%	26	84%	1	3%	**27**	**87%**
		2004-05 (*n*=39)	3	8%	7	18%	25	64%	4	10%	**29**	**74%**
		2005-06 (*n*=43)	4	9%	11	26%	22	51%	6	14%	**28**	**65%**
Elementary 8	Grade 4	2002-03 (*n*=38)	4	11%	1	3%	23	61%	10	26%	**33**	**87%**
		2003-04 (*n*=36)	3	8%	2	6%	24	67%	7	19%	**31**	**86%**
		2004-05 (*n*=36)	2	6%	7	19%	18	50%	9	25%	**27**	**75%**
		2005-06 (*n*=36)	1	3%	4	11%	24	67%	7	19%	**31**	**86%**
Elementary 9	Grade 4	2002-03 (*n*=72)	11	15%	9	13%	39	54%	13	18%	**52**	**72%**
		2003-04 (*n*=70)	9	13%	11	16%	43	61%	7	10%	**50**	**71%**
		2004-05 (*n*=61)	3	5%	6	10%	41	67%	11	18%	**52**	**85%**
		2005-06 (*n*=78)	6	8%	8	10%	50	64%	14	18%	**64**	**82%**

Figure 6.22 (Continued)

Canyon View School District Math Proficiency Levels
Number and Percentage by School and Grade Level, 2002-03 to 2005-06

School	Grade Level	Year	Novice		Nearing Proficiency		Proficient		Advanced		Total Proficient	
			Number	Percent	Number	Percent	Number	Percent	Number	Percent	Number	Percent
Elementary 10	Grade 4	2002-03 (*n*=48)	2	4%	6	13%	26	54%	14	29%	**40**	**83%**
		2003-04 (*n*=53)	5	9%	6	11%	31	58%	11	21%	**42**	**79%**
		2004-05 (*n*=51)	4	8%	3	6%	30	59%	14	27%	**44**	**86%**
		2005-06 (*n*=49)	3	6%	3	6%	28	57%	15	31%	**43**	**88%**
Elementary 11	Grade 4	2002-03 (*n*=35)	4	11%	9	26%	22	63%			**22**	**63%**
		2003-04 (*n*=45)	7	16%	7	16%	25	56%	6	13%	**31**	**69%**
		2004-05 (*n*=35)	6	17%	8	23%	19	54%	2	6%	**21**	**60%**
		2005-06 (*n*=52)	9	17%	8	15%	28	54%	7	13%	**35**	**67%**
Middle 1	Grade 8	2002-03 (*n*=311)	21	7%	33	11%	181	58%	76	24%	**257**	**83%**
		2003-04 (*n*=305)	38	12%	29	10%	178	58%	60	20%	**238**	**78%**
		2004-05 (*n*=315)	34	11%	35	11%	169	54%	77	24%	**246**	**78%**
		2005-06 (*n*=323)	28	9%	34	11%	176	54%	85	26%	**261**	**81%**
Middle 2	Grade 8	2002-03 (*n*=241)	37	15%	37	15%	128	53%	39	16%	**167**	**69%**
		2003-04 (*n*=216	30	14%	34	16%	125	58%	27	13%	**152**	**70%**
		2004-05 (*n*=230)	39	17%	35	15%	123	53%	33	14%	**156**	**68%**
		2005-06 (*n*=219)	34	16%	34	16%	110	50%	41	19%	**151**	**69%**
High 1	Grade 11	2002-03 (*n*=306)	20	7%	41	13%	172	56%	73	24%	**245**	**80%**
		2003-04 (*n*=293)	26	9%	23	8%	158	54%	86	29%	**244**	**83%**
		2004-05 (*n*=297)	28	9%	23	8%	197	66%	49	16%	**246**	**83%**
		2005-06 (*n*=319)	33	10%	33	10%	177	55%	76	24%	**253**	**79%**
High 2	Grade 11	2002-03 (*n*=321)	22	7%	33	10%	205	64%	61	19%	**266**	**83%**
		2003-04 (*n*=376)	38	10%	40	11%	229	61%	69	18%	**298**	**79%**
		2004-05 (*n*=356)	43	12%	31	9%	207	58%	75	21%	**282**	**79%**
		2005-06 (*n*=333)	56	17%	31	9%	201	60%	45	14%	**246**	**74%**

Figure 6.23 shows the Math proficiency levels for the district by school, grade level, and gender, over time.

Look Fors: **Student proficiency increases/decreases by school, grade level, and gender, over time.**

Planning Implications: **Are all schools effective in serving males and females at all grade levels? Are the scores consistent over time?**

Figure 6.23

Canyon View School District Math Proficiency Levels
Number and Percentage by School, Grade Level, and Gender, 2002-03 to 2005-06

School and Grade Level		Gender	Year	Novice		Nearing Proficiency		Proficient		Advanced		Total Proficient	
				Number	Percent	Number	Percent	Number	Percent	Number	Percent	Number	Percent
ELEMENTARY — Elementary 1	Grade 4	Female	2002-03 (*n*=22)	1	5%	2	9%	16	73%	3	14%	**19**	**86%**
			2003-04 (*n*=20)	2	10%	3	15%	13	65%	2	10%	**15**	**75%**
			2004-05 (*n*=14)	1	7%	3	21%	9	64%	1	7%	**10**	**71%**
			2005-06 (*n*=26)	5	19%	4	15%	14	54%	3	12%	**17**	**65%**
		Male	2002-03 (*n*=13)	1	8%	3	23%	8	62%	1	8%	**9**	**69%**
			2003-04 (*n*=29)	4	14%	5	18%	14	50%	6	21%	**20**	**71%**
			2004-05 (*n*=22)			1	5%	17	77%	4	18%	**21**	**95%**
			2005-06 (*n*=19)	3	16%	2	11%	12	63%	2	11%	**14**	**74%**
Elementary 2	Grade 4	Female	2002-03 (*n*=10)	1	8%	3	23%	9	69%			**9**	**69%**
			2003-04 (*n*=23)	4	17%	6	25%	13	54%	1	4%	**14**	**58%**
			2004-05 (*n*=17)	5	29%	4	24%	8	47%			**8**	**47%**
			2005-06 (*n*=10)	1	10%			8	80%	1	10%	**9**	**90%**
		Male	2002-03 (*n*=26)	7	27%	3	12%	13	50%	3	12%	**16**	**62%**
			2003-04 (*n*=20)	2	10%	4	20%	10	50%	4	20%	**14**	**70%**
			2004-05 (*n*=24)	2	8%	2	8%	18	75%	2	8%	**20**	**83%**
			2005-06 (*n*=20)	2	10%	1	5%	13	65%	4	20%	**17**	**85%**
Elementary 3	Grade 4	Female	2002-03 (*n*=27)	6	22%	3	11%	16	59%	2	7%	**18**	**67%**
			2003-04 (*n*=20)	3	15%	2	10%	13	65%	2	10%	**15**	**75%**
			2004-05 (*n*=26)	1	4%	6	23%	16	62%	3	12%	**19**	**73%**
			2005-06 (*n*=22)	3	14%	6	27%	9	41%	4	18%	**13**	**59%**
		Male	2002-03 (*n*=22)	4	18%	4	18%	12	55%	2	9%	**14**	**64%**
			2003-04 (*n*=24)	4	17%	4	17%	12	50%	4	17%	**16**	**67%**
			2004-05 (*n*=25)	4	16%	3	12%	16	64%	2	8%	**18**	**72%**
			2005-06 (*n*=24)	3	13%	5	21%	15	63%	1	4%	**16**	**67%**
Elementary 4	Grade 4	Female	2002-03 (*n*=39)					31	79%	8	21%	**39**	**100%**
			2003-04 (*n*=28)	3	11%			22	79%	3	11%	**25**	**89%**
			2004-05 (*n*=37)	3	8%			22	59%	12	32%	**34**	**92%**
			2005-06 (*n*=34)	2	6%	1	3%	23	68%	8	24%	**31**	**91%**
		Male	2002-03 (*n*=38)	2	5%	4	11%	19	50%	13	34%	**32**	**84%**
			2003-04 (*n*=47)	1	2%	3	7%	29	63%	14	30%	**43**	**93%**
			2004-05 (*n*=32)	1	3%	3	9%	18	56%	10	31%	**28**	**88%**
			2005-06 (*n*=43)	2	5%	3	7%	27	63%	11	26%	**38**	**88%**
Elementary 5	Grade 4	Female	2002-03 (*n*=20)	1	5%	3	15%	13	65%	3	15%	**16**	**80%**
			2003-04 (*n*=25)	1	4%			21	84%	3	12%	**24**	**96%**
			2004-05 (*n*=18)	2	11%	1	6%	10	56%	5	28%	**15**	**83%**
			2005-06 (*n*=26)	1	4%	2	8%	16	62%	7	27%	**23**	**88%**
		Male	2002-03 (*n*=22)	1	5%	5	24%	13	62%	3	14%	**16**	**76%**
			2003-04 (*n*=21)	1	5%	1	5%	12	57%	7	33%	**19**	**90%**
			2004-05 (*n*=25)			7	28%	13	52%	5	20%	**18**	**72%**
			2005-06 (*n*=16)	2	13%	2	13%	8	50%	4	25%	**12**	**75%**

Figure 6.23 (Continued)

Canyon View School District Math Proficiency Levels
Number and Percentage by School, Grade Level, and Gender, 2002-03 to 2005-06

School and Grade Level			Gender	Year	Novice		Nearing Proficiency		Proficient		Advanced		Total Proficient	
					Number	Percent	Number	Percent	Number	Percent	Number	Percent	Number	Percent
ELEMENTARY	Elementary 6	Grade 4	Female	2002-03 (*n*=10)			1	10%	6	60%	3	30%	**9**	**90%**
				2003-04 (*n*=17)			1	6%	13	76%	3	18%	**16**	**94%**
				2004-05 (*n*=13)			1	8%	8	62%	4	31%	**12**	**92%**
				2005-06 (*n*=7)					6	86%	1	14%	**7**	**100%**
			Male	2002-03 (*n*=21)	1	5%	1	5%	12	57%	7	33%	**19**	**90%**
				2003-04 (*n*=20)	1	5%	1	5%	8	40%	10	50%	**18**	**90%**
				2004-05 (*n*=20)	1	5%			12	60%	7	35%	**19**	**95%**
				2005-06 (*n*=22)	1	5%	1	5%	7	32%	13	59%	**20**	**91%**
	Elementary 7	Grade 4	Female	2002-03 (*n*=31)	1	3%	5	16%	19	61%	6	19%	**25**	**81%**
				2003-04 (*n*=16)	1	6%	1	6%	13	81%	1	6%	**14**	**88%**
				2004-05 (*n*=20)	2	10%	4	20%	13	65%	1	5%	**14**	**70%**
				2005-06 (*n*=20)	1	5%	7	35%	8	40%	4	20%	**12**	**60%**
			Male	2002-03 (*n*=26)	3	12%	3	12%	19	73%	1	4%	**20**	**77%**
				2003-04 (*n*=15)	1	7%	1	7%	13	87%			**13**	**87%**
				2004-05 (*n*=19)	1	5%	3	16%	12	63%	3	16%	**15**	**79%**
				2005-06 (*n*=23)	3	13%	4	17%	14	61%	2	9%	**16**	**70%**
	Elementary 8	Grade 4	Female	2002-03 (*n*=21)	4	19%	1	5%	11	52%	5	24%	**16**	**76%**
				2003-04 (*n*=17)	1	6%			11	65%	5	29%	**16**	**94%**
				2004-05 (*n*=15)			5	33%	7	47%	3	20%	**10**	**67%**
				2005-06 (*n*=20)			3	15%	11	55%	6	30%	**17**	**85%**
			Male	2002-03 (*n*=17)					12	71%	5	29%	**17**	**100%**
				2003-04 (*n*=19)	2	11%	2	11%	13	68%	2	11%	**15**	**79%**
				2004-05 (*n*=21)	2	10%	2	10%	11	52%	6	29%	**17**	**81%**
				2005-06 (*n*=16)	1	6%	1	6%	13	81%	1	6%	**14**	**88%**
	Elementary 9	Grade 4	Female	2002-03 (*n*=39)	6	15%	8	21%	21	54%	4	10%	**25**	**64%**
				2003-04 (*n*=36)	3	8%	6	17%	24	67%	3	8%	**27**	**75%**
				2004-05 (*n*=28)			3	11%	19	68%	6	21%	**25**	**89%**
				2005-06 (*n*=44)	3	7%	5	11%	30	68%	6	14%	**36**	**82%**
			Male	2002-03 (*n*=33)	5	15%	1	3%	18	55%	9	27%	**27**	**82%**
				2003-04 (*n*=34)	6	18%	5	15%	19	56%	4	12%	**23**	**68%**
				2004-05 (*n*=33)	3	9%	3	9%	22	67%	5	15%	**27**	**82%**
				2005-06 (*n*=34)	3	9%	3	9%	20	59%	8	24%	**28**	**82%**
	Elementary 10	Grade 4	Female	2002-03 (*n*=22)	1	5%	4	18%	13	59%	4	18%	**17**	**77%**
				2003-04 (*n*=24)	1	4%	3	13%	16	67%	4	17%	**20**	**83%**
				2004-05 (*n*=29)	1	3%	2	7%	16	55%	10	34%	**26**	**90%**
				2005-06 (*n*=28)	2	7%	1	4%	16	57%	9	32%	**25**	**89%**
			Male	2002-03 (*n*=26)	1	4%	2	8%	13	50%	10	38%	**23**	**88%**
				2003-04 (*n*=29)	4	14%	3	10%	15	52%	7	24%	**22**	**76%**
				2004-05 (*n*=22)	3	14%	1	5%	14	64%	4	18%	**18**	**82%**
				2005-06 (*n*=21)	1	5%	2	10%	12	57%	6	29%	**18**	**86%**

Figure 6.23 (Continued)

Canyon View School District Math Proficiency Levels
Number and Percentage by School, Grade Level, and Gender, 2002-03 to 2005-06

School and Grade Level			Gender	Year	Novice		Nearing Proficiency		Proficient		Advanced		Total Proficient	
					Number	Percent	Number	Percent	Number	Percent	Number	Percent	Number	Percent
ELEMENTARY	Elementary 11	Grade 4	Female	2002-03 (*n*=21)	3	14%	3	14%	15	71%			**15**	**71%**
				2003-04 (*n*=19)	2	11%	4	22%	11	58%	2	11%	**13**	**68%**
				2004-05 (*n*=18)	3	17%	4	22%	10	56%	1	6%	**11**	**61%**
				2005-06 (*n*=23)	3	13%	5	22%	13	57%	2	9%	**15**	**65%**
			Male	2002-03 (*n*=14)	1	7%	6	43%	7	50%			**7**	**50%**
				2003-04 (*n*=26)	5	19%	3	12%	14	54%	4	15%	**18**	**69%**
				2004-05 (*n*=17)	3	18%	4	24%	9	53%	1	6%	**10**	**59%**
				2005-06 (*n*=29)	6	21%	3	10%	15	52%	5	17%	**20**	**69%**
MIDDLE	Middle 1	Grade 8	Female	2002-03 (*n*=156)	9	6%	17	11%	91	59%	39	25%	**130**	**84%**
				2003-04 (*n*=151)	15	10%	15	10%	95	63%	26	17%	**121**	**80%**
				2004-05 (*n*=139)	14	10%	13	9%	82	59%	30	22%	**112**	**81%**
				2005-06 (*n*=168)	13	8%	14	8%	99	59%	42	25%	**141**	**84%**
			Male	2002-03 (*n*=155)	12	8%	16	10%	90	58%	37	24%	**127**	**82%**
				2003-04 (*n*=154)	23	15%	14	9%	83	54%	34	22%	**117**	**76%**
				2004-05 (*n*=176)	20	11%	22	13%	87	50%	47	27%	**134**	**77%**
				2005-06 (*n*=155)	15	10%	20	13%	77	50%	43	28%	**120**	**77%**
	Middle 2	Grade 8	Female	2002-03 (*n*=132)	11	8%	20	15%	79	60%	22	17%	**101**	**77%**
				2003-04 (*n*=97)	12	12%	14	14%	61	63%	10	10%	**71**	**73%**
				2004-05 (*n*=107)	16	15%	18	17%	60	57%	13	12%	**73**	**69%**
				2005-06 (*n*=110)	19	17%	13	12%	60	55%	18	16%	**78**	**71%**
			Male	2002-03 (*n*=109)	26	24%	17	16%	49	45%	17	16%	**66**	**61%**
				2003-04 (*n*=119)	18	15%	20	17%	64	54%	17	14%	**81**	**69%**
				2004-05 (*n*=123)	23	19%	17	14%	63	51%	20	16%	**83**	**67%**
				2005-06 (*n*=109)	15	14%	21	19%	50	46%	23	21%	**73**	**67%**
HIGH	High 1	Grade 11	Female	2002-03 (*n*=163)	11	7%	19	12%	98	60%	35	21%	**133**	**82%**
				2003-04 (*n*=139)	6	4%	12	9%	81	58%	40	29%	**121**	**87%**
				2004-05 (*n*=152)	8	5%	9	6%	109	72%	26	17%	**135**	**89%**
				2005-06 (*n*=159)	12	8%	15	9%	100	63%	32	20%	**132**	**83%**
			Male	2002-03 (*n*=143)	9	6%	22	15%	74	52%	38	27%	**112**	**78%**
				2003-04 (*n*=154)	20	13%	11	7%	77	50%	46	30%	**123**	**80%**
				2004-05 (*n*=145)	20	14%	14	10%	88	61%	23	16%	**111**	**77%**
				2005-06 (*n*=160)	21	13%	18	11%	77	48%	44	28%	**121**	**76%**
	High 2	Grade 11	Female	2002-03 (*n*=165)	10	6%	21	13%	115	70%	19	12%	**134**	**82%**
				2003-04 (*n*=187)	17	9%	19	10%	129	69%	22	12%	**151**	**81%**
				2004-05 (*n*=175)	18	10%	19	11%	105	60%	33	19%	**138**	**79%**
				2005-06 (*n*=169)	20	12%	13	8%	119	70%	17	10%	**136**	**80%**
			Male	2002-03 (*n*=156)	12	8%	12	8%	90	58%	42	27%	**132**	**85%**
				2003-04 (*n*=189)	21	11%	21	11%	100	53%	47	25%	**147**	**78%**
				2004-05 (*n*=181)	25	14%	12	7%	102	56%	42	23%	**144**	**80%**
				2005-06 (*n*=164)	36	22%	18	11%	82	50%	28	17%	**110**	**67%**

Figure 6.24 shows the Math proficiency levels for the district by grade level and ethnicity from 2002-03 to 2005-06. *Note:* the numbers in some of the student groups are very small. These analyses are for district/school review only.

Look Fors:	**Changes in Math performance by ethnicity, over time.**
Planning Implications:	**Are the instructional needs of all ethnicities being met in each school and at each grade level?**

Figure 6.24

Canyon View School District Math Proficiency Levels
Number and Percentage by Grade Level and Ethnicity, 2002-03 to 2005-06

Grade Level and Ethnicity		Year	Novice		Nearing Proficiency		Proficient		Advanced		Total Proficient	
			Number	Percent	Number	Percent	Number	Percent	Number	Percent	Number	Percent
GRADE 4	American Indian	2002-03 (*n*=23)	6	26%	3	13%	13	57%	1	4%	**14**	**61%**
		2003-04 (*n*=29)	6	21%	3	10%	18	62%	2	7%	**20**	**69%**
		2004-05 (*n*=30)	6	20%	5	17%	17	57%	2	7%	**19**	**63%**
		2005-06 (*n*=34)	9	26%	2	6%	19	56%	4	12%	**23**	**68%**
	Asian	2002-03 (*n*=2)					1	50%	1	50%	**2**	**100%**
		2003-04 (*n*=7)	1	14%			6	86%			**6**	**86%**
		2004-05 (*n*=5)					4	80%	1	20%	**5**	**100%**
	Black	2002-03 (*n*=2)					2	100%			**2**	**100%**
		2003-04 (*n*=4)			1	25%	2	50%	1	25%	**3**	**75%**
		2004-05 (*n*=7)			1	14%	6	86%			**6**	**86%**
		2005-06 (*n*=6)	4	67%	1	17%	1	17%			**1**	**17%**
	Hispanic	2002-03 (*n*=11)	1	9%	3	27%	5	45%	2	18%	**7**	**64%**
		2003-04 (*n*=8)			1	13%	6	75%	1	13%	**7**	**88%**
		2004-05 (*n*=11)			3	27%	6	55%	2	18%	**8**	**73%**
		2005-06 (*n*=12)	2	17%	3	25%	5	42%	2	17%	**7**	**58%**
	Pacific Islander	2002-03 (*n*=2)					1	50%	1	50%	**2**	**100%**
		2003-04 (*n*=1)					1	100%			**1**	**100%**
		2005-06 (*n*=1)	1	100%							**0**	
	White	2002-03 (*n*=483)	43	9%	59	12%	294	61%	87	18%	**381**	**79%**
		2003-04 (*n*=481)	45	9%	53	11%	296	62%	87	18%	**383**	**80%**
		2004-05 (*n*=442)	32	7%	53	12%	267	60%	90	20%	**357**	**81%**
		2005-06 (*n*=474)	32	7%	55	12%	285	60%	102	22%	**387**	**82%**
GRADE 8	American Indian	2002-03 (*n*=18)	4	22%	2	11%	12	67%			**12**	**67%**
		2003-04 (*n*=31)	5	16%	5	16%	19	61%	2	6%	**21**	**68%**
		2004-05 (*n*=21)	7	33%	4	19%	9	43%	1	5%	**10**	**48%**
		2005-06 (*n*=31)	5	16%	6	19%	17	55%	3	10%	**20**	**65%**
	Asian	2002-03 (*n*=9)			4	44%	5	56%			**5**	**56%**
		2003-04 (*n*=10)	1	11%	1	11%	7	78%	1	11%	**8**	**89%**
		2004-05 (*n*=7)	1	14%	1	14%	4	57%	1	14%	**5**	**71%**
		2005-06 (*n*=5)	1	20%			2	40%	2	40%	**4**	**80%**
	Black	2002-03 (*n*=2)					2	100%			**2**	**100%**
		2003-04 (*n*=2)	1	50%					1	50%	**1**	**50%**
		2004-05 (*n*=4)			2	50%	2	50%			**2**	**50%**
		2005-06 (*n*=6)	1	17%	1	17%	4	67%			**4**	**67%**
	Hispanic	2002-03 (*n*=4)	1	25%			2	50%	1	25%	**3**	**75%**
		2003-04 (*n*=8)	2	25%			5	63%	1	13%	**6**	**75%**
		2004-05 (*n*=8)	1	13%	2	25%	2	25%	3	38%	**5**	**63%**
		2005-06 (*n*=13)			6	46%	4	31%	3	23%	**7**	**54%**
	Pacific Islander	2002-03 (*n*=1)			1	100%					**0**	
	White	2002-03 (*n*=521)	54	10%	65	13%	288	55%	114	22%	**402**	**77%**
		2003-04 (*n*=470)	59	13%	57	12%	272	58%	82	17%	**354**	**75%**
		2004-05 (*n*=506)	64	13%	61	12%	275	55%	106	21%	**381**	**76%**
		2005-06 (*n*=491)	55	11%	55	11%	259	53%	122	25%	**381**	**78%**

Figure 6.24 (Continued)

Canyon View School District Math Proficiency Levels
Number and Percentage by Grade Level and Ethnicity, 2002-03 to 2005-06

Grade Level and Ethnicity		Year	Novice		Nearing Proficiency		Proficient		Advanced		Total Proficient	
			Number	Percent	Number	Percent	Number	Percent	Number	Percent	Number	Percent
GRADE 11	American Indian	2002-03 (*n*=14)	2	14%	2	14%	10	71%			**10**	**71%**
		2003-04 (*n*=19)	4	21%	2	11%	12	63%	1	5%	**13**	**68%**
		2004-05 (*n*=27)	4	15%	5	19%	15	56%	3	11%	**18**	**67%**
		2005-06 (*n*=19)	4	21%	3	16%	12	63%			**12**	**63%**
	Asian	2002-03 (*n*=2)			1	50%	1	50%			**1**	**50%**
		2003-04 (*n*=4)					2	50%	2	50%	**4**	**100%**
		2004-05 (*n*=15)	2	13%	1	7%	7	47%	5	33%	**12**	**80%**
		2003-04 (*n*=11)	3	27%	2	18%	5	45%	1	9%	**6**	**55%**
	Black	2002-03 (*n*=1)					1	100%			**1**	**100%**
		2004-05 (*n*=2)					2	100%			**2**	**100%**
		2005-06 (*n*=2)					2	100%			**2**	**100%**
	Hispanic	2002-03 (*n*=4)	1	25%	1	25%	2	50%			**2**	**50%**
		2003-04 (*n*=5)	2	40%			3	60%			**3**	**60%**
		2004-05 (*n*=8)	1	13%			7	88%			**7**	**88%**
		2005-06 (*n*=6)	3	50%			3	50%			**3**	**50%**
	White	2002-03 (*n*=625)	45	7%	74	12%	371	60%	135	22%	**506**	**81%**
		2003-04 (*n*=663)	64	10%	67	10%	380	57%	152	23%	**532**	**80%**
		2004-05 (*n*=633)	79	12%	55	9%	383	61%	116	18%	**499**	**79%**
		2005-06 (*n*=620)	80	13%	62	10%	358	58%	120	19%	**478**	**77%**

Figure 6.25 shows the Math proficiency levels for the district by school, grade level, and ethnicity from 2002-03 to 2005-06. *Note:* the numbers in some of the student groups are very small. These analyses are for district/school review only.

Look Fors: **Changes in Math proficiency by ethnicity, over time, by school.**

Planning Implications: **Do different schools' teachers require professional learning to meet the needs of all students?**

Figure 6.25

Canyon View School District Math Proficiency Levels
Number and Percentage by School, Grade Level, and Ethnicity, 2002-03 to 2005-06

School, Grade Level, and Ethnicity			Year	Novice		Nearing Proficiency		Proficient		Advanced		Total Proficient	
				Number	Percent	Number	Percent	Number	Percent	Number	Percent	Number	Percent
ELEMENTARY 1	Grade 4	American Indian	2002-03 (*n*=2)					2	100%			**2**	**100%**
			2003-04 (*n*=3)			1	33%	2	67%			**2**	**67%**
			2004-05 (*n*=2)					1	50%	1	50%	**2**	**100%**
			2005-06 (*n*=7)	4	57%			3	43%			**3**	**43%**
		Asian	2002-03 (*n*=1)					1	100%			**1**	**100%**
			2003-04 (*n*=2)					2	100%			**2**	**100%**
		Black	2004-05 (*n*=1)					1	100%			**1**	**100%**
			2005-06 (*n*=1)			1	100%					**0**	
		Hispanic	2002-03 (*n*=3)			2	67%	1	33%			**1**	**33%**
			2003-04 (*n*=2)					1	50%	1	50%	**2**	**100%**
			2005-06 (*n*=2)	1	50%	1	50%					**0**	
		Pacific Islander	2002-03 (*n*=1)							1	100%	**1**	**100%**
		White	2002-03 (*n*=29)	2	7%	3	10%	21	72%	3	10%	**24**	**83%**
			2003-04 (*n*=43)	6	14%	7	17%	23	55%	7	17%	**30**	**71%**
			2004-05 (*n*=31)	1	3%	4	13%	22	71%	4	13%	**26**	**84%**
			2005-06 (*n*=35)	3	9%	4	11%	23	66%	5	14%	**28**	**80%**
ELEMENTARY 2	Grade 4	American Indian	2002-03 (*n*=2)	1	50%	1	50%					**0**	
			2003-04 (*n*=3)					3	100%			**3**	**100%**
			2004-05 (*n*=5)	2	40%			3	60%			**3**	**60%**
			2005-06 (*n*=3)					2	67%	1	33%	**3**	**100%**
		Asian	2002-03 (*n*=2)					1	50%	1	50%	**2**	**100%**
		Black	2002-03 (*n*=1)			1	100%					**0**	
			2003-04 (*n*=3)			1	33%	2	67%			**2**	**67%**
		Hispanic	2003-04 (*n*=1)					1	100%			**1**	**100%**
			2004-05 (*n*=1)					1	100%			**1**	**100%**
			2005-06 (*n*=1)					1	100%			**1**	**100%**
		White	2002-03 (*n*=35)	7	20%	5	14%	21	60%	2	6%	**23**	**66%**
			2003-04 (*n*=39)	6	15%	9	23%	19	49%	5	13%	**24**	**62%**
			2004-05 (*n*=32)	5	16%	5	16%	20	63%	2	6%	**22**	**69%**
			2005-06 (*n*=26)	3	12%	1	4%	18	69%	4	15%	**22**	**85%**
ELEMENTARY 3	Grade 4	American Indian	2002-03 (*n*=5)	3	60%			2	40%			**2**	**40%**
			2003-04 (*n*=1)	1	100%							**0**	
			2004-05 (*n*=1)			1	100%					**0**	
			2005-06 (*n*=3)	2	67%			1	33%			**1**	**33%**
		Black	2004-05 (*n*=1)					1	100%			**1**	**100%**
			2005-06 (*n*=1)	1	100%							**0**	
		Hispanic	2003-04 (*n*=2)			1	50%	1	50%			**1**	**50%**
			2004-05 (*n*=2)					2	100%			**2**	**100%**
		White	2002-03 (*n*=44)	7	16%	7	16%	26	59%	4	9%	**30**	**68%**
			2003-04 (*n*=41)	6	15%	5	12%	24	59%	6	15%	**30**	**73%**
			2004-05 (*n*=47)	5	11%	8	17%	29	62%	5	11%	**34**	**72%**
			2005-06 (*n*=42)	3	7%	11	26%	23	55%	5	12%	**28**	**67%**

Figure 6.25 (Continued)

Canyon View School District Math Proficiency Levels
Number and Percentage by School, Grade Level, and Ethnicity, 2002-03 to 2005-06

School, Grade Level, and Ethnicity			Year	Novice		Nearing Proficiency		Proficient		Advanced		Total Proficient	
				Number	Percent	Number	Percent	Number	Percent	Number	Percent	Number	Percent
ELEMENTARY 4	Grade 4	American Indian	2002-03 (*n*=2)					1	50%	1	50%	**2**	**100%**
			2003-04 (*n*=3)					3	100%			**3**	**100%**
			2004-05 (*n*=6)	1	17%			4	67%	1	17%	**5**	**83%**
			2005-06 (*n*=3)					3	100%			**3**	**100%**
		Asian	2003-04 (*n*=1)	1	100%							**0**	
		Black	2002-03 (*n*=1)					1	100%			**1**	**100%**
			2005-06 (*n*=2)	1	50%			1	50%			**1**	**50%**
		Hispanic	2002-03 (*n*=2)					1	50%	1	50%	**2**	**100%**
			2003-04 (*n*=1)					1	100%			**1**	**100%**
			2005-06 (*n*=4)	1	25%	1	25%	1	25%	1	25%	**2**	**50%**
		White	2002-03 (*n*=72)	2	3%	4	6%	47	65%	19	26%	**66**	**92%**
			2003-04 (*n*=70)	3	4%	3	4%	47	68%	17	25%	**64**	**93%**
			2004-05 (*n*=63)	3	5%	3	5%	36	57%	21	33%	**57**	**90%**
			2005-06 (*n*=68)	2	3%	3	4%	45	66%	18	26%	**63**	**93%**
ELEMENTARY 5	Grade 4	American Indian	2002-03 (*n*=2)			1	50%	1	50%			**1**	**50%**
			2003-04 (*n*=2)	1	50%			1	50%			**1**	**50%**
			2004-05 (*n*=2)	1	50%			1	50%			**1**	**50%**
			2005-06 (*n*=2)					2	100%			**2**	**100%**
		Asian	2003-04 (*n*=1)					1	100%			**1**	**100%**
			2004-05 (*n*=2)					1	50%	1	50%	**2**	**100%**
		Black	2002-03 (*n*=1)					1	100%			**1**	**100%**
			2005-06 (*n*=1)	1	100%							**0**	
		Hispanic	2003-04 (*n*=1)					1	100%			**1**	**100%**
			2004-05 (*n*=3)			1	33%	2	67%			**2**	**67%**
			2005-06 (*n*=2)					2	100%			**2**	**100%**
		White	2002-03 (*n*=39)	2	5%	7	18%	24	63%	6	16%	**30**	**79%**
			2003-04 (*n*=42)	1	2%	1	2%	30	71%	10	24%	**40**	**95%**
			2004-05 (*n*=36)	1	3%	7	19%	19	53%	9	25%	**28**	**78%**
			2005-06 (*n*=37)	2	5%	4	11%	20	54%	11	30%	**31**	**84%**
ELEMENTARY 6	Grade 4	American Indian	2003-04 (*n*=2)					2	100%			**2**	**100%**
			2004-05 (*n*=1)					1	100%			**1**	**100%**
		Hispanic	2002-03 (*n*=1)					1	100%			**1**	**100%**
		White	2002-03 (*n*=30)	1	3%	2	7%	17	57%	10	33%	**27**	**90%**
			2003-04 (*n*=35)	1	3%	2	6%	19	54%	13	37%	**32**	**91%**
			2004-05 (*n*=32)	1	3%	1	3%	19	59%	11	34%	**30**	**94%**
			2005-06 (*n*=29)	1	3%	1	3%	13	45%	14	48%	**27**	**93%**

Figure 6.25 (Continued)

Canyon View School District Math Proficiency Levels
Number and Percentage by School, Grade Level, and Ethnicity, 2002-03 to 2005-06

School	Grade Level	Ethnicity	Year	Novice		Nearing Proficiency		Proficient		Advanced		Total Proficient	
				Number	Percent	Number	Percent	Number	Percent	Number	Percent	Number	Percent
ELEMENTARY 7	Grade 4	American Indian	2002-03 (*n*=2)					2	100%			**2**	**100%**
			2003-04 (*n*=1)					1	100%			**1**	**100%**
			2004-05 (*n*=1)					1	100%			**1**	**100%**
			2005-06 (*n*=3)	1	33%	1	33%	1	33%			**1**	**33%**
		Asian	2003-04 (*n*=1)					1	100%			**1**	**100%**
		Black	2005-06 (*n*=1)	1	100%							**0**	
		White	2002-03 (*n*=55)	4	7%	8	15%	36	65%	7	13%	**43**	**78%**
			2003-04 (*n*=29)	2	7%	2	7%	24	83%	1	3%	**25**	**86%**
			2004-05 (*n*=38)	3	8%	7	18%	24	63%	4	11%	**28**	**74%**
			2005-06 (*n*=39)	2	5%	10	26%	21	54%	6	15%	**27**	**69%**
ELEMENTARY 8	Grade 4	American Indian	2003-04 (*n*=1)	1	100%							**0**	
		Asian	2003-04 (*n*=1)					1	100%			**1**	**100%**
		Hispanic	2005-06 (*n*=1)			1	100%					**0**	
		White	2002-03 (*n*=38)	4	11%	1	3%	23	61%	10	26%	**33**	**87%**
			2003-04 (*n*=34)	2	6%	2	6%	23	68%	7	21%	**30**	**88%**
			2004-05 (*n*=36)	2	6%	7	19%	18	50%	9	25%	**27**	**75%**
			2005-06 (*n*=35)	1	3%	3	9%	24	69%	7	20%	**31**	**89%**
ELEMENTARY 9	Grade 4	American Indian	2002-03 (*n*=4)	2	50%			2	50%			**2**	**50%**
			2003-04 (*n*=3)	1	33%			2	67%			**2**	**67%**
			2004-05 (*n*=5)			2	40%	3	60%			**3**	**60%**
			2005-06 (*n*=6)	1	17%	1	17%	3	50%	1	17%	**4**	**67%**
		Asian	2003-04 (*n*=1)					1	100%			**1**	**100%**
			2004-05 (*n*=1)					1	100%			**1**	**100%**
		Black	2003-04 (*n*=2)					1	50%	1	50%	**2**	**100%**
			2004-05 (*n*=1)					1	100%			**1**	**100%**
		Hispanic	2002-03 (*n*=3)	1	33%			2	67%			**2**	**67%**
			2004-05 (*n*=3)			2	67%	1	33%			**1**	**33%**
			2005-06 (*n*=1)							1	100%	**1**	**100%**
		White	2002-03 (*n*=65)	8	12%	9	14%	35	54%	13	20%	**48**	**74%**
			2003-04 (*n*=64)	8	13%	11	17%	39	61%	6	9%	**45**	**70%**
			2004-05 (*n*=51)	3	6%	2	4%	35	69%	11	22%	**46**	**90%**
			2005-06 (*n*=71)	5	7%	7	10%	47	66%	12	17%	**59**	**83%**

Figure 6.25 (Continued)

Canyon View School District Math Proficiency Levels
Number and Percentage by School, Grade Level, and Ethnicity, 2002-03 to 2005-06

School, Grade Level, and Ethnicity			Year	Novice		Nearing Proficiency		Proficient		Advanced		Total Proficient	
				Number	Percent	Number	Percent	Number	Percent	Number	Percent	Number	Percent
ELEMENTARY 10	Grade 4	American Indian	2002-03 (*n*=3)					3	100%			**3**	**100%**
			2003-04 (*n*=5)	1	20%	1	20%	2	40%	1	20%	**3**	**60%**
			2004-05 (*n*=2)	1	50%			1	50%			**1**	**50%**
			2005-06 (*n*=6)	1	17%			3	50%	2	33%	**5**	**83%**
		Black	2003-04 (*n*=1)					1	100%			**1**	**100%**
			2004-05 (*n*=1)					1	100%			**1**	**100%**
		Hispanic	2002-03 (*n*=2)			1	50%			1	50%	**1**	**50%**
			2003-04 (*n*=1)					1	100%			**1**	**100%**
			2004-05 (*n*=1)							1	100%	**1**	**100%**
			2005-06 (*n*=1)					1	100%			**1**	**100%**
		Pacific Islander	2003-04 (*n*=1)					1	100%			**1**	**100%**
		White	2002-03 (*n*=43)	2	5%	5	12%	23	53%	13	30%	**36**	**84%**
			2003-04 (*n*=45)	4	9%	5	11%	26	58%	10	22%	**36**	**80%**
			2004-05 (*n*=47)	3	6%	3	6%	28	60%	13	28%	**41**	**87%**
			2005-06 (*n*=42)	2	5%	3	7%	24	57%	13	31%	**37**	**88%**
ELEMENTARY 11	Grade 4	American Indian	2002-03 (*n*=1)			1	100%					**0**	
			2003-04 (*n*=5)	1	20%	1	20%	2	40%	1	20%	**3**	**60%**
			2004-05 (*n*=5)	1	20%	2	40%	2	40%			**2**	**40%**
			2005-06 (*n*=1)					1	100%			**1**	**100%**
		Asian	2003-04 (*n*=1)					1	100%			**1**	**100%**
		Hispanic	2004-05 (*n*=1)							1	100%	**1**	**100%**
		Pacific Islander	2002-03 (*n*=1)					1	100%			**1**	**100%**
			2005-06 (*n*=1)	1	100%							**0**	
		White	2002-03 (*n*=33)	4	12%	8	24%	21	64%			**21**	**64%**
			2003-04 (*n*=39)	6	16%	6	16%	22	58%	5	13%	**27**	**71%**
			2004-05 (*n*=29)	5	17%	6	21%	17	59%	1	3%	**18**	**62%**
			2005-06 (*n*=50)	8	16%	8	16%	27	54%	7	14%	**34**	**68%**

Figure 6.25 (Continued)

Canyon View School District Math Proficiency Levels
Number and Percentage by School, Grade Level, and Ethnicity, 2002-03 to 2005-06

School	Grade Level	Ethnicity	Year	Novice Number	Novice Percent	Nearing Proficiency Number	Nearing Proficiency Percent	Proficient Number	Proficient Percent	Advanced Number	Advanced Percent	Total Proficient Number	Total Proficient Percent
MIDDLE 1	Grade 8	American Indian	2002-03 (*n*=7)			1	14%	6	86%			**6**	**86%**
			2003-04 (*n*=7)	1	14%	1	14%	5	71%			**5**	**71%**
			2004-05 (*n*=9)	4	44%	1	11%	3	33%	1	11%	**4**	**44%**
			2005-06 (*n*=18)	1	6%	4	22%	10	56%	3	17%	**13**	**72%**
		Asian	2002-03 (*n*=4)			1	25%	3	75%			**3**	**75%**
			2003-04 (*n*=5)	1	25%			3	75%	1	25%	**4**	**80%**
			2004-05 (*n*=3)					2	67%	1	33%	**3**	**100%**
			2005-06 (*n*=3)					2	67%	1	33%	**3**	**100%**
		Black	2002-03 (*n*=1)					1	100%			**1**	**100%**
			2003-04 (*n*=1)	1	100%							**0**	
			2004-05 (*n*=2)					2	100%			**2**	**100%**
			2005-06 (*n*=3)					3	100%			**3**	**100%**
		Hispanic	2002-03 (*n*=2)					2	100%			**2**	**100%**
			2003-04 (*n*=5)	1	20%			4	80%			**4**	**80%**
			2004-05 (*n*=5)			1	20%	1	20%	3	60%	**4**	**80%**
			2005-06 (*n*=10)			3	30%	4	40%	3	30%	**7**	**70%**
		Pacific Islander	2002-03 (*n*=1)			1	100%					**0**	
		White	2002-03 (*n*=296)	21	7%	30	10%	169	57%	76	26%	**245**	**83%**
			2003-04 (*n*=287)	34	12%	28	10%	166	58%	59	21%	**225**	**78%**
			2004-05 (*n*=296)	30	10%	33	11%	161	55%	72	24%	**233**	**79%**
			2005-06 (*n*=289)	27	9%	27	9%	157	54%	78	27%	**235**	**81%**
MIDDLE 2	Grade 8	American Indian	2002-03 (*n*=11)	4	36%	1	9%	6	55%			**6**	**55%**
			2003-04 (*n*=24)	4	17%	4	17%	14	58%	2	8%	**16**	**67%**
			2004-05 (*n*=12)	3	25%	3	25%	6	50%			**6**	**50%**
			2005-06 (*n*=13)	4	31%	2	15%	7	54%			**7**	**54%**
		Asian	2002-03 (*n*=5)			3	60%	2	40%			**2**	**40%**
			2003-04 (*n*=5)			1	20%	4	80%			**4**	**80%**
			2004-05 (*n*=4)	1	25%	1	25%	2	50%			**2**	**50%**
			2005-06 (*n*=2)	1	50%					1	50%	**1**	**50%**
		Black	2002-03 (*n*=1)					1	100%			**1**	**100%**
			2003-04 (*n*=1)							1	100%	**1**	**100%**
			2004-05 (*n*=2)			2	100%					**0**	
			2005-06 (*n*=3)	1	33%	1	33%	1	33%			**1**	**33%**
		Hispanic	2002-03 (*n*=2)	1	50%					1	50%	**1**	**50%**
			2003-04 (*n*=4)	1	33%			1	33%	1	33%	**2**	**50%**
			2004-05 (*n*=3)	1	33%	1	33%	1	33%			**1**	**33%**
			2005-06 (*n*=3)			3	100%					**0**	
		White	2002-03 (*n*=222)	32	14%	33	15%	119	54%	38	17%	**157**	**71%**
			2003-04 (*n*=183)	25	14%	29	16%	106	58%	23	13%	**129**	**71%**
			2004-05 (*n*=209)	34	16%	28	13%	114	55%	33	16%	**147**	**71%**
			2005-06 (*n*=198)	28	14%	28	14%	102	52%	40	20%	**142**	**72%**

Figure 6.25 (Continued)

Canyon View School District Math Proficiency Levels
Number and Percentage by School, Grade Level, and Ethnicity, 2002-03 to 2005-06

School, Grade Level, and Ethnicity			Year	Novice		Nearing Proficiency		Proficient		Advanced		Total Proficient	
				Number	Percent	Number	Percent	Number	Percent	Number	Percent	Number	Percent
HIGH 1	Grade 11	American Indian	2002-03 (*n*=4)	1	25%	1	25%	2	50%			**2**	**50%**
			2003-04 (*n*=9)	1	11%	1	11%	7	78%			**7**	**78%**
			2004-05 (*n*=6)	1	17%			5	83%			**5**	**83%**
			2005-06 (*n*=9)	2	22%	2	22%	5	56%			**5**	**56%**
		Asian	2002-03 (*n*=1)			1	100%					**0**	
			2003-04 (*n*=2)					1	50%	1	50%	**2**	**100%**
			2004-05 (*n*=5)			1	20%	4	80%			**4**	**80%**
			2005-06 (*n*=3)			1	33%	2	67%			**2**	**67%**
		Black	2004-05 (*n*=1)					1	100%			**1**	**100%**
			2005-06 (*n*=1)					1	100%			**1**	**100%**
		Hispanic	2003-04 (*n*=3)	1	33%			2	67%			**2**	**67%**
			2004-05 (*n*=4)					4	100%			**4**	**100%**
			2005-06 (*n*=2)					2	100%			**2**	**100%**
		White	2002-03 (*n*=301)	19	6%	39	13%	170	56%	73	24%	**243**	**81%**
			2003-04 (*n*=279)	24	9%	22	8%	148	53%	85	30%	**233**	**84%**
			2004-05 (*n*=281)	27	10%	22	8%	183	65%	49	17%	**232**	**83%**
			2005-06 (*n*=304)	31	10%	30	10%	167	55%	76	25%	**243**	**80%**
HIGH 2	Grade 11	American Indian	2002-03 (*n*=8)	1	13%			7	88%			**7**	**88%**
			2003-04 (*n*=9)	2	22%	1	11%	5	56%	1	11%	**6**	**67%**
			2004-05 (*n*=17)	2	12%	4	24%	8	47%	3	18%	**11**	**65%**
			2005-06 (*n*=10)	2	20%	1	10%	7	70%			**7**	**70%**
		Asian	2002-03 (*n*=1)					1	100%			**1**	**100%**
			2003-04 (*n*=2)					1	50%	1	50%	**2**	**100%**
			2004-05 (*n*=9)	1	11%			3	33%	5	56%	**8**	**89%**
			2005-06 (*n*=7)	3	43%			3	43%	1	14%	**4**	**57%**
		Black	2002-03 (*n*=1)					1	100%			**1**	**100%**
			2004-05 (*n*=1)					1	100%			**1**	**100%**
			2005-06 (*n*=1)					1	100%			**1**	**100%**
		Hispanic	2002-03 (*n*=4)	1	25%	1	25%	2	50%			**2**	**50%**
			2003-04 (*n*=2)	1	50%			1	50%			**1**	**50%**
			2004-05 (*n*=4)	1	25%			3	75%			**3**	**75%**
			2005-06 (*n*=4)	3	75%			1	25%			**1**	**25%**
		White	2002-03 (*n*=307)	20	7%	32	10%	194	63%	61	20%	**255**	**83%**
			2003-04 (*n*=363)	35	10%	39	11%	222	61%	67	18%	**289**	**80%**
			2004-05 (*n*=325)	39	12%	27	8%	192	59%	67	21%	**259**	**80%**
			2005-06 (*n*=311)	48	15%	30	10%	189	61%	44	14%	**233**	**75%**

Figure 6.26 shows the Math proficiency levels for the district by grade level and lunch status, over time.

Look Fors: **Differences in Math proficiency levels for students who pay for their lunches, versus those who receive free/reduced lunch.**

Planning Implications: **Do teachers at the different grade levels know how to teach Math to students who live in poverty? Is professional learning required?**

Figure 6.26

Canyon View School District Math Proficiency Levels
Number and Percentage by Grade Level and Lunch Status, 2002-03 to 2005-06

Grade Level	Lunch Status	Year	Novice		Nearing Proficiency		Proficient		Advanced		Total Proficient	
			Number	Percent	Number	Percent	Number	Percent	Number	Percent	Number	Percent
Grade 4	Paid	2002-03 (*n*=383)	23	6%	46	12%	229	60%	85	22%	**314**	**82%**
		2003-04 (*n*=373)	30	8%	30	8%	231	62%	82	22%	**313**	**84%**
		2004-05 (*n*=332)	11	3%	34	10%	210	63%	77	23%	**287**	**86%**
		2005-06 (*n*=353)	23	7%	34	10%	206	58%	90	25%	**296**	**84%**
	Free/Reduced	2002-03 (*n*=139)	27	20%	19	14%	86	62%	7	5%	**93**	**67%**
		2003-04 (*n*=156)	22	14%	28	18%	97	63%	9	6%	**106**	**69%**
		2004-05 (*n*=155)	26	17%	26	17%	86	55%	17	11%	**103**	**66%**
		2005-06 (*n*=156)	25	16%	24	15%	92	59%	15	10%	**107**	**69%**
Grade 8	Paid	2002-03 (*n*=450)	29	6%	56	12%	259	58%	106	24%	**365**	**81%**
		2003-04 (*n*=438)	44	10%	50	11%	266	61%	78	18%	**344**	**79%**
		2004-05 (*n*=436)	41	9%	50	11%	240	55%	105	24%	**345**	**79%**
		2005-06 (*n*=414)	29	7%	40	10%	230	56%	115	28%	**345**	**83%**
	Free/Reduced	2002-03 (*n*=83)	23	28%	14	17%	39	47%	7	8%	**46**	**55%**
		2003-04 (*n*=83)	24	29%	13	16%	37	45%	9	11%	**46**	**55%**
		2004-05 (*n*=98)	29	30%	15	15%	48	49%	6	6%	**54**	**56%**
		2005-06 (*n*=118)	30	25%	26	22%	49	42%	13	11%	**62**	**53%**
Grade 11	Paid	2002-03 (*n*=626)	44	7%	75	12%	375	60%	132	21%	**507**	**81%**
		2003-04 (*n*=636)	56	9%	63	10%	373	59%	144	23%	**517**	**81%**
		2004-05 (*n*=626)	70	11%	54	9%	383	61%	119	19%	**502**	**80%**
		2005-06 (*n*=593)	72	12%	61	10%	343	58%	117	20%	**460**	**78%**
	Free/Reduced	2002-03 (*n*=20)	4	20%	3	15%	10	50%	3	15%	**13**	**65%**
		2003-04 (*n*=50)	13	26%	5	10%	22	44%	10	20%	**32**	**64%**
		2004-05 (*n*=54)	14	26%	7	13%	29	54%	4	7%	**33**	**61%**
		2005-06 (*n*=48)	13	27%	5	10%	26	54%	4	8%	**30**	**63%**

Figure 6.27 shows the Math proficiency levels for the district by school, grade level, and lunch status, over time. *Note:* the numbers in some of the student groups are very small. These analyses are for district/school review only.

Look Fors:	**Differences in proficiency levels for free/reduced lunch students by school and over time.**
Planning Implications:	**How are the schools teaching Math students? Do teachers require professional learning in how to teach students who live in poverty?**

Figure 6.27

Canyon View School District Math Proficiency Levels
Number and Percentage by School, Grade Level, and Lunch Status, 2002-03 to 2005-06

School, Grade Level, and Lunch Status			Year	Novice		Nearing Proficiency		Proficient		Advanced		Total Proficient	
				Number	Percent	Number	Percent	Number	Percent	Number	Percent	Number	Percent
ELEMENTARY 1	Grade 4	Paid	2002-03 (*n*=24)	2	8%	2	8%	16	67%	4	17%	**20**	**83%**
			2003-04 (*n*=28)	2	7%	3	11%	15	54%	8	29%	**23**	**82%**
			2004-05 (*n*=24)			2	8%	17	71%	5	21%	**22**	**92%**
			2005-06 (*n*=22)	3	14%	3	14%	13	59%	3	14%	**16**	**73%**
		Free/Reduced	2002-03 (*n*=11)			3	27%	8	73%			**8**	**73%**
			2003-04 (*n*=21)	4	19%	5	24%	12	57%			**12**	**57%**
			2004-05 (*n*=12)	1	8%	2	17%	9	75%			**9**	**75%**
			2005-06 (*n*=19)	5	26%	3	16%	10	53%	1	5%	**11**	**58%**
ELEMENTARY 2	Grade 4	Paid	2002-03 (*n*=18)	1	6%	4	22%	12	67%	1	6%	**13**	**72%**
			2003-04 (*n*=20)	2	10%	3	15%	11	55%	4	20%	**15**	**75%**
			2004-05 (*n*=16)	1	6%	2	13%	11	69%	2	13%	**13**	**81%**
			2005-06 (*n*=11)					9	82%	2	18%	**11**	**100%**
		Free/Reduced	2002-03 (*n*=21)	7	33%	2	10%	10	48%	2	10%	**12**	**57%**
			2003-04 (*n*=23)	4	17%	7	30%	11	48%	1	4%	**12**	**52%**
			2004-05 (*n*=25)	6	24%	4	16%	15	60%			**15**	**60%**
			2005-06 (*n*=19)	3	16%	1	5%	12	63%	3	16%	**15**	**79%**
ELEMENTARY 3	Grade 4	Paid	2002-03 (*n*=28)	2	7%	5	18%	17	61%	4	14%	**21**	**75%**
			2003-04 (*n*=30)	5	17%	3	10%	17	57%	5	17%	**22**	**73%**
			2004-05 (*n*=37)	2	5%	7	19%	24	65%	4	11%	**28**	**76%**
			2005-06 (*n*=30)	4	13%	8	27%	13	43%	5	17%	**18**	**60%**
		Free/Reduced	2002-03 (*n*=21)	8	38%	2	10%	11	52%			**11**	**52%**
			2003-04 (*n*=14)	2	14%	3	21%	8	57%	1	7%	**9**	**64%**
			2004-05 (*n*=11)	3	27%	1	9%	6	55%	1	9%	**7**	**64%**
			2005-06 (*n*=15)	2	13%	3	20%	10	67%			**10**	**67%**
ELEMENTARY 4	Grade 4	Paid	2002-03 (*n*=65)	2	3%	4	6%	39	60%	20	31%	**59**	**91%**
			2003-04 (*n*=61)	4	7%	1	2%	42	69%	14	23%	**56**	**92%**
			2004-05 (*n*=49)	1	2%	2	4%	31	63%	15	31%	**46**	**94%**
			2005-06 (*n*=58)	2	3%	3	5%	37	64%	16	28%	**53**	**91%**
		Free/Reduced	2002-03 (*n*=12)					11	92%	1	8%	**12**	**100%**
			2003-04 (*n*=14)			2	14%	9	64%	3	21%	**12**	**86%**
			2004-05 (*n*=19)	3	16%	1	5%	8	42%	7	37%	**15**	**79%**
			2005-06 (*n*=15)	2	13%	1	7%	11	73%	1	7%	**12**	**80%**
ELEMENTARY 5	Grade 4	Paid	2002-03 (*n*=35)	2	6%	7	20%	21	60%	5	14%	**26**	**74%**
			2003-04 (*n*=42)			1	2%	31	74%	10	24%	**41**	**98%**
			2004-05 (*n*=33)	1	3%	6	18%	17	52%	9	27%	**26**	**79%**
			2005-06 (*n*=30)			4	13%	16	53%	10	33%	**26**	**87%**
		Free/Reduced	2002-03 (*n*=7)			1	14%	5	71%	1	14%	**6**	**86%**
			2003-04 (*n*=4)	2	50%			2	50%			**2**	**50%**
			2004-05 (*n*=9)	1	11%	2	22%	6	67%			**6**	**67%**
			2005-06 (*n*=11)	3	27%			7	64%	1	9%	**8**	**73%**

Figure 6.27 (Continued)

Canyon View School District Math Proficiency Levels
Number and Percentage by School, Grade Level, and Lunch Status, 2002-03 to 2005-06

School	Grade Level	Lunch Status	Year	Novice		Nearing Proficiency		Proficient		Advanced		Total Proficient	
				Number	Percent	Number	Percent	Number	Percent	Number	Percent	Number	Percent
ELEMENTARY 6	Grade 4	Paid	2002-03 (*n*=26)			1	4%	15	58%	10	38%	**25**	**96%**
			2003-04 (*n*=33)	1	3%	1	3%	19	58%	12	36%	**31**	**94%**
			2004-05 (*n*=29)			1	3%	19	66%	9	31%	**28**	**97%**
			2005-06 (*n*=25)	1	4%	1	4%	10	40%	13	52%	**23**	**92%**
		Free/Reduced	2002-03 (*n*=5)	1	20%	1	20%	3	60%			**3**	**60%**
			2003-04 (*n*=4)			1	25%	2	50%	1	25%	**3**	**75%**
			2004-05 (*n*=4)	1	25%			1	25%	2	50%	**3**	**75%**
			2005-06 (*n*=3)					2	67%	1	33%	**3**	**100%**
ELEMENTARY 7	Grade 4	Paid	2002-03 (*n*=42)	2	5%	6	14%	28	67%	6	14%	**34**	**81%**
			2003-04 (*n*=24)	2	8%	2	8%	19	79%	1	4%	**20**	**83%**
			2004-05 (*n*=24)	1	4%	4	17%	16	67%	3	13%	**19**	**79%**
			2005-06 (*n*=26)	3	12%	2	8%	16	62%	5	19%	**21**	**81%**
		Free/Reduced	2002-03 (*n*=15)	2	13%	2	13%	10	67%	1	7%	**11**	**73%**
			2003-04 (*n*=7)					7	100%			**7**	**100%**
			2004-05 (*n*=13)	1	8%	2	15%	9	69%	1	8%	**10**	**77%**
			2005-06 (*n*=12)	1	8%	6	50%	4	33%	1	8%	**5**	**42%**
ELEMENTARY 8	Grade 4	Paid	2002-03 (*n*=29)	1	3%	1	3%	18	62%	9	31%	**27**	**93%**
			2003-04 (*n*=23)	1	4%	1	4%	14	61%	7	30%	**21**	**91%**
			2004-05 (*n*=24)	1	4%	3	13%	11	46%	9	38%	**20**	**83%**
			2005-06 (*n*=28)			4	14%	19	68%	5	18%	**24**	**86%**
		Free/Reduced	2002-03 (*n*=9)	3	33%			5	56%	1	11%	**6**	**67%**
			2003-04 (*n*=13)	2	15%	1	8%	10	77%			**10**	**77%**
			2004-05 (*n*=11)	1	9%	4	36%	6	55%			**6**	**55%**
			2005-06 (*n*=8)	1	13%			5	63%	2	25%	**7**	**88%**
ELEMENTARY 9	Grade 4	Paid	2002-03 (*n*=62)	8	13%	8	13%	33	53%	13	21%	**46**	**74%**
			2003-04 (*n*=51)	7	14%	9	18%	28	55%	7	14%	**35**	**69%**
			2004-05 (*n*=43)	1	2%	1	2%	33	77%	8	19%	**41**	**95%**
			2005-06 (*n*=62)	5	8%	4	6%	40	65%	13	21%	**53**	**85%**
		Free/Reduced	2002-03 (*n*=9)	3	33%	1	11%	5	56%			**5**	**56%**
			2003-04 (*n*=19)	2	11%	2	11%	15	79%			**15**	**79%**
			2004-05 (*n*=18)	2	11%	5	28%	8	44%	3	17%	**11**	**61%**
			2005-06 (*n*=15)	1	7%	4	27%	9	60%	1	7%	**10**	**67%**
ELEMENTARY 10	Grade 4	Paid	2002-03 (*n*=36)	2	6%	4	11%	17	47%	13	36%	**30**	**83%**
			2003-04 (*n*=39)	3	8%	3	8%	23	59%	10	26%	**33**	**85%**
			2004-05 (*n*=37)	1	3%	2	5%	22	59%	12	32%	**34**	**92%**
			2005-06 (*n*=37)			2	5%	21	57%	14	38%	**35**	**95%**
		Free/Reduced	2002-03 (*n*=12)			2	17%	9	75%	1	8%	**10**	**83%**
			2003-04 (*n*=14)	2	14%	3	21%	8	57%	1	7%	**9**	**64%**
			2004-05 (*n*=14)	3	21%	1	7%	8	57%	2	14%	**10**	**71%**
			2005-06 (*n*=12)	3	25%	1	8%	7	58%	1	8%	**8**	**67%**

Figure 6.27 (Continued)

Canyon View School District Math Proficiency Levels
Number and Percentage by School, Grade Level, and Lunch Status, 2002-03 to 2005-06

School	Grade Level	Lunch Status	Year	Novice Number	Novice Percent	Nearing Proficiency Number	Nearing Proficiency Percent	Proficient Number	Proficient Percent	Advanced Number	Advanced Percent	Total Proficient Number	Total Proficient Percent
ELEMENTARY 11	Grade 4	Paid	2002-03 (*n*=18)	1	6%	4	22%	13	72%			**13**	**72%**
			2003-04 (*n*=22)	3	14%	3	14%	12	55%	4	18%	**16**	**73%**
			2004-05 (*n*=16)	2	13%	4	25%	9	56%	1	6%	**10**	**63%**
			2005-06 (*n*=24)	5	21%	3	13%	12	50%	4	17%	**16**	**67%**
		Free/Reduced	2002-03 (*n*=17)	3	18%	5	29%	9	53%			**9**	**53%**
			2003-04 (*n*=23)	4	17%	4	17%	13	57%	2	9%	**15**	**65%**
			2004-05 (*n*=19)	4	21%	4	21%	10	53%	1	5%	**11**	**58%**
			2005-06 (*n*=27)	4	15%	5	19%	15	56%	3	11%	**18**	**67%**
MIDDLE 1	Grade 8	Paid	2002-03 (*n*=276)	13	5%	30	11%	161	58%	72	26%	**233**	**84%**
			2003-04 (*n*=268)	29	11%	23	9%	161	60%	55	21%	**216**	**81%**
			2004-05 (*n*=265)	20	8%	31	12%	141	53%	73	28%	**214**	**81%**
			2005-06 (*n*=270)	18	7%	20	7%	151	56%	81	30%	**232**	**86%**
		Free/Reduced	2002-03 (*n*=35)	8	23%	3	9%	20	57%	4	11%	**24**	**69%**
			2003-04 (*n*=37)	9	24%	6	16%	17	46%	5	14%	**22**	**59%**
			2004-05 (*n*=50)	14	28%	4	8%	28	56%	4	8%	**32**	**64%**
			2005-06 (*n*=53)	10	19%	14	26%	25	47%	4	8%	**29**	**55%**
MIDDLE 2	Grade 8	Paid	2002-03 (*n*=172)	16	9%	24	14%	98	57%	34	20%	**132**	**77%**
			2003-04 (*n*=170)	15	9%	27	16%	105	62%	23	14%	**128**	**75%**
			2004-05 (*n*=170)	21	12%	19	11%	99	58%	31	18%	**130**	**76%**
			2005-06 (*n*=140)	11	8%	20	14%	79	56%	30	21%	**109**	**78%**
		Free/Reduced	2002-03 (*n*=47)	14	30%	11	23%	19	40%	3	6%	**22**	**47%**
			2003-04 (*n*=46)	15	33%	7	15%	20	43%	4	9%	**24**	**52%**
			2004-05 (*n*=48)	15	31%	11	23%	20	42%	2	4%	**22**	**46%**
			2005-06 (*n*=65)	20	31%	12	18%	24	37%	9	14%	**33**	**51%**
HIGH 1	Grade 11	Paid	2002-03 (*n*=288)	16	6%	38	13%	164	57%	70	24%	**234**	**81%**
			2003-04 (*n*=278)	21	8%	23	8%	150	54%	84	30%	**234**	**84%**
			2004-05 (*n*=281)	27	10%	21	7%	185	66%	48	17%	**233**	**83%**
			2005-06 (*n*=303)	30	10%	28	9%	171	56%	74	24%	**245**	**81%**
		Free/Reduced	2002-03 (*n*=18)	4	22%	3	17%	8	44%	3	17%	**11**	**61%**
			2003-04 (*n*=15)	5	33%			8	53%	2	13%	**10**	**67%**
			2004-05 (*n*=16)	1	6%	2	13%	12	75%	1	6%	**13**	**81%**
			2005-06 (*n*=15)	3	20%	4	27%	6	40%	2	13%	**8**	**53%**
HIGH 2	Grade 11	Paid	2002-03 (*n*=321)	22	7%	33	10%	205	64%	61	19%	**266**	**83%**
			2003-04 (*n*=337)	30	9%	34	10%	213	63%	60	18%	**273**	**81%**
			2004-05 (*n*=323)	34	11%	27	8%	191	59%	71	22%	**262**	**81%**
			2005-06 (*n*=287)	41	14%	31	11%	172	60%	43	15%	**215**	**75%**
		Free/Reduced	2003-04 (*n*=34)	7	21%	5	15%	14	41%	8	24%	**22**	**65%**
			2004-05 (*n*=29)	8	28%	4	14%	14	48%	3	10%	**17**	**59%**
			2005-06 (*n*=30)	10	33%			18	60%	2	7%	**20**	**67%**

Figure 6.28 shows the Math proficiency levels for the district for grade four gifted students, over time.

Look Fors:	**How students who participate in the gifted program score in Math. The percentage of gifted students who score *Advanced.***
Planning Implications:	**If not all "gifted" students are proficient, what needs to change to improve their performance?**

Figure 6.28

Canyon View School District Math Proficiency Levels Number and Percentage by Grade Level and Gifted Status, 2004-05 to 2005-06

Grade Level	Year	Novice		Nearing Proficiency		Proficient		Advanced		Total Proficient	
		Number	Percent	Number	Percent	Number	Percent	Number	Percent	Number	Percent
Grade 4	2004-05 (*n*=57)			1	2%	27	47%	29	51%	**56**	**98%**
	2005-06 (*n*=42)					16	38%	26	62%	**42**	**100%**

Figure 6.29 shows the Math proficiency levels for the district for grade four gifted students by school from 2004-05 to 2005-06. *Note:* the numbers in some of the student groups are very small. These analyses are for district/school review only.

Look Fors:	**The number/percentage of students who participate in the gifted program that score *Proficient* or *Advanced*, by school.**
Planning Implications:	**Are all schools able to meet the needs of their gifted students?**

Figure 6.29

Canyon View School District Math Proficiency Levels
Number and Percentage by School, Grade Level, and Gifted Status, 2004-05 to 2005-06

School	Grade Level	Year	Novice		Nearing Proficiency		Proficient		Advanced		Total Proficient	
			Number	Percent	Number	Percent	Number	Percent	Number	Percent	Number	Percent
Elementary 1	Grade 4	2004-05 (*n*=3)					2	67%	1	33%	3	100%
		2005-06 (*n*=4)					1	25%	3	75%	4	100%
Elementary 2	Grade 4	2004-05 (*n*=1)							1	100%	1	100%
		2005-06 (*n*=3)					1	33%	2	67%	3	100%
Elementary 3	Grade 4	2004-05 (*n*=18)			1	6%	15	83%	2	11%	17	94%
		2005-06 (*n*=7)					3	43%	4	57%	7	100%
Elementary 4	Grade 4	2004-05 (*n*=4)					1	25%	3	75%	4	100%
		2005-06 (*n*=4)					2	50%	2	50%	4	100%
Elementary 5	Grade 4	2004-05 (*n*=8)					4	50%	4	50%	8	100%
		2005-06 (*n*=3)							3	100%	3	100%
Elementary 6	Grade 4	2004-05 (*n*=7)					2	29%	5	71%	7	100%
		2005-06 (*n*=4)					2	50%	2	50%	4	100%
Elementary 7	Grade 4	2004-05 (*n*=3)							3	100%	3	100%
		2005-06 (*n*=2)							2	100%	2	100%
Elementary 8	Grade 4	2004-05 (*n*=2)					1	50%	1	50%	2	100%
		2005-06 (*n*=2)					1	50%	1	50%	2	100%
Elementary 9	Grade 4	2004-05 (*n*=5)					1	20%	4	80%	5	100%
		2005-06 (*n*=8)					4	50%	4	50%	8	100%
Elementary 10	Grade 4	2004-05 (*n*=5)					1	20%	4	80%	5	100%
		2005-06 (*n*=3)					1	33%	2	67%	3	100%
Elementary 11	Grade 4	2004-05 (*n*=1)							1	100%	1	100%
		2005-06 (*n*=2)					1	50%	1	50%	2	100%

Figure 6.30 shows the Math proficiency for the district for IEP students by grade level, over time.

Look Fors: **The number and percentage of students with IEPS who scored at the different proficiency levels, by grade level.**

Planning Implications: **Is Math instruction meeting the needs of all students with IEPs? Do teachers know how to teach Math to students with IEPs?**

Figure 6.30

Canyon View School District Math Proficiency Levels
Number and Percentage of IEP Students by Grade Level, 2002-03 to 2005-06

Grade Level	Year	Novice		Nearing Proficiency		Proficient		Advanced		Total Proficient	
		Number	Percent	Number	Percent	Number	Percent	Number	Percent	Number	Percent
Grade 4	2002-03 (*n*=80)	26	33%	12	15%	40	50%	2	3%	**42**	**53%**
	2003-04 (*n*=82)	31	38%	15	18%	32	39%	4	5%	**36**	**44%**
	2004-05 (*n*=79)	26	33%	22	28%	25	32%	6	8%	**31**	**39%**
	2005-06 (*n*=73)	23	32%	17	23%	27	37%	6	8%	**33**	**45%**
Grade 8	2002-03 (*n*=49)	24	49%	10	20%	13	27%	2	4%	**15**	**31%**
	2003-04 (*n*=50)	25	50%	9	18%	15	30%	1	2%	**16**	**32%**
	2004-05 (*n*=67)	31	46%	15	22%	20	30%	1	1%	**21**	**31%**
	2005-06 (*n*=58)	25	43%	17	29%	16	28%			**16**	**28%**
Grade 11	2002-03 (*n*=33)	12	36%	10	30%	11	33%			**11**	**33%**
	2003-04 (*n*=34)	16	47%	9	26%	9	26%			**9**	**26%**
	2004-05 (*n*=53)	24	45%	9	17%	18	34%	2	4%	**20**	**38%**
	2005-06 (*n*=49)	31	63%	5	10%	13	27%			**13**	**27%**

Figure 6.31 shows the Math proficiency for the district of IEP students by school and grade level, over time.

Look Fors: **Differences in proficiency levels for students with IEPS by school and over time.**

Planning Implications: **Are all schools effective in assuring that IEP goals are attainable? Are all students with IEPs improving? Are students with IEPs included in regular classes?**

Figure 6.31

Canyon View School District Math Proficiency Levels
Number and Percentage of IEP Students by School and Grade Level, 2002-03 to 2005-06

School	Grade Level	Year	Novice		Nearing Proficiency		Proficient		Advanced		Total Proficient	
			Number	Percent	Number	Percent	Number	Percent	Number	Percent	Number	Percent
Elementary 1	Grade 4	2002-03 (*n*=4)			1	25%	3	75%			**3**	**75%**
		2003-04 (*n*=5)	2	40%	1	20%	2	40%			**2**	**40%**
		2004-05 (*n*=2)			2	100%					**0**	
		2005-06 (*n*=6)	2	33%	2	33%	2	33%			**2**	**33%**
Elementary 2	Grade 4	2002-03 (*n*=9)	5	56%	2	22%	2	22%			**2**	**22%**
		2003-04 (*n*=7)	5	71%	1	14%			1	14%	**1**	**14%**
		2004-05 (*n*=13)	5	38%	3	23%	5	38%			**5**	**38%**
		2005-06 (*n*=6)	2	33%			3	50%	1	17%	**4**	**67%**
Elementary 3	Grade 4	2002-03 (*n*=7)	5	71%			2	29%			**2**	**29%**
		2003-04 (*n*=8)	3	38%			4	50%	1	13%	**5**	**63%**
		2004-05 (*n*=7)	4	57%	2	29%	1	14%			**1**	**14%**
		2005-06 (*n*=7)	3	43%	1	14%	3	43%			**3**	**43%**
Elementary 4	Grade 4	2002-03 (*n*=15)	2	13%	2	13%	10	67%	1	7%	**11**	**73%**
		2003-04 (*n*=9)	1	11%	1	11%	7	78%			**7**	**78%**
		2004-05 (*n*=12)	4	33%	1	8%	5	42%	2	17%	**7**	**58%**
		2005-06 (*n*=11)	3	27%	1	9%	5	45%	2	18%	**7**	**64%**
Elementary 5	Grade 4	2002-03 (*n*=7)	1	14%	3	43%	3	43%			**3**	**43%**
		2003-04 (*n*=7)	1	14%	1	14%	5	71%			**5**	**71%**
		2004-05 (*n*=5)	1	20%	4	80%					**0**	
		2005-06 (*n*=7)	2	29%	1	14%	3	43%	1	14%	**4**	**57%**
Elementary 6	Grade 4	2002-03 (*n*=4)	1	25%	1	25%	2	50%			**2**	**50%**
		2003-04 (*n*=3)					1	33%	2	67%	**3**	**100%**
		2004-05 (*n*=5)					3	60%	2	40%	**5**	**100%**
		2005-06 (*n*=4)					3	75%	1	25%	**4**	**100%**
Elementary 7	Grade 4	2002-03 (*n*=9)	3	33%	1	11%	5	56%			**5**	**56%**
		2003-04 (*n*=1)	1	100%							**0**	
		2004-05 (*n*=6)	1	17%	2	33%	3	50%			**3**	**50%**
		2005-06 (*n*=4)	1	25%	2	50%	1	25%			**1**	**25%**
Elementary 8	Grade 4	2002-03 (*n*=5)	1	20%			4	80%			**4**	**80%**
		2003-04 (*n*=9)	3	33%	2	22%	4	44%			**4**	**44%**
		2004-05 (*n*=5)	1	20%	2	40%			2	40%	**2**	**40%**
		2005-06 (*n*=5)	1	20%	3	60%	1	20%			**1**	**20%**
Elementary 9	Grade 4	2002-03 (*n*=11)	5	45%			6	55%			**6**	**55%**
		2003-04 (*n*=17)	6	35%	5	29%	6	35%			**6**	**35%**
		2004-05 (*n*=11)	2	18%	3	27%	6	55%			**6**	**55%**
		2005-06 (*n*=13)	4	31%	5	38%	4	31%			**4**	**31%**
Elementary 10	Grade 4	2002-03 (*n*=4)	1	25%			2	50%	1	25%	**3**	**75%**
		2003-04 (*n*=9)	4	44%	3	33%	2	22%			**2**	**22%**
		2004-05 (*n*=9)	4	44%	3	33%	2	22%			**2**	**22%**
		2005-06 (*n*=6)	2	33%	1	17%	2	33%	1	17%	**3**	**50%**
Elementary 11	Grade 4	2002-03 (*n*=5)	2	40%	2	40%	1	20%			**1**	**20%**
		2003-04 (*n*=7)	5	71%	1	14%	1	14%			**1**	**14%**
		2004-05 (*n*=4)	4	100%							**0**	
		2005-06 (*n*=4)	3	75%	1	25%					**0**	

Figure 6.31 (Continued)

Canyon View School District Math Proficiency Levels
Number and Percentage of IEP Students by School and Grade Level, 2002-03 to 2005-06

School	Grade Level	Year	Novice		Nearing Proficiency		Proficient		Advanced		Total Proficient	
			Number	Percent	Number	Percent	Number	Percent	Number	Percent	Number	Percent
Middle 1	Grade 8	2002-03 (*n*=20)	6	30%	6	30%	7	35%	1	5%	**8**	**40%**
		2003-04 (*n*=34)	20	59%	3	9%	11	32%			**11**	**32%**
		2004-05 (*n*=46)	18	39%	11	24%	16	35%	1	2%	**17**	**37%**
		2005-06 (*n*=34)	14	41%	12	35%	8	24%			**8**	**24%**
Middle 2	Grade 8	2002-03 (*n*=29)	18	62%	4	14%	6	21%	1	3%	**7**	**24%**
		2003-04 (*n*=16)	5	31%	6	38%	4	25%	1	6%	**5**	**31%**
		2004-05 (*n*=21)	13	62%	4	19%	4	19%			**4**	**19%**
		2005-06 (*n*=24)	11	46%	5	21%	8	33%			**8**	**33%**
High 1	Grade 11	2002-03 (*n*=14)	6	43%	4	29%	4	29%			**4**	**29%**
		2003-04 (*n*=17)	10	59%	4	24%	3	18%			**3**	**18%**
		2004-05 (*n*=22)	8	36%	5	23%	9	41%			**9**	**41%**
		2005-06 (*n*=18)	10	56%	3	17%	5	28%			**5**	**28%**
High 2	Grade 11	2002-03 (*n*=19)	6	32%	6	32%	7	37%			**7**	**37%**
		2003-04 (*n*=17)	6	35%	5	29%	6	35%			**6**	**35%**
		2004-05 (*n*=27)	14	52%	2	7%	9	33%	2	7%	**11**	**41%**
		2005-06 (*n*=30)	20	67%	2	7%	8	27%			**8**	**27%**

Study Questions for Where Are We Now?

As you review Canyon View's data, use either the margins in the text, this page, or print this page from the CD to write down your early thinking. These notes, of course, are only placeholders until all the data are analyzed. (Ch6Qs.pdf)

1. What are the student learning *strengths* and *challenges* for Canyon View School District?

Strengths	*Challenges*

2. What are some *implications* for the Canyon View improvement plan?

3. Looking at the data presented, what other student learning data would you want to answer the question *Where are we now?* for Canyon View School District?

What I Saw in the Example: Canyon View School District

Using the study questions as an outline, what I saw in the data for Chapter 6 appears below and on the next page. When applicable, I have referenced the figure or page number that gave me my first impression of strengths and challenges. CD-ROM (Ch6Saw.pdf)

Student Learning Strengths	***Student Learning Challenges***
Reading • Overall, the proficiency scores are high. While grade 4 had historically higher percentages of students proficient, grades 8 and 11 saw slight increases in the percent proficient in the most recent year. (Figure 6.8) • While Elementary School 6's percentage of students proficient has decreased each year, those percentages are in the 90s. Plus there were no students scoring *Novice* any of those years. (Figure 6.10) • The highest percentages of proficient students were in Elementary Schools 4, 6, 8, and 10. (Figure 6.10) • All grade 4 girls in Elementary School 6 were proficient in 2002-03 and 2005-06, and all males were proficient in 2004-05. One hundred percent of the fourth-grade females were proficient in elementary school 8 in 2003-04 and 2005-06. (Figure 6.11) • There is an increase in the percent of American Indian and Asian fourth graders who were proficient from 2004-05 to 2005-06. (Figure 6.12) • Eighth and eleventh grades percent proficient increased (or stayed the same) for free/reduced lunch students in 2005-06. (Figure 6.14) • There were a lot of grade two Title 1 reading students that were not proficient in 2005-06.	*Reading* • Grade 4 had a lower percentage of students proficient in the most recent year, after increases in the previous year. (Figure 6.8) • There is not a lot of difference in the percentage proficient by gender, until the last couple of years. More girls than boys were proficient. A slight gender gap appears in grades 8 and 11. (Figure 6.9) • Only four elementary schools had higher percentage of proficient students in 2005-06 than 4 years earlier: Elementary Schools 2, 4, 7, and 8. (Figure 6.10) • The lowest percent proficient students were in Elementary School 1 (72%) and Elementary 11 (75%). (Figure 6.10) • All middle and high schools had a smaller percentage of proficient students in 2005-06 than four years earlier. (Figure 6.10) • Males dropped 4, 6, and 5 percentage points between 2004-05 and 2005-06 in grades 4, 8, and 11, respectively. (Figure 6.9) • Elementary Schools 1 and 11 males had the largest drops in percent proficient in 2005-06. (Figure 6.11) • Eleventh grade Black and Hispanic students scored the lowest. (Figure 6.12) • There is a difference in scores between paid and free/reduced lunch students at all three grades. (Figure 6.11) • There is a difference in percent proficient between paid and free/reduced lunch students in every school (some Ns are very small, however.). (Figure 6.15) • Although the Ns get too small to analyze by school, students with IEPs do not have a high percentage of proficiency. (Figures 6.18 and 6.19) • The percentage of IEP students who are proficient drops dramatically after grade 4. (Figure 6.18)

What I Saw in the Example: (Continued)

Student Learning Strengths	Student Learning Challenges
Math • The proficiency scores for math are relatively high, but not as high as reading. (Figure 6.20) • Only one gifted fourth grader was not proficient in math. (Figure 6.28)	*Math* • The percent proficient is lower than reading. (Figure 6.20) • Only grade 8 had a higher percent of students proficient in 2005-06 than the previous year. (Figure 6.20) • Elementary Schools 1, 3, and 7, and High Schools 1 and 2 had the largest decreases in percent proficient. (Figure 6.22) • In grade 4, the percentage of males proficient in Math was slightly greater than females. In grades 8 and 11, proportionately more females than males were proficient. (Figure 6.23) • The Ns are so small for the different ethnicities with schools that it is difficult to compare results, meaningfully. (Figure 6.25) • There is a difference in percent proficient at each tested grade level for paid and free/reduced lunch students.. (Figure 6.26) • Fewer than 28% of high school students with IEPs were proficient in 2005-06. (Figure 6.31)

Implications for Canyon View's improvement plan

- Do staff members have the professional learning they need to work with students with special needs, such as learning disabilities, ethnic diversity, those living in poverty, etc.? Are both genders taught the same way in all classes?
- Are the programs being implemented completely and effectively? How are they evaluated?

Other desired student learning data or information

- It would be nice to see how the district's formative assessments support the state results.
- Individual student growth analyses.

Summary

Answering the question, *Where are we now?*, takes the data analysis work into the student learning realm. Analyzing required norm-referenced and/or criterion-referenced tests and disaggregating by school, grade level, gender, ethnicity, free/reduced lunch status, and special education is an excellent way to begin answering the question, *How are we doing?* Looking across measures can be useful and informative—another way to think about what students know and are able to do, giving us a glimpse at *how* students learn.

As one looks at the trends, she/he can begin to see discrepancies and areas for further and deeper analyses, which we follow in the next chapter. The study questions can help guide us to these next levels.

Analyzing required norm-referenced and/or criterion-referenced tests and disaggregating by school, grade level, gender, ethnicity, and lunch status is an excellent way to begin answering the question, "How are we doing?"

On the CD Related to this Chapter

- Study Questions Related to *Where Are We Now?* (Ch6Qs.doc)
  These study questions will help you understand the information provided in Chapter 6. This template file can be printed for use with staff as you begin to explore your own student learning results.
- *Arguments For and Against Standardized Testing* (TestArgu.pdf)
  This table summarizes the most common arguments for and against the use of standardized testing.
- *Standardized Test Score Terms, Their Most Effective Uses, and Cautions for Their Uses* (TestTerm.pdf)
  This table shows the different standardized testing terms, their effective uses, and cautions for their uses.
- *Arguments For and Against Performance Assessments* (PerfArgu.pdf)
  This table shows the most common arguments for and against the use of performance assessments.
- *Arguments For and Against Teacher Grading* (GradeArg.pdf)
  This table shows the most common arguments for and against the use of teacher grading.
- *Terms Related to Analyzing Student Learning Results, Descriptively, Their Most Effective Uses, and Cautions for Their Uses* (SAterms1.pdf)
  This table shows the different terms related to analyzing student learning results, descriptively, their effective uses, and cautions for their uses.

- *Terms Related to Analyzing Student Learning Results, Inferentially, Their Most Effective Uses, and Cautions for Their Uses* (SAterms2.pdf)
  This table shows the different terms related to analyzing student learning results, inferentially, their effective uses, and cautions for their uses.
- *What I Saw in the Example* (Ch6Saw.pdf)
  What I Saw in the Example is a file, organized by the student learning study questions, that summarizes what the author saw in the student learning data provided by Canyon View School District.
- Student Learning Graphing Templates (DistrSA_Math.xls and DistrSA_Read.xls)
  All of the *Microsoft Excel* files that were used to create the Reading and Math student learning tables in the Canyon View example (Chapter 6) appear on the CD. Use these templates to create your data tables.
- Other-size District Student Learning Graphing/Table Templates (Folder)
  All of the *Microsoft Excel* files that were used to create the student learning tables/graphs in the district A and C examples appear on the CD. Use these templates similar to your district size by entering your data in the tables or graphs.
  - *Sample District A (30,941 students)* (DistrictSA_A.xls)
  - *Sample District C (180 students)* (DistrictSA_C.xls)
- *Questions to Guide the Analysis of Student Learning Data* (QsSLearn.doc)
  This *Microsoft Word* file consists of questions to guide the interpretation of your district student learning data. You can input your responses into this file.

Analyzing the Data:

What Are the Gaps?

What Are the Root Causes of the Gaps?

7

Chapter

Gaps are the differences between "where the district wants to be" and "where the district is right now."

A vision is what the district would look like, sound like, and feel like when it is carrying out its purpose and mission.

Goals are the outcomes of the vision. Goals are stated in broad, general, abstract, and measurable terms.

Gaps are the differences between *where the school district wants to be* and *where it is right now. Where the district wants to be* can be defined through the district's vision and goals.

A *vision* is what the district would look like, sound like, and feel like when it is carrying out its purpose and mission. To be effective in getting all staff members in all schools implementing the same concepts, a vision must be spelled-out in specific terms that everyone can commit to and understand in the same way. The vision of Canyon View School District is shown in Chapter 8. The tools to assist in creating a vision are located on the CD. (*Creating a Shared Vision* Folder)

Goals are the outcomes of the vision. Goals are stated in broad, general, abstract, and measurable terms. (*Objectives* are much more specific.) School districts and schools often want to attempt too many goals, and very few get implemented. There should be only three or four overall goals that reflect the results the district wants to achieve by implementing the vision. (See *Goal Setting* and *Gap Analysis and Objectives Activities* on CD.) (ACTGoals.pdf and ACTGap.pdf)

Where the school district is right now are the results—specifically what the data say about strengths, challenges, and areas for improvement. To uncover *gaps*, one must review the data and dig deeper. Just looking at one level of analysis could be misleading. One must dig deeper to uncover those students not meeting the standards and where they rank on the scoring scale. The reason for digging deeper is that a large gap may not seem as large when one discovers that the students in the area with the largest gap scored only one or two points away from mastery, while the students not mastering the subtest with the smallest gap could be on the very bottom of the distribution—a long way from mastery.

Once district and school personnel see the gaps, they typically want to start implementing solutions *without discovering the root causes.* When root causes are not discussed, we often see programs added-on to "fix" the kids. Systems thinking research tells us that most of what needs to change to get different results lies with the system and not with the people. We need to study all the data to understand how the *system* is creating the results we are getting.

Root causes are real reasons that "problems" or "challenges" exist. School districts must uncover the root causes of their undesirable results to alleviate the problem and to get desirable results that will last over time. (ACTRoot.pdf) If they do not understand the root causes, districts could merely be treating a symptom and never get to the real reason for the results. Analyses completed for Canyon View School District are on the pages that follow. Several activities/processes for working with staff to uncover root causes are on the CD. (ACTCause.pdf and ACTCycle.pdf)

Please note the study questions on page 319 to assist in studying the data. (Ch7Qs.pdf) Also note that there is space in the margins on the data pages to write your impressions as you review the data. At the end of the chapter, I have shared what I saw in the data.

Where the district is right now are the results—specifically what the data say about strengths, challenges, and areas for improvement.

Systems thinking research tells us that most of what needs to change to get different results lies with the system, and not the people.

Root causes are real reasons that "problems" or "challenges" exist.

Our Example District: Canyon View School District

What are the Gaps?

Figures 7.1 and 7.2 show the number and percentage of students who scored at *Proficient* or *Advanced* levels, defined as "proficient" in this state, in Reading and Math. While showing the percentage of *Proficient* students by NCLB student groups, the shaded cells in the figures represent the largest gaps (50% and lower of that student group). Noticing the percentage of proficient students by NCLB student groups, one can quickly calculate the percentage of students who must become proficient by 2013-14, the date given for school districts and states to achieve 100% proficiency.

Note: Some of the student group numbers are very small for Canyon View and are not shown in these tables. While these small numbers should never be reported publicly, a district must monitor these students' performance to make sure no child is left behind. The numbers of students with IEPs are shown here, however, as this is the one student group that needs the most improvement.

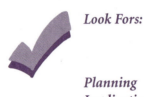

Look Fors:	**The student groups that have the highest and lowest percentage scoring *Proficient*. The gaps.**
Planning Implications:	**Are there professional learning programs that all teachers need in order to meet the needs of all students? What other services can be provided for student groups that are not scoring *Proficient?***

Proficiency Gaps by District

Figure 7.1 shows the number and percentage of students scoring proficient on the STBS Reading and Math tests for the district total and for NCLB student groups with more than 40 students, by grade level. Overall, the district is doing very well. In fact, for the past four years, the district has been doing well, and about the same, so we can estimate gaps accurately even though next year's fourth, eighth, and eleventh graders will be different students.

Figure 7.1

Summary of Canyon View School District Reading STBS Number and Percentage Proficient, 2002-03 to 2005-06

			Reading Proficiency											
			Grade 4			Grade 8			Grade 11			District		
			Number Tested	Proficient Number	Proficient Percent	Number Tested	Proficient Number	Proficient Percent	Number Tested	Proficient Number	Proficient Percent	Number Tested	Proficient Number	Proficient Percent
Overall	All Students	2002-03	523	447	85%	554	456	82%	649	543	84%	1,726	1,446	84%
		2003-04	529	446	84%	532	426	80%	694	572	82%	1,755	1,444	82%
		2004-05	494	424	86%	549	424	77%	684	552	81%	1,727	1,400	81%
		2005-06	527	447	85%	562	444	79%	655	539	82%	1,744	1,430	82%
By Gender	Female	2002-03	266	234	88%	286	239	84%	340	284	84%	892	757	85%
		2003-04	247	216	87%	260	215	83%	338	284	84%	845	715	85%
		2004-05	235	201	86%	250	200	80%	348	295	85%	833	696	84%
		2005-06	261	228	87%	287	238	83%	332	283	85%	880	749	85%
	Male	2002-03	257	213	83%	268	217	81%	309	259	84%	834	689	83%
		2003-04	282	230	82%	272	211	78%	356	288	81%	910	729	80%
		2004-05	259	223	86%	299	224	75%	336	257	76%	894	704	79%
		2005-06	266	219	82%	275	206	75%	323	256	79%	864	681	79%
By Ethnicity	White	2002-03	483	416	86%	520	431	83%	628	528	84%	1,631	1,375	84%
		2003-04	481	407	85%	479	384	80%	666	551	83%	1,626	1,342	83%
		2004-05	440	382	87%	509	399	78%	632	513	81%	1,581	1,294	82%
		2005-06	475	411	87%	506	407	80%	617	511	83%	1,598	1,329	83%
By Lunch Status	Paid	2002-03	384	348	91%	451	391	87%	630	529	84%	1,465	1,268	87%
		2003-04	376	325	86%	447	371	83%	640	536	84%	1,463	1,232	84%
		2004-05	331	302	91%	432	355	82%	626	518	83%	1,389	1,175	85%
		2005-06	353	322	91%	429	358	83%	591	495	84%	1,373	1,175	86%
	Free/Reduced	2002-03	138	98	71%	81	48	59%	19	14	74%	238	160	67%
		2003-04	152	120	79%	85	55	65%	49	33	67%	286	208	73%
		2004-05	155	115	74%	105	61	58%	53	31	58%	313	207	66%
		2005-06	156	108	69%	119	74	62%	47	32	68%	322	214	66%
By IEP		2002-03	80	43	54%	50	22	44%	35	12	34%	165	77	47%
		2003-04	79	40	51%	54	18	33%	34	8	24%	167	66	40%
		2004-05	76	42	55%	72	26	36%	52	19	37%	200	87	44%
		2005-06	63	26	41%	56	20	36%	48	20	42%	167	66	40%

Note: Number Tested = the number of students in that student group and grade level who took the test.
Number Proficient = the number of students who scored *Proficient* or *Advanced* on the test.
Percent Proficient = the number of students who scored *Proficient* or *Advanced* on the test, divided by the number taking the test.
Shaded cells represent the student groups and grade levels with 50% or fewer students scoring "proficient".

Figure 7.1 (Continued)

Summary of Canyon View School District Math STBS Number and Percentage Proficient, 2002-03 to 2005-06

			Math Proficiency											
			Grade 4			Grade 8			Grade 11			District		
			Number Tested	Proficient Number	Proficient Percent	Number Tested	Proficient Number	Proficient Percent	Number Tested	Proficient Number	Proficient Percent	Number Tested	Proficient Number	Proficient Percent
Overall	All Students	2002-03	523	408	78%	555	424	76%	646	520	80%	1,724	1,352	78%
		2003-04	530	420	79%	521	390	75%	691	552	80%	1,742	1,362	78%
		2004-05	495	395	80%	546	403	74%	685	538	79%	1,726	1,336	77%
		2005-06	527	418	79%	546	416	76%	658	501	76%	1,731	1,335	77%
By Gender	Female	2002-03	257	200	78%	267	193	72%	304	247	81%	838	640	76%
		2003-04	282	221	78%	271	198	73%	356	277	78%	909	696	77%
		2004-05	260	211	81%	298	217	73%	337	257	76%	895	685	77%
		2005-06	267	213	80%	267	196	73%	326	232	71%	860	641	75%
	Male	2002-03	265	208	78%	287	231	80%	340	273	80%	892	712	80%
		2003-04	245	199	81%	248	192	77%	335	275	82%	828	666	80%
		2004-05	235	184	78%	246	186	76%	348	281	81%	829	651	79%
		2005-06	260	205	79%	279	220	79%	332	269	81%	871	694	80%
By Ethnicity	White	2002-03	482	381	79%	520	402	77%	623	506	81%	1,625	1,289	79%
		2003-04	478	383	80%	469	354	75%	663	532	80%	1,610	1,269	79%
		2004-05	442	357	81%	504	381	76%	633	499	79%	1,579	1,237	78%
		2005-06	474	387	82%	491	381	78%	620	478	77%	1,585	1,246	79%
By Lunch Status	Paid	2002-03	383	314	82%	449	365	81%	624	507	81%	1,456	1,186	81%
		2003-04	373	313	84%	436	344	79%	636	517	81%	1,445	1,174	81%
		2004-05	332	287	86%	435	345	79%	626	502	80%	1,393	1,134	81%
		2005-06	353	296	84%	414	345	83%	593	460	78%	1,360	1,101	81%
	Free/Reduced	2002-03	138	93	67%	83	46	55%	20	13	65%	241	152	63%
		2003-04	153	106	69%	83	46	55%	50	32	64%	286	184	64%
		2004-05	155	103	66%	97	54	56%	54	33	61%	306	190	62%
		2005-06	156	107	69%	118	62	53%	48	30	63%	322	199	62%
By IEP		2002-03	80	42	53%	49	15	31%	33	11	33%	162	68	42%
		2003-04	82	36	44%	50	16	32%	34	9	26%	166	61	37%
		2004-05	79	31	39%	67	21	31%	53	20	38%	199	72	36%
		2005-06	73	33	45%	58	16	28%	49	13	27%	180	62	34%

Note: Number Tested = the number of students in that student group and grade level who took the test.
Number Proficient = the number of students who scored *Proficient* or *Advanced* on the test.
Percent Proficient = the number of students who scored *Proficient* or *Advanced* on the test, divided by the number taking the test.
Shaded cells represent the student groups and grade levels with 50% or fewer students scoring "proficient".

As an entire district, the NCLB goal of getting all students proficient in Reading by 2013-14 seems to be obtainable with 82% of the students proficient in 2005-06. The district has eight years to move 18% more students to proficiency—about 2.25% a year. The task looks a lot harder when one begins to look at the student groups involved and the amount of movement that is needed to fill some gaps.

Students with IEPs have the lowest percentage of proficiency. Currently, only 40% of the students with IEPs in the district scored proficient in Reading. To reach proficiency in Reading by 2013-14, 60% more students with IEPs will need to become proficient—about 7.5% each year for the next eight years.

Within the proficiency disaggregations in Chapter 6, one can also see that the minority populations and students that qualify for free/reduced lunch had proficiency percentages much lower than the district total.

As a district, the NCLB goal of getting all students proficient in Mathematics by 2013-14 also seems to be obtainable with 77% of the students proficient in 2005-06. The district has eight years to move 23% more students to proficiency—about 3% each year. Again, the task looks a lot harder when one begins to look at the student groups involved and the amount of movement that is needed to fill some gaps.

Students with IEPs have the lowest percentage of proficiency in Mathematics, as well as in Reading. Currently, only 34% of the students with IEPs in the district scored proficient in Mathematics. To reach proficiency in Mathematics by 2013-14, 66% more students with IEPs will need to become proficient—over 8.25% each year for the next eight years.

Note: The gaps are estimates based on the grades assessed in 2005-06. In 2006-07, students in grades 3 through 11 will be assessed on the same assessment instrument, and the gaps will need to be recalculated. It is then that the district will be able to follow the same students over time and truly understand the impact of its processes on student learning and what it can do differently to get different results.

Proficiency Gaps by School

Figure 7.2 shows the number and percentage of students scoring proficient on the STBS Reading and Math subtests for the schools in the district by grade level and NCLB student groups.

Within the proficiency disaggregations in Chapter 6, one can see that the minority populations, students that qualify for free/reduced lunch, and students with IEPs had percentages of proficiencies much lower than the district/school totals. Most student group numbers are too small for the individual schools to be held accountable according to NCLB requirements. These student groups will need to become proficient, however, in order to get the entire populations in each school proficient by 2013-14.

Figure 7.2

Summary of Canyon View School District Reading and Math STBS by School Number and Percentage Proficient, 2002-03 to 2005-06

Elementary 1		Reading Proficiency			Math Proficiency		
		Grade 4			Grade 4		
		Number Tested	Proficient Number	Proficient Percent	Number Tested	Proficient Number	Proficient Percent
All	2002-03	35	30	86%	35	28	80%
	2003-04	49	38	78%	49	35	71%
	2004-05	36	31	86%	36	31	86%
	2005-06	46	33	72%	45	31	69%
Female	2002-03	22	21	95%	22	19	86%
	2003-04	20	15	75%	20	15	75%
	2004-05	14	11	79%	14	10	71%
	2005-06	27	20	74%	28	17	65%
Male	2002-03	13	9	69%	13	9	69%
	2003-04	29	23	79%	29	20	71%
	2004-05	22	20	91%	22	21	95%
	2005-06	19	13	68%	19	14	74%
White	2002-03	29	25	87%	29	24	83%
	2003-04	43	33	77%	43	30	71%
	2004-05	31	26	84%	31	26	84%
	2005-06	36	28	78%	35	28	80%
Paid Lunch	2002-03	24	21	88%	24	20	83%
	2003-04	29	23	79%	28	23	82%
	2004-05	24	22	92%	24	22	92%
	2005-06	22	17	77%	22	16	73%
Free/Reduced Lunch	2002-03	11	9	82%	11	8	73%
	2003-04	20	15	75%	16	12	75%
	2004-05	12	9	75%	12	9	75%
	2005-06	20	12	60%	19	11	58%
IEP	2002-03	4	2	**50%**	4	3	75%
	2003-04	5	3	60%	5	2	**40%**
	2004-05	2	0	**0%**	2	0	**0%**
	2005-06	5	1	**20%**	6	2	**33%**

Figure 7.2 (Continued)

Summary of Canyon View School District Reading and Math STBS by School Number and Percentage Proficient, 2002-03 to 2005-06

Elementary 2		Reading Proficiency Grade 4			Math Proficiency Grade 4		
		Number Tested	Proficient Number	Proficient Percent	Number Tested	Proficient Number	Proficient Percent
All	2002-03	39	27	69%	39	25	64%
	2003-04	44	36	82%	44	28	64%
	2004-05	41	31	76%	41	28	68%
	2005-06	30	25	83%	30	26	87%
Female	2002-03	13	11	85%	13	9	69%
	2003-04	24	20	83%	24	14	58%
	2004-05	17	11	65%	17	8	47%
	2005-06	10	9	90%	19	8	42%
Male	2002-03	26	16	62%	26	16	62%
	2003-04	20	16	80%	20	14	70%
	2004-05	24	20	83%	24	20	83%
	2005-06	20	16	80%	20	17	85%
White	2002-03	35	24	71%	35	23	66%
	2003-04	39	31	79%	39	24	62%
	2004-05	32	24	75%	32	22	69%
	2005-06	26	21	81%	26	22	85%
Paid Lunch	2002-03	18	15	83%	18	13	72%
	2003-04	20	18	90%	20	15	75%
	2004-05	16	14	88%	16	13	81%
	2005-06	11	11	100%	11	11	100%
Free/Reduced Lunch	2002-03	21	12	57%	21	12	57%
	2003-04	23	17	74%	23	12	52%
	2004-05	25	17	68%	25	15	60%
	2005-06	19	14	74%	19	15	79%
IEP	2002-03	9	4	44%	9	2	22%
	2003-04	7	1	14%	7	1	14%
	2004-05	13	6	46%	13	5	38%
	2005-06	6	4	67%	6	4	67%

Figure 7.2 (Continued)

Summary of Canyon View School District Reading and Math STBS by School Number and Percentage Proficient, 2002-03 to 2005-06

Elementary 3		Reading Proficiency Grade 4			Math Proficiency Grade 4		
		Number Tested	Proficient Number	Proficient Percent	Number Tested	Proficient Number	Proficient Percent
All	2002-03	48	39	81%	49	32	65%
	2003-04	42	38	90%	44	31	70%
	2004-05	49	46	94%	51	37	73%
	2005-06	46	40	87%	46	29	63%
Female	2002-03	27	21	78%	27	18	67%
	2003-04	20	18	90%	20	15	75%
	2004-05	26	25	96%	26	19	73%
	2005-06	22	20	91%	22	13	59%
Male	2002-03	21	18	86%	22	14	64%
	2003-04	22	20	91%	24	16	67%
	2004-05	23	21	91%	25	18	72%
	2005-06	24	20	83%	24	16	67%
White	2002-03	43	37	86%	44	30	68%
	2003-04	40	36	90%	41	30	73%
	2004-05	44	42	95%	47	34	72%
	2005-06	42	39	93%	42	28	67%
Paid Lunch	2002-03	28	26	93%	28	21	75%
	2003-04	29	26	90%	30	22	73%
	2004-05	35	33	94%	37	28	76%
	2005-06	30	27	90%	30	18	60%
Free/Reduced Lunch	2002-03	20	13	65%	21	11	52%
	2003-04	13	12	92%	14	9	64%
	2004-05	11	10	91%	11	7	64%
	2005-06	15	12	80%	15	10	67%
IEP	2002-03	6	3	**50%**	7	2	**29%**
	2003-04	6	5	83%	8	5	63%
	2004-05	4	3	75%	7	1	**14%**
	2005-06	6	3	**50%**	7	3	**43%**

Figure 7.2 (Continued)

Summary of Canyon View School District Reading and Math STBS by School Number and Percentage Proficient, 2002-03 to 2005-06

Elementary 4		Reading Proficiency Grade 4 Number Tested	Reading Proficient Number	Reading Proficient Percent	Math Proficiency Grade 4 Number Tested	Math Proficient Number	Math Proficient Percent
All	2002-03	77	68	88%	77	71	92%
	2003-04	74	70	95%	75	68	91%
	2004-05	70	64	91%	69	62	90%
	2005-06	77	71	92%	77	69	90%
Female	2002-03	39	35	90%	39	39	100%
	2003-04	28	27	96%	28	25	89%
	2004-05	38	36	95%	37	34	92%
	2005-06	34	30	88%	34	31	91%
Male	2002-03	38	33	87%	38	32	84%
	2003-04	46	43	93%	47	43	93%
	2004-05	27	28	88%	32	28	88%
	2005-06	43	41	95%	43	38	88%
White	2002-03	72	63	88%	72	66	92%
	2003-04	69	66	96%	70	64	93%
	2004-05	64	60	94%	63	57	90%
	2005-06	68	65	96%	68	63	93%
Paid Lunch	2002-03	65	57	88%	65	59	91%
	2003-04	61	58	95%	61	56	92%
	2004-05	50	49	98%	49	46	94%
	2005-06	58	56	97%	58	53	91%
Free/Reduced Lunch	2002-03	12	11	92%	12	12	100%
	2003-04	13	12	92%	14	12	86%
	2004-05	19	14	74%	19	15	79%
	2005-06	15	12	80%	15	12	80%
IEP	2002-03	15	9	60%	15	11	73%
	2003-04	9	8	89%	9	7	78%
	2004-05	12	8	67%	12	7	58%
	2005-06	8	4	50%	11	7	64%

Figure 7.2 (Continued)

Summary of Canyon View School District Reading and Math STBS by School Number and Percentage Proficient, 2002-03 to 2005-06

Elementary 5		Reading Proficiency Grade 4 Number Tested	Reading Proficient Number	Reading Proficient Percent	Math Proficiency Grade 4 Number Tested	Math Proficient Number	Math Proficient Percent
All	2002-03	41	35	85%	42	32	76%
	2003-04	46	43	93%	46	43	93%
	2004-05	43	35	81%	43	33	77%
	2005-06	42	35	83%	42	35	83%
Female	2002-03	20	17	85%	20	16	80%
	2003-04	25	24	96%	25	24	96%
	2004-05	18	15	83%	18	15	83%
	2005-06	26	22	85%	26	23	88%
Male	2002-03	21	18	86%	22	16	73%
	2003-04	21	19	90%	21	19	90%
	2004-05	25	20	80%	25	18	72%
	2005-06	16	13	81%	16	12	75%
White	2002-03	38	33	87%	39	30	79%
	2003-04	42	40	95%	42	40	95%
	2004-05	36	30	83%	36	28	78%
	2005-06	37	32	86%	37	31	84%
Paid Lunch	2002-03	35	30	86%	35	26	74%
	2003-04	42	41	98%	42	41	98%
	2004-05	33	28	85%	33	26	79%
	2005-06	30	28	93%	30	26	87%
Free/Reduced Lunch	2002-03	6	5	83%	7	6	86%
	2003-04	4	2	**50%**	4	2	**50%**
	2004-05	9	6	67%	9	6	67%
	2005-06	11	6	55%	11	8	73%
IEP	2002-03	7	1	**14%**	7	3	**43%**
	2003-04	7	5	71%	7	5	71%
	2004-05	5	1	**20%**	5	0	**0%**
	2005-06	6	2	**33%**	7	4	57%

Figure 7.2 (Continued)

Summary of Canyon View School District Reading and Math STBS by School Number and Percentage Proficient, 2002-03 to 2005-06

Elementary 6		Reading Proficiency Grade 4			Math Proficiency Grade 4		
		Number Tested	Proficient Number	Proficient Percent	Number Tested	Proficient Number	Proficient Percent
All	2002-03	31	30	97%	31	28	90%
	2003-04	37	35	95%	37	34	92%
	2004-05	33	31	94%	33	31	94%
	2005-06	29	27	93%	29	27	93%
Female	2002-03	10	10	100%	10	9	90%
	2003-04	17	16	94%	17	16	94%
	2004-05	13	11	85%	13	12	92%
	2005-06	7	7	100%	7	7	100%
Male	2002-03	21	20	95%	21	19	90%
	2003-04	20	19	95%	20	18	90%
	2004-05	20	20	100%	20	19	95%
	2005-06	22	20	91%	22	20	91%
White	2002-03	30	29	97%	30	27	90%
	2003-04	35	33	94%	35	32	91%
	2004-05	32	30	94%	32	30	94%
	2005-06	29	27	93%	29	27	93%
Paid Lunch	2002-03	26	26	100%	26	25	96%
	2003-04	33	31	94%	33	31	94%
	2004-05	29	27	93%	29	28	97%
	2005-06	25	25	100%	25	23	92%
Free/Reduced Lunch	2002-03	5	4	80%	5	3	60%
	2003-04	4	4	100%	4	3	75%
	2004-05	4	4	100%	4	3	75%
	2005-06	3	1	**33%**	3	3	100%
IEP	2002-03	4	3	75%	4	2	**50%**
	2003-04	3	2	67%	3	3	100%
	2004-05	5	5	100%	5	5	100%
	2005-06	4	4	100%	4	4	100%

Figure 7.2 (Continued)

Summary of Canyon View School District Reading and Math STBS by School Number and Percentage Proficient, 2002-03 to 2005-06

Elementary 7		Reading Proficiency Grade 4			Math Proficiency Grade 4		
		Number Tested	Proficient Number	Proficient Percent	Number Tested	Proficient Number	Proficient Percent
All	2002-03	58	47	81%	57	45	79%
	2003-04	31	25	81%	31	27	87%
	2004-05	39	33	85%	39	29	74%
	2005-06	43	36	84%	43	28	65%
Female	2002-03	31	28	90%	31	25	81%
	2003-04	16	14	88%	16	14	88%
	2004-05	20	17	85%	20	14	70%
	2005-06	20	18	90%	20	12	60%
Male	2002-03	27	19	70%	26	20	77%
	2003-04	15	11	73%	15	13	87%
	2004-05	19	16	84%	19	15	79%
	2005-06	23	18	78%	23	16	70%
White	2002-03	56	45	80%	55	43	78%
	2003-04	29	23	79%	29	25	86%
	2004-05	38	32	84%	38	28	74%
	2005-06	39	33	85%	39	27	69%
Paid Lunch	2002-03	42	37	88%	42	34	81%
	2003-04	24	19	79%	24	20	83%
	2004-05	24	23	96%	24	19	79%
	2005-06	26	23	88%	26	21	81%
Free/Reduced Lunch	2002-03	16	10	63%	15	11	73%
	2003-04	7	6	86%	7	7	100%
	2004-05	13	9	69%	13	10	77%
	2005-06	12	8	67%	12	5	**42%**
IEP	2002-03	10	4	**40%**	9	5	56%
	2003-04	1	1	100%	1	0	**0%**
	2004-05	6	2	**33%**	6	3	**50%**
	2005-06	4	0	**0%**	4	1	**25%**

Figure 7.2 (Continued)

Summary of Canyon View School District Reading and Math STBS by School Number and Percentage Proficient, 2002-03 to 2005-06

Elementary 8		Reading Proficiency Grade 4			Math Proficiency Grade 4		
		Number Tested	Proficient Number	Proficient Percent	Number Tested	Proficient Number	Proficient Percent
All	2002-03	38	33	87%	38	33	87%
	2003-04	35	30	86%	36	31	86%
	2004-05	35	29	83%	36	27	75%
	2005-06	36	33	92%	36	31	86%
Female	2002-03	21	17	81%	21	16	76%
	2003-04	16	16	100%	17	16	94%
	2004-05	14	10	71%	15	10	67%
	2005-06	20	20	100%	20	17	85%
Male	2002-03	17	16	94%	17	17	100%
	2003-04	19	14	74%	19	15	79%
	2004-05	21	19	90%	21	17	81%
	2005-06	16	13	81%	16	14	88%
White	2002-03	38	33	87%	38	33	87%
	2003-04	33	29	88%	34	30	88%
	2004-05	35	29	83%	36	27	75%
	2005-06	35	32	91%	35	31	89%
Paid Lunch	2002-03	29	28	97%	29	27	93%
	2003-04	23	20	87%	23	21	91%
	2004-05	23	21	91%	23	20	83%
	2005-06	28	27	96%	28	24	86%
Free/Reduced Lunch	2002-03	9	5	56%	9	6	67%
	2003-04	12	10	83%	13	10	77%
	2004-05	11	7	64%	11	6	55%
	2005-06	8	6	75%	8	7	88%
IEP	2002-03	5	3	60%	5	4	80%
	2003-04	8	3	**38%**	9	4	**44%**
	2004-05	5	4	80%	5	2	**40%**
	2005-06	5	3	60%	5	1	**20%**

Figure 7.2 (Continued)

Summary of Canyon View School District Reading and Math STBS by School Number and Percentage Proficient, 2002-03 to 2005-06

Elementary 9		Reading Proficiency Grade 4 Number Tested	Reading Proficient Number	Reading Proficient Percent	Math Proficiency Grade 4 Number Tested	Math Proficient Number	Math Proficient Percent
All	2002-03	73	66	90%	72	52	72%
	2003-04	73	62	85%	70	50	71%
	2004-05	61	53	87%	61	52	85%
	2005-06	78	65	83%	78	64	82%
Female	2002-03	40	36	90%	39	25	64%
	2003-04	39	34	87%	36	27	75%
	2004-05	28	26	93%	28	25	89%
	2005-06	44	38	96%	44	36	82%
Male	2002-03	33	30	91%	33	27	82%
	2003-04	34	28	82%	34	23	68%
	2004-05	33	27	82%	33	27	82%
	2005-06	34	27	79%	34	28	82%
White	2002-03	66	60	91%	65	48	74%
	2003-04	67	57	85%	64	45	70%
	2004-05	51	46	90%	51	46	90%
	2005-06	71	60	85%	71	59	83%
Paid Lunch	2002-03	63	58	92%	62	46	74%
	2003-04	53	44	83%	51	35	69%
	2004-05	43	39	91%	43	41	95%
	2005-06	62	53	85%	62	53	85%
Free/Reduced Lunch	2002-03	9	7	78%	9	5	56%
	2003-04	20	18	90%	19	15	79%
	2004-05	18	14	78%	18	11	61%
	2005-06	15	11	73%	15	10	67%
IEP	2002-03	11	9	82%	11	6	55%
	2003-04	17	10	59%	17	6	**35%**
	2004-05	11	8	73%	11	6	55%
	2005-06	10	3	**30%**	13	4	**31%**

Figure 7.2 (Continued)

Summary of Canyon View School District Reading and Math STBS by School Number and Percentage Proficient, 2002-03 to 2005-06

Elementary 10		Reading Proficiency Grade 4			Math Proficiency Grade 4		
		Number Tested	Proficient Number	Proficient Percent	Number Tested	Proficient Number	Proficient Percent
All	2002-03	48	43	90%	48	40	83%
	2003-04	53	40	75%	53	42	79%
	2004-05	51	42	82%	51	44	86%
	2005-06	48	43	90%	49	43	88%
Female	2002-03	22	19	86%	22	17	77%
	2003-04	24	22	92%	24	20	83%
	2004-05	29	25	86%	29	26	90%
	2005-06	28	24	86%	28	25	89%
Male	2002-03	26	24	92%	26	23	88%
	2003-04	29	18	62%	29	22	76%
	2004-05	22	17	77%	22	18	82%
	2005-06	20	19	95%	21	18	86%
White	2002-03	43	38	88%	43	36	84%
	2003-04	45	33	73%	45	36	80%
	2004-05	47	39	83%	47	41	87%
	2005-06	42	37	88%	42	37	88%
Paid Lunch	2002-03	36	34	94%	36	30	83%
	2003-04	39	31	79%	39	33	85%
	2004-05	37	32	86%	37	34	92%
	2005-06	37	36	97%	37	35	95%
Free/Reduced Lunch	2002-03	12	9	75%	12	10	83%
	2003-04	14	9	64%	14	9	64%
	2004-05	14	10	71%	14	10	71%
	2005-06	11	7	64%	12	8	67%
IEP	2002-03	4	4	100%	4	3	75%
	2003-04	9	0	**0%**	9	2	**22%**
	2004-05	9	4	**44%**	9	2	**22%**
	2005-06	5	2	**40%**	6	3	**50%**

Figure 7.2 (Continued)

Summary of Canyon View School District Reading and Math STBS by School Number and Percentage Proficient, 2002-03 to 2005-06

Elementary 11		Reading Proficiency Grade 4 Number Tested	Reading Proficiency Grade 4 Proficient Number	Reading Proficiency Grade 4 Proficient Percent	Math Proficiency Grade 4 Number Tested	Math Proficiency Grade 4 Proficient Number	Math Proficiency Grade 4 Proficient Percent
All	2002-03	35	29	83%	35	22	63%
	2003-04	45	29	64%	45	31	69%
	2004-05	36	29	81%	35	21	60%
	2005-06	52	39	75%	52	35	67%
Female	2002-03	21	19	90%	21	15	71%
	2003-04	18	10	56%	19	13	72%
	2004-05	18	14	78%	18	11	61%
	2005-06	23	20	87%	23	15	65%
Male	2002-03	14	10	71%	14	7	**50%**
	2003-04	27	19	70%	26	18	69%
	2004-05	18	15	83%	17	10	59%
	2005-06	29	19	66%	29	20	69%
White	2002-03	33	28	85%	12	21	64%
	2003-04	39	26	67%	39	27	71%
	2004-05	30	24	80%	29	18	62%
	2005-06	50	37	74%	50	34	68%
Paid Lunch	2002-03	18	16	89%	18	13	72%
	2003-04	23	14	61%	22	16	73%
	2004-05	17	14	82%	16	10	63%
	2005-06	24	19	79%	24	16	67%
Free/Reduced Lunch	2002-03	17	13	76%	17	9	53%
	2003-04	22	15	68%	23	15	65%
	2004-05	19	15	79%	19	11	58%
	2005-06	27	19	70%	27	18	67%
IEP	2002-03	5	1	**20%**	5	1	**20%**
	2003-04	7	3	**43%**	7	1	**14%**
	2004-05	4	1	**25%**	4	0	**0%**
	2005-06	4	0	**0%**	4	0	**0%**

Figure 7.2 (Continued)

Summary of Canyon View School District Reading and Math STBS by School Number and Percentage Proficient, 2002-03 to 2005-06

Middle 1		Reading Proficiency Grade 8			Math Proficiency Grade 8		
		Number Tested	Proficient Number	Proficient Percent	Number Tested	Proficient Number	Proficient Percent
All	2002-03	312	260	83%	311	257	83%
	2003-04	314	254	81%	305	238	78%
	2004-05	314	243	77%	315	246	78%
	2005-06	338	269	80%	323	261	81%
Female	2002-03	155	128	83%	156	130	84%
	2003-04	162	135	83%	151	121	80%
	2004-05	141	113	80%	139	112	81%
	2005-06	176	147	84%	168	141	84%
Male	2002-03	158	132	84%	155	127	82%
	2003-04	153	119	78%	154	117	76%
	2004-05	174	130	75%	176	134	77%
	2005-06	162	122	75%	155	120	77%
White	2002-03	298	246	83%	296	245	83%
	2003-04	294	237	81%	287	225	78%
	2004-05	297	232	78%	296	233	79%
	2005-06	304	245	81%	289	235	81%
Paid Lunch	2002-03	280	238	85%	276	233	84%
	2003-04	277	231	84%	268	216	81%
	2004-05	262	212	81%	265	214	81%
	2005-06	284	234	82%	270	232	86%
Free/Reduced Lunch	2002-03	33	22	67%	35	24	69%
	2003-04	38	23	61%	37	22	59%
	2004-05	53	31	60%	50	32	64%
	2005-06	54	35	65%	53	29	55%
IEP	2002-03	22	10	45%	20	8	40%
	2003-04	35	13	37%	34	11	32%
	2004-05	47	19	40%	46	17	37%
	2005-06	32	9	28%	34	8	24%

Figure 7.2 (Continued)

Summary of Canyon View School District Reading and Math STBS by School Number and Percentage Proficient, 2002-03 to 2005-06

Middle 2		Reading Proficiency Grade 8			Math Proficiency Grade 8		
		Number Tested	Proficient Number	Proficient Percent	Number Tested	Proficient Number	Proficient Percent
All	2002-03	239	194	81%	241	167	69%
	2003-04	218	172	79%	216	152	70%
	2004-05	234	180	77%	230	156	68%
	2005-06	220	171	78%	219	151	69%
Female	2002-03	132	111	84%	132	101	77%
	2003-04	98	80	82%	97	71	73%
	2004-05	109	86	80%	107	73	69%
	2005-06	110	90	82%	110	78	71%
Male	2002-03	107	83	78%	109	66	61%
	2003-04	122	92	77%	119	81	69%
	2004-05	126	94	75%	123	83	67%
	2005-06	110	81	74%	109	73	67%
White	2002-03	220	183	83%	222	157	71%
	2003-04	187	147	79%	183	129	71%
	2004-05	213	166	78%	209	147	71%
	2005-06	198	158	80%	198	142	72%
Paid Lunch	2002-03	170	151	89%	172	132	77%
	2003-04	173	140	82%	170	128	75%
	2004-05	170	142	84%	170	130	76%
	2005-06	141	120	85%	140	109	78%
Free/Reduced Lunch	2002-03	47	26	55%	47	22	47%
	2003-04	47	32	68%	46	24	52%
	2004-05	53	30	57%	48	22	46%
	2005-06	65	39	60%	65	33	51%
IEP	2002-03	28	12	43%	29	7	24%
	2003-04	19	5	26%	16	5	31%
	2004-05	25	7	28%	21	4	19%
	2005-06	24	11	46%	24	8	33%

Figure 7.2 (Continued)

Summary of Canyon View School District Reading and Math STBS by School Number and Percentage Proficient, 2002-03 to 2005-06

High 1		Reading Proficiency Grade 11 Number Tested	Reading Proficient Number	Reading Proficient Percent	Math Proficiency Grade 11 Number Tested	Math Proficient Number	Math Proficient Percent
All	2002-03	307	264	86%	306	245	80%
	2003-04	293	248	85%	293	244	83%
	2004-05	297	247	83%	297	246	83%
	2005-06	317	267	84%	319	253	79%
Female	2002-03	164	144	88%	163	133	82%
	2003-04	139	117	84%	139	121	87%
	2004-05	153	135	88%	152	135	89%
	2005-06	159	132	83%	159	132	83%
Male	2002-03	143	120	84%	143	112	78%
	2003-04	154	131	85%	154	123	80%
	2004-05	144	112	78%	145	111	77%
	2005-06	158	135	85%	160	121	76%
White	2002-03	302	261	86%	301	243	81%
	2003-04	279	238	85%	279	233	84%
	2004-05	281	234	83%	281	232	83%
	2005-06	302	254	84%	304	243	80%
Paid Lunch	2002-03	289	251	87%	288	234	81%
	2003-04	278	236	85%	278	234	84%
	2004-05	282	235	83%	281	233	83%
	2005-06	302	256	85%	303	245	81%
Free/Reduced Lunch	2002-03	18	13	72%	18	11	61%
	2003-04	15	12	80%	15	10	67%
	2004-05	15	12	80%	16	13	81%
	2005-06	14	10	71%	15	8	53%
IEP	2002-03	14	3	**21%**	14	4	**29%**
	2003-04	17	5	**29%**	17	3	**18%**
	2004-05	21	8	**38%**	22	9	**41%**
	2005-06	17	7	**41%**	18	5	**28%**

Figure 7.2 (Continued)

Summary of Canyon View School District Reading and Math STBS by School Number and Percentage Proficient, 2002-03 to 2005-06

High 2		Reading Proficiency Grade 11 Number Tested	Proficient Number	Proficient Percent	Math Proficiency Grade 11 Number Tested	Proficient Number	Proficient Percent
All	2002-03	325	270	83%	321	266	83%
	2003-04	380	312	82%	376	298	79%
	2004-05	355	289	81%	356	282	79%
	2005-06	332	269	81%	333	246	74%
Female	2002-03	165	133	81%	165	134	82%
	2003-04	190	163	86%	187	151	81%
	2004-05	174	150	86%	175	138	79%
	2005-06	169	149	88%	169	136	80%
Male	2002-03	172	138	95%	156	132	85%
	2003-04	190	149	78%	189	147	78%
	2004-05	181	139	77%	181	144	80%
	2005-06	163	120	74%	164	110	67%
White	2002-03	313	259	83%	307	255	83%
	2003-04	367	302	82%	363	289	80%
	2004-05	324	265	82%	325	259	80%
	2005-06	310	255	82%	311	233	75%
Paid Lunch	2002-03	327	270	83%	321	266	83%
	2003-04	342	288	84%	337	273	81%
	2004-05	322	270	84%	323	262	81%
	2005-06	286	238	83%	287	215	75%
Free/Reduced Lunch	2002-03	33	21	64%	34	22	65%
	2004-05	29	16	55%	29	17	59%
	2005-06	30	20	67%	30	20	67%
IEP	2002-03	21	9	43%	19	7	37%
	2003-04	17	3	18%	17	6	35%
	2004-05	27	9	33%	27	11	41%
	2005-06	31	13	42%	30	8	27%

What are the Root Causes of Canyon View's Gaps?

To begin to uncover root causes and/or contributing causes, Canyon View District staff members did two things. They asked a representative group of teacher, and school and district administrators to use: 1) the problem-solving cycle to uncover why certain "gaps" exist, and 2) a table approach to review the data they collected to help them understand more about the root causes. The results of these two activities are shown below.

The Problem-solving Cycle: Canyon View School District

Canyon View district administrators pulled together a representative group of teachers and school administrators, the district assessment team, the newly created *District Literacy Instructional Leadership Focus Group,* and the *Mathematics Teachers on Special Assignment* (TOSA) to uncover root causes for not enough students scoring *Proficient* and/or *Advanced* on the Reading and Math sections of the *State Test of Basic Skills* (STBS). CD-ROM (ACTCycle.pdf) (The group decided that the results would be the same if the problem-solving cycle was completed for Reading and Math separately, so they chose to work the problem for both content areas together.)

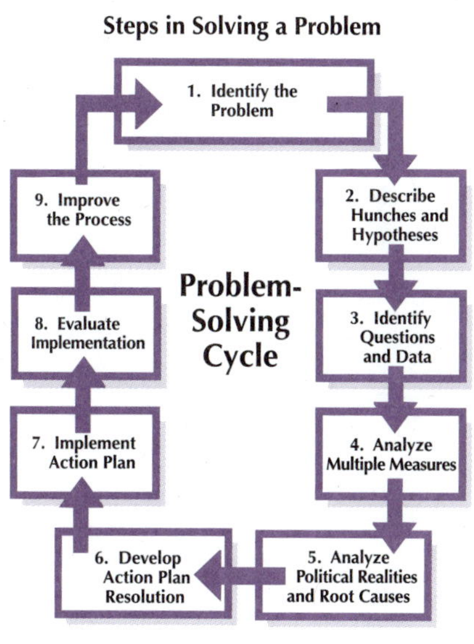

The "problem" was stated objectively as: *Not enough students are proficient in Reading and Math, as measured by the STBS.* The group members brainstormed 20 reasons they think this problem exists, withholding any judgments, while encouraging all ideas. The problem and the 20 brainstormed reasons follow.

Problem:
Not enough students are proficient in Reading and Math, as measured on the STBS.

Brainstormed reasons this problem exists, in the order mentioned:

1. Students in high school don't care how well they do.
2. There is a lack of parent support in some schools.
3. Too many students live in poverty.
4. Middle and high school teachers are not doing enough to get all students reading at a proficient level.
5. Students don't want to read or do math homework.
6. There are not enough interesting books for the students to read.
7. We need better measures that will help teachers diagnose skills throughout the year.
8. Teachers do not know how to use the assessment data.
9. Teachers do not get assessment data soon enough to make a difference.

10. Not all our curriculum is aligned to the standards, although the district thinks all areas of the curriculum are aligned.
11. Too many teachers are not teaching to the standards.
12. Too many teachers do not know how to set-up lessons to teach to the standards.
13. There are not enough programs to provide direct instruction for students with specific needs.
14. Teachers don't care enough about all students at the middle and high school levels.
15. There is not good articulation between grade levels to make sure students are being challenged and to make sure the standards are being implemented.
16. Teachers need more professional development to know how to differentiate instruction for all students.
17. Teachers need more professional development to know how to work with special needs students.
18. The district does not monitor standards implementation.
19. We need cross-grade-level meetings to calibrate standards.
20. Teachers need more opportunities and time for meetings with administrators and other teachers, schoolwide and districtwide.

Following the brainstorming, staff members were asked if they thought #20 represented the root cause. The group said that #6 through #20 are contributing causes: until there is instructional coherence, a shared vision for implementing the standards in all classrooms, and the use of data to improve instruction, the district would not get to 100% proficiency.

Instead of creating questions that need to be answered with data, as suggested in the problem-solving cycle, the group members decided to review what the data that had been collected and analyzed could tell them about the problem of getting all students to proficiency. The group then listed questions that still needed to be answered with data.

Review of the Data: Canyon View School District

The committee that gathered to explore root causes also reviewed what the comprehensive data analysis revealed about the "problem": *Not enough students are proficient in Reading and Math, as measured by the STBS.* A summary of key findings are shown as Figure 7.3. A summary of key data elements for the district and schools is displayed in Figure 7.4. CD-ROM (KeyData.pdf)

Figure 7.3

What the Data Tell Us About the Problem

PROBLEM:

Not enough students are proficient in Reading and Math as measured by the STBS

Demographics

- There are 2% more males than females each year.
- Not all HS students are accurately identified for free/reduced lunch status.
- The percentage of students identified for Sp. Ed. has increased each year.
- HS does not seem to be serving the identified special education population.
- Twice as many males than females get identified for special education.
- The higher the grade level, the lower the attendance rate.
- The mobility rate is increasing.

Student Achievement

- Grade 4 had a lower percentage of students proficient in the most recent year, after an increase in the previous year.
- Students who qualify for free/reduced lunch have a lower percentage of proficiency than those who pay for their lunches.
- All middle and high schools had smaller percentages of proficient students in 2005-06 than four years earlier.
- Minority students had lower percentages of proficiency than Caucasian students.
- The percentage of students proficient is lower for Math than Reading.
- Students with IEPs have a relatively low percentage of proficiency in both subject areas.
- Males typically had lower percentages of proficiency than females in Reading and Math.

Processes

- Staff needs training in data analysis and how to effectively use data.
- An assessment tool to measure progress and curriculum alignment is needed.
- District needs to improve consistency across schools with respect to curriculum and assessment alignment.
- The implementation of standards needs to be monitored and measured at the district level.
- Professional learning in how to implement standards is needed.
- Professional learning is needed for teachers in how to teach all types of students.
- Teachers think cross-grade-level meetings about standards would improve student learning.
- Teachers want to collaborate in grade levels and cross-grade levels about the standards, schoolwide, and districtwide.

Perceptions

- Students do not feel that they have freedom or choices in what they learn.
- Middle school students struggle with students and adults treating them fairly and with respect.
- HS students do not feel that the adults in the school care about them.
- HS students do not feel that time is spent in classes doing work they find meaningful.
- HS students do not think school is fun.
- Teachers admit to not knowing the state content standards.
- Elementary teachers know a little about ELA and Math standards at their grade levels only.
- Middle school and high school staffs do not feel supported with standards implementation.

Continuous Improvement Continuums

- Communication about data needs to improve K-12.
- Principals need to share more data with teachers.
- Teachers and administrators need data analysis training.
- We need assessment tools to ensure alignment of curriculum, instruction, and assessment to the standards and STBS.
- We need a shared vision for standards implementation.
- We need to understand the learning gaps.
- The district needs to help schools get a shared vision and plan.
- The district must monitor and measure the implementation of standards, the district goals, and plans.
- We need to commit to staying with our continuous improvement framework.
- We need to celebrate the things we are doing well.
- Professional learning must be about implementing the standards districtwide, and giving instructional staff the knowledge and skills to better meet the needs of students.
- The above needs to tie into teacher evaluations.
- The district must create a leadership structure that seeks input from all.
- We need to confirm the connection of partners to the district vision and to student learning standards.
- District staff needs to decide what to assess, how to assess it, and what to do with the data. All schools and departments need to be congruent—everyone going in the same direction.
- Someone in the district office will be assigned to each piece of data. She/he will own it and ensure its accuracy, intentions, and effectiveness.

Figure 7.4

Canyon View School District Summary of Key Data Elements 2002-03 to 2005-06

School	and Year	Enroll	Male	White	F/R Lunch	Mobility	Discipline Referrals	SpEd	Days Present	Reading Proficiency				Math Proficiency			
										Novice	Nearing Proficient	Proficient	Advanced	Novice	Nearing Proficient	Proficient	Advanced
DISTRICT	2002-03	8,114	51%	93%	17%	19%	7,723	10%	94%	7%	9%	57%	27%	9%	12%	59%	20%
	2003-04	7,983	51%	92%	20%	17%	7,139	12%	95%	7%	11%	60%	23%	11%	11%	59%	19%
	2004-05	7,901	51%	92%	22%	20%	8,106	13%	94%	9%	10%	57%	24%	11%	11%	58%	19%
	2005-06	7,909	51%	91%	23%	17%	6,060	15%	94%	8%	10%	57%	25%	12%	11%	56%	21%
ELEM 1	2002-03	266	52%	83%	36%	27%	10	10%	96%	9%	6%	66%	20%	6%	14%	69%	11%
	2003-04	281	50%	86%	40%	14%	0	11%	96%	6%	16%	59%	18%	12%	16%	55%	16%
	2004-05	281	55%	87%	43%	15%	0	13%	94%	6%	8%	64%	22%	3%	11%	72%	14%
	2005-06	270	53%	86%	42%	21%	0	11%	96%	13%	15%	52%	20%	18%	13%	58%	11%
ELEM 2	2002-03	230	54%	85%	57%	28%	62	13%	94%	15%	15%	51%	18%	21%	15%	56%	8%
	2003-04	263	56%	81%	61%	21%	384	22%	93%	11%	7%	80%	2%	14%	23%	52%	11%
	2004-05	242	53%	85%	60%	29%	514	25%	94%	17%	7%	54%	22%	17%	15%	63%	5%
	2004-05	238	61%	82%	63%	31%	225	31%	94%	10%	7%	57%	27%	10%	3%	70%	17%
ELEM 3	2002-03	317	51%	91%	34%	17%	0	12%	95%	15%	4%	50%	31%	20%	14%	57%	8%
	2003-04	297	51%	91%	31%	13%	0	15%	95%	5%	5%	62%	29%	16%	14%	57%	14%
	2004-05	271	49%	91%	31%	13%	60	16%	95%	4%	2%	61%	33%	10%	18%	63%	10%
	2004-05	273	51%	88%	29%	14%	10	18%	96%	4%	9%	59%	28%	13%	24%	52%	11%
ELEM 4	2002-03	482	50%	95%	17%	6%	1	10%	96%	1%	10%	56%	32%	3%	5%	65%	27%
	2003-04	468	52%	92%	21%	8%	0	13%	93%	1%	4%	73%	22%	5%	4%	68%	23%
	2004-05	485	52%	92%	23%	15%	40	15%	92%	0%	9%	57%	34%	6%	4%	58%	32%
	2004-05	497	52%	91%	20%	14%	49	16%	91%	3%	5%	52%	40%	5%	5%	65%	25%
ELEM 5	2002-03	235	53%	88%	16%	14%	34	14%	96%	5%	10%	49%	37%	5%	19%	62%	14%
	2003-04	252	52%	88%	18%	5%	19	15%	95%	0%	7%	63%	30%	4%	2%	72%	22%
	2004-05	253	54%	89%	17%	13%	47	18%	91%	12%	7%	51%	30%	5%	19%	53%	23%
	2004-05	261	51%	88%	22%	13%	157	14%	91%	2%	14%	57%	26%	7%	10%	57%	26%
ELEM 6	2002-03	232	58%	95%	17%	20%	51	8%	95%	0%	3%	48%	48%	3%	6%	58%	32%
	2003-04	218	64%	94%	16%	8%		11%	96%	0%	5%	59%	35%	3%	5%	57%	35%
	2004-05	200	64%	93%	14%	21%	91	9%	92%	0%	6%	58%	36%	3%	3%	61%	33%
	2004-05	201	65%	93%	18%	30%	225	15%	92%	0%	7%	66%	28%	3%	3%	45%	48%
ELEM 7	2002-03	270	52%	95%	24%	13%	113	9%	95%	3%	16%	71%	10%	7%	14%	67%	12%
	2003-04	273	52%	93%	26%	7%	70	11%	95%	13%	6%	61%	19%	6%	6%	84%	3%
	2004-05	260	55%	94%	27%	12%	130	13%	95%	8%	8%	67%	18%	8%	18%	64%	10%
	2004-05	258	58%	94%	21%	19%	54	14%	95%	5%	12%	58%	26%	9%	26%	51%	14%

Note: Schools with shading in the table indicate one feeder pattern. The unshaded schools are another feeder pattern.

Figure 7.4 (Continued)

Canyon View School District Summary of Key Data Elements 2002-03 to 2005-06

School and Year		Enroll	Male	White	F/R Lunch	Mobility	Discipline Referrals	SpEd	Days Present	Reading Proficiency				Math Proficiency			
										Novice	Nearing Proficient	Proficient	Advanced	Novice	Nearing Proficient	Proficient	Advanced
ELEM 8	2002-03	246	47%	94%	24%	8%	5	11%	96%	8%	5%	53%	34%	11%	3%	61%	26%
	2003-04	234	49%	96%	29%	15%	62	14%	96%	6%	9%	57%	29%	8%	6%	67%	19%
	2004-05	228	50%	95%	28%	15%	99	13%	96%	3%	14%	57%	26%	6%	19%	50%	25%
	2005-06	223	48%	92%	23%	15%		18%	96%	3%	6%	58%	33%	3%	11%	67%	19%
ELEM 9	2002-03	480	51%	91%	20%	13%	353	17%	91%	5%	4%	67%	23%	15%	13%	54%	18%
	2003-04	481	51%	94%	20%	9%	336	17%	94%	3%	12%	64%	21%	13%	16%	61%	10%
	2004-05	457	53%	92%	23%	15%	50	19%	91%	7%	7%	56%	31%	5%	10%	67%	18%
	2005-06	438	50%	93%	22%	20%	157	18%	92%	8%	9%	56%	27%	8%	10%	64%	18%
ELEM 10	2002-03	302	48%	91%	22%	17%		15%	96%	4%	6%	50%	40%	4%	13%	54%	29%
	2003-04	308	49%	87%	26%	19%		18%	95%	13%	11%	55%	21%	9%	11%	58%	21%
	2004-05	293	45%	90%	28%	19%	8	20%	95%	6%	12%	53%	29%	8%	6%	59%	27%
	2004-05	297	48%	89%	27%	24%		19%	95%	6%	4%	50%	40%	6%	6%	57%	31%
ELEM 11	2002-03	275	55%	90%	40%	8%	863	7%	95%	14%	3%	77%	6%	11%	26%	63%	0%
	2003-04	270	53%	91%	36%	15%	439	13%	94%	16%	20%	53%	11%	16%	16%	56%	13%
	2004-05	291	54%	89%	40%	10%	374	17%	90%	11%	8%	72%	8%	17%	23%	54%	6%
	2004-05	286	52%	92%	48%	27%	380	18%	90%	8%	17%	60%	15%	17%	15%	54%	13%
MIDD 1	2002-03	1,002	52%	94%	16%	4%	590	10%	94%	5%	12%	58%	26%	7%	11%	58%	24%
	2003-04	1,004	50%	93%	18%	4%	676	12%	94%	7%	12%	61%	20%	12%	10%	58%	20%
	2004-05	1,037	49%	92%	19%	5%	754	16%	94%	8%	15%	57%	20%	11%	11%	54%	24%
	2004-05	1,085	49%	92%	21%	4%	709	17%	94%	9%	12%	60%	19%	9%	11%	54%	26%
MIDD 2	2002-03	762	52%	88%	26%	8%	2,121	16%	92%	9%	10%	60%	21%	15%	15%	53%	16%
	2003-04	725	53%	87%	28%	7%	1,804	14%	92%	11%	11%	60%	19%	14%	16%	58%	13%
	2004-05	703	52%	88%	32%	10%	2,013	15%	92%	13%	11%	56%	21%	17%	15%	53%	14%
	2004-05	674	50%	88%	34%	13%	934	18%	91%	10%	12%	60%	17%	16%	16%	50%	19%
HIGH 1	2002-03	1,353	51%	99%	7%	10%	612	7%	91%	7%	7%	55%	31%	7%	13%	56%	24%
	2003-04	1,314	50%	97%	6%	9%	423	7%	93%	5%	10%	56%	29%	9%	8%	54%	29%
	2004-05	1,297	51%	94%	6%	9%	1,343	8%	94%	7%	10%	61%	23%	9%	8%	66%	16%
	2004-05	1,334	51%	95%	9%	10%	721	11%	94%	5%	11%	55%	29%	10%	10%	55%	24%
HIGH 2	2002-03	1,598	51%	94%		15%	2,908	7%	92%	7%	10%	54%	30%	7%	10%	64%	19%
	2003-04	1,551	44%	94%	9%	15%	2,924	8%	92%	6%	12%	58%	24%	10%	11%	61%	18%
	2004-05	1,549	50%	93%	13%	16%	2,583	8%	93%	9%	10%	51%	30%	12%	9%	58%	21%
	2004-05	1,527	51%	90%	14%	14%	2,359	10%	93%	11%	8%	58%	23%	17%	9%	60%	14%

Note: Schools with shading in the table indicate one feeder pattern. The unshaded schools are another feeder pattern.

In summary, the schools are getting very good results overall. However, the lower performing student groups in the district are also the fastest growing—students that qualify for free/reduced lunch, minorities, special education, and males. Mobile students are also increasing, although we do not know how they are scoring. We also do not know how many groups some of these students fall into, and how far they score from "proficiency." We need to know what they know and don't know, and how they prefer to learn.

On the student questionnaires, there are enough student comments about not feeling that adults and students treat them with respect and fairly that we must do something about that. This could impact the discipline numbers. Possibly related are the comments from students about their time being spent in classes doing work they do not find meaningful.

Teachers' comments to the open-ended questions were explicit about what it would take to improve student learning. Those comments were related to getting all teachers teaching to the standards, getting training for aligning curriculum, instruction, and materials, and on-going assessments to the standards and the state test. The teachers want professional learning and want to work more closely with their colleagues by grade level and cross-grade level, school-wide and district-wide. These comments are consistent with the findings of the *Continuous Improvement Continuums.*

The information gathered provides the district with several areas that must be considered in developing a continuous improvement plan.

More data are needed to answer some questions as shown in the table that follows (Figure 7.5).

Figure 7.5

Questions That Need More Data

Questions that still need to be answered with data.	*What data do we need to gather/analyze to answer the question?*
How do the mobile students score?	Student achievement by those students who have been in the system for less than one year.
How many of the students who are scoring as *novice* or *nearing proficiency* in each of these groups are the same students?	Isolate students scoring *novice* or *nearing proficiency* on the STBS, and determine their demographic composition,.
How far from *proficient* are the students who are scoring *novice* or *nearing proficiency*?	Isolate students scoring *novice* or *nearing proficiency* on the STBS, and look at their scores.
How do these students prefer to learn?	Learning styles inventory or individual interviews.
What do the students know and what do they not know?	Students achievement by standards and skills for each student.
Why are Math scores lower than Reading scores? Is there a relationship?	Student achievement results for Reading and Math by student demographics. (Also related to the program evaluation question, below.)
What strategies work with students with IEPs?	Student achievement results for each IEP student over time, compared to the goals for learning and processes used.
Who owns the data? Who is ensuring the data's accuracy and its programmatic implications, especially special education, attendance, discipline, mobility, free/reduced lunch qualifiers?	Someone in the central office needs to own each piece of data and lead the schools in accurately identifying students for these programs.
How effective are our programs and approaches to teaching Reading and Math? Which approaches are most successful with high needs students?	Student achievement results by teacher by processes, by student demographics.
How are our graduates doing in college and careers?	We need to survey alumni.

Review of the Implications of the Data Analysis for the Continuous Improvement Plan: Canyon View School District

After analyzing Canyon View's data, the gaps, the root cause analyses, the implications for the continuous improvement plan from all the data analyses, the root cause committee came up with the idea that there are many contributing causes to the "problem" that *Not enough students are proficient in Reading and Math, as measured by the STBS.* The committee also felt that it is very clear what has to happen at the district and school levels to improve the results the district is getting.

Implications for the district continuous improvement plan derived from the data analysis in Chapters 4 through 7 were organized by commonalities. The specific recommendations for district improvement were organized by topic and are shown below.

Recommendations for Improvement

Demographics:

- Someone in central office must be assigned to own each element of data to ensure that all data are accurate, clean, and understood. In addition, this person needs to lead what the data "ought to look like," as well as how the data will be monitored and measured. This is especially true for attendance, mobility, discipline, free/reduced lunch, special education, all programs, graduation and dropout rates.
- Questionnaires need to continue to be administered each year. In addition, we must administer an alumni questionnaire. We need to establish a focus group model for seeking community input.
- We need to assess on the *Continuous Improvement Continuums* each year and follow-up on the next steps.
- Staffs need training in data analysis and how to effectively use the data collected.
- Administration needs to keep the improvement process (School Portfolio) and issues active for all teaching staff.

Standards Implementation:

- Consistency among and within schools needs to improve with respect to assessments and curriculum alignment. A systematic approach to analyzing school improvement goals, strategies, and assessment plans is desirable. An assessment tool to measure learning progress and curricular/standards alignment is needed. All schools and departments need to be congruent—everyone going in the same direction.

- Professional learning related to how to teach to the standards is needed. Structures need to be put into place to support teachers in their implementation of the standards.
- The district office needs to figure out strategies to monitor and measure how standards are being implemented in each classroom.
- The administrative team needs to develop a means to ensure communication among curriculum committees and the rest of the teaching population.

Professional Learning:

- In addition to professional learning in standards implementation, the district must help teachers and administrators learn:
  - How to incorporate diversity in their classrooms.
  - How to differentiate instruction.
  - How to teach students who live in poverty, with special needs, males, and minorities.
  - How to create a positive learning environment.
  - How to treat students effectively.
  - How to create a shared vision for the school.
- The district needs to develop strategies and processes to ensure schools/curriculum connect the use of data to professional development goals and evaluation, and school improvement plans. Time needs to be restructured for professional development to be included during the workweek so teachers can talk about student instruction and assessment.
- District cross-grade-level and grade-level meetings must be set-up to calibrate the curriculum and standards implementation.

Planning:

- District needs to support the implementation of building plans. The district can provide incentives for schools for keeping their School Portfolios up to date and using their data and plans.

Recruitment:

- Can more male teachers and teachers of other ethnicities be recruited? Maybe younger teachers as well?

Programs and Program Evaluation:

- Each program the district and the schools operate must be evaluated in terms of the intention for the program, whom it is attracting, how it is being implemented, and the results. (Particularly, special education, advanced placement, gifted, alternative, after school, summer school.) Programs that are not effective will be dropped.

Partnerships:

- Staffs need to reconfigure the guidelines and expectations for partnerships to include their connection to student curriculum standards and student learning. We need to confirm the connection of our partnerships to the district vision.
- Staffs need to recognize and acknowledge the partnerships with students, staff, parents, and community as a district.

Study Questions for What Are the Gaps? and What Are the Root Causes of the Gaps?

As you review Canyon View's data, use either the margins in the text, this page, or print this page from the CD to write down your early thinking. CD-ROM (Ch7Qs.pdf) These notes, of course, are only hunches or placeholders until all the data are analyzed and verified with the staff.

1. **What are Canyon View's *gaps*?**

2. **What are the root causes of the gaps?**

3. **What are the implications for the district improvement plan?**

What I Saw in the Example: Canyon View School District

Using the study questions as an outline, what I saw in the data for Chapter 7 appears below. When applicable, I have referenced the figure or page number that gave me my first impression of strengths and challenges. CD-ROM (Ch7Saw.pdf)

What are Canyon View's gaps?

- The gaps: 18% more students need to become proficient in Reading in the next 8 years.
- The group with the lowest percentage of proficiency is the students with IEPs. Currently, only 40% of the students with IEPs in the district scored proficient in Reading. To reach proficiency by 2013-14, 60% more students with IEPs will need to become proficient – about 7.5% each year for the next eight years. (Figure 7.1)
- Within the proficiency disaggregations in Chapter 6, one can also see that the minority populations and students that qualify for free/reduced lunch had percentage of proficiencies much lower than the district total.
- As a district, the NCLB goal of getting all students proficient in Mathematics by 2013-14 also seems to be obtainable with 77% of the students proficient in 2005-06. The district has eight years to move 23% more students to proficiency.
- The students with the lowest percentage of proficiency in Mathematics are those with IEPs. Currently, only 34% of the students with IEPs in the district scored proficient in Mathematics. To reach proficiency by 2013-14, 66% more students with IEPs will need to become proficient—over 8% each year for the next eight years. (Figure 7.1)

What are the root causes of the gaps?

According to the data analyses conducted in Chapters 4 though 7, it appears that the contributing causes are related to the fact that:

- Teachers are not all teaching to the state content standards.
- Training is needed for aligning curriculum, instruction, materials, and ongoing assessments to the standards and the state test.
- Teachers need professional learning in how to meet the needs of students with special needs.
- Teachers need to work more closely with their colleagues by grade level and cross-grade level, schoolwide and districtwide to learn how to teach to the standards and to ensure a continuum of learning that makes sense for the students.
- Teachers need to assess student abilities in an ongoing fashion and determine how to get all students proficient.
- The district needs to monitor and measure standards implementation.
- Teachers need the time and opportunities to work together and with administrators, schoolwide and districtwide.

What are the *implications* for the district improvement plan?

The district must provide:

- Professional learning opportunities for teachers to learn about Reading and Math curriculum, instructional strategies, and materials that are aligned to the state content standards, as well as how to meet the needs of students with different learning styles, and that qualify for free/reduced lunch, have IEPs, and are non-Caucasian.
- Time for teachers to meet in professional learning communities in their schools, and by grade level and cross-grade levels across the district, and model the way.
- Monitoring and measurement of standards instruction implementation at every grade level.

Summary

Gap analyses are critical for answering the question, *What are the gaps?* Gap analyses help districts and schools see the difference between *where they are* (current results) and *where they want to be* (vision and goals). To be effective, gap analyses must dig layers deep into the data to truly understand the results and to begin to uncover root causes.

Root causes, as used in this continuous improvement planning model, refer to the deep underlying reasons for the occurrence of a specific situation, the gap. While a symptom may become evident from a needs assessment or gap analysis—the symptom (low student scores) is not the cause. To find a root cause, one often has to ask *Why?* at least five levels down to uncover the root cause of the symptom. One will know if she/he found the root cause when she/he can answer *no* to the following questions:

- *Would the problem have occurred if the cause had not been present?*
- *Will the problem reoccur if the cause is corrected?* (Preuss, 2003)

If the answers to these questions are *maybe,* you are probably looking at contributing causes, not one root cause. Most problems within districts are caused by systems rather than people. Improvement of the system will result in reduction or removal of the problem. Teams that include processes in their analyses tend not to jump to solutions or conclusions as quickly as those who do not. At some point, when searching for the root cause, one must realize that the "problem" is really a result. What we are trying to do with these analyses is to uncover how we get our results. These very same processes can be used to uncover how we get our successes.

Root causes are not easy to uncover, but the information that is uncovered is well worth the effort.

Canyon View staff members used a couple of quick but analytical brainstorming approaches—the problem-solving cycle and a simple table of results—to study why *Not enough students are proficient in Reading and Math, as measured by the STBS.* The next chapter will show how they took this information and created a plan to continuously improve their results.

Gap analyses help districts and schools see the difference between where they are (current results) and where they want to be (vision and goals).

To find a root cause, one often has to ask "Why?" at least five levels down to uncover the root cause of the symptom.

On the CD Related to this Chapter

- *Creating a Shared Vision* (Folder)

  Templates and examples for planning and creating your district shared vision are provided on the CD.

  - *Shared Vision Template* (VTemplte.doc)

    This is a template for staffs to use when creating their shared vision. It allows staffs to document their personal ideas before they are merged into core principles for the entire district.

  - *Facilitator's Agenda for Creating a Shared Vision* (AgendaFa.pdf)

    This read-only file provides an annotated agenda for taking staffs through a visioning process in one day. Typical time requirements for the different activities are provided.

  - *Agenda for Creating a Shared Vision* (Agenda.pdf)

    This is an example agenda for creating a vision in one day. It accompanies the facilitator's agenda for creating a vision.

  - *Ground Rules* (GrndRule.pdf)

    This read-only file provides example ground rules for staff meetings and professional development sessions.

  - *Vision Quote Posters* (VPosters.pdf)

    These read-only files contain motivating quotes to have enlarged for visioning day. The quotes show how to get to the vision, ground rules, and contain words of wisdom by Peter Senge and Joel Barker.

- *Goal Setting Activity* (ACTGoals.pdf)

  By setting goals, a school or district can clarify end targets for its vision. This activity will help a learning organization set goals for the future.

- *Gap Analysis and Objectives Activity* (ACTGap.pdf)

  The purpose of this activity is to look closely at differences between current results and where the school or district wants to be in the future. It is this gap that gets translated into objectives that guide the development of the action plan.

- *Root Cause Analysis Activity* (ACTRoot.pdf)

  Root causes are the real causes of our educational problems. We need to find out what they are so we can eliminate the true cause and not just address the symptom. This activity asks staff teams to review and analyze data and ask probing questions to uncover the root cause(s).

- *Cause and Effect Analysis Activity* (ACTCause.pdf)
  This activity will help teams determine the relationships and complexities between an effect or problem and all the possible causes.
- *Problem-solving Cycle Activity* (ACTCycle.pdf)
  The purpose of the *Problem-solving Cycle Activity* is to get all staff involved in thinking through a problem before jumping to solutions.
- *Problem-solving Cycle Handout Template* (CycleTmp.doc)
  This *Microsoft Word* file is the last three pages of the problem-solving cycle activity. Use this template to fill-in hunches and hypotheses about why the problem exists, determine the questions needed to answer with data to know more about the problem, and what data are needed to support those answers.
- *Canyon View School District Summary of Key Data Elements* (KeyData.pdf)
  This is the table in Figure 7.4 that shows the key data elements for Canyon View Schools and the district. The table enables one to look across all data elements to understand relationships.
- Study Questions Related to the Gaps and the Root Causes of the Gaps (Ch7Qs.doc)
  These study questions will help you better understand the information provided in Chapter 7. This template file can be printed for use with staffs as they analyze data to determine the gaps and the root causes of the gaps.
- *What I Saw in the Example* (Ch7Saw.pdf)
  What I Saw in the Example is a file, organized by the questions related to gaps and root causes, that summarizes what the author saw in the analyses conducted by the school district.
- *No Child Left Behind* (NCLB) Table Templates (Folder)
  Table templates for analyzing student learning data for NCLB are provided on the CD.
  - *NCLB Student Learning Reading Results Template* (ProfRead.xls)
    This *Microsoft Excel* file is a table template to use in summarizing your NCLB disaggregated student learning Reading proficiency results.
  - *NCLB Student Learning Math Results Template* (ProfMath.xls)
    This *Microsoft Excel* file is a table template to use in summarizing your NCLB disaggregated student learning Math proficiency results.

- Group Process Tools and Activities.

  The files include read-only documents, examples, templates, tools, activities, and strategy recommendations. Many of the group process tools and activities can be used throughout the analysis of data.

  - *Affinity Diagram Activity* (ACTAfnty.pdf)

    The affinity diagram encourages honest reflection on the real underlying root causes of a problem and its solutions, and encourages people to agree on the factors. This activity assists teams in discussing and resolving problems, using a nonjudgmental process.

  - *Fishbowl Activity* (ACTFish.pdf)

    This activity can be used for dynamic group involvement. The most common configuration is an inner ring, which is the discussion group, surrounded by an outer ring, which is the observation group. Just as people observe the fish in the fishbowl, the outer ring observes the inner ring.

  - *Forcefield Analysis Activity* (ACTForce.pdf)

    The *Forcefield Analysis Activity* helps staffs think about the ideal state for the district or school and the driving and restraining forces regarding that ideal state.

  - *Placemat Activity* (ACTPlace.pdf)

    The *Placemat Activity* was developed to invite participants to share their knowledge about the school portfolio, data, a standard, an instructional strategy, a concept, etc.

  - *T-Chart Activity* (ACTTChrt.pdf)

    A *T-Chart* is a simple tool to organize material into two columns. Use a T-Chart to compare and contrast information or to show relationships. Use it to help people see the opposite dimension of an issue.

  - *"X" Marks the Spot Activity* (ACTXSpot.pdf)

    This activity helps staffs understand levels of expertise or degrees of passion about a topic.

  - *Quadrant Diagram Activity* (ACTQuadr.pdf)

    A quadrant diagram is a method to determine which solution best meets two goals at once, such as low cost and high benefit.

Analyzing the Data:

Where Do We Want to Be?

How Can We Get to Where We Want to Be?

Chapter 8

Action plans need to clarify how decisions will be made, identify professional learning required for staffs to acquire new skills and gain new knowledge, and to clarify the use of partners to achieve the vision.

We know the gaps in Canyon View School District's school and student achievement results, and we have a better idea of the root causes. So now, *Where do we want to be?* and *How can we get to where we want to be?* The answers to these questions are the key to unlocking the vision, how the vision will be implemented, and how gaps will be eliminated. A mission and vision clarify why the school district exists; an action plan consisting of strategies, actions, person(s) responsible, measurement, due dates, and timelines needs to be created to achieve the vision and to eliminate the root causes of the gaps.

Visions, created from the *mission* and *purpose* of the school district, begin with school-community values and beliefs about what impacts learning for the students in Canyon View School District.

Action plans need to clarify how decisions will be made, identify professional learning required for staffs to acquire new skills and gain new knowledge, and incorporate the use of partners, such as parents, businesses, and the community, to achieve the vision, and spell-out how all parts of the plan will be evaluated. A district's leadership structure, professional learning strategies, and partnership development plan are important components of the answer to the questions, *Where do we want to be?* and *How can we get to where we want to be?*

This chapter shows how Canyon View School District created an improvement plan, using the data gathered and analyzed, to close its gaps and implement its guiding principles to improve student learning across the district.

Our Example District: Canyon View School District *Where Do We Want to Be?*

The Canyon View Vision

The data (demographics, student learning, the *Continuous Improvement Continuums*, perceptions, and gap analysis) showed Canyon View staff members that they needed to revisit the district vision. The following are the *Guiding Principles*, core values and beliefs, purpose, mission, and vision that staff district staff created in the spring before implementing their plan that would commence in the fall of 2006. CD-ROM (DVVision.pdf)

Canyon View School District
Guiding Principles, May 2006

A system of fundamental motivating assumptions, principles, values, and tenets that leads to a tangible vision.

Values and Beliefs

We believe…

- Canyon View Schools are here to serve *students.*
- Canyon View Schools are accountable to the community for the education of *all* students.
- Public education is a cooperative effort among students, parents, staff, and community.
- Canyon View Schools must meet the unique needs of each student so that each student can reach her/his potential.
- Students must develop intellectual curiosity, critical thinking skills, problem-solving abilities, and aesthetic appreciation to function successfully in a rapidly changing, highly competitive world.
- All students can learn and should be taught according to their individual learning preferences.
- Students should develop habits and skills necessary to maintain life-long learning, self-esteem, physical fitness, and mental health.
- Tolerance is expected toward students, teachers, and staff.
- Students, teachers, and staff should value creativity and diversity.
- An environment that challenges students, teachers, and staff to meet high expectations produces high achievement.
- Curriculum must be responsive, current, proactive, and flexible.
- All school district activities should be conducted with respect for the environment.
- We must invest our limited resources in programs and management systems and ensure the achievement of goals and objectives.
- Our schools must be a safe, non-threatening environment for students to learn and employees to work.
- Technology must be integrated into instruction and curriculum to enhance student learning and teaching.
- Canyon View Schools must anticipate and be responsive to the changes and needs of society.

Canyon View School District Purpose

The purpose of Canyon View School District is to help each student become a competent, productive, responsible, caring citizen.

Canyon View School District Mission

The mission of Canyon View School District is to challenge and empower each student to maximize individual potential and become a competent, productive, responsible, caring citizen.

Canyon View School District Vision

The Canyon View mission and vision will be supported through the wise use of resources to meet students' needs regardless of interests and talents. Students, families, educators, and the community are committed to sharing the responsibility for creating a student-centered education community that acknowledges learning as a life-long process. The mission and vision will be carried out in the following fashion in the Canyon View schools:

Curriculum/Learning

Canyon View Schools will provide relevant, integrated and meaningful learning experiences that will prepare students for life in a rapidly changing, highly competitive world. All curriculum, materials, and instructional strategies will be aligned to the content standards.

Staff Support and Relationships

Canyon View Schools will enhance the learning opportunities for students by providing professional learning and collaboration for all employees and encouraging innovative instructional practices.

Environment

All schools and work sites will be safe and foster positive and productive environments for students and staff.

Technology

Technology will be implemented in the Canyon View Schools to enrich student learning, to complement teacher instructional practices, and to deliver efficient administrative services.

Community Partnerships

Canyon View School District will encourage excellence in its schools by maintaining a positive and productive relationship with parents, employers, community members, and members of the higher education community.

Fiscal Planning

A budget development process is established so the allocation of resources has the greatest positive impact on the performance of students and staff.

Canyon View School District Goals

The Canyon View School District Board of Education and the administrative staff are committed to the achievement of the goals of *No Child Left Behind* (NCLB) and adopted the following four goals—the *outcomes* of the district vision:

1. All students will reach high standards, at a minimum attaining proficiency or better in Reading and Mathematics, by 2013-14.
2. By 2006-07, all students will be taught by highly qualified teachers.
3. All students will be educated in learning environments that are conducive to learning.
4. All students will graduate from high school.

How Can We Get to Where We Want to Be?

The District Improvement Plan

Using its newly revisited values and beliefs, mission, vision, and goals, and the results of its comprehensive data analysis, Canyon View School District created this first draft of its continuous improvement plan (Figure 8.1).

Figure 8.1

Canyon View School District Quality Plan, 2005-06

Performance Goal 1: ***All students will reach high standards, at a minimum, attaining proficiency or better in Reading and Mathematics, by 2013-14***

Planned Improvement in Student Performance in Reading:

- Canyon View School District will increase the percentage of students who perform at the Proficient and Advanced levels on the *State Test of Basic Skills Criterion Referenced Test* (CRT) in Reading by 2.25% each year for the next eight years.
- Canyon View School District will decrease the percentage of students who perform at *Novice* and *Nearing Proficient* on the CRT in Reading by 2.25% each year for the next eight years.
- Canyon View School District will increase the percentage of students with disabilities who perform at the Proficient and Advanced levels on the CRT in Reading by 7.5% each year for the next eight years.
- Canyon View School District will decrease the percentage of students with disabilities who perform at *Novice* and *Nearing Proficient* on the CRT in Reading by 7.5% each year for the next eight years.

Description of Specific Actions to Improve Education Practice in READING	Person(s) Responsible	Measurement	Due Date	Timeline
1. Alignment of instruction with content standards: *The District Literacy Instructional Leadership Focus Group will:* • Support schools in analyzing and using their Reading assessment data, by teacher, to understand which teachers and schools need support with standards-based instruction. • Support schools in analyzing and using their Reading assessment data, by student, to understand which students need additional support on standards-based content. • Provide professional learning where individual teachers and schools require additional support.	District Literacy Instructional Leadership Focus Group District Assessment Director	Reading assessment data disaggregated by teacher-school, and by student-teacher-school. Evidence that the students requiring additional support received the support, and the impact of the support. Evidence that the teachers and schools were given appropriate learning opportunities, and that they participated. Evaluations by participants of the professional learning and how they are using it.	Begin September 2006	Ongoing beginning with 2006-07 school year
2. Use of standards-aligned instructional materials and strategies: • All district instructional materials and strategies acquired/used for teaching Reading will be aligned to the standards. A list of approved materials and strategies will be created and circulated to all schools and teachers. • Professional learning on standards-aligned instructional materials and strategies will be offered for college credit and /or Continuing Education Units (CEU).	District Literacy Instructional Leadership Focus Group	The use of these materials and strategies will be monitored for use and evaluated for effectiveness. The number of teachers taking professional learning and getting college credit or CEUs.	August 2006	Ongoing
3. Extended learning time: • The District Literacy Instructional Leadership Focus Group will provide individual teachers, and groups of teachers, professional learning on interventions for identified students and in areas of students' needs. • Each school will determine how students requiring, and wanting, extra help will get extended learning time.	District Literacy Instructional Leadership Focus Group Expert Facilitator	Professional learning sessions developed by the district and attended by teachers. Evaluations by participants of the professional learning, and how they are using it. Evidence that programs have been established for extended learning time and evaluated for effectiveness.	August 2006	Ongoing

Figure 8.1 (Continued)

Canyon View School District Quality Plan, 2005-06

Description of Specific Actions to Improve Education Practice in READING	Person(s) Responsible	Measurement	Due Date	Timeline
4. Professional learning and collaboration aligned with standards-based instructional materials: *The District Literacy Instructional Leadership Focus Group will provide high quality professional development for classroom teachers, principals, administrators, and other school or community-based personnel:* a. designed to improve the instruction and assessment of children who live in poverty; b. designed to enhance the ability of teachers to understand and use curriculum, assessment measures, and instructional strategies for students with special needs; c. based on scientifically-based research demonstrating the effectiveness of the professional development in increasing teachers' subject matter knowledge; teaching knowledge, and teaching skills; and d. designed to result in positive and lasting impact on teacher performance in the classroom. *The District Literacy Instructional Leadership Focus Group will also:* ♦ Support schools in establishing structures for professional learning and professional collaboration aligned with standards-based instructional materials. ♦ Offer professional learning, by grade level and cross-grade level, across the district, to enhance collaboration across the district.	District Literacy Instructional Leadership Focus Group	Professional learning sessions developed by the district and attended by teachers. Evaluations by participants of the professional learning, and how they are using it. Improvements in student achievement as measured by the STBS CRT, for all student groups. Teacher responses to the Standards Assessment Questionnaire show improvement in the implementation of standards. Evidence that each school has a leadership structure in place to support ongoing professional learning and collaboration. Evidence of regularly scheduled meetings by district level grade level and cross-grade level to calibrate the teaching of learning standards.	Begin September 2006	Ongoing beginning with 2006-07 school year Professional learning will be revamped as necessary
5. Involvement of staff, parents, and community: ♦ The district will provide example notification procedures to reach out to parents about their children's expectations and performance. ♦ In professional learning training, teachers will learn how to describe to parents their children's assessment results.	District Literacy Instructional Leadership Focus Group	Parent follow-up on the effectiveness of the procedures developed to involve and inform parents. Professional learning attended and evaluated by teachers.	September 2006	Completed and evaluated by 2008
6. Monitoring program effectiveness: ♦ The District Literacy Instructional Leadership Focus Group, in conjunction with the District Research and Evaluation Group, will conduct a program evaluation of all components of the District Literacy Program, which will include the degree to which each program is being implemented, and will make recommendations on how to improve.	District Literacy Instructional Leadership Focus Group Research and Evaluation Group	Evaluation plan is developed and implemented.	Begin September 2006	Ongoing, 2006–2014. Revamped yearly, if necessary

Figure 8.1 (Continued)

Canyon View School District Quality Plan, 2005-06

Performance Goal 1: ***All students will reach high standards, at a minimum, attaining proficiency or better in Reading and Mathematics, by 2013-14***

Planned Improvement in Student Performance in Mathematics:

- Canyon View School District will increase the percentage of students who perform at the Proficient and Advanced levels on the *State Test of Basic Skills Criterion Referenced Test* (CRT) in Mathematics by3% each year for the next eight years.
- Canyon View School District will decrease the percentage of students who perform at *Novice* and *Nearing Proficient* on the CRT in Mathematics by 3% each year for the next eight years.
- Canyon View School District will increase the percentage of students with disabilities who perform at the Proficient and Advanced levels on the CRT in Mathematics by 8.25% each year for the next eight years.
- Canyon View School District will decrease the percentage of students with disabilities who perform at *Novice* and *Nearing Proficient* on the CRT in Mathematics by 8.25% each year for the next eight years.

Description of Specific Actions to Improve Education Practice in MATH	Person(s) Responsible	Measurement	Due Date	Timeline
1. Alignment of instruction with content standards: *The District Mathematics Instructional Leadership Focus Group will:* ♦ Support schools in analyzing and using their Math assessment data, by teacher, to understand which teachers and schools need support with standards-based instruction. ♦ Support schools in analyzing and using their Math assessment data, by student, to understand which students need additional support on standards-based content. ♦ Provide professional learning where individual teachers and schools require additional support.	District Math Instructional Leadership Focus Group District Assessment Director	Math assessment data disaggregated by teacher-school, and by student-teacher-school. Evidence that the students requiring additional support received the support, and the impact of the support. Evidence that the teachers and schools were given appropriate learning opportunities, and that they participated. Evaluations by participants of the professional learning and how they are using it.	Begin September 2006	Ongoing beginning with 2006-07 school year
2. Use of standards-aligned instructional materials and strategies: ♦ All district instructional materials and strategies acquired/used for teaching Math will be aligned to the standards. A list of approved materials and strategies will be created and circulated to all schools and teachers. ♦ Professional learning on standards-aligned instructional materials and strategies will be offered for college credit and /or Continuing Education Units (CEU).	District Math Instructional Leadership Focus Group	The use of these materials and strategies will be monitored for use and evaluated for effectiveness. The number of teachers taking professional learning and getting college credit or CEUs.	August 2006	Ongoing
3. Extended learning time: ♦ The District Math Instructional Leadership Focus Group will provide individual teachers, and groups of teachers, professional learning on interventions for identified students and in areas of students' needs. ♦ Each school will determine how students requiring, and wanting, extra help will get extended learning time.	District Math Instructional Leadership Focus Group Expert Facilitator	Professional learning sessions developed by the district and attended by teachers. Evaluations by participants of the professional learning, and how they are using it. Evidence that programs have been established for extended learning time and evaluated for effectiveness.	August 2006	Ongoing

Figure 8.1 (Continued)

Canyon View School District Quality Plan, 2005-06

Description of Specific Actions to Improve Education Practice in MATH	Person(s) Responsible	Measurement	Due Date	Timeline
4. Professional learning and collaboration aligned with standards-based instructional materials: *The District Math Instructional Leadership Focus Group will provide high quality professional development for classroom teachers, principals, administrators, and other school or community-based personnel:* a. designed to improve the instruction and assessment of children who live in poverty; b. designed to enhance the ability of teachers to understand and use curriculum, assessment measures, and instructional strategies for students with special needs; c. based on scientifically-based research demonstrating the effectiveness of the professional development in increasing teachers' subject matter knowledge; teaching knowledge, and teaching skills; and d. designed to result in positive and lasting impact on teacher performance in the classroom. *The District Math Instructional Leadership Focus Group will also:* ♦ Support schools in establishing structures for professional learning and professional collaboration aligned with standards-based instructional materials. ♦ Offer professional learning, by grade level and cross-grade level, across the district, to enhance collaboration across the district.	District Math Instructional Leadership Focus Group	Professional learning sessions developed by the district and attended by teachers. Evaluations by participants of the professional learning, and how they are using it. Improvements in student achievement as measured by the STBS CRT, for all student groups. Teacher responses to the Standards Assessment Questionnaire show improvement in the implementation of standards. Evidence that each school has a leadership structure in place to support ongoing professional learning and collaboration. Evidence of regularly scheduled meetings by district level grade level and cross-grade level to calibrate the teaching of learning standards.	Begin September 2006	Ongoing beginning with 2006-07 school year Professional learning will be revamped as necessary
5. Involvement of staff, parents, and community: ♦ The district will provide example notification procedures to reach out to parents about their children's expectations and performance. ♦ In professional learning training, teachers will learn how to describe to parents their children's assessment results.	District Math Instructional Leadership Focus Group	Parent follow-up on the effectiveness of the procedures developed to involve and inform parents. Professional learning attended and evaluated by teachers.	September 2006	Completed and evaluated by 2008
6. Monitoring program effectiveness: ♦ The District Math Instructional Leadership Focus Group, in conjunction with the District Research and Evaluation Group, will conduct a program evaluation of all components of the District Math Program, which will include the degree to which each program is being implemented, and will make recommendations on how to improve.	District Literacy Instructional Leadership Focus Group Research and Evaluation Group	Evaluation plan is developed and implemented.	Begin September 2006	Ongoing, 2006–2014. Revamped yearly, if necessary

Figure 8.1 (Continued)

Canyon View School District Quality Plan, 2005-06

Performance Goal 2: *By 2006-07, all students will be taught by highly qualified teachers.*

In 2005-06, all teachers in the Canyon View School District were fully credentialed to teach in their subject areas. The district will continue to ensure that all teachers are highly qualified to effectively differentiate instruction, teach to the state standards, and assess student progress to ensure all students are learning.

Description of Specific Actions to Ensure HIGHLY QUALIFIED TEACHERS	Person(s) Responsible	Measurement	Due Date	Timeline
1. Revision of the district's recruitment, selection, and retention process to ensure highly qualified teachers: ♦ Review and revise teacher recruitment process. ♦ Review and revise teacher selection process. ♦ Review and revise teacher retention process.	Human Resources Director	District's recruitment, selection, and retention processes reflect the data analysis findings.	Begin September 2006	Ongoing
2. Professional learning activities will have a substantial, measurable, and positive impact on student academic achievement and will be used as part of a broader strategy to eliminate the achievement gap that separates low-income and minority students from other students: *The district will provide training to enable teachers to:* ♦ Teach and address the needs of students with different learning styles, particularly students with disabilities, students with special learning needs (including students who are gifted and talented), and students with limited English proficiency. ♦ Improve student behavior in the classroom and identify early and appropriate interventions to help all students learn. ♦ Involve parents in their child's education. ♦ Understand and use data and assessments to improve classroom practice and student learning.	District Administrators Literacy and Math Instructional Leadership Focus Groups	Professional Learning Calendar will be developed and disseminated to all staff. Evidence that the teachers were given appropriate learning opportunities, and that they participated. Impact on student achievement.	Begin September 2006	Ongoing

Performance Goal 3: *All students will be educated in learning environments that are conducive to learning.*

The district will continue to ensure that all students are taught in environments conducive to learning.

Description of Specific Actions to Ensure that ALL STUDENTS WILL BE EDUCATED IN LEARNING ENVIRONMENTS THAT ARE CONDUCIVE TO LEARNING	Person(s) Responsible	Measurement	Due Date	Timeline
1. District administrators will ensure through data analysis, school plans, and school observations that: ♦ All district schools are supporting students physically, socially, emotionally, intellectually, and psychologically. ♦ All district schools know what the acceptable ranges are that indicate the above. ♦ Teachers and school administrators have the professional learning they need to support student needs. ♦ Schools know how attendance, mobility, and behavior numbers "ought" to look. ♦ Schools know how to accurately record and analyze attendance, mobility, and behavior data.	District Administrators Building Administrators	Questionnaire and school observations will show that students are supported physically, socially, emotionally, intellectually, and psychologically in environments that are conducive to learning. Attendance, mobility, and behavior incidents are within acceptable ranges, as identified by district leadership.	September 2006	Ongoing

Figure 8.1 (Continued)

Canyon View School District Quality Plan, 2005-06

Performance Goal 4: *All students will be educated in learning environments that are conducive to learning.*

Planned improvements: High School Graduation and Dropout Rates.

- The current graduation rate of 80% will increase to 100% by 2013-14.
- The current dropout rate of 20% will decrease to 0% by 2013-14.

Description of Specific Actions to Ensure that ALL STUDENTS WILL GRADUATE FROM HIGH SCHOOL	Person(s) Responsible	Measurement	Due Date	Timeline
1. Decrease the number of dropouts: District will study who and why students are dropping out of Canyon View's high schools. • Develop a plan to interview each student who is dropping out; try to ascertain what could have been done to prevent her/him from dropping out. • Identify early, and intercept, potential dropouts.	Research and Evaluation Department	Number and percentage of students who dropout from high school disaggregated by race/ethnicity, gender, disability status, English proficiency, and status as economically disadvantaged. Calculate dropouts in the same manner as used in National Center for Education Statistics reports on Common Core of Data. Reveal early potential dropouts through a study of district data variables.	Begin September 2006	Ongoing
2. Increase the number of graduates: District will study the need for more program offerings to keep students in school. (e.g., advanced placement, dual credits, vocational education, mentoring, internships with businesses, alternative, independent study, transition programs from elementary to middle and middle to high schools, counselors.) • Study whether to eliminate 120-hour "seat time" requirement for course credit and allow students to graduate early. • Develop a system to maintain contact with graduates, to find out how successful they are in their chosen careers and colleges. • Develop an alumni questionnaire and a system for implementing it.	Deputy Superintendent	A study of program offerings will be completed and appropriate programs implemented. A study of seat time and early graduation will be presented to the Board of Education. Design, administer, and analyze an alumni/follow-up questionnaire. Retrieve and analyze college records of Canyon View graduates to see if they complete college, if they need remediation, etc.	Begin September 2006	Ongoing

Research shows that there are three preconditions to school / district performance improvement: instructional coherence, a shared vision for school improvement, and data-driven decision making.

Implementing the Plan: The Leadership Structure

Research shows that there are three preconditions to school/district performance improvement: instructional coherence, a shared vision for school improvement, and data-driven decision making (Armstrong, 2002). All three must work together. Canyon View district administration believes the link among these three preconditions is leadership, specifically, the district administrators. Administrators must lead the way, challenging processes through the study of school and district results; inspiring the shared vision; enabling others to act through planning, professional learning, and partnerships; modeling the way through consistent actions; encouraging the heart by reminding teachers and school administrators of the purpose of the school and why they got into teaching in the first place; and celebrating successes (Kouzes & Posner, 2002). A district's performance cannot improve without the administrators and teachers being totally dedicated to and engaged in these processes.

Canyon View School District reorganized its instructional leadership structure to support the implementation of the vision throughout the district and within each school. The instructional leadership structure now shows relentlessness to the implementation of the content standards, quality instructional practices, and on-going assessments aligned to the state standards and assessment. (*Note:* Facilities and business operations are beyond the scope of this book.)

Changes in district leadership are described, by Continuous Improvement Continuum categories, below:

Information and Analysis

Someone in the district office used to be assigned to gather data when there was a "problem to solve" or a "fire to put out." In the new leadership structure of Canyon View, each district administrator is the owner of the data related to her/his program. This means that that administrator is responsible for the accuracy of the data and cleanliness of the reporting of the data. It also means that the administrator sets performance measures for the data she/he owns, and leads the cause by guiding the way the numbers look. It also means that each administrator knows about the data longitudinally, and how to use each data element to predict and ensure successes.

Student Achievement

The district office used to tell schools that they needed to implement the state content standards and figure out how to get all students proficient—with district support. They felt that the schools did not want district leadership to be "too heavy handed."

Beginning with the new continuous improvement plan, the district instructional leadership adopted a framework which included:

- Support for each school to create and implement a vision that is congruent with the district vision.
- A districtwide curriculum aligned to the content standards.
- Training for all teachers in the curriculum, instructional strategies, assessments, and materials aligned to the content standards.
- Professional learning and support for teachers to understand and use ongoing assessment data to improve student learning.
- The monitoring and measurement of the implementation of the standards in each grade level and classroom.

Quality Planning

In the past, the district required schools to create annual school improvement plans. The plans were seldom revisited or implemented in full. They pretty much looked the same each year. Based on the feedback provided in the *Continuous Improvement Continuum* assessment, the schools requested that the district become the primary supporter of the implementation of school plans through School Portfolios. The schools want to keep their School Portfolios up-to-date, and use them with district administrators in any conversations about the school, so their school improvement efforts can continually move forward.

Leadership

The district always wanted principals and teacher leaders to become strong instructional leaders. With little explicit support, the leadership looked different at each school. A network of teacher leaders has been created, and given professional learning on how to provide support to teachers, principals, and district administrators, to implement the district vision.

Professional Development

The district leadership went from giving money to schools to choose their own professional development, to ensuring districtwide research-based professional learning, focused on implementing the standards and creating instructional coherence throughout the district, including:

- Professional learning in how to understand diversity, how to teach students from diverse backgrounds, students who live in poverty, who have special needs, males, and minorities, how to differentiate instruction, and how to create positive learning environments..
- Strategies and processes to ensure that schools connect the use of data to professional learning goals and school improvement plans.
- Time restructured during the workweek for teachers to talk about student instruction and assessment.
- District cross-grade-level and grade-level meetings to calibrate the curriculum and standards implementation.

Partnership Development

Canyon View School District knows that students, parents, businesses, and the community, are important for helping get all students proficient. The district will lead the way in acknowledging the partnerships that exist in the district, and will confirm their connections to the district vision. Guidelines and expectations for new win-win partnerships will be established.

Continuous Improvement and Evaluation

Continuous Improvement and Evaluation is required to assess the alignment of all parts of the system to the vision and to check the results the learning organization is getting compared to what is being implemented. With the comprehensive data analyses described in their School Portfolios, the schools already have comprehensive evaluations. The schools just need to learn to use them that way, and to systematically evaluate every program for effective implementation. This will take reorganizing the data already analyzed, or simply answering questions, using the data already analyzed. The District will reorganize districtwide data to evaluate programs, as well.

Implementing the Plan: Professional Learning

In ensuring districtwide research-based professional learning focused on implementing the standards and creating instructional coherence throughout the district, the district leadership established a professional learning structure that includes:

- Professional learning in how to understand diversity, how to teach students from diverse backgrounds, students who live in poverty, who have special needs, males, and minorities, how to differentiate instruction, and how to create positive learning environments.
- Strategies and processes to ensure that schools connect the use of data to professional learning goals and school improvement plans.
- Time restructured during the workweek for teachers to talk about instruction and assessment. Resources have been allotted to create time for teachers to collaborate to improve teaching and learning.
- Model lessons developed by teacher leaders, who will demonstrate in classrooms of other teachers. The lessons will also be videotaped so they can be reviewed and used for reinforcement.
- District cross-grade-level and grade-level meetings to calibrate the curriculum and standards implementation.
- A *District Induction Program* that provides newly hired professionals with the information and skills needed for success in the classroom.

While the focus during the 2006-07 school year is Reading and Mathematics, the calibration of Science and Social Studies standards will begin in 2007-08.

On the CD is a table on Powerful Professional Development Designs and a folder of activities related to these designs. CD-ROM (Designs.pdf and *Powerful Professional Development Designs* Folder). Most improvement plans that get implemented include at least thirty *Powerful Professional Development Designs* to assist with implementation.

Evaluating the Plan

In the Canyon View Quality Plan is a column indicating how specific actions/strategies and activities will be monitored and evaluated by condensing the *Measurement* column into a comprehensive evaluation plan (Figure 8.2), the persons responsible for the measurement of the plan can see the overall evaluation separate from the plan. CD-ROM (EvalPlan.pdf) It is good to look at the evaluation holistically. If one looks only at the measurement of individual strategies and activities in isolation of each other, she/he could miss ways to efficiently measure the entire plan.

Figure 8.2

Canyon View School District Evaluation Plan

The Canyon View School District administrative staff and the Board of Education approved the evaluation of their adopted goals:

1. All students will reach high standards, at a minimum attaining proficiency or better in Reading and Mathematics, by 2013-14.
2. By 2006-07, all students will be taught by highly qualified teachers.
3. All students will be educated in learning environments that are conducive to learning.
4. All students will graduate from high school.

How each goal will be evaluated in shown in the plan and summarized below.

Goal 1: *All students will reach high standards, at a minimum attaining proficiency or better in Reading and Mathematics, by 2013-14.*

Planned Improvement in Student Performance in Reading

- Canyon View School District will increase the percentage of students who perform at the *Proficient* and *Advanced* levels on the *State Test of Basic Skills Criterion Referenced Test* (CRT) in Reading by 2.25% each year for the next eight years.
- Canyon View School District will decrease the percentage of students who perform at *Novice* and *Nearing Proficient* on the CRT in Reading by 2.25% each year for the next eight years.
- Canyon View School District will increase the percentage of students with disabilities who perform at the *Proficient* and *Advanced* levels on the CRT in Reading by 7.5% each year for the next eight years.
- Canyon View School District will decrease the percentage of students with disabilities who perform at *Novice* and *Nearing Proficient* on the CRT in Reading by 7.5% each year for the next eight years.

Planned Improvement in Student Performance in Mathematics

- Canyon View School District will increase the percentage of students who perform at the *Proficient* and *Advanced* levels on the *State Test of Basic Skills Criterion Referenced Test* (CRT) in Mathematics by 3% each year for the next eight years.
- Canyon View School District will decrease the percentage of students who perform at *Novice* and *Nearing Proficient* on the CRT in Mathematics by 3% each year for the next eight years.
- Canyon View School District will increase the percentage of students with disabilities who perform at the *Proficient* and *Advanced* levels on the CRT in Mathematics by 8.25% each year for the next eight years.
- Canyon View School District will decrease the percentage of students with disabilities who perform at *Novice* and *Nearing Proficient* on the CRT in Mathematics by 8.25% each year for the next eight years.

To achieve this goal and improve Reading and Mathematics performance for all students, Canyon View School District plans to:

1. Align all instruction with Reading and Mathematics content standards.
2. Use only standards-aligned instructional materials and strategies.
3. Extend learning time for students needing and wanting extra time to learn.
4. Provide professional learning and collaboration aligned with standards-based instructional materials and strategies.
5. Involve staff, parents, and community.
6. Monitor program effectiveness.

Figure 8.2 (Continued)

Canyon View School District Evaluation Plan

Align All Instruction with Reading and Mathematics Content Standards

The degree to which teachers are teaching to the Reading and Mathematics content standards will be measured as follows:

- Reading and Mathematics assessment data will be disaggregated, by teacher, within each school, and by student, by teacher, within each school. The results will show which teachers are teaching to the standards and which students are learning the standards, as measured by the Reading and Mathematics assessments. The teacher Standards Implementation Questionnaire will show that all teachers know how to teach and assess to the Reading and Mathematics content standards.
- The number of students requiring additional support as measured by the Reading and Mathematics assessments will be compared to the number of students receiving the support. The impact of the additional support will be measured by the CRT Reading and Mathematics assessments, as well as by teacher developed common assessments that will be given quarterly.
- Evidence that all teachers and schools were given appropriate learning opportunities about teaching to Reading and Mathematics content standards, that all teachers participated, and how they are using the learning will be documented.
- Participants' evaluations of the professional learning will be analyzed and used to improve the professional learning, as well as each school's implementation of the professional learning.
- Student work will show that students are taught and know the standards.
- Principals' classroom observations will show that students know what they are supposed to be learning and that they are learning the content.
- Principals' classroom observations will show that teachers know how to implement the Reading and Mathematics standards.

Use of Standards-aligned Instructional Materials and Strategies

- Principals' classroom observations will show that teachers are using the district approved Reading and Mathematics standards-aligned instructional materials and strategies.
- All district instructional materials and strategies acquired/used for teaching Reading and Mathematics will be monitored for use by each school and districtwide and will be evaluated for effectiveness through teacher interviews, student and teacher questionnaires, and by analyzing student achievement results in these content areas.
- The number of teachers taking professional learning on standards-aligned instructional materials and strategies and taking college credit and/or Continuing Education Units (CEUs) will be documented.

Extended Learning Time

- The number of students requiring additional support, as measured by the Reading and Mathematics assessments, will be compared to the number of students receiving the support. The impact of the additional support will be measured by the Reading and Mathematics assessments.
- How each school determines how students requiring, and wanting, extra help will get extended learning time will be documented, along with how the school plans to evaluate the impact of the extended learning time.
- Professional learning sessions, related to creating extended learning time programs will be attended by teachers and administrators, and evaluated by participants. How they use the learning to create programs will be documented.

Figure 8.2 (Continued)

Canyon View School District Evaluation Plan

Professional Learning and Collaboration Aligned with Standards-based Instructional Materials

- Professional learning sessions developed by the district will be evaluated by the participants with respect to how effective the sessions are in helping them implement the standards-based curriculum and instructional strategies in the classroom.
- The *Standards Assessment Questionnaire* will show schoolwide improvement in the implementation of standards.
- The impact of the professional learning sessions will also be seen in the student learning results, for all student groups.
- The effectiveness of each school's leadership structure to ensure ongoing professional learning and collaboration will be measured through administrator and teacher interviews, and questionnaire responses.
- The effectiveness of district level, grade-level and cross-grade-level meetings to calibrate the teaching of learning standards will be measured through administrator and teacher interviews, questionnaire responses, and by reviewing student achievement results.

Involvement of Staff, Parents, and Community

- The district notification procedures to reach out to parents about their children's expectations and performance will be evaluated through parent follow-up on the effectiveness of the procedures developed.
- Teacher professional learning to describe to parents their children's assessment results will be evaluated for effectiveness.

Monitoring Program Effectiveness

- All components of the *District Literacy and Mathematics Programs* will be analyzed for effectiveness by studying the degree to which each program is being implemented, STBS results by student groups and teachers, and student, staff, and parent questionnaires.

Goal 2: *By 2006-07, all students will be taught by highly qualified teachers.*

In 2005-06, all teachers in the Canyon View School District were fully credentialed to teach in their subject areas. The district will continue to ensure that all teachers are highly qualified to effectively differentiate instruction, teach to the state standards, and assess student progress to ensure all students are learning.

Revision of district's recruitment, selection, and retention process to ensure highly qualified teachers.

- The effectiveness of the District's recruitment, selection, and retention processes will be determined by evidence that all teachers have appropriate credentials, and professional learning in differentiating instruction, teaching and assessing of the state content standards, and can show evidence of effective teaching. The recruitment, selection, and retention processes will be revised on the basis of the evaluation results.

Professional learning activities will have a substantial, measurable, and positive impact on student academic achievement that will be used as part of a broader strategy to eliminate the achievement gap that separates low-income and minority students from other students.

- Evidence that the teachers were given appropriate learning opportunities, and that they participated will be analyzed through questionnaires and school professional development calendars.
- The impact on student learning will be measured by STBS results by student groups and teachers, and student, staff, and parent questionnaires, disaggregated by student groups, over time.

Figure 8.2 (Continued)

Canyon View School District Evaluation Plan

Goal 3: ***All students will be educated in learning environments that are conducive to learning.***

District administrators will ensure through data analysis, school plans, and school observations that all district schools are supporting students physically, socially, emoitonally, intellectually, and psychologically.

- Questionnaire results and school observations will show that students are supported physically, socially, emotionally, intellectually, and psychologically in environments that are conducive to learning.
- Attendance, mobility, and behavior incidents will be measured and monitored over time.
- Evidence will show that teachers and school administrators have the professional learning they need to support student needs.

Goal 4: ***All students will graduate from high school.***

Planned Improvements: High School Graduation and Dropout Rates

- The current graduation rate of 80% will increase to 100% by 2013-14.
- The current dropout rate of 20% will decrease to 0% by 2013-14.

Decrease the number of dropouts

- The number and percentage of students who dropout of high school, disaggregated by race/ethnicity, gender, disability, English proficiency, and economically disadvantaged will be calculated for each school and for the district.
- A district study will reveal early potential drop-outs through appropriate data variables, and a program to intercept potential drop-outs will be implemented and evaluated.

Increase the number of graduates

- A study of program offerings will be completed and appropriate programs implemented.
- A study of seat time and early graduation option will be presented to the Board of Education.
- The analysis of an alumni/follow-up questionnaire will show that the programs developed and implemented to help students graduate are effective from the perspective of the students.
- College records of Canyon View graduates will show the numbers who complete college and need remediation.

A continuous improvement plan includes objectives for reaching the school district goals, strategies, and actions to achieve the objectives, person(s) responsible, how each strategy and action will be measured, resources needed, due dates, and timeline.

Summary

With the strengths, challenges, gap analyses, and root cause analyses complete, one can integrate findings to create a continuous improvement plan that is informed by the data and the school district vision, and that will lead to improved student learning. A continuous improvement plan that is based on quality data can eliminate root causes. Identifying and then eliminating the root causes of the gaps in student achievement by using the data will almost surely guarantee student learning increases.

A continuous improvement plan includes objectives for reaching the school district goals, strategies, and actions to achieve the objectives, person/people responsible, how each strategy and action will be measured, resources needed, due dates, and timelines.

From the overall continuous improvement plan, one can create a leadership structure, evaluation plan, professional learning plan, and even a partnership plan that will reinforce roles, responsibilities, meeting times, and the overall approach to continuous improvement and evaluation.

On the CD Related to this Chapter

- *Canyon View School District Shared Vision* (CVVision.pdf)
  This read-only file is the first draft of the *Canyon View School District Guiding Principles and Shared Vision,* shown on pages 327-329 in Chapter 8.
- *Canyon View School District Plan for Improvement* (SchlPlan.pdf)
  This read-only file is the first draft of the *Canyon View School District Plan* and is shown as Figure 8.1 in Chapter 8.
- *Planning Template* (APForm.doc)
  A quality action plan to implement the vision consists of goals, objectives, strategies, actions, person(s) responsible, resources required, due dates, and timelines. A template with these components is provided in *Microsoft Word,* ready to be completed.
- *Developing a Plan Activity* (ACTDevAP.pdf)
  The purpose of this activity is to take the shared vision to the action level. The steps in creating an action plan are spelled out in this activity.
- *Establishing a Partnership Plan* (EstPPlan.pdf)
  This read-only file describes the steps in creating a partnership plan that will become a part of the continuous improvement plan.
- *Partnership Evaluation Questionnaire* (PaEvalQ.pdf)
  This read-only file, the *Canyon View School District Partnership Evaluation Questionnaire,* is used to assess community members' role in the partnership, perceptions of the impact of the partnership, and satisfaction with the partnership program.
- *Canyon View Evaluation Plan* (EvalPlan.pdf)
  This read-only file, the *Canyon View School Evaluation Plan,* combines the goals, object, and measurement column of the action plan into a comprehensive evaluation plan, and is shown as Figure 8.2 in Chapter 8.
- *Evaluating a Program Activity* (ACTEval.pdf)
  The purpose of this activity is to get many people involved in creating a comprehensive evaluation design to determine the impact of a program and to know how to improve the program.
- *Classroom Observation Tool* (ObvTool.pdf)
  This read-only file is the first draft of the *Big River High School Classroom Observation Tool,* created for assessing where each teacher is in implementing the state content standards and vision.

- *Powerful Professional Development Designs* (Designs.pdf)
  This read-only file describes numerous ways to embed professional development into the learning community.
- *Powerful Professional Development Designs Folder*
  Powerful Professional Development Designs are those that are embedded into the daily operations of a staff. They are ongoing and lead to improvement of instruction and increases in student learning.
  - *Action Research Activity* (ACTRsrch.pdf)
    Teachers and/or administrators raise questions about the best way to improve teaching and learning, systematically study the literature to answer the questions, implement the best approach, and analyze the results.
  - *Cadres or Action Teams Activity* (ACTCdres.pdf)
    Organizing cadres or teams allows for the delegation of responsibilities so teams of educators can study new approaches, plan for the implementation of new strategies or programs, and get work done without every staff member's involvement.
  - *Case Studies Activity* (ACTCases.pdf)
    Staff members review case studies of student work, and/or of another teacher's example lessons, which can lead to quality discussions and improved practices.
  - *Coaching Activity* (ACTCoach.pdf)
    Teachers form teams of two or three to observe each other, plan together, and to talk and encourage each other in meaningful ways, while reflecting on continuously improving instructional practices.
  - *Examining Student Data: Teacher Analysis of Test Scores Table One* (Table1.doc)
    Examining student data consists of conversations around individual student data results and the processes that created the results. This approach can be a significant form of professional development when skilled team members facilitate the dialogue.
  - *Examining Student Work Activity* (ACTSWork.pdf)
    Examining student work as professional development ensures that what students learn is aligned to the learning standards. It also shows teachers the impact of their processes.
  - *Example Lessons: Birds of a Feather Unit Example* (UnitEx.pdf)
    Some teachers need to see what a lesson that implements all aspects of the school vision would look like. Providing examples for all teachers to see can reward the teacher who is doing a good job of implementing

the vision and provide a template for other teachers. It is very effective to store summary examples in a binder or on a website for everyone to peruse at any time.

- *Example Lessons: Unit Template* (UnitTmpl.doc)
  This *Microsoft Word* template provides the outline for creating instructional units that implement the vision.
- *Immersion Activity* (ACTImrsn.pdf)
  Immersion is a method for getting teachers engaged in different content through hands-on experiences as a learner.
- *Journaling Activity* (ACTJourn.pdf)
  Journal writing helps teachers construct meaning for, and reflect on, what they are teaching and learning.
- *Listening to Students Activity* (ACTListn.pdf)
  Students' perceptions of the learning environment are very important for continuous improvement. Focus groups, interviews, and questionnaires can be used to discover what students are perceiving.
- *Needs Assessment: Professional Development Needs Related to Technology Example* (TechnEx.pdf)
  Needs assessments help staff understand the professional development needs of staff. At the same time, if done well, this tool can lead to quality staff conversations and sharing of knowledge.
- *Needs Assessment: Professional Development Plan Related to Technology Template* (TechTmpl.doc)
  This template provides the outline for doing your own professional development needs assessment.
- *Networks Activity* (ACTNtwrk.pdf)
  Purposeful grouping of individuals/schools to further a cause or commitment.
- *Partnerships: Creating Partnerships Activity* (ACTParts.pdf)
  Teachers partnering with businesses in the community, scientists, and/or university professors can result in real-world applications for student learning and deeper understandings of content for the teacher.
- *Process Mapping: Charting School Processes Activity* (ACTProcs.pdf)
  School processes are instruction, curriculum, and assessment strategies used to ensure the learning of all students. Mapping or flowcharting school processes can help staff members objectively look at how students are being taught.

- *Reflection Log Activity* (ACTLog.pdf)
  Reflective logs are recordings of key events in the educators' work days to reflect on improvement and/or to share learnings with colleagues.
- *Scheduling Activity* (ACTSchdl.pdf)
  A real test for whether or not a vision is realistic is to have teachers develop a day's schedule. This will tell them immediately if it is doable, or what needs to change in the vision and plan to make it doable.
- *School Meetings: Running Efficient Meetings* (Meetings.pdf)
  Staff, department, grade level, and cross-grade level meetings can promote learning through study or sharing best practice, while focusing on the implementation of the vision.
- *Self-Assessment: Teacher Assessment Tool Related to the School Vision* (AssessEx.pdf)
  Staff self-assessments on tools to measure progress toward the vision, such as the *Continuous Improvement Continuums,* will help them see where their school is as a system and what needs to improve for better results.
- *Self-Assessment: Teacher Assessment Tool Related to Our School Vision Template* (AssessEx.doc)
  This template file for self-assessments on tools to measure progress toward the vision, such as the *Continuous Improvement Continuums,* will help teachers see where their school is as a system and what needs to improve for better results.
- *Self-Assessment: Our School Shared Vision Implementation Rubric Example* (StRubric.pdf)
  Self-assessments on tools to measure progress toward the vision, such as the *Continuous Improvement Continuums,* will help teachers see where their school is as a system and what needs to improve for better results.
- *Self-Assessment: Our School Shared Vision Implementation Rubric Template* (StRubric.doc)
  This template file for self-assessments on tools to measure progress toward the vision, such as the *Continuous Improvement Continuums,* will help teachers see where their school is as a system and what needs to improve for better results.

- *Self-Assessment: Staff-Developed Rubric Activity* (ACTRubric.pdf)
  This activity for self-assessments on tools to measure progress toward the vision, such as the *Continuous Improvement Continuums*, will help teachers see where their school is as a system and what needs to improve for better results.
- *Shadowing Students Activity* (ACTShadw.pdf)
  Purposefully following students and systematically recording the students' instructional experiences is a wonderful job-embedded approach to understanding what students are experiencing in school.
- *Storyboarding Activity* (ACTStory.pdf)
  Storyboarding is an activity that will allow participants to share previous knowledge, while reflecting on the topic. It is a structure for facilitating conversations.
- *Study Groups Activity* (ACTStudy.pdf)
  Groups of educators meet to learn new strategies and programs, to review new publications, or to review student work together.
- *Teacher Portfolio Activity* (ACTTcher.pdf)
  Teacher portfolios can be built to tell the story of implementing the vision in the classroom, and its impact on student learning. Portfolios are excellent for reflection, understanding, and showing progress. Portfolios can be used for many things including self-assessment, employment, supervision to replace traditional teacher evaluation, and peer collaboration.
- *Train the Trainers Activity* (ACTTrain.pdf)
  Train the Trainers is an approach to saving time and money. Individuals are trained and return to the school or school district with a commitment to train others.
- *Tuning Protocols Activity* (ACTTune.pdf)
  A tuning protocol is a formal process for reviewing, honoring, and fine tuning colleagues' work through presentation and reflection.

Analyzing the Data:
Conclusions and Recommendations

Chapter 9

Most school districts do not need to gather more data—except in the area of school processes. Where effort is needed is in organizing, graphing, analyzing, and using the data they already have.

The main purpose of *Using Data to Improve Student Learning in School Districts* is to show data analyses of four real school districts, using a continuous improvement planning model to understand, explain, and continuously improve learning for all students.

In this book, an analysis of one school district's data has been presented. Many of you might consider the analysis to be massive. However, this example was created using only the state criterion-referenced assessments, some demographics, some student learning, some perceptions, and some process data. The data shown here and on the CD, therefore, are not exhaustive. More comprehensive data analyses would use other measures of student learning in addition to state assessments, such as grades, ongoing assessments, and additional process measures such as classroom observations, degree of program or process implementation. Additionally, comprehensive data analyses would have multiple years of cohort data—ideally, we want to follow students throughout their K-12 education experiences. If this is not feasible for your district at this time, three years of consistent measures are good—five years are better. School districts have plenty of data. Most school districts not need to gather more data—except in the area of school processes. Where effort is needed is in organizing, graphing, analyzing, and using the data they already have. Using the data means getting the information into the hands of school and district administrators and teachers who are actively engaged in teaching and learning.

What the Canyon View School District Example Shows

From the example, you can see how much a person can learn about a school district through data and how these data can lead staffs to appropriate and important conversations about continuous improvement—even when only little data are available. I hope you can also see that one person alone cannot analyze all the data. Everybody sees something different in the results, so many perspectives are necessary and valuable.

The demographic analyses of Canyon View School District, as well as the districts on the CD, show us that we can get a very good understanding of the context of education for students in a district. The way the school district organizes itself to provide for its students is revealed in the demographic data. School district personnel reviewing these data need to take the time to comprehensively analyze their own system's demographic data. There are times when others must read about your district. Remember how easy it would be, when reviewing these data, to start "making up" parts of the story when it is not complete. Your best defense against others drawing incorrect or incomplete assumptions about your school district is to provide complete analyses and to know your data inside and out.

With regard to perceptions data, we viewed six different types of perceptual data—a District *Continuous Improvement Continuum* assessment (also considered process data, school-level student, staff, and parent questionnaire data, district-level administrative questionnaire results, and teacher-level standards-implementation questionnaire. These data helped the district see itself from different perspectives. A major caution in looking at the questionnaire results is to make sure one does not over-interpret differences in student groups—even though a gap in averages appears, there might not be a *real* difference if both averages indicate agreement. It just might be the degree of the agreement that is different. *Real* differences would show agreement-disagreement. We are not concerned with looking for "significant differences." We want to know about "educational or perceptual differences," because these differences are significant in the learning of students.

Done well, data analysis is a massive activity requiring the technical support of knowledgeable people and data analysis tools.

The *Continuous Improvement Continuums* are powerful system analysis tools. These assessments help whole staffs talk the same talk and walk the same walk. Over time, they show staffs that they can get onto the proverbial *same page* in order to make improvements. The indications that they are making improvements through the *Continuous Improvement Continuums* keep staffs engaged in the continuous improvement process and moving forward.

Many districts would be able to analyze school processes more comprehensively than shown in this example. All programs or processes used to deliver instruction could be measured and described so impact can be determined. The way in which instruction is delivered is the one element over which schools/districts have complete control, and the one that is seldom analyzed thoroughly. Demographic, perceptual, and student learning data can also show process data.

In analyzing student learning results, Canyon View used its state criterion-referenced test. Unfortunately, at the time the analyses were created, only grades four, eight, and eleven were assessed, so we do not show analyses for the other grades in the district. We also do not know how well the students did after high school. We would very much want to follow the students through college or post-high-school work to see how they are doing.

As far as gap analyses are concerned, Canyon View School District was able to indicate gaps. The district was able to see contributing causes that, when "fixed," should lead to student learning increases.

Chapter 7 shows strategies for understanding contributing causes to student learning gaps. This information, along with the implications for the continuous improvement plan determined by analyzing demographic, perceptual, student learning, and school process data, led to recommendations for improvement. These recommendations became the plan, that includes strategies for improvement, person(s) responsible, how the strategies will be measured, resources required (not shown in this example), due dates, and timelines.

What School District Leaders Can Do to Ensure Continuous Improvement Throughout the District

Strong district leadership and operations are "essential to advancing equitable and sustainable reform." (McLaughlin and Talbert, 2003, page 3.) Districts must take on continuous improvement with a plan to improve the entire system, including all the parts that make up the system. To do this, the district must know the system and how its parts interrelate to create the system. Comprehensive data analyses show these interrelationships and the impact of the system on the students. These analyses also indicate where leadership and support are needed to improve the system and learning for all students.

One of the first and most important things district leaders can do for schools is to *encourage schools to commit to a continuous improvement framework* that is congruent, or the same as the district's, and stick with it—help schools embrace and implement a framework for continuous improvement, monitor it, and don't change it every time a new idea comes along. Too many districts keep schools from improving by asking them to change their focus annually, or after the schools have committed to a framework. Without a framework, schools tend to lose focus and become inefficient and ineffective with their continuous improvement work: repeating things already done and not doing the things that matter. The framework keeps schools doing the work when the work gets hard. It is a structure for them to rely on and not just spin their wheels.

A good framework for continuous improvement includes the elements shown in Figure 9.1. Each of these elements in a continuous improvement model must be monitored and measured, with next step actions created regularly to keep the improvement continuous.

Figure 9.1

Framework for Continuous Improvement

DATA: Information and Analysis	A framework for continuous improvement must have a strong data analysis component that requires looking at the entire system and the students through different lenses. Student learning data are extremely important. However, these data, by themselves, do not provide, enough information to know how to improve a system. We find schools that use only student learning measures adding on to their days with "before school programs" and "after school programs." What they are telling their students is that we know you are not learning math during the day with our current processes, so just sit there all day; we will use processes that get to your learning needs with before or after school programs. Certainly teachers must have on-going student learning measures available to them at all times to know how their processes are helping students get to the desired outcomes. In our perfect world, all teachers would be clear about what they want students to know and be able to do by the end of the year. They would conduct assessments that would tell them what their students know and do not know at the beginning of the year. They would have short-cycle assessments that would help students learn the content and provide information about how student learning is progressing throughout the year. That way, teachers would know how to adjust their teaching strategies throughout the year to ensure continuous student learning. The assessment information would be shared with students and parents.
A VISION: Student Achievement	The vision clarifies what it will look like, sound like, feel like when the school is carrying out its mission. A vision must be understandable to everyone in the organization in the same way. It should cement commitments, not just compliance. A vision helps a system achieve *Focused Acts of Improvement.* Without a vision, a system could produce *Random Acts of Improvement.* The vision of the school—created from what it expects students to know and be able to do, the values and beliefs of the staff, and the purpose and mission of the school—must be at the center of everything that the school does. When the vision is shared and clear, everything that is planned will focus on implementing the vision. Everything implemented in the school must be about the vision. Everything is evaluated in terms of how it will get the school to its vision, and everything is improved to better implement the vision. 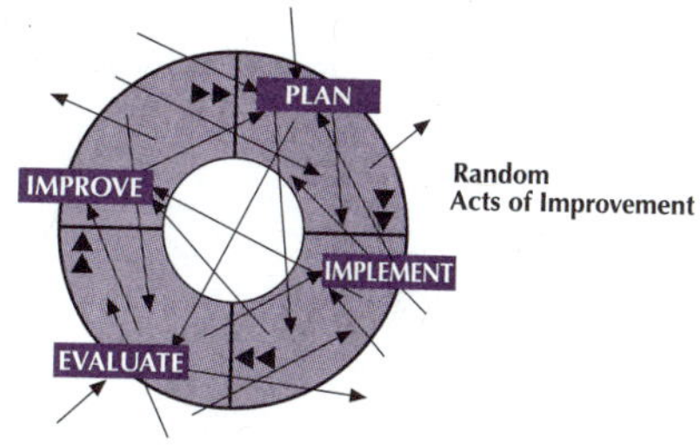 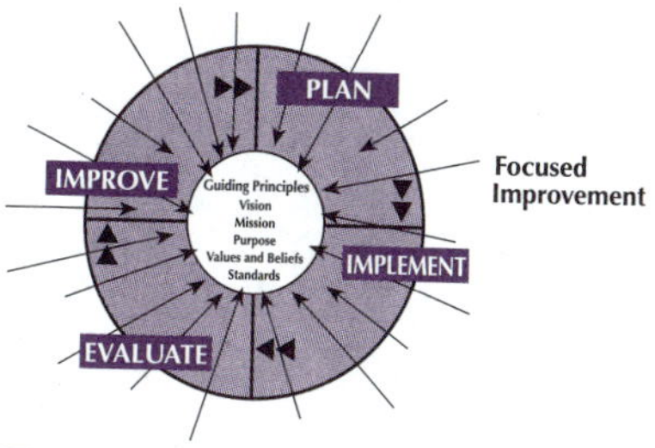 PLAN, IMPROVE, IMPLEMENT, EVALUATE — Random Acts of Improvement PLAN, IMPROVE, IMPLEMENT, EVALUATE; Guiding Principles: Vision, Mission, Purpose, Values and Beliefs, Standards — Focused Improvement
A PLAN: Quality Planning	One plan, aligned to the vision, is a quality plan. A quality plan has goals, strategies, and activities to implement the vision, and eliminate student learning gaps. Each strategy and activity has a person(s) responsible, measurement, resources required, due date, and timelines so the plan and all of its elements can be regularly evaluated.
Leadership	Leadership structures are necessary so everyone knows who is making what decisions, when, and when staff will meet to calibrate the implementation of the vision. We believe the job of leaders is to help everyone in the organization implement the vision and the plan. Teachers must become strong leaders in the organization, not just the administrators. Without strong and supportive leadership to "shepherd" the vision, even the best plans will not result in continuous improvement throughout the district.
Professional Learning	A major component of the plan and a continuously improving school is the professional learning of all staff to implement the vision. Professional learning is about professionals communicating and collaborating about student work and student data to improve student learning. Just as strategies to improve student learning should be implemented throughout the regular school day, professional learning should be embedded throughout the workweek.
Partnership Development	Schools are an important part of any community, and they cannot be successful if they exist in isolation. Starting with what we expect students to know and be able to do, conversations with parents, community, and businesses can lead to win-win partnerships, and improved student learning.
Continuous Improvement and Evaluation	Continuous Improvement and Evaluation is about systems thinking – evaluating all the parts and the whole on a regular basis.

Help the Schools with Data

Another thing districts can do is to help the schools with data. School staffs get very busy with their day-to-day work with students. If the schools and their staffs do not get the support for data from the district, there is a chance that they will not get the data in a timely fashion to be able to use them to improve teaching and learning. What follows are ways the district can help schools with data.

- *Student information system:* get a good system, help the schools clean the data, train personnel in how to input the data consistently and correctly, and establish systems to monitor the data integrity.
- *Help schools study root/contributing causes of their undesirable results, so they can make real changes, not just eliminate the symptoms.*
- *Create appropriate, pre-determined data reports and get them to the schools to use.* We want teachers and principals spending their time using the data, not gathering and organizing the data they receive. Do not overwhelm them with too many data reports. Clarify what is important for them to have, and provide them with the story of their school.
- *Go beyond:* at the district level, look across the data to understand the relationship of the data elements to each other and the impact of processes on student outcomes. Present data to the schools in meaningful ways so they can use them immediately.
- *Get good ongoing assessments into the hands of the teachers.* Looking for, or creating, formative assessments that predict the high stakes assessments is difficult and time-consuming. The district needs to lead the way on this.
- *Help teachers and school administrators understand what the high stakes tests are testing and how the results should be used appropriately.*
- *Technological support:* Make sure all technology equipment and software stay up-to-date and running.
- *Provide leadership by the numbers.* Help schools understand what the numbers mean, what they should look like, and how to achieve those results.
- *Model the use of data:* when requiring schools to gather and use data, district leadership should use data for talking points during frequent monitoring.

Create Incentives for Schools to Do the Work

We want schools to stay committed to continuous improvement. When schools are using a good framework for continuous improvement, they will make progress. Reward the schools for committing to continuous improvement and for making progress. Perhaps fewer district requirements would be reward enough.

Help with Creating a School Vision

It is important for the district to have a vision and each school in the district to have its own vision that reflects the district's vision. District leadership can help schools create a vision and understand how important a vision is to continuous improvement.

Help Schools Align Assessment/Benchmarks to Curriculum/Instruction

Help schools align curriculum, instruction, and formative assessments to what you want students to know and be able to do (also to the high stakes tests, as long as the high stakes tests are testing what you want students to know and be able to do). Help teachers know what it would look like if they were teaching in a totally aligned classroom and school, and then help them measure and reinforce the alignment.

Reinforce One Plan

Reinforce one plan, aligned to the vision. Support the vision by the analysis of data to create the one plan that will get implemented, monitored, and evaluated on a regular basis.

Leadership

Help schools establish leadership structures to implement the school and, thus, the district vision. A school's leadership structure helps all staff know who is making what decisions and when. That leadership structure will require teachers to collaborate and communicate to continuously improve teaching and learning for all students, ensure that the system is set up for success, and help all staff to keep going when the work gets difficult.

Professional Learning

When sponsoring districtwide professional development, the district must make sure all activities will help with the implementation of the district vision and goals. Provide coaches, modeling, demonstration lessons, and observations to support the classroom teachers in knowing what it would look like if they were "doing it." Develop protocols to structure and encourage professional conversations and collaboration.

Never require all schools to do the same professional development just because one school was successful.

Make sure every professional knows how to differentiate instruction, how to treat students with care and respect, how to teach students with learning disabilities, English as a second language learners, and students who live in poverty.

Help schools create the time to collaborate and communicate to improve teaching and learning for all students. Give all staffs the motivation, inspiration, and courage to *implement* the vision.

Partnership Development

District offices can set the tone for constructively including parents, community, and businesses in the learning mission of the school. Beginning with what they expect students to know and be able to do will help all parties to contribute and to benefit. Win-win partnerships are about student learning, and not just about acquiring money and stuff.

Continuous Improvement and Evaluation

Continuous Improvement and Evaluation is about systems thinking and evaluating the system on a continuous basis, from Preschool through Grade 12. Schools need help from the district office in the evaluation of programs and processes. The district can model the way by evaluating its processes on a regular basis.

Data Warehouses

Done well, data analysis is a massive activity requiring the technical support of knowledgeable people and a data warehouse. Districts are coming on board with acquiring data warehouses that will enable the storage of a large number of data elements, and the analysis of data quickly, easily, accurately, and meaningfully. (See *Data Warehousing to Improve Teaching and Learning* [Bernhardt, 2007, in press].) On the accompanying CD are two articles entitled *Databases Can Help Teachers with Standards Implementation* (Bernhardt, 1999), and *Data Tools for School Improvement* (Bernhardt, 2005). CD-ROM (Dbases.pdf and DataTools.pdf)

School districts that do not have such a tool right now must begin looking and preparing to acquire a data warehouse, because they need one. It simply is no longer an option not to have one. When looking for data tools or a data warehouse, districts need to keep at least six considerations in mind:

1. *Accessibility at different levels.* We would like the data stored at the district, possibly even regional or state levels, and have it accessible at the district, school, and classroom levels.
2. *Build graphs automatically.* We want to be able to look over the data tables to check for accuracy; however, we want the data analysis tool to build graphs as well. Because we want staffs to review the data, it is wise to put the data in picture form so everyone can see the resulting information in the same way. Trends are often easier to detect in graphs rather than in tables. However, sometimes we need tables to display the data. (The CD has graphing templates for use with a data analysis tool or paper data.)
3. *Disaggregation on the fly.* When performing analyses that are starting to show interesting data, we want to be able to analyze quickly and easily at the next deeper levels. The easier and quicker this is to do, the deeper one can get into the data, and the more likely we are to get to root causes.
4. *Point and click or drag and drop technology that is intuitive.* We want anyone to be able to use the database without requiring a manual every time it is used.
5. *The ability to create standard reports with a click of a button.* Some reports have to be created every year, such as a *District Accountability Report Card* or a Title 1 report. If the same information is required each year, the programming should allow one to push a button the next year to create the report without spending a lot of time on it.
6. *The ability to follow cohorts.* Following the same groups of students as they progress through their educational careers will provide a great deal of information about one's school processes.

For all four case studies associated with this book and CD, I used a data warehouse tool called *EASE-E Data Analyzer* by *TetraData (www.tetradata.com).* With this tool, I am able to analyze an entire district's data and all of its schools at the same time, as quickly and easily as analyzing one school. I do the analyses for all the schools at the same time, and then use graphing templates, such as the ones provided on the accompanying CD, to build the graphs quickly and easily. (*Point of clarification: EASE-E* builds graphs. I use graphing templates for the fastest production. Teachers and administrators can also access specific school and classroom data from this warehouse.)

Our passion with data analysis is getting the results into the hands of teachers and administrators, providing professional learning to understand the results, and the time to study the results of the analyses, instead of having staffs use their time performing the analyses.

Who Does the Data Analysis Work?

For the types of data analyses shown in the example, or described previously as comprehensive data analyses, it would be ideal if someone at the district level did the major analyses. With a good strong data analysis tool, the district person can analyze the data for all the schools, at all grade levels, for all the subtests, disaggregated by demographics, in one query. A clerk can then copy and paste the individual results into charting templates, perhaps even into the templates provided on the CD with this book.

With a strong data analysis tool, one person can create standard queries and standard reports, such as a *school report card,* for each of the schools. Our passion with data analysis is getting the results into the hands of teachers and administrators, and providing professional learning to understand the results, and the time to study the results of the analyses, instead of having staffs use their time performing or graphing the analyses. In our ideal world, at minimum, teachers would start the school year with historical data on each student in their class(es). They would have the demographic data and would know what the students know and what they need to know with respect to content standards. Also in our ideal world, teachers would be using ongoing measurements in their classrooms to make sure all students are progressing and mastering the standards/outcomes.

Let's say your district does not have a data warehouse and provides only the state assessment results on paper; you can still use these data in meaningful ways. At minimum, schools and districts can use the templates on the CD to graph the content and proficiency levels over time.

Summary: Review of Steps in Using Data to Improve Student Learning in School Districts

Continuous improvement planning for increasing student learning can be organized through answering a series of logical questions.

One of the first questions we want to answer is *Who are we?* Demographic data can answer this question. The answers set the context for the district and its schools, have huge implications for the direction the continuous improvement plan will take, and can help explain how the schools get the results they are getting. In fact, there is no way any school district can understand another number without this context.

The second question, *How do we do business?*, tells us about perceptions of the learning environment from student, staff, administrator, and parent perspectives. Understanding these perceptions can help a district know what is possible and what is appropriate, needed, and doable in the continuous improvement plan.

Answering the question, *How are we doing?* takes the data analysis work into the student learning realm. Analyzing required norm-referenced and/or criterion-referenced tests is an excellent way to begin answering this question. Looking across all measures can be useful and informative—another way to think about what students know and are able to do, giving us a glimpse of how students learn.

Gap analyses are critical for answering the question, *What are the gaps?* Gap analyses help districts see the differences between where they are (current results) and where they want to be (vision and goals). To be effective, gap analyses must dig layers deep into the data to truly understand the results and to begin to uncover root causes.

A root cause, as used in this continuous improvement planning model, refers to the deep underlying reason for the occurrence of a specific situation, the gap. While a symptom may become evident from a needs assessment or gap analysis—the symptom (low student scores) is not the cause. To find a root cause, one often has to ask *why* at least five levels down to uncover the root reason for the symptom. Root causes are not easy to uncover, but the information that is uncovered in the process of uncovering root causes is well worth the effort.

With the strengths, challenges, gap analyses, and root cause analyses complete, one can integrate findings to create a district-level continuous improvement plan that is informed by the data, and that will lead to student achievement increases across the district. Additionally, a continuous improvement plan based on data will eliminate root causes.

Continuous Improvement Planning through Answering Logical Questions

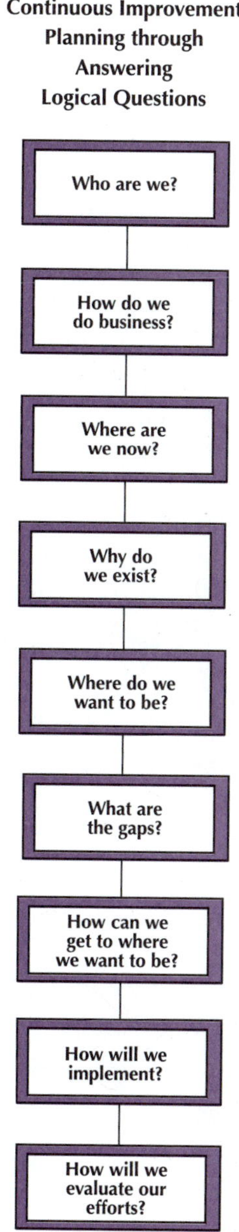
Who are we?
How do we do business?
Where are we now?
Why do we exist?
Where do we want to be?
What are the gaps?
How can we get to where we want to be?
How will we implement?
How will we evaluate our efforts?

> *It's easy to get the players. Getting 'em to play together, that's the hard part.*
>
> Casey Stengel

A continuous improvement plan to eliminate root causes can answer the question, *How will we get there?* A continuous improvement plan focused on data lays out the strategies and activities to implement. Required professional learning, a leadership structure, a design for partnerships with parents, communities, and businesses, and the evaluation of the plan are vital components.

Recommendations

In the past, the usual way typical school district personnel dealt with data was to analyze the dickens out of their annual state assessment results, develop a plan to increase the lowest scores, and then wait for the next year's results to come out to know if their plan made a difference. Many found they could improve their assessment results in that area, only to discover that other subject-area scores declined. With *No Child Left Behind*, this approach is no longer plausible. To move all students to proficiency, district and school personnel must have a complete understanding of the entire system the students experience, and work on improving the systems that create the results.

In the Canyon View example, we started with demographic and perceptual data, which gave us a view of the system that student learning data alone cannot give. There were definite student learning issues that would be missed had we only looked at student learning results. My recommendations for getting student learning increases across districts include the following:

- Gather and analyze your demographic data to understand clearly the students you are serving and who is teaching them by school, by grade level, and by content area. Make sure all processes are set up for success.
- Listen to the *voices* of students, parents, staff, and administrators through questionnaire analyses.
- Align and monitor your curriculum and instructional strategies to meet content standards.
- Provide professional learning for all staff to effectively implement the content standards.
- Incorporate into all teaching ongoing assessments related to standards acquisition (e.g., diagnostics, benchmarking, grade level indicators).
- Measure the implementation of content standards in every classroom, throughout the year.
- Measure the implementation of your desired curriculum and instructional strategies.

- Analyze your student learning results by schools, by student groups, by grade level, by classrooms, and by following student cohorts.
- Pull all your data together to learn what needs to change to get different results.
- Analyze the root causes of undesirable results.
- Create a vision that is shared and a plan to implement the vision and close the gaps.
- Monitor and evaluate the implementation of the vision and plan.

Gather your districtwide data, graph them in a manner similar to the examples in this book and on the CD; this will give you a good look at where your district and where your schools are right now. To understand what to improve in your system, you have to know as much about your system as you possibly can; study your demographic data, and your perceptual and student learning results, along with your current processes—study it all.

Time and time again, the differences in results by classroom or by school come down to the fact that some teachers are teaching to the standards and some are not. I can almost guarantee that if all teachers in your schools know what the students know when they start a grade level and subject area, focus their effective instructional strategies on teaching what they want students to know and be able to do to meet the standards, measure learning in an ongoing fashion to know if the students are improving, student learning results for *all* students will increase in a very short period of time.

Data are not the hardest parts of creating this scenario in all schools. Getting staffs to work together to share and implement the shared vision and plan takes strong and consistent leadership from the district and school administrators, school and district leadership teams. Data can help support this effort.

Best wishes to you as you continuously improve your systems for the students. You are creating the future in which the next generation will live.

On the CD Related to this Chapter

- *Databases Can Help Teachers with Standards Implementation* (Dbases.pdf)
  This read-only article, by Victoria L. Bernhardt, describes how databases can help with standards implementation.
- *Data Tools for School Improvement* (DataTools.pdf)
  This read-only article, by Victoria L. Bernhardt, describes how data tools can help schools analyze and use data effectively.

Appendix A

Overview of the CD Contents

The Appendix provides a list of the files as they appear on the accompanying CD. These files are listed by section, along with a description of the file's content and file type. (This list appears as the Index file [Index.pdf] on the CD.) CD-ROM

▼ CHAPTER 2 – WHAT DATA ARE IMPORTANT?

The files in this section support Chapter 2 in the book and provide an overview of what data are important in understanding if a district is effectively carrying out its purpose and assessing if *all* students are learning.

Multiple Measures of Data Graphic	MMgraphc.pdf	Acrobat Reader

This is Figure 2.1 in a PDF (portable document file) for printing.

Summary of Data Intersections	IntrscTbl.pdf	Acrobat Reader

This is Figure 2.2 in a PDF for your use with staff.

Data Discovery Activity	ACTDiscv.pdf	Acrobat Reader

The purpose of this activity is to look closely at examples of data and to discover specific information and patterns of information, both individually and as a group.

Intersections Activity	ACTIntrs.pdf	Acrobat Reader

The purpose of this activity is to motivate improvement teams to think about the questions they can answer when they cross different data variables. It is also designed to help teams focus their data-gathering efforts so they are not collecting everything and anything.

Creating Intersections Activity	ACTCreat.pdf	Acrobat Reader

This activity is similar to the *Intersections Activity*. The purpose is to have participants "grow" their intersections.

Data Analysis Presentation	DASlides.ppt	Microsoft PowerPoint

This *Microsoft PowerPoint* presentation is an overview to use with your staffs in getting started with data analysis.

Articles (Folder)

These read-only articles, by Victoria L. Bernhardt, are useful in workshops or in getting started on data with staff.

Multiple Measures	MMeasure.pdf	Acrobat Reader

This article by Victoria L. Bernhardt, in read-only format, summarizes why, and what, data are important to continuous district and school improvement.

Intersections: New Routes Open when One Type of Data Crosses Another	Intersct.pdf	Acrobat Reader

This article by Victoria L. Bernhardt, in read-only format, published in the *Journal of Staff Development* (Winter 2000), discusses how much richer your data analyses can be when you intersect multiple data variables.

No Schools Left Behind	NoSchls.pdf	Acrobat Reader

This article by Victoria L. Bernhardt, in read-only format, published in *Educational Leadership* (February 2003), summarizes how to improve learning for *all* students.

It Takes More Than Test Scores	TestScores.pdf	Acrobat Reader

This article by Victoria L. Bernhardt, published in *ACSA Leadership* (Nov/Dec 2004), summarizes why analyzing state assessment results is only the beginning of effective data-driven decision making.

Input/Process/Output (IPO) Diagram | IPODiagrm.pdf | Acrobat Reader

This is Figure 2.3 in a PDF file that shows different types of data in terms of *input, process,* and *outcome.* This diagram helps us know why it is important to analyze all of these data. This read-only file is the handout graphic that goes with the *IPO Activity* (below).

Input/Process/Output (IPO) Activity | ACTIPO.pdf | Acrobat Reader

This is an activity that allows staffs to determine if different data elements are *input, process,* and *outcome* elements. With this activity, you will also need the *headings* and *elements* files below.

IPO Headings | IPOHead.pdf | Acrobat Reader

This file contains the three *headings* to print and cut into strips for use when doing the *Input/Process/Output Activity* with staffs.

IPO Elements | IPOElem.pdf | Acrobat Reader

This file contains the the data *elements* to print and cut into strips for use when doing the *Input/Process/Output Activity* with staffs.

Study Questions Related to *What Data are Important?* | Ch2Qs.doc | Microsoft Word

These study questions will help you understand the information provided in Chapter 2. This file can be printed for use with staffs as they think through the data questions they want to answer and the data they will need to gather to answer the questions.

▼ CHAPTER 3 – GETTING STARTED ON DATA ANALYSIS FOR CONTINUOUS IMPROVEMENT

The files in this section support Chapter 3 in the book and provide an overview of how a district can get started with comprehensive data analysis work.

Continuous Improvement Planning via a School or District Portfolio Graphic | CSIPlang.pdf | Acrobat Reader

This read-only file displays the questions that can be answered to create a continuous improvement plan. The data that can answer the questions, and where the answers would appear in the school or district portfolio, also appear on the graphic. In the book, it is Figure 3.1.

Continuous Improvement Planning via a School or District Portfolio Description | CSIdscr.pdf | Acrobat Reader

This read-only file shows Figure 3.1, along with its description.

The School Portfolio Presentation | SPSlides.ppt | Microsoft PowerPoint

This *Microsoft PowerPoint* presentation is an overview to use with your staffs in getting started on a school or district portfolio.

Overview: The School Portfolio | Overview.pdf | Acrobat Reader

This read-only file summarizes what the school portfolio is, what it does, and describes the purposes for each of the sections of the school portfolio.

Purposes and Uses of a School Portfolio | Purposes.pdf | Acrobat Reader

This read-only file describes the purposes and uses for a school or district portfolio.

Study Questions Related to *Getting Started* | Ch3Qs.doc | Microsoft Word

These study questions will help you understand the information provided in Chapter 3. This file can be printed for use with staffs as they begin continuous improvement planning. Answering the questions will help staff determine the data needed to answer the questions discussed in this chapter.

▼ CHAPTER 4 – ANALYZING THE DATA: *WHO ARE WE?*

The files in this section support Chapter 4 in the book and are tools to create a demographic profile of your district in order to answer the question, *Who are we?*

Study Questions Related to *Who Are We?* — Ch4Qs.doc — Microsoft Word

These study questions will help you understand the information provided in Chapter 4. This template file can be printed for use as you study the case study or to use with staff as they study demographic data.

Canyon View Demographic Graphing Templates — DistrDemog.xls — Microsoft Excel

All of the *Microsoft Excel* files that were used to create the demographic graphs and tables in the Canyon View School District example (Chapter 4) appear on the CD (DistrDemog1 and DistrDemog2). Use these templates by putting your data in the data source table and changing the title/labels to reflect your data, or enter your data in the table templates. This file also explains how to use the templates.

Data Profile Template — DistrProfil.doc — Microsoft Word

This *Microsoft Word* file provides a template for creating your own district data profile like the one for Canyon View School District, using the graphing and table templates provided. Create your graphs and tables in the graphing and table templates, then merge them into the *Data Profile Template.*

Other-size District Demographic Profiles (Folder)

These read-only profiles are examples of other-size districts. The graphing templates used to create these profiles are also provided in this section.

Sample District A (30,941 students)	District_A.pdf	Acrobat Reader
Sample District B (1,373 students)	District_B.pdf	Acrobat Reader
Sample District C (180 students)	District_C.pdf	Acrobat Reader

Other-size District Demographic Templates (Folder)

All of the *Microsoft Excel* files that were used to create the demographic graphs and tables in the other-size district examples appear on the CD. Use the templates similar to your district size by putting your data in the *Excel* data source table and changing the title/labels to reflect your data, or enter your data in the table templates. After you have created your graphs, merge them into the *Word* data profile template (DistrProfil.doc). After you create your tables, print and insert them in the profile document.

Sample District A (30,941 students)	District_A.xls	Microsoft Excel
Sample District B (1,373 students)	District_B.xls	Microsoft Excel
Sample District C (180 students)	District_C.xls	Microsoft Excel

School Profile *(optional)* — ProfilSc.doc — Microsoft Word

The *School Profile* is a template for gathering and organizing data about your schools, prior to graphing, especially for districts without a central database system. Please adjust the profile to add data elements you feel are important for describing the context of your schools and district. This information is then graphed or tabled, and described in narrative form. If creating a district portfolio, the data graphs and narrative will appear in *Information and Analysis.* (If you already have your data organized and just need to graph it, you will want to skip this step and use the graphing templates, described previously.)

Community Profile *(optional)* — ProfilCo.doc — Microsoft Word

The *Community Profile* is a template for gathering and organizing data about your community, prior to graphing. Please adjust the profile to add data elements you feel are important for describing the context of your community. It is important to describe how the community has changed over time, and how it is expected to change in the near future. This information is then added to the narrative. If creating a district portfolio, the data graphs and narrative will appear in *Information and Analysis.* (If you already have your data organized and just need to graph it, you will want to skip this step and use the graphing templates, described previously.)

Administrator Profile *(optional)* ProfilAd.doc Microsoft Word

The *Administrator Profile* is a template for gathering and organizing data about your administrators, prior to graphing. Please adjust the profile to fully describe your administrators. This information is then graphed and written in narrative form. If creating a district portfolio, the data graphs and narrative will appear in the *Information and Analysis* and *Leadership* sections. (If you already have your data organized and just need to graph it, you will want to skip this step and use the graphing templates, described previously.)

Teacher Profile *(optional)* ProfilTe.doc Microsoft Word

The *Teacher Profile* is a template for gathering and organizing data about your teachers, prior to graphing. Please adjust the profile to fully describe your teachers. The synthesis of this information is then graphed and written in narrative form. If creating a district portfolio, the data graphs and narrative will appear in *Information and Analysis.* (If you already have your data organized and just need to graph it, you will want to skip this step and use the graphing templates, described previously.)

Staff (Other than Teacher) Profile *(optional)* ProfilSt.doc Microsoft Word

The *Staff (other than teacher)Profile* is a template for gathering and organizing data about staff who are not teachers, prior to graphing. Please adjust the profile to fully describe your non-teaching staff. The synthesis of this information is then graphed and written in narrative form. If creating a district portfolio, the data graphs and narrative will appear in *Information and Analysis.* (If you already have your data organized and just need to graph it, you will want to skip this step and use the graphing templates, described previously.)

History Gram Activity ACTHstry.pdf Acrobat Reader

The *History Gram* is a team-building activity that will "write" the history of the school or district, which could help everyone see what staff has experienced since coming to the district and how many continuous improvement initiatives have been started over the years. It is helpful for understanding what it will take to keep this continuous improvement effort going.

Questions to Guide the Analysis of Demographic Data QsDemogr.doc Microsoft Word

This *Microsoft Word* file provides a guide for interpreting your demographic data. Adjust the questions to better reflect the discussion you would like to have with your staff about the gathered demographic data.

What I Saw in the Example Ch4Saw.pdf Acrobat Reader

What I Saw in the Example is a file, organized by the demographic study questions, that summarizes what the author saw in the demographic data provided by Canyon View School District.

Demographic Data to Gather to Create the Context of the School DemoData.pdf Acrobat Reader

This file defines the types of demographic data that are important to gather to create the context of the district and describe *Who are we?*

▼ CHAPTER 5 – ANALYZING THE DATA: *HOW DO WE DO BUSINESS?*

The files in this section support Chapter 5 in the book and include tools to help staff understand the organization and climate of the district from the perspective of students, staff, parents, administrators, and schools. The resulting analyses can help answer the question, *How do we do business?*

Continuous Improvement Continuum Tools (Folder)

These files are tools for assessing on the CICs and for writing the CIC report.

Continuous Improvement Continuums for Districts CICs_Dstrct.pdf Acrobat Reader

This read-only file contains the seven *Education for the Future District Continuous Improvement Continuums*. These can be printed as is and enlarged for posting individual staff opinions during staff assessments.

Canyon View School District Baseline CIC Results — CViewBase.pdf — Acrobat Reader

This read-only file is the summary of Canyon View's baseline assessment on the *Education for the Future District Continuous Improvement Continuums.*

Continuous Improvement Continuums for Schools — CICs_Schls.pdf — Acrobat Reader

This read-only file contains the seven *Education for the Future School Continuous Improvement Continuums*. These can be printed as is and enlarged for posting individual staff opinions during staff assessments.

Continuous Improvement Continuums Self-Assessment Activity — ACTCIC.pdf — Acrobat Reader

Assessing on the *Continuous Improvement Continuums* will help staffs see where their systems are right now with respect to continuous improvement and ultimately will show they are making progress over time. The discussion has major implications for the *Continuous Improvement Plan.*

Coming to Consensus — Consenss.pdf — Acrobat Reader

This read-only file provides strategies for coming to consensus, useful when assessing on the *Continuous Improvement Continuums.*

Continuous Improvement Continuums Report Example — ExReprt1.pdf — Acrobat Reader

This read-only file shows a real school's assessment on the *Education for the Future Continuous Improvement Continuums,* as an example.

Continuous Improvement Continuums Report Example for Follow-Up Years — ExReprt2.pdf — Acrobat Reader

This read only file shows a real school's assessment on the *Education for the Future Continuous Improvement Continuums* over time, as an example.

Continuous Improvement Continuums Baseline Report Template — ReptTemp.doc — Microsoft Word

This *Microsoft Word* file provides a template for writing your district's report of its assessment on the *Education for the Future Continuous Improvement Continuums*.

Continuous Improvement Continuums Graphing Templates — CICGraph.xls — Microsoft Excel

This *Microsoft Excel* file is a template for graphing your assessments on the seven *Education for the Future Continuous Improvement Continuums*.

Study Questions Related to *How Do We Do Business?* — Ch5Qs_CICs.doc — Microsoft Word

These district CIC assessment study questions will help you better understand the information provided in Chapter 5. This template file can be printed for use with staffs as they answer the question, *How do we do business?,* through analyzing Canyon View's CIC assessment data.

What I Saw in the Example: CIC Assessment — Ch5Saw_CICs.pdf — Acrobat Reader

What I Saw in the Example is a file, organized by the CIC assessment data study questions, that summarizes what I saw in the CIC data provided by Canyon View School District.

Study Questions Related to *How Do We Do Business?* — Ch5Qs_Qs.doc — Microsoft Word

These district questionnaire study questions will help you better understand the information provided in Chapter 5. This template file can be printed for use with staffs as they answer the question, *How do we do business?,* through analyzing Canyon View's perceptual data.

What I Saw in the Example: Questionnaires — Ch5Saw_Qs.pdf — Acrobat Reader

What I Saw in the Example is a file, organized by the perceptual study questions, that summarizes what I saw in the perceptual data provided by Canyon View School District.

Analysis of Questionnaire Data Table — Distr_QTable.doc — Microsoft Word

This *Microsoft Word* file is a tabular guide for interpreting your district student, staff, and parent questionnaires, independently and interdependently. It will help you see the summary of your results and write the narrative.

Education for the Future ***Questionnaires (Folder)***

These PDF files are for content review purposes only—*not* intended for use in questionnaire administration. For more information about administering and analyzing *Education for the Future* questionnaires, please visit *http://eff.csuchico.edu/questionnaire_resources/.*

Student (Kindergarten to Grade 3) Questionnaire	StQKto3.pdf	Acrobat Reader
Student (Grades 1 to 12) Questionnaire	StQ1to12.pdf	Acrobat Reader
Student (Middle/High School) Questionnaire	StQMidHS.pdf	Acrobat Reader
Teaching Staff Questionnaire	TeachStaffQ	Acrobat Reader
Organizational Learning Questionnaire	OrgLearnQ.pdf	Acrobat Reader
Administrator Questionnaire	AdminQ.pdf	Acrobat Reader
Parent Questionnaire	ParntK12Q.pdf	Acrobat Reader
High School Parent Questionnaire	ParntHsQ.pdf	Acrobat Reader
Alumni Questionnaire	AlumniQ.pdf	Acrobat Reader

Assessing Perceptions Using EFF Questionnaires — EFF_AssessQs.pdf — Acrobat Reader

This read-only file is a document that details the development of *Education for the Future's* questionnaire content, and specifically provides reliability and validity information.

How to Analyze Open-ended Responses — OEanalz.pdf — Acrobat Reader

This read-only file discusses how to analyze responses to the open-ended questions on questionnaires.

Questions to Guide the Analysis of Perceptions Data — PerceptQ.doc — Microsoft Word

This *Microsoft Word* file is a tabular guide for interpreting your district perceptions data. You can change the questions if you like or use the file to write in the responses. It will help you write the narrative for your results.

▼ CHAPTER 6 – ANALYZING THE DATA: *WHERE ARE WE NOW?*

The tools in this section support Chapter 6 in the book, help staffs determine the results of their current processes, particularly student learning results, and can help staffs answer the question, *Where are we now?*

Study Questions Related to *Where Are We Now?* — Ch6Qs.doc — Microsoft Word

These study questions will help you understand the information provided in Chapter 6. This template file can be printed for use with staffs as they begin to explore your own student learning results.

Arguments For and Against Standardized Testing — TestArgu.pdf — Acrobat Reader

This table summarizes the most common arguments for and against the use of standardized testing.

Standardized Test Score Terms — TestTerm.pdf — Acrobat Reader

This table shows the different standardized testing terms, their most effective uses, and cautions for their uses.

Arguments For and Against Performance Assessments — PerfArgu.pdf — Acrobat Reader

This table shows the most common arguments for and against the use of performance assessments.

Arguments For and Against Teacher Grading — GradeArg.pdf — Acrobat Reader

This table shows the most common arguments for and against the use of teacher grading.

Terms Related to Analyzing Student Learning Results, Descriptively — SAterms1.pdf — Acrobat Reader

This table shows the different terms related to analyzing student learning results, descriptively, their most effective uses, and cautions for their uses.

Terms Related to Analyzing Student Learning Results, Inferentially — SAterms2.pdf — Acrobat Reader

This table shows the different terms related to analyzing student learning results, inferentially, their most effective uses, and cautions for their uses.

What I Saw in the Example — Ch6Saw.pdf — Acrobat Reader

What I Saw in the Example is a file, organized by the student learning study questions, that summarizes what I saw in the student learning data provided by Canyon View School District.

Student Learning Graphing Templates — DistrSA.xls — Microsoft Excel

All of the *Microsoft Excel* files that were used to create the Reading and Math student learning tables in the Canyon View example (Chapter 6) appear on the CD (DistrSA_Math.xls and DistrSA_Read.xls). Use these table templates to create your data tables.

Other-size District Student Learning Graphing/Table Templates (Folder)

All of the *Microsoft Excel* files that were used to create the student learning tables/graphs in the district A and C examples appear on the CD. Use these templates similar to your district size by entering your data in the tables or graphs.

Sample District A (30,941 students)	DistrictSA_A.xls	Microsoft Excel
Sample District C (180 students)	DistrictSA_C.xls	Microsoft Excel

Questions to Guide the Analysis of Student Learning Data — QsSLearn.doc — Microsoft Word

This *Microsoft Word* file consists of questions to guide the interpretation of your district student learning data. You can input your responses into this file.

▼ CHAPTER 7 – ANALYZING THE DATA: *WHAT ARE THE GAPS?* AND *WHAT ARE THE ROOT CAUSES OF THE GAPS?*

The tools in this section support Chapter 7 in the book and help staffs analyze their data to determine the gaps and the root causes of the gaps. These files and tools can help answer the questions, *What are the gaps?* and *What are the root causes of the gaps?*

Creating a Shared Vision (Folder)

Templates and examples for planning and creating your district shared vision are provided on the CD .

Shared Vision Template — VTemplte.doc — Microsoft Word

This is a template for staffs to use when creating their shared vision. It allows staff to document their personal ideas before they are merged into core principles for the entire district.

Facilitator's Agenda for Creating a Shared Vision — AgendaFa.pdf — Acrobat Reader

This read-only file provides an annotated agenda for taking staffs through a visioning process in one day. Typical time requirements for the different activities are provided.

Agenda for Creating a Shared Vision — Agenda.doc — Microsoft Word

This is an example agenda for creating a vision in one day. It accompanies the facilitator's agenda for creating a vision.

Ground Rules — GrndRule.pdf — Acrobat Reader

This read-only file provides example ground rules for staff meetings and professional development sessions.

Vision Quote Posters — VPosters.pdf — Acrobat Reader

These read-only files contain motivating quotes to have enlarged for visioning day. The quotes show how to get to the vision, ground rules, and words of wisdom by Peter Senge and Joel Barker.

Goal Setting Activity — ACTGoals.pdf — Acrobat Reader

By setting goals, a school or district can clarify end targets for its vision. This activity will help a learning organization set goals for the future.

Gap Analysis and Objectives Activity — ACTGap.pdf — Acrobat Reader

The purpose of this activity is to look closely at differences between current results and where the school or district wants to be in the future. It is this gap that gets translated into objectives that guide the development of the action plan.

Root Cause Analysis Activity — ACTRoot.pdf — Acrobat Reader

Root causes are the real causes of our educational problems. We need to find out what they are so we can eliminate the true cause and not just address the symptom. This activity asks staff teams to review and analyze data, and ask probing questions to uncover the root cause(s).

Cause and Effect Analysis Activity — ACTCause.pdf — Acrobat Reader

This activity will help teams determine the relationships and complexities between an effect or problem and all the possible causes.

Problem-solving Cycle Activity — ACTCycle.pdf — Acrobat Reader

The purpose of the *Problem-solving Cycle Activity* is to get all staff involved in thinking through a problem before jumping to solutions. This activity can also result in a comprehensive data analysis design.

Problem-solving Cycle Handout Template — CycleTmp.doc — Microsoft Word

This Microsoft Word file is the last three pages of the Problem-solving Cycle Activity. Use this template to fill-in hunches and hypotheses about why the problem exists, determine the questions needed to answer with data to know more about the problem, and what data are needed to support those answers.

Canyon View School District Summary of Key Data Elements — KeyData.pdf — Acrobat Reader

This is the table in Figure 7.4 that shows the key data elements for Canyon View Schools and the district. The table enables one to look across all data elements to understand relationships.

Study Questions Related to the Gaps and the Root Causes of the Gaps — Ch7Qs.doc — Microsoft Word

These study questions will help you understand the information provided in Chapter 7. This template file can be printed for use with staffs as they analyze data to determine the gaps and the root causes of the gaps.

What I Saw in the Example — Ch7Saw.pdf — Acrobat Reader

What I Saw in the Example is a file, organized by the study questions related to gaps and root causes, that summarizes what the author saw in the analyses conducted by the school district.

No Child Left Behind (NCLB) Table Templates (Folder)

Table templates for analyzing student learning data for NCLB are provided on the CD.

NCLB Student Learning Reading Results Template — ProfRead.xls — Microsoft Excel

This *Microsoft Excel* file is a table template to use in summarizing your *No Child Left Behind* (NCLB) disaggregated student learning Reading proficiency results.

NCLB Student Learning Math Results Template — ProfMath.xls — Microsoft Excel

This *Microsoft Excel* file is a table template to use in summarizing your *No Child Left Behind* (NCLB) disaggregated student learning Mathematics proficiency results.

Group Process Tools and Activities (Folder)

The files include read-only documents, examples, templates, tools, activities, and strategy recommendations. Many of the group process tools and activities can be used throughout the analysis of data.

Affinity Diagram Activity — ACTAfnty.pdf — Acrobat Reader

The affinity diagram encourages honest reflection on the real underlying root causes of a problem and its solutions, and encourages people to agree on the factors. This activity assists teams in discussing and resolving problems, using a nonjudgmental process.

Fishbowl Activity — ACTFish.pdf — Acrobat Reader

The *Fishbowl Activity* can be used for dynamic group involvement. The most common configuration is an inner ring, which is the discussion group, surrounded by an outer ring, which is the observation group. Just as people observe the fish in the fishbowl, the outer ring observes the inner ring.

Forcefield Analysis Activity — ACTForce.pdf — Acrobat Reader

The *Forcefield Analysis Activity* helps staffs think about the ideal state for the school or district and the driving and restraining forces regarding that ideal state.

Placemat Activity — ACTPlace.pdf — Acrobat Reader

The *Placemat Activity* was developed to invite participants to share their knowledge about the school portfolio, data, a standard, an instructional strategy, a concept, etc.

T-Chart Activity — ACTTChrt.pdf — Acrobat Reader

A *T-Chart* is a simple tool to organize material into two columns. Use a T-Chart to compare and contrast information or to show relationships. Use it to help people see the opposite dimension of an issue.

"X" Marks the Spot Activity — ACTXSpot.pdf — Acrobat Reader

This activity helps staffs understand levels of expertise or degrees of passion about a topic.

Quadrant Diagram Activity — ACTQuadr.pdf — Acrobat Reader

A quadrant diagram is a method to determine which solution best meets two goals at once, such as low cost and high benefit.

CHAPTER 8 – ANALYZING THE DATA: *HOW CAN WE GET TO WHERE WE WANT TO BE?*

The files in this section support Chapter 8 in the book, helping staffs answer the question, *How can we get to where we want to be?* through comprehensive planning to implement the vision and eliminate the gaps, using powerful professional development, leadership, partnership development, and continuous improvement and evaluation.

Canyon View School District Shared Vision — DistrVision.pdf — Acrobat Reader

This read-only file is the first draft of the Canyon View Guiding Principles and Shared Vision, shown on pages 327-329 in Chapter 8.

Canyon View School District Plan for Improvement — SchlPlan.pdf — Acrobat Reader

This read-only file is the first draft of the Canyon View School District Plan and is shown as Figure 8.1 in Chapter 8.

Planning Template — APForm.doc — Microsoft Word

A quality action plan to implement the vision consists of goals, objectives, strategies, actions, persons responsible, resources required, due dates, and timelines. A template with these components is provided in *Microsoft Word,* ready to be completed.

Developing a Plan Activity — ACTDevAP.pdf — Acrobat Reader

The purpose of this activity is to take the shared vision to the action level. The steps in creating an action plan are spelled out in this activity.

Establishing a Partnership Plan — EstPPlan.pdf — Acrobat Reader

This read-only file describes the steps in creating a partnership plan that will become a part of the continuous improvement plan.

Partnership Evaluation Questionnaire — PaEvalQ.pdf — Acrobat Reader

This read-only file, the Canyon View School District Partnership Evaluation Questionnaire, is used to assess community members' role in the partnership, perceptions of the impact of the partnership, and satisfaction with the partnership program.

Canyon View School District Evaluation Plan — EvalPlan.pdf — Acrobat Reader

This read-only file, the Canyon View School District Evaluation Plan, combines the goals, object, and measurement column of the action plan into a comprehensive evaluation plan, and is shown as Figure 8.2 in Chapter 8.

Evaluating a Program Activity — ACTEval.pdf — Acrobat Reader

The purpose of this activity is to get many people involved in creating a comprehensive evaluation design to determine the impact of a program and to know how to improve the program.

Classroom Observation Tool — ObvTool.pdf — Acrobat Reader

This read-only file is the Big River High School Classroom Observation Tool, created for assessing wher each teacher is in implementing the state content standards and vision.

Powerful Professional Development Designs | Designs.pdf | Acrobat Reader

This read-only file describes numerous ways to embed professional development into the learning community.

Powerful Professional Development Designs Folder

Powerful Professional Development Designs are those that are embedded into the daily operations of a staff. They are ongoing and lead to improvement of instruction and increases in student learning.

Action Research Activity | ACTRsrch.pdf | Acrobat Reader

Teachers and/or administrators raise questions about the best way to improve teaching and learning, systematically study the literature to answer the questions, implement the best approach, and analyze the results.

Cadres or Action Teams Activity | ACTCdres.pdf | Acrobat Reader

Organizing cadres or teams allows for the delegation of responsibilities so teams of educators can study new approaches, plan for the implementation of new strategies or programs, and get work done without every staff member's involvement.

Case Studies Activity | ACTCases.pdf | Acrobat Reader

Staff members review case studies of student work, and/or of another teacher's example lessons, which can lead to quality discussions and improved practices.

Coaching Activity | ACTCoach.pdf | Acrobat Reader

Teachers form teams of two or three to observe each other, plan together, and to talk and encourage each other in meaningful ways, while reflecting on continuously improving instructional practices.

Examining Student Data: *Teacher Analysis of Test Scores Table One* | Table1.doc | Microsoft Word

Examining student data consists of conversations around individual student data results and the processes that created the results. This approach can be a significant form of professional development when skilled team members facilitate the dialogue.

Examining Student Work Activity | ACTSWork.pdf | Acrobat Reader

Examining student work as professional development ensures that what students learn is aligned to the learning standards. It also shows teachers the impact of their processes.

Example Lessons: *Birds of a Feather Unit Example* | UnitEx.pdf | Acrobat Reader

Some teachers need to see what a lesson that implements all aspects of the school vision would look like. Providing examples for all teachers to see can reward the teacher who is doing a good job of implementing the vision and provide a template for other teachers. It is very effective to store summary examples in a binder or on a website for everyone to peruse at any time.

Example Lessons: *Unit Template* | UnitTmpl.doc | Microsoft Word

This template provides the outline for creating instructional units that implement the vision.

Immersion Activity | ACTImrsn.pdf | Acrobat Reader

Immersion is a method for getting teachers engaged in different content through hands-on experiences as a learner.

Journaling Activity | ACTJourn.pdf | Acrobat Reader

Journal writing helps teachers construct meaning for, and reflect on, what they are teaching and learning.

Listening to Students Activity | ACTListn.pdf | Acrobat Reader

Students' perceptions of the learning environment are very important for continuous improvement. Focus groups, interviews, and questionnaires can be used to discover what students are perceiving.

Needs Assessment: *Professional Development Needs Related to Technology Example* | TechnEx.pdf | Acrobat Reader

Needs assessments help staff understand the professional development needs of staff. At the same time, if done well, a tool can lead to quality staff conversations and sharing of knowledge.

Needs Assessment: *Professional Development Needs Related to Technology Template* — TechTmpl.doc — Microsoft Word

This template provides the outline for doing your own professional development needs assessment.

Networks Activity — ACTNtwrk.pdf — Acrobat Reader

Purposeful grouping of individuals/schools to further a cause or commitment.

Partnerships: *Creating Partnerships Activity* — ACTParts.pdf — Acrobat Reader

Teachers partnering with businesses in the community, scientists, and/or university professors can result in real world applications for student learning and deeper understandings of content for the teacher.

Process Mapping: *Charting School Processes Activity* — ACTProcs.pdf — Acrobat Reader

School processes are instruction, curriculum, and assessment strategies used to ensure the learning of all students. Mapping or flowcharting school processes can help staff objectively look at how students are being taught.

Reflection Log Activity — ACTLog.pdf — Acrobat Reader

Reflective logs are recordings of key events in the educators' work days to reflect on improvement and/or to share learnings with colleagues.

Scheduling Activity — ACTSchdl.pdf — Acrobat Reader

A real test for whether or not a vision is realistic is to have teachers develop a day's schedule. This would tell them immediately if it is doable, or what needs to change in the vision and plan to make it doable.

School Meetings: *Running Efficient Meetings* — Meetings.pdf — Acrobat Reader

Staff, department, grade level, and cross-grade level meetings can promote learning through study or sharing best practice, while focusing on the implementation of the vision.

Self-Assessment: *Teacher Assessment Tool Related to the Big River High School Vision* — AssessEx.pdf — Acrobat Reader

This read-only file is shown as Figure 8.3 in Chapter 8. Staff self-assessments on tools to measure progress toward the vision, such as the *Continuous Improvement Continuums,* will help them see where their school is as a system and what needs to improve for better results.

Self-Assessment: *Teacher Assessment Tool Related to Our School Vision* — AssessEx.doc — Microsoft Word

This template file for staff self-assessments on tools to measure progress toward the vision, such as the *Continuous Improvement Continuums,* will help them see where their school is as a system and what needs to improve for better results.

Self-Assessment: *Our School Shared Vision Implementation Rubric Example* — StRubric.pdf — Acrobat Reader

Staff self-assessments on tools to measure progress toward the vision, such as the *Continuous Improvement Continuums,* will help them see where their school is as a system and what needs to improve for better results.

Self-Assessment: *Our School Shared Vision Implementation Rubric Template* — StRubric.doc — Microsoft Word

This template file for staff self-assessments on tools to measure progress toward the vision, such as the *Continuous Improvement Continuums,* will help them see where their school is as a system and what needs to improve for better results.

Self-Assessment: *Staff-Developed Rubric Activity* — ACTRubric.pdf — Acrobat Reader

This activity for staff self-assessments on tools to measure progress toward the vision, such as the *Continuous Improvement Continuums,* will help them see where their school is as a system and what needs to improve for better results.

Shadowing Students Activity | ACTShadw.pdf | Acrobat Reader

Purposefully following students and systematically recording the students' instructional experiences is a wonderful job-embedded approach to understanding what students are experiencing in school.

Storyboarding Activity | ACTStory.pdf | Acrobat Reader

Storyboarding is an activity that will allow participants to share previous knowledge, while reflecting on the topic. It is a structure for facilitating conversations.

Study Groups Activity | ACTStudy.pdf | Acrobat Reader

Groups of educators meet to learn new strategies and programs, to review new publications, or to review student work together.

Teacher Portfolio Activity | ACTTcher.pdf | Acrobat Reader

Teacher portfolios can be built to tell the story of implementing the vision in the classroom, and its impact on student learning. Portfolios are excellent for reflection, understanding, and showing progress. Portfolios can be used for many things including self-assessment, employment, supervision to replace traditional teacher evaluation, and peer collaboration.

Train the Trainers Activity | ACTTrain.pdf | Acrobat Reader

Train the trainers is an approach to saving time and money. Individuals are trained and return to the school or school district to train others.

Tuning Protocols Activity | ACTTune.pdf | Acrobat Reader

A tuning protocol is a formal process for reviewing, honoring, and fine-tuning colleagues' work through presentation and reflection.

▼ CHAPTER 9 – ANALYZING THE DATA: *CONCLUSIONS AND RECOMMENDATIONS*

The files in this section support Chapter 9 in the book and help staffs evaluate their programs and processes.

Databases Can Help Teachers with Standards Implementation | Dbases.pdf | Acrobat Reader

This read-only article, by Victoria L. Bernhardt, describes how databases can help with standards implementation.

Data Tools for School Improvement | DataTools.pdf | Acrobat Reader

This read-only article, by Victoria L. Bernhardt, describes how data tools can help schools analyze and use data effectively.

Appendix B
Continuous Improvement Continuums for Districts

These *Education for the Future Continuous Improvement Continuums,* adapted from the *Malcolm Baldrige Award Program for Quality Business Management,* provide an authentic means for measuring organizational improvement and growth. Districts use these Continuums as a vehicle for ongoing self-assessment. They use the results of the assessment to acknowledge their accomplishments, to set goals for improvement, and to keep staff and partners apprised of the progress they have made in their improvement efforts.

Understanding the Continuums

These Continuums, extending from *one* to *five* horizontally, represent a continuum of expectations related to continuous improvement with respect to an *Approach* to the Continuum, *Implementation* of the approach, and the *Outcome* that results from the implementation. A *one* rating, located at the left of each Continuum, represents a district that has not yet begun to improve. *Five,* located at the right of each Continuum, represents a district that is one step removed from "world class quality." The elements between *one* and *five* describe how that Continuum is hypothesized to evolve in a continuously improving district. Each Continuum moves from a reactive mode to a proactive mode—from fire fighting to prevention. The *five* in *Outcome* in each Continuum is the target.

Vertically, the *Approach, Implementation,* and *Outcome* statements, for any number one through five, are hypotheses. In other words, the implementation statement describes how the approach might look when implemented, and the outcome is the "pay-off" for implementing the approach. If the hypotheses are accurate, the outcome will not be realized until the approach is actually implemented.

Using the Continuums

Use the *Continuous Improvement Continuums* (CICs) to understand where your district is with respect to continuous improvement. The results will hopefully provide that sense of urgency needed to spark enthusiasm for your improvement efforts.

Start the assessment by stating or creating the ground rules, setting the tone for a safe and confidential assessment, and explaining why you are doing this. Provide a brief overview of the seven sections, taking each section one or two at a time, and having each staff member read the related Continuum and make independent assessments of where she/he believes the district is with respect to *Approach, Implementation,* and *Outcome.* We recommend using individual 8 1/2 x 11 copies of the Continuums for individual assessments. CD-ROM (CICs.pdf) Then, have each staff member note where she/he believes the district is with a colorful sticker or marker on a large poster of each Continuum. The markers allow all staff to see how much they are in agreement with one another. If only one color is used for the first assessment, another color can be used for the next assessment, and so forth, to help gauge growth over time, or you can plan to use two different charts for gauging progress over time such as in the photos that follow.

When all dots or marks have been placed on the enlarged Continuum, look at the agreement or disagreement of the ratings. Starting with *Approach,* have staff discuss why they believe the district is where they rated it. Keep discussing until the larger group comes to consensus on one number that reflects where the district is right now. You might need to make a quick check on where staff is with respect to coming to consensus, using a thumbs up, thumbs down "vote." Keep discussing the facts until consensus is reached. CD-ROM (Consenss.pdf) Do not average the results—it does not produce a sense of urgency for improvement. We cannot emphasize this enough! Keep discussing until agreement is reached by everyone on a number that represents where "we" are right now. When that consensus is reached, record the number and move to *Implementation* and then *Outcome.* Determine *Next Steps.* Proceed in the same way through the next six categories.

During the assessments, make sure someone records the discussions of the Continuum assessments. Districts might want to exchange facilitators with a neighboring district to have someone external to the district office facilitate the assessments. This will enable everyone in the district to participate and provide an unbiased and competent person to lead the consensus-building piece. Assessing over time will help staff see that they are making progress. The decision of how often to assess on the *Continuous Improvement Continuums* is certainly up to the district. We recommend twice a year—about mid-fall and mid-spring—when there is time (or has been time) to implement next steps. Over time, once a year might be sufficient.

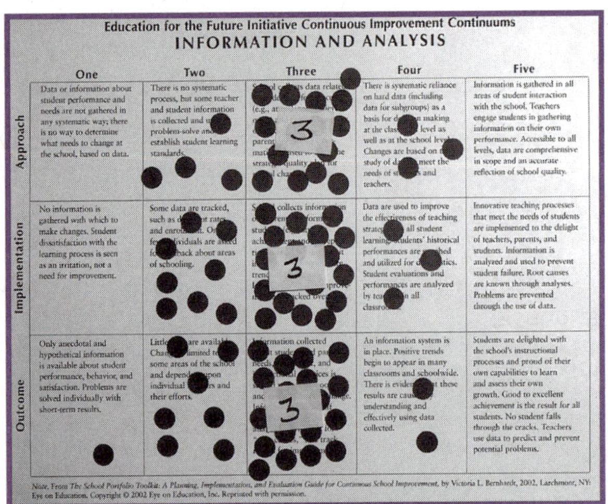

Education for the Future Initiative Continuous Improvement Continuums
INFORMATION AND ANALYSIS

	One	Two	Three	Four	Five
Approach	Data or information about student performance and needs are not gathered in any systematic way; there is no way to determine what needs to change at the school, based on data.	There is no systematic process, but some teacher and student information is collected and u[illegible] problem-solve an[illegible] establish student learning standards.	[illegible]	There is systematic reliance on hard data (including data for subgroups) as a basis for d[illegible] making at the clas[illegible] level as well as at the school lev[illegible] Changes are based on [illegible] study of d[illegible] meet the needs of st[illegible] and teachers.	Information is gathered in all areas of student interaction with the school. Teachers engage students in gathering information on their own performance. Accessible to all levels, data are comprehensive in scope and an accurate reflection of school quality.
Implementation	No information is gathered with which to make changes. Student dissatisfaction with the learning process is seen as an irritation, not a need for improvement.	Some data are tracked, such as d[illegible] rate[illegible] and enro[illegible]. O[illegible] fe[illegible]ividuals are a[illegible] fo[illegible]back about areas of schooling.	[illegible]	Data are used to improve the effectiveness of teaching strat[illegible] all student learning[illegible]udents' historical performances are [illegible]hed and utilized for d[illegible]tics. Student evaluations and performances are analyzed by tea[illegible] all classro[illegible]	Innovative teaching processes that meet the needs of students are implemented to the delight of teachers, parents, and students. Information is analyzed and used to prevent student failure. Root causes are known through analyses. Problems are prevented through the use of data.
Outcome	Only anecdotal and hypothetical information is available about student performance, behavior, and satisfaction. Problems are solved individually with short-term results.	Littl[illegible] are availa[illegible] Cha[illegible]imited to some areas of the school and depend[illegible]upon individual [illegible]rs and their efforts.	[illegible]	An information system is in place. Positive trends begin to appear in many classrooms and schoolwide. There is eviden[illegible]t these results are caus[illegible] understanding and effectively using data collected.	Students are delighted with the school's instructional processes and proud of their own capabilities to learn and assess their own growth. Good to excellent achievement is the result for all students. No student falls through the cracks. Teachers use data to predict and prevent potential problems.

Note. From *The School Portfolio Toolkit: A Planning, Implementation, and Evaluation Guide for Continuous School Improvement,* by Victoria L. Bernhardt, 2002, Larchmont, NY: Eye on Education. Copyright © 2002 Eye on Education, Inc. Reprinted with permission.

Fall Assessment

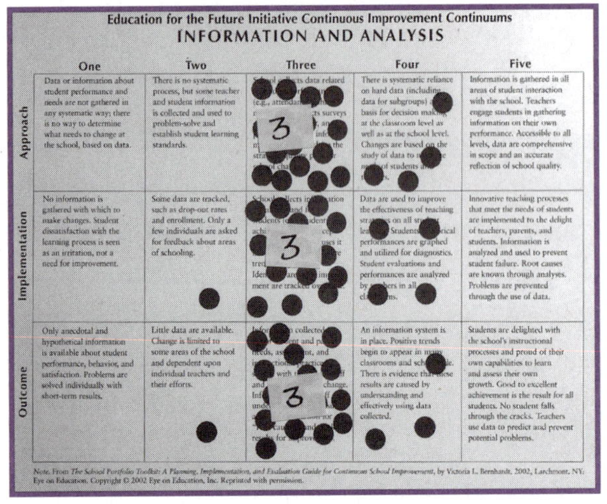

Education for the Future Initiative Continuous Improvement Continuums
INFORMATION AND ANALYSIS

	One	Two	Three	Four	Five
Approach	Data or information about student performance and needs are not gathered in any systematic way; there is no way to determine what needs to change at the school, based on data.	There is no systematic process, but some teacher and student information is collected and used to problem-solve and establish student learning standards.	[illegible]	There is systematic reliance on hard data (including data for subgroups) [illegible] basis for decision mak[illegible] at the classroom level as well as at the school level. Changes are based on the study of data to [illegible] needs of students [illegible]	Information is gathered in all areas of student interaction with the school. Teachers engage students in gathering information on their own performance. Accessible to all levels, data are comprehensive in scope and an accurate reflection of school quality.
Implementation	No information is gathered with which to make changes. Student dissatisfaction with the learning process is seen as an irritation, not a need for improvement.	Some data are tracked, such as drop-out rates and enrollment. Only a few individuals are asked for feedback about areas of schooling.	[illegible]	Data are used to improve the effectiveness of teaching stra[illegible]s on all st[illegible] lea[illegible] Students' [illegible]rical performances are graphed and utilized for diagnostics. Student evaluations and performances are analyzed by [illegible]hers in all cl[illegible]ms.	Innovative teaching processes that meet the needs of students are implemented to the delight of teachers, parents, and students. Information is analyzed and used to prevent student failure. Root causes are known through analyses. Problems are prevented through the use of data.
Outcome	Only anecdotal and hypothetical information is available about student performance, behavior, and satisfaction. Problems are solved individually with short-term results.	Little data are available. Change is limited to some areas of the school and dependent upon individual teachers and their efforts.	[illegible]	An information system is in place. Positive trends begin to appear in ma[illegible] classrooms and sch[illegible]e. There is evidence th[illegible]ese results are caused by understanding and effectively using data collected.	Students are delighted with the school's instructional processes and proud of their own capabilities to learn and assess their own growth. Good to excellent achievement is the result for all students. No student falls through the cracks. Teachers use data to predict and prevent potential problems.

Note. From *The School Portfolio Toolkit: A Planning, Implementation, and Evaluation Guide for Continuous School Improvement,* by Victoria L. Bernhardt, 2002, Larchmont, NY: Eye on Education. Copyright © 2002 Eye on Education, Inc. Reprinted with permission.

Spring Assessment

Using these Continuums will enable you and your district to stay motivated, to shape and maintain your shared vision, and will assist with the continuous improvement of all elements. Take pictures of the resulting charts. Even if your consensus number does not increase, the dots will most probably come together over time showing shifts in whole staff thinking.

Remember that where your district is at any time is just where it is. The important thing is what you do with this information. Continuous improvement is a never-ending process which, when used effectively, will ultimately lead your district toward providing a quality program for all children.

District Continuous Improvement Continuums

INFORMATION AND ANALYSIS

	One	Two	Three	Four	Five
Approach	Data or information about school student performance and needs are not gathered in any systematic way. The district does not provide assistance in helping schools understand what needs to change at the school and classroom levels, based on data.	There is no systematic process for data analysis across the district. Some school, teacher, and student information are collected and used to problem solve and establish student-learning standards across the district.	School district collects data related to school and student performance (e.g., attendance, enrollment, achievement), and surveys students, staff, and parents. The information is used to drive the strategic quality plan for district and school improvement.	There is systematic reliance on hard data (including data for subgroups) as a basis for decision making at the district, school, and classroom levels. Changes are based on the study of data to meet the educational needs of students and teachers.	Information is gathered in all areas of student interaction with the school. The district engages administrators and teachers in gathering information on their own performance. Accessible to all schools, data are comprehensive in scope and an accurate reflection of school and district quality.
Implementation	No information is gathered with which to make district or school changes. Student dissatisfaction with the learning process is seen as an irritation, not a need for improvement.	Some data are tracked, such as attendance, enrollment, and drop-out rates. Only a few individuals are asked for feedback about areas of schooling and district operations.	The district collects information on current and former students (e.g., student achievement and perceptions), analyzes and uses it in conjunction with future trends for planning. Identified areas for improvement are tracked over time.	Data are used to provide feedback to improve the effectiveness of teaching strategies on all student learning. Schools' historical performances are graphed and utilized for diagnosis by the district.	Innovative teaching processes that meet the needs of students are implemented across the district. Information is analyzed and used to prevent student failure. Root causes are known through analyses. Problems are prevented through the use of data.
Outcome	Only anecdotal and hypothetical information are available about student performance, behavior, and satisfaction. Problems are solved individually with short-term results.	Little data are available. Change is limited to some areas of the district and dependent upon individual administrators and their efforts.	Information collected about school needs, effective assessment, and instructional practices are shared with all school and district staff and used to plan for school and district improvement. Information helps staff understand pressing issues, analyze information for "root causes," and track results for improvement.	An information system is in place. Positive trends begin to appear in many schools and districtwide. There is evidence that these results are caused by understanding and effectively using the data collected.	Schools are delighted with their instructional processes and proud of their own capabilities to learn and assess their own growth. Good to excellent achievement is the result for all schools. Schools use data to predict and prevent potential problems. No student falls through the cracks.

District Continuous Improvement Continuums
STUDENT ACHIEVEMENT

	One	Two	Three	Four	Five
Approach	Instructional and organizational processes critical to student success are not identified. Little distinction of student learning differences is made. Some schools believe that not all students can achieve.	Some data are collected on student background and performance trends. Learning gaps are noted to direct improvement of instruction. It is known that student learning standards must be identified.	Student learning standards are identified, and a continuum of learning is created across the district. Student performance data are collected and compared to the standards in order to analyze how to improve learning for all students.	Data on student achievement are used throughout the district to pursue the improvement of student learning. The district ensures that teachers collaborate to implement appropriate instruction and assessment strategies for meeting student learning standards articulated across grade levels. All teachers believe that all students can learn.	The district makes an effort to exceed student achievement expectations. Innovative instructional changes are made to anticipate learning needs and improve student achievement. District makes sure that teachers are able to predict characteristics impacting student achievement and to know how to perform from a small set of internal quality measures.
Implementation	All students are taught the same way. There is no communication between the district and schools about students' academic needs or learning styles. There are no analyses of how to improve instruction.	Some effort is made to track and analyze student achievement trends on a districtwide basis. District begins to understand the needs and learning gaps within the schools.	Teachers across the district study effective instruction and assessment strategies to implement standards and to increase students' learning. Student feedback and analysis of achievement data are used in conjunction with implementation support strategies.	There is a systematic focus on implementing student learning standards and on the improvement of student learning districtwide. Effective instruction and assessment strategies are implemented in each school. District supports teachers supporting one another with peer coaching and/or action research focused on implementing strategies that lead to increased achievement.	All teachers correlate critical instructional and assessment strategies with objective indicators of quality student achievement. A comparative analysis of actual individual student performance to student learning standards is utilized to adjust teaching strategies to ensure a progression of learning for all students.
Outcome	There is wide variation in student attitudes and achievement with undesirable results. There is high dissatisfaction among students with learning. Student background is used as an excuse for low student achievement.	There is some evidence that student achievement trends are available to schools and are being used. There is much effort, but minimal observable results in improving student achievement.	There is an increase in communication among district and schools, students, and teachers regarding student learning. Teachers learn about effective instructional strategies that will implement the shared vision, student learning standards, and how to meet the needs of students. The schools make some gains.	Increased student achievement is evident districtwide. Student morale, attendance, and behavior are good. Teachers converse often with each other about preventing student failure. Areas for further attention are clear.	Schools and teachers conduct self-assessments to continuously improve performance. Improvements in student achievement are evident and clearly caused by teachers' and students' understandings of individual student learning standards, linked to appropriate and effective instructional and assessment strategies. A continuum of learning results. No students fall through the cracks.

District Continuous Improvement Continuums

QUALITY PLANNING

	One	Two	Three	Four	Five
Approach	No quality plan or process exists. Data are neither used nor considered important in planning.	The district realizes the importance of a mission, vision, and one comprehensive action plan. Teams develop goals and timelines, and dollars are allocated to begin the process.	A comprehensive plan to achieve the district vision is developed. Plan includes evaluation and continuous improvement.	One focused and integrated districtwide plan for implementing a continuous improvement process is put into action. All district efforts are focused on the implementation of this plan that represents the achievement of the vision.	A plan for the continuous improvement of the district, with a focus on students, is put into place. There is excellent articulation and integration of all elements in the district due to quality planning. Leadership team ensures all elements are implemented by all appropriate parties.
Implementation	There is no knowledge of or direction for quality planning. Budget is allocated on an as-needed basis. Many plans exist.	School district community begins continuous improvement planning efforts by laying out major steps to a shared vision, by identifying values and beliefs, the purpose of the district, a mission, vision, and student learning standards.	Implementation goals, responsibilities, due dates, and timelines are spelled out. Support structures for implementing the plan are set in place.	The quality management plan is implemented through effective procedures in all areas of the district. Everyone commits to implementing the plan aligned to the vision, mission, and values and beliefs. All share responsibility for accomplishing district goals.	Districtwide goals, mission, vision, and student learning standards are shared and articulated throughout the district and with feeder schools. The attainment of identified student learning standards is linked to planning and implementation of effective instruction that meets students' needs. Leaders at all levels are developing expertise because planning is the norm.
Outcome	There is no evidence of comprehensive planning. Staff work is carried out in isolation. A continuum of learning for students is absent.	The school district community understands the benefits of working together to implement a comprehensive continuous improvement plan.	There is evidence that the district plan is being implemented in some areas of the district. Improvements are neither systematic nor integrated districtwide.	A districtwide plan is known to all. Results from working toward the quality improvement goals are evident throughout the district. Planning is ongoing and inclusive of all stakeholders.	Evidence of effective teaching and learning results in significant improvement of student achievement attributed to quality planning at all levels of the district organization. Teachers and administrators understand and share the district mission and vision. Quality planning is seamless and all demonstrate evidence of accountability.

District Continuous Improvement Continuums
PROFESSIONAL DEVELOPMENT

	One	Two	Three	Four	Five
Approach	There is no professional development. Teachers, principals, and staff are seen as interchangeable parts that can be replaced. Professional development is external and usually equated to attending a conference alone. Hierarchy determines "haves" and "have-nots."	The "cafeteria" approach to professional development is used, whereby individual teachers and administrators choose what they want to take, without regard to an overall district plan.	The shared vision, district plan and student needs are used to target focused professional development for all employees. Staff is inserviced on relevant instructional and leadership strategies.	Professional development and data-gathering methods are used by all teachers and administrators, and are directed toward the goals of the shared vision and the continuous improvement of the district and schools. Teachers have ongoing conversations about student achievement data. All staff members receive training in their content areas. Systems thinking is considered in all decisions.	Leadership and staff continuously improve all aspects of the learning organization through an innovative, data-driven, and comprehensive continuous improvement process that prevents student failures. Effective job-embedded professional development is ongoing for implementing the vision for student success. Traditional teacher evaluations are replaced by collegial coaching and action research focused on student learning standards. Policies set professional development as a priority budget line-item. Professional development is planned, aligned, and leads to the achievement of student learning standards.
Implementation	District staff, principals, teachers, and school staff performance is controlled and inspected. Performance evaluations are used to detect mistakes.	Teacher professional development is sporadic and unfocused, lacking an approach for implementing new procedures and processes. Some leadership training begins to take place.	The district ensures that teachers are involved in year-round quality professional development. The school community is trained in shared decision making, team building concepts, effective communication strategies, and data analysis.	Teachers, in teams, continuously set and implement student achievement goals. Leadership considers these goals and provides necessary support structures for collaboration. Teachers utilize effective support approaches as they implement new instruction and assessment strategies. Coaching and feedback structures are in place. Use of new knowledge and skills is evident.	Teams passionately support each other in the pursuit of quality improvement at all levels. Teachers make bold changes in instruction and assessment strategies focused on student learning standards and student learning styles. *A teacher as action researcher* model is implemented. Staffwide conversations focus on systemic reflection and improvement. Teachers are strong leaders.
Outcome	No professional growth and no staff or student performance improvement. There exists a high turnover rate of employees, especially administrators. Attitudes and approaches filter down to students.	The effectiveness of professional development is not known or analyzed. Teachers feel helpless and unsupported in making schoolwide changes.	Teachers, working in teams, feel supported by the district and begin to feel they can make changes. Evidence shows that shared decision making works.	A collegial school district is evident. Effective classroom strategies are practiced, articulated schoolwide. These strategies, focused on student learning standards, are reflective of professional development aimed at ensuring student learning and the implementation of the shared vision.	True systemic change and improved student achievement result because teachers are knowledgeable of and implement effective, differentiated teaching strategies for individual student learning gains. Teachers' repertoire of skills is enhanced and students are achieving. Professional development is driving learning at all levels.

District Continuous Improvement Continuums

LEADERSHIP

	One	Two	Three	Four	Five
Approach	The School Board is decision maker. Decisions are reactive to state, district, and federal mandates. There is no knowledge of continuous improvement.	A shared decision-making structure is put into place and discussions begin on how to achieve a district vision. Most decisions are focused on solving problems and are reactive.	District leadership team is committed to continuous improvement. Leadership seeks inclusion of all school sectors and supports study teams by making time provisions for their work.	District leadership team represents a true shared decision-making structure. Study teams are reconstructed for the implementation of a comprehensive continuous improvement plan.	A strong continuous improvement structure is set into place that allows for input from all sectors of the district, school, and community, ensuring strong communication, flexibility, and refinement of approach and beliefs. The district vision is student focused, based on data and appropriate for district/school/community values, and meeting student needs.
Implementation	The School Board makes all decisions, with little or no input from administrators, teachers, the community, or students. Leadership inspects for mistakes.	District values and beliefs are identified; the purpose of district is defined; a district mission and student learning standards are developed with representative input. A structure for studying approaches to achieving student learning standards is established.	The district leadership team is active on study teams and integrates recommendations from the teams' research and analyses to form a comprehensive plan for continuous improvement within the context of the district mission. Everyone is kept informed.	Decisions about budget and implementation of the vision are made within teams, by the school board, by the leadership team, by the individual schools, and by the full staff, as appropriate. All decisions are communicated to the leadership team and to the full staff.	The vision is implemented and articulated across all grade levels and into feeder schools. Quality standards are reinforced throughout the district. All members of the district community understand and apply the quality standards. Leadership team has systematic interactions and involvement with district administrators, teachers, parents, community, and students about the district's direction. Necessary resources are available to implement and measure staff learning related to student learning standards.
Outcome	Although the decision-making process is clearly known, decisions are reactive and lack focus and consistency. There is no evidence of staff commitment to a shared vision. Students and parents do not feel they are being heard.	The mission provides a focus for all district and school improvement and guides the action to the vision. The school community is committed to continuous improvement. Quality leadership techniques are used sporadically.	The district leadership team is seen as committed to planning and quality improvement. Critical areas for improvement are identified. Faculty feel included in shared decision making.	There is evidence that the district leadership team listens to all levels of the organization. Implementation of the continuous improvement plan is linked to student learning standards and the guiding principles of the school. Leadership capacity for implementing the vision throughout the district is evident.	Site-based management and shared decision making truly exists. Teachers understand and display an intimate knowledge of how the school and district operate. Schools support and communicate with each other in the implementation of quality strategies. Teachers implement the vision in their classrooms and can determine how their new approaches meet student needs and lead to the attainment of student learning standards. Leaders are standards-driven at all levels.

District Continuous Improvement Continuums
PARTNERSHIP DEVELOPMENT

	One	Two	Three	Four	Five
Approach	There is no system for input from parents, business, or community. Status quo is desired for managing the school district.	Partnerships are sought, but mostly for money and things.	School district has knowledge of why partnerships are important and seeks to include businesses and parents in a strategic fashion related to student learning standards for increased student achievement.	School district seeks effective win-win business and community partnerships and parent involvement to implement the vision. Desired outcomes are clearly identified. A solid plan for partnership development exists.	Community, parent, and business partnerships become integrated across all student groupings. The benefits of outside involvement are known by all. Parent and business involvement in student learning is refined. Student learning regularly takes place beyond the school and district walls.
Implementation	Barriers are erected to close out involvement of outsiders. Outsiders are managed for least impact on status quo.	A team is assigned to get partners and to receive input from parents, the community, and business in the school district.	Involvement of business, community, and parents begins to take place in some schools and after school hours related to the vision. Partners begin to realize how they can support each other in achieving district goals. District staff understand what partners need from the partnership.	There is systematic utilization of parents, community, and businesses districtwide. Areas in which the active use of these partnerships benefit student learning are clear.	Partnership development is articulated across all district groupings. Parents, community, business, and educators work together in an innovative fashion to increase student learning and to prepare students for the Twenty-first Century. Partnerships are evaluated for continuous improvement.
Outcome	There is little or no involvement of parents, business, or community at-large. The district is a closed, isolated system.	Much effort is given to establishing partnerships. Some spotty trends emerge, such as receiving donated equipment.	Some substantial gains are achieved in implementing partnerships. Some student achievement increases can be attributed to this involvement.	Gains in student satisfaction with learning and school are clearly related to partnerships. All partners benefit.	Previously non-achieving students enjoy learning with excellent achievement. Community, business, and home become common places for student learning, while school becomes a place where parents come for further education. Partnerships enhance what the school district does for students.

District Continuous Improvement Continuums

CONTINUOUS IMPROVEMENT AND EVALUATION

	One	Two	Three	Four	Five
Approach	Neither goals nor strategies exist for the evaluation and continuous improvement of the district organization or for elements of the organization.	The approach to continuous improvement and evaluation is problem-solving. If there are no problems, or if solutions can be made quickly, there is no need for improvement or analyses. Changes in parts of the system are not coordinated with all other parts.	Some elements of the district organization are evaluated for effectiveness. Some elements are improved on the basis of the evaluation findings.	All elements of the district's operations are evaluated for improvement. Efforts are consistently made to ensure congruence of the elements with respect to the continuum of learning that students experience.	All aspects of the district organization are rigorously evaluated and improved on a continuous basis. Students, and the maintenance of a comprehensive learning continuum for students, become the focus of all aspects of the school district improvement process.
Implementation	With no overall plan for evaluation and continuous improvement, strategies are changed by individual schools, teachers, and/or administrators only when something sparks the need to improve. Reactive decisions and activities are a daily mode of operation.	Isolated changes are made in some areas of the district organization in response to problem incidents. Changes are not preceded by comprehensive analyses, such as an understanding of the root causes of problems. The effectiveness of the elements of the district organization is not known.	Elements of the district organization are improved on the basis of comprehensive analyses of root causes of problems, client perceptions, and operational effectiveness of processes.	Continuous improvement analyses of student achievement and instructional strategies are rigorously reinforced within each classroom and across learning levels to develop a comprehensive learning continuum for students and to prevent student failure.	Comprehensive continuous improvement becomes the way of doing business throughout the district. Teachers continuously improve the appropriateness and effectiveness of instructional strategies based on student feedback and performance. All aspects of the district organization are improved to support teachers' efforts.
Outcome	Individuals struggle with system failure. Finger pointing and blaming others for failure occur. The effectiveness of strategies is not known. Mistakes are repeated.	Problems are solved only temporarily and few positive changes result. Additionally, unintended and undesirable consequences often appear in other parts of the system. Many aspects of the school district are incongruent, keeping the district from reaching its vision.	Evidence of effective improvement strategies is observable. Positive changes are made and maintained due to comprehensive analyses and evaluation.	Teachers become astute at assessing and in predicting the impact of their instructional strategies on individual student achievement. Sustainable improvements in student achievement are evident at all grade levels due to continuous improvement supported by the district.	The district becomes a congruent and effective learning organization. Only instruction and assessment strategies that produce quality student achievement are used. A true continuum of learning results for all students and staff. The impact of improvements is increasingly measurable.

Appendix C
Continuous Improvement Continuums for Schools

These *Education for the Future Continuous Improvement Continuums,* adapted from the *Malcolm Baldrige Award Program for Quality Business Management,* provide an authentic means for measuring schoolwide improvement and growth. Schools use these Continuums as a vehicle for ongoing self-assessment. They use the results of the assessment to acknowledge their accomplishments, to set goals for improvement, and to keep school districts and partners apprised of the progress they have made in their school improvement efforts.

Understanding the Continuums

These Continuums, extending from *one* to *five* horizontally, represent a continuum of expectations related to continuous improvement with respect to an *Approach* to the Continuum, *Implementation* of the approach, and the *Outcome* that results from the implementation. A *one* rating, located at the left of each Continuum, represents a school that has not yet begun to improve. *Five,* located at the right of each Continuum, represents a school that is one step removed from "world class quality." The elements between *one* and *five* describe how that Continuum is hypothesized to evolve in a continuously improving school. Each Continuum moves from a reactive mode to a proactive mode—from fire fighting to prevention. The *five* in *outcome* in each Continuum is the target.

Vertically, the *Approach, Implementation,* and *Outcome* statements, for any number one through five, are hypotheses. In other words, the implementation statement describes how the approach might look when implemented, and the outcome is the "pay-off" for implementing the approach. If the hypotheses are accurate, the outcome will not be realized until the approach is actually implemented.

Using the Continuums

Use the *Continuous Improvement Continuums* (CICs) to understand where your school is with respect to continuous improvement. The results will hopefully provide that sense of urgency needed to spark enthusiasm for your improvement efforts.

The most beneficial approach to assessing on the Continuums is to gather the entire staff together for the assessment. When assessing on the Continuums for the first time, plan for three hours to complete all seven categories.

Start the assessment by stating or creating the ground rules, setting the tone for a safe and confidential assessment, and explaining why you are doing this. Provide a brief overview of the seven sections, taking each section one at a time, and having each staff member read the related Continuum and make independent assessments of where she/he believes the school is with respect to *Approach, Implementation,* and *Outcome.* We recommend using individual 8 1/2 x 11 copies of the Continuums for individual assessments. CD-ROM (CICs.pdf) Then, have each staff member note where she/he believes the school is with a colorful sticker or marker on a large poster of each Continuum. The markers allow all staff to see how much they are in agreement with one another. If only one color is used for the first assessment, another color can be used for the next assessment, and so forth, to help gauge growth over time, or you can p to use two different charts for gauging progress over time such as in the photos that follow.

When all dots or marks have been placed on the enlarged Continuum, look at the agreement or disagreement of the ratings. Starting with *Approach,* have staff discuss why they believe the school is where they rated it. Keep discussing until the larger group comes to consensus on one number that reflects where the school is right now. You might need to make a quick check on where staff is with respect to coming to consensus, using a thumbs up, thumbs down "vote." Keep discussing the facts until consensus is reached. CD-ROM (Consenss.pdf) Do not average the results—it does not produce a sense of urgency for improvement. We cannot emphasize this enough! Keep discussing until agreement is reached by everyone on a number that represents where "we" are right now. When that consensus is reached, record the number and move to *Implementation* and then *Outcome.* Determine *Next Steps.* Proceed in the same way through the next six categories.

During the assessments, make sure someone records the discussions of the Continuum assessments. Schools might want to exchange facilitators with a neighboring school to have someone external to the school facilitate the assessments. This will enable everyone in the school to participate and provide an unbiased and competent person to lead the consensus-building piece. Assessing over time will help staff see that they are making progress. The decision of how often to assess on the *Continuous Improvement Continuums* is certainly up to the school. We recommend twice a year—about mid-fall and mid-spring—when there is time (or has been time) to implement next steps. Over time, once a year might be sufficient.

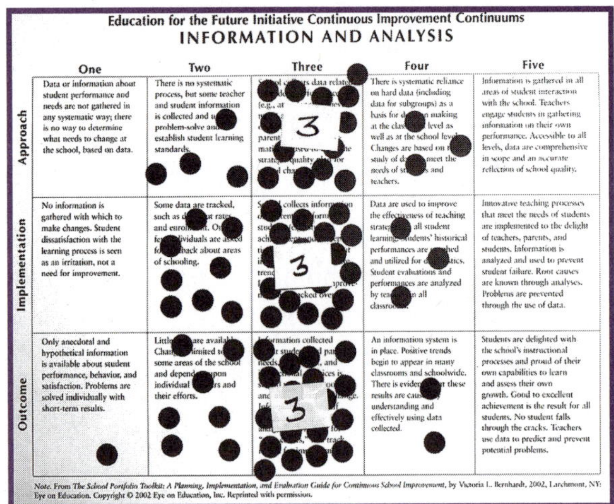
Education for the Future Initiative Continuous Improvement Continuums
INFORMATION AND ANALYSIS
One | Two | Three | Four | Five
Approach | Implementation | Outcome

Fall Assessment

Education for the Future Initiative Continuous Improvement Continuums
INFORMATION AND ANALYSIS
One | Two | Three | Four | Five
Approach | Implementation | Outcome

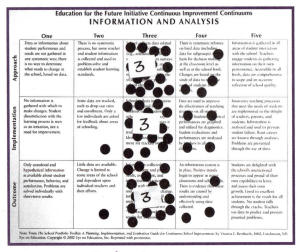

Spring Assessment

Using these Continuums will enable you and your school to stay motivated, to shape and maintain your shared vision, and will assist with the continuous improvement of all elements. Take pictures of the resulting charts. Even if your consensus number does not increase, the dots will most probably come together over time showing shifts in whole staff thinking.

Remember that where your school is at any time is just where it is. The important thing is what you do with this information. Continuous improvement is a never-ending process which, when used effectively, will ultimately lead your district toward providing a quality program for all children.

School Continuous Improvement Continuums

INFORMATION AND ANALYSIS

	One	Two	Three	Four	Five
Approach	Data or information about student performance and needs are not gathered in any systematic way; there is no way to determine what needs to change at the school, based on data.	There is no systematic process, but some teacher and student information is collected and used to problem solve and establish student learning standards.	School collects data related to student performance (e.g., attendance, achievement) and conducts surveys on student, teacher, and parent needs. The information is used to drive the strategic quality plan for school change.	There is systematic reliance on hard data (including data for subgroups) as a basis for decision making at the classroom level as well as at the school level. Changes are based on the study of data to meet the needs of students and teachers.	Information is gathered in all areas of student interaction with the school. Teachers engage students in gathering information on their own performance. Accessible to all levels, data are comprehensive in scope and an accurate reflection of school quality.
Implementation	No information is gathered with which to make changes. Student dissatisfaction with the learning process is seen as an irritation, not a need for improvement.	Some data are tracked, such as drop-out rates and enrollment. Only a few individuals are asked for feedback about areas of schooling.	School collects information on current and former students (e.g., student achievement and perceptions), analyzes and uses it in conjunction with future trends for planning. Identified areas for improvement are tracked over time.	Data are used to improve the effectiveness of teaching strategies on all student learning. Students' historical performances are graphed and utilized for diagnostics. Student evaluations and performances are analyzed by teachers in all classrooms.	Innovative teaching processes that meet the needs of students are implemented to the delight of teachers, parents, and students. Information is analyzed and used to prevent student failure. Root causes are known through analyses. Problems are prevented through the use of data.
Outcome	Only anecdotal and hypothetical information is available about student performance, behavior, and satisfaction. Problems are solved individually with short-term results.	Little data are available. Change is limited to some areas of the school and dependent upon individual teachers and their efforts.	Information collected about student and parent needs, assessment, and instructional practices is shared with the school staff and used to plan for change. Information helps staff understand pressing issues, analyze information for "root causes," and track results for improvement.	An information system is in place. Positive trends begin to appear in many classrooms and schoolwide. There is evidence that these results are caused by understanding and effectively using data collected.	Students are delighted with the school's instructional processes and proud of their own capabilities to learn and assess their own growth. Good to excellent achievement is the result for all students. No student falls through the cracks. Teachers use data to predict and prevent potential problems.

School Continuous Improvement Continuums
STUDENT ACHIEVEMENT

	One	Two	Three	Four	Five
Approach	Instructional and organizational processes critical to student success are not identified. Little distinction of student learning differences is made. Some teachers believe that not all students can achieve.	Some data are collected on student background and performance trends. Learning gaps are noted to direct improvement of instruction. It is known that student learning standards must be identified.	Student learning standards are identified, and a continuum of learning is created throughout the school. Student performance data are collected and compared to the standards in order to analyze how to improve learning for all students.	Data on student achievement are used throughout the school to pursue the improvement of student learning. Teachers collaborate to implement appropriate instruction and assessment strategies for meeting student learning standards articulated across grade levels. All teachers believe that all students can learn.	School makes an effort to exceed student achievement expectations. Innovative instructional changes are made to anticipate learning needs and improve student achievement. Teachers are able to predict characteristics impacting student achievement and to know how to perform from a small set of internal quality measures.
Implementation	All students are taught the same way. There is no communication with students about their academic needs or learning styles. There are no analyses of how to improve instruction.	Some effort is made to track and analyze student achievement trends on a school-wide basis. Teachers begin to understand the needs and learning gaps of students.	Teachers study effective instruction and assessment strategies to implement standards and to increase their students' learning. Student feedback and analysis of achievement data are used in conjunction with implementation support strategies.	There is a systematic focus on implementing student learning standards and on the improvement of student learning schoolwide. Effective instruction and assessment strategies are implemented in each classroom. Teachers support one another with peer coaching and/or action research focused on implementing strategies that lead to increased achievement and the attainment of the shared vision.	All teachers correlate critical instructional and assessment strategies with objective indicators of quality student achievement. A comparative analysis of actual individual student performance to student learning standards is utilized to adjust teaching strategies to ensure a progression of learning for all students.
Outcome	There is wide variation in student attitudes and achievement with undesirable results. There is high dissatisfaction among students with learning. Student background is used as an excuse for low student achievement.	There is some evidence that student achievement trends are available to teachers and are being used. There is much effort, but minimal observable results in improving student achievement.	There is an increase in communication between students and teachers regarding student learning. Teachers learn about effective instructional strategies that will implement the shared vision, including student learning standards, and meet the needs of their students. They make some gains.	Increased student achievement is evident schoolwide. Student morale, attendance, and behavior are good. Teachers converse often with each other about preventing student failure. Areas for further attention are clear.	Students and teachers conduct self-assessments to continuously improve performance. Improvements in student achievement are evident and clearly caused by teachers' and students' understandings of individual student learning standards, linked to appropriate and effective instructional and assessment strategies. A continuum of learning results. No students fall through the cracks.

School Continuous Improvement Continuums
QUALITY PLANNING

	One	Two	Three	Four	Five
Approach	No quality plan or process exists. Data are neither used nor considered important in planning.	The staff realize the importance of a mission, vision, and one comprehensive action plan. Teams develop goals and timelines, and dollars are allocated to begin the process.	A comprehensive school plan to achieve the vision is developed. Plan includes evaluation and continuous improvement.	One focused and integrated schoolwide plan for implementing a continuous improvement process is put into action. All school efforts are focused on the implementation of this plan that represents the achievement of the vision.	A plan for the continuous improvement of the school, with a focus on students, is put into place. There is excellent articulation and integration of all elements in the school due to quality planning. Leadership team ensures all elements are implemented by all appropriate parties.
Implementation	There is no knowledge of or direction for quality planning. Budget is allocated on an as-needed basis. Many plans exist.	School community begins continuous improvement planning efforts by laying out major steps to a shared vision, by identifying values and beliefs, the purpose of the school, a mission, vision, and student learning standards.	Implementation goals, responsibilities, due dates, and timelines are spelled out. Support structures for implementing the plan are set in place.	The quality management plan is implemented through effective procedures in all areas of the school. Everyone commits to implementing the plan aligned to the vision, mission, and values and beliefs. All share responsibility for accomplishing school goals.	Schoolwide goals, mission, vision, and student learning standards are shared and articulated throughout the school and with feeder schools. The attainment of identified student learning standards is linked to planning and implementation of effective instruction that meets students' needs. Leaders at all levels are developing expertise because planning is the norm.
Outcome	There is no evidence of comprehensive planning. Staff work is carried out in isolation. A continuum of learning for students is absent.	The school community understands the benefits of working together to implement a comprehensive continuous improvement plan.	There is evidence that the school plan is being implemented in some areas of the school. Improvements are neither systematic nor integrated schoolwide.	A schoolwide plan is known to all. Results from working toward the quality improvement goals are evident throughout the school. Planning is ongoing and inclusive of all stakeholders.	Evidence of effective teaching and learning results in significant improvement of student achievement attributed to quality planning at all levels of the school organization. Teachers and administrators understand and share the school mission and vision. Quality planning is seamless and all demonstrate evidence of accountability.

School Continuous Improvement Continuums
PROFESSIONAL DEVELOPMENT

	One	Two	Three	Four	Five
Approach	There is no professional development. Teachers, principals, and staff are seen as interchangeable parts that can be replaced. Professional development is external and usually equated to attending a conference alone. Hierarchy determines "haves" and "have-nots."	The "cafeteria" approach to professional development is used, whereby individual teachers choose what they want to take, without regard to an overall school plan.	The shared vision, school plan, and student needs are used to target focused professional development for all employees. Staff is inserviced on relevant instructional and leadership strategies.	Professional development and data-gathering methods are used by all teachers and are directed toward the goals of the shared vision and the continuous improvement of the school. Teachers have ongoing conversations about student achievement data. Other staff members receive training in their content areas. Systems thinking is considered in all decisions.	Leadership and staff continuously improve all aspects of the learning organization through an innovative, data-driven, and comprehensive continuous improvement process that prevents student failures. Effective job-embedded professional development is ongoing for implementing the vision for student success. Traditional teacher evaluations are replaced by collegial coaching and action research focused on student learning standards. Policies set professional development as a priority budget line-item. Professional development is planned, aligned, and lead to the achievement of student learning standards.
Implementation	Teacher, principal, and staff performance is controlled and inspected. Performance evaluations are used to detect mistakes.	Teacher professional development is sporadic and unfocused, lacking an approach for implementing new procedures and processes. Some leadership training begins to take place.	Teachers are involved in year-round quality professional development. The school community is trained in shared decision making, team building concepts, effective communication strategies, and data analysis at the classroom level.	Teachers, in teams, continuously set and implement student achievement goals. Leadership considers these goals and provides necessary support structures for collaboration. Teachers utilize effective support approaches as they implement new instruction and assessment strategies. Coaching and feedback structures are in place. Use of new knowledge and skills is evident.	Teams passionately support each other in the pursuit of quality improvement at all levels. Teachers make bold changes in instruction and assessment strategies focused on student learning standards and student learning styles. A teacher as action researcher model is implemented. Staffwide conversations focus on systemic reflection and improvement. Teachers are strong leaders.
Outcome	No professional growth and no staff or student performance improvement. There exists a high turnover rate of employees, especially administrators. Attitudes and approaches filter down to students.	The effectiveness of professional development is not known or analyzed. Teachers feel helpless about making schoolwide changes.	Teachers, working in teams, feel supported and begin to feel they can make changes. Evidence shows that shared decision making works.	A collegial school is evident. Effective classroom strategies are practiced, articulated schoolwide, are reflective of professional development aimed at ensuring student achievement, and the implementation of the shared vision, that includes student learning standards.	True systemic change and improved student achievement result because teachers are knowledgeable of and implement effective, differentiated teaching strategies for individual student learning gains. Teachers' repertoire of skills are enhanced, and students are achieving. Professional development is driving learning at all levels.

School Continuous Improvement Continuums
LEADERSHIP

	One	Two	Three	Four	Five
Approach	Principal as decision maker. Decisions are reactive to state, district, and federal mandates. There is no knowledge of continuous improvement.	A shared decision-making structure is put into place and discussions begin on how to achieve a school vision. Most decisions are focused on solving problems and are reactive.	Leadership team is committed to continuous improvement. Leadership seeks inclusion of all school sectors and supports study teams by making time provisions for their work.	Leadership team represents a true shared decision-making structure. Study teams are reconstructed for the implementation of a comprehensive continuous improvement plan.	A strong continuous improvement structure is set into place that allows for input from all sectors of the school, district, and community, ensuring strong communication, flexibility, and refinement of approach and beliefs. The school vision is student focused, based on data, and appropriate for school/community values, and meeting student needs.
Implementation	Principal makes all decisions, with little or no input from teachers, the community, or students. Leadership inspects for mistakes.	School values and beliefs are identified; the purpose of school is defined; a school mission and student learning standards are developed with representative input. A structure for studying approaches to achieving student learning standards is established.	Leadership team is active on study teams and integrates recommendations from the teams' research and analyses to form a comprehensive plan for continuous improvement within the context of the school mission. Everyone is kept informed.	Decisions about budget and implementation of the vision are made within teams, by the principal, by the leadership team, and by the full staff as appropriate. All decisions are communicated to the leadership team and to the full staff.	The vision is implemented and articulated across all grade levels and into feeder schools. Quality standards are reinforced throughout the school. All members of the school community understand and apply the quality standards. Leadership team has systematic interactions and involvement with district administrators, teachers, parents, community, and students about the school's direction. Necessary resources are available to implement and measure staff learning related to student learning standards.
Outcome	Decisions lack focus and consistency. There is no evidence of staff commitment to a shared vision. Students and parents do not feel they are being heard. Decision-making process is clear and known.	The mission provides a focus for all school improvement and guides the action to the vision. The school community is committed to continuous improvement. Quality leadership techniques are used sporadically.	Leadership team is seen as committed to planning and quality improvement. Critical areas for improvement are identified. Faculty feel included in shared decision making.	There is evidence that the leadership team listens to all levels of the organization. Implementation of the continuous improvement plan is linked to student learning standards and the guiding principles of the school. Leadership capacities for implementing the vision among teachers are evident.	Site-based management and shared decision making truly exists. Teachers understand and display an intimate knowledge of how the school operates. Teachers support and communicate with each other in the implementation of quality strategies. Teachers implement the vision in their classrooms and can determine how their new approach meets student needs and leads to the attainment of student learning standards. Leaders are standards-driven at all levels.

School Continuous Improvement Continuums
PARTNERSHIP DEVELOPMENT

	One	Two	Three	Four	Five
Approach	There is no system for input from parents, business, or community. Status quo is desired for managing the school.	Partnerships are sought, but mostly for money and things.	School has knowledge of why partnerships are important and seeks to include businesses and parents in a strategic fashion related to student learning standards for increased student achievement.	School seeks effective win-win business and community partnerships and parent involvement to implement the vision. Desired outcomes are clearly identified. A solid plan for partnership development exists.	Community, parent, and business partnerships become integrated across all student groupings. The benefits of outside involvement are known by all. Parent and business involvement in student learning is refined. Student learning *regularly* takes place beyond the school walls.
Implementation	Barriers are erected to close out involvement of outsiders. Outsiders are managed for least impact on status quo.	A team is assigned to get partners and to receive input from parents, the community, and business in the school.	Involvement of business, community, and parents begins to take place in some classrooms and after school hours related to the vision. Partners begin to realize how they can support each other in achieving school goals. School staff understand what partners need from the partnership.	There is a systematic utilization of parents, community, and businesses schoolwide. Areas in which the active use of these partnerships benefit student learning are clear.	Partnership development is articulated across all student groupings. Parents, community, business, and educators work together in an innovative fashion to increase student learning and to prepare students for the 21st Century. Partnerships are evaluated for continuous improvement.
Outcome	There is little or no involvement of parents, business, or community at-large. School is a closed, isolated system.	Much effort is given to establishing partnerships. Some spotty trends emerge, such as receiving donated equipment.	Some substantial gains are achieved in implementing partnerships. Some student achievement increases can be attributed to this involvement.	Gains in student satisfaction with learning and school are clearly related to partnerships. All partners benefit.	Previously non-achieving students enjoy learning with excellent achievement. Community, business, and home become common places for student learning, while school becomes a place where parents come for further education. Partnerships enhance what the school does for students.

School Continuous Improvement Continuums

CONTINUOUS IMPROVEMENT AND EVALUATION

	One	Two	Three	Four	Five
Approach	Neither goals nor strategies exist for the evaluation and continuous improvement of the school organization or for elements of the school organization.	The approach to continuous improvement and evaluation is problem solving. If there are no problems, or if solutions can be made quickly, there is no need for improvement or analyses. Changes in parts of the system are not coordinated with all other parts.	Some elements of the school organization are evaluated for effectiveness. Some elements are improved on the basis of the evaluation findings.	All elements of the school's operations are evaluated for improvement and to ensure congruence of the elements with respect to the continuum of learning students experience.	All aspects of the school organization are rigorously evaluated and improved on a continuous basis. Students, and the maintenance of a comprehensive learning continuum for students, become the focus of all aspects of the school improvement process.
Implementation	With no overall plan for evaluation and continuous improvement, strategies are changed by individual teachers and administrators only when something sparks the need to improve. Reactive decisions and activities are a daily mode of operation.	Isolated changes are made in some areas of the school organization in response to problem incidents. Changes are not preceded by comprehensive analyses, such as an understanding of the root causes of problems. The effectiveness of the elements of the school organization, or changes made to the elements, is not known.	Elements of the school organization are improved on the basis of comprehensive analyses of root causes of problems, client perceptions, and operational effectiveness of processes.	Continuous improvement analyses of student achievement and instructional strategies are rigorously reinforced within each classroom and across learning levels to develop a comprehensive learning continuum for students and to prevent student failure.	Comprehensive continuous improvement becomes the way of doing business at the school. Teachers continuously improve the appropriateness and effectiveness of instructional strategies based on student feedback and performance. All aspects of the school organization are improved to support teachers' efforts.
Outcome	Individuals struggle with system failure. Finger pointing and blaming others for failure occurs. The effectiveness of strategies is not known. Mistakes are repeated.	Problems are solved only temporarily and few positive changes result. Additionally, unintended and undesirable consequences often appear in other parts of the system. Many aspects of the school are incongruent, keeping the school from reaching its vision.	Evidence of effective improvement strategies is observable. Positive changes are made and maintained due to comprehensive analyses and evaluation.	Teachers become astute at assessing and in predicting the impact of their instructional strategies on individual student achievement. Sustainable improvements in student achievement are evident at all grade levels, due to continuous improvement.	The school becomes a congruent and effective learning organization. Only instruction and assessment strategies that produce quality student achievement are used. A true continuum of learning results for all students and staff. The impact of improvements is increasingly measurable.

Glossary of Terms

The *Glossary* provides brief definitions of data analysis and testing terms used throughout *Using Data to Improve Student Learning in School Districts.*

▼ Achievement

The demonstration of student performance measured against learning goals, learning objectives, or standards.

▼ Achievement Gap

The difference between how well low-income and minority children perform on standardized tests, as compared with their peers. For many years, low-income and minority children have been falling behind their white peers in terms of academic achievement.

▼ Accountability

The act of being responsible to somebody else or to others. It also means capable of being explained.

▼ Action

Specific steps, tasks, or activity used to implement a strategy.

▼ Action Plan

The part of continuous school improvement planning that describes the tasks that must be performed, when they will be performed, who is responsible, and how much they will cost to implement.

▼ Action Research

Teachers and/or administrators raise questions about the best way to improve teaching and learning, systematically study the literature to answer the questions, implement the best approach(es), and analyze the results.

▼ Adequate Yearly Progress (AYP)

An individual state's measure of yearly progress toward achieving state academic standards. *Adequate Yearly Progress* is the minimum level of improvement that states, school districts, and schools must achieve each year to fulfill the requirement of the *No Child Left Behind Act.*

▼ Affinity Diagram

A visual picture or chart of reflective thinking. The result is that more participants are likely to deal with problems that emerge.

▼ Aggregate

Combining the results of all groups that make up the sample or population.

▼ Alignment

An arrangement of groups or forces in relation to one another. In continuous school improvement planning, we align all parts of the system to the vision. With curriculum, we align instruction and materials to student learning standards.

▼ Analysis

The examination of facts and data to provide a basis for effective decisions.

▼ **Analysis of Variance (ANOVA)**

ANOVA is an inferential procedure to determine if there is a significant difference among sample means.

▼ **Anticipated Achievement Scores**

An estimate of the average score for students of similar ages, grade levels, and academic aptitude. It is an estimate of what we would expect an individual student to score on an achievement test.

▼ **Articulation**

The varied process of integrating the district/school aligned curriculum across disciplines and between grade levels and connecting it to real-life situations; also presenting it to all stakeholders and implementing it district/school wide.

▼ **Assessment**

Gathering and interpretation of student performance, primarily for the purpose of enhancing learning. Also used for the improvement of a program and/or strategies.

▼ **Authentic Assessment**

Refers to a variety of ways to assess a student's demonstration of knowledge and skills. Authentic assessments may include performances, projects, exhibitions, and portfolios.

▼ **Bar Graph**

A pictorial representation that uses bars to display data, usually frequencies, percentages, and averages.

▼ **Baseline Data**

Information collected to comprise a reference set for comparison of a second set of data collected at a later time; used to interpret changes over time, usually after some condition has been changed for research purposes that sets the standard for any research that follows in the same project.

▼ **Benchmark**

A standard against which something can be measured or assessed.

▼ **Brainstorming**

The act of listing ideas without judgment. Brainstorming generates creative ideas spontaneously.

▼ **Cadres or Action Teams**

Groups or teams of educators who agree to accept responsibility to study new approaches, plan for the implementation of new strategies or programs, and get work done without every staff member's involvement.

▼ **Case Studies**

Reviewing student's work, and/or another teacher's example lessons, which can lead to quality discussions and improved practices.

▼ **Cause and Effect**

The relationship and complexities between a problem or effect and the possible causes.

▼ **Coaching**

Teachers form teams of two or three to observe each other, plan together, and talk and encourage each other in meaningful ways while reflecting on continuously improving instructional practices.

▼ **Cognitive Abilities or Skills Index**

An age-dependent, normalized standard score based on a student's performance on a cognitive skills test with a mean of 100 and standard deviation of 16. The score indicates a student's overall cognitive ability or academic aptitude relative to students of similar age, without regard to grade level.

▼ **Cohort**

A group of individuals sharing a particular statistical or demographic characteristic, such as the year they were in a specific school grade level. Following cohorts over time helps teachers understand the effects particular circumstances may have on results. Matched cohort studies follow the same individuals over time, and unmatched cohort studies follow the same group over time.

▼ **Cohort Analysis**

The reorganization of grade level data to look at the groups of students progressing through the grades together over time.

▼ **Collaboration**

Evidence of two of more concerned groups (i.e., teachers, aides, itinerant and resource teachers, parents, community representatives, etc.), working together to improve the school program.

▼ **Collaborative**

Working jointly with others, especially in an intellectual endeavor.

▼ **Comprehensive Action Plan**

Defining the specific actions needed to implement the vision, setting forth when the actions will take place, designating who is responsible for accomplishing the action, how much it will cost, and where to get the funds.

▼ **Confidence Interval**

Used in inferential statistics, a range of values that a researcher can estimate, with a certain level of confidence, where the population parameter is located.

▼ **Congruent**

Corresponding to, or consistent with, each other or something else.

▼ **Consensus**

Decision making where a group finds a proposal acceptable enough that all members can support it; no member actively opposes it.

▼ **Content Standard**

Description of the knowledge or skills that educators want students to learn.

▼ **Continuous**

In the context of continuous improvement, continuous means the ongoing review of the data, the implementation of the plan, and the progress being made.

▼ **Continuous Improvement**

Keeping the process of planning, implementing, evaluating, and improving alive over time.

▼ Continuous Improvement and Evaluation

The section of the school portfolio that assists organizations to further understand where they are and what they need to do to move forward in the big picture of continuous school improvement.

▼ Continuous Improvement Continuums (CICs)

As developed by *Education for the Future Initiative*, CICs are seven rubrics that represent the theoretical flow of systemic school or district improvement. The *Continuous Improvement Continuums* take the theory and spirit of continuous school improvement, interweave educational research, and offer practical meaning to the components that must change simultaneously and systematically.

▼ Continuous Improvement Plan

A plan for improvement, based on data, that will help create and manage change. The process of answering the following questions: *Who are we? How do we do business? What are our strengths and areas for improvement? Why do we exist? Where do we want to be? What are the gaps? What are the root causes of the gaps? How can we get to where we want to be? How will we implement? How will we evaluate our efforts?*

▼ Control Groups

Control groups serve as a baseline in making comparisons with treatment groups and are necessary when general effectiveness of the treatment is unknown. During an experiment, the control group is studied the same as the experimental groups, except that it does not receive the treatment of interest.

▼ Convenience Sampling

Convenience sampling is done when one wants to survey people who are ready and available, and not hassle with trying to get everyone in the population ready and willing to complete the questionnaire.

▼ Correlation

A statistical analysis that helps one see the relationship of scores in one distribution to scores in another distribution. Correlation coefficients have a range of –1.0 to +1.0. A correlation of around zero indicates no relationship. Correlations of .8 and higher indicate strong relationships.

▼ Criteria

Characteristics or dimensions of student performance.

▼ Criterion-referenced Tests

Tests that judge how well a test taker does on an explicit objective, learning goal, or criteria relative to a pre-determined performance level. There is no comparison to any other test takers.

▼ Culture

Attitudes, values, beliefs, goals, norms of behavior, and practices that characterize a group.

▼ Curriculum Alignment

A curriculum in which what is taught, how it is taught, and how it is assessed is intentionally based on, but not limited to, the state *Core Curriculum Content Standards and Assessment*—the sequence of learning in an aligned curriculum is articulated and constantly discussed, monitored, and revised.

Curriculum Development and Implementation

The way content is designed and delivered. Teachers must think deeply about the content, student-learning standards, and how it must be managed and delivered, or put into practice.

Curriculum Implementation

Putting the curriculum into practice.

Curriculum Mapping and Webbing

Approaches that require teachers to align the curriculum and student learning standards by grade levels, and then across grade levels, to ensure a continuum of learning that makes sense for all students.

Data Cleansing

The process of ensuring that all values in a database are consistent and correctly recorded.

Data-driven Decision Making

Making decisions based on demographic, student learning, perceptions, and school process data. True data-driven decision making has the guiding principles of the learning organization at the center of every decision.

Data Mining

Techniques for finding patterns and trends in large data sets. The process of automatically extracting valid, useful, previously unknown, and ultimately comprehensible information from large databases. Just doing common data analysis is not data mining.

Data Table

The source of data for tables and graphs. In building graphs with a software program, one would need to create a data table from which to create the graphs or tables.

Data Warehouse

A single, large database that has collected relevant information from several other sources into a single, accessible format designed to be used for decision making. The data warehouse is created to house data imported from many other data sources that are not designed to work together or to share information.

Database

A storage mechanism for data that eliminates redundancy and conflict among multiple data files. Data is entered once and is then available to all programs that need it.

Deciles

The values of a variable that divide the frequency distribution into ten equal frequency groups. The ninth decile shows the number (or percentage) of the norming group that scored between 80 and 89 NCE, for example.

Demographics

Statistical characteristics of a population, such as average age, number of students in a school, percentages of ethnicities, etc. Disaggregation with demographic data allows us to isolate variations among different subgroups.

Derived Score

A score that is attained by performing some kind of mathematical operation on a raw score for comparison within a particular grade (e.g., T-scores, NCE, etc.).

▼ Descriptive Statistics

Direct measurement (i.e. mean, median, percent correct) of each member of a group or population. Descriptive statistics can include graphing.

▼ Diagnostic

Assessment/evaluation carried out prior to instruction that is designed to determine a student's attitude, skill, or knowledge in order to identify specific student needs.

▼ Diagnostic Tests

Usually standardized and normed, diagnostic tests are given before instruction begins to help the instructor(s) understand student learning needs. Many different score types are used with diagnostic tests.

▼ Different Ways of Knowing (DWOK)

A standards-based, interdisciplinary, arts-infused curriculum that promotes collaborative learning and higher–order thinking.

▼ Disaggregate

Separating the results of different groups that make up the sample or population.

▼ Disaggregated Data

To *disaggregate* means separating the results of different groups or separating a whole into its parts. In education, this term means that test results are sorted into groups of students by gender, those who are economically disadvantaged, by racial and ethnic minority groups, disabilities, or by English fluency. This practice allows administrators and teachers to see more than just the average score for the school. Instead, administrators and teachers can see how each student group is performing.

▼ Diverse/Diversity

The inclusion of differences based on gender, race, disability, age, national origin, color, economic status, religion, geographic regions, and other characteristics. Achieving diversity requires respect of differences; valuing differences; supporting, encouraging, and promoting differences; and affirmation initiatives, such as recruitment, placement, and retention.

▼ Educationally Significant

Gains in student learning, school, or program results can be considered educationally significant, even though they are not statistically significant.

▼ Evaluation

Making judgments about the quality of overall student performance for the purpose of communicating student achievement. Evaluation also is the study of the impact of a program or process.

▼ Examining Student Data

Conversations around individual student data results and the processes that created the results. This approach can be a significant form of professional development when skilled team members facilitate the discussions.

▼ Examining Student Work

Ensures that what students learn is aligned to the learning standards. It also shows teachers the impact of their actions.

Exemplars

Models or examples of excellent work that meet stated criteria or levels of performance.

Experimental Design

The detailed planning of an experiment, made beforehand, to insure the data collected is appropriate and obtained in a way that will lead to an objective analysis, with valid inferences. Preferably, the design will maximize the amount of information that can be gained, given the amount of effort expended.

Fluency

The capacity to read text accurately and quickly.

Flow Chart

A flowchart illustrates the steps in a process. By visualizing the process, a flow chart can quickly help identify bottlenecks or inefficiencies where a process can be streamlined or improved.

Focus Group

A group convened to gather information about processes or practices that need to be examined.

Formative

Assessments at regular intervals of a student's progress, with accompanying feedback in order to help the student's performance and to provide direction for improvement of a program for individual students or for a whole class.

Frequency

The number of times a given score occurs in a distribution.

Frequency Distribution

Describes how often observations fall within designated categories. It can be expressed as numbers, percents, and deciles, to name just a few possibilities.

Gain Score

The difference between two administrations of the same test. Gain scores are calculated by subtracting the previous score from the most recent score. One can have negative gains, which are actually losses.

Gaps

The difference between where the school is now and where the school wants to be in the future. It is this gap that gets translated into goals, objectives, strategies, and actions in the action plan.

Goals

Achievements or end results. Goal statements describe the intended outcome of the vision and are stated in terms that are broad, general, abstract, and non-measurable. Schools should have only two or three goals.

Grade-level Analysis

Looking at the same grade level over time.

Grade-level Equivalent

The grade and month of the school year for which a given score is the actual or estimated average. Based on a 10-month school year, scores would be noted as 6.1 for grade six, first month, 8.10 for grade eight, tenth month, etc.

▼ **Grades**

Subjective scores given by teachers to students for performance.

▼ **Guiding Principles**

The vision of the school, or district, that is based on the purpose and mission of the organization, created from the values and beliefs of the individuals to make up the organization. Everything that is done in the organization ought to be aligned to its guiding principles.

▼ **Holistic**

Emphasizing the organic or functional relation between parts and the whole.

▼ **Horizontal Articulation or Coordination**

Indicates that the curriculum is carefully planned within grade levels. In effect, this would mean that every primary grade throughout the school/district will teach the same curriculum—also every grade six social studies class; every grade ten health class; every grade twelve physics class, and so on.

▼ **Inferential Statistics**

Statistical analysis concerned with the measurement of only a sample from a population and then making estimates, or inferences, about the population from which the sample was taken; inferential statistics help generalize the results of data analyses.

▼ **Information and Analysis**

Establishes systematic and rigorous reliance on data for decision making in all parts of the organization. This section of the school portfolio sets the context of the learning organization.

▼ **Intersections**

Analyzing the intersections or overlapping of measures (demographics, perceptions, school processes, student learning) enables schools to predict what they must do to meet the needs of all the students they have, or will have in the future.

▼ **Interval Scale**

Intervals are meaningful with a relative zero point. Can calculate mode, median, mean, range, standard deviation, etc.

▼ **Item Analysis**

Reviewing each item on a test or assessment to determine how many students missed the particular item. A general term for procedures designed to access the usefulness of a test item.

▼ **Latent Trait Scale**

A scaled score obtained through one of several mathematical approaches collectively known as Latent-trait procedures or Item Response Theory. The particular numerical values used in the scale are arbitrary, but higher scores indicate more knowledgeable test takers or more difficult items.

▼ **Leadership**

Providing needed assistance to schools to think through and plan for their vision, shared decision making, and other structures that will work with their specific population.

▼ **Learner-Centered**

An environment created by educators focusing on the needs and learning styles of all students.

Learning

A process of acquiring knowledge, skills, understanding, and/or new behaviors.

▼ **Learning Environment**

Any setting or location, inside or outside the school, used to enhance the instruction of students.

▼ **Learning Goal**

A target for learning: a desired skill, knowledge, or behavior.

▼ **Line Graph**

Line graphs give a lot of flexibility and are exceptionally good for showing a series of numbers over time. Line graphs can display complex data more effectively than bar graphs.

▼ **Matched Cohorts**

Looking at the same students (individual, not groups) progressing through the grades over time.

▼ **Maximum**

The highest actual score or the highest possible score on a test.

▼ **Mean**

Average score in a set of scores; calculated by summing all the scores and dividing by the total number of scores.

▼ **Means**

Methods, strategies, actions, and processes by which a school plans to improve student achievement.

▼ **Measures**

A way of evaluating something; how we know we have achieved the objective.

▼ **Median**

The score that splits a distribution in half: 50 percent of the scores lie above and 50 percent of the scores lie below the median. If the number of scores is odd, the median is the middle score. If the number of scores is even, one must add the two middle scores and divide by two to calculate the median.

▼ **Minimum**

The lowest score or the lowest possible score on a test.

▼ **Mission**

A brief, clear, and compelling statement that serves to unify an organization's efforts. A mission has a finish line for its achievement and is proactive. A mission should walk the boundary between the possible and impossible.

▼ **Mobility**

The reference to the movement of students in and out of a school or district.

▼ **Mode**

The score that occurs most frequently in a scoring distribution.

▼ **Multiple Measures**

Using more than one method of assessment, gathered from varying points of view, in order to understand the multifaceted world of school from the perspective of everyone involved.

▼ **N**

The number of students in the group being described, such as the number taking a test or completing a questionnaire.

Needs Assessment

Questions that help staff understand their professional development needs. At the same time, if done well, this assessment can lead to quality staff conversations and sharing of knowledge.

No Child Left Behind (NCLB)

The No Child Left Behind Act of 2001 reauthorized the 1965 Elementary and Secondary Education Act. NCLB calls for increased accountability for states, school districts, and schools; choices for parents and students; greater flexibility for states, school districts, and schools regarding Federal education funds; establishing a Reading First initiative to ensure every child can read by end of grade three; and improving the quality of teachers.

Nominal Scale

Qualitative, categorical information. Numbers represent categories, e.g., 1=male, 2=female.

Normal Curve

The bell-shaped curve of the normal distribution.

Normal Curve Equivalent (NCE)

Equivalent scores are standard scores with a mean of 50, a standard deviation of 21.06, and a range of 1 to 99.

Normal Distribution

A distribution of scores or other measures that in graphic form has a distinctive bell-shaped appearance. In a normal distribution, the measures are distributed symmetrically about the mean. Cases are concentrated near the mean and decrease in frequency, according to a precise mathematical equation, the farther one departs from the mean. Also known as a normal curve.

Normalized Standard Score

A transformation procedure used to make scores from different tests more directly comparable. Not only are the mean and the standard deviation of the raw score distribution changed, as with a linear standard score transformation, but the shape of the distribution is converted to a normal curve. The transformation to a normalized z-score involves two steps: 1) compute the exact percentile rank of the raw score; and 2) determine the corresponding z-score for that exact percentile rank from a table of areas under the normal curve.

Norming Group

A representative group of students whose results on a norm-referenced test help create the scoring scales with which others compare their performance. The norming group's results are professed to look like the normal curve.

Norm-referenced Test

Any test in which the score acquires additional meaning by comparing it to the scores of people in an identified norming group. A test can be both norm- and criterion-referenced. Most standardized achievement tests are referred to as norm-referenced.

Norms

The distribution of test scores and their corresponding percentile ranks, standard scores, or other derived scores of some specified group called the norming group. For example, this may be a national sample of all fourth graders, a national sample of all fourth-grade males, or perhaps all fourth graders in some local district.

Norms versus Standards

Norms are not standards. Norms are indicators of what students of similar characteristics did when confronted with the same test items as those taken by students in the norming group. Standards, on the other hand, are arbitrary judgments of what students should be able to do, given a set of test items.

Objectives

Goals that are redrafted in terms that are clearly tangible. Objective statements are narrow, specific, concrete, and measurable. When writing objectives, it is important to describe the intended results, rather than the process or means to accomplish them, and state the time frame.

Observation

Teacher and observer agree on what is being observed, the type of information to be recorded, when the observation will take place, and how the information will be analyzed. The observee is someone implementing strategies and actions that others want to know. Observer might be a colleague, a supervisor, or a visitor from another location.

Open-ended Response Items

Questions that require students to combine content knowledge and application of process skills in order to communicate an answer.

Ordinal

Ordinal provides information about size or direction; numbers ordered along underlying dimension, but no information about distance between points.

Outcome

Successful demonstration of learning that occurs at the culmination point of a set learning experiences.

Over Time

No less than three years.

Parameter

A parameter is a population measurement that characterizes one of its features. An example of a parameter is the mode. The mode is the value in the population that occurs most frequently. Other examples of parameters are a population's mean (or average) and its variance.

Partnerships

Teachers developing relationships with parents, businesses in the community, scientists, and/or university personnel to help students achieve student learning standards, and to bring about real world applications for student learning and deeper understandings of content.

Pearson Correlation Coefficient

The most widely-used correlation coefficient determines the extent to which two variables are proportional to each other; measures the strength and direction of a linear relationship between the x and y variables.

Percent Correct

A calculated score implying the percentage of students meeting and exceeding some number, usually a cut score, or a standard. Percent passing equals the number passing the test divided by the number taking the test.

Percent Proficient

Percent Proficient, Percent Mastery, or Percent Passing are terms that represent the percentage of students who pass a particular test at a level above a cut score, as defined by the test creators or the test interpreters.

Percentile

A point on the normal distribution below which a certain percentage of the scores fall. For example, if 70 percent of the scores fall below a raw score of 56, then the score of 56 is at the 70th percentile. The term *local percentile* indicates that the norm group is obtained locally. The term *national percentile* indicates that the norm group represents a national group.

Percentile Rank (PR)

Percentage of students in a norm group (e.g., national or local) whose scores fall below a given score. Range is from 1 to 99. A 50th percentile ranking would mean that 50 percent of the scores in the norming group fall below a specific score.

Perceptions Data

Information that reflects opinions and views of questionnaire respondents.

Performance Assessment

Refers to assessments that measure skills, knowledge, and ability directly—such as through performance. In other words, if you want students to learn to write, you assess their ability on a writing activity.

Performance Standard

Identification of the desired level of proficiency at which educators want a content standard to be mastered.

Pie Chart or Pie Graph

A graph in a circular format, used to display percentages of something, such as the percentage of a school or district population, by ethnicity.

Population

Statisticians define a population as the entire collection of items that is the focus of concern. Descriptive Statistics describe the characteristics of a given population by measuring each of its items and then summarizing the set of measures in various ways. Inferential Statistics make educated inferences about the characteristics of a population by drawing a random sample and appropriately analyzing the information it provides.

Press Release

Article written by school public information official or an education reporter for a local newspaper.

Process Mapping

School processes are instruction, curriculum, and assessment strategies used to ensure the learning of all students. Mapping or flow charting school processes can help staff objectively look at how students are being taught.

Processes

Measures that describe what is being done to get results, such as programs, strategies, and practices.

Professional Development

Planned activities that help staff members, teachers, and administrators change the manner in which they work, i.e., how they make decisions; gather, analyze, and use data; plan, teach, and monitor achievement; evaluate personnel; and assess the impact of new approaches to instruction and assessment on students.

Program Evaluation

The examination of a program to understand its quality and impact.

Purpose

The aim of the organization; the reason for existence.

Quality Planning

Developing the elements of a strategic plan including a vision, mission, goals, action plan, outcome measures, and strategies for continuous improvement and evaluation. Quality planning is a section of the school portfolio.

Quality

A standard for excellence.

Quartiles

Three quartiles—Q1, Q2, Q3—divide a distribution into four equal groups (Q1=25th percentile; Q2=50th percentile; Q3=75th percentile).

Query

A request one makes to a database that is returned to the desktop. Understanding and knowing how to set up queries or to ask questions of the database is very important to the information discovery process.

Quota Sampling

Divides the population being studied into subgroups such as male and female, or young, middle, and old, to ensure that you set a quota of responses.

Range

A measure of the spread between the lowest and the highest scores in a distribution, calculated by subtracting the lowest score from the highest score.

Ratio

A proportional relationship between two different numbers or quantities.

Raw Scores

A person's observed score on a test or subtest. The number of questions answered correctly on a test or subtest. A raw score is simply calculated by adding the number of questions answered correctly.

Regression

An analysis that results in an equation that describes the nature of the relationship among variables. Simple regressions predict an object's value on a criterion variable when given its value on one predictor variable. Multiple regressions predict an object's value on a criterion variable when given its value on each of several predictor variables.

▼ **Relational Database**

A type of database that allows the connection of several databases to each other. The data and relations between them are stored in table form. Relational databases are powerful because they require few assumptions about how data are related and how they will be extracted from the database.

▼ **Relationships**

Looking at two or more sets of analyses to understand how they are associated or what they mean to each other.

▼ **Reliability**

The consistency with which an assessment measures what it intends to measure.

▼ **Research**

The act of methodically collecting information about a particular subject to discover facts or to develop a plan of action based on the facts discovered.

▼ **RIT Scale Scores**

Named for George Rasch, who developed the theory of this type of measurement, RIT scores are scaled scores that come from a series of tests created by the Northwest Evaluation Association (NWEA). The tests that draw from an item bank are created to align with local curriculum and state standards.

▼ **Root Cause**

As used in the continuous school improvement plan, root cause refers to the deep underlying reason for a specific situation. While a symptom may be made evident from a needs assessment or gap analysis—the symptom (low student scores) is not the cause. To find a root cause or causes one often has to ask Why? at least five levels down to uncover the root reasons for the symptom.

▼ **Rubric**

A scoring tool that rates performance according to clearly stated levels of criteria. The scales can be numeric or descriptive.

▼ **Sample**

In statistical terms, a random sample is a set of items that have been drawn from a population in such a way that each time an item is selected, every item in the population has an equal opportunity to appear in the sample. In practical terms, it is not so easy to draw a random sample.

▼ **Scaled Scores**

A mathematical transformation of a raw score. It takes the differences in the difficulty of test forms into consideration and is useful for teaching changes over time.

▼ **School Improvement Planning**

Planning to implement the vision requires studying the research, determining strategies that will work with the students, and determining what the vision would look like, sound like, and feel like when the vision is implemented, and how to get all staff members implementing the vision.

▼ **School Portfolio**

A professional development tool that gathers evidence about the way work is done in the school and a self-assessment tool to ensure the alignment of all parts of the learning organization to the vision. A school portfolio can also serve as a principal portfolio.

School Processes

Instruction, curriculum, and assessment strategies used to ensure the learning of all students.

School Profile

A two to four page summary that presents a picture of a school. Usually includes demographic and achievement information, as well as analysis of other available data.

Scientifically-based Research

The revised *Elementary and Secondary Education Act,* recently approved by Congress and also known as the *No Child Left Behind Act of 2001,* mandates that educators base school programs and teaching practices on Scientifically Based Research. This includes everything from teaching approaches to drug abuse prevention. Scientifically Based Research means research that involves the application of rigorous, systematic, and objective procedures to obtain reliable and valid knowledge relevant to education activities and programs.

Self-assessment

Assessment by the individual performing the activity.

Shared Decision Making

A process whereby all stakeholders within a school are engaged and meaningfully involved in the planning and decision-making process of that school.

Simple Sample

A smaller version of the larger population that can be considered representative of the population. One classroom of students can be a simple sample, or one school in the district. This is typically used when administering a very large questionnaire.

Skewed Distribution

Most of the scores are found near one end of the distribution. When most of the scores are grouped at the lower end, it is positively skewed. When most of the scores are grouped at the upper end, it is negatively skewed.

Snowball Sampling

Relies on members of one group completing the questionnaire to identify other members of the population to complete the questionnaire.

Socioeconomic Status (SES)

An indication of the level of poverty in which a student lives. Most school districts use whether or not a student qualifies for free/reduced lunch as an indicator. Other school districts use more complex equations that include mother's level of education and the like.

Standard

A guideline or description that is used as a basis for judgment—exemplary performance; an objective ideal; a worthy and tangible goal.

Standard Deviation

Measure of variability in a set of scores. The standard deviation is the square root of the variance. Unlike the variance, the standard deviation is stated in the original units of the variable. Approximately 68 percent of the scores in a normal distribution lie between plus one and minus one standard deviation. The more scores cluster around the mean, the smaller the variance.

Standard Scores

A group of scores having a desired mean and standard deviation. A z-score is a basic standard score. Other standard scores are computed by first converting a raw score to a z-score (sometimes normalized), multiplying the transformation by the desired standard deviation, and then adding the desired mean to the product. The raw scores are transformed this way for reasons of convenience, comparability, and ease of interpretation.

Standardized Tests

Tests that are uniform in content, administration, and scoring. Standardized tests can be used for comparing results across classrooms, schools, school districts, and states.

Standards

Consistent expectations of all learners.

Standards-based Assessments

A collection of items that indicate how much students know and/or are able to do with respect to specific standards.

Stanines

A nine-point normalized standard score scale. It divides the normal curve distribution of scores into nine equal points: 1 to 9. The mean of a stanine distribution is 5, and the standard deviation is approximately 2.

Statistically Significant

Statistical significance of a result is the probability that the observed relationship in a sample occurred by pure chance; indicates that there is at least a 95% probability of the result that did not happen by chance.

Strategies

Procedures, methods, or techniques to accomplish an objective.

Stratified Random Sample

One which divides the population into subgroups, and then a random sample is selected from each of the groups. This approach would be used when you want to make sure that you hear from all the groups of people you want to study.

Student Learning Data

Information that reflects a level of knowledge, skill, or accomplishment, usually in something that has been explicitly taught.

Study Groups

Teams or groups of educators meet to learn new strategies or programs, to review new publications, or to review student work together.

Summative

Assessment or evaluation designed to provide information; used in making judgments about a student's achievement at the end of a period of instruction.

Symptom

A symptom is the outward (most visible) indicator of a deeper root cause.

System

A system is the sum of the interactions between and among its component parts. School districts are systems.

Systemic

Affecting or relating to a system as a whole.

Systematic

Refers to approaches that are repeatable and that use data and information so that improvement and learning are possible.

Systems Perspective

Viewing the school or school district as a whole or perceiving the combination of related structures/components of the school and community (i.e., indicators and standards for school improvement), organized into a complex whole.

Systems Thinking

Systems thinking would have continuous improvement teams focusing on improving how the parts of the system interact and support one another towards achievement of common goals.

T-Chart

Used to compare and contrast information or to show relationships. It is used to help people see the opposite dimension of an issue.

T-Scores

A calculated standard score with a mean of 50 and a standard deviation of 10. T-scores are obtained by the following formula: $T=10z+50$. T-scores are sometimes normalized.

Table

A data structure comprised of rows and columns, like a spreadsheet.

Teacher Portfolios

The process and product of documenting a teacher as learner; includes reflections, observations, and evidence. Portfolios can be used for many things, such as, self-assessment, employment, supervision to replace traditional teacher evaluation, and for peer collaboration.

Tests of Significance

Procedures that use samples to test claims about population parameters. Significance tests can estimate a population parameter, with a certain amount of confidence, from a sample.

Trends

Direction that is given from a learning organization's data. Usually need three years of data to see a trend.

Triangulation

The term used for combining three or more student achievement measures to get a more complete picture of student achievement.

Validity

The degree to which an assessment strategy measures what it is intended to measure.

Values and Beliefs

The core of who we are, what we do, and how we think and feel. Values and beliefs reflect what is important to us; they describe what we think about work and how we think it should operate. Core values and beliefs are the first step in reaching a shared vision.

Variance

A measure of the dispersion, or variability, of scores about their mean. The population variance is calculated by taking the average of the squared deviations from the mean—a deviation being defined as an individual score minus the mean.

Variation

All systems and processes vary. It is essential to understand what type of variation is present before trying to correct or improve the system. Two types of variation are *common cause* and *special cause.* Special cause variation must be eliminated before a system can be improved.

Vertical Articulation or Alignment

Indicates that the curriculum is carefully planned and sequenced from beginning learning and skills to more advanced learning and skills. Vertical articulation speaks to what is taught from pre-school through upper grades and is sometimes noted simply as "K-12 Curriculum."

Vision

A specific description of what the learning organization will be like when the mission is achieved. A vision is a mental image. It must be written in practical, concrete terms that everyone can understand and see in the same way.

Weighted Mean

The overall average of two or more individual averages when the individual averages are made up from differing amounts of contributors, so that each individual average is weighted according to its respective number it contributes (e.g., students, teachers).

z-Scores

A standard score with a mean of zero and a standard deviation of one. A z-score is obtained by the following formula: z = raw score (x) minus the mean, divided by the standard deviation (sd). A z-score is sometimes normalized.

References and Resources

The references used in this book, along with other resources that will assist busy district and school administrators and teachers in conducting quality data analyses, appear below.

Airasian, P. W. (1994). *Classroom assessment.* New York, NY: McGraw-Hill, Inc.

Ammerman, M. (1998). *The root cause analysis handbook: A simplified approach to identifying, correcting, and reporting workplace errors.* New York, NY: Quality Resources.

Annenberg Foundation. (2003). *Rethinking accountability: Voices in urban education.* Providence, RI: Author.

Ardovino, J., Hollingsworth, J., & Ybarra, S. (2000). *Multiple measures: Accurate ways to assess student achievement.* Thousand Oaks, CA: Corwin Press, Inc.

Armstrong, J. (2002). *What is an accountability model?* Denver, CO: Education Commission of the States. Available: http://www.ecs.org.

Armstrong, J., & Anthes, K. (2001). How data can help: Putting information to work to raise student achievement. In *American School Board Journal,* 38-41.

Arter, J. (1999). *Teaching about performance assessment.* Portland, OR: Northwest Regional Educational Laboratory.

Arter, J., & The Classroom Assessment Team, Laboratory Network Program. (1998). *Improving classroom assessment: A toolkit for professional developers: Alternative Assessment.* Aurora, CO: MCREL.

Arter, J., & Busick, K. (2001). *Practice with student-involved classroom assessment.* Portland, OR: Assessment Training Institute, Inc.

Arter, J., & McTighe, J. (2001). *Scoring rubrics in the classroom: Using performance criteria for assessing and improving student performance.* In Guskey, T.R., & Marzano, R.J. (Series Eds.). *Experts in Assessment.* Thousand Oaks, CA: Corwin Press, Inc.

Aschbacher, P. R., & Herman, J. L. (1991). *Guidelines for effective score reporting.* (CSE Technical Report No. 326). Los Angeles, CA: University of California, Center for Research on Evaluation, Standards and Student Testing (CRESST).

Baldrige National Quality Program. (2004). *Education criteria for performance excellence.* Gaithersburg, MD: National Institute of Standards and Technology. Available: www.quality.nist.gov.

Barth, P., Haycock, K., Jackson, H., Mora, K., Ruiz, P., Robinson, S., & Wilkins, A. (Eds.). (1999). *Dispelling the myth: High poverty schools exceeding expectations.* Washington, DC: Education Trust in Cooperation with the Council of Chief State School Officers and partially funded by the U.S. Department of Education.

Bernhardt, V. L. (2005). Data tools for school improvement. *Educational Leadership,* 62(5), 66-69.

Bernhardt, V. L. (2005). *Using data to improve student learning in high schools.* Larchmont, NY: Eye on Education, Inc.

Bernhardt, V. L. (2004). Data analysis. In L. Easton (Ed.), *Powerful Designs for Professional Development.* Oxford, OH: National Staff Development Council (NSDC).

Bernhardt, V. L. (2004). *Data analysis for continuous school improvement* (2nd ed.). Larchmont, NY: Eye on Education, Inc.

Bernhardt, V. L. (2004). *Using data to improve student learning in middle schools.* Larchmont, NY: Eye on Education, Inc.

Bernhardt, V. L. (2003). No schools left behind. *Educational Leadership,* 60(5), 26-30.

Bernhardt, V. L. (2003). *Using data to improve student learning in elementary schools.* Larchmont, NY: Eye on Education, Inc.

Bernhardt, V. L. (2002). *The school portfolio toolkit: A planning, implementation, and evaluation guide for continuous school improvement.* Larchmont, NY: Eye on Education, Inc.

Bernhardt, V. L. (2000). *Designing and using databases for school improvement.* Larchmont, NY: Eye on Education, Inc.

Bernhardt, V. L. (2000). Intersections: New routes open when one type of data crosses another. *Journal of Staff Development,* 21(1), 33-36.

Bernhardt, V.L. (1999, June). *Databases can help teachers with standards implementation.* Monograph No. 5. California Association for Supervision and Curriculum Development (CASCD).

Bernhardt, V. L. (1999). *The school portfolio: A comprehensive framework for school improvement* (2nd ed.). Larchmont, NY: Eye on Education, Inc.

Bernhardt, V. L., von Blanckensee, L., Lauck, M., Rebello, F., Bonilla, G., & Tribbey, M. (2000). *The example school portfolio, A companion to the school portfolio: A comprehensive framework for school improvement.* Larchmont, NY: Eye on Education, Inc.

Blythe, T., & Associates. (1998). *The teaching for understanding guide.* San Francisco, CA: Jossey-Bass, Inc.

Bobko, P. (2001). *Correlation and regression: Applications for industrial/organizational psychology and management.* (2nd ed.). Thousand Oaks, CA: Sage Publications, Inc.

Boudett, K. P., City, E., & Murname, R. (Ed.). (2005) *Data wise: A step-by-step guide to using assessment results to improve teaching and learning.* Cambridge, MA: Harvard Education Press.

Carr, N. (2001). Making data count: Transforming schooling through data-driven decision making. *American School Board Journal,* 34-37.

Cawelti, G. (Ed.). (2004). *Handbook of research on improving student achievement* (3rd ed.). Arlington, VA: Educational Research Service.

Celio, M. B., & Harvey, J. (2005). *Buried treasure: Developing a management guide from mountains of school data.* Center on Reinventing Public Education (CRPE).

Chenoweth, T., & Everhart, R.B. (1993). *The restructured school: How do you know if something is happening* (Report No. ISSN-0032-0684). East Lansing, MI: National Center for Research on Teacher Learning. (ERIC Document Reproduction Service No. EJ462413)

Clarke, D. (1997). *Constructive assessment in mathematics: Practical steps for classroom teachers.* Berkeley, CA: Key Curriculum Press.

Clune, B., & Webb, N. (2001-02). WCER Highlights. Madison, WS: University of Wisconsin-Madison, Wisconsin Center for Education Research.

Cohen, M. (2001). *Transforming the American high school.* Washington, DC: Aspen Institute.

Commission on Instructionally Supportive Assessment. (2001). *Building tests to support instruction and accountability.* Available: http://www.aasa.org.

Conzemius, A., & O'Neill, J. (2001). *Building shared responsibility for student learning.* Alexandria, VA: Association for Supervision and Curriculum Development.

Creighton, T. B. (2001). *Schools and data: The educator's guide for using data to improve decision-making.* Thousand Oaks, CA: Corwin Press, Inc.

Creswell, J. W. (2003). *Research design: Qualitative, quantitative, and mixed methods approaches.* Thousand Oaks, CA: SAGE publications.

Cross City Campaign for Urban School Reform. (2004). *A delicate balance: District Policies and Classroom Practice.* Chicago, IL: Author.

Danielson, Charlotte. (2002). *Enhancing student achievement: A framework for student improvement.* Alexandria, VA: Association for Supervision and Curriculum Development.

Dann, R. (2002). *Promoting assessment as learning.* New York, NY: RoutledgeFalmer.

Darling-Hammond, L., Berry, B., & Toreson, A. (2001). Does Teacher Certification Matter? Evaluating the Evidence. *Educational Evaluation and Policy Analysis,* 23(1), 57-77.

Deming, W. E. (1986). *Out of the crisis.* Cambridge, MA: MIT Press.

Dickinson, T. (Ed). (2001). *Reinventing the middle school.* New York, NY: RoutledgeFalmer.

DuFour, R., & Eaker, R. (1998). *Professional learning communities at work: Best practices for enhancing student achievement.* Alexandria, VA: Association for Supervision and Curriculum Development.

Eaker, R., DuFour, R., & Burnett, R. (2002). *Getting started: Reculturing schools to become professional learning communities.* Bloomington, IN: National Educational Service.

Education Trust. (2002). *Dispelling the myth: Lessons from high-performing schools.* Washington, DC: Author.

Educators in Connecticut's Pomperaug Regional School District 15. (1996). *A teacher's guide to performance-based learning and assessment.* Alexandria, VA: Association for Supervision and Curriculum Development.

Ellis, A. K. (2001). *Teaching, learning, and addressing together.* Larchmont, NY: Eye on Education, Inc.

Elmore, R. F. (2006). What (so-called) low-performing schools can teach (so-called) high-performing schools. *Journal of Staff Development,* 27(2), 43-45.

Elmore, R. F. (2000). *Building a new structure for school leadership.* Washington, DC: The Albert Shanker Institute.

English, F. W. (2000). *Deciding what to teach and test: Developing, aligning, and auditing the curriculum.* Thousand Oaks, CA: Corwin Press, Inc.

Falk, B. (2000). *The heart of the matter: Using standards and assessment to learn.* Portsmouth, NH: Heinemann.

Fashola, O. S. (2004). Being an informed consumer of quantitative educational research. *Phi Delta Kappan,* 85(7), pp. 532-538.

Fullan, M. (2001). *Leading a culture of change.* New York, NY: Jossey-Bass/Pfeiffer.

Fullan, M. (2002). *Changing forces with a vengeance.* New York, NY: RoutledgeFalmer.

Garmston, R.J., & Wellman, B.M. (1999). *The adaptive school: A sourcebook for developing collaborative groups.* Norwood, MA: Christopher-Gordon Publishers, Inc.

Glatthorn, A. A. (1999). *Performance standards & authentic learning.* Larchmont, NY: Eye on Education, Inc.

Glatthorn, A. A., & Fontana, J. (Eds.). (2000). *Coping with standards, tests, and accountability: Voices from the classroom.* Washington, DC: National Education Association.

Glickman, Carl D. (2000). *Leadership for learning: How to help teachers succeed.* Alexandria, VA: Association for Supervision and Curriculum Development.

Gredler, M. (1999). *Classroom assessment and learning.* Needham Heights, MA: Allyn & Bacon.

Gupta, K. (1999). *A practical guide to needs assessment.* San Francisco, CA: Jossey-Bass, Inc.

Guskey, T. (2000). *Evaluating professional development.* Thousand Oaks, CA: Corwin Press, Inc.

Guskey, T. R., & Bailey, J. M. (2001). Developing grading and reporting systems for student learning. In Guskey, T.R. & Marzano, R.J. (Series Eds.). *Experts in assessment.* Thousand Oaks, CA: Corwin Press, Inc.

Haladyna, T. M., Nolan, S. B., & Haas, N. S. (1991). Raising standardized achievement test scores and the origins of test score pollutions. *Educational Researcher,* 20(5), 2-7.

Haycock, K. (1999). *Results: Good teaching matters.* Oxford, OH: National Staff Development Council.

Henry, G. (1997). *Creating effective graphs: Solutions for a variety of evaluation data.* Editor-in-chief. New Directions for Evaluation, a publication of the American Evaluation Association..

Henry, T. (2001, June 11). Lawmakers move to improve literacy, the 'new civil right.' *USA Today,* pp. A1-2.

Herman, J. L., & Golan, S. (1991). *Effects of standardized testing on teachers and learning—another look.* (CSE Technical Report No. 334). Los Angeles, CA: University of California, Center for Research on Evaluation, Standards and Student Testing (CRESST).

Holcomb, E. L. (1999). *Getting excited about data.* Thousand Oaks, CA: Corwin Press, Inc.

Holly, P.J. (2003). *Conceptualizing a new path: Data-driven school improvement series.* Princeton, NJ: Educational Testing Service.

Hord, S. (2003). *Learning, leading together: Changing schools through professional learning communities.* Austin, TX: Southwest Educational Development Laboratory.

Isaac, S., & William, B. M. (1997). *Handbook in research and evaluation for education and the behavioral sciences* (3rd ed.). San Diego, CA: Educational and Industrial Testing Services.

Johnson, D. W., & Johnson, R. T. (2002). *Introduction: Cooperative learning and assessment.* Needham Heights, MA: Allyn & Bacon.

Johnson, R. S. (2002). *Using data to close the achievement gap: How to measure equity in our schools.* Thousand Oaks, CA: Corwin Press, Inc.

Joint Commission Resources. (2002). *Root cause analysis in healthcare: Tools and techniques.* Indianapolis, IN: Joint Commission Resources.

Kachigan, S. K. (1991). *Multivariate statistical analysis: A conceptual introduction* (2nd ed.). New York, NY: Radius Press.

Kain, D. L. (1996). *Looking beneath the surface: Teacher collaboration through the lens of grading practices.* Teachers College Record, Summer, 569-587.

Kelehear, Z. (2004). Focused improvement. *American School Board Journal.* Alexandria, VA: National School Boards Association.

Kifer, E. (2000). *Large-scale assessment: Dimensions, dilemmas, and policy.* Thousand Oaks, CA: Corwin Press, Inc.

Killion, J. (2002). *Assessing impact: Evaluating staff development.* Oxford, OH: National Staff Development Council.

Koretz, D., Stecher, B., Klein, S., & McCaffrey, D. (1994). The Vermont portfolio assessment program: Finding and implications. *Educational Measurement: Issues and Practice,* 13(3), 5-16.

Kosslyn, S. (1994). *Elements of graph design.* New York, NY: W. H. Freeman and Company.

Kouzes, J. M., & Posner, B. Z. (2002). *The leadership challenge: How to keep getting extraordinary things done in organizations.* (2nd Ed.). San Francisco, CA: Jossey-Bass, Inc.

Krueger, R. A. (2000). *Focus groups: A practical guide for applied research.* (3rd ed.). Thousand Oaks, CA: Sage Publications, Inc.

Kubiszyn, T., & Borich, G. (1996). *Educational testing and measurement: Classroom application and practice.* (5th ed.) New York, NY: HarperCollins.

Lambert, L. (2003). *Leadership capacity for lasting school improvement.* Alexandria, VA: Association for Supervision and Curriculum Development.

Lambert, L. (1998). *Building leadership capacity in schools.* Alexandria, VA: Association for Supervision and Curriculum Development.

Lazear, D. (1998). *The rubrics way: Using MI to assess understanding.* Tucson, AZ: Zephyr Press.

Linn, R. L., Baker, E. L., & Dunbar, S. B. (1991). *Complex, performance-based assessment: Expectations and validation guide.* (CSE Technical Report No. 331). Los Angeles, CA: University of California, Center for Research on Evaluation, Standards and Student Testing (CRESST).

Lissitz, R. W., & Schafer, W. D. (2002). (Eds.). *Assessment in educational reform: Both means and ends.* Needham Heights, MA: Allyn & Bacon.

Marsh, J. A., Kerr, K., Ikemoto, G., Darilek, H., Suttorp, M., Zimmer, R., & Barney, H. (2005). *The role of districts in fostering instructional improvement.* Santa Monica, CA: Rand Education.

Marzano, R. J. (2000). *Transforming classroom grading.* Alexandria, VA: Association for Supervision and Curriculum Development.

Marzano, R. J., Pickering, D., & McTighe, J. (1993). *Assess student outcomes: Performance assessment using dimensions of learning model.* Alexandria, VA: Association for Supervision and Curriculum Development.

Marzano, R. J., Pickering, D., & Pollock, J. E. (2001). *Classroom instruction that works: Research-based strategies for increasing student achievement.* Alexandria, VA: Association for Supervision and Curriculum Development.

McIntyre, C.V. (1992). *Writing effective news releases: How to get free publicity for yourself, your business, or your organization.* Colorado Springs, CO: Piccadilly Books.

McLaughlin, M., & Talbert, J. (2003). *Reforming districts: How districts support school reform.* Seattle, WA: Center for the Study of Teaching and Policy.

McMillian, J. H. (2001). *Classroom assessment: Principles and practice for effective instruction* (2nd ed.). Needham Heights, MA: Allyn & Bacon.

McMillian, J. H. (2001). *Essential assessment concepts for teachers and administrators.* In Guskey, T.R. & Marzano, R.J. (Series Eds.). Experts in Assessment. Thousand Oaks, CA: Corwin Press, Inc.

McREL. (1995-2002). *Classroom assessment, grading, and record keeping.* Aurora, CO: Author.

McTighe, J., & Ferrara, S. (1998). *Assessing learning in the classroom.* Washington, DC: National Education Association.

Merrow, J. (2001). *"Good enough" schools are not good enough.* Lanham, MD: Scarecrow Press.

Microsoft. (2003). Available: http://www.microsoft.com.

National Association of Secondary School Principals. (2004). *Breaking ranks II: Strategies for leading high school reform.* Reston, VA: Author.

National Education Association. (2001). *School dropouts in the United States: A policy discussion.* Washington, DC: Author.

National Staff Development Council (NSDC) *Journal of research in professional learning.* [online]. Available from *http://www.nsdc.org/library/publications/research/index.cfm.*

National Staff Development Council. (2002, October). Scientifically-based research as defined by NCLB. *Results.* Oxford, OH: Author.

Newman, F. (Ed.). (1992). *Student engagement and achievement in American secondary schools.* New York: Teachers College Press.

Noguera, P.A. (2004). Transforming high schools. *Educational Leadership,* Volume 61, No. 8.

Northley, S. (2005). *Handbook on differentiated instruction for middle and high schools.* Larchmont, NY: Eye on Education.

Northwest Evaluation Association (NWEA). (2002). Available: http://www.nwea.org.

O'Connor, K. (1999). *The mindful school: How to grade for learning.* Arlington Heights, IL: Skylight Professional Development.

Oshry, B. (2000). *Leading systems: Lessons from the power lab.* San Francisco, CA: Berrett-Koehler Publishers.

Oosterhof, A. (1999). *Developing and using classroom assessments* (2nd ed.). Upper Saddle River, NJ: Prentice Hall, Inc.

Parsons, B. A. (2002). *Evaluative Inquiry: Using evaluation to promote student success.* Thousand Oaks, CA: Corwin Press, Inc.

Patten, M. L. (1997). *Understanding research methods: An overview of the essentials.* Los Angeles, CA: Pyrczak Publishing.

Payne, R. K., & Magee, D. S. (1999). *Meeting standards and raising test scores when you don't have much time or money.* Highlands, TX: RFT Publishing Company.

Perone, V. (Ed.). (1991). *Expanding student assessment.* Alexandria, VA: Association for Supervision and Curriculum Development.

Peterson, K. D. (1999). *Shaping school culture: The heart of leadership.* San Francisco, CA: Jossey-Bass, Inc.

Petrides, L., Nodine, with T., Nguyen, T., Karaglani, A., Gluck, R. (2005). *Anatomy of school system improvement: Performance-driven practices in urban school districts.* San Francisco, CA: NewSchools Venture Fund.

Peterson, R. A. (2000). *Constructing effective questionnaires.* Thousand Oaks, CA: Sage Publications, Inc..

Popham, W. J. (1999). *Classroom assessment: What teachers need to know* (2nd ed.). Needham Heights, MA: Allyn & Bacon.

Popham, W. J. (2001). Standardized achievement tests: Misnamed and misleading. *Education Week,* 21(3), 46.

Preuss, P. G. (2003). *School leader's guide to root cause analysis: Using data to dissolve problems.* Larchmont, NY: Eye on Education, Inc.

Quellmalz, E., & Burry, J. (1983). Analytic scales for assessing students' expository and narrative writing skills. (CSE Technical Report No. 5). Los Angeles, CA: University of California, Center for Research on Evaluation, Standards and Student Testing (CRESST).

Rauhauser, B., & McLennan, A. (1995). *America's schools: Making them work.* Chapel Hill, NC: New View.

Rauhauser, B., & McLennan, A. (1994). *America's schools: Meeting the challenge through effective schools research and total quality management.* Lewisville, TX: School Improvement Specialists.

Rauhauser, B., & McLennan, A. (1995). *Research design: Qualitative, quantitative, and mixed methods approaches.* Thousand Oaks, CA: SAGE publications.

Reeves, Douglas. (2004). *Assessing educational leaders: Evaluating performance for improved individual and organizational results.* Thousand Oaks, CA: Corwin Press, Inc.

Rogers, S., & Graham, S. (2000). *The high performance toolbox: Succeeding with performance tasks, projects, and assessments* (3rd ed.). Evergreen, CO: Peak Learning Systems.

Sanders, J. R. (2000). *Evaluating school programs: An educator's guide.* Thousand Oaks, CA: Corwin Press, Inc.

Saphier, J., King, M., & D'Auria, J. (2006). Three strands form strong school leadership. *Journal of Staff Development,* 27(2), 51-57.

Schafer, W. D., & Lissitz, R. W. (1987). Measurement training for school personnel: Recommendations and reality. *Journal of Teacher Education,* 38(3), 57-63.

Schmoker, M. (2001). *The results fieldbook: Practical strategies from dramatically improved schools.* Alexandria, VA: Association for Supervision and Curriculum Development.

Senge, P., Cambron-McCabe, N. H., Lucas, T., Smith, B., Dutton, J., & Kleiner, A. (2000). *Schools that learn: A fifth discipline fieldbook for educators, parents, and everyone who cares about education.* New York, NY: Doubleday Dell Publishing Group, Inc.

Senge, P., Kleiner, A., Roberts, C., Ross, R. B., & Smith, B. (2000). *The fifth discipline fieldbook: Strategies and tools for building a learning organization.* New York, NY: Doubleday Dell Publishing Group, Inc.

Shapiro, A. (2003). *Creating contagious commitment: Applying the tipping point to organizational change.* Hillsborough, NC: Strategy Perspective.

Shepard, L. A. (2000). *The role of classroom assessment in teaching and learning.* (CSE Technical Report No. 517). Los Angeles, CA: University of California, Center for Research on Evaluation, Standards and Student Testing (CRESST).

Smith, J. K., Smith, L. F., & DeLisi, R. (2001). *Natural classroom assessment: Designing seamless instruction & assessment.* In Guskey, T.R. & Marzano, R.J. (Series Eds.). Experts in Assessment. Thousand Oaks, CA: Corwin Press, Inc.

Solomon, P. (2002). *The assessment bridge: Positive ways to link tests to learning, standards, and curriculum improvement.* Thousand Oaks, CA: Corwin Press, Inc.

Statistica. (2003). Available: http://www.statsoft.com.

Stiggins, R. J. (2000). *Student-Involved classroom assessment* (3rd ed.). Englewood Cliffs, NJ: Prentice Hall.

Stiggins, R. J. (1999). Assessment, student confidence, and school success. *Phi Delta Kappan,* November, 191-198.

Stigler, J. W., & Hiebert, J. (1999). *The teaching gap: Best ideas from the world's teachers for improving education in the classroom.* New York, NY: The Free Press.

Strong, R. W., Silver, H. F., & Perini. M. J. (2001). *Teaching what matters most: Standards and strategies for raising student achievement.* Alexandria, VA: Association for Supervision and Curriculum Development.

TetraData. (2002). Available: http://www.Tetradata.com.

Togneri, W. (2003). *Beyond islands of excellence: What districts can do to improve instruction and achievement in all schools.* Washing DC: Learning First Alliance.

Trice, A. D. (2000). *A handbook of classroom assessment.* Needham Heights, MA: Allyn & Bacon.

Tufte, E. R. (2001). *The visual display of quantitative information.* (2nd ed.). Cheshire, CT: Graphics Press.

Tufte, E. R. (1997). *Visual explanations: Images and quantities, evidence and narrative.* Cheshire, CT: Graphics Press.

Tufte, E. R. (1990). *Envisioning information.* Cheshire, CT: Graphics Press.

U. S. Department of Education. *No child left behind.* Available: http://www.ed.gov.

Visual Mining, Inc. (2003). Available: http://www.visualmining.com.

Wahlstrom, D. (1999). *Using data to improve student achievement: A handbook for collecting, analyzing, and using data.* Virginia Beach,VA: Successline Publications.

Wellman, B., & Lipton, L. (2004). *Data-driven dialogue: A facilitator's guide to collaborative inquiry.* Sherman, CT: MiraVia, LLC.

WestEd. (2002). *Improving districts: Systems that support learning.* San Francisco, CA: WestEd, with McCREL and NCREL

Whitaker, T., Whitaker, B., & Lumpa, D. (2000). *Motivating and inspiring teachers: The educational leader's guide for building staff morale.* Larchmont, NY: Eye on Education.

White, Stephen H. (2005). *Beyond the numbers: Making data work for teachers and school leaders.* Englewood, CO: Advanced Learning Press.

Wiggins, G. (1998). *Educative assessment: Designing assessments to inform and improve student performance.* San Francisco, CA: Jossey-Bass, Inc.

Wiggins, G., & McTighe, J. (1998). *Understanding by design.* Alexandria, VA: Association for Supervision and Curriculum Development.

Wilson, L. W. (2002). *Better instruction through assessment: What your students are trying to tell you.* Larchmont, NY: Eye on Education, Inc.

Wittrock, M. C., & Baker, E. L. (Eds.). (1991). *Testing and cognition.* Englewood Cliffs, NJ: Prentice Hall.

Wormeli, R. (2003). *Day one & beyond: Practical matters for new middle-level teachers.* Portland, ME: Stenhouse Publishers.

Worthen, B. R., White, K. R., Fan, X., & Sudweeks, R. R. (1999). *Measurement and assessment in the schools* (2nd ed.). Needham Heights, MA: Allyn & Bacon.

Yero, J. L. (2002). *Teaching in mind: How teacher thinking shapes education.* Hamilton, MT: MindFlight Publishing.

Yin, R. K. (2003). *Case study research: Design and methods.* (3rd ed.). Thousand Oaks, CA: Sage Publications, Inc.

Zemelman, S., Daniels, H., & Hyde, A. (1998). *Best practice: New standards for teaching and learning in America's schools* (2nd ed.). Portsmouth, NH: Heinemann.

Zepeda, S.J. (1999). *Staff development practices that promote leadership in learning communities.* Larchmont, NY: Eye on Education.

Zmuda, A., Kuklis, R., & Kline, E. (2004). *Transforming schools: Creating a culture of continuous improvement.* Alexandria, VA: Association for Supervision and Curriculum Development.

Index

E

F

G

H

I

L

M

EYE ON EDUCATION and EDUCATION FOR THE FUTURE INITIATIVE
END-USER LICENSE AGREEMENT

READ THIS

You should carefully read these terms and conditions before opening the software packet(s) included with this book ("Book"). This is a license agreement ("Agreement") between you and EYE ON EDUCATION. By opening the accompanying software packet(s), you acknowledge that you have read and accept the following terms and conditions. If you do not agree and do not want to be bound by such terms and conditions, promptly return the Book and the unopened software packet (s) to the place you obtained them for a full refund.

1. License Grant

EYE ON EDUCATION grants to you (either an individual or entity) a nonexclusive license to use the software and files (collectively, the "Software") solely for your own personal or business purposes on a single computer (whether a standard computer or a workstation component of a multiuser network). The Software is in use on a computer when it is loaded into temporary memory (RAM) or installed into permanent memory (hard disk, CD-ROM, or other storage device). EYE ON EDUCATION reserves all rights not expressly granted herein.

2. Ownership

EYE ON EDUCATION is the owner of all rights, title, and interests, including copyright, in and to the compilation of the Software recorded on the CD-ROM ("Software Media"). Copyright to the individual programs recorded on the Software Media is owned by the author or other authorized copyright owner of each program. Ownership of the Software and all proprietary rights relating thereto remain with EYE ON EDUCATION and its licensers.

3. Restrictions On Use and Transfer

(a) You may only (i) make one copy of the Software for backup or archival purposes, or (ii) transfer the Software to a single hard disk, provided that you keep the original for backup or archival purposes. You may not (i) rent or lease the Software, (ii) copy or reproduce the Software through a LAN or other network system or through any computer subscriber system or bulletin-board system, or (iii) adapt or create derivative works based on the Software.

(b) You may not reverse engineer, decompile, or disassemble the Software. You may transfer the Software and user documentation on a permanent basis, provided that the transferee agrees to accept the terms and conditions of this Agreement and you retain no copies. If the Software is an update or has been updated, any transfer must include the most recent update and all prior versions.

4. Restrictions On Use of Individual Programs

You must follow the individual requirements and restrictions detailed for each individual program on the Software Media. These limitations are contained in the individual license agreements recorded on the Software Media. By opening the Software packet, you will be agreeing to abide by the licenses and restrictions for these individual programs that are detailed on the Software Media. None of the material on this Software Media or listed in this Book may ever be redistributed, in original or modified form, for commercial purposes.

5. Limited Warranty

(a) EDUCATION FOR THE FUTURE INITIATIVE warrants that the Software and Software Media are free from defects in materials and workmanship under normal use for a period of thirty (30) days from the date of purchase of this Book. If EDUCATION FOR THE FUTURE INITIATIVE receives notification within the warranty period of defects in materials or workmanship, EDUCATION FOR THE FUTURE INITIATIVE will replace the defective Software Media.

(b) **EYE ON EDUCATION, EDUCATION FOR THE FUTURE INITIATIVE, AND THE AUTHOR OF THIS BOOK DISCLAIM OTHER WARRANTIES, EXPRESSED OR IMPLIED, INCLUDING WITHOUT LIMITATION IMPLIED WARRANTIES OF MERCHANTABILITY AND FITNESS FOR A PARTICULAR PURPOSE WITH RESPECT TO THE SOFTWARE AND FILES, AND/OR THE TECHNIQUES DESCRIBED IN THIS BOOK. EYE ON EDUCATION DOES NOT WARRANT THAT THE FUNCTIONS CONTAINED IN THE SOFTWARE WILL MEET YOUR REQUIREMENTS OR THAT THE OPERATION OF THE SOFTWARE WILL BE ERROR FREE.**

(c) This limited warranty gives you specific legal rights, and you may have other rights that vary from jurisdiction to jurisdiction.

6. Remedies

(a) EYE ON EDUCATION's entire liability and your exclusive remedy for defects in materials and workmanship shall be limited to replacement of the Software Media, which may be returned to EDUCATION FOR THE FUTURE INITIATIVE with a copy of your receipt at the following address: EDUCATION FOR THE FUTURE INITIATIVE, ATTN: Brad Geise, 400 West 1st. St., Chico, CA 95929-0230, or call 1-530-898-4482. Please allow three to four weeks for delivery. This Limited Warranty is void if failure of the Software Media has resulted from accident, abuse, or misapplication. Any replacement Software Media will be warranted for thirty (30) days.

(b) In no event shall EYE ON EDUCATION, EDUCATION FOR THE FUTURE INITIATIVE, or the author be liable for any damages whatsoever (including without limitation damages for loss of business profits, business interruption, loss of business information, or any other pecuniary loss) arising from the use of or inability to use the Book or the Software, even if EYE ON EDUCATION, EDUCATION FOR THE FUTURE INITIATIVE, or the author has been advised of the possibility of damages.

(c) Because some jurisdictions do not allow the exclusion or limitation of liability for consequential or incidental damages, the above limitation or exclusion may not apply to you.

7. U.S. Government Restriction Rights

Use, duplication, or disclosure of the Software by the U.S. Government is subject to restrictions stated in paragraph (c) (1)(ii) of the Rights in Technical Data and Computer Software clause of DFARS 252.227-7013, and in subparagraphs (a) through (d) of the Commercial Computer—Restricted Rights clause at FAR 52. 227–19, and in similar clauses in the NASA FAR supplement, when applicable.

8. General

This Agreement constitutes the entire understanding of the parties and revokes and supersedes all prior agreements, oral or written, between them and may not be modified or amended except in writing signed by both parties hereto that specifically refers to this Agreement. This Agreement shall take precedence over any other documents that may be in conflict herewith. If any one or more provisions contained in this Agreement are held by any court or tribunal to be invalid, illegal, or otherwise unenforceable, each and every other provision shall remain in full force and effect.

INSTALLATION INSTRUCTIONS

Windows

Step 1 Set up a folder on your desktop (or in your documents folder) labeled ***District Data Tools*** for capturing the files that you wish to download.

Step 2 Make sure your monitor is set to 800 by 600 or higher to view the entire CD contents. (When you are on the main menu page of the CD and cannot see the top menu bar, your monitor must be moved to a higher setting. Do this by going into ***Start / Settings / Control Panel / Display.*** Open ***Display,*** and click on ***Settings.*** Move the arrow on the screen area to at least 800 by 600 pixels.)

Step 3 The CD should start automatically. The introduction will run up to the ***Main Menu*** page. If the CD does *not* start automatically, follow steps 3a. and 3b. below:

3a. Open/Explore ***My Computer*** and Open/Explore the CD ***District.***

3b. With the CD contents showing, click on ***Click Here.exe.*** The CD will begin.

Step 4 After the introduction, you will come to the ***Main Menu.*** If you do not have ***Adobe Reader*** v.5 or above, download it by pressing ***Adobe Acrobat.*** After installing, go back to the ***Main Menu.***

Step 5 By placing your cursor on the section titles, you will be able to see what is on the CD. Click on the section that you want to know more about and read the descriptions of the files in that section.

Step 6 To download the tools from that section, press the ***Download*** button.

Step 7 When ***Extract Archive Files*** appears, click ***Next.***

Step 9 **Note:** When ***Destination Directory*** appears, click ***Browse*** to locate the folder in which you want the files to download. If you put a folder entitled ***District Data Tools*** on your desktop, you will see it in the ***Desktop Folder.*** (This may vary slightly depending upon the version of ***Windows*** you are using.)

Step 9 Open ***The District Data Tools*** folder and click ***Next.*** The files will extract and ask you if it is okay to download. Click ***Yes*** and the files will extract into your ***District Data Tools*** folder. Click ***Finish.***

Step 10 Go back to the ***INFO* window.** Select the ***Back to Main Menu*** button to return to the ***Main Menu.***

Step 11 Continue exploring and downloading. You must quit the CD to view the documents that you download.

Mac

Step 1 Create a folder on your desktop (or your hard drive) labeled ***District Data Tools*** for capturing the files that you wish to download.

Step 2 Make sure your monitor is set to 800 by 600 or higher to view the entire CD contents. (When you are on the main menu page of the CD and cannot see the top menu bar, your monitor must be moved to a higher setting. Change the settings in the ***Monitors Control Panel.***)

Step 3 The CD will start automatically. The introduction will run up to the ***Main Menu*** page. If the CD does *not* start automatically, follow steps 3a. and 3b. below:

3a. Open the CD by double-clicking the CD icon on your desktop.

3b. Select the icon for ***Classic OS 9*** or ***OS X,*** depending upon which operating system you use. The CD will begin.

Step 4 By placing your cursor on the section titles, you will be able to see what is on the CD. Click on the section that you want to know more about and read the descriptions of the files.

Step 5 To download the tools from that section, press the ***Download* button.**

Step 6 When a dialog box appears, click ***Continue.***

Step 7 **Note:** A ***Save*** window will appear. Locate your ***District Data Tools*** folder, or if you did not make a folder when you started, create a new folder. Save the section's files to the ***District Data Tools*** folder.

Step 8 Go Back to ***INFO* window.** Select the ***Back to Main Menu*** button to return to the ***Main Menu.***

Step 9 Continue exploring and downloading. You must quit the CD to view the documents that you download.

Please see our website for more information:

http://eff.csuchico.edu/home/

To contact *Education for the Future,* please call:

(530) 898-4482